online resource centre
www.oxfordtextbooks.co.uk/orc/horsey2e/

Tort Law is accompanied by a wealth of online resources for students and lecturers. This is just a sample of the support available; turn to pages xiv–xvii for further information or go to **www.oxfordtextbooks.co.uk/orc/horsey2e/**.

For lecturers

Test bank

A fully-customisable resource containing ready-made assessments with which to test your students and aid their learning. Offering versatile testing tailored to the content of this book, each answer is accompanied by feedback to explain to the student why their answer is correct or incorrect and where in this book they can find further information. Particularly useful for part-time or distance-learning courses, test banks are also invaluable to supplement traditional modes of teaching and assessment on more conventional courses.

On the way home from work, Colin experiences his first epileptic fit during which he completely loses consciousness. Colin's car careers into a cyclist who suffers multiple fractures. Which of the following is correct?

○ People with epilepsy are not allowed to drive, therefore Colin is liable in negligence to the cyclist.
○ The standard of care expected of drivers does not take into account any illness or disability they may have unless that condition places the driver into a state of automatism so that it can be said he had no control over the vehicle. Colin is therefore liable in negligence for the cyclist's injury.
◉ Colin is not liable to the cyclist: the defendant is not liable if he was unaware of the disabling condition from which he was suffering, whether its onset was sudden or gradual.
○ Colin is not liable as the standard of care is that of the reasonable driver taking into account any idiosyncrasies or illnesses that the driver suffers.

1 out of 1
Correct. In the case of illness or disability affecting driving the defendant will not be regarded as negligent he could not reasonably have known of the relevant illness or disability. See *Mansfield v Weetabix*

For students

Flashcard glossary

Test yourself on the legal terms used in the book: click on a term and the 'card' will flip to reveal the definition – or vice versa! You can even download these to your iPod or similar small screen device to use on the move.

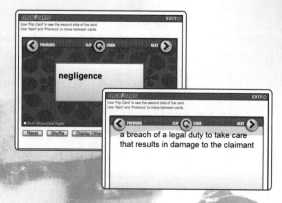

Tort Law

Second Edition

Kirsty Horsey and **Erika Rackley**

OXFORD
UNIVERSITY PRESS

OXFORD
UNIVERSITY PRESS

Great Clarendon Street, Oxford OX2 6DP

Oxford University Press is a department of the University of Oxford.
It furthers the University's objective of excellence in research, scholarship,
and education by publishing worldwide in

Oxford New York

Auckland Cape Town Dar es Salaam Hong Kong Karachi
Kuala Lumpur Madrid Melbourne Mexico City Nairobi
New Delhi Shanghai Taipei Toronto

With offices in

Argentina Austria Brazil Chile Czech Republic France Greece
Guatemala Hungary Italy Japan Poland Portugal Singapore
South Korea Switzerland Thailand Turkey Ukraine Vietnam

Oxford is a registered trade mark of Oxford University Press
in the UK and in certain other countries

Published in the United States
by Oxford University Press Inc., New York

Contains public sector information licensed under the
Open Government Licence v1.0 (http://www.nationalarchives.gov.uk/doc/
open-government-licence/open-government-licence.htm)

Crown Copyright material reproduced with the permission of the
Controller, HMSO (under the terms of the Click Use licence)

Database right Oxford University Press (maker)

First edition 2009

British Library Cataloguing-in-Publication Data
Data available

Library of Congress Cataloging-in-Publication Data
Horsey, Kirsty.
Tort law / Kirsty Horsey, Erika Rackley.—2nd ed.
p. cm.
ISBN 978–0–19–960077–9 (pbk.)
1. Torts—England. 2. Torts—Wales. I. Rackley, Erika. II. Title.
KD1949.H67 2011
346.4203—dc23   2011027595

Typeset by Newgen Imaging Systems (P) Ltd, Chennai, India
Printed in Great Britain
on acid-free paper by
Ashford Colour Press Ltd, Gosport, Hampshire

ISBN 978–0–19–960077–9

3 5 7 9 10 8 6 4

Kirsty Horsey

Kirsty Horsey studied law at Kent Law School and followed this with a PhD in the area of medical/family law. She is currently a Lecturer in law at Kent Law School, teaching contract and tort law to undergraduate students across all years. Her main research interests lie in tort, as well as the overlap of medical and family law, particularly in the area of assisted reproduction.

Erika Rackley

Erika Rackley is a Senior Lecturer in the Law School at Durham University. She studied law at Cardiff University and for her PhD at Kent Law School. She has taught tort at Kent, Leicester, and Durham Universities. Her research interests are broadly in the field of feminism, gender, and law, particularly in relation to judicial diversity.

Preface

Given the verbosity of the preface to our first edition, we'll keep this one brief. As anyone who's ever written an essay, article or book will know, redrafting a document is a very different (and often far more pleasurable) experience from the initial writing process. We've taken the opportunity not only to include developments and changes in the law but also to revise and (hopefully) improve the structure and argument of a number of the chapters. This process has benefitted enormously from the comments of colleagues, students and reviewers on the first edition. We are grateful for the time that was spent doing this and, though we do not know who all of you are, we thank you. Among the new cases included in this edition are *Gray v Thames Trains* [2009] (illegality), ***British Chiropractic Association v Singh*** [2010] (honest comment), ***Spiller and another (Appellants) v Joseph and others (Respondents)*** [2010] (honest comment), *Shell UK Ltd and others v Total UK Ltd and others* [2010] (economic loss), *LNS v Persons Unknown* [2010] (privacy and super-injunctions), ***Star Energy Weald Basin Limited and another v Bocardo SA*** [2010] (trespass to land), as well as the recent Supreme Court decision in ***Sienkiewicz (Administratrix of the Estate of Enid Costello Deceased) (Respondent) v Greif (UK) Limited (Appellant)*** [2011] (causation). We've also included a number of reports including Lord Young's report on health and safety (*Common Sense; Common Safety* (October 2010)) and Lord Justice Jackson's *Review of Civil Litigation Costs: Final Report* (2010), and have been able to incorporate brief reference to the measures included in the Draft Defamation Bill (CP3/11) published in March 2011.

As well as new content, our new edition also had a new editor at OUP, Helen Swann. We're thankful for her support, and her patient extension of deadlines. We are also rather shame-faced at our failure to thank last time our copy-editor, Joy Ruskin-Tompkins. Joy has now worked with us on both editions, we're grateful for her keen eye and grammatical knowhow—her knowledge as to when an adjectival compound does and does not have a hyphen is second to none (for those who are interested 'newly-wed' is the only exception to the general rule that they don't).

However, despite all these changes, one thing remains unchanged. Mike, Frank and Charlie—you rock!

We have done our best to state the law as of 31 January 2011 though as noted above we have been able to include a few selected developments after this date.

Kirsty Horsey
Erika Rackley

Preface to first edition

Despite (or maybe because of) its colourful characters and scenarios—itchy under-pants, decomposing snails, wayward cricket balls, noisy neighbours and lively parish council meetings—students often find tort law a difficult subject to grasp. Legal principles often appear fluid and few and far between and those they do encounter can seem inconsistent or contradictory. Yet while all this (and more) may make tort law a difficult subject to study, it also makes it a great subject to teach. Importantly, this book grew out of our *teaching* of tort law and the difficulties we saw our students encountering. We wanted to write a book which might go some way to making the study of tort a more enjoyable and intellectually satisfying experience.

To this end, our purpose has been to try to make tort law as *accessible* as possible by encouraging our student readers to *engage* with it. While the overall structure of the book is fairly traditional, we have sought in its content to set out the law 'as it is' and have utilised various pedagogical features (many of which we have gratefully adopted from Mindy Chen-Wishart's *Contract Law*) in order to highlight to students the types of questions that can be asked about the way tort law *is*, *why* it is this way and *how* it might be different.

Parts I to IV of the book are structured around various discrete torts with Part V exploring some more general principles, primarily related to damages and compensation. The book begins by looking at the tort of negligence—a position which highlights both its practical importance and the increasing tendency of its principles to infiltrate other torts. It forms a significant part of the text as it does most tort law courses. After this, the book is broadly structured according to 'interests'. Part II considers various 'special liability regimes' that have been developed to deal with employers', occupiers' and product liability, while Part III discusses the 'personal torts'—here trespass to the person, defamation and the emerging 'tort' of privacy. Finally, Part IV explores the land torts—trespass to land, nuisance and the rule in **Rylands v Fletcher [1868]**.

While we hope our structure and coverage is coherent, we make no claims of completeness—many torts (indeed on Bernard Rudden's figure almost as many as fifty) have fallen by the wayside. We hope, however, to have included the majority of torts studied on most tort law courses.

Our purpose, in writing this book, is to counter the idea that tort law (or indeed law generally) is something to be learnt rather than understood—to encourage students to critically reflect on and assess the law. Some further explanation may be needed. In our experience students are often told that they need to 'think critically' about the law without ever *really* being told what this means or, *crucially*, how to achieve it. Critical thinking is not synonymous with criticism; it is not necessarily negative or cynical. Rather, critical thinking is 'a *process* which involves you in thinking independently and evaluatively about the law'.[1] It requires you to ask questions about what you are reading—for example, *why* is this the rule here? *Whose* interests are served by this decision? And so on.

---

1. 'Critical Thinking' in Carr, Carter and Horsey *Skills for Law Students* (OUP, 2009), pp 100–1.

In our book, we have adopted a number of pedagogical features in order to help you do this.[2]

Each chapter begins with a **problem question** and **list of scenarios**—tasters, if you like, of some of the issues that lie ahead. We do not expect you to be able to answer the problem questions immediately. As with all problem questions they require detailed knowledge of, and the ability to apply, legal concepts and relevant case law. Rather, we hope that you will keep the problem questions and scenarios in the back of your mind as you continue reading so that by the end of the chapter you will recognise the case or issue we were referring to. We have tried, as far as possible, to make the characters and facts familiar and, therefore, the legal issues raised (hopefully) more memorable. **Annotated versions of the problem questions** with 'hints' about the issues you need to be thinking about can be found in the Appendix at the end of the book. **Outline answers** to the problem questions are available on the Online Resource Centre. These are not model answers, but rather more detailed guidance which breaks the question down into more manageable pieces and points you in the right direction. To get the most out of the problem questions, you should try to draft an answer to them before looking online. We hope that these questions will be particularly useful when you come to your revision.

We have also used **pause for reflection** and **counterpoint** boxes in order to encourage you to think beyond the basic text and fully engage with the complexity of the issues. **Pause for reflection** boxes appear regularly throughout the text. Their purpose is to provide you with an opportunity to stop and reflect on the law as has just been described. You should come to expect them as you read through the book and become attuned to their questioning approach so that, as your understanding of tort law deepens, you adopt their reflectively critical approach for yourself as you continue reading the book. **Counterpoint** boxes differ from these slightly. In these boxes we identify areas of controversy in the current law and consider possibilities for reform.

Remember—there is **no correct answer or opinion** to the questions raised in these boxes. In order to help you think about the questions, we have often provided pointers as to things you might like to consider while thinking about the issues raised. You do not have to agree with us. Our opinions are, at times, deliberately provocative in order to ensure that you are constantly challenging your own conclusions and assumptions.

At various stages throughout the book, you will come across **context or background** boxes. It is crucial to the development of your critical understanding of tort law that you experience it as a dynamic and fluid process, as a body of progressive rather than static, ahistorical rules (*Conaghan & Mansell* p 82). The purpose of these boxes is to fill you in on some of the background to the cases or legislation you are studying; to give you a sense of historical perspective so that you can begin to recognise the role of the context and history of the development of legal doctrine. It is important that you begin to ask questions about why things started to happen when they did. To consider, for example, whether is it significant that the nascent 'tort' of privacy has developed in a so-called 'age of celebrity' or that ***Donoghue v Stevenson*** [1932] was decided at the time of increasing mass-production of consumer goods.

---

2. Some of which you may be familiar with if you are using/have used Mindy Chen-Wishart's *Contract Law* (3rd edn, OUP, 2010).

These boxes supplement the final group of boxes—the **case** boxes. In each chapter, we have highlighted a number of key cases which we think are crucial to your understanding of tort law, as we have explained it. Importantly, these are *in no way* the *only* cases you will need to look at but rather provide a starting point into the case law of a particular topic. Where there is a case box for a particular case the name of that case will appear in bold throughout the text—for example, ***Donoghue v Stevenson*** [1932]. Remember, often cases raise different issues, many of which will overlap and interconnect, this means that the case box for a particular case may be in a different chapter to the one you are reading. You can find out where the case box is by looking at the table of cases at the front of the book.

You will also encounter a few **diagrams** and an **annotated judgment and statutes**. The **diagrams** explain the relationship between different torts or provide an overview of particular areas. Crucially, we recognise that people learn in different ways. If you don't find the diagrams helpful, ignore them, the text can stand on its own. The **annotated judgment and statutes** are intended to help you engage directly and closely with these important primary materials. In our annotations we have highlighted key passages and made links back to the text or to key cases.

At the end of the chapter you will find some suggested **further reading** and **questions**. Another aspect of critical thinking is that you are able to ground your argument in authoritative evidence. This requires you to consider *and evaluate* what academics, judges and other commentators say about the topic. The **further reading** (together with the references in the footnotes) covers a variety of sources—including academic journal articles and case notes, monographs (that is non-student texts), articles from practitioner journals, Law Commission reports, even newspaper articles and websites. The **end-of-chapter questions** are meant to be challenging. Many of them are typical of exam essay questions, which require you to critically analyse the law. Again, 'hints' as to how to answer these questions can be found on the **Online Resource Centre**.

On the **Online Resource Centre** you will also find links to **recent cases**, **legislation and law reports**, **annotated judgments**, a **glossary** and general **guidance on how to approach problem questions and essays** (along with sample problem questions with sample answer plans). Finally, we have provided **annotated web links** to topical sites of legal interest. For **lecturers**, we have provided **video clips** and a customisable **test bank** of multiple choice questions to test students' understanding, with page references back to the textbook.

There is one further point to make. An obvious danger in adopting such an explicit pedagogy is that substance may give way to style (as cases and principles are squeezed into boxes they don't really fit into) or that format distracts from purpose (as opportunities to 'think' break rather than develop a particular train of thought). While there may be other criticisms that might be made of the book, we trust that this is not one of them and, for those of you who do find them helpful (we recognise that the features used in our book may not appeal to everyone), we hope that they nurture and develop your understanding and that our book encourages you to bring a multi-dimensional and critical approach to your study of tort law.

The book has benefitted greatly from the many conversations we have had about tort with colleagues and students. Particular thanks are due to Joanne Conaghan, Karen

Devine, Janice Richardson and, especially, to Alan Thomson, for taking the time to comment on earlier drafts of many of the chapters.

We are also very grateful to the many academics and students who anonymously reviewed (sometimes very) early drafts often under considerable pressure of time.

Jack Anderson, Lecturer in Law, Queen's University Belfast
Darren Calley, Lecturer in Law, University of Essex
Dennis Dowding, Lecturer in Law, Bournemouth University
Jesse Elvin, Lecturer in Law, City Law School
Sirko Harder, City Solicitors Educational Trust Lecturer, University of Leicester
Andrew Harries, Senior Lecturer in Law, Lancashire Law School
José Miola, Senior Lecturer in Law, University of Leicester
Colm O'Cinneide, Reader in Laws, University College London
Chris Pawlowska, Senior Lecturer in Law, University of Greenwich
Shilan Shah-Davis, Senior Lecturer in Law, Bristol Law School
Avis Whyte, Senior Research Fellow and Senior Lecturer, Westminster School of Law
Rebecca Wong, Senior Lecturer in Law, Nottingham Law School
Christine Ferst, undergraduate law student, Liverpool Law School
Sarah Flanagan, undergraduate law student, University of Plymouth
Katerina Ktatunkova, undergraduate law student, University of Surrey
Helen Measures, undergraduate law student, Nottingham Law School

The book is stronger for all of their insights, comments, criticism and suggestions. Thanks are also due to our editor at Oxford University Press, Francesca Griffin, who has been gently but firmly supportive, and Sarah Viner, without whose initial enthusiasm for the idea this book would not have come about.

Kirsty Horsey's special thanks go to Mike and Frank Walters, particularly for spending the majority of another summer without her, and Erika Rackley's to Charlie Webb for his willingness to spend far too many Sunday afternoons discussing tort law rather than reading the newspaper.

While we stand jointly behind the book, the initial drafting was inevitably shared. After intense negotiations, Kirsty Horsey took primary responsibility for the chapters on omissions, public bodies, economic loss, causation, product liability, privacy, the land torts and damages, and Erika Rackley for the introductions to the book and negligence, psychiatric harm, breach, defences, occupiers' and employers' liability, trespass to the person, and defamation.

We have done our best to state the law as of 1 September 2008.

Kirsty Horsey
Erika Rackley

Guided tour of pedagogical features

Tort Law is a pedagogically-rich learning resource. This 'guided tour of pedagogical features' will show you how to make the most of your text by illustrating each of the features used by the authors to explain the key concepts of tort law.

Problem-based approach to learning

The authors use an innovative problem-based approach to teaching tort law. This will enable you to recognise and practise the skills you will need for exams, and help you to begin to think about how you might apply the law in a real-life situation.

Problem question

Read this problem question carefully, and keep it in mind while you are working through the chapter that follows. At the end of the chapter, you will be able to apply what you have learnt to the problem question and advise the relevant parties.

Margaret, who is 75 years old, is doing her weekly supermarket shop on a busy Saturday afternoon when she begins to feel pains in her chest. It transpires she is having a heart attack and she collapses to the floor. Although the supermarket is crowded, no one comes to help her.

Each chapter starts with a problem question of the type you might expect to see in an exam. Don't worry about answering this question right away—it's just to give you a taste of the kind of topics and issues covered.

✱ End-of-chapter questions

After reading the chapter carefully, try answering the questions below. If you would like to know what we think visit the Online Resource Centre (www.oxfordtextbooks.co.uk/orc/horsey2e/).

1. Should a 'Good Samaritan' statute be passed in this country? What are the benefits of *not* having one?
2. Do the concepts of liberal individualism and personal autonomy carry more weight than collective or social responsibility? Should they?
3. In his speech in *Smith v Littlewoods* [1987], Lord Goff indicated that the legal treatment of omissions may one day need to be reconsidered. Was he correct?
4. Consider the problem question at the start of this chapter. Now having read about the topic, what would be your advice to the various injured parties? If you need some pointers in thinking about how to answer this question, turn to the Appendix (p XXX) where

Keep the question in mind while you read the chapter, and at the end of the chapter you will be asked to try and answer it.

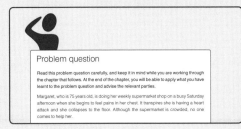

If you need some pointers in thinking about how to tackle this question, you can turn to the Appendix where each problem is annotated with issues and cases to consider.

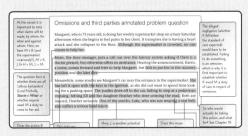

Next, you can try to write your own answer and, finally, you can log on to our Online Resource Centre (**www.oxfordtextbooks.co.uk/orc/horsey2e/**) to check your ideas against the authors' suggested outline answer.

In each chapter

List of brief scenarios

After the problem question, each chapter opens with a bullet-pointed list of scenarios, such as 'A pedestrian is knocked down and seriously injured by a speeding motorist' or 'A student collapses unconscious after an evening of heavy drinking. His housemates decide to lock him in the garden shed overnight.' Like the problem questions, these are designed to get you thinking about the issues at stake; the scenarios will be referred to later in the chapter (in the text and/or footnotes) where the authors will outline what they think is the most likely outcome in each case.

> **5.1 Introduction**
>
> Consider the following examples:
>
> → A grandfather watches as his grandchild is hit and killed by a car driven by a drunk driver. He later develops severe depression.
>
> → A woman is diagnosed with cancer and told she only has weeks to live. Distraught, she settles her affairs, plans her funeral and waits to die. Six months later she is still alive and further medical tests reveal that there has been a misdiagnosis—her X-rays became mixed up with another patient's and she is not sick after all. She is deeply embarrassed about seeing the people she told she was dying and has become severely agoraphobic.
>
> → A teenage boy is involved in a car accident. Though he escapes physical injury, he suffers a reoccurrence of chronic fatigue syndrome.
>
> → An elderly man is trapped in a poorly serviced lift for 12 hours. During the

Pause for reflection boxes

These boxes are ideally placed to help you stop, reflect on and assess the law described. They help you to consider how the law works in practice, as well as look more closely at its logic and its consistency with other principles, its policy ramifications and how it relates to other key issues.

> 🔲 **Pause for reflection**
>
> It has been argued that the notion of 'ordinary phlegm or fortitude' not only allows for the incorporation of evaluative judgments (and possible gender bias) as to what is a 'normal' reaction to any given event, but also perpetuates the false assumption that there is (or can be) a reasonable response to a tragic event. Do you agree? Consider, again, the facts of *Bourhill*. To what extent are the characteristics of the claimant significant here? What degree of fortitude is to be expected of an 'ordinary pregnant woman'? Or is a pregnant woman, by definition, not 'ordinary'?

Counterpoint boxes

These boxes highlight critiques of the law, identify areas of controversy or problems with the current law and suggest possible options for reform.

Most of the 'Pause for reflection' and 'Counterpoint' boxes end with questions to consider. Hints as to how to answer some of the more challenging questions are provided on the Online Resource Centre.

Whenever you see this icon in the margin, *@*
go to **www.oxfordtextbooks.co.uk/orc/horsey2e/** for some pointers.

> ◆◆ **Counterpoint**
>
> The Law Commission considered arguments for limiting liability for negligently inflicted psychiatric illness in its *Report on Liability for Psychiatric Illness* (1998). It concluded that most of the arguments for restricting liability do not stand up to close scrutiny. In particular, it suggested that many apply equally well to claims for physical injury. Consider, for example, the momentarily careless car driver—the absence of proportionality between culpability and consequences in this situation is as prominent and problematic whether a claim following an accident is for physical or psychiatric injury (although, of course, it is important to note that, unlike psychiatric harm, physical injuries are likely to be limited to those in physical proximity to the accident). Moreover, despite a general distrust of psychiatric illnesses, fraudulent or exaggerated claims are just as likely in relation to physical harm; although medically it can be determined that an injury has occurred it often cannot establish

Additional boxed features

Boxes are also used throughout the chapters to highlight particularly important cases (though remember that the boxed cases aren't the only ones you need to know!) and to provide some context about events such as the Hillsborough stadium disaster and the Thalidomide tragedy.

> vast number of potential claimants and this mood was cemented—the Hillsborough Stadium disaster.[25]
>
> **The Hillsborough Stadium disaster**
>
> 'The tragedy that claimed the lives of 96 Liverpool football fans shattered a community and shook the world of football took a matter of minutes to unfold. In its simplest terms, Hillsborough was a case of overcrowding in the central standing area allocated to Liverpool fans at the FA Cup semi-final match against Nottingham Forest ... The disaster →

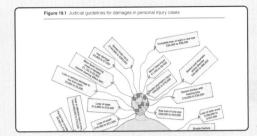

Tables and diagrams

Overviews are given and key concepts are explained visually using clear and colourful tables and diagrams. All the tables and diagrams included in the book are available for you to download from the Online Resource Centre.

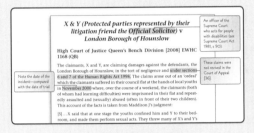

Annotated statutes and judgments

Some chapters (Introduction to negligence, Occupiers' liability and Product liability) also contain annotated judgments or statutes. The annotations explain the more difficult points of law and/or prompt you to think about whether you agree with the judges at various points. The annotations are designed to help you develop the invaluable skill of reading, interpreting and analysing judgments and statutes—essential throughout your degree and especially in relation to your coursework and exams. The annotated judgment and statutes from the book are also provided online, so that you can refer to these while reading the relevant chapters without flipping back and forth between different pages of the book. Read on-screen or print off: whatever suits you best.

End of the chapter

Conclusions

Each chapter ends with a 'Conclusion' paragraph which draws together the main threads of the chapter and leaves you with clear key points to remember.

End-of-chapter questions

Use these questions to test your understanding and prepare for seminars and exams. Each list starts with more factual questions and moves on to more discursive, essay-type questions. Pointers as to how to answer some of the questions appear on the Online Resource Centre (**www.oxfordtextbooks.co.uk/orc/horsey2e/**).

Further reading

Select titles from the further reading lists at the end of each chapter in order to broaden your knowledge of the individual topics covered. The authors introduce each further reading list with an indication of the best place to start your reading if time is short.

Guided tour of ORC resources

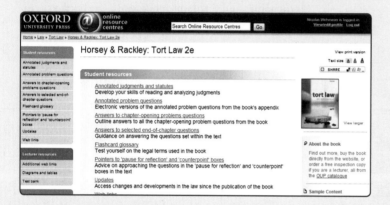

www.oxfordtextbooks.co.uk/orc/horsey2e/

Lecturer resources

OUP's Online Resource Centres are developed to provide lecturers and students with ready-to-use teaching and learning resources. They are free of charge, designed specifically to complement the textbook and offer additional materials which are suited to electronic delivery.

Using an Online Resource Centre saves you time by providing you with ready-made teaching and testing materials, while facilitating blended learning and enhancing the student experience. Use these resources to complement your own teaching notes or as a platform to update and restructure your course.

While the student resources are open-access, the lecturer resources are only available to lecturers who are adopting the book, to safeguard the investment the authors and OUP have made in developing the site. (This also means that students cannot gain access to these resources.)

If you are thinking of adopting this book and would like to take a look at the resources available to lecturers, please contact your local sales representative (via **http://www.oup.co.uk/contactus/academic/sales/hecontact/**) to request an inspection password.

If you have already adopted this book, do register for a year's access to the online resources – otherwise you are missing out on a wealth of tools to use in your teaching! Contact your local sales rep and also complete our simple online registration form (follow the links from **www.oxfordtextbooks.co.uk/orc/horsey2e/**). You can choose your own username and password, and access will be granted within three working days (subject to verification).

Once you have access, all the resources can be downloaded and are fully customisable allowing them to be incorporated into your institution's existing virtual learning environment if you wish – meaning no separate passwords or logins are required and everything is in the same place for quick and easy access. (You can ask your OUP sales rep and/or your university's e-learning co-ordinator for assistance in downloading the resources or incorporating them into your VLE.) Alternatively, you can continue accessing the resources directly from **www.oxfordtextbooks.co.uk/orc/horsey2e/** if this is easier.

If you would like advice or help at any point, don't hesitate to contact our ORC helpdesk at: orc.help@oup.com.

On the way home from work, Colin experiences his first epileptic fit during which he completely loses consciousness. Colin's car careers into a cyclist who suffers multiple fractures. Which of the following is correct?

○ People with epilepsy are not allowed to drive, therefore Colin is liable in negligence to the cyclist.
○ The standard of care expected of drivers does not take into account any illness or disability they may have unless that condition places the driver into a state of automatism so that it can be said he had no control over the vehicle. Colin is therefore liable in negligence for the cyclist's injury.
◉ Colin is not liable to the cyclist; the defendant is not liable if he was unaware of the disabling condition from which he was suffering, whether its onset was sudden or gradual.
○ Colin is not liable as the standard of care is that of the reasonable driver taking into account any idiosyncrasies or illnesses that the driver suffers.

1 out of 1
Correct. In the case of illness or disability affecting driving the defendant will not be regarded as negligent he could not reasonably have known of the relevant illness or disability. See *Mansfield v Weetabix*.

Test bank

A fully customisable resource containing ready-made assessments with which to test your students and aid their learning. Offering versatile testing tailored to the content of this book, each answer is accompanied by feedback to explain to the student why their answer is correct or incorrect and where in this book they can find further information. The test bank is downloadable into Questionmark Perception, Blackboard, WebCT and most other virtual learning environments capable of importing QTI XML. The test bank is also available in print format.

Particularly useful for part-time or distance-learning courses, test banks are also invaluable to supplement traditional modes of teaching and assessment on more conventional courses.

Figure 17.1a Weighing up the factors in a private nuisance claim (1)

Diagrams and tables

All of the diagrams and tables in the textbook are available to download electronically. These can be used in PowerPoints during lectures and seminars to aid student understanding.

Student resources

OUP's Online Resource Centres (ORCs) are developed to provide students and lecturers with ready-to-use teaching and learning resources. They are free of charge, designed specifically to complement the textbook and offer additional materials which are suited to electronic delivery.

Using an Online Resource Centre increases the value you get from your textbook, by providing you with additional materials to check your understanding, extend your knowledge and ensure you are up-to-date with the latest developments in the field, allowing you to maximise your achievements in exams and coursework. The student resources are completely open-access with no registration or password required, meaning you can use them whenever and wherever suits you best. Bookmark the url (**www.oxfordtextbooks.co.uk/orc/horsey2e/**) on your computer now (i.e. make it a 'favourite') so that you can access it in just a couple of clicks. Use the site to consolidate your learning after each lecture, to prepare for seminars, as a starting point to research a coursework essay, and of course during your revision.

Page 196
Viasystems was applied in the case of *Hawley v Luminar Leisure Ltd [2006] IRLR* where the Court of Appeal said employee remains an employee of the general employer for the purposes of vicarious liability or whether he is de the hirer, turns on the facts of the individual case. The general employer has the burden of showing that respons employer. It was noted by the court that this is a heavy burden. Luminar had contracted with ASE Security Servic for their nightclub. In the course of an incident outside Luminar's nightclub, one of these doormen, Warren, went attempt to show he wanted no trouble, Warren punched him so hard in the face that he fell to the ground and suff damage. Hawley sued Luminar and ASE on the basis that they were each responsible for failing to carry out a pr was a suitable person to be employed as a doorman and for failing to train or supervise him.

In determining the question of vicarious liability, the Court of Appeal considered a number of factors including wh who paid them and to whom they were responsible while working at Luminar's clubs. In this case, the *prima facie* shifted from ASE, the general employer, to Luminar, the temporary employer, because Luminar had exercised cor carried out his duties.

Regular updates

An indispensable resource allowing you to access changes and developments in this fast-moving area of law that have occurred since publication of the book. Added to the ORC at the beginning of each semester, and with page references to enable you to easily identify which material has been superseded, they allow you to keep up-to-date with new developments without buying a new book. Pages are available in Word format and can be printed for easy reference.

Annotated web links

A selection of annotated web links, chosen by the authors and organized by chapter, allowing you to research those topics that are of particular interest to you. The sites linked to include video and audio clips of news reports and 'talking heads' with politicians, claimants, and lawyers. The authors also include deep links on BAILII to many cases included in case boxes: with just one click you can access the full text of the case being discussed.

> Chapter 5
>
> **THE HILLSBOROUGH STADIUM DISASTER**
>
> There is a lot of material on the web about the Hillsborough Stadium disaster. Here is just a taster.
>
> **From the BBC News archives:**
>
> On This Day: 15 April 1989: Football fans crushed at Hillsborough
> http://news.bbc.co.uk/onthisday/hi/dates/stories/april/15/newsid_2491000/2491195.stm
>
> Hillsborough 10 Years On
> http://news.bbc.co.uk/1/hi/special_report/1999/04/99/hillsborough/319303.stm
>
> BBC Audio Clip on discussing the House of Lords' decision in *White*
> http://news.bbc.co.uk/1/hi/uk/226855.stm

Hints on answering questions from the end of Counterpoint and Pause for Reflection boxes, and from the end of each chapter

A handy way to check you are on the right track. Offers advice on how to tackle selected questions set within the text and at the end of chapters, along with guidance on what you should consider in your answer.

> **3. Does the law relating to psychiatric damage apply coherent principles?**
>
> This exam question requires you to bring together the issues you've been considering in the previous que
>
> As with all essay questions it is important that you establish your argument or thesis at the beginning of yo
>
> It is widely agreed by both academic commentators and judges that the law in this area has developed in a described this area of law as 'a patchwork quilt of distinctions which are difficult to justify'. Similarly, Lord Ho principle' in this area of law has been 'called off'. Even the Law Commission recognised that the law in rela psychiatric injury has 'taken a wrong turn'. Too much appears to turn upon the 'primary'/'secondary' victim actions by those deemed to be in the latter category has, arguably, led to unjust results.
>
> A basic answer will then go through the additional hurdles necessary to establish liability and will discuss th It should also examine the Law Commission recommendations and whether these would make the law mor courts have attempted to address this.
>
> Stronger answers will consider whether we can justify placing limitations on recovery for those who suffer p apply such or similar limitations in respect of *physical* injuries. Even if we do consider that psychiatric injur example, for the reasons given by Lord Steyn in *White*), there is still a question of whether English law is c does.

Outline answers to essay questions

An essay question is included in every list of end-of-chapter questions. Outline answers to many of these essay questions are provided online.

Outline answers to problem questions

Outline answers to all the chapter-opening problem questions are available online, so that you can check the answer you have drafted and gain pointers on how to improve your grade.

> *Following months of speculation the legendary indie guitar band – Blinking Idiot – are about to embark on a reuni a warm-up gig at a small intimate venue when a spotlight falls onto the stage causing a massive explosion killing th and Dave. Unfortunately, the lighting rig (onto which the spotlight was fitted) had been negligently maintained by R particularly gruesome.*
>
> You are asked to advise various parties.
>
> The best way to answer this question is to work through each of the potential claimants one by one. Use headings defendants – Rack & Horse Lighting – owe a duty of care to those who have suffered psychiatrically injured as a r so, the parties need to establish that they are either *primary* or secondary victims.
>
> Hannah
> Pete

General guidance on how to answer problem questions and essays

The authors have provided essential guidance on how to approach both types of question you will encounter during your degree: essays and problem questions.

> General guidance on answering essay-type questions
>
> Many students are wary of answering essay questions. Compared to a problem-type question there can appear to question itself as to the sort of issues the assessor is wishing the student to address. In fact, an essay gives far m own ideas than does a problem-type question.
>
> I therefore recommend that students attempt essay questions when a question appears which is based on a subjec feels confident in. The scope for achieving a very good mark in an essay is enhanced because of the flexibility that Whereas even a good student will find it hard to answer a problem in a *distinctive* way within the allotted time, the s answer a distinctive flavour and take the opportunity to make original observations. You may even go into the exa mind, ready prepared, to say about each of the major topics you have studied.

Further annotated judgments

Further judgments annotated with explanatory notes and points for students to consider. This innovative resource will help you to develop the skills of reading and analysing judgments.

Electronic versions of annotated judgment and statutes from the book

The annotated judgment and statutes from the book are also provided online, so that you can refer to these while reading the relevant chapters without flipping back and forth between different pages of the book. Read on-screen or print off: whatever suits you best.

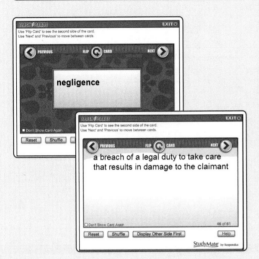

Flashcard glossary

Test yourself on the legal terms used in the book: click on a term and the 'card' will flip to reveal the definition – or vice versa! You can even download these to your iPod or similar small screen device to use on the move.

Contents in brief

Contents in full

PART V Liability, damages and limitations — 549

Tables of cases

The case names in **bold** indicate that the case features in a 'case box' (which can be found on the page numbers given in red)

Tables of legislation

List of abbreviations of commonly cited works

Atiyah	Atiyah, Patrick *The Damages Lottery* (Hart Publishing, 1997)
Cane	Cane, Peter *Atiyah's Accidents, Compensation and the Law* (7th edn, CUP, 2006)
Conaghan & Mansell	Conaghan, Joanne and Wade Mansell *The Wrongs of Tort* (2nd edn, Pluto Press, 1999)
Harlow	Harlow, Carol *Understanding Tort Law* (Sweet & Maxwell, 2005)
Ibbetson	Ibbetson, David *A Historical Introduction to the Law of Obligations* (OUP, 1999)
Lunney & Oliphant	Lunney, Mark and Ken Oliphant *Tort Law: Text and Materials* (4th edn, OUP, 2010)
Markesinis & Deakin	Deakin, Simon, Angus Johnston and Basil Markesinis *Markesinis and Deakin's Tort Law* (6th edn, OUP, 2007)
McBride & Bagshaw	McBride, Nicholas and Roderick Bagshaw *Tort Law* (3rd edn, Pearson Education, 2008)
Rogers	Rogers, WVH *Winfield and Jolowicz on Tort* (18th edn, Sweet & Maxwell, 2006)
Steele	Steele, Jenny *Tort Law: Text, Cases, and Materials* (2nd edn, OUP, 2010)
Weir	Weir, Tony *An Introduction to Tort Law* (2nd edn, OUP, 2006)

Introduction

1.1 **Introduction**

Consider the following examples:

→ A pedestrian is knocked down and seriously injured by a speeding motorist.

→ An office worker suffers psychiatric injury after being subjected to a campaign of transphobic bullying by his supervisor.

→ An elderly resident catches her foot in a small hole on the village green left by a maypole, breaking her ankle.

→ A school fails to diagnose a student's dyslexia believing the student's poor performance is simply down to laziness. The student fails their GCSEs.

→ A house is burnt down as a result of an explosion at a nearby oil refinery.

→ A prisoner is kept in their cell for 24 hours after the prison guards walk out on an unofficial strike.

→ A group of ramblers take a short cut over a farmer's field without the farmer's permission.

→ A student collapses unconscious after an evening of heavy drinking. His housemates decide to lock him in the garden shed overnight while he sobers up.

→ A first-time buyer buys a house on the basis of an inaccurate survey. As a result the property is worth significantly less than they paid for it.

→ A professional footballer wants to stop a national newspaper from publishing allegations about his private life.

→ The lead singer of a Smiths tribute band is branded a 'meat-eating wannabe who can't hold a note' on their former management's website.

In each of these examples there is a potential tort claim. In fact, most of these scenarios (as with many of those that begin the following chapters) are drawn from cases you will be studying during your tort law course. Such tales—often tragic and bizarre in equal measure—are the very stuff of tort. There are few, if any, other subjects where you will encounter wayward cricket balls, learner drivers driving into lampposts and misjudged electro-convulsive therapy within the space of a few pages. And yet, despite its varied case law, many students often find tort law a difficult subject to grasp—at least initially. (Something we acknowledge here in a spirit of supportive openness (we hope!) rather than with smug condescension.) Indeed, even before you begin your adventures into a subject where general principles at times appear to point one way and common sense the other, the title of the book might present a more immediate obstacle: what is 'tort law'?[1]

1.2 What is tort law?

A 'tort' is a civil (as opposed to criminal) wrong for which the law provides a remedy to the injured party. The origins of the word 'tort' come indirectly from the Latin *tortus* (meaning crooked or twisted), although the more usual translation is that from modern French where it corresponds with 'wrong'. Thus, at its simplest, the law of tort is the law of non-criminal wrongs.[2] The plural 'wrongs' here is deliberate. Tort law is the name given to a diverse collection of legal wrongs. Some of which will, no doubt, be familiar—the torts of negligence, trespass to land, assault, battery, libel, and so on often feature in the news. Others may be less familiar (such as, the tort of nuisance, which protects an individual's use and enjoyment of their land or those named after the cases from which they stem, such as the rule in **Rylands v Fletcher (1868)**, which holds a landowner liable when something he collects on his land escapes and does damage to his neighbour's land). Beyond this, however, there is no general agreement on what defines, and distinguishes, a 'tort'. Moreover, no one really knows quite how many torts there are (although Bernard Rudden back in the early 1990s counted 70 individual torts).[3] The boundaries between torts are fluid and the popularity of individual torts can change—'old' torts die out (the rule in *Wilkinson v Downton* may be a case in point here) while new ones emerge (such as the 'tort' of invasion of privacy). So, it is clear that tort law covers a lot of ground. What is less clear is the extent to which the various individual torts—and so the law of torts as a whole—share common features, principles and justifications. The best view may be that of *Weir*, who has observed that '[t]ort is what is in the tort books, and the only thing holding it together is the binding' (ix).

1. This chapter draws on and develops the ideas, insights and structure of Alan Thomson's introduction to tort law lectures given at the University of Kent. We both worked with Alan, who retired in 2010, at Kent and are grateful for his collegiate support. In particular, we thank him for his permission to use his case example of **Woodroffe-Hedley v Cuthbertson**.

2. There are, of course, other civil wrongs which fall outside the remit of tort—including breach of contract and equitable obligations. The principal distinction between torts and breaches of contract is that the contracts are voluntarily undertaken obligations, whereas the wrongs which make up the law of torts are breaches of imposed obligations—in other words, obligations which we have not chosen to be subjected to. For instance, my obligation not to hit you is an obligation I am subjected to whether I like it or not. By contrast, if I contract to sell my car to you, my obligation to hand over the car is an obligation I have chosen to be subjected to. The distinction between torts and breaches of equitable obligations is less straightforward, essentially turning on an outdated jurisdictional division between the types of court which first recognised these obligations. These days it is increasingly common to see some equitable wrongs, such as breach of confidence, being increasingly treated as a tort (**Campbell v MGN Ltd [2004]**).

3. Bernard Rudden 'Torticles' (1991–2) 6/7 *Tulane Civil Law Forum* 105.

It is certainly true that in comparison to, say, contract law (tort law's 'other half' in the law of obligations)[4] which is said to be grounded, *inter alia,* in the morality of promise-keeping, tort law appears to lack any such common theme or ambition, and resembles little more than a miscellaneous collection of relatively self-contained wrongs. As we shall see, in recent years one particular tort—the tort of negligence—has gained prominence, and started to gain ground from the other, older torts. If this development continues it may be possible that we will end up with a law of tort sharing a similar unity and coherence as is found in contract law. However, this move has not been universally welcomed and, in any case, we are not there yet.

Moreover, definitions in the abstract may not be particularly helpful. The description of tort law as 'a collection of civil wrongs for which the law provides a remedy' or, alternatively, as Peter Cane suggests, as a way of protecting people's interests through 'a system of precepts about how people may, ought and ought not to behave in their dealings with others' (Cane 1997, p 13) simply prompts another question: what wrongs or interests are we talking about?

1.2.1 **What interests does tort law protect?**

To return to the examples above of situations where an action in tort law might arise, in each case someone has suffered an unwanted harm. Some involve **physical injury** (for example, the damage caused by the elderly resident getting her foot caught in a hole) or even **death** (in the case of the pedestrian killed by the speeding motorist). In others the harm is **psychiatric injury** (such as that suffered by the office worker). However, clearly not all cases involve physical or mental injury to the potential claimant, other types of harm include **damage to property** (for example, that caused by the explosion at the oil refinery) and **financial loss** (for example, the buyer whose house is not worth as much as they thought or, more controversially, the student who has not been recognised as dyslexic).

In some of these examples, there does not appear to be any damage or harm at all. However, even assuming for the sake of argument, the ramblers walk over the farmer's land without causing damage (they do not, for example, tear up the ground or pick flowers) and that the housemates unlock the shed door before the drunk student wakes up the next morning and so he is unaware that he's been locked in all night, we can still say that in these cases there is an interference with the individual's **rights**. So, you have a right to determine who has access to or makes use of your land—in other words, the law says that you get to control the use, if any, that others may make of your property. Similarly, each of us has a right to bodily freedom and autonomy. Others are not entitled to touch us or confine our movements (subject to certain exceptions) without our consent. Therefore, even if the farmer or the drunk student may not have been *harmed*, in the sense of being left worse off, as a result of these actions, we can say that they have been *wronged*.

As such, tort law is not just, or indeed primarily, concerned with harm as much as it is with rights. So what rights do we have? We have mentioned already rights to **bodily freedom and autonomy**, which we can also regard as embracing physical and

---

4. Though we should also acknowledge that it is now common to identify 'unjust enrichment' or 'restitution' as a third branch of the law of obligations.

psychological integrity. We have also noted rights to or **interests in property**, such as land. Others include rights to **reputation**—as in the example of the lead singer of the tribute band—and, more controversially, rights to **privacy**—as with the professional footballer. This list is not, or need not be regarded as, closed, and one of the main roles of tort law is to mark out what rights or interests the law will recognise and protect.

There are three further points to make in relation to an understanding of tort law as a system of rules protecting our rights or interests.

First, while an understanding of tort law enables us to present it in a neat, linear form, it also involves something of a mis-description of the way the distinct torts are arranged and how they interrelate. What we mean by this is that while some torts exist and are defined only to protect a single interest (for example, defamation protects a person's reputation, nuisance protects an individual's interest in enjoying their land), the tort of negligence—the biggest and most important of the torts—offers protection to *all* our legally recognised rights and interests.[5] What this means is that often, for any single harm or injury, there will often be more than one tort upon which a claim may be founded. So, if you punch me I may have a claim for battery (a tort specifically designed to protect my right to bodily integrity) *and* a claim in negligence.

Moreover, it is possible to define the rights and interests the law recognises and protects in broader or narrower terms. We could say that we have a single interest in our physical integrity, embracing both bodily and mental wellbeing. Alternatively, we could separate these into two. As we shall see, the law is somewhat ambivalent here; for some purposes it draws just such a distinction, yet for others it does not (see, for instance, *Page* v *Smith* [1996]). The same goes for our interest in our assets or property. As *Steele* notes:

> Property interests *of different sorts* are protected *against invasion of different types* by various torts. So negligence protects against damage to property; private nuisance over-laps with negligence but more broadly protects against interference with use and enjoy-ment of land [and]; trespass to land protects against interference with possession of land and need not involve any diminution in value at all. (p 13)

The position is muddied further when we note that even where a tort is designed to protect a single interest (such as defamation and nuisance), if a claim is successful the claimant can also recover for other sorts of harms which they suffer as a consequence of their interest having been infringed. For example, if you defame me, the basis of my claim is that you have harmed my reputation. However, if my claim is successful I can also recover for any financial losses I suffer as a result of my reputation having been tarnished (for instance, if it led to me losing my job and hence a loss of income). As such, we may say that even these 'single interest' torts end up protecting a variety of interests and remedying a variety of harms.

Secondly, tort law does not recognise *all* interferences with an individual's inter-ests as actionable harms. Typically tortious liability is limited when it is thought to be undesirable for policy reasons. For example, we all have an interest in our mental

---

5. As a result, any attempt to study tort according to protected interest (see e.g. Cane 1997 and more recently Robert Stevens' suggestion for a tort textbook structured according to 'rights' (*Torts and Rights* (OUP, 2007), p 303)) would inevitably involve breaking up the tort of negligence, since this protects and so cuts across all such interests.

Table 1.1 Interests protected by the torts discussed in this book

Interest	Tort
Personal (both physical and mental) integrity including the right to self-determination	Negligence (including occupiers' liability, employers' liability) Product liability Trespass to the person (assault, battery, false imprisonment) The rule in *Wilkinson* v *Downton* Claims under the Protection from Harassment Act 1997 Nuisance (public)
Damage to property	Negligence (including occupiers' liability, employers' liability) Product liability Trespass to land Nuisance (public and private) The rule in **Rylands** v **Fletcher**
'Pure' financial loss (that is, loss *not* consequent on other injuries) 'Consequential' financial loss	Negligence Negligence Product liability Defamation (libel and slander) Nuisance (public and private)
Possession, use and enjoyment of land	Trespass to land Nuisance (public and private) The rule in **Rylands** v **Fletcher** Negligence Claims under the Protection from Harassment Act 1997
Reputation	Defamation (libel and slander) Breach of confidence
Privacy	Negligence Trespass to land Nuisance (public and private) Breach of confidence 'Tort' of invasion of privacy Claims under the Protection from Harassment Act 1997

wellbeing, but the courts have placed significant limitations on the availability of claims in respect of such harm.[6] Of course, the absence of tort liability does not mean that a defendant can act without fear of legal consequences. In particular, there may still be a criminal sanction. The speeding motorist who does *not* hit the pedestrian commits no tort (assuming they cause no other harm), however they may well still be guilty of a criminal offence in relation to their dangerous driving.[7]

We may also note that tort law does not protect the interests it does recognise *equally*—sexual harassment and (until recently) a person's interest in their private life have, traditionally, been weakly protected by tort in comparison with, say, physical injury or damage to an individual's reputation.[8]

Finally, and following on from the previous point, to say that the law of tort protects an individual's rights or interests does *not* mean that a claimant will succeed simply by showing that the defendant harmed them or infringed their rights. Tort law lays down a set of rules stating when exactly a harm or infringement of one's interest will give rise to legal liability. Moreover, these rules—the hurdles a claimant must get over for their claim to succeed—vary from tort to tort. As such, we can speak only in very loose terms about there being general principles in the law of tort. So, although we can say that all claims in tort share the common feature that they concern infringements with a claimant's rights or interests, in reality you will gain a better understanding of how tort law actually operates in practice by recognising the individual torts as largely distinct.

Policy

At a number of points in your study of tort law you will come across references to 'policy'. For instance, judges or commentators sometimes explain decisions on the basis that they give effect to particular 'policy' considerations. As such, policy tends to be used to describe a certain type of factor or consideration which courts do or may take into account when deciding cases and framing legal rules. But what types of factors fall under the heading 'policy'?

The difficulty here is that the language of 'policy' appears to be used by different people at different times to mean different things. Even worse, those who make reference to 'policy' often fail to explain exactly what they mean by this.

Sometimes, the language of 'policy' is used to describe *all* factors which may have a bearing on how a case should be decided and how the law should develop. So, on this approach, every argument you might make about the law—what rules we should have,

→

---

6. Discussed in Chapter 5.

7. Examples of torts which overlap with/are crimes include the torts of assault and battery and public nuisance (discussed in Chapters 14 and 17 respectively). Conversely, there are many torts where there is either no corresponding crime or where a criminal prosecution is very rare—e.g. medical negligence. The key difference between tort law and criminal law is that while actions in criminal law are brought by the state to punish the defendant, in tort law actions are by an individual (usually the injured party) to provide a remedy (i.e. compensation) for loss or harm.

8. See generally Conaghan 2003.

→

who should win a given case—is an argument of policy.[9] Policy here covers arguments of morality or justice, economic considerations, questions of resource allocation—in short, *everything*. The question here then is not what role policy should play in the law—all law is necessarily driven by policy of some sort. Rather, the question is simply what particular policies the law should advance or embody.

More commonly, however, 'policy' tends to be used to describe a particular subset of factors or arguments that the courts may employ when deciding cases. Here, policy is simply one thing the courts may turn to when determining the shape of the law, and is to be contrasted with other sorts of factors or considerations. This was most famously articulated by the legal philosopher Ronald Dworkin,[10] who distinguished 'policy' from 'principle'. His distinction was essentially that between moral standards and other sorts of arguments—principles are based on notions of individual fairness and justice, policy by contrast covers so-called collective goals such as wealth maximisation or the encouragement of particular activities or trades. As such, policy is essentially defined by reference to what it is not. Policy is anything other than arguments of justice and morality.

The same point has been made by *Conaghan & Mansell*, who describe policy as a '"catch-all" phrase, used by judges and commentators alike, to describe judicial considerations which are "non-legal", that is not based on a recognised legal principle or an established precedent' (p 204). Typically then, when we make policy arguments we are looking beyond the particular facts of the case at hand, and the relationship and dealings between the particular claimant and defendant, to consider the wider social, economic and political impact of imposing liability. In other words, we are not asking simply 'would it be fair to make the defendant liable to the claimant?' but 'what would be the consequences for society at large for imposing liability in situations such as this?' Unsurprisingly, perhaps, such arguments tend in practice to be used more commonly to deny rather than to allow claims.

Whether the courts should take policy considerations into account when deciding cases (and, if so, to what extent) is a hugely controversial question. Some lawyers argue that courts should *never* base their decisions on policy factors. This was Dworkin's argument and has, more recently, been repeated by Robert Stevens: 'We should not ask our judges to resolve questions of policy and, if asked, they should decline to provide answers that they have neither the ability nor legitimacy to give. Judges should adjudicate on rights and leave issues of policy to be discussed by academics and resolved by the legislature'.[11]

What this assumes is that there are certain types of argument and consideration which are within the (democratic and/or intellectual) competence of judges and others which are not, and that judges should therefore base their decisions only on those factors

→

---

9. e.g. Lord Browne-Wilkinson in *X (Minors)* v *Bedfordshire County Council* [1995] seemed to be using 'policy' in this sense when he said that 'the public policy consideration which has first claim on the loyalty of the law is that wrongs should be remedied' (at 749).

10. *Taking Rights Seriously* (Duckworth, 1977).

11. Stevens, above, p 311. See also Peter Cane's discussion of this in his review of Stevens's *Torts and Rights* ((2008) 71(4) *Modern Law Review* 641, 644–6).

➡

which they are competent to evaluate. But how do we draw this line? And is it tenable in practice?

In many ways, the distinction between policy and principle draws a questionable dichotomy. Everyone is agreed that sometimes the courts modify or develop the law. In other words, sometimes courts do more than simply follow the decisions reached and rules set down in previous decisions and statute. As such, courts have a 'creative' (quasi-)legislative function. This means that courts will sometimes have to look beyond the established case and statute law—to 'extra legal' considerations of fairness or justice, economic efficiency and the like—to determine how a case should be decided.[12] The question then is why should we consider, as the likes of Dworkin and Stevens argue, that some of these 'extra legal' considerations are acceptable for courts to take into account, while others must be excluded?

The democratic argument—that it is the business of Parliament and not the courts to decide what the law should be—is an argument against *all* judicial creativity. It does not matter whether the courts are employing moral arguments or other sorts of considerations. In each case the law is open to the challenge that key decisions about our rights and liabilities are not being taken by a democratically elected body. And, in each case, the answer to this is that this may not be democratically ideal but this is the way the law has always been and always will be.

Similarly, the argument that judges are not 'experts' on policy matters, and so should consider only 'moral' rights or questions of fairness and justice when deciding new points of law, makes little sense unless we can say that judges *are* experts on such moral questions. Otherwise, judges' lack of expertise should prevent them from making arguments of policy *or* of moral principle. And yet it seems that there is no reason to view our judges as having any particular understanding or competence in relation to questions of morality and justice or that, by contrast, their understanding of policy matters is noticeably weaker. As such, it is far from apparent why certain types of argument—of morality, fairness, etc—can be entrusted to judges while others—policy considerations—cannot.

Therefore, in the end the argument that courts should not take policy considerations into account when deciding cases appears rather dogmatic. Moreover, irrespective of whether courts really *should* take policy into account, it is clear that, at least on occasion, they *do*. However, here too we see a number of conflicting views as to what the correct role of policy should be in judicial decision-making. Compare the following:

Public policy is 'a very unruly horse, and once you get astride of it you never know where it will carry you'. (Burrough J in *Richardson* v *Mellish* (1824) at 252)

With a good man [or presumably woman] in the saddle, the unruly horse can be kept in control. It can jump over obstacles. (Lord Denning MR in *Enderby Town Football Club Ltd* v *The Football Association Ltd* [1971] at 606)

12. Although cf Allan Beever *Rediscovering the Law of Negligence* (Hart Publishing, 2007).

1.3 **The disparate aims of tort law: a case study on *Woodroffe-Hedley* v *Cuthbertson***

Tort law has both backward and forward looking elements. It looks backward at what happened—the 'wrong'—and addresses the harm done, while also looking to the future and at ways of regulating behaviour and developing a response to the risk of harm. It seeks to protect an individual's interests both *prospectively*, that is to prevent or deter future harm, and *retrospectively* through the provision of compensation for past harms and the distribution of losses. Thus, tort law has a number of disparate functions or purposes—typically identified under the broad headings of compensation, deterrence, (corrective) justice and, less often, vindication, that is inquiry and/or publicity. It is to these that we now turn through an analysis of the little-known, and unreported, case of ***Woodroffe-Hedley* v *Cuthbertson*** [1997]. We are mindful of *Weir*'s warning that before 'discussing the purpose of "tort", it is surely desirable to become familiar with what the ragbag actually contains: otherwise we shall be like adolescents spending all night discussing the meaning of life before, perhaps instead of, experiencing it' (p ix).

Woodroffe-Hedley v *Cuthbertson* (20 June 1997) QBD

This case involved a negligence claim following a climbing accident on the North Face of the Tour Ronde (one of the peaks of the Mont Blanc Massif). Gerry Hedley was an experienced rock climber. He hired David Cuthbertson, an experienced alpine climber, to guide him to the summit of the Tour Ronde—a steep ice climb of about 350 metres. At the time of the accident, Cuthbertson was leading (that is, going first). Concerned about the heat of the sun on the snow and the danger of rock fall, he decided to protect Hedley on a single ice screw belay in order to save time. Cuthbertson had no recollection of the accident, however another climber on the mountain described how a large sheet of ice broke away from under his feet, dragging him down with it. The shock of the fall wrenched out the single ice screw and Hedley was also dragged down the mountain. The rope caught on a rocky outcrop and Hedley was killed instantly. Cuthbertson survived with a fractured knee.

The question for the court was whether Cuthbertson had negligently caused Hedley's death.

The evidence was that had two ice screws been used (as was good practice), Hedley would not have died. In response, Cuthbertson argued that given pressures of time it was reasonable to use a single screw. Dyson J disagreed. Cuthbertson, in deciding to dispense with a second screw and not to use a running belay, had fallen below the standard of care expected of a reasonably competent and careful alpine guide.[13]

The claimant (Hedley's young son) was awarded £150,000 in damages.

Woodroffe-Hedley is of no great legal significance (although Dyson J's (now Lord Dyson JSC) clear exposition of the elements of a claim in the tort of negligence deserves careful reading) and is unlikely to appear on your tort law reading lists. It is, nevertheless,

13. See further Chapter 8.

indicative and revealing about the diverse purposes and functions of tort law. Our reason for introducing it here is to use it as an illustration of what tort law is about and how the courts balance its—at times competing—objectives.

1.3.1 **Doing (corrective) justice**

The facts of the case paint a fairly bleak picture:

> Mr Cuthbertson made a serious mistake with tragic consequences which will live in his memory for the rest of his life. I am sure that he had Mr Hedley's best interests in mind when he made that fateful decision to move across the rocks, without taking the elementary and fundamental precaution of making the belay safe for Mr Hedley by driving in a second screw. Objectively viewed, this was not a situation of emergency. Mr Cuthbertson had time to reflect. He reached a decision which, even without the benefit of hindsight, could not reasonably be justified. (Dyson J)

In short, the accident was Cuthbertson's fault; he was to blame for causing the accident and therefore, the argument goes, he should pay.[14]

The argument here is one of justice, specifically corrective justice.[15] Justice requires that we do not unreasonably interfere with others—their person and their property—when we go about our daily lives. So if we were to ask why we should not go around punching each other or destroying one another's property, the (or at least an) answer is that this is simply, morally wrong. It is a requirement of justice that we do not treat each other in this way. Similarly, if I do punch you or destroy your property, justice requires me to do something about this—to correct or make good your loss.

This latter demand of justice is what is called corrective justice, and (as typically formulated) is built on two key elements—fault and causation. A defendant is liable to make good a claimant's losses because they (a) factually caused the claimant to suffer those losses and (b) were to blame in so acting. By contrast, where either the defendant did not cause the claimant's losses or where they were not at fault in causing them, then, as a matter of justice, we have no particular reason to require the defendant to bear them. In the first case, the defendant can simply say 'it was nothing to do with me!'; in the second their defence is 'I couldn't help it!'

As such, corrective justice seems to provide a fairly good account of the typical tort claim. For the most part, defendants are liable in the law of tort only where they caused the claimant's loss and (though there are more exceptions here) where they were at fault in so doing. This, then, is what looks to be happening in **Woodroffe-Hedley**. However, even on the comparatively simple facts of this case, how corrective justice actually applies may not be clear.

Corrective justice essentially identifies a notion of individual responsibility. If I am responsible for harming you, then justice requires me to put things right. However, in **Woodroffe-Hedley**, it was not only Cuthbertson who was in some way responsible

---

14. It should be noted that the professional standards committee of the British Mountain Guides found that David Cuthbertson was 'not at fault'. The climbing community has never accepted the *legal* decision in this case (Stephen Goodwin 'Climbers "acquit" colleague' *Independent* 2 October 1997).

15. Ernest Weinrib's *The Idea of Private Law* (Harvard University Press, 1995) is generally seen as setting out the 'purest' account of corrective justice.

for what happened. Hedley also played a role. After all, as Dyson J also acknowledged, 'mountain climbing is extremely dangerous. That is one of the reasons why so many risk their lives every year on mountains.' Hedley, as an experienced climber, knew this and willingly took the risk.

So even if we treat the role of a tort claim as being to determine who (if anyone) was (morally) responsible for the claimant's injuries, there may be no clear or single answer. To put the point another way, a case like **Woodroffe-Hedley** seems to present the court with a choice between the justice of righting a wrong (assuming this can be established) and avoiding the (possible) injustice of making someone else pay for another's self-chosen risk.[16] The court, in this case, through the mechanisms of negligence, allocated the loss to Cuthbertson. However, had the court found the situation to be an emergency, it would have been open to it to find his actions reasonable and the loss would have lain where it fell (that is, with the claimant).

1.3.2 **Compensation**

In **Woodroffe-Hedley**, as in the majority of tort cases, corrective justice is achieved by requiring the defendant to compensate the claimant for the losses they have caused them. This may make it appear that corrective justice and compensation are effectively synonymous—to say that tort law is concerned with corrective justice is to say that it is about compensating harms. But this is not quite right.

While corrective justice often requires the payment of compensation, as we have seen, it does so only where the defendant is morally, and legally, responsible for the claimant's losses. This (typically) requires both causation and fault. As such, corrective justice requires the payment of compensation only where the defendant culpably caused the claimant's losses. Moreover, corrective justice is actually done only where it is *the defendant* who pays that compensation—otherwise it will not be *the defendant* who is making good the loss they have wrongfully caused—and that this money goes to *the claimant*—since otherwise it will not be *the claimant* who is then 'made good'.[17] This seems to impose a significant limit on the role of tort law as a means for compensating losses. If tort law is simply about 'doing' corrective justice, then the law of tort can do nothing to remedy accidents and to make good losses which are nobody's fault or where the party who is at fault cannot themselves pay compensation.

But then look again at **Woodroffe-Hedley**. The claimant was not the climber's estate but his young son, who was not even born at the time of the accident. It is not impossible to say that, by not using a second ice screw or a running belay, Cuthbertson was wronging Hedley's unborn son (as well as wronging Hedley himself), but nor is this self-evident. So, even here, whether the claim can really be said to have given effect to corrective justice is far from clear.

Moreover, the extent to which tort law is really concerned with corrective justice can be challenged when we look at the motives of those who bring tort claims. In

16. Though, as we shall see, the law has a mechanism for splitting losses in such cases through the defence of contributory negligence (see Chapter 10).

17. Indeed, Patrick Atiyah has argued that tort law no longer operates as a system of personal responsibility or corrective justice as the actual tortfeasor never pays ('Personal Injuries in the 21st Century: Thinking the Unthinkable' in Peter Birks (ed) *Wrongs and Remedies in the 21st Century* (OUP, 1996)).

newspaper interviews at the time of the case, Hedley's widow was quoted as saying she felt deeply sorry for Cuthbertson.[18] It was clear that she was looking to allocate blame only in so far as was necessary to gain compensation for her son. Moreover, any compensation that Cuthbertson would be required to pay would be covered by his liability insurance. As such, it would not be *Cuthbertson* paying but his insurance company. Thus, while on the surface tort law works to make the blameworthy pay, its corrective justice purposes are undercut by the reality of insurance.

Indeed, claiming in tort can be seen often to be, in practice, conditional on the defendant having insurance. After all, there is no point suing someone who will not in the end be able to pay:

> . . . it is seldom worth suing an uninsured negligent defendant.[19] Because of the operation of insurance, the plaintiff's loss is distributed, not to the careless defendant but, through insurance premiums, to all those who were not careless but who had insured against the possibility of being so. By the back door, the presence of insurance goes someway to the destruction of the central fault principle itself. (*Conaghan & Mansell* p 12)

In such circumstances, the principles of corrective justice give way to the practicality of distributing losses. And, more fundamentally, the loss-*shifting* credentials and justifications of tort law (moving losses onto those who have culpably caused others to suffer such losses) are undermined. Losses, rather than being moved from one individual to another, are instead *spread* over a larger number of people. Tort law, while retaining its rhetoric of individual responsibility, effectively forces people to contract into the collective responsibility strategies of the welfare state (*Conaghan & Mansell* p 12).[20]

Tort law and the individual

Tort law, like all law, is political. By this we do not mean political in the party politics sense (although they may be relevant), but rather as 'being characterised by policy'.[21] Put simply, tort law embodies a philosophical perspective which prioritises individual over social or collective responsibility. Consider, for example, the decision in *Roe* v *Ministry of Health* [1954][22] or the fact that there exists no general legal duty to rescue.[23] The difficulty is that the politics of this understanding of tort law are rarely made explicit—they are, instead, presented as the way things are, as 'common sense'.

---

18. Gary Younge 'Go tell it on the mountain' *Guardian* 21 June 1997.

19. Though the case of *A* v *Hoare* [2008], involving the so-called 'lottery rapist' may be the exception that proves the rule here (Batty, David 'Victim wins right to sue Lotto rapist' *Guardian* 30 January 2008).

20. Most notably in the contexts of employment and road traffic accidents where statutory requirements that employers and motorists have liability insurance have been described by Jonathan Morgan as a '*partial* move towards a state-sanctioned compensation scheme' ('Tort, Insurance and Incoherence' (2004) 67(3) *Modern Law Review* 384, 400).

21. Wade Mansell, Belinda Meteyard and Alan Thomson *A Critical Introduction to Law* (Cavendish Publishing, 2004), p 2.

22. Discussed in Chapter 8, p 210.

23. Discussed in Chapter 4, pp 74–78.

➡️

This understanding of tort law is not unproblematic: Joanne Conaghan and Wade Mansell argue that:

if the basic subject matter of tort is concerned with how the law responds, or fails to respond, to the misfortunes which afflict individuals in our society, it can be strongly argued that the tort system represents a political solution which is undesirable both because of the arbitrariness of its results and because of the underlying callousness of its ideology. (1992)

This critique is, of course, itself political. It reflects a view which emphasises the importance of social or collective responsibility for an individual's misfortune and which questions the effectiveness of the tort law system—and in particular the centrality of the fault-principle—as a mechanism for compensation and/or loss distribution (*Conaghan & Mansell* pp 3–4).

Our purpose here, however, is not to argue for one understanding of tort law over another. Rather, it is simply to make clear from the outset that there is more going on beneath the surface of tort law than might, at first, be apparent and, in so doing, to encourage you to approach your study of it with a critical eye.

There is, however, another difficulty with tort law as a mechanism for compensation. As we have seen, the idea of corrective justice which underlies tort law's general requirements of causation and fault calls only for losses to be made good where they are the responsibility of someone else. However, while it might seem fair that Hedley's young son is in some way compensated for the loss of his father, what about the many other children who lose a parent but have no one to blame for their death and, therefore, no one to sue in tort? Are they any less deserving of compensation? Similarly, would Hedley's son have been any *less* in need of compensation if the court had found the guide *not* to be negligent—if they had found one ice screw, in the circumstances of the case, to be sufficient?

The point here is not to question the requirements of corrective justice, but to ask whether the law of tort should put all its eggs in this one basket. Corrective justice provides *one* good reason for providing a claimant with compensation, but it does not follow that there are not other, equally good, reasons for compensating accident victims. If so, why should the law generally, and through the law of tort in particular, prioritise corrective justice? Should not the law also provide compensation for those who suffer losses but who cannot find a defendant on which to pin them? Moreover, even where losses *are* caused by another's culpable conduct—and hence where corrective justice would seem to apply—as we have seen, the loss will often be borne either by an insurer or will not be made good at all (because the defendant does not have the resources to pay). In the end, corrective justice actually seems to cover very little ground, and to protect only a small minority of those whom we might feel should be compensated for their injuries.

> ### Pause for reflection
>
> Consider the following situations:
>
> (a) Leslie, an affluent 80-year-old, while drunk crashes his car and loses a leg.
>
> (b) Joan, an 18-year-old single parent, loses a leg when, while working as a traffic warden, she is struck by an unidentified hit and run driver.
>
> (c) Mary as a result of a congenital defect, is born with only one leg. She is now 5.
>
> (d) Dillon loses a leg as a result of contracting a serious disease.
>
> (e) John, a 'career burglar', loses a leg after being shot by a householder during a break-in.
>
> Which of these people should receive compensation? Who or where should the compensation come from?
>
> There is no 'right' answer to this exercise. Its purpose is simply to get you thinking about the variety of harms you will encounter in your study of tort law. Think about why you believe a person who loses a leg as the result of someone else's fault is more or less deserving of compensation than someone who, say, loses a leg after contracting a serious disease— what assumptions about the comparative severity of these harms and, importantly, the purpose of tort law, underpin your decision? You should keep these questions (and your responses to them) in mind as you continue reading this and the following chapters so that you can re-assess your position as you learn more about tort law.

As such it has been argued that the operation of tort law is largely arbitrary—a lottery if you like (*Atiyah*). Tort law's effectiveness as a mechanism for compensation is limited by its allegiance to fault over need. In the absence of fault, tort victims are thrown back onto alternative sources of compensation and support: social security, insurance policies and other compensation schemes such as the Criminal Injuries Compensation Scheme.

> ### A compensation culture?
>
> In recent years there has been much debate about the existence, and eradication, of a so-called 'compensation culture' in the UK, a culture that encourages us all to 'blame and claim'.[24] Certainly, a cursory glance at the news media will provide any number of examples of its (supposed) effects.[25] Moreover, this is something that courts have, for
>
> →

---

24. Hand (2010); Williams, Kevin 'State of Fear: Britain's "Compensation Culture" Reviewed' (2005) 25(3) *Legal Studies* 500; Richard Lewis et al 'Tort Personal Claim Statistics: Is There a Compensation Culture in the UK' (2006) 14 TLJ 158–75.

25. See e.g. Jaya Navin 'Ridiculous compensation culture claims and pay-outs burden on tourist attractions' *Daily Mail* 26 April 2010; Sandra Laville and Sally James Gregory 'How a puppy, a paving slab and a passing cyclist made a bad break worth thousands: No-win no-fee firms blamed for compensation culture that costs £10bn a year' *Guardian* 23 October 2004. It is worth reading these articles alongside Annex D of Lord Young's *Common Sense, Common Safety* report which details the 'real' story behind the 'myth' of what it calls health and safety 'hysteria' (Cabinet Office, 2010), pp 49–50.

→

some time now, been conscious of and which they have sought to distance themselves from when imposing liability. For instance, Dyson J in **Woodroffe-Hedley** was careful to stress the following:

> Many accidents occur on guided climbs where no one is to blame. This decision should not be seen as opening the floodgate of claims against mountain guides whenever such accidents happen...Anyone who climbs with a guide is, as a matter of law, treated as consenting to the ordinary dangers of mountain climbing.

But why should we be concerned about a compensation culture? After all, surely all this means is that accident victims are compensated for their losses. Similarly, in so far as tort law is concerned with effecting corrective justice, more tort claims simply means more justice. What could be undesirable about that?

At the root of concerns about the existence and effects of 'an unrestrained culture of blame and compensation' (*Tomlinson* v *Congleton Borough Council* [2004] [81]), is a discomfort with the apparent unwillingness of individuals to take personal responsibility for their actions.[26] This may seem a strange argument to make. After all, as we have seen, tort law appears to be built on notions of individual responsibility, by holding people responsible for their actions and the harm they have caused. If so, how can an increase in the availability of tort claims be understood to *discourage* individual responsibility? The answer is that there is a danger that if we provide tort claims and compensation *too* readily—that is, if we make it too easy for people to demand that others make good losses they suffer—it may discourage people from taking responsibility *for themselves*.

That would, of course, be a bad thing. But is there any evidence that this is really happening? While the conclusion of the Labour Government's Better Regulation Task Force inquiry in 2004 was that the 'compensation culture is a myth, but the cost of this belief is very real',[27] more recently the Prime Minister, David Cameron, has taken a different view:

> A damaging compensation culture has arisen, as if people can absolve themselves from any personal responsibility for their own actions, with the spectre of lawyers only too willing to pounce with a claim for damages on the slightest pretext. We simply cannot go on like this.[28]

Both views, however, share the same concern. Whether there really is an unhealthy expectation that all losses or injury ought to be compensated, or whether rather the real danger lies in the *perception* that such a culture exists, the consequence of *both* is that people become over-cautious, abandoning activities which, though risky, also bring societal benefits. In other words, the *fear* of liability leads people to simply refuse to engage in generally beneficial activities—hence the cancellation of school trips, village fetes and so on for fear of being sued if things go wrong.

This is the problem of *over*-deterrence (discussed further below). As James Hand notes:

---

26. Morgan, above, p 384.
27. Better Regulation Task Force Better Routes to Redress (2004), p 3. See also Hand pp 572–5.
28. Young, p 5.

The compensation culture cliché may not be a reality, but if it discourages people from pursuing truly legitimate claims—or undertaking valuable activities—then it is, nevertheless, a very real cause for concern.[29]

The most recent governmental response to this has been Lord Young's *Common Sense, Common Safety* report published in October 2010. Commissioned by David Cameron to 'put the common sense back into health and safety',[30] Lord Young made a number of recommendations including the simplification of the health and safety checks needed before a school trip could go ahead and a single consent form covering *all* activities that a child might undertake during his or her time at school, better routes for redress for individuals who wish to challenge an official's decision to ban an event on health and safety grounds and stricter controls of 'where there's blame, there's a claim' type advertising.

Pause for reflection

If tort law does such a bad job of compensating those whom we feel should be compensated, what are the alternatives?

One is simply to extend state provision for those who suffer misfortunes. In other words, the state should compensate those who suffer losses and should not limit such compensation to those injured as a result of another's fault. However, the costs of this might be considered prohibitive. So, while the state does make some provision for the disadvantaged, there is no prospect of it taking over responsibility for protecting us from all our losses.

An even more radical solution has been proposed by Patrick Atiyah. In *The Damages Lottery*, Atiyah notes that, in a system where people have a strong financial incentive to blame others for injury and where welfare support is increasingly provided through insurance and personal support systems, the solution to the inadequacy of the tort system to compensate for accidental harm lay in *personal*—that is first-party—*insurance*. The idea is that those engaged in risky activities would take out insurance to cover themselves should they be involved in an accident. People would be able to insure themselves against *any* risks—from being run over to insuring against congenital disabilities that may affect our children (*Atiyah* p 191).

Do you think this is a good idea? Think about the other purposes and functions tort law serves. Or has Atiyah, as Joanne Conaghan and Wade Mansell argue 'simply substituted one system of arbitrary and fortuitous distribution for another'.[31] What would happen, for example, to those who could not—or would not—buy insurance?

1.3.3 Deterrence

Tort law also plays a role in deterring future tortious activity. The imposition of liability in relation to a particular activity enables others to regulate their behaviour accordingly. Thus, it is argued, following the decision in **Woodroffe-Hedley v Cuthbertson**,

---

29. P 591.
30. Young, p 5.
31. Joanne Conaghan and Wade Mansell 'From the Permissive to the Dismissive Society: Patrick Atiyah's Accidents, Compensation and the Market' (1998) 25(2) *Journal of Law and Society* 284–93, 291.

mountain guides are more likely to use two ice screws rather than risk liability by relying on one. Moreover, one might think that anything that encourages safe practices is, in itself, a good thing.

The problem is that sometimes the effect of the imposition of tortious liability in such circumstances is not to deter potentially negligent conduct but to stop the activity altogether 'just in case'. Hence school trips are cancelled, horse chestnut trees are stripped of their conkers and competitors are banned from running in pancake races.[32] The deterrent effect of tort law is also weakened by the presence of insurance as it, once again, subverts that which it is said to reinforce. After all, the incentive to be careful is somewhat weaker when the result will be a rise in insurance premiums rather than having to bear a hefty compensation payout oneself. The financial impact on careless drivers of losing their 'no claims bonus' coupled with higher premiums for those who fall into certain 'risky' categories—young men, for example—does not, at present, appear to have a significant deterrent effect. However, there may be more of a deterrent effect where insurance companies, as perhaps in relation to employers' or occupiers' liability, themselves put pressure on defendants to comply with safety regulations and meet other standards before agreeing to provide insurance.

1.3.4 **Vindication**

Finally, sometimes tort actions are brought to find out 'what really happened'. What happened in the operating theatre? Or on the streets of Omagh?[33] Indeed, another reason Hedley's widow sued in **Woodroffe-Hedley** was because she wanted to know what had happened up on the mountain (the French police had refused to give her the accident report).

 Counterpoint

The tort system does little to encourage cooperation between the parties. It is, after all, dangerous—and, more importantly, costly—to apologise or admit responsibility (however limited) for an accident when litigation is likely (*Harlow* p 38). However, the Compensation Act 2006 attempts to go some way to remedying this by explicitly separating any admission of culpability from simply 'saying sorry': 'An apology, an offer of treatment or other redress, shall not in itself amount to an admission of negligence' (s 2).

This function of tort is often coupled with a wish to gain publicity about what has happened—to 'stop it from ever happening again'. This is often the line taken by

---

32. Curtis, Polly 'Children denied school trips over teachers' fears of being sued' *Guardian* 6 October 2009; BBC News 'Conkers removed over safety fears in Nottingham' 1 October 2010; Anon 'Health and safety officers ban running in pancake race' *Telegraph* 7 February 2010.

33. Twenty-nine people were killed by a Real IRA bomb in Omagh in August 1998. As no one has been convicted in a criminal court in relation to the bombing, relatives of those killed are now bringing a civil action against the five people they believe are behind the bombing (BBC News 'Omagh civil case "unprecedented"' 7 April 2008).

relatives of those killed and injured by another's negligence, including Gerry Hedley's wife, Lydia.[34] Consider also the claims of the friends and family of those killed in the Hillsborough Stadium disaster (***Alcock*** v ***Chief Constable of South Yorkshire Police* [1992]**) or that of Dwayne Brooks against the Metropolitan Police following the murder of his friend, Stephen Lawrence (*Brooks* v *Commissioner of Police for the Metropolis* [2005]).[35]

However, unsurprisingly, this strategy does not always work; answers are not always forthcoming. Speaking out against the voluntary payments made by the police to some of the relatives of the Hillsborough victims, Phil Scraton, a lawyer for the support group argued:

> in one of the most televised, monitored and photographed disasters in the UK...no individual, no corporate body has had to admit even negligence. The law and the legal process will be the final victims of Hillsborough—for the loss of faith among all those involved will never be restored.[36]

A variant on this can be seen in *League Against Cruel Sports* v *Scott* [1986] a case about stag hunting on Exmoor. While formally this is a case about trespass to land, in reality it has very little to do with protecting interests in land. Rather, it was a mixture of publicity and activism, of mobilising and using the law to further collectively held ends, in this case the desire of those opposed to stag hunting to put a stop to it on Exmoor by strategically buying up parcels of land so that the hunt, in passing over them, could be sued in trespass.

1.4 Tort law and the Human Rights Act 1998

The Human Rights Act 1998 (HRA) incorporates the majority of the European Convention on Human Rights (ECHR) into UK law.[37] What is the significance of this for tort law?

In the first instance, it imposes a duty on the state to respect and act consistently with the human rights set down in the Convention. These rights include: the right to life (Art 2), the right not to be subjected to inhuman or degrading treatment (Art 3), the right to liberty and security (Art 5), the right to a fair trial (Art 6), the right to respect for private and family life (Art 8) and the right to freedom of expression (Art 10). Accordingly, where the state does not do so the HRA enables an individual to make a claim against the state (s 7). This is what is known as 'vertical effect'.[38]

---

34. Young, above.

35. Which, it should be noted, also sparked a government inquiry: Sir William Macpherson of Cluny, *Report on the Stephen Lawrence Inquiry* (Cm 4262–I, 1999).

36. Phil Scraton 'Justice: Hillsborough's Final Victim' [1992] Apr *Legal Action* 7.

37. On the relationship between tort law and the HRA, see generally Jane Wright *Tort Law and Human Rights* (Hart Publishing, 2001).

38. It is important to note that this is not a claim in tort. It is a public, not a private, law claim; i.e. it creates a remedy in *public* law to enforce a Convention right.

More significantly, for our purposes, the HRA may have an influence on tort law claims between private individuals. This stems from section 6 of the HRA which makes it 'unlawful for a public authority to act in a way which is incompatible with a Convention right' (s 6(1)). Why is this relevant to tort law? What this appears to suggest is that courts (as 'public authorities' by virtue of s 6(3)) when deciding cases or framing legal rules are under a duty to respect the litigants' human rights (just as they are under an *express* obligation to read and give effect to legislation in a way that is HRA compliant (s 3(1)). This is significant for the purposes of tort law because it would seem to mean that when determining the existence and scope of liability in tort, that the courts must ensure that their decisions are HRA compatible. That in turn would seem to suggest that the content of the law of tort, and hence the rights and duties which exist between private individuals, must include adequate protection of the rights provided for in the Act (this is what is meant by the HRA having 'horizontal' effect).

To see how this might work, take the following example. One convention right in respect of which English tort law has failed to offer much protection is the right to privacy (Art 8). As such, before the HRA, a claimant who went to court complaining that the defendant had interfered with their privacy would more than likely see their claim dismissed on the basis that it disclosed no cause of action. How might the HRA change this? The HRA allows for a claimant, bringing such a claim, to say that if the court does not recognise their claim it will be failing in its duty as a public body to protect their right to privacy. In other words, effective protection of the defendant's right to privacy would require the courts to recognise that an invasion of the claimant's privacy is an actionable wrong.

Note that this does *not* mean that the HRA itself imposes duties on private individuals to respect each other's human rights. The House of Lords has emphasised that the HRA does not provide a remedy in tort *per se* (*R (Greenfield)* v *Secretary of State for the Home Department* [2005]). The HRA itself only imposes duties on public bodies. What the claimant is arguing, however, is that if the court does not recognise them as having a claim against the defendant in the law of tort, the court will be failing *its* duty to ensure that the claimant's right to privacy is respected.

The courts have yet fully to recognise this argument and, in particular, have thus far refused to recognise any *new* torts in response to the HRA. It is clear though that the courts are willing to modify existing torts to ensure that they are HRA compatible:

> [The] obligation on the court does not seem to me to encompass the creation of a free-standing cause of action based directly upon the articles of the convention . . . The duty of the court, in my view, is to act compatibly with the Convention rights in adjudicating upon existing causes of action, and that includes a positive as well as a negative obligation. (Butler-Sloss P, *Venables* v *News Group Newspapers Ltd* [2001] at 918)

This view was confirmed in **Campbell v Mirror Group Newspapers [2004]** where the House of Lords refused to recognise a new cause of action on the basis of the HRA but amended an existing action to protect the claimant's privacy.

1.5 **A note on terminology**

Since 1999 the victim or wronged party has been known in England and Wales as the **claimant**.[39] They were previously called the 'plaintiff' (and still are in some common law jurisdictions). You will therefore encounter both terms in your reading. In this book, we use 'claimant' whenever we are discussing the victim (even in relation to pre-1999 cases), reserving the term 'plaintiff' for when we quote directly from texts which pre-date the change.

On the other side, is the **defendant** who is also usually (but need not be) the alleged wrongdoer or **tortfeasor** (that is, the person said to have committed the tort). It is important that you recognise, and remember, this. The distinction between tortfeasor and defendant usually arises where an action is brought on the basis of **vicarious liability**, that is against an employer (the defendant) who, it is argued, should be held vicariously liable for the torts of their employee (the tortfeasor).[40] However, it may also arise where the case is brought against an insurer under the Third Parties (Rights Against Insurers) Act 1930, which allows the victim to sue an insolvent defendant's liability insurer directly.

1.6 **Conclusion**

In this introductory chapter we have considered the obvious, but essential, question: What is tort law? The answer has taken us from its origins in the simple mispronunciation of the French word for 'wrong'—tort—imported into England with the Norman Conquest to the recent and ongoing concerns about the so-called 'compensation culture'. Tort law is, then, the name given to a diverse collection of legal wrongs for which the law provides a remedy. These wrongs—or torts—protect an individual's interest in, for example, their personal integrity, their property, their use and enjoyment of their land or their reputation. Many, but not all, of these interests are protected in different ways by a number of torts and, similarly, while some torts—for example negligence—protect a wide variety of interests, others—for example libel or slander—protect a single interest, in this case reputation.

Before considering the effects of the HRA on tort law, we explored the many—and at times conflicting—purposes and functions of tort law and the extent to which it is able to meet them. Tort law tends to be about righting wrongs. It can be seen to operate as a mechanism of loss-shifting, ensuring that the victim of the tort is returned to the position they would have been in had the tort not occurred (usually through an award of damages). However, as we have seen, the corrective justice aspect of tort law is somewhat undercut by the presence of insurance liability which ensures the loss is spread amongst the policy holders. Tort law is also forward looking. It can also act as a deterrent, shaping the potential wrongdoer's behaviour as they seek to avoid liability, as well as providing an avenue for publicity and inquiry.

39. Civil Procedure Rules 1998 (which implemented the Woolf reforms designed to speed up and simplify civil litigation).
40. Discussed in Chapter 12.

✱ End-of-chapter questions

After reading the chapter carefully, try answering the questions below. If you would like to know what we think visit the Online Resource Centre (www.oxfordtextbooks.co.uk/orc/horsey2e/).

1. What is tort law and how does it differ from contract or criminal law?
2. What is the purpose of compensating for injury?
3. What is meant by the term 'compensation culture' and what does the use of the term imply?
4. Are the disparate aims of tort law conflicting or complementary? Give reasons for your answer.

✱ Further reading

The best place to start your reading is with Tony Weir's excellent introductory chapter in his 'Introduction to Tort Law'.

Cane, Peter *The Anatomy of Tort Law* (Hart Publishing, 1997)

Conaghan, Joanne 'Tort Law and Feminist Critique' (2003) *Current Legal Problems* 175

Conaghan, Joanne and Wade Mansell 'Tort Law' in Ian Grigg-Spall and Paddy Ireland *The Critical Lawyer's Handbook* (Pluto Press, 1992), pp 83–90 (available online via the 'Critical Lawyers' Group website)

Hand, James 'The Compensation Culture: Cliché or Cause for Concern?' (2010) 37(4) *Journal of Law and Society* 569

Harlow, Carol *Understanding Tort Law* (Sweet & Maxwell, 2005), Ch 2

Hershovitz, Scott 'Harry Potter and the Trouble with Tort Law' (2011) 63 *Stanford Law Review* 67

Hutchinson, Allan and Derek Morgan 'The Canengusian Connection: A Kaleidoscope of Tort Theory' (1984) 22 *Osgoode Hall Law Journal* 69

Weir, Tony *An Introduction to Tort Law* (OUP, 2006), Ch 1

Williams, Glanville 'The Aims of the Law of Tort' (1951) 4 *Current Legal Problems* 137

The tort of negligence

Introduction to Part I

1. The tort of negligence provides a remedy where injury or loss is caused to the injured party by the wrongdoer's failure to keep to a legal duty to take reasonable care (*Donoghue* v *Stevenson* [1932]). It plays a central role in the law of tort: more tort law claims are brought in the tort of negligence than in any other tort and it has influenced the interpretation of other torts.

2. Part I begins with two introductory chapters—**Introduction to the tort of negligence** and **Duty of care: introduction and basic principles**. The first of these chapters introduces the origins of the modern law of negligence and some of the key themes underpinning the tort. It outlines the essential ingredients of a claim in negligence—a duty of care, a breach of that duty and the damage caused by that breach—before going on to explore these in practice using *X & Y* v *London Borough of Hounslow* [2008]. The second introductory chapter tracks the development of the **duty of care**. It considers the various general tests developed and used by the courts in order to establish when a duty of care is owed. In new cases where there is no existing precedent, since the decision of the House of Lords in *Caparo Industries* v *Dickman* [1990], the defendant will owe the claimant a duty of care only where there are positive reasons for them to do so (either because the circumstances of the case are very similar to another where a duty is already owed or because there is sufficient proximity and foreseeability between the parties and the harm suffered to make it fair, just and reasonable to impose a duty).

3. Chapters 4 to 7 consider the circumstances in which the courts have developed specific rules as to when a duty of care is owed. These fall into three broad groups: liability in relation to particular harms—**psychiatric injuries** and **economic loss**; claims against **public bodies**, for example local authorities, the police and other emergency services; and, finally, those relating to the way in which the harm was caused—either indirectly, such as through a failure to act (an **omission**), or where the immediate cause of the harm was the **act of a third party** (someone other than the claimant or defendant). As we shall see, duty of care is often used as a control mechanism in these cases to *deny* liability on the basis that the defendant was not, or ought not to be, held responsible for the claimant's injury.

4. Chapter 8 focuses exclusively on the second of the requirements necessary to establish a claim in the tort of negligence—**breach** of duty. **Breach** occurs where a defendant has fallen below the particular standard of care demanded by the law. This is largely an objective test and is determined by comparing the actions of the defendant to those imagined to be done in the same circumstances by the so-called 'reasonable man'.

5. The final 'hurdle' for the claimant to overcome in the tort of negligence is **causation**. This is considered in Chapter 9. The claimant must prove that their injuries were caused by the defendant's actions in both *fact* and *law*. This is not always as straightforward as might be expected, especially in circumstances where there are multiple defendants and/or possible causes of the claimant's injury.

6. Finally, even if all the elements of a claim in negligence have been met, the defendant may still be able to avoid liability by raising a defence. In Chapter 10, we consider three key defences in the tort of negligence: **consent** (more specifically, *volenti non fit injuria*), **contributory negligence** and **illegality**. It is important to note that although these defences are discussed in the context of the tort of negligence they are all (to a greater or lesser extent) applicable throughout tort law.

2

Introduction to the tort of negligence

2.1 **Introduction**

Consider the following examples:

→ **A cyclist is knocked down and killed by a speeding car.**
→ **A junior doctor mistakenly injects their patient with the wrong antibiotic causing permanent paralysis.**
→ **An elderly woman breaks her hip tripping over a raised paving slab outside her local shop.**
→ **A young child falls down a manhole left uncovered by Post Office employees earlier in the day and seriously injures his leg.**

In each of these examples the accident or injury suffered appears to be the fault (at least in part) of someone other than the injured party. The speeding motorist, the junior doctor, the local authority and the Post Office employees have all been, in some way, negligent, in the sense of having acted carelessly or neglectfully. They may therefore be liable for damages in the *tort of* negligence—defined by Percy H Winfield as 'the breach of a legal duty to take care by an inadvertent act or omission that injures another'.[1] It is important to distinguish at the outset between negligence in the former everyday or colloquial sense—whereby it is synonymous with carelessness or neglect—and negligence in the legal sense—that is, the type of liability which the law attaches to people who fall below a standard of care imposed by the law. Not all actions which are negligent in the first sense will be negligent in the second. It is only sometimes that the law *requires* us to act carefully and, therefore, it is important always to bear in mind that a person is not *automatically* liable for all (or indeed any) of the consequences of their negligent (in the sense of careless) actions. (Moreover, as we shall see, a person may be liable in the tort of negligence even when their actions cannot realistically be described as careless.)

---

1. Percy H Winfield 'The History of Negligence in the Law of Torts' (1926a) 42 *Law Quarterly Review* 184. You should note now, however, that the tort of negligence is not limited to acts of inadvertence. Deliberate infliction of harms can also give rise to liability in the tort of negligence.

'Negligence', in tort law, therefore refers to a tort which, since the landmark case of ***Donoghue* v *Stevenson*** [1932], provides a remedy (usually in the form of damages) where injury or loss is caused to the injured party by the wrongdoer's failure to keep to a legal duty to take reasonable care.

Negligence liability may arise in relation to a range of diverse types of harm or injury—personal injury (physical and psychiatric), property damage, financial loss—and covers a wide range of activities—driving a car, giving financial advice, running a hospital operating theatre, playing football and so on. However, some harms or injuries are better protected by the tort of negligence than others. The courts have limited the operation of negligence in relation to some injuries which they view with suspicion—particularly psychiatric injuries and economic loss—and in claims against certain defendants—most notably public bodies, for example local authorities, the police and other emergency services. As such, though there is a single tort of negligence covering, potentially, all possible harms in all possible contexts, the courts have developed different approaches to deal with different sorts of harm in different contexts. We shall see examples of this in Chapters 4 to 7.

However, this should not obscure the general principle of the tort of negligence: to make people pay for the damage they cause when their conduct falls below an acceptable standard or level. It is this feature that makes the tort of negligence so important. The other torts we shall be looking at in this book are all identified by the type of interest or right they protect—for example, the tort of defamation protects the interest you have in your reputation, the trespass to the person torts protect rights to bodily freedom and safety. The tort of negligence is different. It is not defined by, and so is not limited to the protection of, any single type of right or interest. Instead, the focus of the tort of negligence is the 'quality' of the defendant's conduct—what must be shown is that the defendant acted unreasonably.

Of course, this is not to suggest that the actual harm caused by the wrongdoer is unimportant—far from it. It is crucial. Unlike, for example, the trespass torts which are actionable *per se*—that is, the claimant need not show that they have suffered any loss for their claim to succeed—liability in negligence can only be established where the defendant's breach has resulted in harm: 'Negligence in the air will not do; negligence, in order to give a cause of action, must be the neglect of some duty owed to the person who makes the claim' (Greer LJ in *Haynes* v *Harwood* [1935] at 152).

It is, therefore, misleading to talk about 'liability for negligence' in the abstract—the wrongdoer will not be liable *in the tort of negligence* if no injury results from their careless action—the elderly woman who *doesn't* trip over the broken paving slap as she does her weekly shop, has no claim in negligence. Moreover, even where the claimant has suffered harm, it doesn't mean that they will necessarily have a claim—the harm must be one that is *legally recognised*. The law does not provide compensation for *every* loss; harms which do not fall within the scope of negligence law, no matter how great and notwithstanding a defendant's clear breach of duty, will ground no liability in negligence. As Lord Rodger notes in ***D* v *East Berkshire Community NHS Trust*** [2005]: 'the world is full of harm for which the law furnishes no remedy' (at [100]). Thus, to use Lord Rodger's examples, there is nothing to stop the owner of the local shop from injuring his rivals by destroying their businesses. Similarly, 'a young man whose fiancée deserts him for his best friend may become clinically depressed as a result, but in the circumstances the fiancée owes him no duty of care to avoid causing this suffering. So he too will have no right to damages for his illness. The same goes for a middle-aged woman whose husband runs off with a younger woman...However badly one of them may have treated the other, the law does not get involved in awarding damages' (at [100]).

 Pause for reflection

Consider again the examples at the start of the chapter. What would happen if the speeding driver had at the last moment avoided hitting the cyclist or if the doctor's mistake had caused the patient no ill effects? In such cases, although the wrongdoer's actions are in fact just as careless or negligent, in law the driver and doctor would not be liable. Is the presence or absence of harm—in these types of cases more often than not a matter of luck rather than judgement—really the appropriate measure or dividing line between liability and no liability? If not, why not? You may find it helpful to refer again to the purposes of tort law (Chapter 1, pp 9–18) and the tort of negligence in particular when thinking about your answer.

The tort of negligence plays a central role in the law of tort. This is for two reasons:

(1) It is by far the most important tort in practice. More tort law claims are brought in the tort of negligence than in any other tort.

(2) Its influence extends beyond the tort itself; the ideas and principles of negligence have influenced the interpretation of other torts—such as the infusion of the notion of foreseeability into private nuisance and the previously strict liability imposed by the rule in *Rylands v Fletcher* [1868] by the House of Lords in *Cambridge Water Co Ltd v Eastern Counties Leather plc* [1994] and in defamation where the privilege defences have been redefined in terms of the defendant's fault (*Reynolds v Times Newspapers* [2001]).[2]

The tort of negligence therefore usually forms a substantial part of tort law modules and textbooks. This book is no exception. The law relating to the tort of negligence occupies the whole of Part I (Chapters 2 to 10) and much of Part II on 'special liability regimes'. The purpose of this chapter is to explore the origins of the modern law of negligence and to introduce you to some of the key themes underpinning the tort before outlining the essential ingredients of a claim in negligence.

2.2 Mapping the historical development of the tort of negligence

The tort of negligence is a relatively modern tort. Unlike trespass which by the 1270s has begun to develop a 'more sharply focused legal meaning' (*Ibbetson* p 39), the general principle of negligence as liability for conduct falling below a particular standard

2. Discussed further in Chapters 17, 18 and 15 respectively.

of care was fully articulated only in the early twentieth century in the House of Lords' groundbreaking decision in **Donoghue v Stevenson** in the 1930s.

So-called 'internal histories' of the development of the tort of negligence expounded by academics and legal historians such as Percy Winfield, Bob Hepple and, more recently, David Ibbetson, typically adhere to the following form.[3] Originally, negligence was understood *as a way of* committing and understanding other torts rather than as a distinctive tort in itself.[4] The tort of negligence was 'thoroughly fragmented' (*Ibbetson* p 188). A duty of care was recognised only in very limited circumstances—for example, if someone had control of some dangerous thing, say a gun, they had a duty of care to prevent it from causing harm (*Langridge v Levy* [1837])—and in relation to particular relationships, such as between innkeeper and guest. Thus though throughout the nineteenth century there were isolated pockets of negligence liability, there was no general principle of negligence (*Winterbottom v Wright* [1842]).

As the century progressed these 'pockets' began to join up and by the end of the century the judges were beginning to move towards the articulation of a general principle of a duty of care. This can be seen most notably in the judgment of Brett MR in *Heaven v Pender* [1883]:

> Whenever one person is by circumstances placed in such a position with regard to another that every one of ordinary sense who did think would at once recognise that if he did not use ordinary care and skill in his own conduct with regard to those circumstances he would cause danger of injury to the person or property of the other, a duty arises to use ordinary care and skill to avoid such danger. (at 509)

However, by the time **Donoghue v Stevenson** reached the House of Lords in 1932, there was still no *general* principle of negligence in tort law. Private law thinking continued to be dominated by contractual understandings of responsibilities and obligations between parties. This meant that, outside the limited pockets of liability mentioned above, an individual owed a duty of care to another only in situations where *they had specifically agreed to do so*—usually through a contract. As a result many people who were injured through another's carelessness had no claim. Take, for example, the situation where a consumer is injured by a defective and dangerous product. A contract would exist between the manufacturer and whoever had bought the article from them, say a shop owner. There would also be a contract between the shop owner and the person who had bought the article from them. This then enabled the shop owner to sue the manufacturer and the buyer to sue to shop owner. But the lack of any general tort of negligence, combined with the doctrine of privity of contract—which, broadly speaking, means that only the parties to a contract could sue or be sued under it—meant that the consumer would have no claim against the manufacturer, whose carelessness was the cause of their injuries but with whom they had no contract. Moreover, if the injury was suffered by someone other than the person who had bought the article, that person would have no claim against *anyone*, since they had no contractual relationship on which to ground it.

---

3. Winfield (1926a) above; Bob Hepple 'Negligence: The Search for Coherence' (1997) 50 *Current Legal Problems* 69; *Ibbetson*.
4. Winfield (1926a) above.

This was the stumbling block facing the claimant in ***Donoghue* v *Stevenson*.**[5]

Donoghue v *Stevenson* [1932] HL

Mrs Donoghue and a friend were enjoying a drink in a café in Paisley, near Glasgow. Mrs Donoghue had already consumed some of her ginger beer (brought by her friend) when said friend poured the remainder of the beer, from its dark opaque glass bottle, into a glass tumbler together with what appeared to be the remains of a decomposed snail. The shock of what she saw, together with the thought of what she had already drunk, led Mrs Donoghue to suffer shock and serious gastro-enteritis. She sought compensation for the shock and her illness from Stevenson, the manufacturer of the ginger beer, claiming that they were negligent in their production of the bottle of ginger beer. (She could not sue the café owner as, having not brought the drink, she had no contract with him on which to sue.)

The difficulty was that Mrs Donoghue also appeared to have no legal relationship with the manufacturer, who argued that this was not one of those pockets of 'exceptional cir- cumstances'—such as where a product was inherently dangerous—where a duty of care was recognised outside a contractual relationship.

Eventually the case made its way to the House of Lords where the law lords heard prelim- inary arguments on whether the alleged facts could give rise to a legal claim.[6] A split house (3:2) believed they did and allowed Mrs Donoghue's claim. Ultimately, the case was settled out of court—one result of which is that in the absence of any findings of fact, which would only have happened at trial, it was never established whether there was *in fact* a snail in Mrs Donoghue's bottle of ginger beer.

Why is this case so important? We can identify three separate conclusions or aspects of the decision of the majority (*Ibbetson* pp 190–1).

First, at its most narrow, ***Donoghue***, overruling *Winterbottom* v *Wright* [1842], recog- nised the existence of a new 'pocket' of liability, that is a further, isolated, situation where a duty of care was owed outside a contractual relationship:

> a manufacturer of products, which he sells in such a form as to show that he intends them to reach the ultimate consumer in the form in which they left him with no reason- able possibility of immediate examination, and with the knowledge that the absence of reasonable care in the preparation or putting up of the product will result in injury to the consumer's life or property, owes a duty to the consumer to take that reasonable care. (Lord Atkin at 599)

This understanding of the case, consistent with the reasoning of Lords Thankerton and Macmillan (who were in the majority with Lord Atkin), was the one preferred at the time.

---

5. The full title in the Law Reports reads *'M'Alister (or Donoghue) (Pauper)* v *Stevenson'* reflecting the Scottish practice of referring to a married woman in legal documents by both her married and maiden surnames. The correct citation is that which states her married surname (Donoghue) alone.

6. This means they were not deciding whether Mrs Donoghue's claim succeeded but rather whether *in law* she had an arguable case.

Secondly, and following on closely from this, the decision demonstrates that the 'categories of negligence are never closed' (Lord Macmillan at 619). In other words, the courts were prepared to recognise that new duty situations may arise, even if they are not necessarily closely analogous to previously recognised duties.

Finally, and most broadly, *Donoghue v Stevenson* can be seen to establish a single, universal requirement to take reasonable care as articulated, most obviously, in Lord Atkin's so-called 'Neighbour Principle' (discussed further below). It is for this reason that *Donoghue v Stevenson* is regarded as so important to the development of the tort of negligence.

The significance, and innovative reasoning, of the majority opinions in *Donoghue v Stevenson* can be best seen in contrast with the dissent of Lord Buckmaster—the most senior law lord present on a bench otherwise entirely comprised of law lords who had been appointed within the preceding five years. Rejecting any possibility of Mrs Donoghue's claim succeeding, he sought to restrict such claims to those who entered into a contractual relationship in line with current practice. He went on to quote with approval from the judgment of Lord Anderson in *Mullen v Barr & Co* [1929]:

> where the goods of the defenders are widely distributed throughout Scotland, it would seem little short of outrageous to make [the manufacturers] responsible to members of the public for the condition of the content of every bottle which issues from their works. (at 578)

Donoghue v Stevenson was a landmark decision. In particular, it established for the first time—and at a time of huge expansion of the market in consumer goods—that a manufacturer could be held liable to the ultimate consumer of their goods.[7] This expansion of liability beyond the contractual relationship and rejection of the so-called privity fallacy (which prevented tort claims where *any* contract existed between *any* of the parties) laid the crucial foundations for the subsequent developments in consumer protection.[8]

More fundamentally, Lord Atkin's opinion represents a watershed in the tort of negligence. Despite a preface to the contrary—'[t]o seek a complete logical definition of the general principle is probably to go beyond the function of the judge, for the more general the definition the more likely it is to omit essentials or to introduce non-essentials' (Lord Atkin at 580)—his leading majority opinion has since provided the foundations of a general principle of negligence liability. He noted that the courts had previously been 'engaged upon an elaborate classification of duties' as they existed in various factual scenarios (at 579). Instead, he argued that 'the duty which is common to all the cases where liability is established must logically be based upon some element common to the cases where it is found to exist' (at 580).

Lord Atkin's Neighbour Principle

It is hard to discuss the significance which judges and authors since 1932 have attached to the neighbour principle without writing the whole history of the tort of negligence (Heuston 1957, p 14).

→

7. Most notably in the opinion of Lord Macmillan (at 609–11).
8. See Chapter 13, pp 347–354.

→

As discussed above, Lord Atkin was not the first judge to attempt to formulate a general principle of negligence liability in tort law. Almost 50 years earlier, Brett MR (latterly Lord Esher), in *Heaven* v *Pender* [1883] had articulated a broad test grounded in the concept of foreseeability and again, ten years later, somewhat more narrowly, in *Le Lievre* v *Gould* [1893]: 'If one man is near to another, or is near to the property of another, a duty lies upon him not to do that which may cause a personal injury to that other, or may injure his property' (at 509).

This latter formulation met with more judicial and academic support, and ultimately formed the basis of Lord Atkin's neighbour principle:

> The rule that you must love your neighbour becomes in law: You must not injure your neighbour, and the lawyer's questions: Who is my neighbour? receives a restricted reply. You must take reasonable care to avoid acts or omissions which you can reasonably foresee would be likely to injure your neighbour. Who then in law is my neighbour? The answer seems to be—persons who are so closely and directly affected by my act that I ought reasonably to have them in contemplation as being so affected, when I am directing my mind to the acts or omissions which are called in question. (at 580–1)

In short, an individual must take reasonable care to avoid injuring those they can (or should) reasonably foresee will be injured if they do not take such care. Note, however, that Lord Atkin makes no reference to the specific type of damage in relation to which a duty of care may arise or to the way that damage may be caused.

Initially, despite the rhetorical flair of Lord Atkin's speech, which appeared to allow judges to come to more or less any conclusion they wished (*Ibbetson* p 191), it was Lord Macmillan's more measured approach (that limited the ratio of **Donoghue v Stevenson** to claims between manufacturers and consumers) that won the day. However, gradually thinking began to change and, by the 1970s, the tort of negligence had come to be seen as 'an ocean of liability for carelessly causing foreseeable harm, dotted with islands of non-liability, rather than as a crowded archipelago of individual duty situations' (*Ibbetson* pp 192–3). That is, rather than a gradual widening of specific duties, the courts appeared to be operating from an (excessively) broad principle of (almost) default liability wherever harm was caused by a defendant's careless conduct. See, for example, **McLoughlin v O'Brian** [1982] (psychiatric injury); **Anns v Merton London Borough Council** [1978] (economic loss) (overruled by **Murphy v Brentwood District Council** [1990]); *Benarr* v *Kettering HA* [1988] (where the claimants were awarded damages for the costs of bringing up a child, including the private school fees, where a child was born after a negligently performed sterilisation procedure); and **Home Office v Dorset Yacht Co Ltd** [1970] (liability imposed on the Home Office for damage inflicted by escaping young offenders).

Foreshadowing the 'compensation culture' claims of the early 1990s, it was increasingly being argued that far too many people were being made liable in too many situations. Thus throughout the 1980s and 1990s there was a general retrenchment of the tort of negligence, primarily by cutting back the situations in which a duty of care was held to arise (discussed in detail in the next chapter). There was a move by the judiciary to keep the tort of negligence in check by exercising greater caution and imposing liability only where there were clear precedents to do so or by relatively small incremental steps (*Caparo Industries plc v Dickman* [1990]). As such, negligence law appeared to have gone almost full circle. Rejecting a single general principle, the judges once more adopted a more restrictive approach to claims, working from established pockets of liability.

Since the late 1990s, however, the mood has appeared generally to be a little more expansive. The judicial retrenchment of the 1980s and early 1990s has gradually been relaxed and allowed increasingly for the expansion of negligence liability into a number of new situations—for example in relation to the 'messed up lives' claims (such as, *Phelps v Hillingdon London Borough Council* [2001] (negligent failure to diagnose dyslexia); *W v Essex County Council* [2000] (abusive foster child)).

 Pause for reflection

It is important to keep this legal context in mind as you learn more about the tort of negligence. The tort of negligence, like all legal rules and principles, is not 'timeless' or 'ageless'. Nor does each case stand in isolation from the others. As discussed further below (and throughout this book), much of tort (and negligence) law has been shaped by the political, social and economic context of the time in which various cases were decided. Consider, for example, the deliberate reigning in of tortious liability during the rampant individualism of the Thatcher years (1979–90), particularly in response to financial losses, or the impact of the unfortunate spate of significant public disasters—the sinking of the *Herald of Free Enterprise* in Zeebrugge harbour, the fire in the underground station at King's Cross, the destruction of the Piper Alpha oil rig, the Hillsborough Stadium disaster—or of the environmental movement on the torts of nuisance or trespass to land.

2.3 Explaining the historical development of the tort of negligence

The historical map described above provides an important backdrop to the development of the tort of negligence and a starting point from which to begin to understand and contextualise contemporary debates and difficulties within it. It also suggests, contrary to some accounts, that the development of the tort of negligence was not seamless, nor can it be regarded as inevitable or logically necessary. As *Conaghan & Mansell* point out, there is a tendency to paint a picture of this process of development by which:

> Negligence emerges from the chaos of the discredited writ system to form a new order based on the apparent self-evident soundness of the principle of reasonable care…Nineteenth-century judges are presented as moving 'subconsciously' towards the negligence principle while scarcely aware of it, directed inexorably and unerringly by the demands of logic and reason. (*Conaghan & Mansell* p 88)

So, just as interesting (and certainly as, if not more, important) as *what* happened is *why* it happened—why did negligence triumph as a principle of liability? What was its intended (as opposed to actual) function? What effect, if any, did the values and influences of the society from which this 'new' tort emerged have on its form and structure? Why did this fledgling tort prioritise 'fault' over the more historically common place strict liability?

A number of arguments have been made in the academic literature. We will look, briefly, at three:

(1) The influence of social and political thinking in an age of principles.

(2) A positive response to victims of workplace injuries.

(3) Strategic economic subsidisation of infant industries.[9]

2.3.1 The influence of social and political thinking in an age of principles

G Edward White, in his book *Tort Law in America—An Intellectual Tradition*, points to the importance of nineteenth-century intellectual trends and changing jurisprudential thought in reshaping the tort of negligence.[10] In the nineteenth century increased classification, conceptualisation and individualism were the order of the day—after all if Charles Darwin had uncovered the hidden order of the natural and social worlds (*On the Origins of the Species* was published in 1859) why, the 'lawyer-intellectuals' argued, should the same not be true for the legal world? Developments in America took the lead,[11] and then in 1887 some 45 years before **Donoghue v Stevenson**, Sir Frederick Pollock attempted to articulate a general theory of English tort law in his textbook *The Law of Torts*.

In a similar vein, Patrick Atiyah has drawn attention to the overlap between the fault principle and the individualistic principles of Victorian society and liberal individualism.[12] The prioritisation of individual responsibility and minimal state interference meant that the fault principle was far more attractive than the strict imposition of liability for all injuries caused by one's actions. The fault principle is liberal individualism made law. No one is responsible for the fate of others unless there is a positive reason for making them so. One such reason is the responsibilities arising out of a contract; another is where the individual is at fault (the fact that they could have chosen to act in another way, and thereby avoided creating a risk or harm, is sufficient to establish liability).

2.3.2 A positive response to victims of workplace injuries

Other commentators stress the importance of increased industrialisation in the development of the tort of negligence: 'the explosion of torts law and negligence in

---

9. For a more detailed exploration of the argument outlined here, the best place to start is *Conaghan & Mansell*'s discussion and critique of 'Historical Perspectives on Negligence', pp 81–104.

10. G Edward White *Tort Law in America—An Intellectual Tradition* (OUP, 2003, originally published in 1980), p 3.

11. Francis Hilliard *The Law of Torts* (2 vols, 1859); and Oliver Wendell Holmes 'Theory of Torts' (1873) 7 *American Law Review* 652.

12. Patrick Atiyah *The Rise and Fall of Freedom of Contract* (Clarendon Press, 1979).

particular must be entirely attributed to the age of engines and machines'.[13] However, opinions differ on the precise nature of this causal connection.

On one view the development of the tort of negligence was a positive response to the victims of industrialisation and a way of shifting the loss from one party to another at a time when there was little or no state support or system of insurance. The development of railways, road, factories, mines, quarries and such like had not only led to a vast rise in the numbers of accidents but also to changes in the nature of the relationship between the claimant and the defendant. Accidental injuries between strangers—in both the everyday and legal sense—were increasingly becoming the norm. Increasing mass production made it less likely that individuals would have a direct, contractual relationship with the manufacturer or producer of the goods they used. Whereas requiring them to establish a special relationship with those who injured them would have significantly restricted their ability to recover, the recognition of these claims within the scope of the new general duty of care facilitated the expansion of liability.

2.3.3 **Supporting infant industries**

In contrast to the positive conception of a positive and humane widening of negligence principles described above, Morton Horwitz adopts an explicitly 'instrumentalist' stance arguing that liability was *restricted* by the courts during this period through the prioritisation of the fault principle in order to protect and nurture fledging industries.[14] The essential basis of liability of tort in the eighteenth century was strict liability.[15] This meant that, though liability only arose in limited circumstances, where it did so, wrongdoers were liable for all injuries their actions caused even if they were not at fault. Were the new industries held to the same standard, Horwitz argues, the ensuing liability would have seriously impaired their growth and development. Thus, far from being a humane response to personal injuries, the development of the fault principle within the tort of negligence was an attempt by the courts to protect new industries from the crippling liability that would have followed had strict liability been imposed (*Conaghan & Mansell* p 91). Instead, they had to pay only when the victim established 'fault' on the part of the defendant, which was not easy to do.

This view gains some support from the doctrine of common employment, which, until its abolition by the Law Reform (Personal Injuries) Act 1948, prevented claims by employees against their employers for injuries sustained at work where their injury was caused by other employees.[16] Similarly, the defence of contributory negligence, until the Law Reform (Contributory Negligence) Act 1945, acted as an absolute bar to recovery in cases where the defendant was able to show that the claimant had (however slightly) contributed to their own injury.

---

13. Lawrence Friedmann *A History of American Law* (Simon & Schuster, 1972), p 261.

14. Morton Horwitz *The Transformation of American Law, 1780–1860* (Harvard University Press, 1977).

15. Although cf Winfield's criticism of this (Percy H Winfield 'The Myth of Absolute Liability' (1926b) 41 *Law Quarterly Review* 437).

16. Though the effects of this doctrine were somewhat reduced by the introduction of the Workmen's Compensation Act 1897. See Chapter 12, pp 311–312.

Counterpoint

It is, of course, possible to respond to Horwitz's arguments with the more balanced suggestion that while, on the one hand, in so far as liability is fault-based (as opposed to strict), then this does represent a lowering of the protection offered to an individual, on the other hand, a broad principle of negligence makes this (albeit) lower standard available to a greater number of people. If the courts were really concerned with insulating industry from legal liability, then it would have had no reason for expanding tort law in general, and the tort of negligence in particular, *at all*.

2.4 **The role of the modern law of negligence**

Today, despite greater state support for accident victims through social security payments and the NHS, the tort of negligence retains its place as the primary legal mechanism of accident compensation for personal injuries in the UK.[17] Moreover, alongside its role in determining compensation for accident victims, negligence—often treated as synonymous with 'accident law'—plays an important role in the *prevention* of accidents. The threat of a hefty compensation payout can have significant deterrent effects.[18] Unlike social security or other accident compensation schemes, awards of damages following a successful tort claim are (at least notionally) paid by the defendant responsible for inflicting the relevant harm.[19]

Despite its loss-shifting credentials, the tort of negligence operates more frequently as a loss-*spreading* device. Although the loss is shifted from the accident victim, the increasing availability of liability insurance means that it rarely falls on the individual defendant directly (indeed it is rarely worth suing an uninsured defendant, although the National Lottery winning defendant in *A v Hoare* [2008] may be the exception that proves the rule). Rather, it is shifted once again to the defendant's insurance company and, from there, spread across all those who have, and shall take out, policies with the company:

> Thus from the very outset negligence proves paradoxical. The goal to which it claims to aspire (loss shifting on the grounds of fault), it rarely attains and the idea against which it stands in opposition (loss spreading among those who are not at fault), is its most commonplace effect. (*Conaghan & Mansell* pp 12–13)

We may consider that this move away from the fault principle is no bad thing. Presumably, the increased use of insurance means that more claims are likely to be met. Moreover, those claims will end up being met by those in the best position to pay. Finally, in so far as the imposition of tort liability might otherwise lead to undesirable practices—for instance, the fear that holding doctors liable could lead to 'defensive medicine' (see Denning LJ in *Roe v Ministry of Health* [1954])—the fact that such

17. See generally *Cane*.
18. On the deterrence aspect of tort law see further *Harlow* pp 37–41.
19. Though, it should be noted that there are exceptions to this—see, in particular, the discussion of vicarious liability in Chapter 12, pp 324–338.

losses are often passed on by insurance provides further benefits. Nevertheless, the fact that in many instances it is not the 'wrongdoer' who ends up compensating the claimant seems to clash significantly with the tort of negligence's intellectual and moral underpinnings (*Ibbetson* pp 196–9).

2.5 The elements of the tort of negligence

As established above, the tort of negligence is, according to Percy H Winfield's enduring definition, 'the breach of a legal duty to take care resulting in damage, undesired by the defendant, to the claimant'.[20] His three-fold presentation remains the mainstay of most tort textbooks and neatly encapsulates the three essential elements of the tort. Thus, in order to establish a successful claim in the tort of negligence there needs to be:

(1) a legal **duty** owed by the defendant to the claimant to take care;

(2) a **breach** of this duty by the defendant; and

(3) damage to the claimant, **caused** by the breach, which is not considered by the courts to be too remote.

A number of preliminary points need to be made here before looking at each of these elements in more detail.

First, the defendant may be able to raise a defence which may either defeat the claim entirely or reduce the amount of damages paid.[21] Secondly, each element of a negligence claim is necessary, but not sufficient, in order to establish liability. Without a recognised legal duty of care between the defendant and claimant, for example, no liability will attach to even the most extreme acts of neglect; similarly, if no damage is caused by the defendant's breach of their duty of care—or the damaged caused is too remote—the defendant will not be liable.

Finally, in any given claim there may be more than one defendant, as well as multiple claimants. Where two or more parties act together in pursuit of a common design or plan and cause the same damage, each will be *jointly and severally liable*. This means that the claimant may choose to sue each party separately for the entirety of the damage or sue both jointly in the same action.[22] *Several concurrent* liability arises where the negligent actions of two or more parties acting independently cause the same damage—for example, where the claimant's car is hit by two cars both causing the claimant to suffer whiplash.[23] In this case, as with joint defendants, each party is liable separately for the entirety of the damage (although the claimant can only recover once). The distinction between the two types of defendants is largely historical; there is, in fact, very little substantive or practical difference between joint and several defendants.[24]

---

20. Winfield (1926a) above.

21. See Chapter 10.

22. The Civil Liability (Contribution) Act 1978 allows the court to apportion damages between the parties responsible (or leave them to do this for themselves).

23. See further *Fitzgerald* v *Lane* [1987].

24. Contribution between defendants is discussed further in Chapter 19.

2.5.1 **Duty**

A defendant will only be liable for their carelessness if they owe the claimant a legal duty to take care. Carelessness alone (however great) is not enough:

> The law takes no cognizance of carelessness in the abstract. It concerns itself with carelessness only where there is a duty to take care and where failure in that duty has caused damage. (Lord Macmillan, *Donoghue* v *Stevenson* at 618)

The existence (or otherwise) of a duty of care essentially acts as a control mechanism restricting or extending liability. In most cases, however, establishing a duty will be straightforward. It is, for example, well established that a car driver owes a duty of care to other road users and that a doctor owes a duty of care to patients in their care (*Pippin* v *Sheppard* [1822]). Such cases are more likely to give rise to *factual* uncertainties—for example, how fast was the car going? What did/did not the doctor do?—as opposed to specific *legal* difficulties. These questions raise issues of breach, and, occasionally, causation (see further below).

However, occasionally (but significantly), a court will have to consider whether a duty of care is or should be owed on the facts. As we have seen already, despite the broad statement of Lord Atkin in **Donoghue**, the courts have latterly placed significant limitations on the situations in which a duty to take care will arise. This is particularly apparent in what might be called 'problematic' duty areas—for example, where the injury suffered by the claimant is psychiatric or purely economic, where the defendant is a public body, where the harm is caused by someone for whom the defendant was responsible (acts of third parties) or where injury is suffered as a result of the defendant's failure to act (an omission) rather than any 'positive' actions. In these areas, the courts have in general either held that there is no duty on the part of the defendants or severely restricted its scope (often for 'public policy' reasons) in an effort to contain liability. Put another way, the courts employ the concept of the duty of care as a means to *deny* liability (often in the context of significant carelessness) where they consider that it would be inappropriate to hold the defendant liable.

2.5.2 **Breach**

To say that the defendant owes a duty of care is also to say that their conduct must meet a certain standard—the standard of 'reasonable care'. Accordingly, a defendant will breach their duty of care where their conduct falls below the standard the law has set. The requirement that a defendant will be liable in the tort of negligence only where they have failed to exercise reasonable care suggests that negligence liability is both premised and dependent upon *fault*. It is not enough to show that the defendant harmed the claimant; liability depends on the defendant having harmed the claimant as a result of failing to show reasonable care.

The fault principle lies at the heart of the tort of negligence. It works in two ways:

> first, . . . a person who causes loss or damage to another by fault should be required to compensate that other; and, secondly, . . . a person who causes loss or damage to another without fault should *not* be required to compensate that other. (*Cane* p 35)

Though most would agree that liability should follow where fault is present, the reverse is more problematic. The principle of 'no liability without fault' works well for defendants. It is, however, less attractive for claimants who, in the absence of fault, may be left to bear the entirety of their losses.

Finally, we may note that, since negligence in law is a failure to meet a standard of care, 'negligence' here does not describe a particular state of mind but rather the 'quality' of their conduct. A defendant who deliberately runs over a claimant with their car is just as negligent—in the sense of having failed to show reasonable care for the claimant—as one who runs down the claimant inadvertently when changing the station on their car radio.

 Pause for reflection

Though it is useful to talk about negligence law being fault-based, the concept of fault employed in the tort of negligence is a *legal*, and not necessarily a *moral*, standard. Only certain moral 'wrongs' give rise to liability in tort. Hence, it is possible to deliberately walk past the ubiquitous child drowning in a puddle without (usually) fearing any *legal* consequences (see Chapter 4, pp 74–77). But what of the driver who forgets to indicate right as they pull out into the outside lane of the M25 causing a major road accident? By contrast, sometimes liability will attach in the tort of negligence to people whom most would consider in no way morally culpable (an example of which is provided by *Nettleship v Weston* [1971]). Moreover, even where those liable in negligence are morally blameworthy, the consequences of liability can appear entirely disproportionate to their moral blame. For example, a single, momentary lapse of concentration will lead to extraordinary legal culpability (*Cane* p 175). Do you think this is fair? Think again about the role the concept of 'duty of care' plays (see further discussion in Chapter 3).

2.5.3 Causation and remoteness

The final element of a claim in the tort of negligence is causation—the damage suffered by the claimant must have been *caused* by the defendant's breach of their duty. The claimant must prove not only that the defendant was at fault (that they breached their duty of care) and that they suffered a recognisable harm, but also that this was *as a result* of the defendant's actions—that is, that there is a causal link between the defendant's fault and the damage caused, which means both that the defendant factually *caused* the claimant's loss (factual causation) and that the loss caused is not too *remote* (sometimes called legal causation). This is not as straightforward as one might think. What constitutes a causal link is often one of the trickiest questions in this area of law.

2.5.4 Putting it all together

Establishing liability in the tort of negligence breaks down into three questions:

(1) Does the defendant owe the claimant a **duty of care**?

(2) Has the defendant **breached this duty** by falling below the required standard of care in the circumstances of the case? (Or, more roughly, is the defendant at fault?)

(3) Is the defendant's breach of their duty both the factual and legal **cause** of the claimant's injury?

To this can be added a fourth question:

(4) Is the defendant able to raise any partial or full **defences** to the claimant's action?

The elements of the tort of negligence

Duty + Breach + (Causation – Remoteness) – Defences = the tort of negligence

---

We will look at each question in turn in Part I of this book, however, it is important to recognise from the outset that the elements of the tort of negligence are not as self-contained as Winfield's checklist suggests.

 Counterpoint

The presentation of the tort in this way is theoretically problematic—it suggests the elements to the tort of negligence have clearer boundaries than they actually have. In fact, as we shall see, certain ideas and concepts—notably foreseeability—crop up at a number of different stages, and cut across these supposedly distinct elements. Moreover, this linear presentation of the elements of a negligence claim suggests a logic and consistency of approach which, some argue, fails to represent what the courts are actually doing, and the reasoning they are really employing when deciding cases. Indeed, sometimes the judges have admitted as much. Consider the following extracts from Lord Denning MR's judgments in *Spartan Steel* v *Martin & Co* [1973] and *Lamb* v *Camden London Borough Council* [1981]:

> The more I think about these cases, the more difficult I find it to put each into its proper pigeon-hole. Sometimes I say: 'There was no duty.' In others I say: 'The damage was too remote.' So much so that I think the time has come to discard those tests which have proved so elusive. (*Spartan Steel* v *Martin & Co* at 37)

> The truth is that all these three, duty, remoteness and causation, are all devices by which the courts limit the range of liability for negligence … As I have said … 'it is not every consequence of a wrongful act which is the subject of compensation'. The law has to draw a line somewhere. Sometimes it is done by limiting the range of persons to whom a duty is owed. Sometimes it is done by saying that there is a break in the chain of causation. At other times it is done by saying that the consequence is too remote to be a head of damage. All these devices are useful in their way. But ultimately it is a question of policy for the judges to decide. (*Lamb* v *Camden London Borough Council* at 636)

It may be that Lord Denning is overstating things somewhat. It is simply wrong to think that judges are entitled and do habitually choose to disregard legal rules and/or precedent (although they do, of course, have considerable freedom in their interpretation).

However, it does show that those looking for a clear equation which determines when liability in negligence arises are likely to be left empty-handed. The tests and elements developed by the courts to analyse and decide such claims are not entirely meaningless, but nor are they (at least in practice) concrete, clear and distinct.

Finally, in so far as we can meaningfully distinguish the various elements of a negligence claim, though each—duty, breach, causation—are essential for a claim to succeed, they are not always *all* at issue. Sometimes duty is straightforward (for example in road traffic accidents), while at other times is it more problematic (for example in relation to claims for psychiatric injury). Similarly, while it is clear that the speeding driver (absent exceptional circumstances, such as transporting an accident victim) will be in breach of their duty of care, it may be more difficult to establish, for example, the appropriate standard of care required of a doctor in any given case and a causal link between the doctor's actions and the harm suffered by the claimant. Put another way, the legal 'hurdles' of duty, breach and causation may be easier or harder for the claimant to scale depending on the facts of the case.

Some examples may help here:

Alcock v *Chief Constable of South Yorkshire Police* [1992]

Alcock is one of a number of cases arising out of the Hillsborough Stadium disaster (see box on pp 105–106). The claimants were friends and family of people who had died in the disaster and who suffered psychiatric injury. The question for the court was whether the police owed them a duty of care. Although the House of Lords held that the police did not owe the claimants a duty of care in relation to the psychiatric injury they suffered, had they decided otherwise, the issues of breach and causation would have been relatively straightforward. In other words, it was clear that the defendants had failed to show reasonable care and that their carelessness had caused the claimants' loss. What was at stake was whether the law did indeed regard the defendants as under an obligation to take reasonable care. This can be represented (rather crudely) by the diagram below.

Figure 2.1 Case example: *Alcock* v *Chief Constable of South Yorkshire Police* [1992]

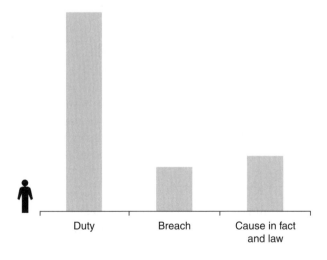

Duty   Breach   Cause in fact and law

Bolton v *Stone* [1951]

In *Bolton* v *Stone* the claimant was hit on the head outside her house by a cricket ball hit by a player from an adjacent cricket pitch. It was clear that the defendant cricket club owed her a duty of care not to cause her physical injury. Moreover, there was no doubt that it was because of their activities—allowing cricket to be played at the ground—that the claimant suffered her injury. The key question for the court was one of breach—had the defendant fallen below the appropriate standard of care? The focus of the case was on the breach stage, with the duty and causation questions being more straightforward.

Figure 2.2 Case example: *Bolton* v *Stone* [1951]

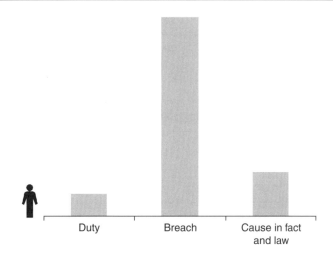

| Duty | Breach | Cause in fact and law |

Fairchild v *Glenhaven Funeral Services* [2002]

This case involved claims by three employees who had developed mesothelioma as a result of being exposed to asbestos dust while working for the defendants. It is well established that employers owe their employees a duty of care. Moreover, it was plain on the facts that, by exposing the claimants to asbestos dust, the defendants had failed to take reasonable care for their safety. The key question was one of causation. Since each of the claimants had worked for a number of different employers, each of which had exposed them to asbestos fibres, the claimants had difficulty showing which employer was responsible for their illness given that their condition may have stemmed from inhaling a single asbestos fibre on one isolated occasion. In other words, though each of the defendant employers *could have* caused the relevant harm, it was much harder (indeed impossible) to prove which one actually *did*.

Morris v *Murray* [1991]

Morris and Murray had spent the afternoon drinking in the pub after which they decided to take Murray's light airplane for a spin. Morris drove them both to the airfield and helped to prepare the plane for take-off. Shortly after the plane took off it

Figure 2.3 Case example: *Fairchild* v *Glenhaven Funeral Services* [2002]

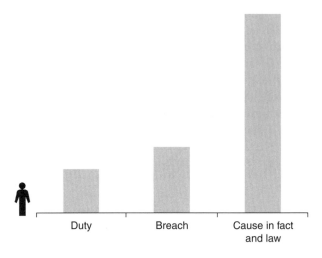

Figure 2.4 Case example: *Morris* v *Murray* [1991]

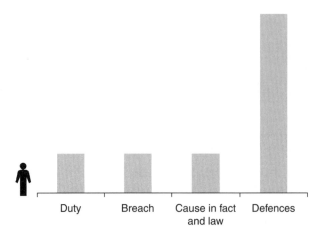

crashed, killing Murray (who was flying the plane) and seriously injuring Morris. It was clear that Murray had been negligent, however his estate successfully met Morris's claim for compensation with the defence that he had voluntarily assumed the risk of injury by Murray's negligence.

 Pause for reflection

The purpose of these very straightforward diagrams is simply to illustrate the varying importance of, or difficulty in establishing, each element of the tort of negligence in these →

cases. They are not in any way mathematical and have no numerical scale—they are purely to give the reader a general impression of the relative importance of each 'hurdle'. What they show is that, though in *every* case each element of the tort must be present for the claim to succeed, in practice only one or two are likely to be at issue. The uncontroversial aspects of the case will be glossed over relatively quickly.[25]

Of course, these diagrams cannot convey the details of the case. Nevertheless, readers may find it helpful as they begin thinking about the tort of negligence to consider where the 'hurdle' or 'hurdles' arise in the cases they are reading and what a similarly constructed diagram of these cases would look like.

2.6 Case example: *X & Y* v *London Borough of Hounslow*

In order for there to be a successful claim in the tort of negligence duty, breach and causation must be established. This is clearly demonstrated in *X & Y* v *London Borough of Hounslow* [2008].[26] Though the decision of Maddison J has since been overruled by the Court of Appeal (*X & Y* v *London Borough of Hounslow* [2009]),[27] his judgment remains an excellent example of how the ingredients of a negligence claim fit together. For this reason we have annotated *the first instance judgment*, making reference to where the view of the Court of Appeal differed (see comments in bold).[28]

 Pause for reflection

In his comment on the case Richard Mullender notes:

The body of negligence doctrine applied by Maddison J and the Court of Appeal in *X and Y* is fraught with tension. Judges are sensitive to the demands of corrective justice . . . But judges are also aware that they may, by imposing liability on public bodies, deflect them from the pursuit of the public interest . . . [Both] were at work in *X and Y*. The Court of Appeal's response was to read the relevant doctrine narrowly and to emphasise the Council's many responsibilities to the public . . . [The alternative was to conclude] that the close relationship between the couple and the Council made them neighbours in Lord Atkin's sense.[29]

---

25. The same is true of problem questions in tort courses and exams. These will tend to focus on particular issues in or aspects of the tort of negligence. However, again, it should not be forgotten that all these elements must be proved and so a complete answer must address each stage.

26. The legal issues raised by this case, and the Court of Appeal judgment, are discussed further in Chapter 6, pp 164–165.

27. Although permission to appeal to the Supreme Court was refused, the claimants (and 'Z', X's mother) have taken their case to the ECtHR alleging violations of Arts 3 and 8.

28. For a concise summary and discussion of the different approaches adopted by the trial judge and Court of Appeal see Richard Mullender 'Negligence, Neighbourliness, and the Welfare State' (2009) *Cambridge Law Journal* 507.

29. Ibid, p 509.

➡

X & Y is then also an excellent example of the differing priorities of judges and the way in which legal rules can be interpreted to reach very different conclusions depending on their understanding of the issues at stake. Mullender suggests the Court of Appeal's decision ought to be understood in a context in which the growth of the welfare state is such that 'neighbourliness is a luxury that society cannot afford' (p 509).

As you read the judgment below, think about whether Maddison J would agree with Mullender's view.

X & Y (Protected parties represented by their litigation friend the Official Solicitor) v London Borough of Hounslow

An officer of the Supreme Court who acts for people with disabilities (see Supreme Court Act 1981, s 90).

High Court of Justice Queen's Bench Division [2008] EWHC 1168 (QB)

Note the date of the incident—compared with the date of trial.

The claimants, X and Y, are claiming damages against the defendants, the London Borough of Hounslow, in the tort of negligence and under sections 6 and 7 of the Human Rights Act 1998. The claims arose out of an 'ordeal' which the claimants suffered in their council flat at the hands of local youths in November 2000 where, over the course of a weekend, the claimants (both of whom had learning difficulties) were imprisoned in their flat and repeatedly assaulted and (sexually) abused (often in front of their two children). This account of the facts is taken from Maddison J's judgment:

These claims were not revived in the Court of Appeal [36].

[5]...X said that at one stage the youths confined him and Y to their bedroom, and made them perform sexual acts. They threw many of X's and Y's possessions over the balcony. They forced pepper and fluid into X's eyes. They locked him in the bathroom for a time, in the dark. They made him drink urine, eat dog biscuits, dog faeces and the faeces of one of the youths, threatening him that he would be stabbed if he did not. They made him put a vibrator up his bottom, and then lick it. They sprayed kitchen cleaner in his mouth, face and hair. They slashed him repeatedly all over his body with a knife or knives. Y's statement was to similar effect, adding that she too was made to put the vibrator in her mouth. The children too were abused, assaulted and locked in their bedroom from time to time. Even the family dog was abused. It is unnecessary to go into further detail, or into the physical and psychological injuries suffered by the Claimants as a result.

The claimants argued that, amongst other things, the defendant should have foreseen that they were in imminent physical danger at their flat and should have arranged for them to be accommodated elsewhere. The claimants and their family were known to the defendants. Although they lived as a unit in the community, the family was seen as vulnerable and two sections of the defendant's Social Services Department had been engaged with the family prior to the relevant weekend. These were the Community Team for People with Learning Disabilities ('CTPLD') and the Children and Families section ('C & F').

The defendant strongly contested liability. They denied they owed the claimants a duty of care, pointing out that in no previous case had a local

➡

authority been held to be under a duty of care to protect vulnerable adults from abuse by third parties and that any failings in this regard are only justiciable, if at all, within the forum of public law, and not by way of actions for damages of the kind brought here. Still less, argued the defendant, did it breach any such duty of care: what happened during the relevant weekend was caused by third parties, and was not reasonably foreseeable.

After setting out the background to the case in detail, Mr Justice Maddison turned to the law:

The Law

[84] The liability of local authorities in negligence and under the Human Rights Act 1998 and the European Convention on Human Rights is a complex and developing area of the law. It is perhaps for this reason that I have been referred by Counsel to well over 40 authorities. I have found some helpful, but by no means all. In one of them, *Midland Bank Trust Co. Ltd and Another v Hett Stubbs & Kemp (a firm)* [1979] 1 Ch 384 at 405B Oliver J said

> I have been lead by counsel through a bewildering complex of authorities many of which are not easily reconciled with the principles established in subsequent cases in superior courts or, in some case, with one another. The task of a judge of the first instance faced with this situation is not an easy one.

That observation, with which I sympathise, has provided some relief and comfort during my trawl of the authorities cited to me. Otherwise, I have not found the *Midland Bank* case helpful.

The Test to be Applied

[85] I first consider the test that should be applied to determine whether or not the Defendant owed the Claimants a duty of care. I have been taken to authorities in which it has been observed that the courts may be prepared to find that a duty of care exists more readily in cases involving injury or damage to person or property than in those involving only economic loss. (See e.g. *Caparo Industries Ltd v Dickman* [1990] 2 AC 605 at page 618, per Lord Bridge.) I have also been referred to authorities illustrating that important if not determinative factors in deciding whether or not a duty of care exists may be the assumption by the defendant concerned of responsibility toward the claimant concerned (see e.g. *Hedley Byrne v Heller & Partners* [1964] AC 465) or the degree of proximity between the parties (see e.g. *Perrett v Collins* [1998] 2 Lloyd's Rep 255 at page 261 per Hobhouse L.J.). In the event, I do not need to consider such authorities in any detail because, at the conclusion of the oral argument, counsel appeared to accept that the proper test to apply in this case was the familiar tri-partite test deriving from the *Caparo* case referred to above. I agree with this approach. Given that I am dealing, as

→

[Margin notes:]

Essentially what the defendants are arguing is that the court is not in a position to judge or adjudicate on the case—that it falls outside its remit. See further Chapter 6, pp 156–160.

This is true. The 'public bodies' chapter (Chapter 6) is one of the longest, and most complicated, chapters in this book.

Establishing a duty of care is the first element of any claim in the tort of negligence.

This is the leading case on establishing a duty of care in novel areas of the tort of negligence.

It is worth noting here that Sir Anthony Clarke MR who gave the judgment of the court in the Court of Appeal did not approach the case in this way—rather he focused on whether the defendants had 'assumed responsibility' for the claimants noting that this claim falls outside cases where the courts have previously imposed negligence liability [60].

'per' here means that the principle or dictum is quoted on 'the authority of' (that is, can be found in) Lord Bridge's opinion.

This is the Caparo three-stage 'test' for establishing a duty of care (used when it is not possible to find a duty 'incrementally'):

(1) the injury or loss is reasonably foreseeable;
(2) there is sufficient proximity between the parties; and
(3) it is fair, just and reasonable to impose a duty. See further Chapter 3, pp 61–69.

As this is a 'new' duty area, it is not possible to find a duty of care using the so-called 'incremental approach'. See further Chapter 3, pp 66–68.

→ stated above, with a difficult and developing area of the law, and given that no previous case has established that a local authority owes a duty of care to adults in circumstances such as those arising in this case, I think it right that I should find that a duty of care existed only if I am satisfied that the injury and loss suffered by the Claimants was reasonably foreseeable; that their relationship with the Defendant was sufficiently proximate to warrant the imposition of the duty of care; and that it would be just, fair and reasonable to impose such a duty.

This is the *Caparo* three-stage 'test' for establishing a duty of care (used when it is not possible to find a duty 'incrementally').

[Maddison J then established that the defendant could be treated as a single entity.]

This aspect of Maddison J's judgment was rejected by the Court of Appeal [67].

Was the Injury and Loss Reasonably Foreseeable?

[93] I therefore turn to consider whether the Defendant should reasonably have foreseen the injury and loss which the Claimants suffered. The authorities cited to me establish that the Claimants must show that it was reasonably foreseeable that they would suffer an assault by local youths at their home of the general kind that actually happened; but need not show that the Defendant should have envisaged "the precise concatenation of circumstances" which led up to the incident (see *Hughes v Lord Advocate* [1963] AC 837 at p 853 per Lord Morris) or the precise form the assault would take (see by way of analogy *Jolley v London Borough of Sutton* [2000] 1 WLR 1082). The fact that the injury and loss resulted from the acts of third parties would not by itself prevent that injury and loss from being foreseeable but it would be reasonable to expect someone to foresee such third party intervention only if it was highly likely or probable (see e.g. *Smith v Littlewoods Organisation Ltd* ([1987] 1 AC 241 at p 261 E to G per Lord Mackay of Clashfern).

This is the first stage of the *Caparo* test.

This is what needs to be established as reasonably foreseeable in order for the first stage of the *Caparo* test to be satisfied—the injury must be of the same general kind. This is clarified in relation to the acts of third parties in the next sentence. We discuss issues relating to the establishment of a duty of care for the acts of third parties in more detail in Chapter 4.

[94] The chronology of events…seems to me to point a picture of gradually mounting concern about the welfare and safety of the Claimants and their family. It is true that in some respects the Claimants could lead normal lives. It is also true that they were anxious to preserve their independence, to the extent that they sometimes resented and resisted the efforts of the Defendant's Social Services Department to help them. However, the repeated concerns, expressed by Z and the Defendant's own Social Services Department about the Claimants' vulnerability, their ability to keep themselves and their children safe, the unsuitability of their home and the condition in which they kept it, the way in which the children were being looked after, and the suspicion that the children had been sexually abused by others, tell their own story. In addition, there was information from Z that X had been attacked from time to time both in Wandsworth and Hounslow; and although there may have been times when the Defendant regarded Z as a thorn in its side, I see no reason why the information she provided should have been seen as unreliable.

'Z' is X's mother.

[95] In my judgment, these mounting concerns made it reasonably foreseeable from an early stage that the Claimants and/or the children might in some manner come to some sort of harm. However, despite the number and variety of different concerns and the frequency with which they were expressed, they would not in my judgment be sufficient to satisfy the first of the three *Caparo* conditions as explained…above. What needs to be asked is whether, and if so when, events gathered pace to the extent that the harm

This seems to suggest foreseeability.

→

that was reasonably foreseeable changed from harm of a general ill-defined nature to harm resulting from an attack of the kind that happened during the relevant weekend. In my judgment, this development did indeed take place, and the events that made critical difference began early in September 2000. They took the form of the infiltration and ultimately the taking-over of the Claimants' flat by local youths; the development of a state of disorder and then of chaos or near-chaos at the flat; the assault on X at McDonalds; the making of threats to the Claimants; the obtaining of keys to the flat by youths who did not live there; and the reluctance of the Claimants through fear to complain about what was happening to them. That is not to say that the events occurring before September 2000 are irrelevant. Though insufficient by themselves in my view to establish the required degree of foreseeability, they did provide the background against which the events occurring in and after September 2000 could and should have been considered and assessed. [...]

[*The judge then went on to detail the incidents of violence and intimidation against the claimants (known to the defendants) between September and November 2000.*]

[106] ... it was in my judgment reasonably, indeed clearly foreseeable that either or both of the Claimants would suffer a serious physical attack from local youths in their flat. In my judgment the danger of this happening should have been foreseen at the very latest by 7th November when, to the Defendant's knowledge, the prior assaults, threats, infiltration of the Claimants' home, dumping of stolen goods and arrests had been followed by the variety of complaints from neighbours referred to above. However, in my judgment it could and should reasonably have been foreseen by 20th October when Tajinder Hayre's letter of 18th October was received by the Defendant's Housing Department, given what was already known to the Defendant by then.

Was there a Relationship of Sufficient Proximity?

[107] The Claimants having thus cleared the first hurdle, as it were, I consider whether they and the Defendant were in a relationship sufficiently proximate to warrant the imposition of the duty of care. In my judgment they were, for reasons that can be explained comparatively briefly. The Defendant was the Claimants' landlord. More importantly, the Defendant, aware of the Claimants' disabilities, provided social services for them and indeed for their children. [...]

Just, Fair and Reasonable

[108] I therefore turn to consider whether it would be just fair and reasonable to impose a duty of care on the Defendant. It is convenient to begin by considering the scope of the duty contended for. The more widely based this is, the more difficult it might be to argue that it would be just, fair and reasonable to impose it.

[109] Vulnerable though they were, the Claimants do not suggest that the Defendant was under a general duty to protect them from harm. They were living independent lives in the community, and life is not free from risk and danger. The Defendant did not purport to provide policing or security

---

However, in order for the claimant's injury to be 'reasonably foreseeable' it must be established that the defendants had (or should have had) *more* than a general awareness that the family might come to some sort of harm. That is, the defendants must have been aware of the possibility of the claimants suffering a serious physical assault.

This aspect was considered by the Court of Appeal which held that: 'Given our view that there was here no relevant assumption of responsibility or other considerations such as those discussed in the *Gorringe* [relating to statutory duties] and *Mitchell* cases we have reached a different conclusion on the question whether it would be fair, just and reasonable to impose a duty of care of the kind suggested on the council. We do not think that it would' [93].

This is a point not often acknowledged—the narrower the scope of the duty is (if found), the less likely it is that allowing it will 'open the floodgates' to future claims.

The first stage of the *Caparo* test is met.

One of the claimants' social workers.

This is the second aspect of the *Caparo* test. It is easily established.

The final stage of the *Caparo* test is whether the imposition of a duty of care is 'fair, just and reasonable'. This essentially allows the court to consider matters of policy etc that might weigh against (or for) there being a duty of care.

→

services. It would plainly not be fair, just and reasonable to impose such a broadly-based duty on the Defendant.

[110] However the Claimants do contend in essence that the Defendant became under a duty to protect them in a particular way, namely by moving them out of their flat and into some form of alternative accommodation at some stage before the relevant weekend. All parties accept that in practical terms there was nothing else the Defendant could have done to prevent the Claimants from being assaulted and abused as they were during the relevant weekend.

[*The judge considers arguments as to when the defendants should have moved the claimants out of their flat.*]

This is the potential scope of the defendant's duty—it is not a general duty to take care but rather a specific duty to move the claimants to alternative accommodation.

[116]...if it was not the Defendant's duty to move the Claimants out of the flat long before the relevant weekend, it certainly became their duty to protect them by doing so in response to the developing crisis towards the end of 2000. I accept that submission. I return to my earlier findings that by about 20th October 2000 an attack of the kind that the Claimants suffered during the relevant weekend was reasonably foreseeable, and that the Defendant had the power and the procedures in place to move the Claimants on an emergency basis. Subject to the further discussion below, in those circumstances I would regard it as fair, just and reasonable to impose upon the Defendant a narrowly-defined duty to move the Claimants out of the flat in response to the unusual but dangerous situation which had developed.

The third stage of establishing a duty seems to be met...cf **the view of the Court of Appeal [91–93].**

Having established that the defendants might owe the claimants a narrowly framed duty to move them out of their flat once the dangerous situation had become apparent, Maddison J then goes on to consider arguments to the contrary.

[117] I now consider whether there are any other features of the case which would suggest that it would or would not be fair, just and reasonable to impose a duty of care. I have borne in mind the absence of any previous decided case establishing liability in similar circumstances. That is not of course determinative of the present case. However, regard must be had to the following dictum of Brennan J. in *Sutherland Shire Council v Heyman* (1985) ALR 1, at p 44:

> It is preferable, in my view, that the law should develop novel categories of negligence incrementally and by analogy with established categories, rather than by a massive extension of a prima facie duty of care restrained only by indefinable considerations which ought to negative or to reduce or to limit the scope of the duty or the class of persons to whom it is owed.

[118] This dictum has often been cited with approval in the courts of England and Wales, for example by Lord Bridge in the *Caparo* case at p 618.

[119] It is well-established that local authorities may, in certain circumstances, owe a duty of care to children, for example in relation to the investigation of suspected child abuse and the initiation and pursuit of care proceedings (see *JD and others v East Berkshire NHS Trust and Others* [2003] Lloyd's Law Reports 552) and in relation to the return of children previously placed in foster care to their natural parents (see *Pierce v Doncaster MBC* [2007] EWHC 2968). In the present case the Claimants, though adults, both functioned in many ways like children. No adult of normal intellect and understanding was living in their household. The Defendant knew this, and

This refers to the so-called 'incremental approach' to establishing a duty of care (see further Chapter 3, pp 61–66). The difficulty with this approach is that if we were to take it seriously, if a party is unfortunate enough to suffer an injury in a unique way, so that no case similar to theirs has been brought to court, then its claim will fail, not because it is unmeritorious, but for the simple, and highly unsatisfactory, reason that they are the first person to bring such a claim. It is usually taken to mean that the three-stage test ought to be used to develop the law incrementally (indeed this is how Maddison J uses it). The relationship between the two ways of establishing a duty of care is discussed further in Chapter 3.

→

had allocated a social worker to both their cases. In my judgment, the extension of a duty of care to the Claimants would involve a small step rather than a giant leap forward, and would not offend the "incremental" principle enunciated by Brennan J. This is so particularly since, for the reasons explained above, the duty to be imposed, if any, would be of a very narrow and case-specific nature, and as such would not open the gates to a flood of future claims that would not otherwise have been brought.

[120] I have not overlooked the fact that in the *JD* case it was held by the Court of Appeal (and indeed by the House of Lords on a further appeal) that no separate duty of care was owed to the adult parents of the children concerned; and that a similar conclusion was reached by the Court of Appeal in *Lawrence v Pembrokeshire County Council* [2007] 1 WLR 2991. However, the position of the Claimants is in my judgment much closer akin to that of the children concerned in those cases than to that of their parents; and this case does not involve any conflict of interest between parent and child that prompted the refusal of the parents' claims in the cases just cited.

[121] Does the fact that the direct cause of the Claimants' injury and loss was the actions of third parties over whom the Defendant had no control mean that it would be unjust, unfair or unreasonable to impose a duty of care? In my view, it does not. It is clear from the *Littlewoods* case referred to in paragraph 93 above that the actions of such third parties are capable of founding an action in the tort of negligence. The Defendant is protected by the principle that a high degree of foresight is required in such cases.

[122] A further factor which it seems to me can properly be taken into account, though by itself it is not determinative of the issue, is the advent of the Human Rights Act 1998 and its incorporation of the European Convention on Human Rights into domestic law. The authorities appear to show a greater willingness to find the existence of duties of care subsequent to the passing of the Act.

[*The judge then looks at two cases by way of example and dismisses the relevance of the defendant's apology to the claimants.*]

[126] Accordingly, I find that it would be just, fair and reasonable to impose on the Defendant a duty of care of the kind contended for.

Breach of Duty

[127] The next question to be considered is whether or not the Defendant was in breach of its duty of care to the Claimants. In the context of this case, the question becomes whether or not the Defendant could and should have moved the Claimants out of their flat before the relevant weekend.

[*First the judge considered whether the defendants could have moved the claimants and their procedures for doing so.*]

[132] ... Given my earlier conclusion (which some might see as generous to the Defendant) that an assault of the kind that occurred during the relevant weekend first became reasonably foreseeable on or about 20th October 2000, in my judgment this emergency system was the only one available to the Defendant which could have been deployed to move the Claimants out of their flat before the relevant weekend.

Often, as we shall see, it is hard to establish a duty of care when the harm was caused by the actions of third parties (such as the youths in this case)—see Chapter 4.

Again the Court of Appeal came to a different conclusion in relation to this: 'If anyone assumed responsibility towards the claimants it was [the social worker] and, in our judgment, if anyone was at fault it was her. In our judgment, it follows from the fact that no such suggestion has been made that it is accepted that [the social worker's] approach was one which a reasonable social worker could reasonably take. It further follows that it is accepted that she could not be in breach of duty because of the principles in *Bolam v Friern Hospital Management Committee* [1957]' [98].

Here Maddison J is distinguishing the facts of *JD* and *Lawrence* from those in this case.

The considerations above only established a **duty**. The second hurdle in every claim in negligence is whether the defendant was 'at fault'. There are two questions that need to be addressed: (1) What is the standard of care required of the defendant? (2) Have they fallen below it?

So, the defendants *could* have moved the claimants out of their flat, which leads to a second question—*should* they have done so?

[133] I therefore turn to consider whether the Defendant *should* have invoked the emergency transfer system to move the Claimants from their flat. [...]

[137]...I find that the Defendant should have invoked its emergency procedure to remove the claimants from their flat on or very shortly after 20th October, 2000 but at the very latest on or very shortly after 7th November. The fact that this did not happen in my judgment pointed to and resulted from a lack of proper cooperation and communication between the Social Services and Housing Departments; a failure within those Departments sufficiently to appreciate the gravity and urgency of the situation which the Claimants faced (to which both Z and Tajinder Hayre were doing their best to draw attention); and a failure to give the Claimants' case the priority it deserved.

[138] Accordingly, I find that the Defendant was in breach of its duty of care to the Claimants.

Causation

[139] Finally, in the context of the tort of negligence I have to consider whether the Defendant's breach of its duty of care caused the injury and loss in respect of which this claim is brought. I can come clearly to the conclusion that it did. Self-evidently, had the Claimants left their flat before the relevant weekend, the assault of which they complain would not have happened. However, the Defendant has advanced two arguments in this regard.

Do the Claimants have a Right of Action at All?

[142] I have thus far assumed that the Claimants do in fact have a right of action for damages based on the tort of negligence. The Defendant submits, however that the Claimants do not. Though it may appear strange to leave this matter until this stage of the judgment, I have done so because it needs to be considered against the background of the matters already dealt with.

[143] Ultimately, it is said on behalf of the Defendant, the Claimants are complaining about the failure of the Defendant to re-house them; and decisions taken by local authorities in relation to the provision of social housing can be challenged only by way of an application for judicial review. In this connection, reliance is placed on the case of *O'Rourke v Camden London Borough Council* [1998] AC 188, in which the House of Lords held that the Plaintiff's claim for damages, arising out of the Council's failure to accommodate him as a homeless person pursuant to section 63(1) of the Housing Act 1985, should be struck out. Section 63(1) was part of a scheme involving the provision of social housing for the benefit of society in general, and created no private law duty sounding in damages, but was enforceable solely by way of judicial review.

[...]

[148]...The present case is distinguishable [from *O'Rourke*]. The Claimants were well-established tenants of the Defendant. The Defendant had already exercised its powers as to social housing in relation to the Claimants. Their

---

Put simply, the defendants could and should have moved the claimants out of their flat and so by failing to do so the defendants fell below the standard of care expected of them, that is they breached their duty to the claimants to move them out of their flat once it became reasonably foreseeable that they were likely to suffer a serious physical assault.

Put simply, the defendants are arguing that the claimants ought not be allowed to claim in the tort of negligence (private law) about something which is essentially a public law matter and which has a public law remedy (judicial review). *O'Rourke* is considered in the context of the tort of breach of statutory duty in Chapter 12, p 322.

This is the final element that needs to be addressed. It can sometimes be tricky to establish that the *defendant's* actions *in fact* caused the claimant's loss or injury. Alternatively, it may be clear that the defendant caused the claimant's injury in fact, but not *in law*—that is their injury or loss is considered to be too remote. However, here Maddison J deals with causation quickly, rejecting arguments made by the defendants in relation to whether the claimants would have agreed to move or have maintained contact with their eventual abusers. The defendant was unable to establish on the balance of probabilities that the claimants would have been assaulted even had they moved before the relevant weekend [141].

And therefore already had a relationship that the law might recognise.

claim is that they should have been moved *from* that accommodation, and not necessarily into further Council accommodation. Their claim is not based on narrow considerations of housing policy. There is, for example, no complaint that, being literally homeless, the Claimants were wrongly denied housing; or, being already housed by the Defendant, were wrongly placed in a transfer list below competing candidates. Their claim involves both the Housing and Social Services Departments; the interaction between them; and the manner in which these departments together reacted (or failed to react) to information they received about the Claimants' predicament.

[149] Finally, the evidence in and the reality of this case is that, by virtue of whatever statutory provisions, the Defendant actually had in place an emergency transfer procedure which it could have used before the relevant weekend, and which it did in fact use though only after that weekend.

> Essentially, it would have been **easy** for the defendant to do more than they did.

[150] I therefore regard the Claimants as having a valid cause of action.

The Claim under the Human Rights Act, 1998

[151] In addition to their claim based on the tort of negligence, the Claimants claim damages under the Human Rights Act, 1998 sections 6 and 7. This is on the basis that, in the circumstances already discussed, the Defendant failed to protect them from inhuman and degrading treatment, and to maintain the integrity of their private and family life, thus breaching Articles 3 and 8 respectively of the European Convention on Human Rights.

> Claims under s 7 of the HRA 1998 are **not** claims in tort law. They are *public* law claims against the state for not ensuring that your rights under the HRA are protected. Courts (as public bodies) are obliged under s 6 of the HRA to ensure that all their decisions are HRA compatible. Both claims are considered in more detail in the introduction to the book (pp 18–19) and in the course of discussion of public body liability (see Chapter 6).

[…]

[153] However, I do not think that it is necessary for me to determine the claim, for several reasons. The first is that I have already found the Defendant liable in the tort of negligence. In doing so, incidentally, I have taken into account the impact of the Human Rights Act, albeit amongst many other factors when deciding that the Defendants owed a duty of care to the Claimants. The second reason is that in the course of argument the parties agreed (as do I) that in the circumstances of this case it is difficult to see how the claim under the Human Rights Act might succeed if that based on the tort of negligence failed. If the negligence claim failed, so would the Human Rights Act claim fail. Not having heard full argument on the point, however, it occurs to me that the converse may not necessarily apply. I have in mind that the 1998 Act came into force of the 2nd October, 2000 so that, on my earlier findings, the Claimants could rely on it only in relation to the period beginning on that date and ending on or about 20th October or, at the latest 7th November, 2000. Since I have found that the significant deterioration in the Claimants situation began in September, 2000 and that developments after that month should have been assessed against the background of what had gone before, the claim in relation to the Human Rights Act is not without its complications. However, for the reasons I have given, I do not think it is necessary to extend any further what is already a lengthy judgment by detailed consideration of this claim.

> As noted above the claimants (and 'Z', X's mother) have taken their case to the ECtHR alleging violations of Articles 3 and 8 (Application no 32666/10).

Conclusion

[154] I therefore give judgment for the Claimants on the question of liability. Damages have been almost entirely agreed, any remaining issues can be resolved when the court convenes for the handing down of this judgment.

> The claimants win.

> These were agreed at £97,000. Of course, these will not now be paid.

> Compensation in the form of money—the primary remedy available in tort law. See further Chapter 19.

2.7 **Conclusion**

The tort of negligence has a central role in the law of tort. This is for two reasons: more claims are brought under the tort of negligence than any other tort and its influence extends beyond the tort itself as in recent years it has gained prominence, and started to steal ground from other, older torts. The purpose of this chapter has been to explore the origins of the modern law of negligence, to highlight some of the key themes underpinning the tort, and to outline the essential ingredients of a claim in negligence. To this end, the chapter began by mapping and explaining the historical development of the tort of negligence. It located the development of the tort within its political, social and economic context and against a backdrop of increasing industrialisation. It then went on to explore the origins of the modern tort of negligence in the landmark decision of the House of Lords in *Donoghue* and Lord Atkin's neighbour principle. Finally, the chapter outlined the three components—duty, breach and causation (including remoteness) (four, if including defences)—which need to be established in order to succeed in a claim in the tort of negligence. Although in reality cases—and hence judgments—will tend to focus on one or two of these elements, with the uncontroversial aspects of the case being glossed over very quickly, in every case every element of the tort must be present for the claim to succeed. A 'real life' application of these elements was considered in the case of *X & Y* v *London Borough of Hounslow*.

✱ End-of-chapter questions

After reading the chapter carefully, try answering the questions below. If you would like to know what we think visit the Online Resource Centre (www.oxfordtextbooks.co.uk/orc/horsey2e/).

1. How do negligence in the everyday or general sense and the tort of negligence differ?
2. What must be established in order for there to be a successful claim in the tort of negligence?
3. Why would the courts ever want to deny a claim when someone is injured through another's carelessness?
4. What is the *ratio* of *Donoghue* v *Stevenson*?

✱ Further reading

The readings below provide a general introduction to development and purposes of the tort of negligence and the leading case of **Donoghue v Stevenson**. The best place to start is with the chapters in *Cane* or *Conaghan & Mansell*.

Cane, Peter *Atiyah's Accidents, Compensation and the Law* (7th edn, CUP, 2006), Chs 2 and 3

Conaghan & Mansell, *The Wrongs of Tort* (2nd edn, Pluto Press, 1999), Chs 4 and 5

Harlow, Carol *Understanding Tort Law* (3rd edn, Sweet & Maxwell, 2005), Ch 3

Heuston, Robert '*Donoghue* v *Stevenson* in Retrospect' (1957) 20 *Modern Law Review* 1–24

Ibbetson, David *A Historical Introduction to the Law of Obligations* (OUP, 1999), Ch 10

3

Duty of care: introduction and basic principles

3.1 Introduction

Consider the following examples:

→ A lorry driver crashes into a queue of traffic while talking on his mobile phone, killing the occupants of the car in front.

→ A nurse misreads a doctor's handwriting and, as a result, gives a patient the wrong drug, causing them to suffer a serious allergic reaction.

→ A university law lecturer fails to check departmental files properly before writing a reference to accompany a student's application to join an Inn of Court—unfortunately this means that a strong candidate ends up with a weak reference and their application is refused.

→ A school caretaker injures their back falling off a step ladder while putting up decorations for the end of term play—the step ladder had not been properly maintained by his employer.

In each of these cases the defendant owes the claimant a duty of care. The concept of the duty of care is central to the tort of negligence. As discussed in the previous chapter, duty is one of three elements in the tort of negligence—the first 'hurdle' if you like—that must be established in order for a claim to be successful. Carelessness alone does not give rise to liability; the defendant must not only be 'at fault' but also in a relationship to the claimant where their carelessness can carry legal consequences. If the defendant owes no duty of care to the claimant, then the defendant will incur no liability regardless of how carelessly they acted and how much loss they caused to the claimant. Moreover, if no duty of care is owed *in respect of the injury suffered* (and it is vital always to bear in mind that we are concerned with whether there is a duty in respect of the particular type of harm suffered, and that a defendant may owe a given claimant a duty of care in respect of one type of loss and none in respect of another) there is no need to address the other elements of a negligence claim—that is breach, causation and remoteness. This makes the question as to when the defendant *does* owe such a duty crucial. However, the courts have had great difficulty in setting down a *single* test to determine when a duty of care is owed to the claimant.

This does not mean, however, that it is *never* clear when a duty of care is owed. Far from it; in many situations establishing a duty will be straightforward. It is clear that, for example, an employer owes their employees a duty of care not to cause them foreseeable physical (and increasingly psychiatric) injury at work, a driver owes a similar duty to other road users, including cyclists and pedestrians, and a doctor owes a duty to his patients (in both treating and, increasingly, advising them). In these, and many other cases, a duty of care is established by clear precedent or common sense. So, for example, no one would dream of arguing in a road traffic accident case that road users do not owe a duty of care to one another. In such cases the key issue is usually breach—that is, whether the defendant has fallen below the standard of care expected in all the circumstances of the case.[1]

The question of whether we can formulate a general test for determining the existence of a duty of care only matters in the comparatively rare cases where it is unclear whether a duty is, or should be, owed. It is in such 'novel' situations—those where there is no established precedent or authority—that the courts need some sort of test or guidance as to whether the situation is one in which a duty of care should be found. To be clear, when considering whether a duty of care is owed, the starting point is *always* to look to existing precedent. If the cases give a clear answer one way or the other—that is, if they reveal whether a duty is or is not owed—then that is the end of the matter. It is only where the cases give no clear answer that the courts must fall back on a more general test and revert to first principles.

It follows from this that there is no universal duty to take care not to harm or injure each other: indeed 'whereas Lord Atkin seems to have put forward the neighbour principle[2] as a way of *expanding* the scope of liability for negligence, the duty of care concept is most commonly used in modern cases as a means of justifying *refusal* to impose liability' (*Cane* p 69, emphasis added). In other words, the law does not *always* require us to show reasonable care for those who may be harmed—however foreseeably—by our conduct. In particular, there are a number of situations where the law either denies a duty of care outright or makes establishing such a duty more onerous for claimants. These relate to particular types of harm (such as where the defendant's actions cause psychiatric injury or economic loss), how the harm is suffered (for example, where the claimant's loss or injury has been caused by the acts of a third party or through an omission rather than a positive act) and who the defendant is (such as where the defendant is a public body—for example, a local authority, the police or other emergency services). This, of course, prompts a further question as to why the courts might wish to deny a duty of care in such cases.

There are any number of reasons why the courts might be reluctant to impose a duty of care (Stapleton 1998). These may include a wish to avoid imposing on a particular individual or class of defendants so-called 'crushing' liability—'liability in an indeterminate amount for an indeterminate time to an indeterminate class' (*Ultramares Corporation* v *Touche, Niven & Co* [1931]). Related to this may be a wish to prevent a 'flood' of claims—either in relation to one specific event or, more generally, in relation to a particular type of injury, which may in turn clog-up or slow down the tort system as a mechanism for compensation. The courts may also seek to avoid the more negative aspects of deterrence—that is the danger of 'overkill'—whereby beneficial yet 'risky'

---

1. See Chapter 8.
2. See discussion in Chapter 2, pp 32–33.

activities are restricted as would-be defendants overly self-regulate. Finally, the courts may well recognise that in some circumstances the defendant has simply done nothing wrong—that is, that it is sometimes entirely reasonable to act in ways that leave others worse off.[3] For example, failing a student's exam paper will inevitably leave them worse off both in terms of their future employment prospects as well as their current mental state. However, the examiner (assuming the paper is not of a sufficient standard to pass) is under no duty to prevent this from happening by not failing the student.[4]

 Pause for reflection

Cane argues that the main function of the duty of care element in the tort of negligence is to:

> define the boundaries of liability for damage caused by negligent conduct by reference to what are commonly called 'policy considerations'...To say that a person owes a duty of care means (and means only) that the person will be liable for causing damage by negligence in that situation. (p 69)

Nicholas McBride disagrees. He argues that tort law's regulatory function—that is the extent to which tort law tells people how they *ought* to behave—is *at least as* important. So viewed, it is wrong to say the imposition of a duty of care 'means only' that the defendant will be liable for carelessly harming the claimant. Rather we should take the notion of a duty of care seriously—it requires and directs a defendant to act with reasonable care (2004, pp 418–19).

This distinction, described by McBride as that between those who adopt a 'cynical' as opposed to 'idealist' view of the tort of negligence, is an important one. On one view tort law is about attributing or shifting losses, and hence the key question is: Do we want to impose liability in these circumstances, on this defendant, for this injury? On this basis the purpose of the duty of care inquiry is simply to weigh up the pros and cons of requiring the defendant to bear the claimant's losses. By contrast, the idealist view suggests that tort law is concerned primarily with telling people how they may and may not act. So, to impose a duty of care on a defendant is not simply to say that they will be liable if they carelessly injure someone, but that they must actually 'take care'.

You should keep this distinction in mind as you read more about the tort of negligence and, particularly, when reading Chapters 4 to 7, which deal with the types of claims in which the courts have struggled with the duty concept. To what extent, if any, can this distinction provide an explanation for some of the courts' more controversial decisions in relation to establishing a duty of care?

---

3. See e.g. in relation to economic losses and freedom of speech, Robert Stevens *Torts and Rights* (OUP, 2007), p 21 and also Chapter 2, pp 28–29.

4. This is not to say that an examiner is not under a duty of care to mark papers *fairly* or *accurately*—i.e. to give better papers better marks (it is also probably the case that the student's teachers owed a duty of care to teach them adequately so as to enable them to pass the exam in the first place). The point is rather that when an examiner gives a bad paper a bad mark, they are, consciously, leaving that student worse off than if they had awarded a higher mark. Nonetheless, as long as the mark is fair, no liability will attach since there is no duty to avoid causing such harm.

All this means is that it is important to know how, and in what circumstances, the courts will determine that a duty of care is established and it is to this that we shall now turn.

3.2 From *Donoghue* to *Caparo*—a brief history of the duty of care

Unsurprisingly the starting point in any consideration of the concept of a duty of care is *Donoghue* v *Stevenson* [1932]. As discussed in detail in Chapter 2, the House of Lords set down a single test which could be applied in all cases to answer the question whether a duty was owed—Lord Atkin's 'neighbour principle':

> You must take reasonable care to avoid acts or omissions which you can reasonably foresee would be likely to injure your neighbour. Who then, in law, is my neighbour? The answer seems to be persons who are so closely and directly affected by my act that I ought reasonably to have them in contemplation as being so affected when I am directing my mind to the acts or omissions which are called in question. (at 580)

In many ways, Lord Atkin's statement is 'extraordinarily empty' (*Conaghan & Mansell* p 13). It simply prompts the question: what is, or ought to be, reasonably foreseeable? This is something which may ultimately depend on the imagination of the individual judge; what one judge may believe to be reasonably foreseeable, another may consider unusual and so on.

A more modern reformulation of this can be found in the dictum of Lord Wilberforce in *Anns* v *Merton London Borough Council* [1978]:

> ...the question has to be approached in two stages. First one has to ask whether, as between the alleged wrongdoer and the person who has suffered damage there is a sufficient relationship of proximity or neighbourhood such that, in the reasonable contemplation of the former, carelessness on his part may be likely to cause damage to the latter, in which case a prima facie duty of care arises. Secondly, if the first question is answered affirmatively, it is necessary to consider whether there are any considerations which ought to negative, or to reduce or limit the scope of the duty or the class of person to whom it is owed or the damages to which a breach of it may give rise. (at 751–2)

The position was this: the defendant owed the claimant a duty to take reasonable care (provided that it was *reasonably foreseeable* that a failure to take reasonable care by the defendant would cause damage to the claimant) *unless* there was some policy reason why, nonetheless, no duty should be held to be owed. This prompted Lord Goff in *Smith* v *Littlewoods* [1987] to acknowledge 'the broad general principle of liability for foreseeable damage is so widely applicable that the function of the duty of care is not so much to identify cases where liability is imposed as to identify those where it is not' (at 280).

The first stage of the test appeared to present almost no hurdle—almost everything is foreseeable if you think about it long enough. This meant that most of the work when it came to restricting claims was left to the second stage—policy. The fact that the first hurdle of Lord Wilberforce's test was so readily jumped was at the heart of the huge expansion of the tort of negligence in the late 1970s and early 1980s (discussed in Chapter 2) during which the courts seemed reluctant to refuse claims of any vaguely sympathetic claimant who came before them. *McLoughlin v O'Brian* [1982] is a case in point.

Mrs McLoughlin suffered psychiatric injury after her husband and three children were injured (one fatally) in a serious car accident caused by the defendant. She was not at the crash site. Instead, she was told about the accident an hour or so later by a friend, who then drove her to hospital, where she arrived approximately two hours after the accident. There she encountered circumstances that were 'distressing in the extreme' (at 417). Her husband and children, still covered in the grime and dirt from the accident, were cut and bruised; she could also hear her son, George, shouting and screaming in the room next door before he lapsed into unconsciousness.

Until this point, recovery for negligently psychiatric injuries had usually been limited to claimants who had actually and directly witnessed the traumatic event or happened upon its 'immediate aftermath' (usually within a few minutes). Mrs McLoughlin's claim was then 'on the margins' of recovery—requiring a significant widening of the concept of the 'immediate aftermath' in order for her to succeed. The House of Lords allowed her claim, and, in so doing, challenging the policy arguments that might have been used to deny it—'I believe the "floodgates" argument…is, as it always has been, greatly exaggerated' (Lord Bridge at 422).[5]

Lord Wilberforce's two-stage test soon fell into disfavour. It was seen to be behind the unprecedented, and increasingly unpopular, expansion of the tort of negligence (see, for example, Lord Roskill's leading opinion in *Junior Books v Veitchi* [1983]). The test was rejected in *Yuen Kun-yeu v Attorney General of Hong Kong* [1987] and *Anns* itself was subsequently overruled by *Murphy v Brentwood District Council* [1990].[6]

 Counterpoint

Though many modern accounts tend to hide this, the decision in *Anns* was not universally derided. Ward J had this to say:

> As I have tried to navigate my fragile craft to judgment, I have become aware that it is a tidal sea which flows as causes of action are extended and then ebbs as limitations are placed upon them. I can only console myself that if I am cast up among the flotsam and jetsam at the high water mark on the beach, I shall lie, I hope unnoticed but among such battered treasures as *Anns* v *Merton London Borough Council*. (*Ravenscroft* v *Rederiaktiebolaget Transatlantic* [1991] at 76)

Moreover, it is far from clear that the test in *Anns* *necessitated* any expansion of liability. It may be that it was a victim of association—a casualty of the backlash against an increasing number of decisions (for example, *McLoughlin*; *Home Office* v *Dorset Yacht*

➡

---

5. Unsurprisingly, the decision in *McLoughlin v O'Brian* was an early victim of the so-called 'retreat from *Anns*' and no longer represents the law in this area. *Alcock v Chief Constable of South Yorkshire Police* [1992] is now the authority on this point (see further Chapter 5, pp 109–110).

6. Discussed further in Chapter 7, pp 177–181.

Co [1970]; even the decision in *Anns* itself) which appeared to threaten the principles of individual freedom and responsibility at a time when these were high on the political and governmental agenda (*Conaghan & Mansell* pp 17, 20).[7]

What do you think led the courts to the conclusion that the potential for liability had become too widespread? Think, in particular, about the so-called 'problematic' duty situations in relation to omissions, pure economic loss, public authorities, psychiatric harm and so on.

3.3 Establishing a duty of care: *Caparo Industries* v *Dickman*

At present, the leading case on the duty of care in tort is ***Caparo Industries plc* v *Dickman*** [1990] in which the House of Lords detailed two approaches that courts should adopt when seeking to determine whether, on the facts of a particular case, a duty of care was owed:

(1) a three-stage 'test';

(2) an incremental approach.

In so doing, the House of Lords sought to reassert the limits that were traditionally placed on liability—heralding the beginning of what became known as the 'retreat from *Anns*' (discussed further below).

3.3.1 The three-stage 'test'

The House of Lords in *Caparo* was determined to effect a shift away from attempts to articulate a general principle of duty.[8] They sought to move away from the position of *Donoghue* and *Anns* whereby foreseeability of damage was enough to raise a *prima facie* duty of care, which would be negated only if there were public policy considerations which militated against such a duty. They favoured instead a return to 'the more traditional categorisation of different specific situations as guides to the existence, the scope and the limits of the varied duties of care which the law imposes' (at 618). Lord Bridge continued:

> . . . in addition to the foreseeability of damage, necessary ingredients in any situation giving rise to a duty of care are that there should exist between the party owing the duty and the party to whom it is owed a relationship characterised by the law as one of 'proximity' or 'neighbourhood' and that the situation should be one in which the court considers it fair, just and reasonable that the law should impose a duty of a given scope on the one party for the benefit of the other. (at 617)

7. See also *Atiyah* Ch 8.
8. The facts of *Caparo* are not relevant to this discussion. The case, which concerned economic loss following reliance on information provided by auditors, is explored in detail in Chapter 7, p 186.

According to this approach, now commonly referred to as the '*Caparo* three-stage test', in order to find that a duty of care is owed in a given situation, the following must be established:

(1) it was reasonably foreseeable that the defendant's failure to take care could cause damage to the claimant; **and**

(2) there was a relationship of proximity between the claimant and the defendant; **and**

(3) it is fair, just and reasonable that the law should recognise a duty on the defendant to take reasonable care not to cause that damage to the claimant.

As with the test in *Anns*, the first requirement is that the claimant must fall within a class of individuals put at **foreseeable risk** by the defendant's action—the defendant does not owe a duty of care to the world at large. The most famous articulation of this principle can be found in the American case of *Palsgraf* v *Long Island Railroad Co* [1928]. In this case, the defendant dropped a box of fireworks, which in turn caused an explosion, the shockwaves of which (it was alleged) caused heavy metal scales to fall onto the claimant. Denying her claim, the New York Court of Appeals held that the claimant was not a foreseeable victim; it was simply not enough that the defendant's negligence had exposed her to the risk of injury, nor that their negligence would cause foreseeable harm to others.

The second stage—the requirement of **proximity** marks a departure from the *Anns* test. Though the language of 'proximity' was used in *Anns* and indeed in *Donoghue*, it appears that Lord Wilberforce, and (less clearly) Lord Atkin, did not intend the term to add anything to the notion of reasonable foreseeability. In other words, to say that there was 'proximity' between the claimant and defendant was to say no more than that it was reasonably foreseeable that the defendant's carelessness could cause the claimant harm. As such, 'proximity' did not describe a hurdle or requirement additional to the requirement of reasonable foreseeability. *Caparo* changed this. By employing 'proximity' as a second, additional, element to the test for establishing the existence of a duty of care it is plain that the House of Lords were using the term to mean something more than simple reasonable foreseeability of harm. The key question then is what does this more refined understanding of 'proximity' mean.

The first thing to say is that, in contrast to everyday understandings, proximity does not describe simple physical closeness—a defendant can owe a duty of care to a claimant who is thousands of miles away (indeed in *Donoghue* itself the claimant and defendant were not close in space and time). Rather proximity is what Alistair Mullis and Ken Oliphant describe as a 'legal term of art'[9] which gives a generic name to the more specific tests through which the existence of a duty of care is established in particular cases—for example the so-called *Alcock* control mechanisms which limit duty of care in relation to psychiatric injuries suffered by 'secondary victims'.[10] So understood, 'proximity', Lord Oliver notes, is a 'convenient expression so long as it is realised that it is no more than a label which embraces not a definable concept but merely a

---

9. *Tort* (3rd edn, Palgrave Macmillan, 2003), p 25.
10. See Chapter 5, pp 107–111.

description of circumstances from which, pragmatically, the courts conclude that a duty of care exists' (*Caparo* at 632).

As such, the proximity requirement tells us that, before a duty of care can arise, a certain type of relationship or connection must exist between the parties. However, importantly, and as Lord Oliver's quote reveals, *Caparo* itself tells us very little about what precise relationship or connection amounts to a relationship of proximity on any given set of facts. *Donoghue* and *Anns* both suggested that the only connection or relationship that needed to exist between the parties was that it was reasonably foreseeable that the claimant might be harmed by the defendant's carelessness. *Caparo* tells us that this is not true (since otherwise this second stage of the **Caparo** 'test' would add nothing to the first) and that something more is needed. However, it is not made clear what this 'something more' is.

 Pause for reflection

One constant in the quest for a general test for establishing duties of care is the requirement of foreseeability—that is, the claimant must be said to fall into a particular class of people in relation to whom it is reasonably foreseeable that the defendant's failure to take care could cause them damage. However, as we shall see, foreseeability also crops up as a requirement or relevant factor in other elements of the tort of negligence. To recap, establishing a claim in negligence requires the claimant to prove not just that the defendant owed them a duty of care, but also that the defendant breached that duty, that the breach caused the claimant a loss and that this loss is not too remote. When we come to look at breach, we shall see that one of the key factors in determining whether the defendant did indeed act reasonably is the likelihood and gravity of the harm that could reasonably have been foreseen—so, for instance, the greater the likelihood of harm, the more care we expect the defendant to take to prevent it. Moreover, when determining whether the loss suffered by the claimant is too remote, we again turn to reasonable foreseeability—a loss is too remote if was not reasonably foreseeable that a loss of that kind might follow from the defendant's breach (*The Wagon Mound (No 1)* [1961]) (Howarth 2006, pp 457–63)).

This all appears rather confusing. If the claimant's loss was not reasonably foreseeable, then no duty of care can arise and so their claim will fail before we get to questions of breach, causation and remoteness. By contrast, if a court has held that harm was reasonably foreseeable when looking at whether a duty arose, then it seems unnecessary to re-inquire into foreseeability when looking at breach and remoteness since that issue has already been addressed at the duty stage. To put much the same point another way, if it is held that the claimant's loss was *not* a reasonably foreseeable consequence of the defendant's carelessness, then it seems we can deny their claim on a variety of grounds: we could say that no duty was owed, that the defendant was not in breach or that the claimant's loss was too remote. So, not only does it seem as though we are asking the same question two or three times but this also appears to muddy the relationship between the supposedly distinct elements of a negligence claim. The same point has on occasion been made by the courts. For instance in *Lamb* v *Camden London Borough Council* [1981] Lord Denning MR had this to say:

→

> ↦
>
> The truth is that all these three, duty, remoteness and causation, are all devices by which the courts limit the range of liability for negligence...As I have said...'it is not every consequence of a wrongful act which is the subject of compensation'. The law has to draw a line somewhere. Sometimes it is done by limiting the range of persons to whom a duty is owed. Sometimes it is done by saying that there is a break in the chain of causation. At other times it is done by saying that the consequence is too remote to be a head of damage. All these devices are useful in their way. But ultimately it is a question of policy for the judges to decide. (at 636)
>
> The best way to make sense of this all is to understand that at each stage—duty, breach, remoteness—we are, or should be, asking a slightly different question in relation to foreseeability. So, at the duty stage, we are asking whether harm of some broad variety—personal injury, psychiatric harm, property damage, pure economic loss, etc—was a reasonably foreseeable consequence of the defendant's carelessness. If a duty is established, we move on to breach. This involves asking whether the foreseeable harm was sufficiently grave or likely that the defendant should have done more than they did to avoid it happening. As such, the inquiry into foreseeability here is a little more detailed or focused—we are asking not only 'Was harm foreseeable?' but 'How likely was it that harm might be caused?' and 'How serious was the harm that the defendant could reasonably have foreseen?'. Finally, when addressing remoteness, we are looking at the foreseeability of the specific harms that the claimant did in fact suffer. So, while at the duty stage we ask whether, for instance, physical harm, as broadly defined, was foreseeable, when turning to remoteness we look at the precise injury suffered by the claimant (and sometimes, too, the way in which they were injured), and we ask whether this was the *type of* physical harm that could reasonably have been foreseen (see, for example, *Tremain* v *Pike* [1969] and *Hughes* v *Lord Advocate* [1963], although compare *Page* v *Smith* [1996]).

The final stage of the *Caparo* test—that is whether it is **fair, just and reasonable** to find that the defendant owed the claimant a duty to take reasonable care not to cause them damage—returns, once again, to notions of policy. In so doing, it has been argued that it leaves the courts with an inevitable 'residual discretion as to whether or not a duty of care should be recognised' (Witting 2005, p 62). Traditionally, judges have sought to play down this aspect of their role (especially during the period of retreat following *Anns*). However, more recently, they have been more willing to engage in frank discussions about the fairness or otherwise of imposing a duty of care. For example, in *Marc Rich & Co* v *Bishop Rock Marine Co Ltd* [1996] (also known as *The Nicholas H*) the House of Lords denied a duty of care on the part of the defendants on the basis that it was not 'fair, just and reasonable' to disturb the contractual allocation of risks between the claimant cargo holders and the ship owner (who was not party to the action) and which might threaten to undermine the terms on which international trade was conventionally conducted. Other policy reasons for refusing to impose a duty of care on the grounds that it would not be 'fair, just and reasonable' include a reluctance on the part of the courts to second guess the priorities, decisions and resource allocations of public bodies—including the police (**Hill v Chief Constable of West Yorkshire Police [1989]**), local authorities (*X (Minors)* v *Bedfordshire County Council* [1995]) and armed forces (*Mulcahy* v *Ministry of Defence* [1996]). This all seems very open-ended.

However, as Lord Browne-Wilkinson in *X (Minors)* v *Bedfordshire County Council* reminded us, we should not lose sight of the compensatory purposes of the tort of negligence: 'the public policy consideration which has first claim on the loyalty of the law is that wrongs should be remedied and that very potent counter-considerations are required to override that policy' (at 749).

3.3.2 The *Caparo* three-stage test—uncovered

The three-stage test, gleaned from Lord Bridge's opinion in *Caparo*, is not unproblematic. Its principal flaw or limitation is that it tells us remarkably little about when a duty of care will arise or even how courts should go about determining when such duties arise. This, as we have seen, is the very thing we need a general test for establishing duties of care to do. However, it seems clear that it was never the intention of the House of Lords to set down a test that could be used by courts in future cases to provide concrete answers to whether a duty of care arose on a given set of facts. At the same time as endorsing the requirements of foreseeability, proximity and fairness, justice and reasonableness as relevant to determining the existence of a duty of care, the House of Lords in *Caparo* stressed the impossibility of finding *any* single test which, in practice, could be used to identify those situations in which a duty of care will be owed. Lord Oliver put it thus:

> I think that it has to be recognised that to search for any single formula which will serve as a general test of liability is to pursue a will-o'-the wisp. The fact is that once one discards, as it is now clear one must, the concept of foreseeability of harm as the single exclusive test, even a *prima facie* test, of the existence of the duty of care, the attempt to state some general principle which will determine liability in an infinite variety of circumstances serves not to clarify the law but merely to bedevil its development in a way which corresponds with practicality and common sense. (at 632)

Moreover, not only did the House of Lords reject the possibility of formulating any single, practicable test (effecting a judicial U-turn in respect of the development of a general principle of negligence in tort law), they also went on to deny the utility of the very concepts of 'foreseeability', 'proximity' and 'fairness, justice and reasonableness' that are adopted in the three-stage test:

> [T]he concepts of proximity and fairness embodied in these additional ingredients are not susceptible of any such precise definition as would be necessary to give them utility as practical tests, but amount in effect to little more than convenient labels to attach to the features of different specific situations in which, on a detailed examination of all the circumstances, the law recognises pragmatically as giving rise to a duty of a given scope. (Lord Bridge at 618)

Lord Oliver went even further, suggesting that the three stages outlined above are, in fact, 'merely facets of the same thing' (at 633).

The *Caparo* three-stage test is, then, at best, 'shorthand' for the *types of factors* which determine whether a given defendant owes a duty of care to a particular claimant in respect of a particular type of harm—a framework or guide for inquiries into the existence of a duty rather than a reliable test whereby a duty arises when all the conditions are satisfied. In the same way, 'foreseeability', 'proximity' and 'fairness, justice and reasonableness' are simply suitable (that is, judicially acceptable) language through which the court can formulate its decision that a duty was or was not owed (see, for example, *X (Minors)* v *Bedfordshire County Council* at 371). In other words, once the court has concluded that there is no duty, it can choose to express this conclusion by saying that there was no proximity between the parties or that it was not fair, just and reasonable to impose a duty. But in reaching its decision in the first place these concepts are essentially redundant.

So viewed, it may be that the ***Caparo*** three-stage test amounts to little more than a change in the rhetoric used to justify the outcome of a case—'reasonableness', 'proximity' and so on being far more judicially friendly than 'policy', legal or otherwise—rather than effecting a wholesale rejection of the *criteria* by which the existence of a duty of care is determined (*Conaghan & Mansell* p 17).

 Pause for reflection

> The trend of authorities has been to discourage the assumption that anyone who suffers loss is *prima facie* entitled to compensation from a person (preferably insured or a public authority) whose act or omission can be said to have caused it. The default position is that he is not. (Lord Hoffmann, *Stovin* v *Wise* [1996] at 949)

The ***Caparo*** three-stage test, then, changes the starting point from which decisions on whether the defendant owes the claimant a duty to take reasonable care not to cause them injury. Whereas Lord Wilberforce's test in ***Anns*** started from the presumption that, where harm was reasonably foreseeable, there *was* a duty (unless there were sufficient policy reasons to deny it); the ***Caparo*** three-stage test starts from the position that *no* duty is owed in respect of reasonably foreseeable harms, unless there are further reasons for imposing liability.

What do you think about the creation of an assumption *against* the existence of a duty of care? Think again about McBride's understanding of the purpose of a duty of care. Why do the courts persist in utilising the concepts of 'fairness' and 'proximity' despite their lack of substance—what are the alternatives?

3.3.3 The incremental approach

Having dismissed the utility of the questions posed in the three-stage test discussed above, how then did the House of Lords consider that courts ought to approach the task of determining whether a duty of care is owed? Apart from stressing that these things have to be decided 'pragmatically', the principal indication their lordships gave of their preferred approach was their adoption of a dictum of Brennan J in the Australian case of *Sutherland Shire Council* v *Heyman* [1985]: 'It is preferable, in my view, that the law should develop novel categories of negligence incrementally and by analogy with established categories' (at 481).

What this amounts to is the rejection of the need for a general test for the existence of a duty of care in negligence. Rather, a duty of care will exist where (and only where) one has already been found to exist (that is, there is existing precedent) or in a situation which can be regarded as analogous to one in which a duty has already been found. This heralds a return to the pre-*Donoghue* approach and 'the more traditional categorisation of distinct and recognisable situations as guides to the existence, the scope and the limits of the varied duties of care which the law imposes' (Lord Bridge, *Caparo* at 618).

The suggestion that we should recognise duties of care in situations identical or analogous to those where the courts have recognised a duty of care previously (and that we should reject duties of care in situations where the courts have previously denied their existence) is clearly sensible and is hardly revolutionary. Indeed, it involves little more than an application of the doctrine of precedent. However, the problem with this approach is that it also suggests that, where no analogy can be found—that is, where no previously decided case exists which can be viewed as analogous to the case at hand—a duty of care will be denied since the recognition of a duty of care cannot be understood as an incremental development of the law from existing, analogous authorities. In other words, if the law is to develop incrementally, we can *only* recognise duties of care in situations analogous to those where a duty of care has *already* been recognised.

But, if this is true, it then means that the outcome of cases depends not upon legal principle and the substantive merits of the case but upon the accidents of legal history or, in other words, whether you are fortunate enough that an analogous case has already been decided by the courts. If we take the incremental by analogy approach seriously, if a party is unfortunate enough to suffer an injury in a unique way, so that no case similar to theirs has been brought to court before, then their claim will fail not because it is unmeritorious but for the simple (and highly unsatisfactory) reason that they are the first person to bring such a claim. Indeed, it is just this type of arbitrary and unfair result that the majority of the House of Lords in *Donoghue* rejected. The incremental and by analogy approach requires us to say that the minority in that case were right after all.

Perhaps unsurprisingly, the courts have shown little enthusiasm for this approach. In *The Nicholas H* the House of Lords, faced with a novel type of negligence claim, rejected the utility of the incremental by analogy approach on the basis that, if there had been no analogous cases previously decided, then the past cases could offer no guidance either way as to whether a duty should be held to exist. Instead, the court decided the case pragmatically by analysing the reasons for and against the recognition of a duty and deciding whether on balance a duty ought to be recognised.

This is not to suggest that there is no worth in the incremental by analogy approach. If there *is* a previous decision which does cover, directly or by analogy, the case at hand, then that will decide the case, without any need to have recourse to the three-stage test. Also, certain situations are governed by more exact tests than those set down in *Caparo*. So, for example, if the claimant suffers psychiatric injury, the courts will look to cases such as *Alcock* v *Chief Constable of South Yorkshire Police* [1992] and *Page* v *Smith* [1996], rather than *Caparo*, to answer the duty of care question. Similarly, where public authority liability in respect of children in care is concerned, the courts will examine the rules set down in *D* v *East Berkshire Community NHS Trust* [2005] and *Barrett* v *Enfield London Borough Council* [2001]. Furthermore, where personal injuries, and possibly property damage, is concerned, it will generally be the case that foreseeability of such injury will suffice to establish a duty, in other words the test set down in **Donoghue** will be used (although see *The Nicholas H* for an exception to this). The point we are making is that where there is no clear precedent governing the case at hand, in contrast to the implication of the incremental by analogy approach, the courts do not—and should not—simply reject the claim without consideration of its merits.

3.4 **Where does this leave us?**

It is important to remember that ultimately it is only a small minority of cases—where the courts are asked to determine whether new categories of claim should be recognised or existing precedents should be extended—which call for the application of a general test such as those propounded in **Donoghue**, **Anns** and **Caparo**. As such, the relationship between the two approaches detailed by the House of Lords in **Caparo**—that is whether, for example, the three-stage test is to be applied 'incrementally' or only when the incremental by analogy approach fails—is relatively unimportant and may even be positively misguided. **Caparo** does not set out clear guidance as to *how* judges should decide future cases. On the contrary, all it does set out is the simple proposition that foreseeability alone is not sufficient to impose liability and it maps out two approaches through which liability may instead be achieved. This reluctance toward prescription is born out in the subsequent case law (for example in *The Nicholas H*) in which judges have felt free to ignore both the three-stage test and the incremental by analogy approach in favour of a more general consideration of the fairness or otherwise of imposing a duty of care in the circumstances of the case. Indeed, some recent cases show that the House of Lords may be moving away from a rigid reliance on the three-stage test but not necessarily distancing themselves from the language of *Caparo*. In *Customs and Excise Commissioners v Barclays Bank plc* [2006], for example, Lord Walker said that there is an 'increasingly clear recognition that the three-fold test...does not provide an easy answer to all our problems, but only a set of fairly blunt tools' (at [25]). Similar comments were made by Lord Hoffmann (at [14]) and Lord Bingham (at [7]).

But, while the practical significance of a general test should not be overplayed, the issue of how we should decide when a duty of care is owed is central to the conceptual foundations, as well as to our understanding, of the tort of negligence. With this is mind, it may be helpful to begin to think about establishing a duty of care in novel situations along the lines of the 'five-stage approach' we have outlined in Figure 3.1.

Nevertheless, important questions remain: What should we be looking for in a test for the duty of care? Why do we need the duty of care at all? Are we criticising the actual decisions in these cases or simply the language that the courts have been using to explain their decisions? These are some of the questions you should be thinking about as you read the chapters that follow (which discuss situations where the law either denies a duty of care outright or makes establishing such a duty more onerous) and as you begin to learn more about duty and the tort of negligence as a whole.

Figure 3.1 Establishing a duty of care in new cases: a five-stage approach

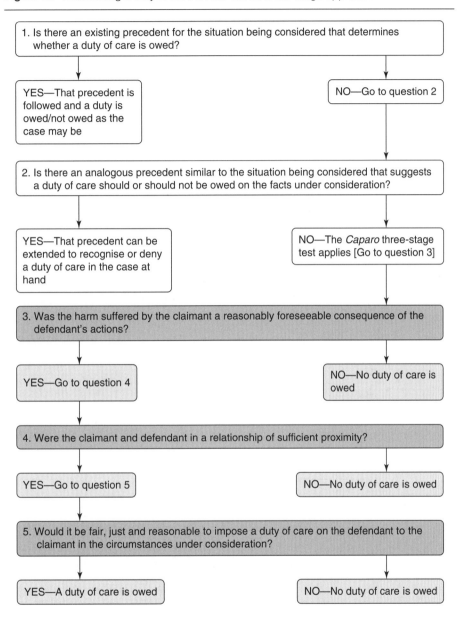

1. Is there an existing precedent for the situation being considered that determines whether a duty of care is owed?

YES—That precedent is followed and a duty is owed/not owed as the case may be

NO—Go to question 2

2. Is there an analogous precedent similar to the situation being considered that suggests a duty of care should or should not be owed on the facts under consideration?

YES—That precedent can be extended to recognise or deny a duty of care in the case at hand

NO—The *Caparo* three-stage test applies [Go to question 3]

3. Was the harm suffered by the claimant a reasonably foreseeable consequence of the defendant's actions?

YES—Go to question 4

NO—No duty of care is owed

4. Were the claimant and defendant in a relationship of sufficient proximity?

YES—Go to question 5

NO—No duty of care is owed

5. Would it be fair, just and reasonable to impose a duty of care on the defendant to the claimant in the circumstances under consideration?

YES—A duty of care is owed

NO—No duty of care is owed

Pause for reflection

The House of Lords in *Caparo* was determined to effect a shift away from the position of *Donoghue* and *Anns* whereby foreseeability of damage was enough to raise a *prima facie* duty of care, which would be negated only if there were public policy considerations which militated against such a duty. Do you think this shift has gone too far? Think about *Caparo* and the cases that have followed it (discussed in the following chapters). Are the courts now paying too little attention to the principle that negligently caused harm should be compensated?

3.5 **Conclusion**

In this chapter, we have looked at the concept of **duty** in negligence claims. We have considered attempts by the courts to establish general 'tests' through which to establish when a duty of care is owed, focusing on the most important of these—the three-stage test and incremental approach from *Caparo*. We concluded by noting that although we should not downplay the significance of these general tests, they are used in a small minority of cases where the judges are being asked to develop a new area of the law and they are best approached using the five-stage approach outlined above. Thus, over the course of the next four chapters we shall consider the circumstances in which the courts have developed specific rules in order to establish when a duty of care is owed.

✳ End-of-chapter questions

After reading the chapter carefully, try answering the questions below. If you would like to know what we think visit the Online Resource Centre (www.oxfordtextbooks.co.uk/orc/horsey2e/).

1. What purpose does the concept of duty of care serve? Why shouldn't everyone who falls below the standard of care of the reasonable person be liable if they injure someone?

2. In what situations is the issue of whether or not there is a duty of care unproblematic and when is it problematic? Why is this?

3. In each of the following situations consider both whether there **is** a legal duty of care **and** whether there **should** be:

  (i) Neil, a 2-year-old child, falls into two feet of water. Gavin, an adult, walks by and offers no assistance. Neil drowns.

  (ii) In (i) above, what if Gavin is Neil's father?

  (iii) Doreen, an elderly woman, lives alone in an isolated farmhouse. Recently there have been a number of burglaries in the neighbourhood so she decides to protect herself by digging a hole beneath her front window, which she then covers with leaves. Unfortunately, Charlie, a postman, falls down this hole while looking through her window to see if Doreen is in to collect a parcel.

  (iv) Dr Smith is a well-know magician. One night while performing his signature trick, which involves 'cutting' his assistant, Pip, in half, he accidently slices into her side causing her to bleed heavily. On seeing this, Pip's new boyfriend, Dan, who is in the audience, faints and falls and hits his head—he suffers severe concussion.

  (v) While out shopping, Kate's 7-year-old daughter slips out of her hand and runs into the road causing a serious accident.

  (vi) Helen negligently leaves the door of her fireworks factory unlocked one night. Some boys enter the factory and steal a large quantity of fireworks, which they light in the nearby park. This causes an explosion that seriously injures Ben who is walking his dog in the park.

4. '[T]he postulate of a simple duty to avoid any harm, that is, with hindsight, reasonably capable of being foreseen becomes untenable without the imposition of some intelligible limits to keep the law of negligence within the bounds of common sense and practicability (**Caparo**, Lord Oliver at 633)'.

How have the courts sought to place limits upon the duty of care owed in negligence and to what extent do you consider that such limits are 'intelligible'?

✳ Further reading

Much of the writing in this area focuses on the role of duty as an ingredient in the tort of negligence and asks the 'big questions' such as: 'Do duties of care exist?' 'If so, how many are there?' 'Do we need the concept of a duty of care?' and so on. The best place to start is with Nicholas McBride's discussion of the 'idealist' and 'cynical' views of negligence.

Cane, Peter *Atiyah's Accidents, Compensation and the Law* (7th edn, CUP, 2006), Ch 3

Hepple, Bob 'Negligence: The Search for Coherence' (1997) 50 *Current Legal Problems* 69

Howarth, David 'Many Duties of Care—Or A Duty of Care? Notes from the Underground' (2006) 26(3) *Oxford Journal of Legal Studies* 449

McBride, Nicholas 'Duties of Care—Do They Really Exist?' (2004) 24(3) *Oxford Journal of Legal Studies* 417

Stapleton, Jane 'Duty of Care Factors: A Selection from the Judicial Menus' in Peter Cane and Jane Stapleton (eds) *The Law of Obligations: Essays in Honour of John Fleming* (OUP, 1998), p 59

Witting, Christian 'Duty of Care: An Analytical Approach' (2005) 25(1) *Oxford Journal of Legal Studies* 33

4

Omissions and acts
of third parties

Problem question

Read this problem question carefully, and keep it in mind while you are working through
the chapter that follows. At the end of the chapter, you will be able to apply what you have
learnt to the problem question and advise the relevant parties.

Margaret, who is 75 years old, is doing her weekly supermarket shop on a busy Saturday
afternoon when she begins to feel pains in her chest. It transpires she is having a heart
attack and she collapses to the floor. Although the supermarket is crowded, no one
comes to help her.

Brian, the store manager, puts a call out over the tannoy system asking if there is a doctor
present, but otherwise offers no assistance. Hearing the announcement, a nurse comes
forward and tries to help Margaret, but fails to put her in the recovery position and she
later dies.

Meanwhile, some youths see Margaret's car near the entrance to the supermarket. She
has left it open with the keys in the ignition, as she did not want to spend time looking
for a parking space. The youths drive off in the car, failing to stop at a pedestrian crossing, hitting Jill and her daughter Heather who were crossing the road. Both are injured,
Heather seriously. One of the youths, who was not wearing a seatbelt, also suffers a
serious head injury.

4.1 **Introduction**

Consider the following situations:

→ A small child falls into a pond and is struggling to get out. An adult walking by offers no assistance.

→ A couple hire a motor boat at the seaside and are clearly in difficulties when the boat begins to sink. The owner of the hire shop sits on the beach and does nothing to help them.

→ A doctor is driving along a road on which there has been a bad accident, but does not stop to help the victims.

→ A man sees another man about to walk off the edge of a cliff, but does nothing to try and stop him.

→ The door to a pub is left open one night by the cleaner. Some teenagers enter the pub, consume a large amount of alcohol and cause lots of damage.

→ The same teenagers, upon leaving the pub, vandalise a car belonging to someone who lives on the same street.

In all of these scenarios the harm suffered by the various individuals can be attributed to a 'third party' or came about because the potential defendant did not do anything (as opposed to doing something to cause harm). Thus, it might seem logical that no liability should arise in any of these situations. As in all situations where negligence is alleged, liability here depends, first, on whether a duty of care was owed in respect of what happened or who it happened to. For example, we need to ask the question 'Does an adult walking past a drowning child owe that child a duty of care?' Whether a duty is owed by one party to another to whom they cause harm often depends on the *manner* in which that harm was inflicted. Generally, subject to other limitations on liability, there is little problem establishing a duty to avoid the direct infliction of physical harm. However, when harm is inflicted indirectly, such as through a failure to act (what the law calls an omission, or non-feasance), or where the immediate cause of the harm was the act of a third party (someone other than the claimant or defendant), it becomes far harder to establish that a duty would—or should—be owed.

This chapter looks at two problematic duty areas. The first section considers when and how the courts have found that a duty of care should be owed by defendants when the harm was the result of their **omission**, while the second section explores the situations when a defendant may owe a duty of care in relation to the **action of a third party**. It might be thought strange that someone would compensate someone else for a harm that was not the result of their own actions. This is the stance the courts have generally taken: ordinarily you can be liable only for things that you do, not things you do not do. However, when someone *does not* do something that they *ought* to have done—perhaps because of the relationship between the parties concerned—a duty might be found in relation to a failure to act (omission). Similarly, while it appears strange that someone may be liable for harms that they did not actually, in any real sense, cause , the courts have nonetheless found that in limited circumstances people who have responsibility for, or control over, others—may incur a duty in respect of the harms caused by these 'third parties'.

4.2 **Acts and omissions**

Although Lord Atkin in **Donoghue v Stevenson [1932]** spoke of a duty of care aris-ing in respect of 'acts or omissions', later interpretations suggest that he only meant omissions in situations where there is a pre-tort relationship giving rise to a positive obligation to act (and, therefore, where any failure to do so would be a breach of that duty). This, broadly, seems to be the position of the law today. A relationship between the parties—for example, between parent and child, or school teacher and pupil, and also contractual relationships or those created by statute—may create a positive duty to act.[1] Outside specific pre-tort relationships, positive duties to do something are not generally present in the tort of negligence and the courts seem unwilling to create them—most likely because negligence law developed against a social and political landscape that favoured individualism over any kind of collective responsibility.

In short, the exclusionary rule operates to prevent a duty being owed in respect of omissions. Lord Goff stated clearly in *Smith v Littlewoods* [1987] that 'the common law does not impose liability for what are called pure omissions' (at 271). And, of course, if there is no duty, there can be no liability, and thus no compensation available for harms caused by the failure of someone to do something. Generally, then, we can say that the duties of care that arise in negligence are duties not to cause harm to others by our actions. These do not extend to an active or positive duty to act to help others, even when to do so would be easy. An example commonly cited in this respect (including in our scenarios, above) is that of a child lying face down in a puddle of water and po-tentially drowning. A stranger who walks by while this is happening does not have a duty to take any steps whatsoever to save that child, even if all it would take would be for them to grab their arm and pull them out of the water to safety. The principle is starkly illustrated by the American case of *Osterlind v Hill* [1928]. In that case, the claimant had rented a canoe from the defendant and took it out into the water. The canoe overturned and the defendant, who was a strong swimmer, did nothing: he sat on the shore and watched the claimant drown. When sued in negligence it was found that he owed no duty of care, despite the fact he had rented out the canoe.[2]

 Pause for reflection

Many people are shocked that the adult in the scenario referred to above would have no duty of care towards the child. Should this be the case, in your opinion? Do you think that the way the law operates would actually discourage people from going to the assistance of others?

---

1. e.g. the Occupiers' Liability Act 1957 fixes a positive duty on occupiers to ensure that their premises are safe for lawful visitors (see p 232) and there are various statutory provisions relating to health and safety that impose positive duties on employers.

2. So, in our scenario above, there would be no duty of care owed by the owner of the hire shop to do anything to assist the couple in trouble. However, in the light of later cases (e.g. the Canadian case of *The Ogopogo* [1970]), a contractual relationship might now be enough to create a positive duty to act, see e.g. *Stansbie v Troman* [1948] and *Bailey and another v HSS Alarms* (2000) *The Times*, 20 June.

It is the 'pure' notion of omissions that concerns us here; that is, not those omissions which happen in the context of a relationship in which there is an obligation to act. In some circumstances there *would* be a duty to go to the rescue of the child in a puddle—if there was a pre-tort relationship that deemed a duty to take positive action to help was in place, such as if the mother or carer of the child was the person walking by.[3] This general exclusion of liability for 'pure' omissions has been restated time and time again in case law—most notably in recent years by Lord Hoffmann in **Stovin v Wise [1996]**:

> There are sound reasons why omissions require different treatment from positive conduct. It is one thing for the law to say that a person who undertakes some activity shall take reasonable care not to cause damage to others. It is another thing for the law to require that a person who is doing nothing in particular shall take steps to prevent another from suffering harm from the acts of third parties . . . or from natural causes. (at 943)

He goes on to say that there are political, moral and economic reasons why no duty should be owed in such circumstances:

> In political terms it is less of an invasion of an individual's freedom for the law to require him to consider the safety of others in his actions than to impose upon him a duty to rescue or protect. A moral version of this point may be called the 'Why pick on me?' argument. A duty to prevent harm to others or to render assistance to a person in danger or distress may apply to a large and indeterminate class of people who happen to be able to do something. Why should one be held liable rather than another? In economic terms, the efficient allocation of resources usually requires an activity should bear its own costs. If it benefits from being able to impose some of its costs on other people (what economists call 'externalities'), the market is distorted because the activity appears cheaper than it really is. So liability to pay compensation for loss caused by negligent conduct acts as a deterrent against increasing the cost of the activity to the community and reduces externalities. But there is no similar justification for requiring a person who is not doing anything to spend money on behalf of someone else. Except in special cases (such as marine salvage) English law does not reward someone who voluntarily confers a benefit on another. So there must be some special reason why he should have to put his hand in his pocket. (at 943–4)

Lord Hoffmann suggests that the rule against liability in the context of pure omissions is an application of the 'Why pick on me?' aspect of modern day life. After all, the argument goes, why should the burden to go to the assistance of anyone else be placed on one particular person purely because they were in that particular place at that particular time?

---

3. See e.g. *Carmarthenshire County Council* v *Lewis* [1955], where the duty of a parent was confirmed in the context of a claim against a school. From *Carmarthenshire* it can be seen that a similar duty arises in respect of schools when children are in their care: see also *Barnes* v *Hampshire County Council* [1969]. This positive obligation can now also be said to extend to ensuring that the educational needs and interests of a child are met (*Bradford-Smart* v *West Sussex County Council* [2002]).

Pause for reflection

If a number of people are in a situation where they *could* prevent someone else from coming to harm, but no one actually does anything, should all of them be potentially liable for failing to help? Or does the fact that so many people *could* have done something indicate that we should not impose a positive obligation on any one of them?

In *Stovin* v *Wise*, Lord Nicholls refers to these people (who do not help) as 'callous bystander[s]' (at 931). However, he goes on to say that 'something more is required than being a bystander. There must be an additional reason why it is fair and reasonable that one person should be regarded as his brother's keeper[4] and have legal obligations in that regard'—do you agree?

While there may be arguments made against a general exclusionary principle in respect of pure omissions, the rule was vigorously reiterated by the House of Lords in *Sutradhar* v *National Environmental Research Council* [2006]. In this case, the claimant was poisoned by arsenic after drinking water from an irrigation well, which had been tested for toxins (but not arsenic) on behalf of the British government by the British Geological Survey (BGS). The claimant tried to assert that BGS had been under a positive duty to test for arsenic (particularly as arsenic-contaminated water was a major environmental problem in Bangladesh, affecting between 35 and 77 million of the country's inhabitants). The House of Lords held that no duty was owed in respect of BGS's failure to test for arsenic. Indeed, Lord Hoffmann found that 'BGS owed no positive duties to the government or people of Bangladesh to do anything. They can only be liable for the things they did…not for what they did not do' (at [27]).

Wrongly not doing something that you should have done (an omission), is to be contrasted with wrongly doing something (an act), that is 'misfeasance'. Whether a case is one or the other depends either on the nature of the relationship between the parties (claimant and defendant) or the activity being undertaken and is closely linked to the notion of proximity (or closeness of relationship) that threads through all aspects of the duty question and in particular the so-called 'problematic' duty areas.

The duties imposed by law are those not to cause injury by your actions; they are not duties actively to help or become involved with others. The courts have found that there is no duty even to go to the rescue of another who is about to injure themselves accidentally, or even to shout to warn them: as Lord Keith said in *Yuen Kun Yeu* v *Attorney General of Hong Kong* [1988], there will be no liability 'on the part of one who sees another about to walk over a cliff with his head in the air and forbears to shout

---

4. The reference to being one's brother's keeper is biblical: God, after Cain had killed Abel, asked Cain where his brother was and Cain replied 'Am I my brother's keeper?' (Genesis 4:9). The answer to Cain's question differs according to one's political and ethical standpoint. While some might answer 'Yes, you are. WE are'—that is, we are all (and should be) responsible, at least to some extent, for the welfare of our brothers and sisters (fellow humans)—others will respond differently, relying on conceptions of individual rather than collective responsibility to support the view that one should not have to expend time, energy or money on those who are not directly related (or proximate) to us in some way.

a warning' (at 192).[5] This stands in direct contrast to most civil law jurisdictions, in which such a duty *is* workably imposed upon citizens, even in relation to strangers. In France, for example, Article 223–6 of the *Code Penal* makes it a *criminal* offence not to try and assist someone in danger (as long as to do so would not mean taking undue risks to your own safety), which also translates into a civil obligation (and therefore potentially a liability) when this does not occur.[6] In the UK, only when someone does act (that is, they begin to attempt a rescue) does a duty become attached to them— they become obliged not to make the (claimant's) situation worse than it already was, though they are not obliged to make it better.[7]

 Pause for reflection

Consider how a duty to rescue *could* work in practice in relation to the example of the drowning child. What would the duty actually *consist* of, if one was to be owed? Would it be a duty to *save* the child or a duty to *try* and save the child by taking reasonable (but not dangerous) steps? Do you think there is a good reason why we should not owe this kind of duty? In any case, could we protect people from liability if they did try to help—by statute, for example? A number of US, Canadian and Australian states and territories have passed what are called 'Good Samaritan' statutes which provide those who try to help with an 'immunity from suit' (that is, they cannot be sued for any consequences of trying to help). Do you think the same should happen here?

The rule that says that you are *not* obliged to go to someone's aid, even when it would be easy for you to do so, surprises a great many law students. It lies behind what we may term 'rescuer anxiety'. Many people, when they see a situation in which they *could* intervene to help someone, are often scared to because they fear that *if* they help, they may end up being held liable for not being able to save the person. In fact, this fear reflects an inaccurate understanding of the law. One can actually only be liable, once stepping in to help, for positive actions that make the situation worse than it was before the intervention. So, in the example of the drowning child, exerting too much pressure while trying to resuscitate the child and breaking a rib while doing so may be 'making the situation worse'. *Liability*, however, is different from owing a duty of care. Liability simply means having legal responsibility for one's actions and only attaches once all the elements of a tort are made out by the claimant. So, for example, while

---

5. We can therefore infer that there would be no obligation in the scenario above for a bystander to take any measures to stop the man walking off the edge of the cliff, unless a special or pre-tort relationship existed between the parties. Nor would a doctor or nurse have to stop at the scene of an accident to help a stranger who might be injured or even dying. If they *did* stop and intervene, however, they may owe a duty not to make the situation worse.

6. The penalties apply to anyone who wilfully fails to offer assistance to a person in danger which he could himself provide without risk to himself or to third parties, or by initiating rescue operations. To give an example of this law in practice, the press photographers at the scene of Princess Diana's fatal car accident in Paris were investigated for deliberately avoiding providing assistance to endangered persons.

7. This is also the position, as will be seen in Chapter 6, that applies to the duty of care that the fire service or coastguard potentially owe to individuals. See p 139 and p 153.

someone who intervenes may owe a duty not to make the situation worse, their actions would still be judged against those of a 'reasonable person' in the circumstances (and so if a reasonable person would have tried to resuscitate the child in the same way, there will be *no breach* of their duty and therefore no *liability* to pay compensation).

 Pause for reflection

Do you think it is right that there should be no duty to act when someone is seen to be in peril? If there was a duty to try and help, what would someone have to do in order to breach that duty? Failing to do anything at all might be a breach but this will depend on the circumstances. For example, say you are walking down the High Street late at night and happen to see a mugging take place. If a general duty to rescue existed, your duty would be to try and do something to help, *if you can*—the least you could do is try to call the police or alert other people to what's happening—you would *not* have to take steps to stop the mugging yourself, as this may put you in danger. Why shouldn't this kind of duty be imposed on people? What does it say about our society and its values that such a duty is not imposed?

All this said, there are—as ever—some limited exceptions to the general exclusionary rule. These can be said to fall under three general headings:

(1) control;

(2) assumption of responsibility;

(3) creation (or adoption) of risks.

In one way or another all of these increase the degree of proximity between the claimant and defendant, creating a relationship between them and therefore providing a reason why the defendant should potentially be liable to that specific claimant for *not doing something* that they could or should have done.

4.2.1 **Control**

When we speak of control in this sense, we mean those situations where it can be said that the defendant *should* owe a duty to the claimant *because* they exercise a high degree of control over them, or have express responsibility for them. A parent or carer of a small child, for example, has a sufficient degree of control over/responsibility for their child such that they *ought* to step in to try and help them if they were drowning in a pool of water.[8] However, the control exception also extends to situations where it can be said that the defendants, because they exercise control over the person harmed, owe them a positive duty to take steps to ensure they are not harmed by themselves or by anyone else (in so doing, it clearly overlaps in part with the 'assumption of responsibility' category, discussed in the next section).

---

8. *Carmarthenshire County Council v Lewis* [1955], though note that this appears not to stretch beyond situations in which there is an express or implied undertaking to care for the child and is not based merely on e.g. a blood relationship.

An example of this can be seen in *Reeves* v *Commissioner of Police for the Metropolis* [2000].[9]

Reeves v *Commissioner of Police for the Metropolis* [2000] HL

In this case, a man called Martin Lynch committed suicide while being held in police custody. His widow claimed that the police had owed him a duty to prevent this from happening. Previous case law (see *Kirkham* v *Chief Constable of Greater Manchester* [1990]) had established that a duty of care was owed in respect of suicide attempts of prisoners known to be mentally ill, but a doctor had found Mr Lynch to be of sound mind. The police, who clearly owed him a duty of care not to physically harm him by their own actions, argued that they owed him no duty of care in respect of his suicide because he was not mentally ill, and had deliberately taken his own life, even though the opportunity for him to do so had only arisen from their own carelessness.

A majority of the House of Lords disagreed, holding that the police's duty to prisoners in custody *did* extend to a positive duty to take reasonable steps to assess the suicide risk of all prisoners. This was justified by the degree of control exercised over prisoners in custody and the known (high) risk of suicide among prisoners, even those without a known mental illness. As it was, the court also took account of the deliberate nature of the prisoner's actions by finding him partially responsible for his own death. The amount of damages awarded to his widow was therefore reduced by 50 per cent.[10]

In a later case also involving the suicide of a man in police custody, however, it was held that the duty found in *Reeves* did not mean that the police have a duty of care requiring them to treat *all* prisoners as a suicide risk. In *Orange* v *Chief Constable of West Yorkshire Police* [2001], a man committed suicide by hanging himself with his belt from a grille on the door in a police cell after being arrested and detained for being drunk and disorderly. His widow claimed that the police had owed a duty to take away any means of suicide from him, such as his belt, and that they should have watched him more carefully. The Court of Appeal held that the duty from *Reeves* was only to take reasonable steps to *assess* whether a prisoner posed a suicide risk, and to act accordingly. As the police had no real reason to think that this particular prisoner would attempt suicide, the duty did not arise in this case. This distinction was later approved by the European Court of Human Rights in *Keenan* v *United Kingdom* [2001].[11] In *Savage* v *South Essex Partnership NHS Trust* [2008], the House of Lords found that a similar positive duty, based on Article 2 ECHR, could be owed to a patient detained in a mental hospital who had negligently been allowed to abscond, later committing suicide.[12]

---

9. Notably, this case is also an exception to the general absence of duty owed by the police as a public body, discussed in Chapter 6, pp 151–152.

10. For an explanation of the principles of contributory negligence, see Chapter 10.

11. The duty of state authorities to protect prisoners with mental health problems has recently been confirmed in *Renolde* v *France* [2009].

12. The daughter of the woman who killed herself was later awarded £10,000 from the NHS in a Human Rights Act claim: *Anna Savage* v *South Essex Partnership NHS Trust* [2010]. Contrast *Rabone* v *Pennine Care NHS Trust* [2010] where a patient was voluntarily receiving inpatient treatment for her mental health.

Pause for reflection

Despite their differing outcomes, the facts of *Reeves* and *Orange* are very similar. In light of what we have said about the concept of duty being used as a 'control device', could it be argued that the Court of Appeal in *Orange* was seeking to 'put the brakes on' what could potentially be an expanding category of liability? Is it realistic to expect the police to owe a duty to all prisoners in their custody (and therefore under their control) to prevent them from attempting suicide? If not, why not? What positive obligations would this impose on the police, and are they unreasonable?

It is certainly arguable that because the risk of suicide in custody is known to be high, the police should monitor all prisoners, even those without a history of mental illness (especially when they are first admitted), should design cells in a way that would minimise the risk of suicide and should remove items from prisoners (such as belts) that they could use to harm themselves. However, this must be balanced against the resources and time available to the police and a respect for the judgements they make in relation to who is at risk and who is not. Imposing an undue burden on the police constantly to monitor every prisoner (particularly when we are talking about acts of individual responsibility) might detract from their other functions. Although, again, it is important to note that imposing a duty of care is not enough to establish liability in the tort of negligence. Similarly, we might again ask what such a duty would *consist* of—would it be a duty to prevent all suicides in custody or merely a duty to take reasonable steps to try and ensure that prisoners did not commit suicide?

4.2.2 Assumption of responsibility

As stated above, this category of exceptions has obvious links with the 'control' category. When the defendant can be said to have 'assumed responsibility' for the claimant's wellbeing or safety, then it seems obvious that positive obligations (in the form of a duty of care) should arise. The most common types of assumed responsibility (as opposed to more naturally arising relationships of responsibility, such as parent/child, which are better thought of as falling into the 'control' category) are those that arise out of a contract or from an employment relationship.

Costello v Chief Constable of Northumbria Police [1999] CA

A female police constable was attacked by a prisoner in a cell. Despite her screams for help, a police inspector who was in the vicinity did nothing to come to her aid. Costello sued, alleging that the police inspector owed a duty to assist a fellow officer when in trouble.

The Court of Appeal agreed. Police officers assume a responsibility to one another to 'watch each other's back'. Where a police officer's omission has lead to avoidable harm being suffered by a fellow officer, a positive duty to act would be imposed. Thus in failing to act, the police inspector was in breach of that duty and the Chief Constable was vicariously liable.[13]

---

13. This case is another example of an exception to the general rule that the police owe no duty of care, as discussed in Chapter 6. See further on vicarious liability Chapter 12.

Another way that someone can assume responsibility for the wellbeing of someone else is by their actions. Put another way, *what* someone does in relation to someone else can indicate, by conduct, an assumption of responsibility. A clear example of this is seen in *Barrett* v *Ministry of Defence* [1995].

Barrett v *Ministry of Defence* [1995] CA

A naval pilot stationed on a remote Norwegian naval base where extreme drunkenness had become commonplace had been celebrating his 30th birthday and a promotion, when he became so drunk that he collapsed. The officer on duty ordered that he be taken to his bed—however, no one stayed to watch over him and make sure he did not choke. He later choked to death on his own vomit.

At first instance, it was ruled that the senior officers had breached their duty to prevent irresponsible drinking by the men on the base, but the damages to be awarded would be reduced by 25 per cent to account for the man's own contributory negligence.

The Court of Appeal agreed. However, to them, the senior officers' duty (and, through the doctrine of vicarious liability, that of the Ministry of Defence) was not owed in relation to the failure to prevent or discourage excessive drinking, as here the court felt that adults should take responsibility for themselves in this respect. Rather, a duty was owed in relation to the duty officer's failure to have someone stationed to watch the drunken man while he slept (a different omission) because by that point, responsibility for the man's safety had been assumed by the officer concerned:

> [i]n the present case I would reverse the judge's finding that the defendant was under a duty to take reasonable care to prevent the deceased from abusing alcohol to the extent he did. Until he collapsed, I would hold that the deceased was in law alone responsible for his condition. Thereafter, when the defendant assumed responsibility for him, it accepts that the measures taken fell short of the standard reasonably to be expected. It did not summon medical assistance and its supervision of him was inadequate. (Beldam LJ at 1225)

The Court of Appeal also considered that more responsibility for his death lay with the deceased than with the officers, and reduced the damages by two-thirds.

 Counterpoint

On closer inspection, the *ratio* of *Barrett* suggests that had no one found the naval officer when he was drunk or—more specifically, as this is what the case turns on—taken him back to his room, no one would have assumed responsibility and therefore no duty of care would or could have arisen. Can this be right? What this means is that if he had fallen unconscious outside (on the Norwegian naval base) and been left to freeze to death, either because he had not been found or because whoever did see him chose to ignore his plight and walk past (a 'pure' omission), no duty of care would have been owed. Would it be better to say that this was a situation in which the superior officers had 'control', and therefore *should* have done what they could to prevent excessive drinking? Or is it right that individual responsibility is taken into account *only until the point when someone else intervenes*?

4.2.3 **Creating or adopting risks**

The final exception to the general exclusionary rule in relation to omissions is based on the creation or adoption of a risk. If it can be said that the defendant—even accidentally—creates a dangerous situation, a positive duty to try and deal with that danger may be imposed. In *Capital & Counties plc* v *Hampshire County Council* **[1997]**, it was found that a fire service, as a public body, will only owe a duty to a property owner when it either created the danger in the first place or where its positive actions upon responding to the fire made the situation worse than it already was. In this case, the county council was vicariously liable for the fire chief's decision to turn off a sprinkler system on the claimant's property, thereby allowing the fire to spread more rapidly than it would have had the sprinkler system still been operational. This general point flows through the law on omissions.

In terms of 'adopting' risks, *Goldman* v *Hargrave* [1967][14] illustrates a similar idea. Here, a tree caught fire after being struck by lightning. The landowner ensured that the tree was cut down, but decided to let it burn itself out and took no further precautions to stop the fire from spreading. Therefore, although he had not caused the risk, in deciding not to take any further steps to completely extinguish the fire he had adopted the risk that the fire might spread (in a similar way to assuming responsibility for someone else he had, in a sense, assumed responsibility for the risk). Extensive damage was caused to a neighbouring property when the fire was revived by the wind and spread. The Privy Council found that a duty of care was owed in relation to adopted dangers existing on one's land when that danger could spread to a neighbour's land.

4.3 **Summary of when a duty of care may be found in respect of omissions**

Table 4.1 Summary of when a duty of care may be found in respect of omissions

Omissions	
General rule: no duty of care *Smith* v *Littlewoods* [1987] **Stovin** v *Wise* **[1996]** *Sutradhar* v *National Environmental Research Council* [2006]	Exceptions:
	Control exercised over claimant by defendant **Reeves** v *Commissioner of Police for the Metropolis* **[2000]**
	Assumption of responsibility for claimant's welfare by defendant *Costello* v *Chief Constable of Northumbria Police* [1999] *Barrett* v *Ministry of Defence* [1995]
	Creation or adoption of a risk *Capital & Counties plc* v *Hampshire County Council* [1997] *Goldman* v *Hargrave* [1967]

14. Discussed in more detail in the section on land torts, see Chapter 18, p 543.

4.4 Liability for acts of third parties: the general rule

There is no general duty to prevent other people causing damage. After all, why should someone owe a duty of care in respect of harm inflicted on another by a third party? Again, however, there are exceptions to this general rule, many of which relate to and overlap with some of the concepts already discussed in the context of omissions, and stem from either a special or pre-tort relationship. For example, it is often because someone has not done something (an omission) that a third party is allowed the chance or opportunity to do something that they otherwise might not have done, this being what leads to the harm suffered.[15] The question for the courts is similar to that in relation to omissions—in what circumstances should we depart from the general rule that people should not be liable for the actions of third parties?

4.5 When is there liability for the acts of third parties?

The law *does* impose liability for the acts of third parties in exceptional circumstances. In such circumstances, one of the logistical problems that might have been encountered—in relation to when or whether a defendant should be liable for the actions of a third party—is broadly met by the *content* of the duty being a 'duty to control the third party' or a 'duty to safeguard a dangerous thing'. However, this does not prevent there being any problems with causation—as we will see, a later act of a third party may actually operate to break the chain of causation back to the defendant (or may affect what damages can be paid if thought to be a supervening, rather than intervening event).[16] It is a very fine line as to whether a third party's actions fall to be considered as a duty issue or a causation issue and often the questions we ask are part and parcel of the same thing.[17] Some guidance on this point can be gleaned from the speech of Lord Reid in *Home Office* v *Dorset Yacht Co Ltd* **[1970]** where he said that an act of a third party:

> must have been something very likely to happen if it is not to be regarded as a *novus actus interveniens* breaking the chain of causation. I do not think that a mere foreseeable possibility is or should be sufficient, for then the intervening human action can more properly be regarded as a new cause than as a consequence of the original wrongdoing. (at 1030)

So, there are some exceptional situations in which a duty has been imposed on a defendant in respect of the actions of a third party. Lord Goff (in *Smith* v *Littlewoods* [1987]) suggested that such a duty can in fact arise in four types of situation:

(1) where there is a special relationship between the defendant and the claimant;

15. See e.g. *Home Office* v *Dorset Yacht Co Ltd* [1970].
16. Chapter 9, p 250.
17. See further *Smith* v *Littlewoods* [1987], as one example of a case that clearly highlights the difficulty courts have in categorising third party actions as either a duty or causation issue.

(2) where there is a special relationship between the defendant and the third party, such as a relationship of control or supervision;

(3) where someone creates a 'source of danger' that may be 'sparked' by a third party;

(4) where there is a failure to take steps to abate a known danger created by a third party.

We will look at examples from each of these categories in turn to explain how a duty might arise in these circumstances.

4.5.1 A special relationship between defendant and claimant

Where the defendant and the claimant have a special (pre-tort) relationship, that is a relationship in which a sufficient degree of proximity can be found to justify the imposition of a duty of care from one to the other, a duty may arise in relation to the activities of a third party. Such a relationship may be defined by a contract between the two parties. For example, in *Stansbie* v *Troman* [1948], the claimant employed the defendant to decorate her premises. When she went out, she specifically requested that the decorator lock up after himself when he left. He failed to do this and she was subsequently burgled. Here, the court found that the contractual relationship between them was enough to create the degree of proximity necessary for the imposition of a duty of care on the defendant. Put simply, because of the relationship between them, he had a duty to lock the premises when he left, in order to prevent a burglary by a third party.[18]

A contrast can be found, however, in *P Perl (Exporters) Ltd* v *Camden London Borough Council* [1984]. Here, two adjoining buildings were owned by Camden Council, one of which was leased by the claimant, the other was empty. The empty building had no lock on the door. As a result, thieves entered the premises, made a hole in the wall separating the two buildings, and burgled the claimant's property. The Court of Appeal found that the council owed no duty of care in respect of the third parties' (the burglars') actions. Even though they could have foreseen that some harm might be caused by leaving their property unlocked, this was not enough to establish the necessary proximity between the defendant and the claimant.

Notably, however, this case falls into a clear group of cases in which property owners were not found—for various reasons—liable for the actions of third parties. This suggests that there may be underlying policy reasons for such decisions, not least the fact that the property-owning claimants might be expected to have insurance.[19] However, presumably, *all* property owners might be expected to have insurance meaning that there are equally valid competing policy reasons in these cases.

The requisite degree of proximity may also stem from an express or implied undertaking made by the defendant to the claimant. In such circumstances—for example where the defendant promised not to do something that may endanger the claimant

---

18. The principle has been more recently confirmed in *Bailey and another* v *HSS Alarms* (2000) *The Times*, 20 June.

19. Indeed, this point was explicitly acknowledged by Lord Denning MR in *Lamb* v *Camden London Borough Council* [1981], a case with similar facts to *P Perl (Exporters) Ltd*.

in some way—it seems right that a duty should be owed. In *Swinney* v *Chief Constable of Northumbria Police* [1997] the Court of Appeal found that the police owed a duty of care not to leak confidential information about the claimant, a police informant, because otherwise she may be harmed by those about whom she had given information. Such undertakings can also be implied, as in **Costello** where it was found that one police officer has a duty to assist another if they come under attack from a third party in police custody.

However, it can also be seen that there has to be a *direct* undertaking by the defendant in order for a duty to arise in these circumstances. In **Hill v Chief Constable of West Yorkshire** [1989] and **Osman v Ferguson** [1993], for example, no duty was owed by the police to the claimants, who were victims of crimes committed by a third party. In both of these cases the police had a general duty to the public at large, but no specific duty existed to protect the claimants from harm, as no promise—express or implied—had been made to this effect.[20] The idea that there must indeed be a specific undertaking can also be seen in a more recent case, **Palmer v Tees Health Authority** [1999].

Palmer v *Tees Health Authority* [1999] CA

Mrs Palmer alleged that the defendant health authority had been negligent in its assessment of a mentally ill patient—Armstrong—who had sexually assaulted, killed and mutilated her 4-year-old daughter Rosie upon his release from a secure unit. While under treatment for his illness, Armstrong stated that he had sexual feelings towards children and had threatened to abduct and murder a child. Post-release, he failed to attend an outpatient's appointment.

The Court of Appeal, relying on *Hill*, found that the health authority owed neither Mrs Palmer nor Rosie a duty of care, as the necessary level of proximity between the claimants and the defendant did not exist. The child was not identifiable as a potential victim (as in *Hill*), meaning the health authority could have done nothing to prevent her murder, other than keep the patient detained, so there was no special relationship that could give rise to a duty of care.

Though we note that in his judgment in **Palmer**, Stuart-Smith LJ said that 'once rules are established, it is not open to the courts to extend the accepted principles of proximity simply because the facts of a given case are particularly horrifying or heart-rending' (at 7), it appears strange to us that the requisite degree of proximity could not be found—or was not even argued on appeal—from the fact that Rosie lived in the same street as Armstrong.

Following **Palmer**, it was argued in *K* v *Secretary of State for the Home Department* [2002] that in situations where 'exceptionally serious' risks are posed by a known third party, a sufficient degree of proximity could exist between an injured claimant and a defendant whose negligence fails to prevent the harm occurring. Here a Kenyan man, who had been imprisoned for a number of violent crimes and was due to be deported,

---

20. It should be noted here that there was a far higher degree of proximity in **Osman v Ferguson** than in **Hill**, though still not enough in the court's opinion to make it 'fair, just and reasonable' to impose a duty on the police (see further p 145).

was released early by the Secretary of State. The claimant, who was subsequently raped by the man, sued the Secretary of State alleging that the decision to release him early was negligent, as he posed a known risk of committing a violent crime. The Court of Appeal found that because the victim was unidentifiable to the defendant, there was no relationship of proximity between the claimant and defendant, following the authority of **Hill** and **Palmer**, and this was not changed by the seriousness of the risk, even if it was clearly known by the defendant that such a risk existed.

 Pause for reflection

Do you think it is right that the claimants in cases like **Palmer** and *K* should have no cause of action? Where a psychiatric patient makes known his wish to harm a child, *should* he be released? *Why* do you think the criminal in *K* was released before deportation? Surely both men did 'the very thing that was likely to happen' upon their release? As we have seen from Lord Reid's comment in **Dorset Yacht**, this is, in slightly different circumstances, enough to create a duty. We would argue that simply because there was no undertaking between the defendant and the claimant, this should not mean that the claimants in cases like **Palmer** and *K* have no cause of action. The crimes committed were just as severe, and the defendant's negligence just as intense, as they would have been if the criminal had told the defendant who he was intending to attack. Arguably, also, preventative measures would have been easy to take in each of the cases.

In any case, as we have seen from cases like **Osman v Ferguson**,[21] even where the victim is clearly identifiable (thus creating the requisite degree of proximity), a duty may not arise for policy reasons. What policy reasons exist in relation to these cases?

A recent case in which the House of Lords underlined the principle that a duty of care will not exist even where a potential victim is known to the defendant unless a specific undertaking has been made is *Mitchell* v *Glasgow City Council* [2009]. A 72-year-old man was attacked and killed with a stick or iron bar by his 60-year-old neighbour, Drummond. Both were tenants of the defendant, who had long been aware of Drummond's anti-social and hostile behaviour, including death threats made to the deceased. Having issued many previous warnings, after a further serious incident the defendant called Drummond to a meeting, where he was told he may be evicted if his anti-social behaviour continued. Leaving the meeting angry, Drummond returned home and attacked Mitchell. Acting on his behalf, Mitchell's widow contended that the council owed the deceased a duty of care to inform him the meeting had taken place and warn both him and the police of the potential danger. The House of Lords found that the council owed the claimant no duty of care:

> [a] duty to warn another person that he is at risk of loss, injury or damage as the result of the criminal act of a third party will only arise where the person who is said to be under that duty has by his words or conduct assumed responsibility for the safety of the person who is at risk. (Lord Hope at [29])

Given the high degree of foreseeability of harm, coupled with the council's proximate relationship (to both the claimant *and* the third party), as well as what looks

---

21. Also see **Smith v Chief Constable of Sussex** [2008].

like assumption of responsibility for the situation, it is not apparent to us that this is a clear-cut case where no duty should be owed.[22]

4.5.2 **A special relationship between defendant and third party**

Again, when we speak of a 'special relationship' in this respect, we are talking about proximity. The more proximate (or close) the relationship between the defendant and the third party who actually caused the damage or harm, the more likely it is that a duty will be imposed on the defendant in respect of the third party's actions. As with liability for omissions, proximate relationships in this context will include those where there is a degree of control exercised over the third party by the defendant, or where it can be said that the defendant has 'assumed responsibility' for the actions of the third party. *Home Office* v *Dorset Yacht Co Ltd* illustrates this principle well.[23]

Home Office v *Dorset Yacht Co Ltd* [1970] HL

In this case, the court had to consider whether the acts of third parties (young offenders detained on Brownsea Island just off the Dorset coast) broke the chain of causation between the defendant's carelessness and the damage suffered by the claimants. The defendants, the boys' supervisors (for whom the Home Office would be vicariously liable), negligently allowed a group of boys to escape and damage the claimants' yachts moored in the harbour. Here, the supervisory nature of the relationship created the requisite degree of proximity between the defendant and the third party. Moreover, the damage suffered by the claimants was the direct consequence of this relationship 'failing'—upon their escape, the boys did the very thing that might be expected of them—they attempted to steal a boat to get off the island. The chain of causation was therefore intact and, correspondingly, a duty of care was owed in respect of the boys' actions. The duty arose because the actions of the boys following their negligent supervision were the thing 'very likely to happen' (Lord Reid at 1030).

 Counterpoint

In the previous section we looked at the cases of *Palmer* and *K*, where no duty was found on the basis that the relationship between the defendants and claimants lacked proximity. In our view, however, it is equally arguable that those cases fit into the category of a special relationship (based on control or an assumption of responsibility) existing between the defendant *and the third party.*

 Did the claimants fail to establish a duty only because the case was being looked at the wrong way? We can see no real differences between these cases; if anything, the case

---

22. Also see *X & Y* v *London Borough of Hounslow* [2009] EWCA Civ 286, discussed in Chapter 2, pp 45–53 and Chapter 6, p 164. The Court of Appeal decision relied heavily on the findings in *Mitchell.*

23. Also see *Vowles* v *Evans and Another* [2003] in the context of sports officials.

⟶

in *Palmer* is stronger than that in *Dorset Yacht*. In the former, not only was the psychiatric patient still under the care of the health authority as an outpatient but he had expressed a *specific* wish to harm a child.

In *Palmer*, the Court of Appeal found that there was no proximity between the defendant and the claimant as there had been no assumption of responsibility toward the victim, who was merely one of a member of a class of people who might be at risk. Is this the right question to ask, given there are four exceptions to the general exclusionary rule to the liability for third parties, as outlined by Lord Goff? Is it better to ask whether the defendant assumed responsibility for the conduct of (or the danger posed by) the third party?

Consider here the Canadian case of *Doe v Metropolitan Toronto (Municipality) Commissioners of Police* [1998], where it was found that a woman *was* owed a duty of care by the police in respect of her rape. She was one of a number of women in the potential target group for the rapist, who operated in a particular area of the city and was known as the 'Balcony Rapist' because he preferred to gain access to women's flats via their balconies. The potential victims were neither warned nor adequately protected owing to a number of significant failings on the part of the police. Was this case decided differently from *Palmer* and *K* because the woman was in a smaller and more readily identifiable group of potential victims? If so, how few potential victims need there be before it can be said a duty would be owed to each of them? In *Palmer*, it should be remembered, the victim lived on the same street as the man who killed her. How difficult would it have been to warn parents of children in the area? Or, if this is not the appropriate response, what else could the health authority have done? In our opinion, the fact that the claimant in *Palmer* could have been classified in a smaller group of potential victims should, like in *Doe*, have weighed more heavily with the court, as it is this feature that marks this case out from a law where the police would owe a duty in respect of all crimes committed by released prisoners and health authorities for psychiatric patients.

4.5.3 Creating a source of danger

If a third party's actions exacerbate a dangerous situation originally created by the defendant, subsequently causing the claimant harm, the defendant may owe the claimant a duty of care. For example, in *Haynes* v *Harwood* [1936], the defendant left his horses untethered on a busy street, and they bolted when some children threw stones at them. A police officer was injured trying to control the horses; it was found that the defendant owed him a duty of care, as he had created a source of danger that was 'sparked' by the third parties.

For a duty to be found in these circumstances, a special risk must be created. In *Topp* v *London Country Bus* [1993], the defendant's employee left an unlocked minibus unattended outside a pub, with the keys in its ignition. Unsurprisingly, when the pub closed, a patron entered the minibus and drove it away carelessly, killing a pedestrian. However, the Court of Appeal found that the minibus was no more a source of danger than any other vehicle parked on the road at that time, therefore leaving the minibus did not create the type of risk that would create a duty of care as in *Haynes*.[24]

 Pause for reflection

Is an unlocked bus with the keys in the ignition, left outside a pub at closing time, really less dangerous than an untethered horse? Is the outcome of this case surprising, particularly as the driver/owners of the bus would be insured?

4.5.4 **A failure to abate a known danger**

In a sense, this is the reverse of the situation outlined above. There, we looked at instances where the defendant created a danger that could be 'sparked' by a third party. Here, we consider the situation where the danger is in fact created by a third party, but the defendant does nothing to abate that danger. However, the key word here is 'known'; unknown (or unknowable) dangers do not fall into this category. It can be summed up as follows: if a defendant knows—or ought to have known— that a third party has created a danger that he *should* do something about (for example because it is on his property), then the defendant will owe a duty of care to anyone injured as a result of that danger.[25] Put simply, the defendant has a duty to do something about the danger in order to prevent injury (to person or property) to anyone else.

In *Smith* v *Littlewoods* [1987], the claimant's property was damaged by fire spreading from a derelict cinema owned by Littlewoods after vandals had entered the empty cinema at night and started a fire there. The House of Lords—in particular Lord Goff— found that only where the danger was known, or foreseeable, would a duty be owed in respect of the danger.[26] On the facts, no such duty was owed as Littlewoods had no reason to suspect the entry of the vandals and the only thing they could have done to prevent such a thing occurring would be to hire round-the-clock security, which would be disproportionate to the level of risk. As they had some security and had taken some precaution against trespassers, they had done all they reasonably should be expected to do. This case illustrates that a duty will arise only when the specific danger is (or ought to be) known—and is therefore foreseeable to the defendant.[27] In this sense it went a long way towards clarifying the law in this area in which liability

---

24. Would the same be true where a cleaner left the door to a pub open one night (as in the scenario at the beginning of the chapter)? The legal question is whether she should be held responsible for the damage to the pub and, also, for the damage to the car parked on the same street. By analogy with *Stansbie* it might be fairly easy to establish the duty in relation to the stolen alcohol and damaged pub—but might *Topp* stand in the way of the car owner claiming successfully?

25. See, in the context of land torts, **Sedleigh Denfield v O'Callaghan** [1940], *Goldman* v *Hargrave* [1967] and *Leakey* v *National Trust* [1980] (pp 542–544).

26. Notably, although *Smith* v *Littlewoods* was a unanimous decision, each of the law lords reached their decision by different means.

27. Compare also Smith LJ's judgment in the context of a knife attack in a nightclub in the more recent case *Everett* v *Comojo (UK) Ltd (t/a The Metropolitan)* [2011], particularly [31]–[33].

had previously been judicially controlled using various other aspects of the law of negligence.[28]

In *Clark Fixing Ltd* v *Dudley Metropolitan Borough Council* [2001], the reasoning from *Smith* v *Littlewoods* was used to find a duty in exactly the extended circumstances envisaged by Lord Goff in that case. In *Clark*, Dudley Council owned property which shared a roof with an adjoining property owned by the claimant. Similarly to *Smith*, trespassers entered the council's property and started a fire, which spread to the claimant's property, causing substantial damage. The council, unlike the cinema owners in *Smith*, was aware that trespassers had entered the premises—and had started fires—on a number of previous occasions, and in fact the claimants had complained about this to the council. Because of this, the Court of Appeal found that a duty should be owed by the council to the claimants, even though the actual harm had been caused by third parties. Similarly, but without actual knowledge of the risk, a duty of care was found in *Sandhu Menswear Co Ltd* v *Woolworths plc* [2006], where the defendants had left piles of flammable material by storage units on an industrial estate, which when set alight had caused damage to the claimant's property. Even though in this case, unlike *Clark*, there was no evidence that fires had previously been lit by third parties, the court held that it was foreseeable that fires *could* be lit by people trespassing in the area and therefore a duty could be found.

 Pause for reflection

As outlined in the introduction to negligence chapter, a claimant not only has to prove that a duty was owed to them, but that this was breached and that the breach *caused* the harm suffered by them. How is it possible, however, when the harm is the result of a third party's actions, to establish that the *defendant* was the *cause* of the claimant's harm?

Generally, this causation difficulty is overcome by the *content* of the duty—for example, it will be a 'duty to control a third party' or a 'duty to safeguard a dangerous thing'. When looked at this way, failure to control a third party or a dangerous thing (the breach) *is* what causes the claimant's harm. Do you agree with this statement? And if so, how do we explain cases like *Palmer* or *K*?

 Counterpoint

According to Claire McIvor, 'third party liability' is a 'novel category of tortious liability' that has 'evolved from a collection of disparate and isolated judicial decisions setting out *ad hoc* exceptions to the entrenched common law rules against liability for omissions and liability for the acts of others' (p 1). We agree, adding that the law defining if and when a defendant can be held to owe a duty of care in respect of either an omission or for the

➔

---

28. Compare, e.g. *Lamb* v *Camden London Borough Council* [1981] (third party's acts too remote a consequence of the defendant's breach (causation in law)), *P Perl* v *Camden London Borough Council*, (no duty because the defendant could not be expected to control the actions of third parties) and *King* v *Liverpool City Council* [1986] (duty found but defendant not in breach as there was nothing they could reasonably have done to prevent the third parties' actions).

→

actions of another seems to be based on judicial perceptions rooted wholeheartedly in the concept of individualism. While it may often be admirable to indicate that people should only take responsibility for their own actions, this approach does not adequately take into account the fact that in many of the cases we have seen it may be more morally justifiable to adopt a broader conception of duty and allow breach to be used as a control on liability. Put simply, we would prefer the approach in these situations to be based on the level of fault or moral blameworthiness that could be attached to the defendant. McIvor is right to contend that due to 'the improvised nature of its development, the current law on third party liability is unstructured, unprincipled and incoherent' (p 1).

4.6 Summary of when a duty of care may be found for the actions of third parties

Table 4.2 Summary of when a duty of care may be found for the actions of third parties

General rule: no duty of care	Exceptions (see *Smith v Littlewoods* [1987])	
	Proximity between defendant and claimant	
	Duty found in *Stansbie* v *Troman* [1948] *Swinney* v *Chief Constable of Northumbria Police* [1997]	But not in *P Perl (Exporters)* v *Camden London Borough Council* [1984] **Palmer v Tees Health Authority [1999]** *K* v *Secretary of State for the Home Department* [2002]
	Proximity between defendant and third party	
	Duty found in **Home Office v Dorset Yacht [1970]**	But not in **Palmer v Tees Health Authority [1999]** *K* v *Secretary of State for the Home Department* [2002]
	Creation of a source of danger	
	Duty found in *Haynes* v *Harwood* [1936]	But not in *Topp* v *London Country Bus* [1993]
	Failure to abate a known danger	
	Duty found in *Clark Fixing Ltd* v *Dudley Metropolitan Borough Council* [2001] *Sandhu Menswear Co Ltd* v *Woolworths plc* [2006]	But not in *Smith* v *Littlewoods* [1987]

4.7 **Conclusion**

In this chapter we have looked at the separate—but closely linked—concepts of liability for **omissions** and liability for the **actions of third parties**. A general exclusionary rule operates in respect of both. However, as usual, there are exceptions to these rules.

In relation to omissions, a duty of care can be established if the defendant and claimant were deemed to be in a relationship that makes it appropriate to depart from the general rule. As we saw, such relationships include those where a degree of control is exercised over the claimant by the defendant, that is, where the responsibility for them is explicit, such as in a parent–child relationship or with people held in custody and known to be a suicide risk. They may also be defined by assumption of responsibility. If the defendant has actively assumed the responsibility for the claimant's wellbeing, this will be enough, in many cases, to mean that a positive duty to act should be imposed. Finally, we saw that there can be positive obligations in respect of omissions in circumstances where a risk is created or adopted by a defendant.

Third party liability is controlled by similar concepts. Relationships between claimants and defendants are important here also, as the courts have held that a high level of proximity is required before a duty will be imposed. This works in two ways: either there is sufficient proximity between the defendant and the claimant (such as in many contractual relationships) that makes it appropriate for the defendant to be liable when a third party causes harm to the claimant, or there is sufficient proximity between the defendant and the third party. As with omissions, this may come from there being a relationship of control and/or responsibility between the defendant and the third party. Again, in a similar way to liability for omissions, a defendant may be liable for the actions of a third party when they have either created a danger that a third party's actions might cause harm or have failed to abate a known danger created by a third party.

✱ **End-of-chapter questions**

After reading the chapter carefully, try answering the questions below. If you would like to know what we think visit the Online Resource Centre (www.oxfordtextbooks.co.uk/orc/horsey2e/).

1. Should a 'Good Samaritan' statute be passed in this country? What are the benefits of *not* having one?

2. Do the concepts of liberal individualism and personal autonomy carry more weight than collective or social responsibility? Should they?

3. In his speech in *Smith* v *Littlewoods* [1987], Lord Goff indicated that the legal treatment of omissions may one day need to be reconsidered. Was he correct?

4. Consider the problem question at the start of this chapter. Now having read about the topic, what would be your advice to the various injured parties? If you need some pointers in thinking about how to answer this question, turn to the Appendix (p 589) where each problem is annotated with issues and cases to consider. Next, try to write your own answer and, finally, log on to our Online Resource Centre (www.oxfordtextbooks.co.uk/orc/horsey2e/) to check your ideas against our suggested outline answer.

✳ Further reading

Modern literature on this area of law tends to focus on reform, highlighting the inconsistencies and inadequacies of the existing law. Claire McIvor's book would be a great starting point from which to critique the law on third party liability, while Joroen Kortmann provides excellent analysis of the principles of altruism and rescue in the context of English law. Chapter 3 of the book contains a particularly good and persuasive critique of Lord Hoffmann's reasoning/justifications in **Stovin v Wise**.

Kortmann, Jeroen *Altruism in Private Law: Liability for Nonfeasance and* Negotorium Gestio (OUP, 2005)

McIvor, Claire *Third Party Liability in Tort* (Hart Publishing, 2006)

Randell, Melanie 'Sex Discrimination, Accountability of Public Authorities and the Public/Private Divide in Tort Law: An Analysis of *Doe* v *Metropolitan Toronto (Municipality) Commissioners of Police*' (2000–01) 26 *Queen's Law Journal* 451

5

Psychiatric harm

Problem question

Read this problem question carefully, and keep it in mind while you are working through the chapter that follows. At the end of the chapter, you will be able to apply what you have learnt to the problem question and advise the relevant parties.

Following months of speculation the legendary indie guitar band—*Blinking Idiot*—are about to embark on a reunion tour of the UK. They are performing a warm-up gig at a small intimate venue when a spotlight falls onto the stage causing a massive explosion killing the band members: Madeleine, Rob and Dave. Unfortunately, the lighting rig (onto which the spotlight was fitted) had been negligently maintained by Rack & Horse Lighting. The sight is particularly gruesome.

Hannah, Rob's wife, is watching the gig from the VIP area of the venue. She is physically unharmed, but later suffers nightmares and depression. This is particularly traumatic for her as she had previously suffered from depression, but had sought help and recovered.

Pete, Madeleine's brother, is listening to the live radio broadcast of the gig from his hotel room in Paris. He hears the explosion and thinks he can hear Madeleine screaming. He rushes to the airport, managing to catch a flight that is just leaving, and arrives at the hospital three hours after the accident. Unfortunately, Madeleine's body has not yet been moved to the morgue and is still covered in blood and grime from the explosion. He develops post-traumatic shock disorder.

→

➡

Lucy has attended every *Blinking Idiot* gig in the UK and has travelled to a number of their overseas concerts. She is a founder member of their fan club and regularly contributes to their fan magazine. She always tries to stand as close as possible to the stage. Miraculously she was not hurt by the explosion but has since been overcome with grief.

Tim was one of the first on the scene. He is a trainee ambulance man and this was his first major incident. He rushes to the stage but quickly sees that there is little he can do. He spends the next two hours comforting distraught fans. He later suffers from recurring nightmares and panic attacks.

Stuart, one of the roadies, is overcome with feelings of guilt and depression. It was his job to fix the lighting and he feels the explosion was his fault. A subsequent investigation completely exonerates him.

5.1 Introduction

Consider the following examples:

→ **A grandfather watches as his grandchild is hit and killed by a car driven by a drunk driver. He later develops severe depression.**

→ **A woman is diagnosed with cancer and told she only has weeks to live. Distraught, she settles her affairs, plans her funeral and waits to die. Six months later she is still alive and further medical tests reveal that there has been a misdiagnosis—her X-rays became mixed up with another patient's and she is not sick after all. She is deeply embarrassed about seeing the people she told she was dying and has become severely agoraphobic.**

→ **A teenage boy is involved in a car accident. Though he escapes physical injury, he suffers a reoccurrence of chronic fatigue syndrome.**

→ **An elderly man is trapped in a poorly serviced lift for 12 hours. During the experience he is very frightened and afterwards suffers from claustrophobia and insomnia.**

→ **The organisers of a gig negligently let too many people into the venue. The gig is being broadcast live and a young teenager sees his boyfriend caught in the crush at the front of the stage. Six hours later his mother tells him that his boyfriend has died. Over the next two months the teenager becomes increasingly withdrawn and is unable to sleep.**

In all these cases, the nature of the harm suffered is not physical but mental or psychological. The distinction between physical and psychiatric injuries is an important one. The courts have been far more cautious in recognising claims in respect of psychiatric harms than they have in relation to physical injuries, developing a body of rules severely limiting the circumstances in which the victim will be able to recover compensation for their mental injuries.[1] Whether this distinction can be justified as a matter of principle or policy—and indeed whether there is in fact any clear and coherent distinction between physical and psychiatric harms—is far from certain.

5.2 What is psychiatric harm?

Psychiatric harm is a form of personal injury. When the courts first started considering claims in respect of psychiatric injuries, they focused on the distinct *ways* in which such harm tends to be caused: that is by an 'assault' on an individual's mind or senses rather than physical impact on the claimant's body. This explains references to this area of law as relating to liability for 'nervous shock'. So construed, this grouped psychiatric harms together with certain physical harms likewise caused by what one has witnessed (for instance a number of the early cases concerned miscarriages suffered by women after traumatic experiences). However, the distinct policy issues raised by psychiatric injuries have seen the focus shift away from the way the harm is caused to the type of harm suffered. As *Ibbetson* notes:

> Before the middle of the twentieth century the courts took a restrictive attitude towards liability for 'nervous shock'; the focus here was not on the type of injury but on the way in which it had been caused. Gradually this twisted round until 'nervous shock' was identified with 'post-traumatic stress disorder'—a type of harm rather than a mode of causation of harm—from which it shifted yet further into 'psychiatric injury'. (p 195)

Nowadays the courts maintain a clear distinction between physical and psychiatric harm with different rules applying to each. This is notwithstanding developing medical knowledge as to the serious and incapacitating nature of mental illnesses and awareness of the difficulties in categorising injuries as either physical or psychiatric, as well as judicial acknowledgement that this distinction is largely unreal and unsustainable.[2] Nonetheless, there continues to be a reluctance to let go of the common perception that mental harm is not just different from but also 'less significant than physical harm, inability to cope through neurosis less serious than inability to walk by reason of amputation' (*Weir* p 49).

Though at first psychiatric harm was recoverable only if accompanied by physical injury, it is now clear that the claimant can recover for pure psychiatric harm so long

---

1. The focus of this chapter is on claims for negligently caused pure psychiatric injuries, that is where the *only* injury suffered by the claimant is psychiatric. Where the claimant suffers psychiatric harm as a result of physical injuries negligently inflicted by the defendant, recovery is straightforward (*Corr* v *IBC Vehicles Ltd* [2008]).

2. See, e.g. Kennedy J in *Dulieu* v *White & Sons* [1901] at 677 and the comment of Lord Lloyd in *Page* v *Smith* [1996]: 'In an age when medical knowledge is expanding fast, and psychiatric knowledge with it, it would not be sensible to commit the law to a distinction between physical and psychiatric injury, which may already seem somewhat artificial, and may soon be altogether outmoded' (at 188).

as it is a recognised psychiatric illness. However, it is not possible to recover in the tort of negligence for mere grief, anxiety or distress (*Hicks* v *Chief Constable of South Yorkshire Police* [1992]).[3] As Lord Steyn noted in **White v Chief Constable of South Yorkshire Police [1998]** 'the law cannot compensate for all emotional suffering even if it is acute and truly debilitating' (at 491). This was confirmed by the House of Lords in **Grieves v FT Everard & Sons [2007]**.[4] In this case, the claimants had developed pleural plaques[5] after being exposed to asbestos dust at work. Upholding the Court of Appeal's decision, the House of Lords held that neither the pleural plaques themselves nor the claimants' anxiety that they might become seriously ill could ground their claim.[6] However, while some conditions such as depression, schizophrenia, post-traumatic stress disorder and anxiety neurosis are clearly recognisable as psychiatric illnesses, in other cases it is difficult to distinguish ordinary feelings of anxiety or distress from an actionable harm. It may be that the question is one of degree, rather than type, of harm.[7]

 Pause for reflection

Consider for a moment the facts of *Hicks*. The claimants, Sarah and Victoria Hicks, were crushed and suffocated to death in the Hillsborough Stadium disaster. The House of Lords rejected a claim for psychiatric harm brought on their behalf (by their father, Trevor Hicks) holding that the police's negligence had only caused the Hicks sisters to suffer 'distress' which was not recoverable. The evidence suggested that they had become unconscious within seconds and died within five minutes. Do you agree with the House of Lords' decision? At what point, if any, should negligently inflicted 'distress' ground a claim for psychiatric injury? Why do you think Trevor Hicks brought this claim? Think again about the purposes of tort law discussed in Chapter 1, pp 9–18.

---

3. A claimant may, however, have a claim under one of the intentional torts, e.g. assault or libel (which are actionable *per se*) or under the rule in *Wilkinson* v *Downton* [1897].

4. Also known as *Rothwell* v *Chemical and Insulating Co Ltd and Johnston* v *NEI International Combustion Ltd*.

5. A lung condition with no real symptoms, but which can come only from exposure to asbestos. While the plaques in themselves do not lead to an increased risk of developing a serious lung disease such as asbestosis and mesothelioma, the mere fact that the plaques had developed would instil the knowledge that contracting either of these more serious diseases was possible.

6. The Government consulted on their response to the decision in *Grieves* (Pleural plaques, CP 14/08) and in February 2010 introduced an extra-statutory scheme which will make payments of £5,000 to individuals *who had started but not resolved* a claim for compensation before the decision in *Grieves*. The payment broadly reflects the level of compensation likely to have been received if pleural plaques had continued to be compensatable (Pleural plaques: Jack Straw statement, Ministry of Justice, 25 February 2010).

7. It is crucial then that the elderly man trapped in a lift (referred to in the examples at the start of this chapter) is able to show that his insomnia and claustrophobia are (or are symptoms of) a recognised psychiatric illness. However, in order to do so, he will have to distinguish *Reilly* v *Merseyside RHA* [1995] where the claimants (an elderly couple) were unable to claim for the fear and claustrophobia suffered whilst trapped in a hospital lift for an hour and 20 minutes.

5.3 **The general exclusionary rule**

The courts have developed a number of control mechanisms in order to restrict recovery for negligently inflicted psychiatric harm. Opinions differ as to the extent to which these mechanisms are problematic. While some see them as necessary in order to protect the defendant from crushing liability, others suggest that they represent a combination of invidious distinctions and convoluted, and often contradictory, rules grounded in shallow and inadequate theoretical foundations (*Conaghan & Mansell* p 36). Why is it, for example, that a house owner was able to recover in respect of psychiatric harm caused by witnessing a fire which extensively damaged his home (*Attia* v *British Gas* [1988]) while a brother who saw his sibling being crushed to death was unable to claim (*Alcock* v *Chief Constable of South Yorkshire Police*)? Similarly, why was a mother who saw her family in hospital a few hours after a tragic road accident (***McLoughlin* v *O'Brian* [1982]**) able to recover when a father who watched his son slowly die over 14 days as a result of medical negligence was unable to claim (*Sion* v *Hampstead Health Authority* [1994])? Why allow recovery to a social worker whose traumatic caseload caused them to have a nervous breakdown (***Walker* v *Northumberland County Council* [1995]**) but not to the traumatised police officers involved in the Hillsborough Stadium disaster (***White***)?

It may be, *Conaghan & Mansell* suggest, that 'all of these outcomes can be explained in terms of the web of rules which have been spun round cases of psychiatric harm but that does not make them any more defensible when placed side by side and considered in terms of justice and basic common sense' (p 36). However, an alternative view is that the application and the development of these control mechanisms has been somewhat haphazard; the courts have largely acted without clear policy goals with the result that their reasoning and, on occasions, decisions have been motivated both towards and away from allowing recovery according to the—typically tragic—circumstances of particular cases.

Arguments for restricting compensation for pure psychiatric harm

The key arguments for restricting compensation in relation to negligently inflicted psychiatric harm were summarised by Lord Steyn in *White*:

(1) The difficulties of drawing a line between acute grief and psychiatric illness and the greater diagnostic uncertainty in relation to psychiatric claims (based on a fear of sham claims and doubts as to causation).

(2) The effect the increased availability of compensation might have on potential claimants, particularly as a disincentive to rehabilitation.

(3) The significant increase in the class of claimants who could recover and the alleged danger of an over-proliferation of claims (the 'floodgates' argument).

(4) The potential unfairness to the defendant of imposing damages out of all proportion to the negligent conduct (including the increased burden on insurers and, ultimately, all insurance policy holders) (at 493–4).

Counterpoint

The Law Commission considered arguments for limiting liability for negligently inflicted psychiatric illness in its *Report on Liability for Psychiatric Illness* (1998). It concluded that most of the arguments for restricting liability do not stand up to close scrutiny. In particular, it suggested that many apply equally well to claims for physical injury. Consider, for example, the momentarily careless car driver—the absence of proportionality between culpability and consequences in this situation is as prominent and problematic whether a claim following an accident is for physical or psychiatric injury (although, of course, it is important to note that, unlike psychiatric harm, physical injuries are likely to be limited to those in physical proximity to the accident). Moreover, despite a general distrust of psychiatric illnesses, fraudulent or exaggerated claims are just as likely in relation to physical harm; although medically it can be determined that an injury has occurred it often cannot establish to any degree of certainty the extent or duration of the pain and suffering it has caused. The classic example here is neck injury (whiplash) usually following a car accident. There is no way of 'proving' the pain the claimant is in—the courts have to go on their word. However, the existence of many specialist whiplash claims companies suggests that this is 'big business'—unsurprisingly as claims for severe whiplash can reach up to £86,500.[8]

5.4 'Primary' and 'secondary' victims

It has become traditional when discussing claims in respect of psychiatric injuries to draw a distinction between 'primary' and 'secondary' victims with different rules applying to each. The distinction reflects different ways that psychiatric harms may be suffered. Very broadly, a claimant may suffer such injuries because of something that has happened to them (for instance being involved in a car accident) or, alternatively, by seeing or hearing about something that has happened to someone else (such as witnessing a car crash involving other people). Though the language of 'primary' and 'secondary' victim is usually traced to Lord Oliver's opinion in *Alcock* the factual distinction between, on the one hand, those who suffer psychiatric injury as a result of being involved in an accident and, on the other hand, those who suffer psychiatric injury through witnessing an accident involving others can be found in the earlier case of *Bourhill* v *Young* [1943].

Alcock was one of a number of cases arising out of the Hillsborough Stadium disaster.[9] Faced with a tragedy involving multiple victims and a huge number of potential claimants, Lord Oliver drew a distinction between cases in which the claimant is 'involved, either mediately or immediately [that is, indirectly or directly], as a participant', and those in which the claimant was 'no more than the passive and unwilling witness of injury caused to others' (at 407). In relation to the latter group of claimants—that is, secondary victims—the House of Lords went on to articulate a number of limits on the availability of claims (detailing what constitutes a relationship of sufficient proximity

---

8. Figure cited on whiplash claims website (www.whiplash-claims.com).
9. The others discussed in this chapter are *Hicks* v *Chief Constable of South Yorkshire Police* [1992] and **White** v **Chief Constable of South Yorkshire Police** [1998].

between the claimant and defendant—the so-called 'nearness hearness and dearness' requirements (Henry LJ in *Frost* at 278[10]).

Since *Alcock* this distinction, particularly in relation to primary victims, has been applied in differing ways. In contrast to Lord Oliver who clearly envisages a fairly wide class of claimants falling within the primary victim category, including rescuers and unwitting agents, Lord Lloyd in *Page* appeared to restrict it to those within the range of foreseeable physical danger. Significantly, Lord Lloyd's restrictive interpretation of the primary victim category was utilised to strategic effect by the majority of the House of Lords in another Hillsborough-related case—*White*.

Nonetheless, and in contrast to the restrictive approach adopted by the House of Lords in *Page*, more recent case law has shown a willingness to widen the class of claimants who can recover for psychiatric harms.

 Counterpoint

This lack of precision as to who is a primary or (less often) a secondary victim is problematic.[11] Though we may consider any such distinction unsatisfactory, if we are to continue to distinguish primary and secondary victims, it is important that we define these terms with a measure of certainty. Moreover, we should be wary of extending them (and their accompanying rules) to cases they don't fit (see, for example, *AB* v *Leeds Teaching Hospital NHS Trust* [2005]). In light of this, while it is important to understand the various uses of the 'primary' and 'secondary' victim classifications as different rules that apply, the terms are, at best, a means to the end of determining what the claimant needs to establish in order to succeed in their claim. As Lord Phillips CJ has noted 'there is no magic in this terminology' (*French* v *Chief Constable of Sussex Police* [2006] [31]). As such, it is more important to be familiar with the substance of these rules rather than to become too sidetracked by this question of classification.[12]

5.5 Primary victims

It has long been established that a claimant is able to recover damages for psychiatric injury stemming from actual physical injury or from a reasonable fear or apprehension of danger to their physical safety (*Dulieu* v *White* [1901]).[13] This was expanded in *Page* v *Smith*—now the key case in this area.

10. As *White* v *Chief Constable of South Yorkshire Police* was known in the Court of Appeal. These requirements are set out fully on pp 107–111.
11. See e.g. Rachael Mulheron (2008), Paula Case (2010) and Harvey Teff, 'Liability for Negligently Inflicted Psychiatric Harm: Justifications and Boundaries' (1998) 57(1) *Cambridge Law Journal* 91. (Note: this article was written *before* the House of Lords' decision in *White*.)
12. Indeed in *Yearworth* v *North Bristol NHS Trust* [2009] the Court of Appeal assumed that the claimants who had banked sperm with the hospital prior to embarking on treatment for cancer could recover for psychiatric harm suffered as a result of the defendant's negligent destruction of their samples without considering whether they were primary or secondary victims.
13. The court refused to follow the earlier case of *Victorian Railways Commissioners* v *Coultas* [1888] in which the Privy Council denied the claimant's claim on the basis that her injuries were too remote.

Page v *Smith* [1996] HL

The claimant's car was involved in a minor road traffic accident caused by the defendant's negligence. Although the claimant suffered no physical injury, the accident triggered the recurrence of the claimant's myalgic encephalomyelitis (ME), a condition which causes severe fatigue, which had been in remission at the time of the accident. The claimant argued that this had become chronic and permanent as a result of the accident.

Although initially successful, the claimant lost in the Court of Appeal on the ground that his injury was not reasonably foreseeable in a person of ordinary courage and fortitude. A bare majority of the House of Lords allowed his appeal. In his leading opinion, Lord Lloyd held that, where it is reasonably foreseeable that the defendant's negligence may cause *physical* harm to the claimant and, as such, the claimant is a primary victim, they could also recover for any *psychiatric* harm they suffer:

> Suppose, in the present case, the plaintiff had been accompanied by his wife, just recovering from a depressive illness, and that she had suffered a cracked rib, followed by an onset of psychiatric illness. Clearly, she would have recovered damages, including damages for her illness, since it is conceded that the defendant owed the occupants of the car a duty not to cause physical harm. Why should it be necessary to ask a different question, or apply a different test, in the case of the plaintiff? Why should it make any difference that the physical illness that the plaintiff undoubtedly suffered as a result of the accident operated through the medium of the mind, or of the nervous system, without physical injury? If he had suffered a heart attack, it cannot be doubted that he would have recovered damages for pain and suffering, even though he suffered no broken bones. It would have been no answer that he had a weak heart. (at 187)

Thus because the claimant was in the zone of physical danger he was able to recover for the psychiatric harm he suffered notwithstanding that (a) no physical harm was in fact suffered *and* (b) the psychiatric injury itself was not reasonably foreseeable. In other words, so long as *some form of* physical injury was foreseeable, it made no difference whether or not it was foreseeable that Page's particular *psychiatric* illness would have occurred in a person of ordinary moral courage and fortitude.[14] In cases where *physical* harm is reasonably foreseeable, physical and psychiatric harms were to be treated as equivalent, so that if the former is foreseeable, the claimant can recover in respect of both physical *and* psychiatric harms, even in cases where the latter is *not* foreseeable.[15]

---

14. This extension of the 'thin' or 'egg shell' skull rule (discussed in more detail in Chapter 9, p 250), whereby, so long as the relevant kind of harm is foreseeable, it does not matter that its precise form or extent is not, puts the primary victim at a considerable advantage over secondary victims. Unlike their secondary victim counterparts, a primary victim can 'recover damages for negligently inflicted pure psychiatric illness, even if it was sustained because he lacked the fortitude or "natural phlegm" of an ordinary person' (Mulheron 2008, p 106). Mulheron goes on to argue for the reintroduction of a rule of normal fortitude in all cases of psychiatric harm (pp 106–9).

15. As Paula Case notes, in so doing Lord Lloyd is clearly seeking to subvert the traditional differing treatment of physical and psychiatric injuries. Unfortunately, his efforts are somewhat undermined by retention of the primary and secondary victim distinction which, as Case notes, 'discriminates between physical and psychiatric harm (those at risk of physical harm were, eg, automatically assigned to the primary victim group to which more generous rules applied)' (2010, p 36).

Page has been the subject of much criticism.[16] Academic criticism has tended to focus on Lord Lloyd's restrictive definition of a primary victim as a party who is necessarily within the zone of physical danger (although, it can also be argued that, in so far as it removes the requirement that the psychiatric harm be foreseeable, the treatment of primary victims in *Page* is extremely generous). As discussed below, this understanding of the primary victim category was used to deny recovery to the claimants in *White*. Opinions differ over whether Lord Lloyd intended to limit the primary victim category to those claimants who were in physical danger, and it remains unclear as to when a claimant *who is not in peril* will be recognised as a primary victim.[17] This was considered by the House of Lords in *Grieves* v *FT Everard & Sons* [2007].

Grieves v *FT Everard & Sons* [2007] HL

The claimant had been exposed to asbestos in the course of his employment and had developed pleural plaques. He was physically healthy and the pleural plaques themselves would not themselves have caused any illness. They were, however, evidence that asbestos had entered his body and showed that the claimant, therefore, might in the future develop an asbestos-related disease. As noted above, this, in and of itself, was not enough to ground a claim. However the claimant was *so* worried about the risk that he became clinically depressed (a recognisable psychiatric illness). He argued that since it was reasonably foreseeable that the defendant's negligence put him at risk of physical injury (of contracting asbestosis or mesothelioma) he was a primary victim and hence should be owed a duty of care in respect of his psychiatric illness on the basis of *Page*.

His claim failed on the ground that his reaction was unforeseeable. While it was to be expected that the developing pleural plaques would cause anxiety to the person of reasonable fortitude, there was no evidence that it would lead them to have such a serious reaction that they would become mentally ill. Moreover, 'the category of primary victim should be confined to persons who suffer psychiatric injury caused by fear or distress resulting from involvement in an accident caused by the defendant's negligence or its immediate aftermath' (Lord Hope at [54]). The claimant's psychiatric injury, which resulted from a fear as to something that might happen in the future, therefore fell within 'an entirely different category' (at [54]). Similarly, Lord Hoffmann confined *Page* to psychiatric injury caused by events (accidents) that had actually occurred, arguing that 'it would be an unwarranted extension of the principle in *Page* to apply it to psychiatric illness caused by apprehension of the possibility of an unfavourable event which had not actually happened' (at [33]).[18]

---

16. See e.g. Bailey and Nolan's conclusion to their detailed exploration of *Page* in which they remark '[f]ortunately, the long-term prospects for *Page*'s survival look slim' and accompanying references (2010, pp 527–8), Lord Goff's dissenting opinion in *White* (at 468–81), and Peter Handford 'A New Chapter in the Foresight Saga' (1996) 4 *Tort Law Review* 5.

17. See Mulheron's comparison of the changing definitions of a primary victim in *Page* [1996], *White* [1998], *W* [2001] and *Grieves* [2007] (2008, pp 84–6).

18. Compare Smith LJ's view in *Boumedien* v *Delta Displays Ltd* [2008] in which she stated that the claimant was a primary victim if 'the defendant can reasonably foresee that his conduct will expose the plaintiff to risk of personal injury, whether physical or psychiatric' (at [7]).

Pause for reflection

Quite why it was necessary to refine *Page* in this way is unclear, although Lord Hope's reference to Lord Steyn's opinion in *White* in which he cautions against judicial expansion in relation to recovery for negligently inflicted psychiatric harm may provide some explanation. It is likely Lord Hope was mindful of the extent of liability should Grieves' claim succeed. Consider the following example. A potentially deadly virus is negligently allowed to escape from a research laboratory. Following *Grieves* will the employees of the laboratory be owed a duty of care in respect of psychiatric illness caused by anxiety for their future health? What about local residents who face a similar risk of contracting a serious illness— should they be able to claim for any subsequent psychiatric harm caused by their fears? If not, why not?

Lord Hope's reading of *Page* is in many ways in line with a developing body of case law which recognises that certain claimants fall outside the traditional categories of primary and secondary victims.[19] The claimant in *Grieves* was held not to be a primary victim (his *apprehension* of physical harm was not enough), but in no sense could he be described as a secondary victim either (since his psychiatric illness was not caused by witnessing or his experience of someone else being harmed).[20]

5.6 **Secondary victims**

A secondary victim who suffers psychiatric injury as a result of witnessing someone else being harmed or endangered.[21] Recovery in such cases is limited by a number of policy-orientated control mechanisms. The first of these is that the psychiatric injury suffered must be reasonably foreseeable in a person of 'ordinary fortitude' in the same circumstances.[22] The notion of ordinary phlegm or fortitude, derived from *Bourhill* **v *Young*** [1943], is invoked as a means of assessing the 'validity' of a claimant's emotional reactions in the face of trauma.

19. See further pp 112–121.

20. It should be noted also that any claims based on the pleural plaques themselves—a recognised lung condition—grounded no claim in negligence for physical injury, due to the asymptomatic nature of the condition. If the condition itself had physical symptoms, he would have been able to recover fully.

21. The first 'secondary victim' case was *Hambrook* v *Stokes Bros* [1925] in which the Court of Appeal refused to follow the bar against recovery in such cases set down by the Divisional Court in *Dulieu* v *White*.

22. As noted above, typically a primary victim does not need to show that their reaction corresponds with that of a person of ordinary fortitude (*Page*) though following *Hatton* v *Sutherland* [2002] it seems that this exception does not apply to employees who suffer psychiatric harm due to stress at work (unless the employer knows of a particular problem or vulnerability on the part of the claimant) or (following *Grieves*) to those who suffer an 'unforeseeable' reaction caused by the apprehension of an illness. See further Mulheron 2008, pp 106–9.

> ### *Bourhill* v *Young* [1943] HL
>
> The claimant, who was eight months pregnant, witnessed a serious motorbike accident. Though she did not see the accident itself, she heard it, and saw the motorcyclist's blood on the pavement. She later suffered serious psychiatric harm and her child was stillborn about a month after the accident. The House of Lords rejected her claim on the grounds that her injuries were not foreseeable—she was never in physical danger *and* that, as a pregnant woman, she was particularly susceptible to shock.

If, therefore, the claimant suffers psychiatric harm in circumstances where the ordinarily courageous person would not, the defendant will not be liable even if a severe psychological reaction results. However once some psychiatric harm is foreseeable, the defendant will—on the basis of the so-called 'egg shell' or 'thin' skull rule —be liable in full, even if a particular vulnerability or susceptibility means that the claimant suffers much greater psychiatric harm than might have been anticipated (*Brice* v *Brown* [1984]).

> ### Pause for reflection
>
> It has been argued that the notion of 'ordinary phlegm or fortitude' not only allows for the incorporation of evaluative judgements (and possible gender bias) as to what is a 'normal' reaction to any given event, but also perpetuates the false assumption that there is (or can be) a reasonable response to a tragic event. Do you agree? Consider, again, the facts of *Bourhill*. To what extent are the characteristics of the claimant significant here? What degree of fortitude is to be expected of an 'ordinary pregnant woman'? Or is a pregnant woman, by definition, not 'ordinary'?

The foundations for the modern approach to secondary victims were laid down in *McLoughlin* v *O'Brian* [1982].

> ### *McLoughlin* v *O'Brian* [1982] HL
>
> Mrs McLoughlin suffered psychiatric harm after happening upon the 'immediate aftermath' of a serious car accident, which killed her daughter and injured her husband and three children. Arriving at the hospital some two hours after the accident, she encountered circumstances that were 'distressing in the extreme and . . . capable of producing an effect going well beyond that of grief and sorrow' (at 417); her husband and children, visibly upset and bruised, were still covered in grime and dirt from the accident.
>
> The House of Lords allowed her claim on the basis that the claimant had come upon 'the immediate aftermath' of the accident. However, their lordships were not in full agreement as to *why* she should be able to recover. In particular, there was tension as to whether the
>
> →

issue of recovery should be determined) as Lord Bridge suggested, on the ordinary principles of *reasonable foreseeability* or by independent *policy-based* factors (including the
closeness of the relationship between the claimant and the accident victim, the *proximity* of
the claimant to the accident itself and whether the shock was induced by what the claimant
saw or experienced as opposed to what she was *told* after the event) as Lord Wilberforce
argued.[23]

Even at the time, **McLoughlin** was viewed as a borderline case—on 'the margin of what
the process of logical progression would allow' (Lord Wilberforce at 419). Nevertheless,
it encapsulated the judicial understanding of the time; a time when the judges were
more generous to claimants in negligence than they are today. However, darker clouds
were beginning to build on the horizon, as the mood within tort law generally shifted
toward a more restrictive approach toward the duty of care (the so-called 'retreat from
Anns').[24] Then the unthinkable happened, a tragedy with multiple victims and a
vast number of potential claimants and this mood was cemented—the Hillsborough
Stadium disaster.[25]

The Hillsborough Stadium disaster

'The tragedy that claimed the lives of 96 Liverpool football fans shattered a community and shook the world of football took a matter of minutes to unfold. In its simplest
terms, Hillsborough was a case of overcrowding in the central standing area allocated to
Liverpool fans at the FA Cup semi-final match against Nottingham Forest…The disaster

---

23. It may be that there is more overlap between the two approaches than this suggests, Lord
Bridge made it clear that the three factors set down by Lord Wilberforce would be taken into
account when determining whether on the fact the shock was reasonably foreseeable (Nolan 2010,
p 282). However, as Paula Case notes, the differing approaches of Lords Bridge and Wilberforce are
'broadly representative of an "assimilation approach" which uses ordinary negligence principles
to determine duty of care (articulated by Lord Bridge) in contrast to Lord Wilberforce's "isolation
approach" which views psychiatric damage as distinct from other harms and needing to be
insulted from ordinary negligence principles. Though the latter approach won the day in *Alcock*,
more recently case law suggests a movement toward a gradual assimilation of psychiatric harm
into mainstream negligence principles in order to determine whether a duty care exists (Case 2010,
pp 34–5).

24. See further Chapter 2, pp 33–34 and Chapter 7.

25. In fact, as Donal Nolan notes, the Hillsborough Stadium disaster was one of a number of
man-made disasters during the UK's 'disaster era' (1985–89), which included the Bradford football
stadium fire in 1985 (40 fatalities), the sinking of the *Herald of Free Enterprise* car ferry (187) and the
King's Cross underground station fire (31) in 1987, the Piper Alpha oil rig fire (167) in 1988 and, in
1989, the East Midland Kegworth plane crash (47) and the sinking of the *Marchioness* pleasure boat
(51). The fact that there were so many man-man disasters in the years preceding *Alcock* (Nolan lists
ten events, totalling 979 fatalities), each giving rise to litigation (including for psychiatric injury),
combined with the 'topicality of trauma-induced psychiatric injury', Nolan suggests 'can only
have reinforced long-standing judicial concerns about the opening of floodgates in nervous shock
litigation' (2010, p 292).

➡

began to unfold at approximately 2.30pm. With half an hour before kick-off, most of the Nottingham Forest supporters were in their seats. Meanwhile the area reserved for the Liverpool supporters—the Leppings Lane end of the stadium—was half empty. But outside, it was a different story, with more than 2,000 Liverpool supporters building up against the turnstiles to the Leppings Lane entrance. Some had arrived late from their journey across the Pennines. Others had stayed outside to make the most of the sunshine. There were also those who had come without tickets to the all-ticket match, hoping to buy them at the ground. But whatever the reason for the late rush, anxiety among both fans and police was mounting as the minutes to kick-off ticked by.

By 2.45pm the crowd had swelled to over 5,000, making entry to turnstiles virtually impossible. Those who did get through were short of breath and sweating profusely from the crush. As the minutes passed, it became increasing clear that, despite police efforts, the mass of people would never get through by 3pm. There was also a more serious risk of some being dangerously hurt. Something had to be done.

Suddenly at 2.52pm, the large blue, concertina steel door—Gate C—in the perimeter wall was slid open by a police officer. Those at its entrance tumbled through. Those at the back pushed harder still. The logjam was unstuck. But things quickly got out of control. Where fans had been entering in ones and twos through the turnstiles, there was now a wave of about 2,000 racing to the see the start of the game. The majority took the most obvious route: straight ahead through the tunnel of gangway 2. They piled into the back of pens 3 and 4, which were already uncomfortably full, crushing those at the front.

At 2.54pm the teams came onto the pitch. Fans at the back of the pens pushed forward for a better view, unaware that people were dying in the front. As the excitement of the game grew, there were more surges, each causing a squeeze more perilous than the last. Finally, with fans spilling through a narrow escape onto the pitch or being lifted to the seating areas above, a policeman realised what was happening. At 3.06pm, six minutes into the game, he ordered the referee to stop the game. Only then did the scale of the disaster become clear. Bodies were lifted forward and laid out on the pitch—many teenagers and children. People screamed for their loved ones as ambulance staff fought to save lives. Advertising hoardings were torn down as makeshift stretchers in a desperate attempt to bring faster relief.

By 4.50pm, the scheduled end of the game, the ground was empty. Abandoned clothing and programmes littered the scene of the disaster. While nearby the bodies of the dead lay in the stadium's gymnasium.'

(BBC News 'Timetable to a tragedy' 14 April 1999 referring to Taylor LJ, *Interim Report on the Hillsborough Stadium Disaster* (Cm 765, 1989))

Ninety-six people were crushed to death and over 400 people were injured at Hillsborough. At the time, it was 'one of the most televised, monitored and photographed disasters in the UK'.[26] Many thousands of people watched the tragedy unfold on live TV or listened to it on the radio, even more saw later news reports and press coverage. The number of potential claims for psychiatric harm was immense. The

---

26. Phil Scraton 'Justice: Hillsborough's Final Victim' (1992) April *Legal Action* 7.

court's response was to abandon its aspiration to 'provide a comprehensive system of corrective justice…in favour of cautious pragmatism' (Lord Hoffmann, *White* at 502).

Alcock v *Chief Constable of South Yorkshire Police* [1992] HL

Alcock was a test case involving representatives of the friends and families of the victims of the disaster at Hillsborough football stadium who had suffered from medically recognised psychiatric illnesses as a result of what they witnessed during the disaster and its aftermath.

None of the claimants was able to recover as primary victims—they had not been *directly* involved in the disaster (in the sense of having been in physical danger)—rather, they were the grandparents, friends, spouses, siblings, and fiancés (some of whom had been at the ground when the incident occurred, others of whom had arrived at the ground later or seen or heard about the incident on the TV or radio) of those injured or killed at Hillsborough who had suffered psychiatric injury as a result of what they saw happen and/or feared had happened to their loved ones.

The defendant, the Chief Constable of South Yorkshire Police, admitted negligence in respect of those who had been killed or injured at Hillsborough but argued that he did not owe a duty of care to those who had suffered psychiatric damage as a result of seeing or hearing the news of what had happened.[27]

Despite limited success at first instance, both the Court of Appeal and House of Lords rejected the claims. The lack of *proximity* between the claimants and the police meant that no duty of care arose such as was necessary to ground a claim in the tort of negligence: they were not 'in contemplation of law, in a relationship of sufficient proximity to or directness with the tortfeasor as to give rise to a duty of care' (at 410). Drawing on and developing the more restrictive approach of Lord Wilberforce in *McLoughlin*, Lord Oliver set out guidelines—subsequently known as the *Alcock* control mechanisms—as to when proximity will be established. These relate to the following issues:

1. the *class of persons* whose claim should be recognised (defined by their relationship to the victim);

2. the *closeness* of the claimant—both physically and temporally—to the accident;

3. the means by which the *shock* is caused.

It is worth spending some time to look at the *Alcock* control mechanisms in a little more detail. We should note once more, however, that in all instances it is necessary for the claimant to establish first that they are suffering from a medically recognised psychiatric illness.

5.6.1 Relationship with the immediate victim

There must be what is described as 'a close tie of love and affection' between the claimant and the accident victim. Despite subsequent criticisms of this requirement, it is

---

27. It was accepted, for the purposes of deciding the law, that the Chief Constable had breached his duty of care and that the claimants were suffering from a recognised psychiatric illness.

clear that the law lords did *not* want to establish a rigid list of categories of relationship within which claimants would succeed (at 415). Instead,

> Whether the degree of love and affection in any given relationship, be it that of relative or friend, is such that the defendant... should reasonably have foreseen the shock-induced psychiatric illness, has to be decided on a case by case basis. (Lord Ackner at 404)

The court held that this will be presumed in the case of spouses, parents and children—although, of course, this can be rebutted if the defendant can show that such closeness did not exist. This does not mean that siblings and other relatives can never claim; however they must bring evidence to prove such ties existed.[28] Thus, Brian Harrison, who watched the scenes at Hillsborough unfold from the West Stand knowing that both his brothers were in pens three and four behind the goal was unable to recover. He did not have—or did not show that he had—a close enough relationship with his late brother, perhaps because he did not know he had to.

 Counterpoint

The 'love and affection' requirement has been subject to widespread and severe criticism:

> That at present claims can turn on the requirement of 'close ties and affection' is guaranteed to produce outrage. Is it not a disreputable sight to see brothers of Hillsborough victims turned away because they had *no more* than brotherly love towards the victim? In future cases will it not be a grotesque sight to see relatives scrabbling to prove their especial love for the deceased in order to win money damages and for the defendant to have to attack that argument?[29]

The Law Commission in its *Report on Liability for Psychiatric Illness* (1998) recommended widening the list of relationships in which a close tie of love and affection was 'conclusive' to include siblings and cohabitees. Other relationships, including that of work colleagues, teacher and student and close friends would fall outside its scope and as such would have to be established on the facts of each case.

 Pause for reflection

The familial relationships of the claimants in *Alcock* are not the only ones which may exhibit close ties of love and affection. Consider *Robertson v Forth Road Bridge Joint Board* [1996]. In this case the claimant suffered psychiatric harm after his colleague died while

---

28. A grandfather (such as the one in the example at the start of the chapter) would as a secondary victim need to establish, alongside the other *Alcock* control mechanisms, that he had a close tie of love and affection with his grandchild—this would not be presumed by their familial relationship.

29. Jane Stapleton 'In Restraint of Tort' in Peter Birks (ed) *The Frontiers of Liability: Volume 2* (OUP, 1994), p 95.

➙

trying to remove a sheet of metal from the Forth Road Bridge in windy conditions. His claim was denied despite evidence showing that he had spent the greater part of his employment working with the victim. They had often walked to and from work together and had gone out socially during the week.

The fact that they were co-workers was not enough to demonstrate a close tie of love and affection, but clearly their relationship went beyond simply working side by side. When should the law recognise this? What more could the claimant in *Robertson* have done?

Although usually the claimant will have to establish a close tie of love and affection with the immediate victim, the House of Lords in **Alcock** did not rule out the possibility of a mere bystander being able to recover if the circumstances were 'particularly horrific' (at 397). Quite what would be more horrific than the events at the Hillsborough stadium disaster is difficult to imagine, although Lord Ackner suggested that witnessing an out-of-control petrol tanker crash into a school may be such an event (at 403). In *McFarlane* v *EE Caledonia Ltd* [1994] the claimant developed post-traumatic stress disorder after witnessing the Piper Alpha oil disaster from a boat which was engaged in trying to fight the fire which had engulfed the rig. He argued the owners of the oil rig (who had admitted responsibility for the disaster) owed him a duty of care, despite the fact he was a mere bystander (he had no relationship with the people injured or killed in the explosion), as the fire was especially horrific. This was rejected by the Court of Appeal. Not only was it impossible to establish a hierarchy of horrific events, but to do so would wrongly reduce establishing a duty in such cases to a question of foreseeability: the more horrific the accident, the more likely psychiatric harm would occur. (His claim as a primary victim also failed, although the boat he was on had come within eighty metres of the oil rig, his fear for his own life was not reasonable.)

5.6.2 **Proximity in time and space**

In relation to the second and third requirements of 'proximity'—proximity to the accident and means by which the shock was caused—Lord Oliver summed up the general position thus:

> The necessary element of proximity between plaintiff and defendant is furnished, at least in part, by both physical and temporal propinquity and also by the sudden and direct visual impression on the plaintiff's mind of actually witnessing the event or its immediate aftermath. (at 416)

Since **McLoughlin**, the claimant must witness the accident or happen upon its 'immediate aftermath'. But how far does the immediate aftermath extend? While Mrs McLoughlin arriving at the hospital two hours after the accident was sufficient, in **Alcock** Robert Alcock's search at the ground and arrival at the temporary mortuary in the stadium's gymnasium around midnight (about eight hours after the match was abandoned) where he identified his brother-in-law's body which was blue with bruising, his chest red, was too late—the blood on his brother-in-law's body said to be already 'too dry' to allow recovery.[30]

However, recently the courts have been more generous. In *Galli-Atkinson* v *Seghal* [2003] the Court of Appeal allowed a mother's claim for psychiatric harm following the death of her daughter in a road traffic accident on the basis that the aftermath of an accident could be viewed as being made up of different component parts, in particular the mother's visit to the scene of the accident and the hospital morgue.

5.6.3 **The means by which the 'shock' is caused**

It is clear that the psychiatric injury harm must be sustained as a result of a 'shock' rather than as the result of a continuous process of dealing with or responding to such events which Lord Ackner described as a 'sudden appreciation by sight or sound of a horrifying event, which violently agitates the mind' (at 401). Thus in *Sion* v *Hampstead Health Authority* [1994], for example, a father was unable to recover for psychiatric harm sustained as a result watching his son die over a period of 14 days while becoming increasingly aware that the hospital were negligent in their treatment of him.

 Counterpoint

This requirement was criticised by the Law Commission in its *Report on Liability for Psychiatric Illness* (1998) and judges have increasingly tried to eschew its more restrictive effects. In *North Glamorgan NHS Trust* v *Walters* [2002] a mother was able to recover as a secondary victim for psychiatric harm she suffered as a result of events leading to the death of her baby son. The court held that such a shocking event was not confined to a single moment in time and, taking a realistic approach to the facts, the 36-hour period prior to her son's death could be classed as a single horrifying event.

The House of Lords made it clear that there would be no liability to a secondary victim who is merely told about the shocking event by a third party (including newspaper coverage and television broadcasts):

> Although the television pictures certainly gave rise to feelings of the deepest anxiety and distress, in the circumstances of this case the simultaneous television broadcasts of what occurred cannot be equated with the 'sight or hearing of the event or its immediate aftermath.' Accordingly shocks sustained by reason of these broadcasts cannot found a claim. (Lord Ackner at 405)[31]

Nevertheless, the law lords left open the possibility that watching a live broadcast could exceptionally ground a claim if it is clear that the victims have died such as, to

---

30. Stapleton, above, p 84. Further, unlike in **McLoughlin**, the purpose of his visit was for identification rather than aid or comfort.

31. None of the live television coverage, in line with broadcasting policy, showed pictures of suffering by recognisable individuals. Had it done so, it was accepted that this would amount to a *'novus actus'* breaking the chain of causation between the defendant's alleged breach of duty and the psychiatric illness (at 410).

use Nolan LJ's example in the Court of Appeal, if a hot air balloon carrying a number of children were to explode live on television (Lord Ackner, *Alcock* at 405).

 Pause for reflection

Without doubt, despite developments in the law relating to primary victims, *Alcock* remains the 'single most important English authority on liability for nervous shock' (Nolan 2010, p 273). It is, in Lord Steyn's words, the 'controlling decision' on secondary victims (*White* at 496).

Nevertheless, it has been the subject of trenchant criticism. See, for example, Lord Hoffmann in *White*, commenting that in *Alcock* 'the search for principle was called off' (at 511); the Law Commission's recognition that the restrictions 'have been almost universally criticized as arbitrary and unfair' (*Report on Liability for Psychiatric Illness* (1998) [6.3]); and Jane Stapleton's description of this area of law as one where 'silliest rules prevail'.[32] The *Alcock* control mechanisms have come to be seen as arbitrary rules designed to restrict recovery and avoid a 'flood' of liability.[33] However, Donal Nolan suggests these have been used in a way that was unintended by the House of Lords in *Alcock*—the law lords did not seek to lay down rigid rules (p 307)—precisely because 'to draw such a line would necessarily be arbitrary and lacking in logic' (Lord Jauncey at 422). In Nolan's view, as well as being a landmark case in tort *Alcock* is also a 'misunderstood decision' (p 308):

> A case that is often painted as retrograde and reactionary was in fact rather conservative, and even in some respects mildly progressive, not least when one takes into account the circumstances in which it was decided. (p 308)

What do you think?

The traditional distinction between primary and secondary victims can be summarised in Table 5.1.

Table 5.1 The traditional distinction between primary and secondary victims

Primary victims	Secondary victims
Physical injury must be foreseeable; however psychiatric injury itself need not be foreseeable. No need for the claimant to be of 'ordinary fortitude' (*Page*)	*Psychiatric* harm must be foreseeable in a person of 'ordinary fortitude' in the same circumstances as the claimant
Application of *Page*—is the claimant in the 'zone of danger'?	Application of *Alcock* control mechanisms: close tie of love and affection; proximity to the accident and means by which the shock is caused
No policy considerations to limit the number of claimants	Policy used to limit the number of claimants

32. Stapleton, above, p 95.
33. See e.g. Lord Steyn in *White* at 493.

5.7 **Beyond primary and secondary victims**

The examples of psychiatric harm claims we have discussed up until now have all arisen in the context of accidents caused by the defendant's careless acts. It is in this context that the distinction between primary and secondary victims was first drawn and makes best sense: primary victims are those involved in, and endangered by, the accident; secondary victims those who were not involved but witnessed or later learned of what happened to the primary victims. It is clear, however, that psychiatric harms can be suffered in other ways besides these. Though the courts have, on occasion, sought to fit all psychiatric injury claims within the framework of primary and secondary victims,[34] the safer approach is to acknowledge that there are some psychiatric harm claimants who suffer their harms other than through being involved in or witnessing an accident, and that such claimants fall outside the classification of primary and secondary victims. The question then is in what other circumstances does the law recognise victims of psychiatric harms as having a claim in negligence.

5.7.1 **Rescuers**

One area where the primary–secondary victim distinction has proved problematic is in relation to rescuers. Those who seek to assist and save those injured in an accident typically will not be exposed to any risk of personal harm, but nor are they mere bystanders. In this sense they are not simply witnesses but participants. For this reason, when the primary–secondary victim distinction was first set down, rescuers who suffered psychiatric injury as a result of their participation were often thought to fall within the class of primary victim. For instance Lord Oliver, in *Alcock*, clearly envisaged primary victims as encompassing a broad range of claimants including rescuers and unwitting agents. However, more recently, the courts have favoured the narrower conception of primary victim set out by Lord Lloyd in *Page* as embracing only those who were at risk of physical injury.

What is clear is that the courts have traditionally treated rescuers favourably. 'Danger invites rescue. The cry of distress is the summons of relief . . . the act, whether impulsive or deliberate, is the child of the occasion' (*Wagner* v *International Railway Co* [1921]). So, where a defendant has endangered someone by their carelessness, the courts have typically held that it is also reasonably foreseeable that others may put themselves at risk by trying to save the victim. As such, defendants have been held to owe a duty of care not just to those they initially endanger by their actions, but also to those who intervene to rescue those initially endangered (see for instance *Ogwo* v *Taylor* [1988] and *Baker* v *TE Hopkins* [1959]). Similarly rescuers' actions will usually not be treated as *novus actus interveniens*, nor will they be held to be contributorily negligent in respect of any harms they suffer in attempting their rescue.

The approach appeared to extend beyond cases where the rescuer was *physically* harmed in their attempted rescue to those where the rescuer suffered *psychiatric* harm.

---

34. This tendency is evident in the dictum of Lord Slynn in *W* v *Essex County Council* [2001]: '[t]he categorisation of those claiming to be included as primary or secondary victims is not as I read the cases finally closed. It is a concept still to be developed in different factual situations' (at 601).

The leading example is *Chadwick* v *British Railways Board* [1967], where the widow of a window cleaner was able to recover for the psychiatric harm suffered by her husband as a result of his particularly harrowing and gruesome experience giving help and relief to victims of a severe rail crash over the course of 12 hours. And as recently as *Alcock,* Lord Oliver recognised the 'well-established' principle that a defendant owes a duty of care to those 'induced to go to the rescue' of those in peril as a result of their negligence (at 408).

This simple proposition can no longer stand in light of another case arising out of the Hillsborough Stadium disaster—*White* v *Chief Constable of South Yorkshire Police*—involving claims by police officers who had suffered psychiatric harm as a result of their work during the Hillsborough Stadium disaster.

White v *Chief Constable of South Yorkshire Police* [1998] HL

All of the claimants were police officers who had been on duty the day of the Hillsborough Stadium disaster. Three were on duty at the ground itself; one had attempted to free spectators while the other two had attended the makeshift morgue in the gymnasium. The two other officers were among those drafted in later that afternoon and were, with the others, witnesses to the chaotic and gruesome scenes. The final officer had worked as a liaison officer at a nearby hospital. All had suffered psychiatric illness as a result of their participation in the events of that day.

The claimants could not satisfy the conditions set out in *Alcock,* nor could they establish that they were in any danger of physical harm, such as to ground liability under *Page*. Instead the six representative police officers in *White* argued that they were entitled to recover on the basis that they were either rescuers or employees and, as such, fell outside the remit of the previous cases.

A bare majority of the House of Lords held that neither a rescuer nor an employee was placed in any special position in relation to recovery for psychiatric harm by virtue of being so defined.

Accepting the narrow definition of primary victim given by Lord Lloyd in *Page*, Lord Steyn in the majority held that a rescuer could only be considered a primary victim if he 'objectively exposed himself to danger or reasonably believed he was doing so' (at 499). On the facts, the police officers were never in (nor did they reasonably believe themselves to be in) actual physical danger. To extend the category of primary victims to include rescuers would be, in Lord Steyn's view, 'unwarranted' (at 500).

A second line of argument in *White* was that as the claimants could recover on the basis that they were employees of the defendant, they were owed a duty of care on that basis. This was also rejected by the majority of the House of Lords. Though employers clearly do owe a duty of care to their employees in respect of physical injuries, it did not follow that there was also a duty in respect of psychiatric harms they suffer in the course of their employment. To establish whether there is such a duty, one has to look to the general law of torts and this says that duties of care in respect of psychiatric injuries suffered by those witnessing horrific events are owed only where the *Alcock* criteria are met.

→

→

Moreover, to allow the claimants to recover on the basis of their employment with the defendants would lead to 'striking anomalies', with the police officers being given rights denied to others, including doctors and ambulance workers, who had assisted the injured at Hillsborough out of a sense of moral, as opposed to legal, obligation (Lord Hoffmann at 506).

Accordingly, the claimants' status as rescuers and as employees made no difference to the legal principles determining recovery for psychiatric harms. Since the claimants were not exposed to any risk of physical harm and could not satisfy the *Alcock* criteria—the claimants had no close ties of love and affection to the victims, nor did they all meet the requirements of proximity in space and time—their claims necessarily failed.

In contrast Lord Goff, in his dissenting opinion, found it 'inconsistent' to make foreseeability of physical injury not merely a sufficient but also a *necessary* condition of liability for psychiatric harm (at 479). To do so is not only inappropriately restrictive, but also in opposition to Lord Lloyd's expansive strategy in *Page* and Lord Oliver's categorisation of rescuers as primary victims in *Alcock*. In a similar vein, Lord Griffiths (who would have allowed the appeal on the basis of the police officers' position as employees) also rejected the distinction between physical and psychiatric injury; '[i]f it is foreseeable that the rescuer may suffer personal injury in the form of psychiatric injury rather than physical injury, why should he not recover for that injury?' (at 464).

 ### Counterpoint

Controversially, in the Court of Appeal, the claims of all but one of the police officers had been successful on the basis that they were rescuers and/or employees. Unsurprisingly, this decision was highly criticised. Many believed it was unfair to allow the police (who, albeit in another capacity, were the defendants in *Alcock* and *White*) to recover when the claims of friends and family had been dismissed in *Alcock*.[35] As Lord Steyn notes 'The claim of the police officers on our sympathy, and the justice of the case, is great but not as great as that of others to whom the law denies redress' (*White* at 498). Moreover, by the time the police officers' case reached the House of Lords, it was clear that the law in this area was in a 'genuine doctrinal muddle' (*Conaghan & Mansell* p 40). It was, in the words of Lord Steyn, so far beyond judicial repair that 'the only sensible general strategy for the courts is to say thus far and no further . . . to treat the pragmatic categories as reflected in the authoritative decisions such as the *Alcock* case . . . and *Page v Smith* as settled for the time being' (*White* at 500). Any further development or reforms to the law were the job of Parliament.

In short, the law lords' acknowledged aim in *White* was one of damage limitation—with the result, we would argue, that the police officers were abandoned within a tangled web of largely arbitrary and illogical distinctions between physical and psychiatric harm, primary and secondary victims.

---

35. See e.g. the reaction of Trevor Hicks, who was at the stadium during the disaster with his daughters (both of whom died). ('Families' Fury at Cash Bid by Hillsbro Cops' *Daily Mirror* 1 November 1996.)

In *White,* therefore, the courts' usual inclination to protect rescuers was trumped by the Lordships' inclination to limit recovery for pure psychiatric harm. Lord Hoffmann puts it thus:

> There does not seem to me to be any logical reason why the normal treatment of rescuers on the issues of foreseeability and causation should lead to the conclusion that, for the purpose of liability for psychiatric injury, they should be given special treatment as primary victims when they were not within the range of foreseeable physical injury...such an extension would be unacceptable to the ordinary person...He would think it wrong that policemen, even as part of a general class of persons who rendered assistance, should have the right to compensation for psychiatric injury out of public funds while the bereaved relatives are sent away with nothing. (at 510)

In light of this the majority considered that the decision in *Chadwick* could be supported only on the basis that the rescuer was in fact in physical danger (even if he did not realise this himself) when he sought to extract the victims from the wreckage of the train.

 Pause for reflection

Lord Hoffmann frames the decision in *White* as a choice between distributive and corrective justice. We are forced to choose between the two constructed alternatives: either the police officers are able to recover (as dictated by the principles of corrective justice) or their claims are denied (in accordance with both the principle of distributive justice and, in line with, the decision in *Alcock*). His (and our) decision is presented as an either/or choice between the police officers and the families and friends in *Alcock*. This dichotomy underpins his refusal to extend liability to rescuers not in physical danger. Corrective justice is abandoned in favour of 'cautious pragmatism' (at 502) as the burden of distributive justice falls on the police officers.[36]

What do you think of this either/or alternative? To what extent, if any, do you believe the House of Lords should have responded to the earlier decision in *Alcock*?

 Counterpoint

In contrast, Lord Goff, in his dissenting opinion in *White*, highlights the constrained and doctrinally flawed character of the majority opinions. In particular, he criticised the introduction of further 'control mechanisms' (akin to the highly criticised *Alcock* restrictions) through the creation of 'unacceptable' and 'unjust' distinctions, which distinguish claimants according to their physical location (at 487). The imposition of a requirement of fear of physical injury in such cases is, he argues, both capricious and misplaced. Drawing on *Chadwick*, and responding to the majority's attempt to distinguish it, he poses the following analogy:

➡

36. Although note Richard Mullender and Alistair Spier's defence of the decision in *White* on the principles of distributive justice ('Negligence, Psychiatric Injury, and the Altruism Principle' (2000) 20(4) *Oxford Journal of Legal Studies* 645).

> ➔
>
> Suppose that there was a terrible train crash and that there were two Chadwick brothers living nearby, both of them small and agile window cleaners distinguished by their courage and humanity. Mr A Chadwick worked on the front half of the train, and Mr B Chadwick on the rear half. It so happened that, although there was some physical danger present in the front half of the train, there was none in the rear. Both worked for 12 hours or so bringing aid and comfort to the victims. Both suffered PTSD in consequence of the general horror of the situation. On the new control mechanism now proposed, Mr A would recover but Mr B would not. To make things worse, the same conclusion must follow even if Mr A was unaware of the existence of the physical danger present in his half of the train. This is surely unacceptable. (at 487–8)[37]

5.7.2 Involuntary participants

Another category of claimants are those known as involuntary participants or unwitting agents. This stems from *Dooley* v *Cammell Laird & Co Ltd* [1951].

> ### *Dooley* v *Cammell Laird & Co Ltd* [1951] Liverpool Assizes
>
> The claimant was operating a crane at the docks where he worked when, as a result of his employer's negligence, the sling connecting the load to the crane-hooks snapped causing the load to fall into the hold of a ship where men were working.
>
>   Dooley successfully recovered for the psychiatric illness he suffered as a result of his fear that the falling load would injure or kill some of his fellow workmen.

Though Lord Oliver held that *Dooley* had been correctly decided in *Alcock*, there was some doubt as to whether it survived the 'thus far and no further' sentiment of Lord Steyn in *White*. His status as a primary victim arose out of his role as a 'participant' in the accident—he 'had been put into the position of being or believing that he is, has been, or is about to be the involuntary cause of another's death or injury' (*Alcock* at 408)—rather than as a result of being in physical danger. Nevertheless in *W* v *Essex County Council* [2000] the House of Lords declined to strike out[38] the possibility of such claims. A number of more recent cases, factually analogous to *Dooley*, have

---

37. An alternative way to distinguish *Chadwick* and *White* would have been to introduce the so-called 'fireman's rule', whereby the police officers in *White* as professional rescuers are considered to be persons 'of extraordinary phlegm' and recovery is restricted accordingly. This solution was rejected by the majority of the Court of Appeal and by Lord Hoffmann in *White*. Moreover in *Hale* v *London Underground* [1992] a fireman involved in rescuing the victims of the King's Cross underground station fire recovered for psychiatric harm despite the fact he was a professional rescuer and, presumably, hardened to horrifying scenes.

38. The striking-out action is used when a defendant believes the claimant has no cause of action. Essentially, it is a pre-trial hearing used to establish—assuming all the alleged facts are true—whether a duty of care would be owed in the particular circumstances of the case. If the claim is struck out, the court is saying that even where extreme carelessness can be shown to have caused the claimant's harm, the defendant owes no duty of care to the claimant and so has no case to answer. Only if the case is not struck out can it proceed to full trial.

sidestepped the requirement of physical imperilment and preferred the view of Lord Oliver in *Alcock* (Case 2010, pp 42–3). In *Monk* v *PC Harrington* [2009], for example, the claimant was a foreman working on a construction site at Wembley Stadium. A temporary working platform became dislodged through the negligence of the first defendant and fell 60ft and hit two workmen below, killing one and injuring the other. The foreman heard of the accident on a portable radio and went to help the injured workmen. He subsequently developed significant psychiatric injury which prevented him from working. He claimed either as a rescuer, who reasonably feared for his own safety or as an 'unwilling participant' in the accident as he believed his actions had caused it. He was the supervisor of the installation of the platform that fell. Denying his claim on both grounds, the court held that though the primary victim category extended to 'unwilling participants', and that this extended to those who reasonably felt that they had put another in danger, on the facts there was no reasonable basis for the claimant's belief that he was responsible for his co-worker's death.

5.7.3 **Communicators of shocking news**

In *Alcock*, the House of Lords made it clear that there would be no liability to a secondary victim who does not witness the accident or its immediate aftermath and is merely told about an accident involving a loved one by a third party. However, could the claimant sue the *communicator* of the news if the *manner* of communication caused subsequent injury? Suppose the live TV broadcasts coming from the Hillsborough Stadium during the disaster had included—in breach of the broadcasters' code of practice—close-up pictures of individuals caught in the crush and close to death. Could the relatives claim that the TV company was at fault in showing the pictures and so should be liable for the psychiatric injury they suffered as a consequence of seeing them? It is far from obvious that the courts would recognise a duty of care in such cases—the public interest in the dissemination of information might well be taken to preclude the imposition of liability for the negligent communication of distressing news.

 Pause for reflection

We may well feel that there should be media freedom to convey important information to the public, even if some find it shocking. Therefore we should not allow people to recover simply on the basis that they have been shocked by what they have seen or heard. Nonetheless, we may not think that this should entitle broadcasters to sensationalise or misrepresent such information particularly where such sensationalism or misrepresentation itself shocks viewers.

So, while we value freedom of expression this need not preclude claims where there has been some sort of abuse of this freedom. Where would you draw the line?

It is clear that where false, but distressing news is communicated *with the intention to shock or harm the claimant*, the teller of the falsehood is liable in negligence for any physical and psychiatric damage caused (*Wilkinson* v *Downton* [1897]; confirmed in the House of Lords in **Wainwright v Home Office** [2004]). What is more problematic is when the distressing news is negligently communicated in circumstances where there is no intention to harm. This situation first arose in *AB* v *Tameside & Glossop Health Authority* [1997]. In this case, the claimants were patients who had been treated by an obstetrics worker who was found to be HIV positive. They objected to the way in which they were informed about this. Although the Health Authority admitted a duty of care in relation to the patients, the Court of Appeal held that they had not been negligent in deciding to break the news by letter rather than in a face-to-face meeting.

A variation on this arises where the defendant passes on *false* information. In *Farrell* v *Avon Health Authority* [2001] the court held a duty of care was owed in respect of the psychiatric injury suffered by a father who was told on arriving at the hospital where his former girlfriend had just given birth that his son had died and was given a baby's corpse to hold. The claimant was subsequently informed that there had been a mistake and that his son was in fact alive.[39]

This position might seem somewhat anomalous in light of *Alcock*. After all as Michael Jones notes 'which event is worse—being told (correctly) that someone has negligently killed your child or negligently being told (incorrectly) that your child has died?'[40]

5.7.4 Self-harm by the defendant

One final category which deserves a mention is where a claimant suffers psychiatric harm as a result of witnessing the defendant negligently placing themselves in danger or causing themselves harm—would, for example, a mother be able to bring a claim against her son for psychiatric harm caused by witnessing his imperilment when he negligently walked in front of an oncoming car (Lord Oliver, *Alcock* at 418)? The reasons for denying such a claim, Lord Oliver continued, can only be grounded in policy 'for it is difficult to visualise a greater proximity or a greater degree of foreseeability' (at 418). The key policy issue here is that of self-determination: a person ought to be free to choose to incur personal risks, without exposing themselves to liability to others.

Thus, in *Greatorex* v *Greatorex* [2000] the court refused to hold the defendant liable for the claimant's psychiatric injuries suffered as a result of witnessing the aftermath of his negligent driving. John Greatorex, the defendant, was involved in a car accident (he had been drinking and crashed the car while driving on the wrong side of the road). When the fire service arrived he was trapped in the car, injured and unconscious. Coincidentally, the lead fire officer was his father, Christopher Greatorex, who later suffered psychiatric harm as a result of what he had seen. He brought a claim against his son (which would have been met by the Motor Insurers' Bureau as his son

---

39. See also *Allin* v *City & Hackney Health Authority* [1996] where the claimant recovered damages for psychiatric injury suffered as a result of being told after a difficult birth that her baby had died; she found out six hours later that the baby had in fact survived.

40. Michael Jones 'Negligently Inflicted Psychiatric Harm: Is the Word Mightier than the Deed?' (1997) 13 *Professional Negligence* 111, 113. Consider again the woman misdiagnosed with cancer (in the examples at the beginning of the chapter). The decisions in *Farrell* and *Allin* suggest that she will be owed a duty of care in these circumstances (assuming her agoraphobia amounts to a recognised psychiatric illness). The issue is then one of breach—that is, whether the defendant been negligent in mixing up her test results.

was uninsured). The father's claim was denied on the grounds that as the defendant's injuries were self-inflicted it was against public policy to hold him liable.[41]

5.7.5 The 'assumption of responsibility' cases

Finally, a claimant will be able to establish that the defendant owes a duty of care not to cause them psychiatric harm where the defendant has 'assumed responsibility' to ensure that the claimant avoids reasonably foreseeable psychiatric injury.[42] Examples of relationships in which such an assumption or responsibility has been found include employer and employee (*Waters* v *Commissioner of Police for the Metropolis* [2000]);[43] bookmaker and gambler (*Calvert* v *William Hill Credit Ltd* [2008]); doctor and patient (*AB* v *Leeds Teaching Hospital NHS Trust* [2005]); police and police informant (*Swinney* v *Chief Constable of Northumbria Police Force* [1997]);[44] and prison officer and prisoners (*Butchart* v *Home Office* [2006]). In the latter case, *Butchart*, the claimant (who the prison authorities knew to be in a depressed and suicidal state) was housed with another suicidal prisoner, who subsequently went on to commit suicide. The claimant woke up to find his cell mate had hanged himself. He suffered serve shock. He was later told that his cell mate's suicide was his fault. The Court of Appeal, in strike-out proceedings, held that prison authorities owed the claimant a duty of care to ensure the health and safety of prisoners and that this could extend to prevent or minimise the risk of a vulnerable prisoner claimant suffering psychiatric harm as a result of being placed in a cell with a suicidal prisoner.

This category also includes occupational stress claims.[45] As with the other assumption of responsibility cases, these do not usually involve the apprehension of physical impact (or danger) rather their psychiatric injury typically stems from direct pressure or stress they feel as employees. An employer was first found liable for their employee's work-related stress in **Walker v Northumberland County Council [1995]**.

> ### *Walker v Northumberland County Council* [1995] QBD
>
> The claimant was a social services manager with a heavy and emotionally demanding caseload of child abuse cases who had suffered a second nervous breakdown as a result of pressure at work (after his earlier breakdown he had been promised additional support, which had not materialised).
>
> Colman J held that there was no logical reason for excluding the risk of psychiatric injury from an employer's duty to provide a safe system of work:[46]
>
> →

41. The Law Commission recommended that such claims be allowed ([5.34]–[5.43]), however, as with the rest of their recommendations, this has not been adopted.
42. The case law here is explored in detail by Mulheron 2008, pp 99–106.
43. *Waters* is discussed in Chapter 12.
44. *Swinney* is discussed in Chapter 6.
45. See, generally, Jesse Elvin 'The Legal Response to Occupational Stress Claims' (2008) 16 *Tort Law Review* 23.
46. See further, Chapter 12, pp 312–317.

Whereas the law on the extent of this duty has developed almost exclusively in cases involving physical injury to the employee as distinct from injury to his mental health, there is no logical reason why risk of psychiatric damage should be excluded from the scope of an employer's duty of care. (at 710)

Though there was no breach on the part of the employer at the time of the first breakdown (as this was unforeseeable on the part of the employer), in light of this, his second breakdown *was* reasonably foreseeable if the claimant's workload was not reduced. The employer was in breach of his duty in respect of the claimant's second breakdown.

 Counterpoint

The approach in *Walker* seems somewhat at odds with the decision in *White*. The former was distinguished by Lord Hoffmann in *White* on the basis that Walker's 'mental breakdown was caused by the strain of doing the work which his employer had required him to do' (at 506). As such, the harm suffered by Walker was, he suggests, distinguishable from that suffered by the police officers, which was seen to stem from their *witnessing* of the death and injury of others. In so doing, Case argues the House of Lords in *White* draws an 'absurd' distinction between employees' claims for psychiatric injury caused by 'occupational stress' and those arising out of a single traumatic incident (Case 2010, p 38). While in the former the employer–employee relationship is sufficient to ground a claim, in 'traumatic incident' claims the claimant/employee is thrown back on the ordinary principle of negligence for recovery for psychiatric harm—that is, the primary and secondary victim distinction (Lord Steyn at 497). As a result, and as seen below, 'the legacies of *White* [including its "exclusive" definition of primary victims] have been routinely ignored, distinguished, qualified or undermined' in the more recent 'stress at work' case law (*Cane* p 34).

Walker was confirmed by the Court of Appeal in *Hatton* v *Sutherland* [2002] in which the Court of Appeal accepted that a duty was owed in respect of psychiatric injury caused by stress at work. Though only one of the claimants was successful on appeal (reported as *Barber* v *Somerset County Council* [2004]), the House of Lords approved the guidance setting out when an employer would be in breach offered by Hale LJ in the Court of Appeal. In line with the ordinary principles of employer's liability, the 'threshold question' was whether the kind of harm to the particular employee was (or ought to have been) reasonably foreseeable. In so assessing, foreseeability depends on the inter-relationship between the individual characteristics of the relevant employee and the requirements made of them by their employer, including (but not limited to) the nature and extent of the work being undertaken, the signs of stress shown by the employee themselves, the size and scope of the business and the availability of resources. However, once the threshold is crossed, it is immaterial whether a person of ordinary fortitude would have suffered the same harm.

Pause for reflection

It has been suggested the foreseeability hurdles in *Hatton* (as approved by the House of Lords in *Barber*) appear to be set at a level which effectively insulates the employer from liability in the quite typical case where the employee will not admit to experiencing stress for fear of appearing unable to cope (*Pratley* v *Surrey County Council* [2002])—do you agree?[47]

5.8 Conclusion

In this chapter we have considered the law in relation to recovery for negligently inflicted pure psychiatric injury. The law in this area has been shaped by prejudice and tragedy. Assumptions that suffering psychiatric harm is less than suffering physical injury and fears of exaggerated and/or fraudulent claims have found support in a perceived need to limit recovery following a number of high-profile, negligently caused disasters. Central to this is the distinction between claimants deemed 'primary' victims, 'secondary' victims and, more recently, those who fit neither category. So understood, Lord Steyn's conclusion in **White** that 'the law on the recovery of compensation for pure psychiatric harm is a patchwork quilt of distinctions which are difficult to justify' (at 500) remains apposite.

✱ End-of-chapter questions

After reading the chapter carefully, try answering the questions below. If you would like to know what we think visit the Online Resource Centre (www.oxfordtextbooks.co.uk/orc/horsey2e/).

1. Why does the law distinguish psychiatric from physical injury? To what extent, if at all, is this distinction justifiable?

2. What is the distinction between primary and secondary victims and does it produce defensible consequences?

3. Does the law relating to psychiatric damage apply coherent principles?

4. Consider the problem question at the start of this chapter. Now having read about the topic what would be your advice to the various parties? If you need some pointers in thinking about how to answer this question, turn to the Appendix (p 589) where each problem is annotated with issues and cases to consider. Next, try to write your own answer and finally, log on to our Online Resource Centre (www.oxfordtextbooks.co.uk/orc/horsey2e/) and check your ideas against our suggested outline answer.

47. See also discussion relating to the use of the Protection from Harassment Act 1997 by claimants in order to avoid the restrictions of the guidelines set down in *Hatton* (Chapter 14, pp 406–407).

✱ Further reading

Numerous articles and case notes have been written on the issues surrounding psychiatric damage. The best place to start is Donal Nolan's excellent chapter on *Alcock*.

Bailey, Stephen and Donal Nolan 'The *Page v Smith* Saga: A Tale of Inauspicious Origins and Unintended Consequences' (2010) *Cambridge Law Journal* 495

Case, Paula 'Now You See It, Now You Don't: Black Letter Reflections on the Legacies of *White v Chief Constable of South Yorkshire Police*' (2010) *Tort Law Review* 33

Chamallas, Martha and Linda Kerber 'Women, Mothers, and the Law of Fright: A History' (1990) 88 *Michigan Law Review* 814 (on the gender dimension to psychiatric harm)

Handford, Peter 'Psychiatric Injury in Breach of a Relationship' (2007) 27 *Legal Studies* 26

Mulheron, Rachael 'The "Primary Victim" in Psychiatric Illness Claims: Reworking the "Patchwork Quilt"' (2008) 19 *Kings Law Journal* 81

Nolan, Donal '*Alcock v Chief Constable of South Yorkshire Police* (1991)' in Charles Mitchell and Paul Mitchell *Landmark Cases in the Law of Tort* (Hart Publishing, 2010), p 273

Teff, Harvey *Causing Psychiatric and Emotional Harm Reshaping the Boundaries of Legal Liability* (Hart Publishing, 2008)

6

Public bodies

Problem question

Read this problem question carefully, and keep it in mind while you are working through the chapter that follows. At the end of the chapter, you will be able to apply what you have learnt to the problem question and advise the relevant parties.

PC Plod and PC Bill both work for the Countyshire Constabulary. They are both involved in investigating a high-profile criminal case involving a bank robbery.

One night, PCs Plod and Bill are on patrol on the M7 motorway, when a car passes them at a fairly high speed. PC Plod, who is driving the patrol car, recognises the car as belonging to one of his neighbours, Mr Smith, with whom he has had a longstanding feud since Mr Smith had an affair with his wife. Determined to get his own back on Mr Smith, PC Plod, despite PC Bill's objection, decides to give chase. As the cars approach 110 mph, PC Plod loses control and the two cars collide. Mr Smith's car turns over several times before eventually coming to a stop. PC Bill is injured.

PC Plod calls an ambulance from the Countyshire Ambulance Service. This takes 30 minutes to arrive and, even then, because of staff shortages, the paramedic on board is an unqualified trainee. He examines Mr Smith and concludes that he is dead, so devotes his attention to a fairly minor leg wound suffered by PC Bill. Half an hour later a doctor arrives at the scene. When he examines Mr Smith he realises he is actually alive, but deeply unconscious. Despite the doctor's best efforts, Mr Smith dies on the way to hospital.

Meanwhile, the criminal gang under investigation take part in another bank robbery in a nearby town, during which a hostage is killed. Witnesses had called the police and been assured that they were on their way. In fact, the call had gone out to PC Plod, who had ignored it because he was more interested in chasing Mr Smith. Bruce, the husband of the hostage who died, believes the police could have done more to prevent her death. The owner of the bank also believes the police were negligent in failing to prevent more bank robberies in the area.

6.1 **Introduction**

Consider the following examples:

→ An educational psychologist employed by the local education authority fails to diagnose a teenager's special learning needs, with the result that she does not get the support necessary to do well enough in her exams to go to university.

→ The police fail to act on multiple reports of harassment of a woman by a man who has become obsessed with her. The man later assaults and kills her.

→ A fire engine turns up late to a scene of a raging fire and is unable to put out the flames because the fire officers did not bring the right tools to connect the hose to the nearby hydrant.

→ Children suffering from abuse at the hands of their parents are not removed from their home and placed in the care of the local authority, despite calls from the teachers and neighbours that suggest the abuse is escalating.

→ A highways authority resurfaces a road then fails to re-paint the road markings exactly as they were before. When wrongly exiting a junction where she should in fact have given way (but the road was not marked as such), a driver is hit and killed by a lorry which simply could not stop in time.

The object of this chapter is to identify when a public body may be held to owe a duty of care to an individual who makes a claim against it in negligence. A public body is a state-funded (that is, through taxes) organisation, including local councils, educational authorities, the emergency services and even the armed forces. Public body liability is an area of negligence law where the volume of case law and other sources has rapidly expanded. This may be due to the introduction of the Human Rights Act (HRA) in 1998, which brought into sharper focus the harms that can be done by public bodies and made people generally more rights-aware. That said, it is not easy to establish liability on the part of a public body. As usual, liability (or otherwise) is established through the mechanism of duty of care—that is, the existence of a duty or, more likely its non-existence, is the tool by which the courts shape whether any liability can be found. As we have seen, in other contentious areas of negligence treated through the concept of duty of care, judges take into account the nature or type of harm, or how it is caused (for instance, by an omission rather than a positive act, see Chapter 4), and it is this that serves to justify limiting the extent of liability that a defendant might owe. Public body liability, however, is the only area of negligence where it is the *type of defendant* that is taken into account in terms of whether recovery is appropriate or should be limited.

This seems counter-intuitive—if tort is (at least partly) about compensating harms suffered due to the wrong of another, why should it matter who that other is? It will become apparent that when the defendant is *a public body,* a general exclusionary rule operates, preventing a duty of care from arising and therefore the claimant's recovery in the majority of cases. This is because the courts have tended to assume that there are a number of 'policy' reasons why public bodies should generally be exempt from negligence liability—and that the most effective way consistently to avoid liability is to deny that a duty of care exists in the first place.

6.2 **The general exclusionary rule**

Is there a good reason for treating public bodies differently from private bodies and individuals when they cause harm by their negligence?[1] As we shall see from the case law, the term 'public bodies' is wide-ranging and encompasses a number of agencies which have great potential to cause harm, both in terms of volume and severity. In fact, a number of cases keenly illustrate the extreme harms public bodies are capable of causing via their negligence. One of the problems here is that, as a public *body*, we are not dealing with a single entity as such—it becomes harder to pin down exactly what the negligent act is or was when we find ourselves looking at a sequence of events (or omissions), all of which add up to the grand total of negligence. It is also difficult to pinpoint exactly who among an organisation staffed by many was actually to blame for what happened in any given situation.

 Counterpoint

Is incompetence—including gross incompetence—enough to amount to negligence? Often not, as the case law proves, even when this amounts to harms such as the loss of life, sexual abuse, or the burning down of a building. If negligence is about accidents—or 'preventable' accidents—then it would appear to us that accidents that can result in this extent of harm are exactly what the law should be protecting us against, particularly given the fact that public bodies have the capacity to harm us in more diverse and severe ways than individual defendants.

Although there are various in-roads into public body liability the courts have not (yet) gone far enough down those roads. Nor does the judicial reasoning in this area always stand up to close scrutiny. A further problem is that the negligence of public bodies or, more so, the liability for it, is often clouded by the *manner* in which it is caused. Omission and neglect are themselves difficult to attach liability to, and harms 'really' caused by the actions of a third party (who the public body may be responsible for) the same. Should, for example, the police be held liable for harm caused to someone by a criminal they negligently failed to apprehend? Furthermore, the *types* of harm that may be caused are seemingly often unrecognisable at law—if someone suffers emotional distress as a result of a health authority's carelessness, should this be compensated?

6.2.1 **Why is the judiciary reluctant to allow recovery?**

Much of the judicial reluctance in this area has to do with the public law notions of parliamentary sovereignty and the separation of powers, resulting in an unwillingness to interfere with statutory provisions. However, there is little or no reluctance on the part of the judiciary to allow claimants to recover in respect of those twin paragons of harm: personal injury and property damage. If either is negligently caused by the direct actions (and often inactions) of a public body or its agent—say a van was

---

1. Although note also that public body liability can also be found when the defendant *fails to* confer a *benefit*.

negligently driven by a council employee and caused property damage or personal injury—then compensation for these sort of easily recognised harms will be available, without difficulty.[2] However, the general exclusionary rule operates where the actions of the public body are *not* direct, do not cause these 'easily recognised' harms, or are not such as to make a situation worse. Despite the fact that a number of (often very high) hurdles have to be overcome by claimants—duty being only the first of these—the courts have tasked themselves with weighing up the 'social contract', asking how far and in what circumstances is it appropriate to provide a private law remedy where the state has not conferred a benefit on an individual and where there may be other (arguably less effective, less attractive) public law remedies already available. In recent years, the courts have appeared keen to stress a difference between public and private and have made it clear on a number of occasions that political, moral and economic reasons exist why tort law should not be used to impose a private law duty on public bodies to confer benefits on individuals (as opposed to the lesser duty to merely refrain from causing direct harm).

It might be thought, reasonably in our opinion, that because public bodies are paid for by the public, that avoidable harms caused by their carelessness (or worse) ought to attract compensation. However, it is often for precisely this reason that the courts shy away from holding that public bodies owe a duty of care—the fact that taxpayers' money funds them and taxpayers are thought unlikely to want to 'fund' their negligence through compensation payouts. Put like this, it does seem an unattractive proposition, but phrased in terms of redressing a wrong committed (with the dual benefit that lessons will be learnt so that—with luck—similar negligent acts will not happen in the future) and alongside the loss-spreading effects and principles of distributive justice, liability in such circumstances may seem more attractive.

However, the counter argument is that making public bodies pay out for their harmful mistakes would put a strain on the public purse and lead to a diversion of resources away from general public services—this argument holds particular force in times of global financial crisis and national cuts to public spending. It is also suggested, often by judges and with little empirical or other evidence to support such claims, that to allow claims would lead inexorably to a flurry of unmeritorious and vexatious claims being made and to dangerous (but undefined) 'defensive' practices being adopted.[3] The negligent action or inaction of a public body has the potential to harm vast numbers of people at once, so it is suggested by the courts, when denying that a duty should be owed, that actions against them are or could become common—that claims will be made precisely *because* the body concerned is viewed as having deep pockets and is able to bear the loss.

It used to be the case that organs of the state could not be sued at all in negligence: the Crown had a general immunity from suit. This changed with *Mersey Docks and Harbour Board Trustees* v *Gibbs* [1866], a position later confirmed in *Geddis* v *Proprietors of the Bann Reservoir* [1878], where Lord Blackburn said that while no action could be

2. This principle is explained well in the Law Commission's recent consultation document on public body liability (2008) (at [3.104]).

3. Although note that not all members of the House of Lords appear to have been swayed by the notion of liability resulting in 'defensive practices'. In **Home Office v Dorset Yacht Co Ltd** [1970], Lord Reid rejected this notion, saying that 'Her Majesty's servants are made of sterner stuff' (at 1033).

taken for harms caused by an agent of the Crown in doing what it was authorised to do by an Act of Parliament if it was done without negligence, if the harm was the result of negligence then an action would lie (at 455). Later, **East Suffolk Rivers Catchment Board v Kent** [1941] considered, for the first time, whether a public body owes a common law duty of care to an individual harmed by its negligent actions where it has been given a public law *power* to act, but not a public law *duty* to do so. In fact, it is this distinction (between powers and duties) that still leads to many of the judicial problems with finding the liability of a public body today.

East Suffolk Rivers Catchment Board v Kent [1941] HL

At high tide, flood waters breached a sea wall maintained by the catchment board. It tried to fix the wall, but took a long time doing so, during which the claimant's land continued to be affected by the flooding sea water. He sued for the losses caused to him as a result, and was at first unsuccessful in the High Court but later recovered in the Court of Appeal.

On the catchment board's appeal to the House of Lords, a line was drawn: the question was whether this was a breach of a public law *duty* or whether the catchment board was simply exercising the *powers* given to it under statute. The Lords held that the latter was clearly the case: there was no existing duty that said that the board should repair the wall—or even to complete the work once started—it merely had been granted the power to do so. So, the question then became whether the exercise of this power could attract a common law (private) duty of care, owed to individuals who suffered harm as a result of the negligent exercise of the power. The law lords found that this was not the case, stating (with one notable dissent from Lord Atkin, who went back to principles he had earlier expounded in *Donoghue* v *Stevenson* [1932]) that a public body would be liable only for the negligent exercise of a statutory power granted to it where it made matters worse.

In **East Suffolk**, the House of Lords determined that no private law duty would be owed to a claimant in respect of the negligent exercise of a power, unless that action made the claimant worse off than they were before. This general exclusionary rule is still in operation, albeit with exceptions, and the particular issue raised in **East Suffolk**—'justiciability'—is something that the courts have come back to time and again, as we will see later in the chapter.

A further 'landmark' case in public body liability is **Home Office v Dorset Yacht Co Ltd** [1970],[4] in which the House of Lords imposed liability on the Home Office for damage caused by escaping young offenders. This case is a good example of the complex nature of public body cases, as it also involved both an omission and the actions of third parties. In fact, Carol Harlow described it as 'setting the scene for a liability revolution as great as, if not greater than, that usually attributed to *Donoghue* v *Stevenson*'.[5]

The rest of this chapter is divided into sections dealing first with the current status of the general law on public body liability, followed by a closer look at the emergency services (as a particular type of public body, responsible by their very nature for the

---

4. The facts of this case are set out in Chapter 4, p 87.
5. *State Liability: Tort Law and Beyond* (OUP, 2004), p 17.

wellbeing of citizens) and armed forces. This is followed by a section on other types of public bodies, encompassing such things as educational, health and highway authorities and child protection services. The final part of this chapter looks at a possible light at the end of what is, in our opinion, a very dark tunnel—the impact of human rights jurisprudence and the passage of the HRA on this contentious area of tort law, particularly in relation to new 'types' of claim.

6.3 **The current position**

It is still the case that a public body will be liable where the negligent exercise of its powers to act makes a situation worse than it already was. However, other cases dealing with public body liability—that is, those where it is not alleged that the public body's actions have made a situation worse—have, over recent years, been affected greatly by jurisprudence from the European Court of Human Rights (ECtHR), as well as by the domestic passage of the HRA 1998 (and its coming into force in 2000).

The current state of the law can be clearly explained using the conjoined cases of *D* v *East Berkshire Community NHS Trust and Another; MAK and Another* v *Dewsbury Healthcare NHS Trust and Another;* and *RK and Another* v *Oldham NHS Trust and Another* [2005]. In these cases, the House of Lords upheld a 2003 ruling of the Court of Appeal, which said that it would be fair, just and reasonable to impose a duty on local authorities in relation to decisions regarding whether children should be removed from their parents and taken into care.[6]

> ### *D* v *East Berkshire Community NHS Trust* and other cases [2005] HL
>
> The first of the three cases, *D*, concerned a mother who had been wrongly suspected of harming her daughter. In *MAK*, the second case, a man and his daughter claimed that the daughter had been wrongly and unjustifiably taken into care because of suspicions (wrongly held) that the father was abusing her. *RK and Another* was a couple who had also been wrongly accused of abusing their daughter, who had been taken into care on the basis of these false allegations.
>
> In each of these cases, the local authority concerned sought to argue that they owed no duty to the claimants, relying on the authority of *X (Minors)* v *Bedfordshire County Council* [1995]. In *X*, the House of Lords had ruled that no duty was owed by local authorities and their child protection services in respect of decisions about whether to take children into care. The law lords felt that to find such a duty would cut across the statutory framework in which such decisions were made and potentially lead to staff in these areas working
>
> →

---

6. The 'fair, just and reasonable' criterion is one part of a judicially created three-limbed test for when a duty of care should arise in novel claims. The other limbs are proximity and foreseeability and the language of this test permeates contentious negligence cases—at least those where the courts find reason not to impose a duty—both before and after *Caparo* in which the test was formalised (see Chapter 3, p 61 for discussion of *Caparo* and its effect on the law of negligence generally).

less effectively as they would always have to keep one eye on the avoidance of liability (commonly referred to as 'defensive practices'). However, given the timing of the case, in *D v East Berkshire* and its conjoined cases, the Court of Appeal ruled that whether a duty should be owed in respect of this type of claim had now to be considered in the light of the HRA (Lord Phillips MR at [79]–[83]). This brought into domestic focus rights contained in the European Convention on Human Rights,[7] giving citizens the right to sue public bodies in a domestic court for violations of these.[8] In addition, the Act deliberately named the *courts* as a public body,[9] meaning that any domestic court would not now be able to make a decision that impinged on a citizen's human rights guaranteed under the Convention.

The Court of Appeal ruled that the effect of the HRA meant that the policy argument that workers would adversely adapt their practices for fear of being sued in negligence no longer stood up in cases where human rights issues were at stake (in these cases Article 8 (at least) on the right to private and family life was almost certainly engaged). In other words, as individuals could sue the state *directly* under the HRA, this kind of risk avoidance was not unique to the tort of negligence and a duty should not be denied on this basis. As a result, there could be no other interpretation than that it *was* 'fair, just and reasonable' to impose a duty on local authorities charged with making decisions about whether to take children into care. However, the court said that this duty was owed only to the *child* and not to its parents (at [86]–[87]). To allow both could amount to a conflict of interests where abuse by a parent was being alleged and/or investigated.[10]

The claimants appealed to the House of Lords on the smaller issue of whether a duty should be owed to the parents as well, arguing that no such conflict of interest arose: it was in *all* parties' interests that the authority concerned acted with care in making decisions about whether it had to remove children from their parents. However, their appeal was unsuccessful: a majority of the House of Lords ruled that although a more general duty was owed to the whole family, where there was a suspicion or allegation of abuse there had to be a duty to the child only to ensure that this was properly and sensitively investigated, and this inevitably might not be in the interests of the parents, meaning that the conflict of interests still existed (Lord Bingham dissented on this point).

Pause for reflection

Is this issue really one of semantics? In other words, in distinguishing between a duty of care which is owed to children, parents or a family as a whole, do you think that that the House of Lords was playing with words deliberately in order to limit the category of people

7. Not all of the Convention rights are directly actionable under the HRA, only those listed in the Appendix to the Act.
8. Section 6.
9. Section 6(3)(a).
10. Also see *Jain v Trent Strategic Health Authority* [2009]. It has recently been held that a parent's interests do not necessarily conflict with those of the child(ren) concerned and that a duty of care may extend to them as well, provided they are not suspected or being investigated for abuse: *Merthyr Tydfil County Borough Council v C* [2010].

→

to whom a duty of care can be owed—and is it right that they should do so? That is, could it be said that an authority charged with investigating abuse should owe a duty to all parties involved to investigate any allegations *carefully*, in which case there would be no conflict of interest, as it would be in both the parents' and the children's interest that decisions are based on a careful investigation? If you only relate a duty to whether the investigations should be *sensitively* conducted, it becomes easier to see where a conflict of interest might arise.

The reason that *D v East Berkshire* and its conjoined cases are so significant is that a duty was found to be owed to *someone* by the public bodies concerned in respect of the negligence alleged to have taken place. Prior cases, as we have indicated above, had more commonly shown there to be no duty, so this ruling represents a marked change of direction for the courts.[11] Some of the judicial comment in *D v East Berkshire* emphasised that more reliance could be placed on using breach as a 'control device' to limit recovery. In dissent, Lord Bingham, for example, said that even where a duty would be recognised and 'breach rather than duty were to be the touchstone of recovery, no breach could be proved without showing a very clear departure from ordinary standards of skill and care' (at [49]). However, despite this argument attracting later courts, the finding of 'no duty to parents' in *D v East Berkshire* has withstood subsequent challenge (see *Lawrence v Pembrokeshire County Council* [2007]).

Counterpoint

It seems unlikely that this change of direction was due to a change in attitude of the House of Lords itself—the law lords seem always to have seen themselves as the protectors of public bodies against liability in negligence, even in cases where decisions denying the existence of a duty in this respect have seemed wholly unjust given the degree of carelessness shown by the public body personnel involved. It is more likely to be the case that such a change was simply unavoidable. The House of Lords could hardly ignore the challenges relating to public body liability before the ECtHR and the climate of domestic change and emergence of a more rights-aware culture in the UK.

Post-*D v East Berkshire*, some claimants have attempted to use the human rights route rather than making a claim in negligence—despite the fact that it should, in theory at least, be a little easier to claim in negligence itself following *D v East Berkshire*, even where the defendant falls into the public body category or even some smaller category within that. An example of this is *Van Colle v Chief Constable of Hertfordshire Constabulary* [2008]. In this case, the claimants were the parents of Giles van Colle, a man shot dead only days before he was due to give evidence for the prosecution in a

---

11. Consider the implications of *D v East Berkshire* in relation to the abused children in the scenario outlined at the start of this chapter. On the basis of this case, which parties would be owed a duty of care and which would not?

criminal trial. In the period before the trial was meant to begin, the accused, a man named Daniel Brougham, was alleged to have intimidated witnesses and evidence was provided to show that the police were (or should have been) aware of this. Despite this, no protection was offered to Giles van Colle and Brougham was subsequently able to shoot him. Brougham was convicted of the murder. Nevertheless, the van Colles argued that the police had put Giles at risk—they could and should have offered him further protection from a man such as Brougham and it was likely that his death could have been prevented had this been given. The van Colles argued that this meant that the police were in breach of Article 2 of the Convention (which guarantees the right to life) and brought their claim under the HRA, instead of via the more traditional route of negligence.

As we will see later in the chapter, taking a negligence claim against the police would have been likely to lead to failure (and it was noted by the court that a negligence claim in this case would have been 'fraught with difficulty'), due to earlier precedents in police negligence cases. The defendants tried to base their defence to the Article 2 claim in terms of these existing precedents and the policy arguments enshrined in them—but the Court of Appeal said that it was exactly these arguments which led to the obligation of the police to provide protection for the life of witnesses, and the claimants succeeded. However, this decision was overturned by the House of Lords which found that there was, in fact, no violation of Article 2 as there had been no 'direct and immediate threat' to van Colle's life. The threshold test for this was high.[12]

6.4 **The background to *D* v *East Berkshire***

6.4.1 **The *Osman* case**

Some background is needed in order to fully explain the significance of the European jurisprudence that preceded the House of Lords' decision in ***D* v *East Berkshire***. The first such case to have a great impact on domestic interpretations of the law was ***Osman* v *UK* [1997]**, which stemmed from the outcome of the decisions in two earlier domestic cases (***Hill* v *Chief Constable of West Yorkshire* [1989]** and ***Osman* v *Ferguson* [1993]**).

> ### *Hill* v *Chief Constable of West Yorkshire* [1989] HL
>
> A woman sued on behalf of her daughter, who had been the final murder victim of serial killer Peter Sutcliffe, better known as 'the Yorkshire Ripper'. She alleged that the police had been negligent in failing to catch him earlier than they actually had. Her claim failed.
>
> The courts held that although it was foreseeable that if the police failed (negligently or otherwise) to apprehend the killer, he would go on to kill another young woman in the
>
> ➜

---

12. The threshold was set in ***Osman* v *UK* [1999]** (below). That the threshold is high has also been confirmed in *Re Officer L* [2007] (considered in *Van Colle*) and *Mitchell* v *Glasgow City Council* [2009].

→

area, there was no proximity between the police and the victim as the police could have no idea exactly who or where the next victim was likely to be—all females within the fairly wide area in which the murders were being committed were equally at risk. On this ground alone the court would have found that no duty of care could be owed to the victim and the claim could proceed no further. However, even though it was technically not necessary to do so, the House of Lords went on to look at the policy reasons upon which a finding of no duty should rest. Confirming the opinion of the Court of Appeal, their lordships held that wrong decisions made when investigating crimes should attract no duty as this might have an 'inhibiting effect' on the judgement to be used by the officers concerned. Furthermore, even though many claims against the police in this respect would be likely to fail, even pre-paring to mount a defence to such claims would be a waste of police resources in terms of time, manpower and financial expenditure.

Osman v Ferguson [1993] CA

In this case, Mrs Osman and her son Ahmet alleged that the police force had been negligent in failing to prevent an attack on the family in which the boy was badly injured and his father was killed. Ahmet Osman and his family had been subjected to a campaign of harassment by Paget-Lewis (a teacher at Ahmet's school, who had become obsessed by the teenage boy), during the course of which he, *inter alia*, crashed his car into the family's car, damaged their home, smeared dog excrement on the door, assaulted one of the boy's friends and verbally abused Ahmet in public. Despite numerous reports to the police, and assurances that the police were 'aware that Paget-Lewis was the perpetrator of those acts and that [the deceased] should not worry for his own safety or that of his family' (at 347), records of the fam-ily's complaints were neither kept nor linked to previous complaints. Paget-Lewis was never cautioned, despite having been interviewed by the police more than once (including on his own instigation) and even though he himself declared his own criminal insanity and claimed that he might 'do a Hungerford' (in reference to a series of killings in the town of that name in the 1980s). Paget-Lewis went on to steal a gun and shoot Ahmet Osman and his father.

The Court of Appeal struck out the Osmans' claims, relying on the policy arguments from *Hill*. Leave to appeal to the House of Lords was refused.

In **Osman v Ferguson**, McCowan LJ stated that the case was 'doomed' to failure because of the policy reasons given in **Hill**, which provided an immunity for the police against negligence claims of this type (at 354). Having exhausted any possibility of a domestic remedy, the Osmans took their case to the ECtHR.

Osman v UK [1999] ECtHR

The Osmans claimed that a number of human rights had been violated when the domestic courts in the UK refused to consider their claim in negligence against the police, stating that no duty of care was owed to them. They claimed that the striking-out procedure had

→

→

denied their case a fair hearing, and went to the European Court of Human Rights to argue violations of Article 2 (the right to life, in relation to the father), Article 6 (the right to a fair trial), Article 8 (the right to private, home and family life) and Article 13 (the right to an effective remedy).

The ECtHR ruled that there had been no violation of the Article 2 right by the UK because there had not been 'a real and immediate risk to the life of an identified individual or individuals from the criminal acts of a third party' (at [116]). Had there been such a risk, the question would have been whether the police had taken the appropriate 'measures within the scope of their powers which, judged reasonably, might have been expected to avoid that risk', but this question did not arise because the risk was not thought to be real or immediate enough. Similarly, the ECtHR found no violation of Article 8, on the basis that the police did not themselves interfere with the Osmans' right to respect for their private and family life.

However, on Article 6, where it was alleged that the rule from *Hill* meant that the police effectively had a 'blanket immunity' against claims in negligence—meaning that the courts would never look at the individual merits of claims relating to police negligence and the prevention of crimes—a violation was found. The ECtHR found that the way the *Hill* rule was used in *Osman v Ferguson* did in effect confer immunity from suit upon the police in this type of claim and was therefore a disproportionate restriction of the Osmans' ability to access a fair hearing. The UK courts had neither looked at the merits of the Osmans' case nor at whether the facts of their case differed sufficiently from those in *Hill* so as to justify making a distinction. The ECtHR thought that proper consideration should have been given to the opposing policy arguments and that these should have been more carefully balanced against those from *Hill* before reaching a decision. In their view, the case had simply been struck out by the Court of Appeal on the grounds that the exclusionary rule from *Hill* was directly applicable, even though the Osmans clearly had a far greater degree of proximity with the police than Hill did and despite the fact that it might be argued that the police had assumed some responsibility for their safety.

Article 6 gives what is known as a qualified right—some exceptions can apply which may justify the violation of the right in some cases. However, in **Osman v UK**, the ECtHR found that no such exception applied. It acknowledged that the policy arguments put forward in **Hill** were legitimate ones to make, but considered that the *way* those arguments had been used in **Osman** violated their Article 6 rights. In particular, potentially competing policy arguments had not been able to be brought forward, such as the fact that the case involved the protection of a minor, that a life had been lost and that the errors on the part of the police amounted to very serious negligence, rather than mere 'incompetence' as there had been in **Hill**. These factors, the ECtHR said, should have been examined, and the police's 'immunity' should have at least been challenged. As the application of the law stood, these factors were automatically excluded from consideration, and this was what in their mind constituted the violation of the Osmans' right to a fair hearing.

In defence, the UK government claimed that the **Hill** rule did not amount to blanket immunity for the police, saying that negligence suits against the police in relation to criminal investigations and the suppression of crime would not inevitably fail. It also argued that there were alternative mechanisms—outside the tort of negligence—whereby compensation could have been claimed by the Osman family. For example, they could have taken a civil action against Paget-Lewis directly, or his psychiatrist (who had concluded that he was not mentally ill before he went on to attack Ahmet Osman and his father), or they could have claimed money from the Criminal Injuries Compensation Board. The ECtHR dismissed these arguments. The Osmans had had good reason to claim against the police. Their purpose in bringing the claim was to draw attention to the police's negligence (rather than simply to receive compensation); having their case against the police heard in court might have meant that the Osmans would have been able to hear the police account for their negligence, whether or not their claim eventually succeeded. The finding of a violation of Article 6 also meant that Article 13 (the right to a remedy) was engaged and the Osmans were ultimately awarded around £30,000 compensation by the British government in recognition of the violation of their Article 13 right.

Table 6.1 Summary of the human rights issues in *Osman* v *UK*

Claim/Article	Reason for claim	ECtHR finding	Result
Article 2—right to life	Claim on behalf of the father who was shot and killed	Article 2 not engaged as there was no 'real and immediate risk' to anyone's life; therefore there could be no violation	No violation
Article 6—right to a fair trial	Claim that the striking out process in the domestic courts did not enable a fair hearing taking into account all the facts of the case	Striking out the case merely on the basis of the 'immunity' established in *Hill* constituted a disproportionate restriction of the right to a court hearing	Violation of this right, therefore 'just satisfaction' should be given, engaging Article 13 (see below)
Article 8—right to private, home and family life	Claim that the actions of the police in failing to do anything about Paget-Lewis amounted to disruption of the family's home and family life	Article 8 not engaged as it was not the police themselves who had interfered with the Osmans' enjoyment of home and family life	No violation

Table 6.1 *Continued*

Claim/Article	Reason for claim	ECtHR finding	Result
Article 13—right to a remedy	Claimed in respect of breaches of the other three rights; if a right had been violated then a remedy must be awarded (there must be 'just satisfaction')	Was engaged because a right had been violated (Art 6) yet no remedy had been provided for this	Approx £30,000 compensation awarded (from the UK government)

 Pause for reflection

Thinking back to the aims of the tort system, and what the interests of claimants might be, do you think that the decision in *Osman v Ferguson* made any sense at all? Is there another way to control liability in this area (in respect of the police and crime) rather than saying it simply cannot come under court scrutiny, even where the level of negligence is as high as in *Osman*? What aim of the tort system, if any, do you think the ECtHR decision in *Osman v UK* achieved?

The implications of the decision in **Osman v UK** for the domestic law on public body negligence were great.[13] Effectively, what the ECtHR had said was that where a high degree of negligence was alleged in respect of a public body's acts or omissions, coupled with a high degree of harm being attributable to that negligence, a case against a public body should not necessarily be struck out on policy grounds, as there may be countervailing policy arguments pushing the opposite way: in *favour* of a duty of care. In practical terms, this would mean that domestic courts would have to consider the merits of every case where public body negligence was alleged and only strike out those cases where they were *absolutely certain* there would be good reason to do so. As a direct result, the courts became a lot more wary of using the striking-out procedure, as can be seen in the number of claims that were *not* struck out in the years immediately following **Osman v UK** that, we suggest, *would have been* had it not been for that decision.[14]

13. In the light of the **Osman v UK** decision, what do you think the position of the woman assaulted by her harasser would be? Would the police owe her a duty of care?

14. Such as e.g. *W v Essex County Council* [1998]; **Barrett v Enfield London Borough Council** [2001]; **Phelps v Hillingdon London Borough Council** [2001]; *Hall v Simons* [2002]; *Kearn-Price v Kent County Council* [2003]. However, in **Palmer v Tees Health Authority** [2000] the opposite decision was reached (though this may, we suspect, be because of the surface similarity with the facts of **Hill**, even though there are clearly a number of distinguishing features that would point towards a duty of care being at least arguable on the facts).

6.4.2 **The Z and TP & KM cases**

The next ECtHR cases to impact on the domestic law of negligence, and in particular the role of the duty of care control device, were *Z v UK* [2001] and *TP & KM v UK* [2001].

Z v UK [2001] and TP & KM v UK [2001] ECtHR

These cases related back to domestic cases that were conjoined under the name of *X* v *Bedfordshire* and decided by the House of Lords in 1995. Two of the cases within *X* had concerned victims of child abuse. In *X* itself, it was alleged that the child protection services of the local council were negligent in failing to remove a group of siblings from their parents, where they were suffering horrendous cruelty and neglect. The children's teachers, as well as neighbours and the police, had at various times been in contact with social services over a period of years, expressing concern about the children. Five years after the first concerns were expressed, the children were finally taken away from their parents and placed in care—and only then at the instigation of the children's mother—but by this time three of the children had suffered psychiatric harm as a result of the way they had been treated by their parents. The Official Solicitor brought a claim on their behalf against the council in respect of the harms they had suffered, the impact on their health and the impairment of their proper development. The House of Lords struck out the children's claims, holding that no duty of care arose between the social services and the children.

In the second case in *X, M* v *Newham*, it was alleged that social services had incorrectly removed a child from her mother and placed her into care. The girl, who was being sexually abused, had told a social worker and psychiatrist interviewing her on behalf of the authority that her abuser was called 'John'. They wrongly assumed that this was the mother's cohabiting boyfriend of the same name, without adequate further investigation. It turned out that John was a cousin who had previously lived with the family and, when the mistake was discovered, the girl was allowed to return home to her mother. Both the mother and child sought compensation from the council (who was vicariously liable for the social worker and psychiatrist's negligence) for the psychiatric harm they suffered as a result of the traumatic experience and imposed separation. These claims were also struck out for want of a duty of care.

On appeal to the ECtHR, *X* v *Bedfordshire* became *Z* v *UK*. Claims were made that the children's rights under Article 3 (the right to be free from inhumane and degrading treatment) and Articles 6, 8 and 13 had been violated. In *M* v *Newham*, now *TP & KM* v *UK*, violations of Articles 6, 8 and 13 were alleged.

In both cases, the ECtHR retreated from its previous position on Article 6, saying that the striking-out procedure used by the UK courts was not, in fact, a violation of the Convention. Whilst Article 6 was concerned with *procedural* blocks to a fair trial (for example, if particular categories of people were arbitrarily prevented from making claims in the first place, or in respect of particular types of harm), it should not be concerned with *legal* barriers. The court now recognised that it was improper to see the striking-out procedure as always conferring 'immunity' on public bodies (such as the police and social services) against

→

→

negligence claims. Instead, they said that they now understood that the decision whether to strike out a claim was part of the substantive law of negligence and as such was a legal barrier to a claim, but did not prevent a claim being made. So, the fact that a domestic court may find that it is not 'fair, just and reasonable' to impose a duty of care in respect of a public body's actions was not a procedural barrier and was in fact the result of a claim being taken and heard by a court. Although such a hearing (in a striking-out application) did not *examine* the facts of the case, it was adversarial and proceeded on the basis that the facts alleged were true and, having assumed this, asked whether there was a case to answer. That is, did a duty arise, given the circumstances and the negligence alleged? If no duty could be found, then the defendants had no case to answer: this was not to say that they were immune from liability, only that in this instance there was no liability that could arise for them to be immune from.

Put simply, the ECtHR said that the *Caparo* criteria merely defined the law and in what circumstances it would be appropriate to extend the categories where a duty of care could be found. This, even where a case was struck out, would not then be a violation of Article 6.

However, the ECtHR did find that, on the established facts, in *Z* there had been a violation of Article 3 and in *TP & KM* that there had been a violation of Article 8.

So, despite the fact that these two cases had been struck out without detailed investigation of the claims as in *Osman v Ferguson*, in a retreat from its position in *Osman v UK*, the ECtHR admitted, perhaps capitulating to the various judicial and academic criticisms of its findings, that it had misinterpreted the English law on negligence when deciding that case—essentially admitting that its decision in *Osman v UK* had been wrong. In *Z* and *TP & KM* the ECtHR found instead that the striking-out action was a *result* of the competing policy arguments (in favour of and against there being a duty of care owed) being carefully considered and was not so much about conferring an immunity as about whether to extend the existing category of cases where a duty of care could be found. As such, according to the ECtHR, this was sufficient to amount to fair access to a court for the purposes of Article 6.

However, in *Z*, Article 3 had been violated due to the local authority's failure to remove the children from a situation in which they suffered 'inhumane and degrading treatment'. In *TP & KM*, Article 8 had been violated because the child concerned had been wrongly removed from her mother. In both cases, the right to an effective remedy had also been denied the parties, so Article 13 was also engaged. These findings, while clearly not as explosive as the finding on Article 6 in *Osman v UK*, still mean that public bodies must be extremely careful in the way they handle certain situations, particularly since the HRA has come into force, and may lead indirectly to a finding that a duty of care should be owed in respect of certain claims.[15]

15. See e.g. *D v East Berkshire* which rests quite considerably on the findings in *Z v UK* and *TP & KM v UK*.

Pause for reflection

In the 'striking out' procedure, the court proceeds as if the alleged facts are all true—that is, that the defendant *was* negligent (i.e. careless), and then decides whether the defendant has a case to answer. What purpose do you think this procedure serves? Why not hear every case and then decide on the facts whether there was liability?

6.4.3 The implications for domestic law

After *Z* and *TP & KM*, the domestic courts were again 'free' to use the striking-out procedure to determine which cases should proceed and be heard in full. This did not mean, however, that the courts went back to striking out as many claims as they had been doing prior to *Osman v UK*. Although the ruling in *Osman v UK* on the Article 6 point was effectively, though not explicitly, overturned by *Z* and *TP & KM*, some points about what the courts actually must do when striking out had clearly been absorbed by the judiciary. Furthermore, the decisions in *Z* and *TP & KM* were not unanimous; five (of 17) dissenting judges believed, even after the legal position had been explained to them, that the *Osman v UK* approach was correct. Now, however, the question for the courts, where there is existing precedent, is: 'Can this case be distinguished?' Are there, for example, competing policy reasons which should outweigh those previously taken into account? Unless the court thinks there are, the claimant's case will be struck out.[16]

However, in cases where no analogous precedent exists, the courts are still 'careful' about which claims they strike out. As a direct result of this, as well as the findings that there *had* been human rights violations in *Z* and *TP & KM*, some claims against public bodies for previously unrecognised 'types' of harm have luckily, in our opinion, been able to proceed through the courts, setting new precedents along the way.

It may well be, also, that the ECtHR will pronounce again on issues regarding the existence of a duty of care in future cases. In *Z*, the ECtHR stated that it would continue to look at any legal rules which have the effect of meaning that defendants cannot be liable domestically. If it is decided that such a rule *is* a procedural rather than a substantive barrier to a claim, then Article 6 will apply and the policy arguments flowing each way will have to be considered to see whether the barrier amounts to a disproportionate impediment to the claimant's ability to have their case heard. In essence, what we are talking about here is whether there is *immunity*, or *blanket immunity* from suit. It seems that some immunity, for example that in relation to a particular aspect of a public body's activities (for example the police's discretion to investigate crimes as they see fit and according to the resources and priorities they currently operate with), will be considered proportionate, as long as this does not close every avenue of claim against that particular public body. Put more simply, public bodies, even particular ones, should not be protected from *every* type of claim that might be made against them.

16. See e.g. *Brooks* and **Smith** (discussed later in this chapter).

6.5 **The emergency services and armed forces**

Despite the clear guidance from the courts in cases such as **D v East Berkshire**, there are some particular categories of public body which have, in a sense, their own particular rules. The latest ruling is unlikely to greatly affect this, subject to an increased carefulness about striking out claims. As indicated in the previous section, where clear precedents exist, the courts tend to rely heavily on these, rather than actively seeking features that might distinguish a new claim from an older case. This is particularly apparent in claims brought against the emergency services and armed forces. We look here at these particular types of public bodies individually, as different rules regarding whether a duty of care can be found to exist have been drawn up for the different services.

6.5.1 **The fire service**

The position as regards whether a duty of care can be owed by the fire service to individuals to whom it responds was considered in the conjoined cases of **Capital & Counties plc v Hampshire County Council** [1997]; *John Munroe (Acrylics) Ltd v London Fire and Civil Defence Authority* [1997]; *Church of Jesus Christ of Latter-Day Saints (Great Britain) v West Yorkshire Fire and Civil Defence Authority* [1997]. In each of these cases against a fire service, the facts were different but the aspect of law that the court had to consider was the same: did the fire service owe a duty of care to the claimants in relation to their negligent acts or omissions? In each case, the claimant's property had been severely damaged by fire and each was claiming that, at least in part, this was the fault of the defendant fire brigade.

Capital & Counties plc v Hampshire County Council and other cases [1997] CA

In *Capital & Counties*, the fire brigade responded to an emergency call to a building on fire. Upon arrival, the officer in charge had instructed that the building's sprinkler system, which was operational, be turned off. This allowed the fire to worsen and cause more damage than it would otherwise have done. In *John Munroe*, smouldering debris from a fire in an adjacent property set light to the claimant's building. The alleged negligence on behalf of the fire brigade was in relation to the inspection of the first property and their satisfaction that all the fires were out: had they visited the claimant's building, they would have found and dealt with the smouldering debris. In the last of the three cases, the fire brigade had been unable to fight a fire in a church because the nearest fire hydrants were poorly maintained (the responsibility of the fire service under statute) and so there was an inadequate amount of water to fight the fire.

   The Court of Appeal considered first whether the fire service had a duty even to respond to emergency calls. Relying on the authority of *Alexandrou v Oxford* [1993], a case in which it was found that the police owed no duty to a member of the public to respond to

→

→

an activated burglar alarm, the court found similarly that the fire service had no duty to respond to an emergency call or to turn up and attempt to fight a fire.

Though, as we shall see, the emergency services do have a duty (once they have turned up) not to *positively* make the situation worse, there is usually no duty in relation to mere omissions—that is, if the situation is made worse by the emergency services *failing* to do something.

 Pause for reflection

What the court effectively said here is that the fire service (like the police before it) owes no private duty of care to individuals who call it in an emergency, meaning that those individuals would have no right to sue the fire service if they are negligent. This is not the same as saying that fire fighters can ignore fires if they want to—there is a duty in public law and also evidently a social or moral obligation for them to do so, as well as duties under fire officers' individual employment contracts. But does this make it sound any better?

Next, the court went on to consider whether, if a fire brigade *did* respond to an emergency call and turned up to fight a fire, it would owe a duty of care in respect of *how* the fire was fought. Or, put another way, if the fire officers were negligent, could they be found liable as a result? In *Capital & Counties*, it was found that the decision to turn off the sprinkler system was a positive act that had the effect of making the fire worse than it would have been had this decision not been taken. So, following *East Suffolk*, it was found that this action had made the claimants worse off than they were before, and therefore a duty was owed. However, in the other two cases, there had been no direct positive action that had made the situation worse than it was before the fire service's arrival.[17] Nevertheless, the claimants tried to argue that by turning up to the fire, the fire brigade had 'assumed responsibility' for the situation and that the claimants had relied on this; as a result the fire brigade had created an obligation to take care. In the language of the courts, the claimants were arguing that this created the necessary proximity between the defendant fire service and the claimants and therefore a duty of care should be found.

The Court of Appeal refused to find a duty in these two cases. They said that the duty of the fire brigade was to the public at large and that if a duty was owed to individual property owners, the two duties could come into conflict, which, for policy and pragmatic reasons, would be undesirable. They also questioned who in fact would be owed such a duty. Would it be only the owner of the building on fire about which the emergency call had been made? If so, they said, this would leave neighbouring property owners outside the sphere of the duty unless they too (or someone on their behalf) had lodged an emergency call. This, the court held, would be an untenable situation, as then other property owners would be unprotected, and the fire service may act to

17. So, would the fire officers' failure to bring the correct equipment to connect their hose be an instance of them making the situation worse (in which case a duty could be established) or merely an example of them failing to make it better (with the result that no duty would exist)?

protect those buildings whose owners were owed a duty of care but not the surrounding properties—and this may be contrary to the way the fire service itself would choose to fight a fire. As professionals, fire fighters would tend to know how best to proceed, and this should not be dictated by whether a duty is owed to a potential claimant. If other building owners were to be included within the duty, this too would cause problems, as then anyone in the environs and potentially at risk ought to be owed a duty, and the fire service could not protect everyone all the time.

 Counterpoint

The claimants' argument in these cases seems eminently sensible, particularly when one thinks of why the fire service exists in the first place (or at least what the public's perception of this would be). Furthermore, the Court of Appeal's decision seems very conservative given that the question is not actually whether the fire service should owe a duty to protect properties on fire when they are called out in an emergency, but to whom they might end up being liable if they are negligent when doing so. Why would the concept of the *standard* of care not be a sufficient control of liability? That is, could the court have said that the fire service owes a *duty* to all of the building owners as outlined above, but that this duty would be *breached* only if the fire service actually performed negligently according to the usual practices of the profession or in comparison with the actions a competent fire service might have taken in the same situation? As we will see, this is what happens when the liability (or otherwise) of doctors and other professionals is considered, where there is usually no question of whether a duty is owed,[18] and it is also the case that the standard of care can be relaxed in emergency situations.[19]

The third reason that the Court of Appeal gave for not holding that the fire service would owe individuals a duty of care was that it would be irrational to impose a duty about how a fire was fought when it had already been decided that there was no duty to turn up and fight the fire in the first place.

 Counterpoint

Where was this principle decided? It might be argued here that the court was talking in circles to convince itself. It could equally have held that the fire service both owed a duty to respond *as best it could* to emergency calls and that, once there, it would have to take care about *how* the fire was fought. Again, with public expectations in mind, wouldn't this seem more logical? As the situation currently stands following the decision in the conjoined *Capital & Counties* cases, there is no obligation to respond *and* no obligation to take care having done so, *unless* there is a negligent positive act on the part of the fire service which makes the situation worse than it would have been if the fire service failed to turn up at all.

18. See Chapter 8, p 205.
19. See Chapter 8, p 212.

Pause for reflection

If a fire brigade negligently fails to turn up at a building with a fire that could easily be contained (but the owners of the building have done nothing, in reliance on the fire service which has answered their call), have they made the situation worse than it would have been? The difficulty here is the distinction between acts and omissions.[20] Not turning up would be an omission, for which the law struggles to find situations in which a duty should be owed, as opposed to positive acts, where a finding of duty is more likely. Does this seem a logical distinction to you in these circumstances?

The public policy ground in *Capital & Counties* is that, as outlined above, the fire service owes a more general duty to property owners and so owing a duty to individuals would cut across this. As a result, a duty of care is owed to an individual only where the situation is made worse, as this establishes the necessary proximity between the parties. However, where a fire service had not made the harm suffered worse than it would have been with no intervention, the court easily—and unusually—rejected the usual public policy argument that is put forward in relation to public bodies: the fact that imposing a duty might lead to a flood of unmeritorious claims or that damages paid out would be funded by taxes and would divert money away from funding other useful activities. These points applied equally to other public and emergency services, such as the ambulance service, yet were not enough to lead to a finding of no duty in those cases.

 Pause for reflection

Even though this wider public policy angle did not have to be considered by the Court of Appeal, it was still mentioned. But does what the court said make sense to you? Why do those arguments apply to the ambulance service and fire service (in theory at least) but *not* always to the police? What role does—or should—insurance play here? Most buildings are insured, so the question comes down to whether we think the owners of property should pay the price (of fire service incompetence) through increased premiums (which are, in the long run, spread across all policy holders) or whether this is better distributed among taxpayers (as it would be if the fire service paid out compensation).

6.5.2 The ambulance service

As noted above, the ambulance service owes a duty of care to individual claimants in certain circumstances. In fact, the ambulance service, unlike the fire service, has a duty to respond to an emergency call. Both of these points come from *Kent v Griffiths* [2001].

20. Chapter 4.

> ### *Kent v Griffiths* [2001] CA
>
> In this case, an emergency call was made by a GP who had been called to the home of a pregnant woman who was having an asthma attack. The GP called for an ambulance and was told that one was on its way. When it failed to arrive promptly, the GP called twice more. In the end the ambulance took 38 minutes to arrive and, as a result of the delay, the woman temporarily stopped breathing. This caused her to lose her baby and subsequently suffer psychiatric harms including personality changes and memory loss. In her claim against the London Ambulance Service, the defendants—who admitted they had no good reason for the failure to turn up promptly—claimed that the case should be struck out because they owed her no duty of care, based on *Capital & Counties*, so they had no case to answer in respect of their admitted negligence.
>
> The Court of Appeal rejected the ambulance service's application to have the claim struck out holding that the ambulance and fire services were distinguishable due to the nature of the service provided. Thus, the ambulance service did owe a duty to respond to the call.

The Court of Appeal found that the ambulance service is distinguishable from the fire service in that it can be seen as an extension of the National Health Service, which is understood to owe a duty of care towards its patients. It said that the service provided by fire fighters and the police is for the benefit of the public as a whole and could not, except in certain situations, extend to a duty owed to an individual member of the public, for the reasons outlined in *Capital & Counties*. In contrast to the fire service, once the ambulance service accepts a call in relation to a named individual, it must be seen as providing a service to that individual and, crucially, that individual is the only one who could be harmed as a result of the ambulance service's negligence when responding. In short, the ambulance service owes a duty of care to individuals, once it has accepted the emergency call in relation to them, both to respond and to respond without carelessness.

Although the issue did not arise in *Kent*, the court went on to draw a distinction between operational or procedural matters and those involving policy or the exercise of discretion. In essence, if a delay was caused by a lack of resources or a decision to deploy the resources the service has to use in a particular way rather than as a result of operational or procedural negligence, it is far less likely—as in other types of case against public bodies where a policy/operational distinction is used—that a duty of care would arise.

> ### Counterpoint
>
> It might at first glance seem sensible that the ambulance service owes a duty of care because an ambulance is sent out to deal with one individual, whereas the fire service responds to fires and is a service to the public at large so it should not be held to owe a duty of care. It may also seem sensible to maintain the policy/operational decision in relation to these services. But consider the following two scenarios:
>
> →

→

1. An emergency call is made and the ambulance service is asked to respond to a multi-car accident on the motorway in which over a dozen people are hurt. It sends five ambulances. It does not send any more as it has decided that staff overtime cutbacks are needed, despite it being the beginning of the busy holiday season on the roads. All the ambulances are delayed, resulting in many deaths and more serious injuries than would have been suffered if there were more ambulances and they had arrived promptly.

2. A man in an isolated grade-2 listed cottage calls the fire service when his cottage is hit by lightning and catches fire. The fire service has a free engine, but does not send it for half an hour. When it does, the cottage is beyond saving and the man has lost everything.

Which of the affected parties, if any, can make a claim?[21]

6.5.3 **The police**

Similar policy/operational distinctions have been raised in claims taken against the police. As ever, when the police, by a direct and positive negligent act, cause property damage or personal injury, then a duty of care is unquestionably owed to that individual. However, a distinction is drawn between operational negligence (that which happens in regard to the way in which they actually do their job), for which the police *can* be held liable, and policy matters (decisions about resource allocation, prioritisation of cases or investigations and so on), for which they generally *cannot*. What we see particularly distinctly in cases against the police (which are brought far more often than those against the fire or ambulance service) is another 'layer' of the general exclusionary rule. This operates to ensure that in respect of day-to-day activities the police must take care not to injure individuals by negligent acts, but in respect of a broader scope of activities—for example the police's primary function of the investigation, prevention and suppression of crimes—no duty of care can usually arise in respect of individuals harmed by even extreme carelessness. This distinction is clearly illustrated by the case of *Rigby* v *Chief Constable of Northampton* [1985], in which the police were sued for causing property damage to the claimant's shop when they used inflammable CS gas to try and drive out a burglar who was hiding on the premises.[22] While it was a policy decision to arm themselves with the CS gas in the first place, as opposed to a non-flammable alternative—so this decision could not give rise to a claim in negligence—the actual action of using the gas without having the necessary equipment to fight any resulting fire, which was clearly foreseeable, was an operational matter, so a duty could be owed. A duty was also found in *Knightly* v *Johns* [1982] in relation to an operational

---

21. In the first scenario, part of the reason for the ambulances being late is operational and part of it is due to policy. Would any of the potential claimants be able to show that they were affected by one and not the other? Clearly, in the second scenario the man would have no claim at all—the fire service eventually responded, but according to the law's definition of 'making things worse', did not do so.

22. It should be noted that this case is one of the few examples where a positive and direct act on the part of the police caused a physical injury.

decision by a police inspector who instructed a constable to drive against the flow of traffic in a tunnel in which the police were dealing with an accident, resulting in injury to the constable (see also *Henry* v *Thames Valley Police* [2010]).

Pause for reflection

As *Rigby* illustrates, it is not always easy to tell the difference between policy and operational matters. It seems that the difference in that case was in the police deciding to arm themselves with the gas versus the actual usage of the gas and how that was done during that particular incident. Does this seem a logical distinction to draw, particularly because if they had chosen to use a non-flammable gas in the first place, the claim could not have arisen?

Although the distinction is often difficult to see, there are some types of case that the courts have clearly identified as falling within the sphere of unquestionable police policy: the way the police choose to conduct and prioritise their investigations of crime. The additional layer of the exclusionary rule in this area stems from **Hill v Chief Constable of West Yorkshire** [1989]. Given that the investigation and suppression of crime must be seen as one of the primary functions of the police force, and the one that could most directly affect a great number of people, it seems strange to us how highly unlikely it is that liability could ever arise in relation to negligent acts or omissions in this area. Like the fire service, the police are only held to owe a general duty to society, or the 'public at large', and so in relation to this particular activity, a private law duty of care is *not* owed to individuals; seemingly no matter how closely connected that individual is to the police's negligence (proximity) and how likely it is that the particular individual may be affected by it (foreseeability). As we shall see, this principle has recently been confirmed by the House of Lords in **Smith v Chief Constable of Sussex Police** [2008].

The policy reasons raised in **Hill** to prevent a duty being owed by the police in respect of these kinds of activities have been relied on in numerous subsequent cases including *Alexandrou* v *Oxford* [1993] and **Osman v Ferguson** [1993].[23] Similar reasons resurfaced in the case of *Brooks* v *Commissioner of Police for the Metropolis* [2005]. In this case, Duwayne Brooks had been attacked alongside his friend Stephen Lawrence, who was murdered in a racially motivated attack.[24] Duwayne Brooks suffered post-traumatic stress disorder, initially as a result of witnessing the murder of his friend, but he claimed that his treatment at the hands of the police had worsened the condition. He sued the Metropolitan Police in negligence, arguing that they owed him a duty of care on three grounds: to take reasonable steps to ascertain whether he was a victim of the attack and, if so, to treat him accordingly; to take reasonable steps to give him adequate and appropriate support as a witness to a serious crime; and to treat his statements

23. Note, however, that the Court of Appeal in **Kent v Griffiths** [2001] later held that *Alexandrou* should be confined to its own facts in order for it to be able to find a duty in respect of the ambulance service (at [21]).

24. Described by Lord Bingham in the House of Lords as 'the most notorious racist killing which our country has ever known' (at [1]).

with reasonable care and attention. The police investigation into Stephen Lawrence's murder was later found by an official inquiry to have been grossly mishandled, and the same inquiry led to findings of 'institutional racism' in the Metropolitan Police.[25] One of the findings of the inquiry was that the police had begun their mishandling of the case whilst at the scene of the attack. When the officers found Duwayne Brooks at the scene he was in a state of high anxiety, agitated and, according to the police officers, 'aggressive'. Because of this, the officers assumed that there had been a fight between the two men rather than that both had been attacked, and they treated Duwayne more like a suspect than a witness or a victim of violent crime. They did not consider that he would understandably be anxious and agitated after being attacked in that way, particularly after having seen his friend murdered. The inquiry report stated that this mistake was made on the basis of racist stereotyping by the officers at the scene and meant that the police, having failed to take his evidence seriously, lost the advantage they might have had in being able to track down the attackers.

While it can be argued that the actions of the police in this case were clearly extremely negligent—far more so than in *Hill*, for example—the House of Lords ruled unanimously that the police owed no duty of care to Duwayne Brooks, relying almost entirely on the policy arguments that stem from *Hill*. They reiterated that the police's primary duty (to the public at large) is to investigate and to suppress crime and that, should they be found to owe a private law duty in the way that Duwayne Brooks was claiming they did, and had to treat victims of crime in the way he was arguing they should every time they dealt with a potential victim or witness, this would eat up valuable police time and resources would be diverted away from these primary functions. In the same breath, however, their lordships acknowledged that it would be *desirable* for victims and witnesses of crime to be treated seriously and with respect, though this was not the same as saying that each individual victim or witness should be owed a duty of care. Imposing such a duty, which could give rise to a claim for damages, was to them a step too far and would be 'bound to lead to an unduly defensive approach in combating crime' (Lord Steyn at 1509). The latest case to uphold these entrenched assumptions is *Smith v Chief Constable of Sussex Police* [2008].

Smith v Chief Constable of Sussex Police [2008] HL

Stephen Smith sued the police in negligence for serious injuries (including three fractures of the skull and associated brain damage, as well as continuing physical and psychological injury) that he sustained when attacked with a claw hammer by his former boyfriend, Gareth Jeffrey, and left for dead. He had informed the police of a series of 'violent, abusive and threatening telephone, text and internet messages, including death threats' (at [23]) that he had received from his ex-partner prior to the attack. According to the facts as laid out by Lord Bingham in the House of Lords:

> There were sometimes ten to 15 text messages in a single day. During February 2003 alone there were some 130 text messages. Some of these messages were very

→

---

25. Sir William Macpherson of Cluny, *Report on the Stephen Lawrence Inquiry* (Cm 4262–I, 1999).

→

explicit: 'U are dead'; 'look out for yourself psycho is coming'; 'I am looking to kill you and no compromises'; 'I was in the Bulldog last night with a carving knife. It's a shame I missed you'. (at [23])

Notwithstanding the severity of the threats, the police officers assigned to the case treated it as a domestic matter and did not take any steps to arrest the man or otherwise protect Mr Smith: 'The officers declined to look at the messages (which Mr Smith had offered to show them), made no entry in their notebooks, took no statement from Mr Smith and completed no crime form' (at [24]). Later, 'Mr Smith told an inspector that he thought his life was in danger ... He offered to show the inspector the threatening messages he had received, but the inspector declined to look at them and made no note of the meeting. He told Mr Smith the investigation was progressing well, and he should call 999 if he was concerned about his safety'. (at [25])

Smith's claim was struck out in the county court on the basis of previous case law (*Hill*; *Brooks*) which the judge decided prevented a claim in negligence from arising. However, the Court of Appeal ruled [2008] that it was at least arguable that the police did owe a duty of care to him as a known potential victim of violent crime—a duty to take reasonable steps to prevent a foreseeable attack by an identified person, thus enabling Smith to sue the police in negligence for compensation for the injuries if that duty was breached. Sedley LJ said that where

someone's life or safety has been so firmly placed in the hands of the police as to make it incumbent on them to at least take elementary steps to protect it, unexcused neglect to do so can sound in damages if harm of the material kind results. (at [27])

In arriving at its decision the Court of Appeal was particularly influenced by a comparable rights-based duty owed by the police as a result of Article 2 of the European Convention on Human Rights,[26] which they considered should influence the content of the common law duty of care in negligence (see e.g. Rimer LJ at [45] and Pill LJ at [55]).

The House of Lords overturned the Court of Appeal's decision and restored the order of the trial judge. Lords Hope, Phillips, Carswell and Brown, in the majority, found that some of the policy reasons outlined in *Hill* and re-stated in *Brooks* applied equally to Smith's case. Their lordships relied on two in particular. First, the danger that a duty of care would detrimentally affect the working practices of the police, causing them to 'act defensively' in order to avoid legal proceedings being brought against them. Secondly, the fact that time and resources would both have to be diverted towards the handling of such claims and away from the ordinary functions of the police in serving the public. These two policy considerations, it was felt, were enough to deny the possibility that a duty could be found, even though some of their lordships expressed regret, concern or difficulty in reaching such an opinion (Lord Phillips at [36]; Lord Carswell at [107]; Lord Brown at [127]).

26. Which was found by the Court of Appeal in *Van Colle*, but later overturned by the House of Lords (which heard *Van Colle* alongside **Smith**) on the Article 2 point. On the Court of Appeal's findings in *Van Colle*, see JR Spencer 'Tort Law Bows to the Human Rights Act' (2008) *Cambridge Law Journal* 15, where ss 6–8 HRA are compared to Heineken, the beer that it is claimed 'refreshes the parts that other beers cannot reach'.

Following **Smith**, the House of Lords' opinion means that the door currently stands only slightly ajar in respect of any future claims to be made against the police that allege negligence in the way that an investigation was conducted (or not conducted). After *Brooks*, the principle was that only an 'outrageous' case would be enough to show that a duty of care should exist to a private individual. The ineptitude of the police in **Smith** *could* have been seen this way—and indeed was by four of the country's most senior judges in the Court of Appeal and House of Lords. Lord Bingham, dissenting in the House of Lords, agreed with the Court of Appeal that the existence of a duty of care was arguable in this case. In fact, he went further, saying that:

> if the pleaded facts are established, the Chief Constable *did* owe Mr Smith a duty of care [emphasis added]...I would hold that if a member of the public (A) furnishes a police officer (B) with apparently credible evidence that a third party whose identity and whereabouts are known presents a specific and imminent threat to his life or physical safety, B owes A a duty to take reasonable steps to assess such threat and, if appropriate, take reasonable steps to prevent it being executed. I shall for convenience of reference call this 'the liability principle'. (at [44])

He went on to say that he did not consider this 'liability principle' to be at all inconsistent with **Hill** and *Brooks*, which he said had been correctly decided. In his view, the three decisions stood independently of each other. He then set out reasons why the policy arguments expounded in **Hill** were not appropriate in the context of **Smith** and, more dramatically, why they would not affect the operation of the 'liability principle' (at [48]–[53]). He did not see that adopting the principle would 'induce a detrimentally defensive frame of mind', for example, as the only thing the police would need to do would be to make a 'reasonable assessment of the threat posed to an identified potential victim by an identified person' (at [49])—this is essentially testing the police on *standard* of care (breach). Nor did he believe that accepting the principle would detract from the police's primary function of investigating and suppressing crime, a factor which had clearly weighed particularly heavily in *Brooks*. Unfortunately, Lord Bingham's 'liability principle' was not accepted by the four other law lords.[27] Lord Hope, for one, plainly believed that the policy reasons in favour of denying the existence of a duty were still as strong in **Smith** as they had been in *Brooks* and this fact, to him, made the 'liability principle' unworkable. This is evident from the fact that he viewed the case as a 'domestic' issue:

> [s]o-called domestic cases that are brought to the attention of the police all too frequently are a product of [the breakdown of relationships]. One party tells the police that he or she is being threatened. The other party may say, when challenged, that his or her actions have been wrongly reported or misinterpreted. The police have a public function to perform on receiving such information. A robust approach is needed...Not every complaint of this kind is genuine...Police work elsewhere may be impeded if the police were required to treat every report from a member of the public that he or she is being threatened with violence as giving rise to a duty of care...(at [76])

---

27. Three of whom (Lords Hope, Carswell and Brown) disagreed specifically with it in their speeches (at [77], [109], and [129] respectively).

Counterpoint

It appears to us that if the starting point is taken that the events in this case arose from a 'domestic issue' then the policy arguments will always be able to be used to justify a finding of no duty. 'Domestic' implies that people should sort things out for themselves (although changes in emphasis for both the police and the courts to 'domestic' violence would seem to suggest some recognition that 'domestic' does not always mean that these issues are easily resolved and that many such problems arise from an imbalance of power within a relationship). Lord Bingham, on the other hand, recognised the seriousness of the facts in *Smith* and, it seems, found it hard to believe that a duty would not be owed when the threats made were so numerous, plainly violent and escalating in severity. His 'liability principle' only creates a duty that mirrors what most of us would *expect* from the police in a situation of that type: where the evidence is 'credible' (as opposed to where it is not) and the threat is 'specific and imminent', 'reasonable steps' must be taken to assess the threat and, if necessary, do something about it.

Instead, following *Smith*, it seems that the police *do* in fact have a type of blanket protection in respect of the way they conduct their investigations (including whether they choose to investigate in the first place), even though four senior judges thought that a duty could (Court of Appeal) or should (Lord Bingham) have been found in this case. This immunity exists despite the doubt that the *Osman* v *UK* decision should still put into the mind of the judiciary when deciding whether a public body owes a duty of care to an individual harmed by virtue of its negligence. We would argue that *Osman* should infuse in the courts more reticence in striking out this type of case, particularly where the negligence can be deemed to be gross or where, as here, it would have been relatively *easy* to take steps to avoid the negligence. However, as cases against the police continue to illustrate (*Brooks*; *Smith*), the principle seems to extend to cases even where the exact harm and the precise victim are clearly foreseeable, making the degree of proximity between the police and the claimant very high.[28] In *Brooks*, the House of Lords said that theirs was an opinion resting solely on the facts of the case and that the 'blanket immunity' that it might be thought was given by *Hill* was not appropriate. To this end, Lord Keith said that there *could* be some 'cases of outrageous negligence by the police' that would fall beyond the general principle and in which a duty could be found. If the facts of *Brooks* and *Smith* were not outrageous enough, however, it is hard to picture exactly the degree of negligence Lord Keith was imagining. Arguably here, what the public might see as outrageous is clearly not what the House of Lords has in mind when using this get-out clause to retain some semblance of there being no blanket immunity for the police. If it must happen, we would at least prefer to see a less disingenuous 'cloak and dagger' approach to the protection of the police force by the courts.

---

28. So, in fact, it seems unlikely that the police would owe the woman assaulted by her harasser a duty of care, despite the high degree of proximity in that scenario, in contrast to the position we might have thought she would be in above, at footnote 13.

Pause for reflection

What do you think was the right decision in *Smith* and why? Compare the facts and decisions of *Hill*, *Osman* v *Ferguson*, *Brooks* and *Smith* to a Canadian case called *Doe* v *Metropolitan Toronto (Municipality) Commissioners of Police* [1998]. In this case, the police negligently mishandled the investigation of a series of rapes in an area of the city. One of the reasons for this was the police force's overall reliance on 'rape myths' and stereotypical assumptions about women who alleged rape, women who had been raped and what women would do if they were warned about a serial rapist operating in their vicinity. The claimant was a woman who had been raped by the serial rapist. She argued that the police were negligent in failing to catch him sooner and, in the alternative, that they should have warned women in the area so that they could take steps to protect themselves. In *Doe*, the judge vehemently refused to follow *Hill*, pointing out that there were clear policy arguments militating in the other direction, meaning that the police *should* owe a duty of care to any woman who was then raped, possibly as a result in part or whole of their failings.[29]

What do you think the policy arguments operating in the other direction would be in *Smith*? Do you think this is the type of 'outrageous negligence' that Lord Keith had in mind in *Brooks*? Or do you find it hard to distinguish this case from *Brooks*? Why do you think *Doe* was not mentioned in either the *Brooks* or *Smith* judgment?[30]

The *Hill* 'immunity' has extended also to cases sitting on the very edge of negligent activities of the police. For example, in *Elguzouli-Daf* v *Commissioner of Police for the Metropolis and Another* [1995], the claimants sued the police and the Crown Prosecution Service on the basis that their prosecutions had been unduly delayed by negligence, as a result of which they had been kept in custody for longer than they ought to have been. However, no duty of care was found in this case, as the Court of Appeal held that to find such would be dealing with 'individualised justice' as opposed to general principles of justice serving the entire community (Steyn LJ at [349]) and would risk defensive practices and a diversion of resources from the CPS. In *Desmond* v *Chief Constable of Nottinghamshire Police* [2011], the Court of Appeal found that no duty could be owed by the police in respect of information disclosed (wrongly) on an Enhanced Criminal Record Certificate in relation to the claimant securing a job as a teacher. Part of the reason for this was the conflict of interest between the claimant's right to gain employment and the general public interest in protecting children. Further, the police had not assumed responsibility

29. In Canada, then, the family of the assaulted woman (in the scenarios at the beginning of the chapter) may well have a claim.

30. Interestingly, the Cambridgeshire police force settled a claim with a woman who took a Human Rights Act claim against them for failing to properly investigate her rape (see 'Rape complaint woman reaches settlement with police', BBC, 1 December 2009). The force paid her £3,500, which came with an apology, but said that this was not an admission of liability. It remains to be seen whether human rights claims will prove to be fruitful in respect of future negligently investigated rapes. Following the arrest and imprisonment of serial 'Black Cab' rapist John Worboys—which, in respect of the police's handling of rape complaints, has many similarities to *Doe*—an Independent Police Complaints Commission (IPCC) report concluded that 'more needs to be done if public confidence in the police's response to reports of rape and sexual offences is to improve'. Five officers involved in the investigations were subject to misconduct procedures.

to the claimant ([49]).[31] That said, there have been cases where a duty of care has been found to be owed by the police to an individual, even where it was not an operational matter in question, arguably proving that *Hill* does not grant immunity from suit.

In *Swinney* v *Chief Constable of Northumbria Police* [1997] the claimant, a pub landlady and police informant, was owed a duty of care in respect of the police's negligence in not keeping her identity safe. She had given information on a violent criminal and had made it known that she could not be identified as the source of the information, as she would be likely to face repercussions if this were the case. Despite this, police documents containing details of the case, including her name, were left in an unlocked police car and were, inevitably perhaps, stolen and eventually reached the criminal against whom the evidence was given. Swinney then was subjected to a vicious campaign of harassment from which she suffered psychiatric harm and had to give up her pub. At first, the police tried to argue that there was no proximity between them and her as a victim and that the policy reasons in *Hill* served equally in her case. The Court of Appeal disagreed with both of these grounds. It found that Swinney's case could clearly be distinguished from *Hill* as it was clearly known by the Northumbria police who might potentially be harmed as a result of their negligence (in fact that was exactly what they were charged with preventing), as opposed to *Hill* where no particular potential victim was identifiable. The court found that the police in this case had assumed the responsibility for the claimant's protection against the criminal she gave evidence against—meaning there was, in fact, a high degree of proximity between them.

In dealing with the policy arguments, the Court of Appeal stated that although many of the arguments put forward in *Hill* were *relevant* to this case, they could not be considered in isolation, and counterbalancing policy arguments had also to be taken into account. In essence, the court performed a balancing act, weighing up policy reasons both for and against there being a duty owed to the claimant. In this case, they found that the policy arguments that existed *for* there being a duty of care outweighed those against. When witnesses came forward as informants they were performing a public duty and deserved the protection of the police. Without such protection in place, the number of people prepared to inform to the police would drop, making the prevention and detection of crime more difficult. Informers were more than ordinary members of the public and the police assumed a responsibility towards them when relying on them for information. Unfortunately, on the facts of *Swinney*, the police were later not found to be in *breach* of the duty that they owed.

Other exceptions to the *Hill* 'immunity' have come in different types of case, though not always easily. In *Kirkham* v *Chief Constable of Manchester* [1990], the police were found to owe a duty to a remand prisoner in respect of whose suicidal tendencies they had failed to tell the prison authorities. He later hanged himself in custody. A similar duty was found to be owed to a prisoner held overnight in police cells in **Reeves v Commissioner of Police for the Metropolis** [2000]. Similarly, the Court of Appeal held in **Costello v Chief Constable of Northumbria Police** [1999] that a police officer was owed a duty of care by her employers in relation to her safety while at work. Costello was attacked by a prisoner in a cell. Despite hearing her scream, the inspector on duty (and who was specifically charged with her protection) had negligently failed to help

---

31. Contrast similar cases relating to pure economic loss. See e.g. *Spring* v *Guardian Assurance* [1995], discussed in Chapter 7, p 193.

her—it was found that he did owe her a positive duty (for which the commissioner would be vicariously liable) to act where his failure to do so would result in a colleague being unnecessarily exposed to an increased risk of injury. However, all of these cases can be easily classified into the category of 'assumption of responsibility'. In other words, why shouldn't the police owe a duty to those actually in their care at the time the negligence is alleged, if they know that there is a risk of harm? It is this known potential harm that seems to exist as a common thread in these cases—reinforced by the fact that the courts have also found that it would be unreasonable to hold that the police had assumed responsibility for every person in police custody in relation to suicide. Only when there is a known risk of this happening will the positive duty be owed (*Orange* v *Chief Constable of West Yorkshire Police* [2001]).

A more difficult case to pigeonhole is *Waters* v *Commissioner of Police for the Metropolis* [2000]. In this case, Eileen Waters, a young female police officer, brought an action in negligence (as well as a discrimination claim which was dismissed) against her employers for negligently failing to prevent a campaign of harassment being mounted against her by fellow officers after she had alleged that she had been raped by one of them in police quarters. Following her allegation, she was snubbed and victimised by her colleagues and bullied and harassed on more than 80 separate occasions. She claimed that her employers had not dealt seriously with either her complaint or the harassment she suffered following it. Relying on **Hill**, the defence argued (and the lower courts agreed) that allowing a negligence action to proceed would divert officers and resources from the police's primary function; the prevention and detection of crimes. However, the House of Lords considered that all relevant circumstances of her case had to be taken into account. Only in the House of Lords, for example, did any judge (Lord Hutton) allude to the actual harms suffered by Eileen Waters, which could only have been exacerbated by the length of time it took for her claim to get to that point (ten years) and not be dismissed. Their lordships eventually found that the policy arguments *for* there being a duty of care owed to Miss Waters by her employer outweighed those against, even though these still had to be considered. If, as happens in a striking-out action (for this was only what this case was until this point), the court had to proceed assuming the facts alleged were true, then public interest *demanded* that a duty should be owed and that the serious problem the police had in dealing with complaints of this nature by one of their own officers should be made public. Showing that the police owed a duty of care would in theory force something to be done to change the way such claims were handled in the future; the knock-on effect of this also had to be considered. How could the public have any confidence in the way the police would handle rape allegations made by an ordinary citizen if it was known that circumstances such as those faced by Eileen Waters were allowed to continue?

 Pause for reflection

Compare what happened in the *Waters* case to the Canadian case of *Doe*. What do the two cases tell you about the way the tort system typically deals with harms suffered primarily by women?[32] Do you think Eileen Waters should have had to fight so hard merely for the right for her case to proceed to trial?

---

32. You could also consider the fact that **Smith** concerned two gay men.

Counterpoint

Overall, it seems that any case taken against the police will be, at best, a fight. *Hill* seems to be (in our view, unreasonably) standing the test of time. There are, it seems to us, clear policy reasons operating counter to those expounded by Lord Keith in *Hill*, notwithstanding their lordships' admission in both *Brooks* and *Smith* that *some* of these can no longer necessarily be relied upon. It is at least arguable that policy issues like those apparent in *Doe* and *Waters* (keeping public faith in the efficacy of the police force, for example) are apparent in *all* these cases (as the MacPherson report would seem to suggest of *Brooks*).

Even exceptions to the rule, which appear to be based on the idea of the defendant police force having 'assumed responsibility' for the wellbeing of the claimant or being in a 'special relationship' with them, do not seem to be consistent. If it is arguable, for example, that an informant should be owed a duty of care so as not to discourage future informants from coming forward, or that a serving police officer should be owed a duty of care in respect of her treatment after making an allegation of rape against another officer, so that the public have more confidence in the way the police generally handle rape cases and— more importantly—potential rape victims, why do they not owe a duty to someone who is a likely victim of a serious physical attack, particularly when he was also the witness to a racist murder? Even before *Smith* was decided by the House of Lords, Markesinis and Deakin commented that 'the pattern of the decided cases suggests that of all the decisions in the area of duty of care, *Hill* comes closest to providing a "safe haven" for public bodies in the exercise of certain functions'.[33] Hopefully, for the sake of public confidence in the police as well as the ability of the courts to deal with police negligence, this safe haven will not last forever. However, in the light of the most recent authorities on the police in terms of both human rights (particularly *Van Colle*) and duty of care in negligence, it seems that a case even more 'outrageous' on its facts will be needed to persuade the majority of their lordships to depart from the safety of *Hill*.

6.5.4 **The coastguard**

Similar restrictions to those that attach to the fire service operate to prevent there being liability attached to the coastguard. In *OLL Ltd* v *Secretary of State for Transport* [1997], the court held that, like the fire service, the coastguard does not owe a general duty of care to respond to calls from people in trouble at sea, only a duty not to make the situation worse if they do respond. In this case children and teachers on a school canoeing trip got into severe difficulties at sea, some of the canoes capsizing and the party becoming separated in the water. The response of the coastguard was both slow and inefficient and, the claimants argued, made the situation worse. However, the court disagreed, so the claims were struck out as disclosing no cause of action.

---

33. *Markesinis & Deakin* p 213.

Pause for reflection

Interestingly, in the opinion of Lord Bingham in **Smith**, this was another case where the duty should have been obvious on the facts, according to his 'liability principle'. After discussing the facts and outcome of the case, he said: 'My Lords, I feel bound to say that a law of delict [as tort is known in Scotland] which denies a remedy on facts such as these, in the absence of any statutory inhibition, fails to perform the basic function for which such a law exists' (at [57]). Think back to what the functions of tort law are. Do you agree with him? Do you think the fact that the coastguard (and the lifeboat service) is funded through charitable donations and relies heavily on volunteers swayed the court in *OLL*?

6.5.5 **The armed forces**

In respect of the armed forces, the cases seem to suggest that a private law duty of care will only be owed to individuals injured as a result of negligence where a highly proximate relationship arising out of an 'assumption of responsibility' exists. In **Barrett v Ministry of Defence** [1995], for example, a drunken naval officer was found to have been owed no duty of care until the point where a superior officer stepped in to order that he was helped back to his room, thus assuming responsibility for his safety.[34] Similarly, in *Jebson v Ministry of Defence* [2000], the Court of Appeal found that the defendants owed a duty to provide suitable transport and provisions for soldiers after a night out. In this case, a drunken soldier had suffered injuries after climbing onto the roof of an army truck and then falling off. The assumption of responsibility idea seemingly extends only to civilian circumstances: in *Mulcahy v Ministry of Defence* [1996], it was found that 'common sense' and policy reasons (including the 'defensive practices' argument) meant that the army should not owe a duty to soldiers while in battle conditions, even though the claimant was injured by friendly fire from his own sergeant.[35]

6.5.6 **Duty: the emergency services and armed forces—at a glance**

Table 6.2 Duty: the emergency services and armed forces—at a glance

Which service/body	When is a duty of care owed?
Fire service	• No duty to respond to emergency call • Once fighting a fire, the duty is only not to, by any positive act, make the situation worse
Ambulance service	• Must respond to an emergency call to a named individual

34. See Chapter 4, p 81.

35. However, contrast *Bici v Ministry of Defence* [2004] where it was established that this 'combat immunity' applies only where soldiers are actively 'under threat'.

Table 6.2 *Continued*

Which service/body	When is a duty of care owed?
Police	• No duty to respond to emergency call • Duty can be owed when the negligent conduct in question is 'operational' • In non-operational matters, such as investigations, duty only exists when there is a special relationship (usually defined by an 'assumption of responsibility' for the wellbeing of the claimant)
Coastguard	• No duty to respond to emergency call • Once responded, duty is only not to, by any positive act, make the situation worse
Armed forces	• Duty owed where the defendant can be said to have 'assumed responsibility' toward the claimant • No duty in battle conditions while 'under threat'

6.6 **Other types of public body**

Other public bodies include local and district councils and authorities (such as health or highways authorities, for example) and the various agencies within these. Such organisations have posed problems for the courts when determining whether a duty of care should arise in relation to harm suffered by individuals as a result of negligence. Even where there is a high degree of foreseeability that a negligent action (or inaction) would cause an individual harm or where, because of the claimant's relationship with the public body concerned, there exists a high degree of 'proximity', the courts have tended to fall back on the fact that it would not be 'fair, just or reasonable' to impose a duty of care.[36]

One reason commonly cited for this reluctance to impose a duty on, for example local councils, is the fact that any compensation paid out to individuals would ultimately be paid by the taxpayer. The courts are always reluctant to spend public money in this way, particularly when that might mean diverting it from other sources and/or eventually leading to a rise in taxation. Similarly, there is a concern that—in a similar vein to the arguments made against holding that the police owe a duty of care to individuals—making public authorities and agencies pay compensation would divert the focus of the employees of such organisations to litigation-avoidance and thereby instil defensive working practices. However, as with the police, it is at least arguable that changed working practices (such as to avoid negligence or, put another way, to ensure that *more care* is taken) are not necessarily as bad as the picture is painted judicially.

36. See e.g. *Mitchell* v *Glasgow City Council* [2009].

6.6.1 **Justiciability**

When it comes to litigation against public bodies, there is a further layer of complexity which causes the courts a problem: 'justiciability'. This has been described as 'the constitutional concept which recognises [that] the capabilities of the courts are limited'[37] and operates only in the context of cases taken against public bodies, in both public and private law. It is an extremely effective control device by which the courts limit claims against public bodies, notably 'because it requires the court to strike out a claim without even proceeding to ask whether a duty of care should be owed'.[38] In other words, because the public bodies under discussion here were created by statute, as a result of the democratic process, the court will often find itself asking the question whether the court is actually *able* to question the actions of these authorities or whether there is a more suitable forum where this could be done. In many cases, according to the justiciability argument, the proper actions and decisions taken by these bodies need to be examined by reference to factors that adversarial court proceedings are not suited to addressing.

What this comes down to, in a very general sense, is the distinction between statutory powers and duties. Under statutes, public bodies can be authorised to take decisions on a particular matter (that is, they have the *power* to do so), but *how* and *when* and *whether* they exercise these powers is a matter for their discretion, and may come down to a number of different factors such as resource allocation, prioritisation of resources or services and so on. We have already looked at this type of distinction when discussing whether operational or policy matters are capable of giving rise to a duty of care. A good example of the justiciability issue can be seen in *Stovin v Wise* [1996].

Stovin v *Wise* [1996] HL

The claimant, a motorcyclist, was injured in a collision with the defendant's car at a junction. The defendant alleged that the collision was due in part also to the negligence of the highways division of the local authority, which he therefore joined to the action as a co-defendant. The defendant claimed that his view of the claimant exiting the junction was obstructed by a bank of earth which had not been moved by the local authority. Although not the landowners, the authority had the power under statute to do this and, in fact, had previously asked the landowners to remove the mound of earth, in response to previous traffic accidents at the same junction, but had failed to follow this up when the landowner had not removed the earth. The claimant alleged that the existence of the statutory power was enough to create the requisite relationship of proximity between road users and the authority. The question was whether the local authority's failure to follow up was an action (or omission) that the court had the right to question. There were worse accident 'black spots' in the area under the authority's control *and* there were other things than accident black spots that needed to be dealt with under the same limited budget.

→

---

37. B Harris 'Judicial Review, Justiciability and the Prerogative of Mercy' (2003) 62 *Cambridge Law Journal* 631, cited in the Law Commission's consultation paper *Administrative Redress: Public Bodies and the Citizen* (2008), [3.121].
38. Law Commission, above, [3.121].

➡️

So, asked the court, what authority would it have to question how these resources were allocated and which aspects of the many tasks undertaken by the authority within its statutory remit and limited budget were examinable in a court? Their lordships were, they said, not equipped with—and nor should they be—the power to decide whether the authority should have put more resources and manpower into ensuring that the obstruction was moved. Striking out the claim, the majority of the House of Lords (Lord Nicholls and Lord Slynn dissenting) said that the situation regarding the exercise of a statutory power was similar to that regarding a statutory duty.[39] Therefore, in order to determine whether this could give rise to the right of an individual to sue in negligence—that is, that a common law duty of care could be owed—it was necessary to examine the statute itself and identify whether Parliament had *intended* to give individuals the right to claim compensation if the power was not exercised or was exercised incorrectly.

This inevitably proved to be a circular argument. The very fact that Parliament had decided to confer a power on a public body to do something, rather than make it a duty to do so, could be taken to indicate that no right for individuals to be able to make claims was intended.[40] Lord Hoffmann admitted as much: 'the fact that Parliament has conferred a discretion must be some indication that the policy of the Act conferring the power was not to create a right to compensation. The need to have regard to the policy of the statute therefore means that exceptions will be rare' (at 953).

In **Stovin**, while it was held that the presence of a statutory power was not enough, in itself, to create a positive duty to act, the House of Lords stopped short of saying that an individual harmed by the negligent exercise of (or failure to exercise) that power would *never* have a right to compensation. In order for this to be the case, they said, two strict requirements would have to be met. First, the non-exercise or negligent exercise of the power must have been irrational (in the public law sense)[41] in all the circumstances and, secondly, there must be what Lord Hoffmann called 'exceptional grounds' for creating the obligation to compensate (at 953). He envisaged that these might include situations in which there is 'general reliance' on the correct exercise of power under consideration, so much so that 'the general pattern of social and economic behaviour' is affected (an example might be the setting of insurance premiums) (at 954). These exceptions, he went on to say, should reflect the general expectations of the wider community, not merely those of the defendant. General reliance, he said, could exist only where the benefit to be provided by the exercise of the power would be 'uniform and routine' in nature (at 954), so that it would be indisputable what the defendant had been expected to do. A claimant could not establish reliance purely by

39. Chapter 12, p 317.

40. So this principle would therefore seem to preclude any claims in respect of the lines not being re-painted on the road in the scenarios at the beginning of the chapter. See *Larner* v *Solihull Metropolitan Borough Council* [2001] and *Gorringe* v *Calderdale Metropolitan Borough Council* [2004].

41. Though Lord Hoffmann later retreated from this in *Gorringe* v *Calderdale Metropolitan Borough Council* [2004] as it would be too difficult to apply irrationality principles to pure omissions (at [32]). For an exception to the rule, see *Yetkin* v *Newham London Borough Council* [2010].

the fact he relied upon it himself; this reliance must be shared more widely among the general public.[42]

Similar issues regarding justiciability had been raised in *X*, in 1995. The authorities concerned applied to have all five of the claims struck out as disclosing no cause of action, because they would not owe the individual claimants a common law duty of care. As we have already seen, the first two claims (*X* itself, and *M* v *Newham*) concerned allegations that the social services arm of the local authority had acted negligently in exercising its powers to prevent and deal with child abuse. The three other claims were made in relation to the authority's power to make provisions for the education of children with special needs.

In *X*, the House of Lords, using the language of **Caparo**, found that it would not be 'fair, just and reasonable' to impose a duty of care on the local authority in respect of the way it exercised its power with relation to child abuse (Lord Browne-Wilkinson at 749). There were a number of reasons for this, which can be generalised as being that in exercising this power the authority had a degree of discretion, and people might well have different opinions on the best way of acting and on the wisdom or otherwise of decisions taken. If a duty of care was attached to the authority towards the children and families it used its discretion in relation to, the employees would always be thinking about whether they might be sued for reaching particular conclusions or taking particular decisions. This would make their practices less efficient and consequently divert resources from child protection services. Moreover, said the law lords, citizens have other ways of challenging the actions of public bodies, including statutory appeals procedures and ombudsmen, and it would cut across this statutory framework if a duty of care was to be imposed.[43]

However, in relation to the claims about special needs education in *X*, their lordships stated that it was at least arguable that a duty of care might arise, as there was not the same risk of defensive practices and because information was provided to individual parents/families from a position of responsibility with the assumption that it would be relied upon.

 Pause for reflection

Is it not at least arguable that there is always a high degree of reliance from the children involved with the child protection services of a local authority? Why isn't the reliance argument made by the courts in this respect?

Some later cases appear to pull back from such strict restrictions on liability towards individuals. But this should not be seen as a change in direction by the courts in favour of a less strict approach to the duty of care issue with regard to public bodies. In fact, we would argue, it has more to do with events subsequent to *X* and **Stovin** which were outside the control of the courts and which bring into stark relief the real issues created

---

42. This principle has recently been affirmed in *Mitchell* v *Glasgow City Council* [2009], again in the context of a public body's omission to act (at [7]).

43. If a case arose now with similar facts, this would not be the case—a duty *would* be found (following ***D* v *East Berkshire*** [2005]).

by denying that public bodies owe no duty of care in negligence. We have already encountered these events and cases above when looking at the background to the current focus of the law in relation to public body liability; they stem from the appeals to the ECtHR in *Osman v UK*.

 Counterpoint

Stephen Bailey has argued that the justiciability issue is a 'blind alley' and only serves to further complicate the law of negligence relating to public bodies. He says that the 'justiciability proposition' should simply be removed, as it is 'difficult to see any proper basis' for it (2006, p 169) and indicates a preference for breach-based considerations. In a 2008 consultation paper published to assess the efficacy of 'mechanisms through which claimants can obtain redress from public bodies for substandard administrative action' ('Administrative Redress: Public Bodies and the Citizen', now abandoned), the Law Commission described the current position regarding justiciability. It stated that the '[c]ourts have struggled to articulate workable criteria for determining what should and should not be justiciable. The most that can be said under the current state of law is that certain matters are deemed "unsuitable for judicial determination" and that these are revealed on a rather unpredictable, case-by-case basis' (at [3.127]). Further, in *Jain v Trent Strategic Health Authority* [2008], Arden LJ in the Court of Appeal indicated that considerations of justiciability when determining duty are less 'likely in the future to be as important or have the same weight' as the 'fair, just and reasonable' consideration from *Caparo* (at [62]). We would agree that the justiciability point seems only to make matters less clear than they need to be, particularly in an area of law which is already markedly confused and confusing. As Bailey points out, it would be better to allow all claims to be judicially determined and then 'the more complex the decision and the more sensitive the relevant considerations, the more difficult it will be for the claimant . . . to establish breach of duty' (p 170). Breach would seem to us to be a sufficient control device for public body liability, particularly given that section 1 of the Compensation Act 2006 now allows courts to adjust the standard of care to take account of the fact that the defendant was undertaking a socially 'desirable activity'.

In its consultation the Law Commission stated that:

> in private law, we consider that the current situation is unsustainable. The uncertain and unprincipled nature of negligence in relation to public bodies, coupled with the unpredictable expansion of liability over recent years, has led to a situation that serves neither claimants nor public bodies. (at [2.7])[44]

We would agree that the law in relation to the liability of public bodies in negligence is both 'uncertain and unprincipled' and proper reform of this area would be welcome. At the core of the Law Commission recommendations for claims in private law lay a requirement to show 'serious fault' on the part of the public body concerned (at [4.145]–[4.147], [4.152]). This looked very much like a move towards a breach-based test and, from our

➡

---

44. The Commission made similar comments in relation to breach of statutory duty.

→

perspective, this much would have been welcomed (at [2.9]).[45] However, the Commission also proposed that certain activities—those regarded as 'truly public' in nature (defined at [4.110]–[4.131])—would be placed in a specialised scheme, whereby claimants would have to first meet public law requirements in order to establish liability (at [4.99]). Only cases not considered 'truly public' would be considered under the ordinary rules of negligence (paras [2.11–2.12], [4.5], [4.10]). This seems a little like the justiciability test and would serve to limit redress against public bodies—although if it had been clearly defined it may have been less problematic—despite the Commission's supposed commitment to a principle of 'modified' corrective justice (paras [4.2], [4.9]). The proposals encountered a great deal of opposition and critique, mainly from academic quarters.[46] For this reason the Commission announced in May 2010 that it would not continue to pursue reform:

> The Commission concludes that there are good arguments for reform but, given the level of opposition to its earlier proposals and the absence of available data on the costs of compensation paid by public bodies, work will not be taken forward on reviewing this area of the law.[47]

6.7 The recognition of new types of claim—'messed up lives'?

Despite the justiciability issue and what seems to be a general desire of the courts to protect public bodies from claims in negligence made against them, the aftermath of *Osman v UK* seemed to lay the foundation for some new types of claim to succeed in principle against public bodies. These claims fall outside the more traditional claims relating to more easily recognised harms and refer to lives being negatively affected or 'messed up' in some way by the negligence of a public body. We have broken these down further in the following two sections: to 'educational' claims in which the claimants essentially allege that negligence has caused them to be less well educated than they ought to be, and 'social' claims which relate to the disturbance of lives in a more general sense.

6.7.1 Education-based claims

In *Phelps* v *Hillingdon London Borough Council* [2001], four cases were jointly considered by the House of Lords, although *Phelps* itself was the only one at full trial: the

45. Though it should be noted that using the standard of care as the threshold test for liability in the context of public bodies is also likely to present difficulties for claimants (*Pierce* v *Doncaster* [2008]; *X & Y* v *London Borough of Hounslow* [2009]).

46. See, in particular, Tom Cornford 'Administrative Redress: The Law Commission's Consultation Paper' (2009) *Public Law* 70; Richard Mullender 'Negligence, Public Bodies, and Ruthlessness' (2009) 72(6) *Modern Law Review* 961. A full summary of the responses to the consultation is available online.

47. The Law Commission 'Administrative Redress: Public Bodies and the Citizen' (Law Com No 322, 25 May 2010). One proposal that does still survive—and may be very useful—is for costs of compensation paid by public bodies to be collated and published by government.

rest were striking out actions in which the House of Lords had to decide whether the claimants had an arguable case.

Phelps v *Hillingdon London Borough Council and other cases* [2001] HL

In the first case (*Phelps*), the claimant, by then an adult, had learning difficulties as a child. At the time an educational psychologist had been employed by the local authority to make an assessment of her educational needs. The resulting report said that the child's difficulties stemmed from emotional and behavioural problems, whereas in fact she was later properly diagnosed with dyslexia. She claimed that the negligent assessment of her led to a failure to provide the right kind of schooling and that this had a consequential effect on her educational development and subsequently her employment prospects as an adult.

The second case (*Jarvis* v *Hampshire County Council*) also concerned a claimant with dyslexia, who alleged not that there was a failure to diagnose the condition, but that the local authority had given the wrong advice about schooling once the diagnosis had been made. In the third case, *G (a child)* v *Bromley London Borough Council*, the local authority had failed to provide the right equipment to the claimant who had a muscle-wasting disease and needed special equipment to be able to communicate. He alleged that as a result of this failure, his education suffered and that this caused him to suffer psychological damage. The final case (*Anderton* v *Clwyd County Council*) concerned a woman who was seeking access to her educational records, claiming that inadequate education had damaged her.

The Court of Appeal dismissed Miss Phelps' claim, finding numerous policy reasons why such a claim should not be allowed—primarily because their lordships thought that to do so would open the door to all manner of vexatious and inconsequential claims being made against education authorities. A seven-member House of Lords, however, refused to dismiss any of the four claims raised in the *Phelps* group, referring back to its own decision in *X*, in which it had ruled that there may well be duties owed by local education authorities to children in respect of the educational services they provide, on the basis of an assumption of responsibility. Here, it said that an authority owes a duty of care in respect of the provision of an education appropriate to a child's needs and that where this fails to materialise due to the negligence of a teacher or another employee of the authority, such as an educational psychologist, the authority could be liable according to the principles of vicarious liability.

This was a novel approach which served to justify the House of Lords' decision as well as paving the way for future cases to be taken on a vicarious liability basis.[48] However, because their lordships decided Phelps' case on this basis it was—unfortunately in our view—not necessary to look at whether the authority could owe a *personal* duty to the children in its care. Their lordships stressed that whether there was liability in such a situation would depend not on whether a child had or had not done badly at school, or if they had not realised their potential, but on whether this was a direct result of

48. See Chapter 12 at 12.4. Though cf *X & Y* v *London Borough of Hounslow* [2009].

a failure of the employee to live up to the standard of care expected of them, which would be governed according to the standard of others in a similar profession (***Bolam v Friern Hospital Management Committee* [1957]**).[49] This, they said, would be enough to prevent a flood of claims to every local education authority, alleging poor educational standards and decreased employment potential.

 Counterpoint

This House of Lords opinion suggests that *breach* could be used as a sufficient control device in *all* educational claims against public bodies (although it is not hard to see the concept being workable in other types of claims, as we have indicated above). Could we then say that public bodies should, in general, owe a duty of care to individuals to deal carefully with their business, in order to avoid harming those whose day-to-day lives could be affected by their actions—but then say that this is a professional (high) standard, as with doctors, thereby using the standard of care to control liability? Again, it seems that imposing a high *standard* of care might serve both to prevent liability in the majority of cases (if this is what is deemed to be desirable) *as well as* improving the quality of the service provided and increasing public confidence.

The breach-based test appears to have been adopted by the courts in educational cases. In *Carty* v *Croydon London Borough Council* [2005], it was confirmed by the Court of Appeal (who it must be remembered were squarely resistant to educational claims in **Phelps**) that the approach now to be taken from **Phelps** applied not only to educational authority employees such as psychologists or teachers, but also to the authority's administrative staff responsible for decisions about education. If such a matter was justiciable, it could be found that the employee concerned had assumed a responsibility to the child to provide services according to their needs. However, only where the decisions made in this respect are obviously wrong (that is, they have fallen clearly below the standard of care expected) will a claim succeed.

Future claims may alternatively be made under the HRA in respect of negligence in educational provision, as the right to education is guaranteed under the European Convention.[50] In *A* v *Essex County Council* [2010], however, a claim of this type failed in the Supreme Court, in relation to a child who had special educational needs and was left without formal educational provision for 18 months. The majority concluded that there was no absolute right to education meeting the claimant's particular special needs, only a right to have access to the education that was actually available. An alternative claim based on him being given *some* education during the 18-month period was thought possible—but it was time-barred.

---

49. Thus it should be fairly easy to establish that a duty of care was owed by the educational psychologist in the scenario at the beginning of the chapter, with the result that the local education authority would be (vicariously) liable for any negligence on her part: breach then becomes the 'control device' used to establish liability.

50. Protocol 1, Article 2 begins 'No person shall be denied the right to education'.

6.7.2 **Social claims**

Barrett v Enfield London Borough Council [2001] HL

The claimant was a 17-year-old boy who was in the care of the local authority and had been since he was 10 months old. While in care, he had been moved around frequently and, as a consequence, had a difficult and unpleasant childhood in which he formed no lasting bonds and which had negatively affected him when older: he had ended up suffering various psychiatric illnesses. He argued that the local authority owed him a duty of care and had breached this in failing to find him suitable adoptive parents, locate suitable foster parents or initiate and supervise a meeting with his biological mother, as it was meant to do.

At trial and in the Court of Appeal, his case was struck out on the authority of the 'abuse' cases (rather than the 'education' cases) in *X*; the courts ruling that there were good policy reasons why it would not be 'fair, just and reasonable' to impose a duty of care in this situation, despite the high degree of proximity and foreseeability of the harm occurring. On appeal to the House of Lords, however, the strike-out application of the local council was refused. The law lords held that without a proper hearing of the facts it was impossible to say whether the actions of the council in respect of the boy's upbringing were policy decisions (conferred via a statutory power) and therefore not justiciable, or operational decisions which would be justiciable and could therefore give rise to a duty of care.

Barrett is an interesting case study in judicial attitude and political comment, as well as forming the basis for future decisions along similar lines. There seem to be several different reasons for the case succeeding. In the House of Lords, the decision was given with a degree of judicial reluctance. It followed *Osman v UK* and is illustrative of a period where the courts—the House of Lords in particular—were generally reluctant to strike cases out as disclosing no duty of care in case this was viewed as a violation of the claimant's Article 6 right to a fair hearing. This is particularly apparent in Lord Browne-Wilkinson's speech (made all the more striking as he also gave the leading opinion in *X*, see in particular the passage at 560). The Court of Appeal had followed *X*, striking out Barrett's claim, saying that it was not fair, just and reasonable to impose a duty in this respect on the local authority concerned and, in any case, that the matter was not justiciable. The House of Lords, however, given the impact of *Osman v UK*, distinguished the facts of *Barrett* from *X* (and other subsequent cases), arguing that while *X* had been concerned with decisions about *whether* to take a child into care, *Barrett* concerned what happened to a boy once he *had* been taken into care, when the authority had clearly assumed responsibility for his wellbeing. Politically, it seems that the law lords felt this was something that they had to do—though the (tenuous) distinction, if one has to be made at all, is in our view correct.

In *W v Essex County Council* [2000], the House of Lords found a duty of care was owed by a local authority to the claimants, who were council foster parents suing on behalf of their own children. Before accepting a foster child into their home, the claimants had specifically told the council that they could not take a child who was a known abuser or suspected of being so. Negligently, and without informing the claimants, the council placed with the couple a 15-year-old boy who they knew had sexually assaulted his sister. While placed with the family, he sexually assaulted the claimants' children and the claimants sued in respect of the council's negligence. This time, however, the Court of Appeal did not strike out the claim. While it could point to policy reasons why a duty should not be owed that were similar to those stemming from *X*, it also acknowledged that there were also some strong opposing arguments—the most pressing being that the council had broken its own express promise to the claimants. The House of Lords upheld this decision on appeal.

Similarly, in *S* v *Gloucestershire County Council* [2000], the Court of Appeal confirmed that no blanket immunity should be thought to exist regarding claims made against local authorities in relation to child abuse. Making a connection to the education cases, they held that only in the clearest of cases, once the whole context of the case had been carefully considered, should any claim of this type be struck out. Later, in *A* v *Essex County Council* [2004], a claim was made by a married couple who had been on the council's adoption register. They had specified to the council that they would take children with relatively mild emotional or behavioural difficulties but could not cope with anything more severe. The council had—similarly to the council in *W* v *Essex*—agreed to this, but later placed a brother and sister with the couple where it was known that the boy had considerable behavioural problems. In the course of his stay, *inter alia*, the boy physically attacked the couple and tried to harm himself by electrocution. The couple sued in negligence alleging that the council had not provided them with correct information about the boy's behavioural problems and as a result their lives had suffered unreasonable disruption. The Court of Appeal upheld their claim saying that although a council did not have a general duty to provide information about children being placed with adoptive parents, once a decision had been made in relation to the type and amount of information that was to be provided to prospective adopters, reasonable care should be taken to ensure that this informational target was met. However, it should be noted that this then becomes an operational matter rather than a policy decision.

More recently, however, the courts appear to be retreating back to a stricter approach on duty.[51] For example, in a case involving vulnerable adults housed by a local authority (*X & Y* v *London Borough of Hounslow* [2009]), an allegation of negligence was made in respect of the authority's failure to re-home the claimants and their two young children after the family was subjected to bullying and harassment by local youths who were known to be entering the premises and preying on the vulnerability of the claimants.[52] The claimants contended that because the authority (or the social worker for whom it would be vicariously liable) had not taken this emergency action, this enabled them to be subjected to a particularly horrendous incident of prolonged serious abuse in their home by the youths. Though their claim succeeded at first instance, this was overturned by the Court of Appeal, which found that the defendant authority could not be said to owe the claimants a duty of care. Partly this was due to the nature of the claim involving both an omission and the actions of a third party (see Chapter 4). The House of Lords had recently confirmed in *Mitchell* v *Glasgow City Council* [2009] that there was no general duty for a defendant to take care to prevent a third party from deliberately causing damage to the claimant. In any case, the Court of Appeal said that

---

51. See e.g. *Jain* v *Trent Strategic Health Authority* [2009].
52. The facts of the case are outlined in full detail in Chapter 2, from p 45.

it could not be established in *X & Y* that there *had* been any lack of care. Permission to appeal was refused—though the claimants have since taken their case to the ECtHR alleging violations of Articles 3 and 8.[53]

6.8 **Conclusion**

In this chapter we have looked at the situations when a **public body** will owe an individual a **private law** duty of care. Often, it seems that this will depend on the nature of the public body itself as the scope of the liability of some has been greatly affected by European jurisprudence and the impact of the HRA.

Of the **emergency services and armed forces**—which are particular types of public body—it can be said that a duty of care is easily established only in relation to the ambulance service which, by analogy to the NHS and medical profession, owes a duty of care towards any individual to whom it responds. By contrast, the fire service, coastguard and armed forces owe a duty of care only when it can be shown that their positive actions (rather than 'mere' failures to act) made a situation worse than it was or where responsibility for the safety or wellbeing of the claimant was assumed. Similarly, the notion of assumption of responsibility can be used to establish a duty on the part of the police, but rarely (and controversially) does this extend into non-operational matters such as the investigation of crimes, even where the negligence alleged is gross and the injuries suffered due to police incompetence are severe.

Greater in-roads have been made in respect of other types of public body, such as child welfare and protection services or the educational services of **local authorities**. Here, it seems, the impact of decisions from the ECtHR have been felt most strongly, with potential breaches of human rights being considered alongside (explicitly or implicitly) claims in negligence. To an extent, it seems that there is movement towards the use of breach as a control device for liability in these areas (particularly in the educational context). Although this idea was not warmly welcomed by the House of Lords in the leading child welfare case of *D* v *East Berkshire*, there are some indications that considerations of this nature may influence decisions in the future.

✱ **End-of-chapter questions**

After reading the chapter carefully, try answering the questions below. If you would like to know what we think visit the Online Resource Centre (www.oxfordtextbooks.co.uk/orc/horsey2e/).

1. Why are the courts reluctant to make a finding that a public body owes a duty of care to individuals harmed by its negligence? Would breach be a better tool to control liability?

2. Should the liability of public bodies be treated any differently from that of private bodies/individuals?

---

53. (*X, Y & Z* v *UK* Application no 32666/10, 8 June 2010).

3. Is there any valid reason to treat the emergency services differently from each other when dealing with whether a duty of care is owed?

4. Why should the police be afforded what seems like a greater degree of protection from negligence claims taken against them, as compared with other emergency services?

5. What effect did *Osman* v *UK* [1997] have and is this effect still felt after the decisions of *Z* v *UK* and *TP & KM* v *UK* in 2001?

6. What impact have the decisions of the European Court of Human Rights and the passage of the Human Rights Act 1998 had on negligence litigation against public bodies?

7. Consider the problem question at the start of this chapter. Now having read about the topic, what would be your advice to the various claimants? If you need some pointers in thinking about how to answer this question, turn to the Appendix (p 589) where each problem is annotated with issues and cases to consider. Next, try to write your own answer and, finally, log on to our Online Resource Centre (www.oxfordtextbooks.co.uk/orc/horsey2e/) to check your ideas against our suggested outline answer.

✱ Further reading

Numerous books, articles and case notes have been written on the liability of public bodies. For an interesting look at five cases in depth, a good starting point would be *Markesinis et al* and, for a relatively up-to-date critique of the inconsistency of the law in this area, Stephen Bailey's article is good, in particular as it questions whether civil claims in negligence are the best place to deal with many of these issues, though care should be taken not to get too bogged down in public law issues. Many of the others are useful for the historical context and analysis they provide, particularly of the 'big' cases such as *Osman* v *UK*.

Bailey, Stephen 'Public Authority Liability in Negligence: The Continued Search for Coherence' (2006) 26(2) *Legal Studies* 155

Conaghan, Joanne 'Law, Harm and Redress: A Feminist Perspective' (2002) 22(3) *Legal Studies* 319

Fairgrieve, Duncan 'Pushing Back the Boundaries of Public Authority Liability: Tort Law enters the Classroom' (2002) *Public Law* 288

Gearty, Conor 'Unravelling *Osman*' (2001) 64(2) *Modern Law Review* 159

Gearty, Conor '*Osman* Unravels' (2002) 65(1) *Modern Law Review* 87

Giliker, Paula '*Osman* and Police Immunity in the English Law of Torts' (2000) 20(3) *Legal Studies* 372

Hartshorne, John, Nicolas Smith and Rosemaire Everton '"*Caparo* under Fire": A Study into the Effects Upon the Fire Service of Liability in Negligence' (2000) 63 *Modern Law Review* 502

Law Commission *Administrative Redress: Public Bodies and the Citizen* (Consultation Paper No 187, 2008)

Law Commission *Administrative Redress: Public Bodies and the Citizen* (Law Com No 322, 2010)

Markesinis, Basil, Jean-Bernard Auby, Dagmar Coester-Waltjen and Simon Deakin *Tortious Liability of Statutory Bodies: A Comparative Analysis of Five English Cases* (Hart Publishing, 1999)

McIvor, Claire 'The Positive Duty of the Police to Protect Life' (2008) *Professional Negligence* 27

McIvor, Claire 'Getting Defensive About Police Negligence: The Hill Principle, the Human Rights Act 1998 and the House of Lords' (2010) 69(1) *Cambridge Law Journal* 133

Mullender, Richard 'Negligence, Neighbourliness and the Welfare State' (2009) *Cambridge Law Journal* 507

Steele, Iain 'Negligence Liability for Failing to Prevent Crime: The Human Rights Dimension' (2008) 67(2) *Cambridge Law Journal* 239

Wright, Jane '"Immunity" No More: Child Abuse Cases and Public Authority Liability in Negligence after *D v East Berkshire Community Health NHS Trust*' (2004) 20(1) *Professional Negligence* 58

7

Economic loss

Problem question

Read this problem question carefully, and keep it in mind while you are working through
the chapter that follows. At the end of the chapter, you will be able to apply what you have
learnt to the problem question and advise the relevant parties.

Rachael and Chris invest in a business after speaking to Amanda, a personal friend who
is also an auditor. Amanda has prepared a financial report for the trustees of Read-Sing-
Sign, a children's charity bookshop that is for sale. The report shows that the bookshop
is doing well and makes a good annual profit. On the basis of the report, which Amanda
showed them 'off the record', Rachael and Chris decided to buy the shop. Each of them
pays £100,000. It later transpires that the audit was inaccurate as Amanda failed to
include some unpaid debts in the figures and the shop is in fact worthless.

Meanwhile, Rachael, who was relying on a £70,000 inheritance from her grandfather in
order to be able to pay for most of her share of the shop, is told by the solicitors dealing
with her grandfather's will that it is invalid and the terms of his previous will, which left
everything to a local cats' home, would have to be followed. This is because he failed
to sign both copies of the latest version of the will. The solicitor's copy was filed without
checking the signature was present.

7.1 **Introduction**

Consider the following situations:

→ **A driver negligently crashes his car in the Dartford Tunnel, blocking both lanes. As a result, a ten-mile tailback develops. Caught in this tailback are:**

   (a) **Guy, a businessman, hurrying to close a lucrative contract for his company;**

   (b) **Vicki, trying to get to the sales early to buy a cheap LCD TV, of which there are a limited number available;**

   (c) **Benny, who needs to get to work on time or his wages will be docked.**

→ **In the same accident, another driver is seriously injured and is unable to work for a year.**

→ **A council workman negligently cuts a power cable supplying a factory. The factory has to shut down for two days, losing profit as a result.**

→ **A financial adviser negligently advises a client to invest in a company, which later goes bankrupt, causing the client to lose his investment.**

→ **A builder negligently constructs the foundations of a house. When new owners move in the walls begin to crack, causing the house's value to decrease.**

→ **A man buys a washing machine and, after only a week, it goes wrong, flooding his kitchen and ruining the flooring. It cannot be fixed.**

Many of the losses we encounter when looking at negligence (and tort law more generally) are in some way 'economic'. Even some non-economic losses may *appear* to be financial in nature because the way tort law 'fixes' the harms caused by negligence is to pay compensation. Because money is usually the answer, there is a tendency to view all harms in an economic way, asking 'how much is that worth?'[1]

In this chapter, we are concerned only with those losses that are truly *only* economic in nature—so-called 'pure' economic losses. These can be distinguished from 'consequential' economic losses, where financial loss is suffered as a secondary consequence of another harm, such as personal injury or damage to property. The tort of negligence distinguishes between these, using duty of care as a device to control whether and when claimants will be able to recover in respect of pure economic losses. It is difficult, as we shall see, to establish that a duty of care is owed in respect of a pure economic loss in tort, even if that loss is indisputably caused by the defendant's negligence. Like psychiatric harm, pure economic loss is a harm that tort law does not easily recognise. One reason for this is that liability for such losses are often regarded as better dealt with elsewhere, such as in contract law or the 'economic torts'.[2]

The object of this chapter is to show when and how the courts have found that a duty of care should be owed by defendants when the harm caused by them is purely economic. As we will see, this depends on the *type* of negligence that the harm originates from, which

---

1. See, e.g. the diagram on p 560.
2. These torts rely on a defendant's intention, rather than carelessness, and are not covered in this book.

in turn stems from the complicated history of liability in this area. Pure economic loss is, generally speaking, recoverable if the loss stems from a carelessly made statement, or negligent advice, but not when it results from what has been termed a careless 'activity'.

7.2 What is 'pure' economic loss?

The starting point for a claim in economic loss is to decide whether such a loss is 'pure' economic loss. Losses caused by negligence can generally be split, initially, into two categories: pecuniary (related to money) and non-pecuniary (that is, loss not susceptible to precise arithmetical calculation, including pain, suffering, mental distress and so on). A further distinction can be made between pecuniary losses that are consequent on another type of harm having occurred (such as lost earnings after being injured in an accident or the cost of repairing a car after someone has crashed into it) and those financial losses that are 'pure'—that is, *not* consequent on any other type of harm. Not all economic losses are 'purely' so. The categorisation of some losses as 'purely' economic is best understood as a judicial construction designed to distinguish between different types of economic losses in order to prevent (or limit) recovery.

Table 7.1 Types of loss in negligence

Pecuniary		Non-pecuniary
Financial/economic losses that can be accurately calculated by being based on a proper and provable cost assessment		Losses for which money is awarded but where the original harm/damage was not financial in nature and cannot therefore be accurately assessed
Pure economic loss	Consequential economic loss	
A financial loss stemming directly from the harm caused by the negligent act or omission	A financial loss suffered as a result of another harm (e.g. personal injury or damage to property) caused by the negligent act or omission	

The difference between pure and other types of economic loss is illustrated well by *Spartan Steel & Alloys Ltd v Martin & Co (Contractors) Ltd* [1973].

Spartan Steel & Alloys Ltd v Martin & Co (Contractors) Ltd [1973] CA

While digging up a road the defendant contractors negligently cut an electricity mains cable supplying power to the claimant's factory, leaving it without power for 14 hours. In this time the factory owners could not operate their steel furnace. There was a possibility

→

➜

that the molten metal inside the furnace (the steel 'melt') would solidify and cause damage; the 'melt' had to be poured away and the factory closed. The factory owners claimed damages under three heads:

(1) **the damage** to the steel in the furnace at the time of the power cut, which had to be thrown away;

(2) the **loss of profit** that could have been made by selling the steel in the furnace; and

(3) **the anticipated lost profit** on other steel that would have been processed during the period in which the factory was closed.

A majority of the Court of Appeal allowed recovery for the first two heads of damage but found that the third, the *anticipated* profit, was not recoverable.

The first loss was straightforward physical damage to property, which poses few problems to recovery in tort. The second loss was consequential economic loss (the lost profit was directly consequent on the damaged property). The third loss, however, was regarded as a pure economic loss (although a result of the negligence it was not consequent on any damage to property) in respect of which no duty of care arose.

Spartan Steel shows that a duty of care is owed only in respect of financial losses relating to property damage directly caused by the defendant's negligence. This includes any additional financial losses (such as lost profit) that are incurred as a *direct* result of the damage to property. However, lost profits which are not a direct result of the defendant's negligence are deemed to be 'purely economic', attracting no duty.[3] On this view, the losses incurred by Guy, Vicki and Benny in the scenarios at the start of the chapter are pure economic losses, whereas the loss of earnings suffered by the man injured in the accident in the tunnel (assuming he has to take some time off work) would be consequential upon his injuries and, therefore, recoverable.

 Pause for reflection

Do you think the outcome of the case would have been any different if the cable supplying the electricity in *Spartan Steel* had been owned *by the factory*?

It appears so. In *Spartan Steel*, had the factory owned the cable then damage caused by the contractors would be recoverable property damage, making all the other losses 'consequential', including the lost profit on the steel that could not be processed while the factory was closed.

Do you think that such a relatively small factual difference (the ownership of the cable) should have such a significant effect on the amount of damages recoverable?

➜

---

3. See also *D Pride & Partners (A Firm)* v *Institute for Animal Health* [2009] in which it was found that no duty of care was owed to livestock farmers who sustained pure economic losses as a result of a negligently caused outbreak of foot and mouth disease which resulted in the establishment of control zones and a ban on exports designed to prevent the spread of the disease.

➡

The ownership idea seems to be supported by *Leigh and Sillivan Ltd* v *Aliakmon Ltd (The Aliakmon)* [1986], where the claimants were purchasers of steel coils being shipped on *The Aliakmon* which were damaged in transit. They had neither legal nor possessory title until after the goods had been paid for so were deemed unable to recover for the economic loss suffered. Explaining the extent of the exclusionary rule, Lord Brandon said:

> in order to enable a person to claim in negligence for loss caused to him by reason of loss of or damage to property, he must have had either the legal ownership of or a possessory title to the property concerned at the time when the loss or damage occurred. (at 809)

In *The Aliakmon*, the claimants argued that they had *equitable* ownership of the goods despite not having legal title and that equitable ownership should be enough to enable them to bring an action for damage to the cargo. Lord Brandon rejected that submission because the legal owner had not been joined as party to the action. In *Shell UK Ltd and others* v *Total UK Ltd and others* [2010] (part of the litigation following the explosions at the Buncefield oil storage depot in 2005), Shell claimed damages for economic losses it suffered because two oil pipelines it used—but did not own—were damaged. This caused it to lose money on aviation fuel it normally delivered to major airports, as well as fuel it usually sent out in tankers. The Court of Appeal distinguished *The Aliakmon* because Shell had a *beneficial* interest in the damaged property, so could claim for economic losses provided they joined the legal owners as parties to the action:

> a duty of care is owed to a beneficial owner of property (just as much as to a legal owner of property) by a defendant, such as Total, who can reasonably foresee that his negligent actions will damage that property. If, therefore, such property is, in breach of duty, damaged by the defendant, that defendant will be liable not merely for the physical loss of that property but also for the foreseeable consequences of that loss, such as the extra expenditure to which the beneficial owner is put or the loss of profit which he incurs. Provided that the beneficial owner can join the legal owner in the proceedings, it does not matter that the beneficial owner is not himself in possession of the property. (at 142)

In **Spartan Steel**, Lord Denning MR articulated various policy considerations that precluded recovery of damages for the anticipated lost profits, not least the fact that power failures were a fact of life:

> This is a hazard which we all run. It may be due to a short circuit, to a flash of lightning, to a tree falling on the wires, to an accidental cutting of the cable, or even to the negligence of someone or other. And when it does happen, it affects a multitude of persons: not as a rule by way of physical damage to them or their property, but by putting them to inconvenience, and sometimes to economic loss. The supply is usually restored in a few hours, so the economic loss is not very large. Such a hazard is regarded by most people as a thing they must put up with—without seeking compensation from anyone. Some there are who install a stand-by system. Others seek refuge by taking out an insurance policy against breakdown in the supply. But most people are content to take the risk on themselves. When the supply is cut off, they do not go running round to their solicitor. They do

not try to find out whether it was anyone's fault. They just put up with it. They try to make up the economic loss by doing more work next day. This is a healthy attitude which the law should encourage. (at 38)

He went on to say that if such claims were allowed, inflated claims might be made for lost profits that were simply not provable losses and for which the level of mitigation attempted could not be established. He was also conscious of the burden of 'crushing liability':

the risk of economic loss should be suffered by the whole community who suffer the losses . . . rather than on the one pair of shoulders, that is, on the contractor on whom the total of them, all added together, might be very heavy. (at 39)

It seems then, that policy considerations are behind the courts' continued reliance on an exclusionary rule in relation to pure economic loss, including the fear that allowing such claims would lead to a flood of further claims of that nature. This, in turn, could lead to what is known as 'crushing liability', where one defendant, from one careless act, ends up being substantially liable to numerous claimants.[4]

Consider again the first scenario outlined at the start of the chapter. While the negligent driver of the car would clearly owe a duty of care to other drivers not to cause them physical harm (and would also be liable for any financial losses consequent on any physical injury caused, such as loss of earnings), if he was found to owe a duty in respect of pure economic losses, he would have to compensate anyone in the tailback behind him who suffered an economic loss of any kind. Thus, if Guy failed to make his meeting and secure his lucrative contract, the driver would be liable for the sum that he expected to make. Similarly, if Vicki failed to make it to the shop before closing time, she would have to be compensated for the difference in price between the sale TV and the usual price.

This argument—often referred to as a 'floodgates' argument—is grounded in the assumption that it is better to prevent *all* claims by denying a duty than to allow a 'flood' of claims. Moreover, it is generally accepted that a role of the law in a market economy is to shape and develop the framework in which the market should operate with maximum efficiency and one way this is achieved is by preventing claims being brought for pure economic losses.[5]

 Counterpoint

Edmund Davies LJ, dissenting in *Spartan Steel,* saw the central question differently:

Where a defendant who owes a duty of care to the plaintiff breaches that duty and, as both a *direct* and a *reasonably foreseeable* result of that injury, the plaintiff suffers only economic loss, is he entitled to recover damages for that loss? (at 39, emphasis added)

➜

---

4. Though this does not always preclude recovery. In relation to the Buncefield oil depot explosions referred to above (*Shell UK Ltd and others* v *Total UK Ltd and others* [2010]), it is estimated that Total will be liable for compensation running to over £600 million (see Chris Green 'Final Cost of Buncefield Fire could hit £1bn' *Independent* 12 December 2008).

5. See e.g. Stapleton 1991.

➡

He sought guidance from a similar earlier case called *Cattle* v *Stockton Waterworks Co* [1875]. In *Cattle*, the defendant's pipes had leaked, causing delay to the construction of the claimant's tunnel, which in turn delayed and caused the claimant a loss of profit on his construction contract. Blackburn J refused to allow the claimant's recovery, but his judgment was interpreted by Edmund Davies LJ as being based on the specific facts of the case and not ruling out recovery of direct and foreseeable economic losses in the future. The facts of *Spartan Steel*, Edmund Davies LJ suggested, were different. It was clearly foreseeable that if the power supply is negligently disrupted, surrounding factories would be *directly* affected and would suffer foreseeable loss. Put simply, it is inevitable that cutting an electricity supply to a factory will cause the owners to lose money. As such, it is not clear to us, as it was not to Edmund Davies LJ, why this foreseeable loss should, as a matter of course, be unrecoverable.

This formulation would arguably put enough restriction on the ability to claim for economic loss. Not all losses will be foreseeable to a party at the time of the negligent act (which is when foreseeability is assessed, see p 247). Thus, rather than saying outright that there is no duty owed in relation to pure economic loss, issues related to crushing liability could be dealt with by saying that the loss suffered was unforeseeable (as acknowledged by Lord Denning MR at 36). Again, consider the Dartford Tunnel car crash scenario at the start of the chapter. While it is clearly foreseeable that people caught in the traffic jam would suffer delays and even that their cars may then overheat and break down (causing foreseeable economic loss if they have to have the cars towed away and repaired), Guy's particular loss is not foreseeable—it would not be foreseeable that a particular person in the ensuing tailback would fail to make a lucrative business contract.

In *Spartan Steel* Lord Denning MR's 'public policy' considerations seem to have won the day. For him, at the heart of the case lies the failure of the factory owners to insure against their loss. However, it is not at all obvious which of the two companies in *Spartan Steel*—the factory or the construction company which, presumably, could be held to foresee the consequences of its (admitted) negligence[6]—was in a better position to insure against such losses.

 Pause for reflection

In *Canadian National Railway Co* v *Norsk Pacific Steamship Co (The Norsk)* [1992], a claim was allowed for 'relational' economic loss when a ship was negligently steered into a railway bridge owned by a third party. The claimant rail company (which had a contractual licence to use the bridge) was unable to use the bridge, suffering economic loss (lost profits) as a result. The claim was allowed on the basis that operations of the claimant and the bridge owner were 'closely allied' (that is, they both wanted to use the bridge for the same thing (to make profits) and each needed the other to do so).

This case is distinguishable from *Spartan Steel* on the ground that there was no close alliance between the interests of the factory owners and the defendant. Do you agree?

➡

---

6. The alternative policy argument that imposing a duty to compensate for foreseeable economic loss might act as a deterrent and encourage workers to take more care at work was rejected.

> ➡
> Couldn't the same be said of the factory and the electricity company? Moreover, even if this distinction can be sustained—should it make a difference to the outcome of the case?

Another reason for the courts' reluctance to extend a duty of care in the tort of negligence to pure financial losses is that these are more traditionally and readily dealt with by contract law. Accordingly, if people want to protect their economic interests, they should use contracts to do so.[7] In fact, in **Spartan Steel** the factory owners were prevented from being able to claim damages from the electricity company for its failure to supply power by an exclusion clause in the contract. Had they been able to recover in tort, this contractual limitation would have been circumvented and, in so doing, the benefits and extent of the contract would have been called into question—something the court was extremely reluctant to encourage.

7.3 Exceptions to the exclusionary rule: *Hedley Byrne* v *Heller*

Although it can be said that there is a general rule *against* recovery in relation to pure economic loss, as we have already seen with the exclusionary rules operating in relation to other aspects of the duty of care in negligence, such a rule does not prevent *all* recovery. There are a few exceptions which a claimant must fall within in order to be able to recover. These stem primarily from **Hedley Byrne v Heller** [1963]. This is an important case in both the law of contract and in tort. It introduced the tort of 'negligent misstatement' into law and set out precise guidelines as to when and how the tort would operate.[8]

---

7. So, in the washing machine example at the start of the chapter, although the cost of replacing the washing machine itself would be considered pure economic loss in tort, it would in fact be recoverable under contract if it was the machine itself that was faulty—a distinction we will return to when looking at product liability in Chapter 13.

8. **Hedley Byrne** was decided at a time when only 'fraudulent' and 'innocent' misrepresentations were legally recognised—in the context of making a statement that induced someone to enter into a contract. Because fraud required proof on the part of the claimant, few cases were decided in this way. But, at the same time, often there was something more than wholesome innocence on the part of the statement-maker. In **Hedley Byrne**, Lord Denning referred back to his dissenting judgment in the Court of Appeal case of *Candler* v *Crane Christmas & Co* [1951], in which he had found that a duty of care could be owed by accountants preparing accounts knowing that the figures they provided would be relied upon by potential investors. In **Hedley Byrne**, he used this to 'create' a new tort of negligent misstatement, increasing the categories of potential claim for misrepresentation in contractual situations by including negligence for the first time. (This was followed shortly afterwards by a statutory form of negligent misrepresentation in the Misrepresentation Act 1967.) It also enabled claims to be made in three-party situations, where a misstatement is made by A to B, which induces B to enter a contract with C (rather than with A).

Hedley Byrne & Co Ltd v *Heller and Partners* [1963] HL

Hedley Byrne, an advertising agency, was asked by a company called Easipower Ltd to buy it some advertising space. To make sure that Easipower could pay for this service, Hedley Byrne decided to credit check the company. Hedley Byrne's bank twice contacted Easipower's bank, Heller, to ask if the company was creditworthy, and both times was given a positive response. The second check included the specific question as to whether Easipower was 'trustworthy, in the way of business, to the extent of £100,000 per annum'. On the basis of Heller's positive responses, Hedley Byrne contracted with Easipower and bought advertising space for them for £17,000. Easipower later collapsed, and Hedley Byrne sought to claim back the £17,000 from Heller on the basis that they had been negligent when preparing the statement about the credit and trustworthiness of Easipower.

However, when issuing its statements, Heller had included a disclaimer saying that each was prepared 'without responsibility on the part of this Bank or its officials'; a clause excluding their liability, should it arise. The House of Lords held that in view of this disclaimer, no liability could arise on the facts of this particular case.

However, the law lords also considered what the position would be in respect of the £17,000 loss had there been no disclaimer. On this, their lordships found (*obiter*) that a duty of care could arise in some situations where advice was given, even where the only harm caused was what would otherwise be regarded as 'pure' economic loss. But, they said, this was limited to situations where the following four conditions were met:

1. a special (or 'fiduciary') relationship of trust and confidence exists between the parties; **and**

2. the party preparing the advice/information has voluntarily assumed the risk (express or implied); **and**

3. there has been reliance on the advice/information by the other party; **and**

4. such reliance was reasonable in the circumstances.

On the facts of *Hedley Byrne*, had there not been a disclaimer attached to the information given, Heller would have owed a duty of care and would have been liable for Hedley Byrne's losses.[9]

Though there have been some departures from this position, the principles established in *Hedley Byrne* continue to form the basis of any duty of care that can be owed in relation to pure economic loss when such loss is based on reliance on a *statement* of some kind. Put another way, it is only where these principles can be applied that an exception to the general exclusionary rule will be made.

But what about economic losses caused by what somebody has done—that is, by the 'activity' of the defendant? After *Hedley Byrne* and until *Caparo Industries* v *Dickman* [1990], there was a period of significant expansion of liability for pure economic loss. During this period recovery extended beyond losses caused by misstatements (that

---

9. Thus, it seems that the financial advisor in the scenarios outlined at the beginning of this chapter would be liable, as long as the four *Hedley Byrne* conditions are met, and there was no disclaimer in his contract of service.

is, poor advice or information) to include 'activity'-related losses (for example, losses caused when the walls of a house crack due to the negligent building (an activity) of the foundations). This particular expansion was curtailed by the House of Lords in **Murphy v Brentwood District Council** [1990], which closed the door on claims for pure economic loss relating to defective products or buildings.

We can now generalise about when and on what basis recovery will be possible for pure economic loss: there is a difference between statement-based losses and activity-based losses. Recovery is allowed for the first, subject to the **Hedley Byrne** criteria being met, but not the second. Put another way, the **Hedley Byrne** criteria *only* apply where the claimant's pure economic loss has been caused by what the defendant has *said* (rather than what they have done), and only then within the context of a fiduciary relationship. However, as we shall see, the distinction between what is 'said' and what is 'done'—between statements and activities—is not always an easy one to draw and is an even harder one to maintain.

 Pause for reflection

Does it make sense to draw a distinction about *how* an economic loss was caused? Why prioritise economic losses that are caused by what someone else *said*, but not what they *did*?

7.4 Claims for pure economic loss in negligence before *Murphy*

Broadly speaking, until the decision in **Murphy**, there had been three 'phases' of judicial development of the duty of care for pure economic loss, which can be roughly summarised, as in Table 7.2.

Table 7.2 Claims for pure economic loss before *Murphy*

Phase 1	Pre-1963 (*Hedley Byrne*)	No recovery of pure economic loss in negligence[10]
Phase 2	*Hedley Byrne–Junior Books v Veitchi* 1963–83	Period of expansion of the type of situation for which pure economic loss was recoverable, following expansion of duty in negligence more generally and of the *Hedley Byrne* principles
Phase 3	Post-*Junior Books* 1983–90	Closing down of the exceptions, a retreat from a more generous position regarding pure economic loss, culminating in *Caparo v Dickman [1990]* and *Murphy*

10. See e.g. *Cattle v Stockton Waterworks* [1875].

Indirectly, the decision in **Hedley Byrne** opened the door to recovery for other types of pure economic loss claim (that is, those not based on statements).[11] In so doing, it coincided with a more general relaxation of the duty of care concept in the tort of negligence as a whole.[12] In particular, the courts began to allow claims for what could be described as economic losses based on defective products (which for these purposes included buildings, each being based on the activity of production). In *Dutton v Bognor Regis Building Co Ltd* [1972], for example, the purchaser of a house successfully sued a local authority in negligence for carelessly approving the foundations, which had turned out to be insecure, rendering the house physically defective with badly cracked walls.[13] Pre-**Hedley Byrne**, entering the contract to buy the house would have been seen merely as a 'bad bargain' (the house was simply worth less than was paid for it) and the purchaser would have had no remedy for the pure economic loss they had suffered as a result: the cost of repairing the cracked walls. Post-**Hedley Byrne**, in a changed climate, it may have been in the court's mind that the local authority concerned had assumed the risk of its building approvals (which were made pursuant to statutory powers) and that the buyer had been entitled to rely on this. Whatever the reason for it, the decision in *Dutton* seemed to call into question whether any distinction could continue to be drawn between defects in property and pure economic losses.

Anns v Merton London Borough Council [1978] HL

The claimant alleged that the local authority had negligently failed to supervise the construction of a building, with the result that cracks had appeared in the walls caused by sinking foundations.

In the House of Lords, Lord Wilberforce classified the harm suffered as 'material physical damage' (as opposed to pure economic loss) meaning that damages for the cost of repairs were recoverable.

Following *Anns*, the distinction between material physical damage and pure economic loss seemed to have been lost entirely. This became even more apparent in *Junior Books Ltd v Veitchi Co Ltd* [1983].

Junior Books Ltd v Veitchi Co Ltd [1983] HL

A claim was made by the owners of land in relation to a factory under construction. A building company had been contracted to build the factory, and was instructed by the claimant to subcontract the defendant, a specialist flooring company, to lay a floor designed to

➡

11. See e.g. *Weller & Co v Foot and Mouth Disease Research Institute* [1966], a case concerned with lost profit after negligence caused the closure of local cattle markets. Undoubtedly this case—though ultimately unsuccessful—was brought in the wake of **Hedley Byrne** to test the extent of the relaxation.
12. See further pp 59–60.
13. Arguably, granting of approval falls somewhere between statements/advice and activity.

→

support heavy machinery. The floor was laid negligently and had to be rebuilt. While this was done the factory had to be closed and the claimants lost profits. As the landowners had no contract with the subcontractors (they only had one with the building company), they sued them in negligence.

The House of Lords allowed a claim to be made in negligence for the pure economic loss (cost of relaying the floor and lost profits),[14] categorising the claim as one where the supply of a defective product (the floor) caused economic loss. They found, drawing on *Hedley Byrne*, that Veitchi, who occupied a position of special skill, had therefore 'assumed responsibility' for the condition of the floor and the claimants had relied upon this.[15]

However, darker clouds were beginning to build on the horizon. Not only was there confusion ensuing from these decisions but, by the late-1980s, the social and economic climate had once again changed and, in simplistic terms, the courts were looking for a way to 'rein in' the situations in which a duty of care in negligence could be owed—in all contentious areas, not only in relation to pure economic loss.[16]

The first indication of this change of approach came in *D & F Estates Ltd* v *Church Commissioners for England and others* [1989]. In this case the claimants were seeking damages for the cost of repairing defective plastering on the walls of a flat they had purchased some 15 years previously, which was part of a building owned by the defendants. The plastering had been done negligently by a plasterer subcontracted by the co-defendant building firm. At first instance, following *Dutton* and *Anns*, the trial judge awarded the claimants damages against the builders. This was reversed at the Court of Appeal who held that the builders owed a duty only to employ competent subcontractors and on the facts this duty had not been breached. The House of Lords agreed, finding also that, in any case, the cost of repairing the defective plaster was not a loss that was recoverable in negligence. It was distinguishable from defective foundations in that it was simply a defect in the product (the flat) itself and could cause no further direct harm. The first seeds of doubt about the correctness of the *Anns* decision were now sown,[17] paving the way for the decision in *Murphy* v *Brentwood District Council* [1990].

14. Their lordships based their decision on Lord Wilberforce's two-stage duty test from *Anns* (see p 59).

15. Although note the dissent of Lord Brandon, who argued that the type of liability being found in this case was one that should only be recoverable in contract.

16. It seems now that the *Junior Books* decision is confined to its own facts and will therefore not be resurrected in future cases (see e.g. *Losinjska Plovidba* v *Transco Overseas Ltd (The Orjula)* [1995]).

17. Interestingly, the High Court of Australia had by this time already declined to follow *Anns* in *Sutherland Shire Council* v *Heyman* [1985]. New Zealand still allows claims from home owners for defective inspections etc that cause economic loss (*Invercargill City Council* v *Hamlin* [1994] most recently confirmed by the New Zealand Supreme Court in *North Shore City Council* v *Body Corporate* [2010]). The *Junior Books* decision was also called into question in *D & F Estates*, particularly by Lord Bridge, who preferred the dissenting opinion of Lord Brandon, and who stated there was such a 'unique scope of the duty of care owed by the defender to the pursuer arising from that relationship that the decision cannot be regarded as laying down any principle of general application in the law of tort' (at 19). Although *Junior Books* has not been explicitly overruled it is unlikely to be followed today. In fact, in a recent case, Burnton LJ said that 'the decision of the House of Lords in *Anns v Merton LBC*, like its...decision in *Junior Books Ltd v Veitchi Co. Ltd* [1983], must now be regarded as aberrant, indeed as heretical' (*Robinson v PE Jones (Contractors) Ltd* [2011] at [92]).

Murphy v *Brentwood District Council* **[1990] HL**

Mr Murphy purchased a semi-detached house in Brentwood, which had been built by a company called ABC Homes. Over ten years later, serious cracks started appearing in the walls. These were found to be caused by a defect in the foundations, the design of which had been approved by the district council. The defect caused the house to become structurally unsound and worth £35,000 less than had been paid for it. At first instance the judge found that the council had owed and breached a duty of care in relation to its buildings approvals.

The House of Lords decided otherwise, also taking the opportunity to reflect on whether *Anns* had been correctly decided. They held that the damage in *Anns* (and therefore in *Murphy*) should properly be considered pure economic loss and not a form of material physical damage. They found that faulty foundations cause no loss or damage, other than a financial loss, unless they are dangerous or cause further physical damage to the 'fabric of the house' by subsidence or collapsing walls—it is merely the cost of repairing the foundations that is at issue. This, in their view, was pure economic loss for which no duty should be owed. Thus, in *Murphy* the House of Lords overturned *Anns* on this point.[18]

 Counterpoint

Much of the reasoning in *Murphy* came down to whether a house could be viewed as a 'complex structure'. Complex structures are those where each part (or some parts) of a whole can be treated as individual pieces of property. This means that if one part is defective (which would be classified as purely economic loss) but *causes damage to another part* (damage to property), the costs of rectifying this damage will be recoverable. This is particularly helpful in the context of product liability. If a faulty component causes damage to another component or to the product itself, recovery is possible for the damaged component but not for the cost of replacing the original faulty component (see Chapter 13).

The application of the 'complex structure' theory was rejected in *Murphy*. Lord Jauncey said that:

> to apply the complex structure theory to a house so that each part of the entire structure is treated as a separate piece of property is unrealistic. A builder who builds a house from foundations upwards is creating a single integrated unit of which the individual components are interdependent. To treat the foundations as a piece of property separate from the walls or the floors is a wholly artificial exercise. If the foundations are inadequate the whole house is affected. (at 497)

→

18. One of the reasons for this, in addition to the general closing down of the scope of liability in negligence, was clearly the passage of the Defective Premises Act 1972, which had not been considered in *Anns*. Section 1 of the Act imposes an obligation on builders of domestic premises in relation to the quality and fitness of their work, which exists for a period of six years after construction is complete. In *Murphy*, Lord Bridge pointed out that '[i]t would be remarkable to find that similar obligations...applicable to buildings of every kind and subject to no such exclusions or limitations as are imposed by the Act of 1972, could be derived from the builder's common law duty of care' (at 480–1).

> →
>
> *Lunney & Oliphant* suggest that this argument in itself poses difficulties when translated to other products. They ask whether:
>
> > the purchaser of a bottle of wine whose contents were ruined by a defective cork suffer property damage (because the cork had damaged the wine) or pure economic loss (because the 'product' included both the wine and cork so the defect only caused the bottle as a whole to lose value)?[19]
>
> Realistically, of course, even if it was the wine manufacturer who was negligent, one could take a bottle of wine back to the retailer, who would be obliged, having sold a product not of 'satisfactory quality', to provide either a refund or a replacement. This is not true of houses. It may be that on policy grounds, particularly given the extent of the potential loss, houses *should* be viewed as complex structures. Perhaps the real problem here is that many of the claims we have seen in relation to houses and other properties were against public authorities—meaning that courts (especially the House of Lords) would be unlikely to want to find liability.[20]

Thus, we can see that the period from **Hedley Byrne** to **Murphy** was a turbulent time in relation to pure economic loss, with a number of important House of Lords decisions relating to the scope and content of the duty of care. This reached a 'high point' with **Anns** and **Junior Books**, which was later retreated from in *D & F Estates* and **Murphy**.

7.5 Extending *Hedley Byrne*

Post-**Murphy**, the only way to claim in negligence for pure economic loss is to rely on the four principles established in **Hedley Byrne**.[21] More recently, however, these principles have been applied in ways which seem to be *extensions* of the principles as they were first formulated. This is particularly notable given the policy reasons elucidated for not recognising claims for pure economic loss in the first place, and the 'closing down' of liability for economic loss described in the previous section. It is to where these principles have (and have not) been applied that we shall turn next.

7.5.1 A special relationship

In **Hedley Byrne** Lord Reid envisaged that a special (or fiduciary) relationship—a relationship of trust and confidence—would arise where it was clear that:

> the party seeking information or advice was trusting the other to exercise such a degree of care as the circumstances required, where it was reasonable for him to do that, and where the other gave the information or advice when he knew that the inquirer was relying on him. (at 486)

19. Page 403.
20. See further Chapter 6.
21. See p 176.

From this definition it is apparent that the four *Hedley Byrne* principles in fact overlap, as the reliance element and the assumption of risk element are clearly both *part* of what makes a special relationship in the first place. The question of whether it 'was reasonable for him to do that' seems to mean that this type of relationship ought only to arise in a business context.[22] Therefore, if we advise you to invest your money in a certain company's shares, no such special relationship could arise in which we would owe you a duty of care in respect of pure economic loss suffered by you even in reliance on our advice.

> ### Pause for reflection
>
> The limitation of the 'special relationship' to business contexts seems appropriate given the closeness of economic loss claims in negligence to contractual claims. Where people are seeking to promote their business interests (and it is someone's job to assist in this, when asked) is there any good reason why that person should not be liable for any negligent advice they give, when they are only being asked to give it for that very reason?
>
> Why, in *Hedley Byrne*, did the claimants not sue for breach of contract?

A good example of the type of special relationship required to be able to sue for economic loss was found in the case of ***Esso Petroleum Co Ltd* v *Mardon* [1976]**.

> ### *Esso Petroleum Co Ltd* v *Mardon* [1976] CA
>
> An employee of Esso, whose job it was to assess the potential output of petrol stations, advised Mr Mardon, who was thinking of leasing a petrol station, that the station in question would sell at least 200,000 gallons of petrol per year. Mr Mardon entered the lease in reliance on this advice, but sold only 78,000 gallons of petrol in the first 15 months of trading. The advice of the Esso employee (for whom Esso would be vicariously liable) was found to be negligent, in the sense that he had fallen below the standard of care required of someone in his position. The question was whether a duty of care could be owed to Mr Mardon in respect of the loss he had suffered, which was purely economic.
>
> The Court of Appeal held that the required special relationship had been created because, in making the statement, Esso's employee had undertaken a responsibility to Mr Mardon based on his expertise in assessing the market for petrol sales, and Mr Mardon had reasonably relied on this. Therefore, a duty of care was owed.

22. Though cf *Chaudry* v *Prabhaker* [1989] where the claimant relied on the advice of a friend who 'had a lot to do with motor cars' to find her a used car. He negligently found and recommended her to buy a car that had been in an accident, rendering it worthless. By a majority, the Court of Appeal agreed that he owed the claimant a duty of care in respect of her economic loss. Presumably this was because she had asked him to act as her agent, bringing this closer to a business arrangement and away from a purely domestic one.

7.5.2 **Voluntary assumption of risk**

It is a reasonable extension of the special relationship idea that where such a relationship exists, any party giving advice given within this context, without a disclaimer, can be said to have assumed the risk that the statement they make is reliable. If they did not want to assume the risk, they could, as in **Hedley Byrne** itself, attempt to exclude their liability.[23]

In *Goodwill* v *British Pregnancy Advisory Service* [1996], the defendants were sued for negligently advising the claimant's partner that a vasectomy performed on him had been successful. The woman had relied on this information and stopped using other methods of contraception, subsequently falling pregnant and giving birth to a child. The claim was for the costs associated with bringing up the child. While they agreed that the relationship in which the advice was given could be held to be one of 'trust and confidence', the Court of Appeal was unwilling to find that the risks of making the statement had been assumed (and particularly not to the man's partner, who only entered a relationship with him after he had already had the vasectomy). Because of this, the court found, the claimant was not entitled to have relied on the advice given and this was not, therefore, a situation in which damages for economic loss should be recoverable.

 Counterpoint

In recent years the courts have generally found against claimants who claim for the costs associated with bringing up an unwanted child (both in negligence and in relation to defective products). In the tort of negligence, one of the ways they have achieved this is by constructing the parents' claim for the costs associated with bringing up their child as pure economic loss.

Do you think that such costs—such as feeding and clothing the child—are *purely* economic? Could the cost of raising a child which was born because of someone else's negligent advice or action be classified as *consequential* economic loss? See, for example, *McFarlane* v *Tayside Health Board* [2000] which had similar facts to *Goodwill* except that the claimants were a married couple who already had four children and were trying to avoid having another precisely *because* they could not afford the costs of bringing up a fifth child. The McFarlanes were also denied recovery. Alongside categorising their loss as purely economic, the parents' harm (having a healthy—albeit unwanted—child) was not one recognisable in law:

> The law must take the birth of a normal, healthy baby to be a blessing, not a detriment…It would be repugnant to [society's] own sense of value to do otherwise. It would be morally offensive to regard a normal, healthy baby as more trouble and expense than it is worth. (Lord Millett at 1347)

→

---

23. This would be, in the context of negligence, subject to s 2 of the Unfair Contract Terms Act 1977, thus any disclaimer could be struck out of the contract if deemed unreasonable by a court or if the negligence resulted in personal injury or death.

> ➡
>
> The decision in *McFarlane* has been subjected to significant academic and judicial criticism and should now be read in light of the later House of Lords' decision in *Parkinson* v *St James & Seacroft University Hospital NHS Trust* [2002] (in which damages were awarded only for the *additional* costs of bringing up an unwanted child who was also disabled) and *Rees* v *Darlington Memorial Hospital NHS Trust* [2003]. In *Rees*, while not allowing recovery of the costs of raising an unplanned yet healthy child (born to a disabled mother), the House of Lords (by a slim 4:3 majority) controversially reconceptualised the harm suffered by the mother as damage to her autonomy for which there should be a 'conventional award', despite this idea having been raised and rejected in *McFarlane*. The award was set at £15,000.

The modern test for determining assumption of responsibility was outlined by the House of Lords in *Henderson* v *Merrett Syndicates Ltd* [1995], a case involving a number of claims by investors (known as 'Names') who, in syndicates, had underwritten insurance policies for Lloyds. They suffered substantial losses when numerous insurance claims were made against Lloyds in the early 1990s, and alleged that the agents who had set out the syndication of the Names had been negligent in doing so. Their lordships found that the agents had assumed responsibility for the financial affairs of the Names, even though there had been no statement or advice that this was based on:[24]

> there is no problem in cases of this kind about liability for pure economic loss; for if a person assumes responsibility to another in the respect of certain services, there is no reason why he should not be liable in damages in respect of economic loss which flows from the negligent performance of those services. (Lord Goff at 238)

An interesting example of the principle in action is found in *Lennon* v *Commissioner of Police of the Metropolis* [2004]. In this case a police officer was negligently advised by a personnel officer about the impact on the terms of his employment contract of transferring from one police force to another, resulting in him permanently losing his housing entitlement. The Court of Appeal found that it was well established that liability for pure economic loss could arise where there was an express voluntary assumption of responsibility on which the claimant had relied. In this case, the personnel officer had expressly assumed responsibility for the claimant's transfer and for giving advice in relation to the housing allowance and had led him to believe that he could rely on her to handle the arrangements; a duty therefore arose in respect of the economic loss he had suffered.[25]

The assumption of responsibility principle was revisited by the House of Lords in **Customs & Excise Commissioners v Barclays Bank [2006]**.

24. The House of Lords also confirmed in this case that when there are concurrent obligations in contract and tort, the claimant can choose which one to sue in (though not if the contract expressly provides that liability may be contractual only: see *Robinson* v *PE Jones (Contractors) Ltd* [2011]). Here, the Names had a contractual relationship with the agents, but sued in tort to take advantage of the longer limitation period (see Chapter 19).

25. Similar points were made in respect of a claim about a pension fund in *Gorham* v *British Telecommunications plc* [2000].

> ### *Customs & Excise Commissioners* v *Barclays Bank* [2006] HL
>
> Customs officers obtained 'freezing orders' on the bank accounts of two companies which were in debt with regards their tax payments. This meant that the bank (Barclays) was legally obliged not to let any payments leave the companies' bank accounts. However, Barclays negligently allowed some withdrawals to be made. Customs & Excise sought to recover this money by suing Barclays in negligence, alleging that this was recoverable economic loss. They contended that, once a freezing order had been received, a bank assumed responsibility for the loss that would be suffered if money was allowed to leave the frozen accounts.
>
> The House of Lords ruled that there had been *no* assumption of responsibility in the required sense, because it could not truly be said that the responsibility assumed was *voluntary* where the bank was obliged by law to accept the freezing order, therefore the claim failed.

In **Barclays Bank**, the reasoning of the law lords suggests that the 'assumption of responsibility' concept is an imprecise tool with which to determine liability for pure economic loss.[26] Rather than being a blunt concept that is either present or not in any given case, it will need to be interpreted flexibly and in accordance with the precise facts and policy considerations in each case:[27] 'although it may be decisive in many situations, the presence or absence of a voluntary assumption of responsibility does not necessarily provide the answer in all cases' (Lord Rodger at [20]).

Thus it seems that the concept, though retained by the House of Lords, will be able to be more loosely relied upon in the future, or may be side-stepped where policy considerations are deemed to override it.[28]

7.5.3 **Reasonable reliance**

Whether the claimant can be said to have relied on a statement, information or advice is also important in providing an exception to the general exclusionary rule. As indicated above, the idea of reliance overlaps with the other **Hedley Byrne** principles. For example, it is often precisely *because* a 'special relationship' exists that one party will rely on the other's advice, particularly when this is given in a professional context (as in **Esso** v **Mardon**).

26. Though Lord Hoffmann continues to believe the existence of a voluntary assumption of risk is 'critical' when establishing a duty of care in respect of economic loss (at [14]) and Lord Mance defined it as 'a core area of liability' (at [28]). *Rogers* describes the test as 'to some extent a rival to the **Caparo** test as the *general* approach to the duty of care question' (p 211, emphasis added). In contrast, *Lunney & Oliphant* suggest that 'the role of assumption of responsibility seems to be a means of satisfying the three-stage test [**Caparo**], but not the only means' (p 457).

27. Similar points were made about the three-stage duty test from **Caparo** (by Lord Walker at [25], Lord Hoffmann at [14] and Lord Bingham at [7]). As we shall see, both the wider impact of **Caparo** (used to incrementally extend the disputed categories of duty) and its narrower *ratio* have to be taken into account in economic loss claims.

28. Compare *Williams and Reid* v *Natural Life Health Foods Ltd and Mistlin* [1998] and *West Bromwich Albion Football Club Ltd* v *Al-Safty* [2006]. Seemingly it matters who makes the statement, in what context and which party is deemed best able to bear the loss.

The nature of the reliance, coupled with the fourth principle from *Hedley Byrne*, which means that the reliance must be reasonable in the circumstances, is important. In *Caparo Industries plc* v *Dickman* [1990] (a case perhaps better known for statements on whether a duty of care exists at all in contentious cases),[29] for example, it was held that the reliance was not reasonable, given the context in which the statement had been made.

Caparo Industries plc v *Dickman* [1990] HL

Caparo was considering a takeover bid of another company, Fidelity. In pursuance of this, Caparo looked at information prepared by Dickman, Fidelity's auditors, which it received because it already held a number of shares in Fidelity. This information showed that Fidelity was doing well and, in reliance on this audit, Caparo launched its takeover bid only to find later that Fidelity was almost completely worthless. Caparo sued Dickman, alleging negligence in the preparation of the audit.

The House of Lords found that no duty of care was owed by Dickman in respect of the economic loss caused by Caparo's reliance on the information provided. The main reason for this was that it was not reasonable for Caparo to have relied on this information when preparing its takeover bid of Fidelity. Company audits were an annual requirement for businesses under the Companies Act 1985, and the information within them was provided for shareholders; not for potential investors as this would include a class of persons of an indeterminate size.[30] Thus, in Caparo's capacity as a shareholder of Fidelity, the information could be relied upon, but in its capacity as a potential investor, it could not be.

In *Caparo*, because the reliance on the information was not *reasonable*, no special relationship could arise between the two companies. Lord Bridge clarified this position further, saying that there would be a difference where:

> the defendant giving advice or information was fully aware of the nature of the transaction which the plaintiff had in contemplation, knew that the advice or information would be communicated to him directly or indirectly and knew that it was very likely that the plaintiff would rely on that advice or information in deciding whether or not to engage in the transaction in contemplation. (at 620–1)

He explained that because audit information under the Companies Act 1985 is put into 'more or less general circulation', it could foreseeably be relied on by anyone for any purpose and those preparing the audit should not owe a duty to anyone and everyone who relied on it. Put another way, the provision of information for one particular purpose should not (or cannot) *reasonably* be relied on for any other purpose, not least because there is no assumption of risk in respect of any alternative purpose for which the information is used. A similar idea was used to deny the existence of a duty of

---

29. See p 61.

30. Therefore, finding the accountants liable in this case would set a precedent potentially exposing accountants and auditors to vast sums in damages. The decision is clearly policy-based, designed to avoid opening the 'floodgates' of liability, perceived knock-on consequences of which would be inflated prices of accountancy services more generally and therefore a deleterious effect on all business transactions in society.

care to a fisherman in *Reeman* v *Department of Transport* [1997], when the certificate of seaworthiness that had been issued for his boat turned out to have been negligently written. The boat in fact was almost worthless. The Court of Appeal, following **Caparo**, held that such certificates were issued to enhance maritime safety, not to establish the commercial value of boats, so should not have been relied on in this way.[31]

 Pause for reflection

Do you think the distinction drawn in *Caparo* is a valid one? If, as an existing shareholder in Fidelity, Caparo would have been entitled to rely on the information provided by Dickman in relation to the investment they already had, why should they not also be able to rely on it in relation to any further investment they might be considering making? If the idea was to curtail the situations in which a duty of care might arise—and this certainly was one of the aims of the House of Lords, given the climate of the time—then to say that the duty would arise only in the context of existing shareholders—but not *prospective* shareholders—would still have this effect, with the exception that Caparo itself would have been owed a duty of care.

In contrast to **Caparo**, in *Law Society* v *KPMG Peat Marwick* [2000], the claimants sued when the defendants—the accountants for a firm of solicitors—failed to discover that a senior partner in the firm was siphoning off money and defrauding many of the firm's clients. When the fraud was discovered, more than 300 of the firm's clients claimed compensation from the Law Society, via a no-fault compensation fund set up for this very purpose. Trying to recover the economic loss it had suffered, the Law Society sued the accountancy firm, saying that it had been negligent in preparing the annual accounts of the firm. Relying on **Caparo**, the accountants contended that their duty was only to the solicitors' firm and not to anyone else who had relied on the accounts prepared for them for any other purpose. However, the Law Society argued that the duty extended as far as them, as law firms had to have their accounts prepared annually for the benefit of the Law Society, and it was known by the accountants involved that the society would rely on the information provided. The Court of Appeal agreed, holding that because the accountants knew the purpose for which such accounts were prepared, and because it was foreseeable that failure to correctly prepare accounts would lead to claims being made against the fund, it was appropriate for a duty to be imposed in these circumstances.

A decision was reached on similar grounds in the case of **Smith v Eric S Bush [1990]**.

Smith v Eric S Bush [1990] HL

The claimant purchased a house, relying on a survey of the property prepared by the defendants. The survey had been carried out negligently and the house was in fact worth much less than was paid for it. The survey, as is normal practice, had been commissioned

→

---

31. Also see *Marc Rich & Co* v *Bishop Rock Marine Co Ltd* [1995].

by the building society with which the claimants had taken out their mortgage—the principal purpose of such a survey is to satisfy the building society that the value of the house being purchased is at least that of the amount of money being lent.

    The House of Lords held that although a contract exists only between the mortgage lender and surveyor, surveyors would owe a duty of care to the buyer, as they would be aware that the buyer would rely on the information provided by them, and it would be reasonable for buyers to do so.

Part of the reasoning in **Smith** is that it is commonly understood that surveys provided primarily for mortgage lenders are often relied on by home buyers as well. While it is possible for buyers to commission their own more detailed survey, this is more expensive, so many purchasers simply rely on the survey carried out by the mortgage lender, especially as it is actually the buyer who has to pay for this survey to be carried out in the first place. In **Smith** this fact was particularly important—the court recognised that Mrs Smith was making one of the most important purchases of her life and, as she was not wealthy, was fully entitled to rely on the valuation provided for the mortgage lender.[32] In **Smith**, the surveyors had used a disclaimer which, as discussed above when looking at **Hedley Byrne**, would ordinarily prevent a duty of care from arising. However, the disclaimer used in **Smith** fell foul of the Unfair Contract Terms Act 1977 and could not therefore be relied on.

 Counterpoint

It is interesting to consider how the notion of *assumption of responsibility* works in *Smith*. It does not seem to us that it can be said that the surveyors assumed responsibility for the accuracy of the information they were providing *to Mrs Smith*. Furthermore, the disclaimer that was included, though falling foul of contract legislation, surely at least points to the fact that no responsibility had *actually* been assumed (as it was in *Hedley Byrne*).[33]

7.6 Beyond *Hedley Byrne*: the 'will cases' and a more flexible approach

Despite the idea behind **Caparo,** and the cases that followed, being to limit the situations in which a duty of care can arise in relation to pure economic loss, some more recent decisions appear to be expanding this area of liability once again, into areas

---

    32. It was probably helpful that her case is distinct from **Caparo** on another ground: that it was only she who would be relying on the information, meaning there was no wider class of people about which to be concerned.

    33. It was this that precluded liability for a statement on a website in *Patchett* v *Swimming Pool & Allied Trades Association Ltd* [2009]. While the Court of Appeal found that online representations could in theory give rise to a duty of care, it also found that the website in question made clear that its information should not be solely relied upon.

which could be defined as relating to the provision of services rather than the making of a statement or the giving of advice. This expansion started with what have become colloquially known as the 'will cases' but, as we shall see, the principle used has been further extended to other services.

The first of the so-called will cases was *Ross* v *Caunters* [1980]. A solicitor negligently drew up a will for his client, so much so that the will ran contrary to the law on probate and the intended beneficiary, the claimant, was unable to inherit under the will's provisions. The claimant's loss, however, was purely economic—in fact it may be better described as a failure to make an anticipated gain, more commonly encountered in contract law.[34] Furthermore, rather than this being a case where 'advice' was given in the form of a *statement*, this was a negligent *action* or *service*. Notwithstanding this difference, the claimant won her case and was able to recover the sum she had lost (or not gained) from the negligent solicitor.

Ross v *Caunters* was not considered particularly significant at the time of its judgment. The case was decided in 1980, a time when, as we have seen, negligence liability was in a period of expansion, with the courts being willing to find a duty of care in new situations following the formula laid out in **Anns**. *Ross* is made more significant because it was later followed in cases that came *after* this period of expansion had been closed down (following **Murphy** and **Caparo**), when any successful case for pure economic loss had to, in theory, be based on the four **Hedley Byrne** principles (and so therefore relate to statements, advice or similar). The first case to do this was **White** v **Jones** [1995].

White v Jones [1995] HL

Two sisters were cut out of their father's will following an argument. Later, the rift in the relationship between the sisters and their father was mended and the father instructed his solicitor to re-draft the will, including an inheritance of £9,000 for each of his daughters. When, after a month, he discovered that this had not yet been done, he re-issued his instruction. After the father died, it was found that the will had not been changed and the daughters sued the solicitor.

The House of Lords found in favour of the claimants, awarding them the economic loss they had suffered as a result of the solicitor's negligence.

Considering that the principles from **Hedley Byrne** supposedly formed the only basis for recovery of economic losses at the time **White** was decided, it is difficult to see how this case fits. In **White**, a *service* was provided and the loss caused to the claimants came as a result of negligent provision of that service rather than as a statement made

---

34. The claimant had no contract with the solicitor and due to the restrictive laws on privity of contract in operation at the time, she would have been entirely unable to sue in contract. The principle of privity of contract is that only the parties to a contract have any rights or obligations under it, thus only they can sue or be sued. After 1999, a claimant in a similar position to the woman in *Ross* v *Caunters* may be able to circumvent the privity rule, as the Contracts (Rights of Third Parties) Act 1999 allows parties outside a contract to sue if they were an intended beneficiary of the contract and were identified as such in the terms of the contract itself.

in the context of a special relationship where the risk of its accuracy was assumed and relied upon. Moreover, though solicitors in the provision of will-drafting services clearly have a special relationship (of trust and confidence) with *their clients*, it would seem to raise the risk of a conflict of interest if this relationship also extended to the intended beneficiaries of wills. The decision truly marks a more flexible approach to the **Hedley Byrne** principles.[35] Similar claims have, however, been denied by the courts where it appears that the interests of the testator and beneficiaries differ (that is, where there is an *actual* conflict of interest). It is only where these interests are identical that the **White** exception comes into play (see, for example, *Clark* v *Bruce Lance & Co* [1988]).

 Pause for reflection

Do you think the House of Lords was swayed by the need to do 'justice' in **White**? Failures in the context of service provision are certainly more familiar territory in contract law. The problem was that the only party in the contract with the solicitors (the father, or more accurately his estate) had suffered no loss as a result of their breach of contract/negligence. The claimants, who *had* suffered loss, were not parties to the contract. Outside a contractual relationship, to be able to sue in negligence the defendant must owe the claimant a duty of care and the 'rules' on pure economic loss in negligence at this time would not have allowed such a duty to arise. In reality the House of Lords in **White**, by extending the **Hedley Byrne** principles, created such a duty. Do you think they did the right thing?

The situation is analogous to **Hedley Byrne** itself. Why shouldn't a solicitor be liable for negligently failing to do what they ought to have done (for example, by not acting on an instruction)? Furthermore, arguably the solicitor's firm is more likely to be able to absorb the losses than those affected by the negligence, who might be people of 'modest means'. Lord Goff referred to this when he spoke of the unfairness that he felt would come from not providing the claimants a remedy:

> The injustice of denying such a remedy is reinforced if one considers the importance of legacies in a society which recognises . . . the right of citizens to leave their assets to whom they please, and in which, as a result, legacies can be of great importance to individual citizens, providing very often the only opportunity for a citizen to acquire a significant capital sum; or to inherit a house, so providing a secure roof over the heads of himself and his family; or to make special provision for his or her old age. (at 260)

In other cases, courts have been keen to stress the importance of insurance. Here, a solicitors' firm could clearly insure against losses of this nature, whereas those who benefit from a will would not be able to do so, often because they will not know that they were supposed to benefit until it is too late.

---

35. Indeed, in his dissent in this case, Lord Mustill says that the extended duty found by the majority went 'far beyond anything so far contemplated by the law of negligence' (at 291).

Counterpoint

White v *Jones* is a case where the law lords seemed to have decided the outcome they wanted to achieve before embarking on their judgment. In order to do so, and to fill what Lord Goff referred to as a 'lacuna in the law which needs to be filled' (at 260), the House of Lords extended the principles from *Hedley Byrne*. Unfortunately, the result is not a perfect fit. The hardest of these were the principles of 'assumption of risk' and 'reliance': it can clearly be said that solicitors preparing wills assume some kind of responsibility to their clients (to do the job properly), but not to the intended beneficiaries (some of whom might not even know they were due to inherit and so cannot be said to rely on the fiduciary nature of the relationship). Acknowledging this fact, Lord Goff stated:

> [T]here is great difficulty in holding, on ordinary principles, that the solicitor has assumed any responsibility towards an intended beneficiary under a will which he has undertaken to prepare on behalf of his client but which, through his negligence, has failed to take effect in accordance with his client's instructions. The relevant work is plainly performed by the solicitor for his client; but, in the absence of special circumstances, it cannot be said to have been undertaken for the intended beneficiary. Certainly, again in the absence of special circumstances, there will have been no reliance by the intended beneficiary on the exercise by the solicitor of due care and skill; indeed, the intended beneficiary may not even have been aware that the solicitor was engaged on such a task, or that his position might be affected. (at 262)

Lord Browne-Wilkinson circumvented this problem by stating that when a solicitor takes on the drafting of a will, they accept responsibility (and therefore all the risks attached) for doing this properly. The *scope* of the responsibility was for the law to decide and that was what the House of Lords had done in extending the duty owed to the intended beneficiaries, according to the principles of *Caparo*, which he said demanded that:

> the law will develop novel categories of negligence 'incrementally and by analogy with established categories.' In my judgment, this is a case where such development should take place since there is a close analogy with existing categories of special relationship giving rise to a duty of care to prevent economic loss. (at 275)

Seen in this sense, the *White* decision is not an extension of principle but remains firmly based on the existing principles established in *Hedley Byrne*. Lord Goff, on the other hand, held that responsibility was factually assumed only to the father but that the law should extend this duty implicitly to the claimants (at 268). Either way, as we have indicated, this seems to be the result of a desire to do practical justice for the claimants, who would otherwise have no means of recovery. It also prevents solicitors 'getting away with negligence', in the sense that they can now be sued by those parties who would actually suffer the loss as a result.

The principle from **White** was later extended even further in *Carr-Glynn* v *Frearsons* [1998]. In this case, a woman instructed her solicitors to prepare a will in which the claimant had been bequeathed a share in some property. The solicitors advised the woman that her will might be ineffective, as the way the property was owned meant that her share of it might automatically pass to the co-owners when she died. However, they also advised her how this situation could be avoided, but she died before this could be done. As a result, the claimant lost out on the property share that was meant to pass under the will and, in contrast to *Ross* and **White**, the woman's estate *also* suffered a loss, as the property share was lost. The Court of Appeal held that although the estate in this case had suffered a loss and a claim would therefore be able to be made in this respect, if this happened, the estate would receive the damages. This would *then* amount to a situation similar to that which arose in **White**—where the intended beneficiary lost out and had no way of seeking a remedy, but in the long term the estate would suffer no loss. On that basis, a duty was found to be owed to the claimant by the solicitor, who should have done what was necessary to make sure the will would operate as required.

 Pause for reflection

While it might seem like a logical extension to find a duty of care to the beneficiary even where the estate could already claim compensation (as this seems merely an intermediate point in the fact of assessing that the estate would end up suffering no loss, but those who were intended to benefit from a will would do so), do you think the solicitor was *actually* negligent in this case? By framing the duty as 'a duty to make sure the will would work as the testator intended it to', there would clearly be a breach, as this is not what eventually occurred. But given that the solicitor advised the woman what she needed to do, is it simply *bad luck* on the claimant's part that she died before it could be done? Should bad luck be compensated in this way?

In *Esterhuizen* v *Allied Dunbar Assurance plc* [1998], the principle of the will-drafting cases was extended beyond solicitors to other companies offering will-making services. This seems a natural extension of the principle guided by market expansion. It would seem odd that one could sue a solicitor for negligently drafting a will that you expected to benefit under, but not a commercial company that does essentially the same job. Similarly, in *Gorham* v *British Telecommunications plc* [2000], the Court of Appeal held that the widow of a man who had been advised to switch pension schemes could sue for the economic loss she suffered when the benefits of the pension could not be transferred to her on the death of her husband. He had opted out of his employer's pension scheme on the negligent advice of an insurance company. Had he stayed with the employer's scheme, there were insurance benefits that would have been paid to his family upon his death. These were lost when he transferred the pension to the new provider. In awarding his widow damages for the economic loss suffered, the Court of Appeal drew analogies with wills, finding that the pension advisor had assumed the risk of his advice, which would be relied on, to the family as well as his client.

Beyond wills, the **Hedley Byrne** principles were extended in **Spring v Guardian Assurance** [1995] to cover the writing of references (perhaps more obviously a statement—albeit of a different type). In this case, Lord Goff clearly outlined the position the House of Lords held on pure economic loss, finding that recovery should not be confined to cases based on statements or advice but could include the provision of a service, where there had been the appropriate assumption of responsibility and reliance (at 318).

Spring v Guardian Assurance [1995] HL

Spring had worked for the defendant company but had been fired. He sought a reference from his previous employers when he was trying to find new employment with a different company. The reference provided stated that he was dishonest and incompetent and, as a result, Spring was not employed. He sued the defendants in negligence for the economic losses caused to him by not getting the new job.

At trial it was found that although the employer genuinely believed in the truth of the reference it had prepared, it had reached these conclusions wrongly and was therefore negligent. A duty of care was owed to take care in providing accurate references. The House of Lords agreed that this duty had been owed and that it had been breached.

Notably, unlike in **Hedley Byrne** and **White**, the claimant was not the person the statement (in the reference) was made to or prepared for—he was the person the statement was *about*. This seems to indicate that the **Hedley Byrne** principles can also operate in a slightly different direction. The other components of 'assumption of responsibility' and 'reasonable reliance' are apparent in this type of situation; it is only the relationship that is different. It is arguable, however, that a comparable relationship of trust and confidence exists when a past employer is asked to provide a reference.

 Counterpoint

It was argued in *Spring* that the claim was essentially one about damage to the claimant's reputation and would therefore be better suited to defamation (see Chapter 15). The defendants argued that to allow a claim in negligence (as well as or instead of a claim in defamation) would undermine the rules and limits of the law on defamation. However, it seems to us that where there *is* negligence that causes harm—as happened in *Spring*—there should be no reason that a claim along those lines should not be viable as long as there is no potential for double-recovery. That is, if a successful claim for damages is made in one area, then a separate claim in the other should be precluded. It seems that in this case the House of Lords merely sought—again—to achieve Lord Goff's 'practical justice'. Perhaps they recognised (here and in *White*, for example) that the radical 'closing down' in the early 1990s of the areas in which a duty of care for economic loss could arise had been too sweeping in its nature.

7.7 Conclusion

The starting point in relation to pure economic losses—those financial losses that are not consequential on another type of loss—was that no recovery can be made for pure economic loss if it was caused by negligence (**Spartan Steel** [1973]). Much of the reasoning behind this was based on policy considerations: a fear of indeterminate or 'crushing' liability and that allowing recovery would interfere too much with contract law and the role of insurance. As we have seen, however, the law on pure economic loss came to be defined more by *how* the loss was caused—by a negligent statement or a negligent activity or defective product. Economic loss stemming from activities (such as building houses) or defective products (including houses) is not recoverable in the tort of negligence, whereas economic loss arising from a negligent statement or service can be, providing certain conditions are met.

Recent case law from the House of Lords (***Barclays Bank***) suggests that there are now three categories of case in which a claimant may be successful in a claim for pure economic loss. The first exception to the general exclusionary rule can occur where there is a clear analogy to an existing situation that has already been recognised by the courts, as in other types of negligence claim. Secondly, if this is not possible, where existing principles cannot be followed and a claimant following ***Caparo*** can fulfil the general test for the incremental expansion of tortious liability into a new area (a claimant must therefore show 'proximity', 'foreseeability' and that it would be 'fair, just and reasonable' to impose liability in that situation).

Lastly, there are situations where the claimant can establish that the four principles from ***Hedley Byrne*** were met in their case. These are based on the special nature of a relationship in which there is an assumption of responsibility coupled with reliance. The principles have, however, in more recent years been applied beyond statements to encompass negligent provision of certain services, reflecting a more flexible approach and a willingness on the part of the courts to do practical justice. In adopting this more flexible approach, the courts have relied heavily on the reformulation of the 'assumption of responsibility' test outlined by Lord Goff in *Henderson* **v** *Merrett*.

✱ End-of-chapter questions

After reading the chapter carefully, try answering the questions below. If you would like to know what we think visit the Online Resource Centre (www.oxfordtextbooks.co.uk/orc/horsey2e/).

1. Is it possible to give a coherent account of the development of the law on pure economic loss in negligence?

2. Jane Stapleton describes the principles on which pure economic loss in negligence can be found to attract a duty of care as 'soft concepts'. Do you agree?

3. Consider the problem question at the start of this chapter—now having read about the topic what would be your advice to Rachael and Chris? If you need some pointers in thinking about how to answer this question, turn to the Appendix (p 589) where each problem is annotated with issues and cases to consider. Next, try to write your own answer and finally, log on to our Online Resource Centre (www.oxfordtextbooks.co.uk/orc/horsey2e/) and check your ideas against our suggested outline answer.

✱ Further reading

A good place to start further reading on this topic is Paula Giliker's article. Although it discusses Canadian law, it provides useful commentary on the issues outlined in this chapter as well as suggestions for reform.

Barker, Kit 'Wielding Occam's Razor: Pruning Strategies for Economic Loss' (2006) 26 *Oxford Journal of Legal Studies* 289

Giliker, Paula 'Revisiting Pure Economic Loss: Lessons to be Learnt from the Supreme Court of Canada' (2005) 25 *Legal Studies* 49

Hughes, Andrew and Nicolas J McBride '*Hedley Byrne* in the House of Lords: An Interpretation' (1995) 15 *Legal Studies* 376

Quill, Eoin 'Consumer Protection in Respect of Defective Buildings' (2006) 14 *Tort Law Review* 105

Stapleton, Jane 'Duty of Care and Economic Loss: A Wider Agenda' (1991) 107 *Law Quarterly Review* 249

8

Breach

Problem question

Read this problem question carefully, and keep it in mind while you are working through the chapter that follows. At the end of the chapter, you will be able to apply what you have learnt to the problem question and advise the relevant parties.

Kate and Troy have spent the afternoon looking at wedding dresses. Before heading home they go to a new champagne bar to celebrate finding 'the one'. Troy offers Kate a lift home in his car, assuring Kate that he's alright to drive as he's 'probably only just over the drink-drive limit'. On the journey home Troy loses control of the car and crashes into a lamp post. Kate suffers minor cuts and bruises and is taken to hospital for a check up. At the hospital Kate contracts an infection in a cut to her right arm. The doctor on duty decides not to treat the infection with antibiotics immediately as he has recently read a report in a little-known medical journal which suggested that it is better to allow the body 'time to heal' following a trauma. Kate's right arm is partially paralysed.

8.1 **Introduction**

Consider the following:

→ **A cricketer hits a ball for six. It flies over the boundary fence hitting a passer-by on the head, causing serious injury.**

→ **A learner driver mistakes the accelerator for the brake and ploughs into a tree, injuring her instructor.**

→ **A stressed junior doctor misreads the instructions on the back of a packet of drugs and injects a patient with 250 ml, rather than 25 ml as stated, paralysing the patient from the neck down.**

There are three vital ingredients of the tort of negligence: duty of care, breach of duty and damage caused by the breach. This chapter focuses exclusively on the second of these requirements—breach of duty. In each of the examples above the defendant may have breached their duty of care not to cause the claimant physical injury. In practical terms, breach is an important factor. Many everyday negligence cases turn on issues of breach—was the defendant driving too fast given the particular road conditions? Did the doctor follow the correct procedure or administer the correct drug? Was sufficient safety equipment provided by the employer, and so on?

Breach occurs where a defendant has fallen below the particular standard of care demanded by the law. It involves making a value judgement on the defendant's behaviour: 'It cannot be *proved* that a person was negligent; one can merely *argue* that a person was negligent and hope to persuade the judge' (*Cane* p 37). The key issue to be addressed is how and where the courts set the acceptable standard or level of care owed towards one's neighbours. There are two questions to be considered:

(1) How the defendant *ought* to have behaved in the circumstances—what was the required standard of care in these circumstances? This is often described as a matter of law.

(2) How the defendant *did* behave—did they (as a matter of fact) fall below the standard of care required?

As the majority of cases depend on the particular or primary facts of the case—what speed was the car travelling at? Was it appropriate for the time of day, location and so on?—it is difficult (although not impossible) to make generalisations about the standard of care the law will require in particular cases. As such, despite its practical importance, there is relatively little to say about breach of duty in negligence—the actual *law* here is relatively limited. The most we can do is identify a few broad and rather open-ended propositions. In fact, *Weir* has argued that 'decisions on breach are not citable as *authorities*; they are merely *illustrations* of the application of the indubitable rule that if one is under a duty at common law such care must be taken as is called for in all the circumstances' (p 57). However, this only goes so far. While clearly the determination of whether a breach has occurred will largely turn on the specific facts of the case at hand, it is nevertheless possible to identify some broad principles that the courts use when seeking to define the appropriate standard of care.

The key question is how much (and what) does the law require us to do in order to avoid causing harm to others?

 Pause for reflection

Perhaps some of the most familiar cases of negligence in recent years have involved train crashes. These have often been followed by public inquiries (which investigate the cause of the tragedy and make recommendations to prevent similar accidents from happening in the future) and tort claims for compensation. In deciding these claims, courts raise similar public policy issues as they seek to strike a balance between ensuring safety and curtailing legitimate activities and commercial interests (*Cane* p 40). As Asquith LJ recognised back in 1946, 'if all the trains in this country were restricted to a speed of five miles an hour, there would be fewer accidents, but our national life would be intolerably slowed down. The purpose to be served, if sufficiently important, justifies the assumption of abnormal risk' (*Daborn* v *Bath Tramways* [1946] at 336). The balance can be a tricky one.

> Accidents happen, and sometimes they are what can be described as pure accidents in the sense that the victim cannot recover damages for the resulting injury because fault cannot be established. If the law were to set a higher standard of care than that which is reasonable . . . the consequences would quickly become inhibited. There would be no fêtes, no maypole dancing and none of the activities that have come to be associated with the English village green for fear of what might conceivably go wrong. (*Cole* v *Davies-Gilbert* at [36])

8.2 A test of reasonableness

The first thing to note about the standard of care in negligence is that it is *not* a standard of perfection. The standard allows for *some* errors and mistakes. As Lord Atkin held in **Donoghue v Stevenson**: 'You must take *reasonable care* to avoid acts or omissions which you can reasonably foresee would be *likely to injure* your neighbour' (580, emphasis added). The key requirement is then that the defendant behaves reasonably. Of course, this simply prompts the question: What standard of care did the circumstances require or, put another way, what behaviour was reasonable in the situation at hand?

The courts answer this question by comparing what the defendant has done to the imagined actions of the so-called 'reasonable man'. The question becomes what would a reasonable man in the position of the defendant have done in the circumstances? The upshot is that if the defendant has done something that the reasonable man *would not* have done or, alternatively, has omitted to do something that the reasonable man *would* have done, they will be in breach of their duty (*Hazell* v *British Transport Commission* [1958] at 171).

> Negligence is the omission to do something which the reasonable man, guided upon those considerations which ordinarily regulate the conduct of human affairs, would do, or doing something which a prudent and reasonable man would not do. (Alderson B, *Blyth v Birmingham Waterworks* [1856] at 784)

So who is this apparent paragon of virtue against whom all others are to be judged? Over the years various descriptions have been attempted often involving some mode of transport: the reasonable man is 'the man on the Clapham omnibus' (Lord Bowen, *Hall* v *Brooklands Auto-Racing Club* [1933] at 224) or, more recently, a 'traveller on the London underground' (Lord Steyn, *McFarlane* v *Tayside Health Board* [1999] at 82). Rather more grandly, he is 'the anthropomorphic conception of justice' (Lord Radcliffe, *Davis Contractors* v *Fareham Urban District Council* [1956] at 728), someone who is neither all-seeing nor all-knowing who at times makes *reasonable* mistakes. The phrase 'reasonable *man*' has undergone a good deal of criticism (especially from feminist legal scholars); however even if we adopt the more politically correct (if not less contentious) 'reasonable *person*' terminology, questions remain: What is his or her race, religion, class, sexual orientation, age, education, and so on?

> Is the reasonable person black, coloured or white? Male or female? Young, middle-aged or old? Christian, Muslim or of some other, or no, religion? Rich, poor or averagely affluent? Perhaps none of these differences between people is relevant, for instance, to questions about how a reasonable person would drive a car, but some or all of them may be thought relevant in some contexts. (*Cane* p 37)

Feminist critiques of the reasonable man

Some feminist legal scholars argue that the standard of the reasonable man embodies a male point of view and as such holds women to a standard devised without them in mind. However, the 'maleness' of the standard goes beyond a dislike of the way the standard is expressed: 'his gender-specificity is not just a linguistic convention, whereby both sexes are denoted by reference to the masculine: the reasonable man is, in fact, male' (Conaghan 1996, p 52).

What does this mean? There are a number of aspects to this critique. One focuses on the fact that the notion of the 'reasonable man' is not based on statistical evidence of what most people actually do think and do. Rather, it is a conception conjured up by the judges themselves, and so embodies a standard set and considered appropriate *by them*. Given the under-representation of women, ethnic minorities and so on within the judiciary, it can be argued that the 'reasonable man' and the standard *he* represents is likely to reflect the particular perspectives, assumptions and (possibly) prejudices of a subset of society— that is, those who make up the judiciary.

More controversially, it can be argued that the standard of reasonableness not only assumes, but *prioritises*, the ability to assume a position of detached objectivity from which to weigh up the costs and benefits of a particular course of action. This ability, it is argued, is one traditionally (and, perhaps, essentially) associated with men. If this is true, the very idea of applying 'a standard of reasonable care' seems to embody a peculiarly male way of thinking, one which does not take into account the different way women think and act. As such, the problem is not with the language of the reasonable 'man', but with the very notion of 'reasonableness'. In fact, it may well be 'dangerously misleading'—attributing to both (albeit in different ways) a 'false universality to what is in fact a partial and loaded standard' (Conaghan 1996, p 58).

The truth of the matter is, of course, that there is no such individual as the reasonable man (or indeed person). The reasonable man is a judicial construct—or shorthand—through which the judges seek to determine what was reasonable conduct in the circumstances of the particular case: the reasonable man is the personification, if you like, of the judicial view of reasonableness. Moreover, while it is likely (though not inevitable) that it will reflect the view of a judiciary that continues to be unrepresentative, this does not mean that the reasonable man is simply the personification of the judges themselves or that the reasonable man is merely a decoy behind which they can and do pursue their own preferences and prejudices.[1] Not least because there is a whole series of different rules that have been developed through the cases that define what we mean by the reasonable person; it is to these that we now turn.

8.3 **An objective standard**

The reasonable man, or person, test is objective. This means that the standard of care expected of the defendant is not dependent on, or skewed in favour of, certain characteristics and/or capabilities of the defendant; the personal idiosyncrasies of the defendant are largely (although, as we shall see, not completely) irrelevant (*Glasgow Corporation v Muir* [1943] at 457). Put simply (except for in a very few, limited, circumstances) the appropriate question is not 'what could *this particular* defendant have done?' but rather 'what level of care and skill did the activity the defendant was undertaking require?' Put another way, even though certain individuals may, due to certain inherent characteristics (for example age, experience and so on), be more or less able to take care, the law (usually) imposes the same standard of care on everyone. The defendant cannot usually argue against, or raise as a defence in response to, the imposition of liability on the grounds that they 'did their best' according to their education, experience, health and so on where their best falls below the standard of care expected of the reasonable man.

As will be seen below, this is not always true. The courts have developed a number of modifications to the general standard, for example in relation to children and people professing to have a particular skill. Nevertheless, the more general point that the reasonable man standard is objective remains valid.

Nettleship v Weston [1971] CA

The claimant had agreed to give the defendant driving lessons. The learner driver was holding the steering wheel and controlling the pedals, while the claimant moved the gear lever and hand brake. Unfortunately, after turning a corner, the defendant failed to straighten up and panicked. Despite her best efforts and the fact that the car was only travelling at walking pace, the car mounted the pavement and hit a lamp post, breaking the claimant's

➡

---

1. Although cf *Cane* (p 39) who argues that the reasonable person is invoked to obscure the role of the judge as a policy-maker.

> ➜
>
> knee cap. The defendant was later convicted of driving without due care and attention. The claimant sued in negligence.
>
> The majority of the Court of Appeal held that all drivers, *including those learning to drive*, are held to the same standard: 'The standard of care...is measured objectively by the care to be expected of an experienced, skilled and careful driver' (at 702). The standard of care in negligence is not dependent on the particular defendant's characteristics and/ or capacities. The fact that, as a learner, she was by definition incapable of meeting this standard was irrelevant: 'The learner driver may be doing his best, but his incompetent best is not good enough. He must drive in as good a manner as a driver of skill, experience and care' (at 699).
>
> The claimant's damages were ultimately reduced by 50 per cent for contributory negligence as he was jointly controlling the car at the time of the accident.

The decision of the Court of Appeal in **Nettleship v Weston** is perhaps a little harsh. As a learner driver she was unable to reach the standard of care to which she was ultimately held.[2] Moreover, the claimant was well aware of her limited driving capabilities. He was in the car *because he had agreed to give the defendant driving lessons.* As Salmon LJ, in dissent, noted, a learner driver cannot owe an instructor a duty to drive with a degree of skill they both know is not possessed (at 705). However, the majority took the opposite view and upheld the objective standard, thereby avoiding the 'endless confusion and injustice' that would follow should the standard of care be varied according to someone's knowledge of another's skill (at 700).

 Counterpoint

The claim is that the decision in *Nettleship* promotes fairness in that it applies the same standard to all drivers, and ensures that victims of road accidents do not lose out simply because they were unlucky enough to be injured by someone who is learning to drive. The alternative is that the innocent victim of a learner driver who had driven as well as could be expected (albeit to a standard somewhat lower than that expected of an experienced driver) would be denied compensation. So viewed, the 'objective standard of care can be understood as the law's attempt to strike a fair balance between the competing interests in freedom of action and personal security that we all share' (*Cane* p 49).

However, we would argue just as strongly that the decision promotes injustice. The reason we make liability in negligence conditional upon the defendant having failed to exercise reasonable care (rather than, for instance, making liability strict) is that it is only where the defendant is at fault in causing the claimant's injuries that the law should require the defendant to pay compensation. Corrective justice does not require that we compensate

➜

---

2. Indeed the High Court in Australia, in a case on very similar facts, refused to follow **Nettleship** describing it as 'contrary to common sense and the concept of what is reasonable in the circumstances' (*Cook* v *Cook* [1986]) (though in this case the defendant had fallen below the (lower) standard of care required of a learner driver).

> ➡
>
> all the harms we cause, only those that we cause through our fault or neglect. The problem with *Nettleship* is that it imposes liability without genuine fault.
>
> It may be that the decision in *Nettleship* is best understood as resting on a much more pragmatic motivating factor—compulsory motor insurance. The majority judges 'see to it' that the defendant is liable so that the claimant can be compensated out of the insurance fund (at 700). In so doing, the Court of Appeal elevates the function of tort as a mechanism of compensation over that of achieving corrective justice, something that Lord Denning MR clearly recognises:
>
> > Thus we are, in this branch of the law, moving away from the concept: 'No liability without fault'. We are beginning to apply the test: 'On whom should the risk fall?' Morally the learner driver is not at fault; but legally she is liable to be because she is insured and the risk should fall on her. (at 700)
>
> Ultimately, of course, the direct loss falls neither on the claimant nor the defendant but on the defendant's insurance company (and in turn other insurance policy holders). The fault principle is subordinated not only to ensure the claimant is compensated, but also to the loss-shifting goals of distributive justice.

The objective standard of care, independent of the characteristics and capacities of the defendant, was taken to an extreme in *Roberts* v *Ramsbottom* [1980]. In this case, the defendant had (unknowingly) suffered a stroke before starting to drive into town (though he realised his consciousness was impaired, he was unaware that he was unfit to drive). As he was driving along, he suddenly began to feel much worse. He subsequently collided with a stationary van, narrowly avoided two men working in the road, knocked a cyclist onto the pavement, before ploughing into the claimant's car, seriously injuring the claimant and damaging the car. The defendant argued that from the moment of his stroke he was unable, through no fault of his own, to control his car properly or appreciate that he was unfit to drive. Neill J disagreed. Though the defendant was in no way morally to blame, he was nonetheless liable in the tort of negligence. He had fallen below the objective standard of the reasonable driver in relation to both in his collision with the claimant and also in continuing to drive despite feeling increasingly unwell and following his earlier collision with the parked van, even though he was, at the time, unable to appreciate their significance (though it was acknowledged that if he had suffered a complete loss of consciousness he may have had a defence of 'automatism').

Nettleship and *Roberts* v *Ramsbottom*, therefore, appear to be cases where liability in negligence was imposed even though the defendant was not (or may not have been) genuinely at fault. However, the relevance of fault was reasserted in a similar case a few years later, *Mansfield* v *Weetabix Ltd* [1998], where the Court of Appeal held that the defendant was not liable for the damage caused to a shop (and shop owner's home) when the lorry he was driving crashed into it. Unknown to the defendant, he had malignant insulinoma, which resulted in a hypoglycaemic state, starving his brain of glucose so that it was unable to function properly. Although the final accident that formed the basis of the claim was the culmination of a gradual lowering of his blood sugar level (in the course of 40 miles the lorry driver had been involved in three distinct incidents, one of which involved the police), at no time had he been aware of his condition (crucially, had he had an inkling of this, he would, following *Roberts* v *Ramsbottom*, have been liable). The standard of care applied by the court was of 'a reasonably competent driver unaware that he is or may be suffering from a condition that impairs his ability to drive' (at 1268) which, on the facts of the case, the actions of the defendant did not fall below.

 Pause for reflection

Of course, the practical result of *Mansfield* v *Weetabix* is that the claimants were left uncompensated; the pot of insurance money (at least on the side of the defendants) remained untouched. However, unlike the Court of Appeal in **Nettleship**, the appeal judges in *Mansfield*, although aware of the harshness of the decision to the claimants, were nevertheless unwilling to find the innocent lorry driver liable simply in order to compensate the claimants (who, after all, should have had their own *household* insurance). Responsibility for any change in the law, they argued, lay at the feet of Parliament (at 1268). Which approach do you prefer? Why? Think again about the arguments made above in relation to **Nettleship**.

As seen in *Mansfield* v *Weetabix*, the courts do modify the general rule that the standard of care is objective to take into account *certain* characteristics of *some* defendants. In the same vein, it is likely that, for example, where a driver is injured trying to avoid a blind or elderly pedestrian, an allowance would be made for their physical disability or infirmity when assessing whether the pedestrian took reasonable care. The situation would, of course, be different if the defendant had not taken all available precautions and was engaging in an activity that, given their condition, was inherently risky.

8.3.1 **Children**

The objective standard of care is relaxed slightly in relation to children. Here the courts acknowledge that the capacity of children to recognise the dangers of a particular activity, take care to avoid them and not hurt others varies according to the age of the child (unlike in criminal law there is no minimum age for liability in tort). The standard of care is that which can be 'objectively expected of a child of that age' (*Orchard* v *Lee* [2009]), that is 'whether any ordinary child of 13½ [for example] can be expected to have done any more than this child did. I say "any ordinary child". I do not mean a paragon of prudence; nor do I mean a scatter-brained child; but the ordinary girl of 13½' (*Gough* v *Thorne* [1966]). The objective standard remains, it is simply scaled according to age.

Orchard **v** *Lee* **[2009] CA**

Two 13-year-old boys were playing a game of tag in a courtyard and walkway designated for their year group during their school lunch break. During the course of the game the defendant was running backwards, taunting the other boy. Unfortunately he ran into the

→

→

claimant, who was working as a lunchtime assistant supervisor at the school. The back of his head hit her cheek and though the injury initially seemed slight, it later became quite serious. The trial judge dismissed the supervisor's claim finding that 'it was a simple accident caused by "horseplay between two 13-year-old boys in and around an outside courtyard...boys doing what boys do"' (at [2]).

The Court of Appeal agreed. A child will only be held liable in negligence if their conduct is careless to a very high degree or falls significantly outside the norm for a child of their age. In assessing whether this is the case 'the question is whether a reasonable 13-year-old boy, in the situation that [the defendant] was in, would have anticipated that some significant personal injury would result from his actions (Aikens LJ at [24]). As there was nothing to suggest that the defendant was playing tag 'in a manner in which a 13-year-old boy would reasonably foresee there was likely to be injury beyond that normally occurring while a game of tag was in progress', the defendant had not fallen below the standard of care required of him (Waller LJ at [12]).

 Pause for reflection

As noted in the Australian case of *McHale* v *Watson*, 'Children, like everyone else, must accept as they go about in society the risks from which ordinary care on the part of others will not suffice to save them. One such risk is that boys of 12 may behave as boys of 12' (at 216). Or, indeed, that 15-year-old schoolgirls will 'play as somewhat irresponsible girls of 15' (*Mullin* v *Richards* at 1312).

The 'reasonable child' standard invoked by the court effectively prevents a child-defendant's action being measured against a standard of care that they are unable to reach. Can this be reconciled with the Court of Appeal's decision in **Nettleship v Weston**?

8.3.2 Common practice and special skills

Where a person professes to have a special skill or competence, the law requires that when dealing with people in the context of a calling or profession they do so with an appropriate level of competence.

> Nobody expects the passenger on the Clapham omnibus to have any skill as a surgeon, a lawyer, a pilot, or a plumber, unless he is one; but if he professes to be one, then the law requires him to show such a skill as any ordinary member of the profession or calling to which he belongs, or claims to belong, would display.[3]

Thus, in *Phillips* v *William Whiteley* [1938] the court denied a claim for damages in respect of an infection the claimant developed after having her ears pierced in a jewellery store. The claimant could expect only that they were pierced to the standard of a reasonably competent jeweller; ear-piercing is not something which requires a surgical level of skill.[4]

---

3. *Rogers* (17th edn, 2006), p 277.

4. See also *Wells* v *Cooper* [1958] in which a do-it-yourself carpenter was not liable for injuries caused by his failure to use adequate screws to fix a door handle. The standard of care expected of a reasonably competent non-professional carpenter is lower than required of a professional carpenter.

Typically, a defendant cannot escape liability in negligence simply by arguing that they followed common practice: 'Neglect of duty does not cease by repetition to be neglect of duty' (*Bank of Montreal* v *Dominion Gresham Guarantee and Casualty Company* [1930] at 666). Thus, for example, in *Thompson* v *Smiths Ship Repairers (North Shields) Ltd* [1984], a group of shipbuilders claimed for loss of hearing as a consequence of their employers failing to provide sufficient (or indeed any) ear protection or to give the necessary advice to encourage the workers to wear it.[5] They had all been working in the ship-building yards since at least 1944. The defendants knew that the level of noise in their yards was such that there was a risk of hearing loss, however there was a general apathy throughout the industry about the risk. Ear muffs or protectors were not provided until the mid to late 1970s. However, since the mid-1960s, official guidance warned of such risks and effective and comfortable ear protectors were available. The court held that the employers could rely only on the general practice of inaction within the industry until the advances of the 1960s. From then on, however, the dangers were well known and the defendants were in breach of their duty of care toward their employees for failing to provide ear protection. This meant that the claimants were unable to claim for the full extent of their hearing loss since much of it had occurred before the defendants were in breach (during the period from 1944 to the mid-1960s). Thus they could recover damages only for the period between the mid-1960s and when ear protection was finally provided.

8.3.2.1 The *Bolam* test

However, there is one important exception to this rule. The courts give wide latitude to professionals, acting in their professional capacity, to determine the standards by which they are to be judged. In cases where the defendant has a special skill or competence (that is, a skill that the reasonable man ordinarily does not have) and the circumstances are such that they are required to exercise that skill or competence, the courts have developed a different approach. In such cases, the actions of the defendant are judged against those of the ordinary skilled man *professing to exercise that skill*— this is the so-called *Bolam* test.

Bolam v *Friern Hospital Management Committee* [1957] QBD

A patient was given electro-convulsive therapy without being given a relaxant drug and without the appropriate physical restraints. In the course of the treatment the patient/claimant sustained a fractured hip, a possible consequence of the treatment about which he had not been warned. At the time, the medical profession held conflicting views on whether it was necessary to administer relaxant drugs before the procedure as a way of reducing the likelihood of injury and whether it was necessary to warn the patient of the risk of injury.

→

This may appear at odds with the decision in *Nettleship* and *Wilsher* (below)—however a DIY enthusiast is not a 'learner' or 'trainee' professional carpenter in the same way as a learner driver or junior doctor.

5. On an employer's duty of care see further Chapter 12, pp 312–317.

> ➡
>
> In assessing the standard of care, the court held:
>
> a man need not possess the highest expert skill...it is sufficient if he exercises the ordinary skill of an ordinary competent man exercising that particular art...[and acts] in accordance with a practice accepted as proper by a responsible body of medical men skilled in that particular art. (McNair J at 586)
>
> As such, the defendant was not in breach of their duty as other responsible doctors would have acted in the same way.

It is clear that **Bolam** applies to *all* professionals exercising a special skill or competence. In *Moy* v *Pettman Smith* [2005], a case involving a claim in negligence against a barrister, Baroness Hale approved Lord Hobhouse's view in *Arthur JS Hall & Co* v *Simons* [2002] that:

> the standard of care to be applied in negligence actions against an advocate is the same as that applicable to any other skilled professional who has to work in an environment where decisions and exercises of judgment have to be made in often difficult and time-constrained circumstances. It requires a [claimant] to show that the error was one which no reasonably competent member of the relevant profession would have made. (at [25])

A distinction is drawn between the defendant's 'rank or status' and the 'post' they hold at the time of the suspected breach (**Wilsher v Essex Area Health Authority** [1988] **(CA)** at 751). Where the defendant is occupying a particular post, their conduct will be assessed according to the standard reasonably expected of someone occupying such a post. The law makes no allowances for inexperience or for the fact that everyone must, to a certain extent, gain practical experience 'on the job'. Thus in **Wilsher**, a junior doctor was held to the standards of the more senior post they were occupying at the time, notwithstanding the fact that this was effectively part of their training: 'the standard is not just that of the averagely competent and well-informed junior houseman (or whatever the position of the doctor) but of such a person who fills a post in a unit offering a highly specialised service' (at 751).[6]

What this means in practice is that the courts generally defer to the standards of a particular profession as to what is considered appropriate behaviour. This is important: 'judges are not qualified to make professional judgements on the practices of other learned professions...A professional should not be penalised, and held to be incompetent, just because a judge fancies at "playing" at being architect, solicitor or doctor' (Brazier and Miola 2000, p 87). However, a balance needs to be struck between respect for expert opinions and showing them undue deference. Traditionally, this is most acute in relation to the medical profession. Following **Bolam**, a doctor will not have fallen below the standard of care expected of a reasonable doctor, if they have acted in accordance with a respectable body of the medical profession (even if it is a minority viewpoint). However, this is qualified by the 'gloss' applied by the House of Lords in *Bolitho* v *City and Hackney Health Authority* [1998]. It is now the case that 'doctor knows

6. Note this is the Court of Appeal decision. This matter was not discussed when the case went to the House of Lords.

best' *only* 'if he [sic] acts reasonably and logically and gets his facts right'.[7] What this means is that the **Bolam** test is now better understood as a two-stage test:

(1) Has the doctor acted in accordance to a practice accepted as proper by a respectable body of medical opinion?

(2) If yes, is the practice itself 'reasonable' and 'logical'.[8]

Importantly, as Mulheron notes, the courts have not added (nor felt able to add) a third stage in which it chooses between two reasonable and logical schools of thought:

> it is *not* for the court to venture into a consideration of two contrary bodies of opinion and to decide the case on the basis of which, of the patient's and the doctor's expert medical opinion, it prefers... Once *Bolam* applies, the fact of differences in expert opinion cannot lead to a rejection of *Bolam* evidence.[9]

The upshot of *Bolitho* is that the common practices of a profession do not go unchecked.[10] If a particular practice, even if widely accepted within a profession, is logically insupportable, a defendant cannot escape liability simply by showing that others would have acted as they did.

 Counterpoint

It has traditionally been argued that the courts are reluctant to impose liability on members of the medical profession for a number of policy-orientated reasons.[11] These include the importance of the doctor's reputation as a member of a respectable and responsible profession, a reluctance to interfere in a specialised branch of knowledge, the view that doctors are motivated by altruistic reasons and that it would therefore be unjust to penalise them for every error and, finally, a fear of increased claims and defensive medical practices (Sheldon 1998, pp 20–1).

In her exploration of the gendered dimensions of the **Bolam** principle and its conflation of *accepted* with *acceptable* practice (p 19), Sally Sheldon suggests a number of alternative policy arguments which could lead to more claims succeeding. These include the need to compensate the victims of medical misadventures, the potential of negligence claims to discourage bad practice and reinforce the accountability of the doctors, especially given their high status and remuneration, the failure to recognise the vulnerability of the patient in the doctor/patient relationship and, crucially, the existence of liability insurance.

Which of these two positions do you find more persuasive?

---

7. Lord Woolf 'Are the Courts Excessively Deferential to the Medical Profession?' (2001) 9 *Medical Law Review* 1–16 at 1.

8. Mulheron 2010, p 613.

9. Mulheron 2010, p 614. See further *Ministry of Justice* v *Carter* [2010] in which the Court of Appeal overturned the decision of a trial judge who had done just this.

10. Though this approach has developed in the context of medical practice it has been held to have 'considerable force' in other professional contexts (*JD Williams & Co Ltd* v *Michael Hyde & Associates Ltd* [2000] at [25]–[26]).

11. In fact, the NHS Litigation Authority reports that fewer than 4 per cent of the cases handled by them end up in court. The remainder settled out of court or abandoned by the claimant. In 2009/10 £787 million was paid by the NHSLA for clinical negligence claims (*NHS Litigation Authority Report and Accounts* 2010).

The assumption that 'doctor knows best' is especially controversial in relation to warning patients of the risks of treatment. In *Sidaway v Bethlem Royal Hospital* [1985], the claimant was paralysed while undergoing an operation on her back. There was no evidence of negligence in the performance of the operation, rather the claimant argued she should have been told of the known (although very small) risk of paralysis and that, had she been told, she would not have had the operation. The majority of the House of Lords held that the doctor was not liable. However, attention should be paid to Lord Scarman's dissent, arguing for a 'prudent patient' test: the courts 'cannot stand idly by if the profession, by an excess of paternalism, denies its patients real choice. In a word, the law will not allow the medical profession to play God' (at 1028). *Sidaway* has been severely criticised and, though it has not be overruled, **Chester v Afshar** [2005] (although on a different issue) appears to show a more generous approach to patient autonomy and greater willingness on the part of the courts to recognise that doctors do not always know best.[12] In this case, the majority of the House of Lords held that a doctor had breached his duty of care by not informing the patient of a very small risk, which accompanied the course of treatment he was suggesting. Moreover, the law lords thought it was so important that a patient be able to make an informed choice about a course of treatment that they were willing to extend the rules on causation in order to allow her claim: 'Her right of autonomy and dignity can and ought to be vindicated by a narrow and modest departure from traditional causation principles' (Lord Steyn at [24]).[13]

8.4 Setting the standard of care

Having determined that the courts generally apply a common standard, we now need to consider how the courts go about *setting* that standard. When seeking to define the standard of care required of the defendant—that is, what the defendant *ought* to have done or what is *reasonable* in the circumstances of the case—the courts take a number of factors into account: probability or risk of the injury; the seriousness of the injury; the cost of taking precautions; and the social value of the activity.

It is important to note that though the courts do not (usually) take into account the characteristics of the individual defendant, they do take into account the circumstances of the situation in which the accident or injury occurred. The standard of care does not exist in the abstract: 'The law in all cases exacts a degree of care commensurate with the risk' (Lord Macmillan, *Read v Lyons Co Ltd* [1947] at 173). So, if we ask what is a reasonable speed to drive, the answer of course will vary—the reasonable car driver will drive at different speeds at different times and according to different circumstances.

Some examples may help here. All things being equal, it is reasonable to drive at 70 mph on a clear motorway but not on residential streets. It will be reasonable to drive faster in clear weather conditions than when it is pouring with rain or foggy. Why is this? The answer is straightforward. The risks posed by driving at 70 mph in a residential street are higher than those on a clear motorway. Similarly, accidents are more likely in adverse weather conditions. The reasonable driver may be expected to

12. See also *Birch v University College Hospital NHS Trust* [2008].
13. On the causation aspects of this case see Chapter 9, pp 237–238.

take more care near a school, where potential injuries may not only be more likely (for example, a child running out from behind a parked car) but more severe (the child is more likely to be more seriously injured than an adult) compared with circumstances where they have an injured friend in the back of their car who they are rushing to hospital (where the social utility of their act may outweigh the risks it creates).

8.4.1 **Probability that the injury will occur**

One of the first factors the courts will take into account is how likely it was that injury would occur? The general rule is the more likely—or foreseeable—the outcome, the greater the possibility that the courts will find the defendants liable for failing to take steps to avoid it.

***Bolton v Stone* [1951] HL**

The claimant was hit on the head outside her house by a cricket ball hit by a player from an adjacent cricket pitch. The hit was substantial, although possibly not exceptional. The ball had travelled some 100 yards (approx 91 m) and over a seven-foot fence (which, due to the slope of the pitch, was in effect 17 feet high). The claimant sued in negligence and nuisance.

The House of Lords, rejecting both claims,[14] held that although there was evidence that over a period of years balls had been hit out of the ground, this was, in fact, very rare (six times in 30 years). Thus, although the possibility of a ball being hit out of the ground was foreseeable, this was not sufficient to establish negligence since the chances of the ball hitting someone were so low that a reasonable person would not have taken precautions to stop it happening.

The standard of care in the law of negligence is the standard of an ordinarily careful man, but in my opinion an ordinarily careful man does not take precautions against every foreseeable risk...He takes precautions against risks which are reasonably likely to happen...there are many footpaths and highways adjacent to cricket grounds and golf courses on to which cricket and golf balls are occasionally driven, but such risks are habitually treated both by the owners and committees of such cricket and golf courses and by the pedestrians who use the adjacent footpaths and highways as negligible and it is not, in my opinion, actionable negligence not to take precautions to avoid such risks. (Lord Oaksey at 863)

In *Harris* v *Perry* [2008], a case involving the liability of a parent for serious injuries sustained by a child using a bouncy castle hired for her children's birthday party, the Court of Appeal, rejecting the claim, held that what mattered was not merely whether *some* harm was foreseeable but also the *severity* of the foreseeable harm:

A reasonable parent could foresee that if children indulged in boisterous behaviour on a bouncy castle, there would be a risk that, sooner or later, one child might collide with

---

14. It was agreed that nuisance could not be established unless negligence is proved (at 860).

another and cause that child some physical injury of a type that can be an incident of some contact sports. We do not consider that it was reasonably foreseeable that such injury would be likely to be serious, let alone as severe as the injury sustained by the claimant. (Lord Phillips CJ at [38])

It is clear from the cases that the conduct of the defendant is assessed from the position the defendant is imagined to be in at the time; it is a test of foresight, not hindsight (***Roe*** **v** ***Ministry of Health*** **[1954]**). If something seems to be acceptable at the time—that is, if the risk of injury is low—then it is unlikely to be considered negligent.

Roe v *Ministry of Health* [1954] CA

The claimants were paralysed after being injected with a contaminated nupercaine (a spinal anaesthetic) during a routine, minor operation. The nupercaine had been contained in sealed glass ampoules and stored in a solution of phenol prior to use. Unknown to the hospital, the phenol had percolated into the ampoules through invisible cracks or molecular flaws, causing the claimants' paralysis.

Rejecting the claims, the Court of Appeal held that, though it was clear in hindsight that the hospital was at fault, *at the time of the operation* neither the anaesthetist nor any of the hospital staff knew of the dangers of storing glass ampoules in the phenol solution. The test applied was the standard of medical knowledge when the accident occurred in 1947: 'We must not look at the 1947 accident with 1954 spectacles' (Denning LJ at 84).

  Pause for reflection

A leading medical textbook published in 1951 (after the accident which formed the basis of the claim in *Roe*) warns medical practitioners to ensure that they 'never place ampoules of local anaesthetic solution in alcohol or spirit. This common practice is probably responsible for some cases of permanent paralysis reported after spinal analgesia' (*Roe* at 86). In fact, it was the extraordinary accident to the two claimants in *Roe* which first alerted the medical profession to the danger. However, the costs of this medical advance were borne solely by the unfortunate men. This apparent injustice was justified by Denning LJ thus:

we should be doing a disservice to the community at large if we impose liability on hospitals and doctors for everything that happens to go wrong... Initiatives would be stifled and confidence shaken... We must insist on due care for the patient at every point, but we must not condemn as negligence that which is only a misadventure. (at 87)

Do you agree? Compare Denning LJ's reasoning here with that in *Nettleship*—why do you think he adopted such a markedly different approach in this case?

8.4.2 **Seriousness of the injury**

The second factor the courts take into account is the seriousness of the injury should it occur. Generally, the more serious the potential injury the more likely the defendant will be found to have fallen below the required standard of care should it materialise: 'the law expects of a man a great deal more care in carrying a pound of dynamite than a pound of butter' (Singleton LJ, quoting Percy H Winfield, in *Beckett* v *Newalls Insulation Co Ltd* [1953] at 15). One illustration from the case law will suffice here.

Paris v *Stepney Borough Council* [1951] HL

A man, employed as a garage hand, suffered serious injury when a metal chip flew into one of his eyes while he was working. Unfortunately, he was already (as his employers knew) blind in his other eye. The injury, therefore, left him effectively blind. He sued his employers, claiming they were negligent in failing to provide safety goggles and to require their use as part of a safe system of work.

The majority of the House of Lords agreed. Though the chance of injury was low, the seriousness of the consequences should an accident occur must also be taken into account when assessing the precautions a reasonable employer should take to ensure the safety of their workforce. The provision of safety goggles was 'obviously necessary when a one-eyed man was put to [this] kind of work' (at 383).

8.4.3 **Cost of taking precautions**

The courts also consider the cost to the defendant of taking precautions against the risk. The lower the cost—whether in terms of time or money—the more reasonable it is that someone should take them. Thus, it is likely (all things being equal) that the courts would consider a driver who fails to slow down while driving near a school at the end of the school day to have fallen below the standard of care required of a reasonable driver; the cost to the driver of driving more slowly is unlikely to be seen as unreasonably high. If, on the other hand, the cost of taking precautions is very onerous, it is less likely that it will be unreasonable for the defendants to guard against it (***Latimer*** v ***AEC Ltd*** [1953];[15] see also *Webster* v *Ridgeway Foundation School* [2010]).

The courts are also reluctant to interfere with the budgetary decisions made in relation to limited resources by public authorities. In *Knight* v *Home Office* [1990], a mentally ill prisoner committed suicide. As a known suicide risk, he had been observed every 15 minutes. The court recognised that while lack of funds could never be a complete defence to insufficient safety precautions, the facilities of a prison hospital were necessarily different to a specialist psychiatric hospital and so, on the facts, there was no breach.

One precaution that is, perhaps, relatively easy to undertake is to give a warning. While it may not avoid the danger completely, it might reduce the damage the danger causes. In *Al-Kandari* v *JR Brown & Co* [1988], a firm of solicitors failed to warn the claimant that her husband (who had previously kidnapped their children and taken them to Kuwait) had obtained his passport from the Kuwaiti Embassy where it had been taken to have the children's names removed. On retrieving his passport, the husband had attacked the claimant, leaving her bound and gagged in a van and taken the children. The claimant had not seen her children since. The Court of Appeal held that the firm had breached their duty of care to the claimant by failing to inform her

---

15. The facts of ***Latimer*** are discussed in Chapter 12, p 317.

that the Embassy had retained the passport or that arrangements had been made for the husband to go there the following day.

8.4.4 **Social value of the activity**

While an assessment of the 'cost of taking precautions' goes to the *private* costs of adhering to a particular standard of care imposed on the individual, this final factor relates to the social costs of the activity.

There is no special exemption for any of the emergency services from the law of negligence.[16] The question remains whether the defendant has behaved as a reasonable man, although, in so deciding, the court takes into account the emergency in which the defendant acts. The standard of care will be lower where the defendant is acting in the 'heat of the moment' or in an emergency or rescue situation (***Watt v Hertfordshire County Council* [1954]**). The greater the social value of the activity, the more likely the courts will find it reasonable to have dispensed with safety precautions.

Watt v Hertfordshire County Council [1954] CA

A fireman was seriously injured by lifting-gear while travelling in the back of a lorry on the way to an accident where a woman was trapped under a heavy vehicle. The lorry had not been specially fitted to carry the gear in an emergency.

The Court of Appeal, rejecting the fireman's claim, held that the public benefit justified taking the risks associated with failing adequately to secure the lifting-gear in the back of the lorry.

> It is well settled that in measuring due care you must balance the risk against the measures necessary to eliminate the risk. To that proposition there ought to be added this: you must balance the risk against the end to be achieved...The saving of life or limb justifies taking considerable risk. (Denning LJ at 838)

If, therefore, the same accident had occurred in pursuit of a commercial end then the claimant would have recovered: 'the commercial end to make a profit is very different from the human end to safe life or limb' (at 838).

Similarly, the courts recognise that participants in sporting events (including 'horse-play' (*Blake* v *Galloway* [2004])) are concentrating on winning the game or race and so are inevitably going to pay less attention to what is going on around them. Thus, in *Wooldridge* v *Sumner* [1963], a photographer who was injured while working at the National Horse Show was unable to recover damages. One of the riders he was photographing had come round the corner of the arena at excessive speed causing the horse to become temporarily out of control and crash into some shrubs near the claimant. The claimant 'took fright' in the commotion, fell into the path of the horse and was seriously injured. Rejecting his claim, the Court of Appeal held that 'provided the competition or game is being performed within the rules and the requirements of the

---

16. See e.g. *Henry* v *Chief Constable of Thames Valley* [2010].

sport and by a person of adequate skill and competence, the spectator does not expect his safety to be regarded by the participant' (at 56). In the absence of recklessness or an intention to harm the claimant, the horse rider was free to concentrate on winning the competition.

However, although the standard of care owed between participants in a sporting event is lower, it is never eliminated entirely (*Caldwell* v *Maguire* [2002]).[17] Thus while a footballer may have to put up with the odd foul or high tackle, where these fall below what could be reasonably expected in anyone playing the game, liability will arise (*Condon* v *Basi* [1985]).[18] The objective standard of care in competitive sports will alter according to the level at which it is played. The standard of care expected of a footballer in a premiership match will be higher than that of a Sunday league player.[19]

It is clear from *Scout Association* v *Barnes* [2010] that the social value of an activity *as a whole* does not mean that *all* examples of that activity are acceptable, whatever the risk (at [46]). In this case, the claimant was injured while playing a game called 'Objects in the Dark' which involved running around a pile of wooden blocks in a scout hall and attempting to grab a block once the lights were switched off (with only minimal lighting provided by emergency exit lights). The majority of the Court of Appeal upheld the trial judge's decision that the defendant had breached its duty—the value of playing the game in the dark as a way of adding 'spice' to increase the boys' enjoyment of the game did not justify the additional risk: 'the particular justification for playing this game in the dark was only that it added excitement. The darkness did not add any other social or educative value but it did significantly increase the risk of injury...the added excitement of playing the game in the dark, which might well encourage boys to attend scouts—a desirable objective—did not justify the increased foreseeable risk' (Smith LJ at 46).

 Pause for reflection

Though it is clear from the majority judgments in *Barnes* that the trial judge had appropriately weighed the costs and benefits of the competing factors at issue in the case, there is considerable force in Ward LJ's opening paragraph:

I have to confess that I have found it uncommonly difficult to reach a confident judgment in this case. Here was a big strong thirteen year old lad, well-used to rough and tumble, playing rugby with distinction for his county, ever ready to take the bumps and the bruises, ever willingly to put his body on the line for the thrill of his sport. For him, you get hurt, you get up, and you get on with it. He brought the same enthusiasm and competitive instincts to his participation in his local Scout troop. He was the least likely boy to need wrapping in cotton wool. So, is awarding him damages for an injury

→

---

17. See in relation to the standard of care expected of referees and organisers of sporting events *Vowles* v *Evans* [2003] and *Watson* v *British Boxing Board of Control Ltd* [2001].

18. In this way *Condon* v *Basi* appears to depart from **Nettleship** (which was not considered by the court).

19. Of course, even if negligence is established, the defendant may still raise a defence (usually *volenti or contributory negligence*) against the claim (see Chapter 10).

> →
>
> suffered playing the game, 'Objects in the Dark', not an example of an overprotective nanny state robbing youth of fun simply because there was some risk involved in the exercise? Is this a decision which emasculates those responsible for caring for our children and in so doing, enfeebles the children themselves? Where do you draw the line? I have found that hard to answer. (at [50])
>
> Do you think that the majority drew the line correctly in this case?

8.5 A balancing act

In essence, when determining the standard of care required by the defendant, the courts are engaged in a balancing act. As Lord Hoffmann noted in **Tomlinson v Congleton Borough Council** [2004]:

> the question of what amounts to 'such care as is in all the circumstances of the case is reasonable' depends upon assessing…not only the likelihood that someone may be injured and the seriousness of the injury which may occur, but also the social value of the activity which gives rise to the risk and the cost of preventative measure. These factors have to be balanced against each other. (at [34])

No factor is viewed in isolation from the others (although one, or more, may be more important in a particular case). In each case the courts weigh up the likelihood of injury and the seriousness of harm against the cost of taking precautions and the social value of the activity before coming to a decision as to what was reasonable in all the circumstances of the case—what the reasonable man would have done. A case example may help here.

> **Overseas Tankship (UK) Ltd v Miller Steamship Co Pty Ltd (The Wagon Mound) (No 2) [1967][20] PC**
>
> The defendants were transferring furnace oil from a nearby wharf onto a vessel, the *Wagon Mound*, which was moored in Sydney Harbour. Due to carelessness on the part of the engineer, a large quantity of the oil spilled into the harbour where it accumulated around the wharf and the claimants' vessels. The owners of the wharf (who were the claimants in the first of the *Wagon Mound* cases) were carrying out repairs on the claimants' ships which caused pieces of hot metal to fly off and into the wharf. On one such occasion it is thought that the metal fell onto some object supporting a piece of inflammable material in the oil-covered water, which ignited. This caused the oil to catch alight and the ensuing fire quickly destroyed the wharf and the claimants' vessels.
>
> →

20. Note this is the second of the *Wagon Mound* cases. The first case, **Overseas Tankship (UK) Ltd v Morts Dock & Engineering Co Ltd (The Wagon Mound) (No 1)** [1961], was brought by the owners of the wharf and is discussed in Chapter 9, pp 247–249.

→

The Privy Council held that although the chance of the oil catching fire was very low it was nevertheless a real one and, given the very grave consequences should the risk materialise, there was no justification for their failure to take steps to eliminate it. Moreover, it was easy for the claimants to prevent the spillage (had they taken reasonable care in the first place when filling up the vessel). On this basis, the defendants had fallen below the standard of care required—the reasonable man would have taken precautions.

If a real risk is one which would occur to the mind of a reasonable man in the position of the defendant's servant and which he would not brush aside as far-fetched . . . then surely he would not neglect such a risk if action to eliminate if it presented no difficulty, involved no disadvantage, and required no expense. (at 643–4)

 Pause for reflection

This process through which the courts distinguish between acceptable and unacceptable carelessness—that is, the balancing of the probability (P) and likely seriousness of injury (L) against the private and social costs[21] (B) of the necessary precautions—was reduced to a quasi-mathematical formula by a US judge named Learned Hand J (*United States* v *Carroll Towing Co* [1947]).

$B < LP$ = a reasonable person would take precautions = defendant liable if they do not take precautions

$B > LP$ = a reasonable person would not take precautions = defendant not liable if they do not take precautions

The 'Learned Hand test' holds that where the private and social costs of taking precautions (B) is less than the probability (P) multiplied by the likelihood of injury (L), the defendant will be held to have fallen below the standard of care of the reasonable man if they fail to take such precautions. Conversely, where the costs of taking precautions (B) are greater than the probability (P) multiplied by the seriousness of the injury (L) occurring, it would be unreasonable to expect the defendant to take such precautions.

Of course, the formula only tells us so much. Nevertheless, it remains a helpful *illustration* of the sort of balancing exercises the courts are undertaking when setting the appropriate standard of care in all the circumstances of the case.

21. 'Social costs' include not only financial but also 'immeasurable "soft" values such as community concepts of justice, health, life and freedom of conduct' (*Western Suburbs Hospital* v *Currie* [1987]). It may be that a measure may be unjustifiable on these grounds even though it does not cost much. However, the assessment of community values can be problematic. How are we to compare, to use *Cane*'s example, the social value of playing cricket with the safety of passers-by so as to decide whether it is negligent to play cricket without a fence (p 42)?

Counterpoint

It has been argued that the Learned Hand test is essentially an economic one: 'If it can be shown that expenditure of £X on avoiding or minimising the risk of an accident will prevent accident costs of £X + Y, then it is clearly desirable that £X should be spent. On the other hand, it is said, there is no point in spending £X to prevent accident costs which are less than £X' (*Cane* p 41). This reduction of value of life and limb to a mathematical formula is described by *Conaghan & Mansell* as 'ideologically objectionable in its shallow and impoverished view of human activity' (p 62). Do you agree? Consider the US case of *Grimshaw* v *Ford Motor Company* [1981], discussed in Chapter 13, p 350.

8.5.1 The Compensation Act 2006

The Compensation Act 2006 was enacted to address the *perception* of a growing compensation culture in the UK:[22]

> [Its purpose is to] clarify the existing common law on negligence to make clear that there is no liability in negligence for untoward incidents that could not be avoided by taking reasonable care or exercising reasonable skill . . . This will send a strong signal and it will also reduce risk-averse behaviour by providing reassurance to those who may be concerned about possible litigation, such as volunteers, teachers and local authorities.[23]

To this end, section 1 of the Act 2006 requires the courts to 'have regard to' the wider impact of their assessment of the appropriate standard of care in a particular case.[24]

The Compensation Act 2006

1. Deterrent effect of potential liability

A court considering a claim in negligence or breach of statutory duty may, in determining whether the defendant should have taken particular steps to meet a standard of care (whether by taking precautions against a risk or otherwise), have regard to whether a requirement to take those steps might—

(a) prevent a desirable activity from being undertaken at all, to a particular extent or in a particular way, or

(b) discourage persons from undertaking functions in connection with a desirable activity.

---

22. Part 2 of the Act addresses the aggressive marketing of the claims management industry, which the government stressed was responsible, alongside irresponsible media reporting, for fostering the *perception* of a compensation culture (see, generally, Chapter 1, pp 14–16 and Herbert 2006).

23. Tony Blair 'Common Sense Culture not Compensation Culture' speech delivered at Institute of Public Policy Research, 26 May 2005.

24. The Compensation Act is discussed in more detail in Chapter 19.

Section 1 adds little to our understanding of the tort of negligence. It simply restates what we already know: that 'the function of the law of tort [is] to deter negligent conduct and to compensate those who are the victims of such conduct. It is not the function of the law of tort to eliminate every iota of risk or to stamp out socially desirable activities' (Jackson LJ, *Barnes* at 34). Its purpose was to 'send a message' that 'desirable activities' should continue to go ahead.[25]

But what 'desirable' activities does this include? The Act's remit clearly extends to injuries caused while scouting, on school trips, maypole dancing, as well as the playing of sports and games and the provision of public amenities more generally. But does it apply to injuries sustained 'in theatre', that is while in a military zone? *Hopps* v *Mott MacDonald Ltd* [2009] suggests it does. The claimant, a civilian electrical engineer, lost his shoulder when he was hit by an improvised explosive device (IED) while travelling on a road known as 'bomb alley' in a civilian vehicle while working on rebuilding projects in Iraq following the invasion in 2003 (at [93]).[26] He sued his employers and the Ministry of Defence who were responsible for his security. The judge, while acknowledging the claimant's contribution 'at much personal cost...to improving the lot of the Iraqi people' (at [133]) rejected his claim. Applying section 1 of the Compensation Act, the judge found that given the small risk of injury and desirability of the rebuilding work, it was not unreasonable for the claimant to have been carried around in an unarmoured vehicle.

8.6 Establishing breach

You will remember in order to establish whether the defendant has breached their duty of care two questions need to be considered:

(1) How the defendant *ought* to have behaved in the circumstances—what was the required standard of care in these circumstances?

(2) How the defendant *did* behave—did they fall below the standard of care required?

So far, this chapter has concentrated solely on the first of these questions. The second question—that is, proof of negligence—is largely a question of fact to be determined by the court on the evidence before them. The burden is on the claimant to establish, on the balance of probabilities—that is, that it is more likely than not—that the defendant's actions fell below the required standard of care.[27] At times this can be extremely difficult. In many cases the claimant will have to rely on the defendant releasing certain information to them (which they may, understandably, be unwilling to do) or the information may be highly technical or simply very dense. This is particularly so in relation to litigation arising out of a defective drug where it can be very

---

25. Kevin Williams 'Legislating in the Echo Chamber' (2005) *New Law Journal* 1938 at 1938.

26. The case also established that s 1 of the Compensation Act 2005 had retrospective effect (at [92]).

27. The claimant must provide evidence of carelessness if an action in negligence is to disclose a good cause of action. If the claimant is unable to do this, the defendant may apply for summary judgment (which means the claim will fail without further argument).

time-consuming and expensive to sift through the scientific and medical evidence.[28] Things are slightly more straightforward in relation to road traffic accidents. Section 11 of the Civil Evidence Act 1968, where it applies, shifts the burden of proof onto the defendant to show that he was *not* negligent, that his conduct (although criminal) does not for whatever reason amount to civil negligence. Thus, where a defendant has been convicted of a criminal offence, say careless driving, is seen as strong evidence that he is also guilty of civil negligence, it does not automatically amount to negligence itself.[29]

The courts may also infer negligence from the circumstances in which the accident took place. This process is usually described by the phrase *res ipsa loquitur* meaning 'the thing or accident speaks for itself'. Academics disagree on the precise status of the 'doctrine'.[30] Some argue that it simply reflects the common sense view that sometimes the likelihood that the accident was caused by the defendant's negligence is such that it is not necessary to explain it, while others suggest it is a more formal doctrine which, in certain circumstances, shifts the burden of proof from the claimant to the defendant (meaning that they will be liable if they are unable to prove, on the balance of probabilities, the absence of fault on their part). It does not. *Res ipsa loquitur* does *not* shift or reverse the burden of proof onto the defendant. It simply means that sometimes the circumstances of the negligence can be evidence of carelessness.

The 'doctrine' stems from the judgment of Erle CJ in *Scott* v *London and St Katherine Docks Co* [1895] where, in response to the claimant's failure to explain how his injury occurred, he stated:

> There must be reasonable evidence of negligence, but, where the thing is shown to be under the management of the defendant, or his servants, and the accident is such as, in the ordinary course of things, does not happen if those who have the management of the machinery use proper care, it affords reasonable evidence, in the absence of explanation of the defendant, that the accident arose from want of care. (at 601)

Two things need to be met in order for the rule to come into play (although these often run together). First, the thing which caused the accident needs to be 'under the management of the defendant, or his servants', that is, the defendant needs to have control of the thing that caused the injury. A defendant will not be liable if, for example, someone steals their car and causes an accident or for a hotel guest throwing furniture out of a hotel window (*Larson* v *St Francis Hotel* [1948]) however they are more likely to be liable if a hanging basket suddenly drops from its hook and injures a passer-by or if a friend borrows their car and the brakes suddenly fail, as neither of these things are unlikely to happen if those in charge have taken proper care. Secondly, the accident must be such as 'in the ordinary course of things, does not happen if those who have

28. This difficulty was addressed by Parliament in Part 1 of the Consumer Protection Act 1987, see Chapter 13.

29. A breach of the Highway Code is not sufficient by itself to determine the standard of care required of drivers (*Brown* v *Paterson* [2010]). The defendant's criminal conviction goes only to breach—a criminal conviction cannot be used to determine issues relating to causation or damage as this was not relevant to the criminal proceedings.

30. Patrick Atiyah 'Res Ipsa Loquitur in England and Australia' (1972) 35 *Modern Law Review* 337. *Steele* describes *res ipsa loquitur* as not so much a doctrine 'so much as a complex name for a common sense inference from the facts' (p 140).

the management of the [things] use proper care'. This will, largely, depend on the circumstances of the case—it will be easier to prove negligence if you slip on a wet floor near a swimming pool or gym (where the occupiers may be expected to know that the floor might be wet and take appropriate precautions) than in a shopping centre (*Ward v Tesco Stores Ltd* [1976]).

The question for the courts is whether the initial inference of liability on the part of the defendant has been rebutted by their evidence taken as a whole: 'the *res*, which previously spoke for itself, may be silenced, or its voice may, on the whole of the evidence become too weak or muted' (*Lloyde* v *West Midlands Gas Board* [1970] at 755). Moreover, even if the defendant is unable to explain how the accident occurred but is able to show that they exercised all reasonable care in the circumstances, they will not be found liable (*J* v *North Lincolnshire County Council* [2000]). Either way, *res ipsa loquitur* is to be welcomed as an effective means of redressing the balance of power between claimant and defendant where evidential difficulties make it difficult for the claimant to establish negligence.

8.7 Conclusion

In this chapter, we have considered the second part of a claim in the tort of negligence—**breach of duty of care**. This occurs where a defendant has fallen below a particular standard of care demanded by the law. The courts seek to balance issues relating to the public benefit against individual freedom and responsibility. This takes the form of two questions: what was the required standard of care in these circumstances? and did the defendant fall below this standard? When setting the standard of care the courts compare the actions of the defendant to those of the 'reasonable man'. This is an objective test (although the courts, on occasions, may incorporate the defendant's age and skills into their assessment). When setting the standard of care required of the defendant—that is, what defendant *ought* to have done or what is *reasonable* in the circumstances of the case—the courts take a number of factors into account: probability or risk of the injury; the seriousness of the injury; the cost of taking precautions; and sometimes the social value of the activity.

The second question—that is, proof of negligence—is largely a question of fact to be determined by the court on the evidence before them. The claimant is sometimes helped when seeking to establish on the balance of probabilities that the defendant breached their duty of care by the 'doctrine' of *res ipsa loquitur*.

✱ End-of-chapter questions

After reading the chapter carefully, try answering the questions below. If you would like to know what we think visit the Online Resource Centre (www.oxfordtextbooks.co.uk/orc/horsey2e/).

1. In *Bolton* v *Stone* the cricket club were not held liable. What was the role of reasonable foreseeability? Do you agree with the outcome of the case?

2. What was the reasoning behind *Nettleship* v *Weston*? Is it a fair decision? Fair (or unfair) to whom?

3. 'It is better to control liability by adjusting the standard of care than by restricting the circumstances in which a duty of care arises.' Discuss.

4. Consider the problem question at the start of this chapter. Now having read about the topic what would be your advice to the various parties? If you need some pointers in thinking about how to answer this question, turn to the Appendix (p 589) where each problem is annotated with issues and cases to consider. Next, try to write your own answer and finally, log on to our Online Resource Centre (www.oxfordtextbooks.co.uk/orc/horsey2e/) to check your ideas against our suggested outline answer.

✳ Further reading

Much of the academic writing in this area focuses on the effect of the **Bolam** principle—the best place to start here is with Rachael Mulheron's article. The other articles listed consider specific issues relating to breach including the feminist critique of reason and the role of breach in sporting related injuries. For a general discussion of the role and purpose of fault as a basis of negligence liability see Chapter 2 of *Cane*.

Brazier, Margaret and Jose Miola 'Bye-Bye Bolam: A Medical Litigation Revolution?' (2000) 8 *Medical Law Review* 85–114

Conaghan, Joanne 'Tort Law and the Feminist Critique of Reason' in Anne Bottomley (ed) *Feminist Perspectives on the Foundational Subjects of Law* (Cavendish, 1996), p 47

Gardiner, Bruce 'Liability for Sporting Injuries' (2008) *Journal of Personal Injury Law* 16

Herbert, Rebecca 'The Compensation Act 2006' (2006) *Journal of Personal Injury Law* 337

Kidner, Richard 'The Variable Standard of Care, Contributory Negligence and *Volenti*' (1991) *Legal Studies* 1

Moran, Mayo *Rethinking the Reasonable Person* (OUP, 2003)

Mulheron, Rachael 'Trumping *Bolam*: A Critical Legal Analysis of *Bolitho's* "Gloss"' (2010) *Cambridge Law Journal* 609

Sheldon, Sally 'A Responsible Body of Medical Men Skilled in that Particular Art: Rethinking the *Bolam* Test' in Sally Sheldon and Michael Thomson (eds) *Feminist Perspectives on Health Care Law* (Cavendish Publishing, 1998)

Stevens, Robert 'An Opportunity to Reflect' (2005) 121 *Law Quarterly Review* 134

9

Causation and remoteness

Problem question

Read this problem question carefully, and keep it in mind while you are working through the chapter that follows. At the end of the chapter, you will be able to apply what you have learnt to the problem question and advise the relevant parties.

Stefaan and Gavin spend the evening drinking in the pub. Stefaan offers Gavin a lift home in his car, assuring Gavin that this will be fine as he is 'probably only just over the limit'. Driving home, Stefaan swerves to avoid a fox and crashes the car. The paramedics who arrive at the scene find that Gavin has broken his arm but otherwise only has minor cuts and bruises. Gavin is taken to hospital to be checked by a doctor.

At the hospital Gavin is seen by Cheryl, the doctor on duty. Cheryl disagrees with the paramedics' opinion and, deciding Gavin's arm is not broken but only sprained, puts it in a sling, without setting it in a cast. As she was so busy that evening, she decided not to bother sending him for an X-ray first. Gavin returns to hospital the following month with pain in his arm. It transpires that his arm *was* in fact broken and, because it was not set in the proper cast, the bones have fused together wrongly, resulting in a permanent disability. An expert witness says that there was a chance this might have happened anyway, even if Cheryl had not been negligent. Gavin has to have an operation to try and re-set the bones, but this will not improve his arm to the condition it was in before the accident.

A week later Gavin is knocked down by a speeding motorist who fails to stop and cannot be traced. His right arm is so badly injured that it has to be amputated.

9.1 **Introduction**

Consider the following examples:

→ Peter goes to hospital complaining of stomach pains after eating some badly-prepared fish. A doctor negligently examines him and sends him home. Later, he dies from the severe food poisoning he suffered. Medical evidence showed that there was nothing the doctor could have done to save him.

→ David negligently causes a collision on a motorway. Pauline, who was driving one of the other vehicles, was dazed by the collision and went to sit on the hard shoulder. A police car, rushing to the scene of the accident, hit and seriously injured Pauline.

→ Judy had pains in her chest and went to hospital. A doctor gave her a cursory examination and told her to stay in the waiting room, where she later had a heart attack and died. Medical evidence suggested that even if the doctor had treated her properly, she would still have had only a 30 per cent chance of living.

→ Bern contracts lung cancer as a result of exposure to asbestos. Medical evidence has proved that the type of cancer he has is caused by a single asbestos fibre entering the lung. Two of Bern's previous employers negligently exposed him to asbestos.

Once a duty of care and a breach have been established, a claimant must also show that the defendant's breach *caused* the harm. Causation is essential to any claim in negligence, as it links the defendant with the claimant's harm. The purpose of establishing causation is to allocate responsibility for (the costs of) harm and, to some extent, risks. There are two parts to causation: 'factual' and 'legal'. The first of these is worked out almost mathematically, using a balance of probabilities test (though there are some exceptions to this, as we will see below) to establish whether the defendant *in fact* caused the harm. The 'legal' aspect of causation (sometimes referred to as 'remoteness') simply asks whether any of all the potential factual causes should be excluded from being seen as a cause in law. If either of these tests 'fails', the defendant escapes liability in the tort of negligence for the claimant's injuries.

Although we use causal language in our everyday speech, it is not always clear what we mean. The answer to a question about the cause of something often depends on who we ask, or why we ask the question in the first place—different people see causes in different ways, particularly when causing an injury (or similar) is associated with *responsibility*. Any given event has numerous (often infinite) causes—that is, factors without which it could not have happened. Put another way, any number of things may have caused it to occur. The same is, of course, true of a tort or harm. The problem of multiple potential causes runs through causation, with the courts having to pin down or 'find' the 'real' cause from one of a number of factors. In so doing, there are two questions that must be addressed:

(1) What are the prerequisite conditions for the harm (factual causation)?

(2) What is the 'relevant' or 'real' cause of it (legal causation)?

Table 9.1 Considering factual and legal causation in negligence

	'Cause in fact'	'Cause in law'
The questions being asked	• What happened factually in the situation as it occurred? • On the balance of probabilities, did the breach cause the harm alleged ('but for' the negligence, would the harm have been suffered)? • If not, have the courts created an exception to the usual rule?	• Even if the breach was the cause in fact of the harm suffered, what is the legal interpretation of the facts? • Are there any policy or other reasons to justify denying liability? • Was there a break in the chain of causation?

In law as in life, it is not always possible to pinpoint the single *factual* cause of a harm. A road accident, for example, may have two or more 'real' causes—both drivers may have been going too fast on a winding country lane in the fog, in which case there are at least three factors—the speed of each driver and the weather conditions—that might have contributed to the harm.

 Pause for reflection

A stolen and abandoned car is set on fire. Consider the following list of potential causes:

• Adam, who stole the car, didn't tell his parents where he was going

• Adam's parents did not check where he was going when he left the house earlier that evening

• There are a lack of facilities for teenagers in the area

• The police have failed to catch car thieves in the area

• Adam and the police were involved in a chase and Adam had to abandon the car so that he could get away

• The police failed to notify the Highway Authority that the car was abandoned

• No one removed the car from the side of the road

• Ben, who set the car on fire, is only 12, but was out unsupervised at night

• Ben's parents don't know that Ben has left the house

• Ben is sold cigarettes and matches at a local newsagent

• Ben thinks it will be fun to throw lit matches in the abandoned car

Which of these is/are *the* cause/causes of the harm?

→

> →
>   Don't worry if you don't know the 'legal' answer at this stage. The purpose of this exercise
> is for you to think quickly about which of these facts, if any, you would consider the cause
> of the harm (and which you would not). Thinking through the issues in this way will help you
> prepare for the material to follow.

As the example above helps to illustrate, the process of determining *factual* causation comes down to one of elimination rather than inclusion. How do we go about reducing the list of possible causes? Or, put another way, are some causes more likely to be legally considered than others? The answer, it seems, is yes. HLA Hart and AH Honoré suggest that we are more likely to find a cause in something that is out of the ordinary or unusual and that if both natural factors and human actions are involved, we will tend to focus on the human actions.[1] Similarly, positive actions, rather than inactions (omissions), are more likely to be considered causative and, when deciding between human actions, we are more likely to focus on those that were voluntary rather than involuntary and those that we deem unreasonable rather than reasonable.

In tort law, the question is more sharply focused than simply asking 'what caused the injury or harm?' After all, if this were the question, then any or all of the potential reasons given in the list in the box above could be said to be a 'cause' of the car burning: the car would not have burnt without—or 'but for'—each of the listed facts. Rather, when seeking to establish a claim in negligence, the question is: 'Did the defendant's negligence (that is, their breach of duty) cause this harm?' Or, more precisely, 'can we say that the act or omission that we have identified as negligent is a "real" cause (it may be one of many) of the harm?' The law approaches this wider question in two stages as identified above:

(1) Was the defendant's action/inaction a necessary pre-condition for the harm to occur (so-called factual causation) and, if so;

(2) Is it therefore *the* cause of the harm (that is, the *legal* cause)?

These two stages are known among tort lawyers as factual causation (or 'cause in fact') and legal causation (or 'cause in law') respectively and, as each contains different principles and tests, will be dealt with separately in this chapter.

9.2 Factual causation—the 'but for' test

The first essential question to be answered when looking at causation is whether the defendant's wrong (that is, their breach of duty) in fact caused the claimant's harm. Only if this is the case can there be liability. This may seem, at first glance at least, to be a question of common sense. If we ask whether the harm was *a consequence* of the defendant's breach then we can reach a yes or no answer quite easily. However, in law, the question of causation is actually more difficult, in part due to the fact that there

1. HLA Hart and AH Honoré *Causation in the Law* (2nd edn, OUP, 1985).

are various *legal* meanings of the word 'cause' which differ from ordinary meanings of the word.

9.2.1 **Explaining the test**

In some cases, liability is established simply by showing that the defendant's actions caused the harm. This is how strict liability systems work. In fault-based systems like negligence, however, this is not enough. We have to establish that the defendant's *breach of duty*, as opposed to simply his *actions*, caused the harm. In other words, the harm suffered by the claimant must be caused by the fact that the defendant's actions fell below the appropriate standard of care.[2]

The question of cause in fact asks whether the defendant's negligent action or inaction (omission)[3] was a necessary condition for the harm to occur. Put differently, if the harm would have occurred *without* the defendant's carelessness, there will be no cause in fact. This is often expressed in the form of a 'but for' test: we ask the question 'but for the defendant's carelessness, would the claimant have escaped harm?' If the answer to this question is 'yes', cause in fact is identified, as no harm would have come to the claimant without the added element of the defendant's carelessness.

Almost all answers to the factual causation question, however, retain an element of uncertainty. It is probably fair to say that we can never be entirely sure how events would have turned out—for example, whether a particular loss would have been suffered—if the circumstances had been different—for example if the defendant had exercised reasonable care. Confusingly, we are asking what would have happened if the circumstances were different, and yet how are we to know, since, by definition, this is not what *did* happen? We can deal with this through the 'burden of proof'. Unlike the criminal law, where the burden of proof must be established beyond reasonable doubt, in tort law all the claimant must establish is that something was, on the balance of probabilities, a necessary condition for the harm occurring. This is a lower standard. To succeed, the claimant need only show that there was more than a 50 per cent chance that the defendant's breach caused their harm. If they cannot establish that the defendant's negligence made the difference between something happening and not happening, then it cannot be a cause of their injuries.[4] Put another way, it is more likely than not that the defendant's breach did not contribute to the harm suffered by the claimant and so was essentially coincidental and unconnected to that harm.

The classic example of the 'but for' test in action is found in ***Barnett v Chelsea and Kensington Hospital Management Committee*** [1969].

---

2. It should also be noted here that the same rule applies in every tort where proof of harm or damage is required, so what is said in this chapter about causation as it relates to negligence should also be remembered in the context of other fault-based torts, as well as some strict liability ones (claims under the Consumer Protection Act 1987, for example).

3. Questions of cause in relation to a defendant's *failure* to do something only arise if there was a duty to act—see further Chapter 4.

4. In this respect the cause in fact test is purely a negative test as it can be said that it merely excludes things that might have been a cause.

> ### *Barnett v Chelsea and Kensington Hospital Management Committee* [1969] HC
>
> A doctor failed to properly examine a man when he presented himself at the casualty department of the hospital. It transpired that the man was suffering from arsenic poisoning from which he subsequently died. The doctor admitted that he had been negligent (in breach of his duty), but said that he had not caused the man's death. *Even if he had have acted properly, the man would have died anyway* as it was too late to do anything to save him. It could not be said that 'but for' the doctor's negligence the man would not have died.
>
> The court held that as the doctor's negligence was not a necessary condition for the man's death, he could not be held liable for it.[5]

9.2.2 **Problems with the test**

As might be imagined, establishing or disproving cause in fact might not always be as easy as it was in *Barnett*. It is not always easy to imagine what would have happened if the defendant had not been negligent. There are two situations in particular where dealing with factual causation becomes complicated. Here, various policy reasons have led, on some occasions, to the judiciary devising ways around—exceptions to—the usual 'but for' test.

The first of these is in situations where there may be multiple potential causes of the harm and a lack of, for example, scientific or forensic knowledge means that it would be too difficult (or even impossible) to establish what would have happened in the absence of negligence. There are some fairly obvious examples of situations where this might lead to an unclear (below 50 per cent) outcome, such as in complex medical situations or accidents involving multiple vehicles. The second complicated factual causation point, perhaps more contentiously, covers situations where we *could* work out the factual cause as a percentage figure, but the result that this gives appears unjust and we therefore want to reject it.

This, of course, prompts questions as to when such exceptions to the 'but for' test of factual causation are to be recognised, their extent and rationale. Answers can be found in careful analysis of the difficult and often contradictory case law and it is to this that we now turn our attention.

9.2.2.1 Multiple potential causes

Where there is more than one potential cause of harm, it becomes factually hard to establish, in the absence of any clear evidence or proof, that any of the potential causes is any more likely (that is, more than 50 per cent) than any other to be *the* cause. For example, where there are two competing potential causes, each seeming equally plausible, each will only be 50 per cent likely to be the cause of the harm suffered, thus neither would satisfy the 'but for' test. Where there are three competing potential

---

5. Thus we would arrive at the same outcome in respect of Peter and his food poisoning in the scenario above. Also, although the facts seem different on first glance, the same would apply to Judy (see *Hotson*).

causes, each of these will only be 33.3 per cent likely to be the cause, and so on. A good example of this type of problem is found in *Wilsher v Essex Area Health Authority* [1988].

Wilsher v Essex Area Health Authority [1988] HL

The claimant, Martin Wilsher, had been cared for in the special care baby unit of a hospital, after being born prematurely. A doctor was negligent (that is, fell below the standard of care expected of a reasonable doctor) in monitoring his blood. As a result, he was, on two separate occasions, given too much oxygen. Wilsher developed a condition known as retrolental fibroplasia (RLF)—an incurable eye condition affecting the retina, which eventually left him blind in one eye and with seriously impaired vision in the other. Too much oxygen in the blood is a known possible cause of RLF. However, the defence pointed out that there were also a number of other 'innocent' potential causes, including the fact that the baby had been born early (RLF is a known risk to premature babies). In total there were five competing causes, each of which was equally probable, thus 20 per cent likely to be the true cause of the harm.

Wilsher's claim succeeded in the lower court and by a majority in the Court of Appeal. However, it failed in the House of Lords, which was not persuaded (as there was not enough conclusive evidence) that, on the balance of probabilities, the doctor's negligence and not any other factor had caused the baby's harm.

From **Wilsher**, it seems that where there is a negligent act that common sense tells us might potentially be the cause of someone's harm, if there are other, alternative possible causes of that harm, especially 'natural' ones, then it cannot be said that 'but for' the negligent act, the claimant would not have suffered harm. As a result, the defendant will escape liability.[6] The practical problem in a case where there are multiple potential causes is always whether enough evidence can be gathered to prove that it was the defendant's negligence that was the cause of the harm and not any other potential cause. Variants of the 'alternatives' issue arise all the time, but this does not always mean that the claimant will be unsuccessful, as the courts have sometimes deviated from the 'but for' test in such situations.

Material contribution to harm

In *Bonnington Castings Ltd v Wardlaw* [1956] (a case predating **Wilsher**), a factory employee contracted pneumoconiosis, a lung condition, from the inhalation of silica dust. He sued his employer in negligence. The problem was that some dust inhalation was an inevitable consequence of the work being done (this dust was therefore deemed to be 'innocent' dust). Nevertheless, the House of Lords found that there was a higher

---

6. Though see the Court of Appeal decision in *Bailey v Ministry of Defence* [2008]. Here, there were two potential causes of the claimant's cardiac arrest and brain damage—one negligent and one 'natural' and it could not be established which was the 'but for' cause. Thus, following **Wilsher**, there should have been no liability. However, the Court of Appeal, treating the case as one of *cumulative* cause (see below), focused on the idea that the hospital's negligence made a 'material contribution' to the harm, relying on cases that had created such an exception in the context of industrial claims, see further below.

level of dust in the air than there should have been, due to the employer's negligence in not adequately ventilating the factory. The law lords deemed this extra quantity of dust 'illegal'. The question for the courts was, then, whether the 'illegal' or 'guilty' dust made any difference to the claimant's chances of contracting the disease.

Medical evidence established that the disease was progressive, or cumulative—it was caused by the *build up* of silica dust in the lungs. It could not be established exactly at what point the disease occurred. As the question was not, therefore, one about how much dust was in the lungs or how long it had been there, it could not be established, on the balance of probabilities, whether the 'guilty' dust was the cause. That is, it could not be said that 'but for' the defendant's negligence in allowing the 'illegal' dust into the air, that the defendant would not have suffered the harm.[7] Nevertheless, the House of Lords found that *in this case*, because it might be argued that *cumulatively* the 'innocent' and 'guilty' dust were *more likely* to cause harm, it was enough to show that the defendant's negligence had made a *material* (in the sense of it being more than *de minimis*) *contribution* to the condition. The law lords effectively bypassed the 'but for' test (perhaps for policy reasons related to the employer–employee relationship and the existence of employers' liability insurance). The key thing to note is that when the 'but for' test produced—according to the House of Lords—unsatisfactory results, they manufactured a way around it.[8]

The extent of the effect of this diversion from the 'but for' test has been somewhat more diluted in recent years by the decision in *Holtby* v *Brigham & Cowan (Hull) Ltd* [2000].[9] Following *Bonnington*, where a disease is contracted as a result of *cumulative* exposure to toxins, it need only be proved that the negligent part of that exposure would materially contribute to the condition, and not that the negligent exposure was *the* likely cause of the condition. In such cases, the claimant could receive full compensation. In *Holtby*, by comparison, the Court of Appeal ruled that the claimant in such situations will only be entitled to recover damages proportionate to the negligence of the defendant. The claimant in this case was negligently exposed to asbestos by a number of employers over a period of years, contracting asbestosis as a result. The Court of Appeal awarded damages proportionately by defendant, based on the extent of exposure (time plus intensity) under each of the negligent employers.[10] The decision can be viewed as significant because the injury (asbestosis) was treated as 'divisible'. However, it is not a divisible injury in the sense that one defendant caused the claimant harm and another defendant caused a different type of harm entirely, and technically it is only for divisible injuries that proportionate damages can be awarded.

7. In fact the medical evidence said that it made a *difference*; but because the case was argued as 'all or nothing', what it could not say is whether the entire disease would have been avoided in the absence of the guilty dust. This case makes much more sense if the language of 'divisible harm' is used (which was not the language used in the 1950s).

8. See also section 9.2.2.2 below.

9. See also *Ellis* v *Environment Agency* [2008]. Cf *Simmons* v *British Steel* [2004] in which the *Bonnington* test was used to hold the defendant fully liable for the (psychiatric) injury suffered by the claimant.

10. See also *Allen* v *British Rail Engineering* [2001], a case relating to 'vibration white finger' and, more controversially, *Rahman* v *Arearose Ltd* [2001] (claimant beaten then later receiving negligent medical treatment, both cumulatively found to have caused him psychiatric harm) and *Hatton* v *Sutherland* [2002] (a stress-at-work case). This approach to apportionment in relation to psychiatric harm has been later doubted: see *Dickins* v *O2 Plc* [2008].

Pause for reflection

Why do you think the Court of Appeal treated asbestosis as a divisible injury in *Holtby*? What would have been the position, with regard to damages, if they had not done so? Do you think the court was looking for the 'fairest' outcome for both the claimant (who would receive full compensation) *and* the defendants (so all of them became liable to pay at least something, but none would be liable for the full amount)? If so, do you think this is an appropriate role for the court? See the judgment of Stuart-Smith LJ for an indication of how he viewed the court's role: 'in my view the court must do the best it can to achieve justice, not only to the claimant but the defendant, and among defendants' (at [20]).

On the other hand, consider the position of the claimant in this kind of 'divisible' claim who cannot locate one of his previous employers, or who finds out that one of them has long ago gone bankrupt? Does the decision to award proportionate damages seem as fair then, particularly when compared with the position of the claimant in *Bonnington, or those where the harm is 'indivisible'*?

Material increase in risk

The 'material contribution' route around the problem caused by the rigidity of the 'but for' test was revisited in *McGhee* v *National Coal Board* [1973]. This case was similar in its facts to *Bonnington* but with an important difference. Again, scientific evidence was unable to determine whether 'innocent' or 'guilty' causes were the factual cause of the claimant's condition, a kind of dermatitis caused by exposure to brick dust. The claimant encountered the 'innocent' dust while he was at work, but this same dust became 'guilty' *after* work (it stayed on the claimant longer than it should have done, as the employers had negligently failed to provide adequate washing facilities for their employees to use at the end of their shift). The question was whether the extra time the dust was on the claimant's skin caused his skin condition to develop. Unlike *Bonnington*, it was recognised that dermatitis was *not* necessarily a cumulative condition—it could be triggered by a single exposure to the dust—it may, therefore, have occurred from working with the 'innocent' dust. Thus, the 'guilty' dust did not materially contribute to the harm itself, but rather only to the *risk* of harm occurring.

The question was then whether the claimant's condition was caused by his innocent exposure to dust *or* by the 'guilty' dust that remained on his body while he cycled home. Only if it could be shown to be the latter would the employer's negligence be the factual ('but for') cause of the claimant's condition. As in *Bonnington*, the evidence was not strong enough to prove it either way. However, what could be shown was that the longer the dust lay on someone's skin, the greater risk that person had of contracting dermatitis. The House of Lords held that this was enough—the fact that the *risk* of the claimant developing the condition was increased was enough to establish causation.

In *McGhee, material increase of risk* was treated by the majority as equivalent to *material contribution*. Once again, the House of Lords apparently circumvented the 'but for' rule to arrive at the decision they wanted to reach. In so doing, on another view, the House of Lords in fact reversed the burden of proof—shifting it onto the *defendant* who then had to show that there was another, more likely, cause than their negligence.[11] Where this cannot be done (as in *McGhee*), the defendant remains liable. It should be noted, however, that there is still a 'but for' calculation involved. To succeed, a claimant has to show, on the balance of probabilities (that is, it is more than 50 per cent likely), that the alleged negligence materially increased the risk of the harm being suffered.

Pause for reflection

The decisions in *Bonnington* and *McGhee* may seem like logical developments to a fairly rigid rule that can, because of its reliance on establishing a probability above 50 per cent, produce some harsh results. However, look again at the dates of the two cases, and then at *Wilsher*.

Both cases pre-date (and, importantly, survive) *Wilsher*. In fact, the *McGhee* argument was raised in *Wilsher* and was rejected by the House of Lords, which did not think that *McGhee* had established a new test for causation.[12] They said that although there *was* a materially increased risk of blindness caused by the doctor's negligence, this was not enough to establish factual causation. There were four other possible 'innocent' causes, any of which may have led to the condition, and the doctor's carelessness was not the most likely cause. Why was there a difference in this case? Does the fact that there was *more than one* other potential cause make the difference? Or is the decision in *Wilsher* based purely in policy, this time (as is often the case in relation to establishing breach—see Chapter 8) showing undue deference to the medical profession? If so, how can the Court of Appeal's decision in *Bailey v Ministry of Defence* [2008] be explained?

A key development in this area came with the House of Lords' decision in **Fairchild v Glenhaven Funeral Services** [2002]. However, despite the clear overlap with issues relating to 'material increase in risk', discussed above, this case fits better into another category of problematic situations: that where the court feels the result of using the 'but for' test is an unjust one.

9.2.2.2 'Unjust' results

Fairchild v Glenhaven Funeral Services [2002] HL

A group of claims were made against multiple defendants by three employees who had developed mesothelioma (an inevitably fatal type of lung cancer), caused by exposure to asbestos dust. Two of the claims failed at first instance, as the claimants could not satisfactorily show where the asbestos that caused their mesothelioma had come from.

→

11. This approach was resoundingly rejected in later cases; see e.g. **Barker v Corus** [2006].
12. See e.g. Lord Bridge at 1090.

➡

In relation to the claim in *Fairchild*, however, there was no problem in establishing that the employer had been negligent in allowing the claimant to be exposed to asbestos—the problem was that the employee had been exposed *by a series* of negligent employers, not just one. Unlike in *Bonnington* (but like *McGhee*), experts agreed that mesothelioma could be caused in a single moment—for example, even by a single asbestos fibre entering the lung—and was not necessarily caused by prolonged exposure.[13] The difficulty was that the claimants could not show *when* that causative exposure occurred, so they could not show, on the balance of probabilities, which of the employers was the factual cause of the harm. On that basis, strictly following the 'but for' test, the Court of Appeal had dismissed the claim, and the claimant appealed to the House of Lords.

The law lords held that the 'but for' test produced an unjust result and the idea that no defendant would be liable for the harms suffered by the claimant, when there was no doubt that the cause had been negligent, clearly sat uncomfortably with them. To get around this, they resurrected *McGhee*, approving the 'material increase of risk' interpretation and stating that in this exceptional type of case (perhaps defined as employment/industry)[14] this would be enough to establish factual causation; the defendants were therefore liable.[15]

In finding in **Fairchild** that each of the defendants had materially increased the risk of the claimant contracting mesothelioma, the House of Lords did not overrule **Wilsher**, which seemed to potentially stand in the way of this interpretation. Instead, they distinguished it, holding that **Wilsher** had been correctly decided on its facts.[16] The law lords said that the **Fairchild** decision was an *exception* to normal causation principles. The outcome of the **Fairchild** decision was, therefore, that each of the negligent employers was jointly and severally liable. It would therefore be up to the employers who had actually been brought before the court to seek contributions from others who had not (under s 1(1) of the Civil Liability (Contribution) Act 1978).

 Pause for reflection

Does the fact that *Wilsher* and *Fairchild* are both good law have any impact on the type of case the 'material increase of risk' test can be applied to in the future? We do not find the explanation that *Wilsher* should be confined to its facts very convincing, and would rather have seen a more carefully stated exposition of the policy and other distinguishing arguments behind the decision to depart from what seemed to be a binding authority. Was

➡

13. Note, however, that the 'single fibre' theory has since been discredited by experts (*Durham v BAI (EL Trigger Litigation)* [2008]). It is enough that the harm is 'indivisible' and that the state of scientific knowledge renders proof of causation impossible.

14. Though now cf *Willmore v Knowsley Metropolitan Borough Council* [2011].

15. This may mean that Bern, in the scenario at the start of this chapter, would have a successful claim.

16. Perhaps it is the small difference in the facts—that there were only two potential causes, rather than five—that led to the Court of Appeal's finding (distinguishing **Wilsher**) that there *could* be liability in *Bailey v Ministry of Defence* [2008].

➡️

it, for example, the difference between finding employers (who were likely to be insured) liable and the NHS? Did the shorter timescale in *Wilsher* indicate a different outcome—the claimants in *Fairchild* had worked and were exposed to asbestos over a long period of time, followed by the slow onset of their disease and the inevitable nature of their death? If this is the case, why was the claimant's situation in *Bailey v Ministry of Defence* [2008] distinguished from *Wilsher*, when it was also a medical scenario?[17]

In **Barker v Corus UK Ltd** [2006], the House of Lords revisited similar issues, though with the added complication of a period of self-exposure and also with a new question regarding apportionment of damages.

Barker v Corus UK Ltd [2006] HL

A number of claims were made on behalf of people who had died from mesothelioma contracted as a result of exposure to asbestos dust at work. Some of the exposure to asbestos was negligent on the part of the employers concerned and the claims were brought against these employers (those that had not gone bankrupt since the injury occurred). These employers, as in *Fairchild*, had been found to be jointly and severally liable. In one of the claims, the exposure to asbestos could be clearly broken down to three distinct periods of time: a period when the claimant was working for a now insolvent employer (who therefore could not be sued); a period when working for the defendant; and a period of self-employment. At both first instance and in the Court of Appeal, the defendants were held, following *Fairchild*, jointly and severally liable. The difference was that, to reflect the claimant's own negligence during the period of self-employment, a finding of contributory negligence (a partial defence, see Chapter 10) was made, with the claimant's damages reduced by 20 per cent to take this into account. The defendants in all of the cases appealed the finding of joint and several liability to the House of Lords, arguing that their liability should be proportionately divided to reflect the actual risk that was caused by their negligence (for example, based on the proportion of time that the claimant was negligently exposed to asbestos dust by the employer).

A majority of the House of Lords agreed that the damages to be awarded ought to be apportioned among the defendants according to their specific contributions to the increased risk.[18] They agreed that the most 'practical' method of apportionment would be based on the amount of time the claimant was negligently exposed to the asbestos dust by each employer, Lord Hoffmann noting that 'allowance may have to be made for the intensity of the exposure and the type of asbestos' (at [48]). Lord Scott, similarly, said:

---

17. A clearer explanation might be found in *Ministry of Defence v AB & others* [2010], which involved claims relating to people harmed by nuclear testing in the 1950s. Here, the Court of Appeal considered there was 'no foreseeable possibility that the Supreme Court would be willing to extend the *Fairchild* exception' in cases where there are multiple potential causes, some of which were impossible to identify (at [154]).

18. The point is that although mesothelioma is indivisible; if the harm is construed as 'risk of damage', that is divisible.

➡️

It might depend also on the intensity of the exposure for which the defendant was responsible compared with the intensity of the exposure for which the defendant was not responsible. The exact type of agent might be a relevant factor in assessing the degree of risk. I have in mind that there are different types of asbestos and some might create a greater risk than others. (at [62])

So, in **Barker**, the House of Lords departed from the idea that the employers, all of whom had contributed by their negligence to an increased risk of the claimant contracting a fatal lung cancer, should be jointly and severally liable to pay the claimant's compensation. Instead they preferred the idea that compensation payments should be based on the period of time (and intensity of exposure, etc) that the claimant worked for the employer and was negligently exposed to asbestos. This issue was never raised in **Fairchild**. In practice this would mean that, in a situation where an employee was negligently exposed to asbestos by a series of four employers, for example, and one of these employers had subsequently gone bankrupt, compensation—but not full compensation—would be divided between the remaining three solvent employers on the basis of the period of time the claimant was employed by them. This means that the claimant cannot fully recover the damages that have been calculated according to his (or his dependants') need. This principle is illustrated in Table 9.2.

Table 9.2 Division of damages between a series of employers

	Risk increased by negligent defendant	Period of time employed by defendant	Defendant solvent or bankrupt	Proportion of damages paid
Harm suffered by claimant (e.g. mesothelioma)	A	10 years	Solvent	20%
	B	20 years	Bankrupt	None
	C	15 years	Solvent	30%
	D	5 years	Solvent	10%
Total proportion of (full) damages recoverable by claimant				60%

 Pause for reflection

In *Fairchild*, the Court of Appeal refused to find any of the defendants liable, as it could not be established, on the balance of probabilities, that any one of them had caused the harm suffered by the claimants. They said that the required 'leap over the evidential gap' would not only defy logic but would be 'susceptible of unjust results':

If we were to accede to the claimants' arguments, we would be distorting the law to accommodate the exigencies of a very hard case. We would be yielding to a

➡️

→
contention that all those who have suffered injury after being exposed to a risk of that injury from which someone else should have protected them should be able to recover compensation even when they are quite unable to prove who was the culprit. (Brooke LJ at [103])

The House of Lords disagreed. Lord Bingham, dealing with this exact point, said that:

There is a strong policy argument in favour of compensating those who have suffered grave harm, at the expense of their employers who owed them a duty to protect them against that very harm and failed to do so, when the harm can only have been caused by breach of that duty and when science does not permit the victim accurately to attribute, as between several employers, the precise responsibility for the harm he has suffered. I am of the opinion that such injustice as may be involved in imposing liability on a duty-breaking employer in these circumstances is heavily outweighed by the injustice of denying redress to a victim. (at [33])

Which of the opinions do you agree with most? How does your opinion fit with the result of the decision in *Barker*?

In his dissenting opinion in **Barker**, Lord Rodger argued that redefining the harm so as to justify the apportionment of damages between defendants would unfairly shift the risk that defendants had gone bankrupt, or were otherwise untraceable, onto the claimants, who had been negligently injured by the defendants in the first place. The decision in **Barker**, unsurprisingly therefore, caused great concern among workers who had been negligently exposed to asbestos dust during the course of their employment.[19] These concerns were recognised by Parliament which, at the time, was debating the (then unrelated) Compensation Bill.[20] As a result of the hostility to **Barker**, the Bill was amended to reverse the effect of the House of Lords' decision. Section 3 of the Compensation Act 2006 now provides that, where the conditions for applying **Fairchild** are met (that is, where there was negligent exposure to asbestos by a series of employers that caused mesothelioma, but it cannot be conclusively shown which of the employers actually, or most likely, caused the disease), the employer will be liable for the whole sum of damages.[21] This applies even if there were other sources of exposure, including from other negligent employers, self-employment or (*obiter*) any other (non-negligent) source, though a reduction in damages for the claimant's own contributory negligence is still possible under section 3(3)(b). It is, of course, open to the liable defendant to seek contributions from others under the same principles that govern joint and several liability.[22]

19. Or, more importantly perhaps, to claimant lawyers and unions.
20. Now the Compensation Act 2006.
21. Section 3(1)(a)–(d). Thus, in the scenarios at the beginning of this chapter, Bern's claim will not be unduly affected by *Barker*.
22. See Chapter 19.

Counterpoint

Had section 3 of the Compensation Act 2006 not been passed, we would, in our opinion, have been left in an undesirable and contradictory position regarding the decisions of the House of Lords in relation to asbestos-related claims. In *Fairchild*, the position was that claimants should be allowed to recover *full* damages for the harm (and it must be remembered that this was a fatal lung cancer), even though they could not possibly have established which of the defendants was the likely cause. In this sense, the *Fairchild* decision is claimant-centred and is based on the fact that the claimant would receive nothing if the 'material increase of risk' exception to the 'but for' rule was not used.

In contrast, the decision in *Holtby*, while giving a good result for the actual claimant in that case, appears to mean that in future, claimants suffering from asbestosis (as opposed to mesothelioma) may not recover in full if one or more of their previous employers has become insolvent.[23] This is a less claimant-friendly decision. The same can be seen in the House of Lords' decision in *Barker* on the same point in relation to mesothelioma.

In *Barker*, Lord Rodger points out that while it may seem harsh that a single defendant becomes liable for the total sum of a claimant's damages, purely because his negligence made a material contribution to the risk that the claimant would suffer mesothelioma, this result was also settled law. He goes on to say that this principle 'is a form of rough justice which the law has not hitherto sought to smooth, preferring instead, as a matter of policy, to place the risk of insolvency of a wrongdoer or his insurer on the other wrongdoers or their insurers' (at [90]). The decision in *Barker*, he claims, means that this risk has to be 'shouldered entirely by the innocent claimant' (at [90]). This does not appear to us to be consistent with the policy-orientated decision made by the House of Lords that sometimes the wrongdoers should pay, even where it cannot be proved that it was actually *their* own wrong that caused the harm. Indeed, in a statement with which we would wholly agree, Lord Rodger points out in *Barker* that 'the desirability of the courts, rather than Parliament, throwing this lifeline to wrongdoers and their insurers at the expense of claimants is not obvious' (at [90]). This is particularly true given the fact that if a claimant who contracted mesothelioma was only ever employed by one negligent employer over the course of his working life, he would be able to recover full damages based on the 'but for' principle. Claimants should not be hindered by the fact they have worked for more than one negligent employer.

Clearly Parliament felt the same way and section 3 of the Compensation Act 2006 now removes the risk from claimants who have contracted or died from mesothelioma. What section 3 does not tell us is what will happen when the *Fairchild* principle is applied *outside* a claim for mesothelioma. It seems that *Barker* will still apply (proportionate liability) in cases *not* involving mesothelioma.[24]

---

23. Though they may have recourse to some damages via the Financial Services Compensation Scheme.

24. Though see the comments (*obiter*) of Smith LJ in *Novartis Grimsby Ltd v Cookson* [2007], a bladder cancer case, in which she indicates she would have applied the *Fairchild* principle in the absence of an (almost straightforward) application of the 'but for' test, as the two potentially causative agents 'act on the body in the same way' (at [72]).

As *Steele* says, 'the breadth of the impact of *Fairchild* and *Barker* is...not entirely clear' (p 232). Probably for that reason there has been a flurry of causation cases in recent years regarding the idea of material increase in risk, though none have succeeded.[25]

The extent of the provisions of section 3 of the Compensation Act 2006 were most recently called into question in ***Sienkiewicz v Greif (UK) Ltd* [2011]**.

Sienkiewicz v Greif (UK) Ltd [2011] SC

An action was brought on behalf of Mrs Costello, who died from mesothelioma in 2006. Mrs Costello had worked in offices at the defendant's factory in Ellesmere Port in Cheshire for nearly 20 years until 1984. Her job required her to enter areas of the factory that were contaminated with asbestos. At first instance, this exposure was found to be negligent. However, the judge also found that the claimant had been exposed to low levels of asbestos in the general atmosphere around Ellesmere Port, which might also have been significant enough to have caused mesothelioma.

The defendants argued that where there was only one employer, the correct test was the 'but for' test, not the *Fairchild* exception. They contended that the claimant must prove, on the balance of probabilities, that the negligent exposure had caused the disease and that to do this she would need to establish that the negligent exposure more than doubled the risk.[26] The judge accepted this argument, finding also that the doubling of risk could not be established on the facts—the negligent exposure had only increased the risk by 18 per cent. The claimant lost.

The claimant appealed, arguing that the judge had failed to properly apply the law. The correct test was whether the occupational exposure had *materially* increased the risk: the increase did not have to be two-fold, only more than minimal. The Court of Appeal agreed.[27] On the issue of apportionment, Smith LJ first acknowledged that the *Fairchild* judges *might* not have thought the exception appropriate where there was only one negligent employer and the other asbestos source was environmental. However, whether this was the case or not, she found that section 3 of the Compensation Act 2006 rendered this irrelevant, as it covered the situation in this case.[28] Lord Clarke added that the case was clearly the type of case considered in *Fairchild*, as interpreted in *Barker* (as the non-occupational exposure could be viewed in a similar way to the period of self-employment in *Barker*). Unanimously, her appeal was allowed.

The defendants appealed to the Supreme Court, which handed down its unanimous opinion in March 2011. The seven-member court carefully considered the 'Fairchild exception', the effect of section 3 of the Compensation Act 2006, how 'material' a material contribution to risk has to be (alongside a rejection of the so-called 'doubling of risk' idea),

→

---

25. See e.g. *Clough v First Choice Holidays* [2006]; *Sanderson v Hull* [2008]; *Wootton v J Docter Ltd* [2008].

26. This principle was used in *Novartis Grimsby Ltd v Cookson* [2007]—but this was not a mesothelioma case.

27. ***Sienkiewicz v Greif (UK) Ltd* [2009]**. Also see *Willmore v Knowsley Metropolitan Borough Council* [2009].

28. Section 3(1)(d) was the point of contention, as the conditions in s 3(1)(a)–(c) were clearly made out.

> →
>
> as well as the importance of epidemiological evidence. The court dismissed the appeal (alongside the defendant's appeal in *Willmore v Knowsley*).[29] Lord Phillips ([98]–[106]) explained that a continuing justification for maintaining the exception is that the gaps in our knowledge as to how mesothelioma is triggered 'justifies the adoption of the special rule of causation that the House of Lords applied in Fairchild and Barker' (at [103]).[30]

What we now know, then, is that the 'Fairchild exception', as it applies to mesothelioma, also applies in cases where only *one* defendant is proved to have negligently exposed the victim to asbestos, even though she was also at risk of developing the disease from a non-negligent exposure.[31] The Supreme Court has held unanimously that this is the case and that proof that the injury would not have happened but for the defendant's negligence is unnecessary in such circumstances. We also know that section 3 will only apply when the defendant has committed a tort. What we still *don't* know is whether the exception is applicable outside mesothelioma. Many of the Supreme Court opinions seem to hint at its application to any other disease in relation to which the same evidential uncertainties were shown (see e.g. Lord Phillips at [104]). Only Lord Barker seemed to think not, saying '[s]ave only for mesothelioma cases, claimants should henceforth expect little flexibility from the courts in their approach to causation' (at [187]).

Outside asbestos-related litigation, another case where the courts appeared to depart from the ordinary principles of 'but for' causation in order to secure a just result is ***Chester v Afshar*** [2005], a case relating to the disclosure of medical risks. In an earlier case, *Sidaway v Board of Governors of the Bethlem Royal Hospital* [1985], a surgeon failed to disclose a 1–2 per cent risk of spinal damage to a patient undergoing an operation on her back, which later materialised. In all probability, the House of Lords agreed, he had failed to disclose the risks. However, other experts said they would not have disclosed the risks in the same situation either, so Sidaway tried to invoke the transatlantic doctrine of 'informed consent'. The House of Lords refused to entertain this (Lord Scarman dissenting), declaring the doctrine impractical and stating that the time was not right to substantially change the rules on informing of risks. However, Lord Templeman noted that if Sidaway had *asked* about the specific risks, she should have been informed of them.

> ### *Chester v Afshar* [2005] HL
>
> The claimant developed a serious and uncomfortable spinal condition (cauda equina syndrome) following an operation on her spine, which she had been advised to undergo by the defendant. The claimant had reluctantly agreed to the operation. The defendant had not warned her of the small risk that she might develop cauda equina syndrome, even if
>
>

29. *Willmore v Knowsley Metropolitan Borough Council* [2011].

30. The implication appears to be that if the evidential uncertainties disappear by future findings that fill the scientific gaps in our knowledge, the mesothelioma exception would also disappear.

31. This seems to fit more closely with *McGhee v National Coal Board* [1973], the case on which *Fairchild* was originally based (see p 229).

→

the operation was performed without negligence. When this risk materialised, the claimant sued in negligence arguing that had she been aware of the risk she would have sought advice on alternatives to surgery and the operation would not have taken place when it did (although it may well have taken place on a later date). The trial judge found the possibility that the claimant might have consented to surgery in the future was not sufficient to break the causal link between the defendant's failure to warn and the damage sustained by the claimant. The Court of Appeal agreed.

So did the majority of the House of Lords. They held that the claimant had not been able to establish sufficient causation on conventional principles. Because she may well have had the operation later, the defendant's failure to warn neither affected the risk nor was the effective cause of the injury she sustained. However, the law lords went on to modify these principles. The defendant doctor owed her a duty to advise her of the disadvantages of the treatment he proposed and this was closely connected with her ability to give consent and make an informed choice as to whether to have treatment. Since the injury she sustained was within the scope of the defendant's duty to warn and was the result of the risk of which she was entitled to be warned, the defendant's failure to warn the claimant was a breach of this duty and the cause of the claimant's injury: 'Her right of autonomy and dignity can and ought to be vindicated by a narrow and modest departure from traditional causation principles' (Lord Steyn at [24]).[32]

9.2.2.3 Indeterminate causes

What is the situation when there is more than one defendant, each of whom has been negligent, but neither of whom can be proved to be the cause of the harm suffered? This is what is known as an 'indeterminate cause'. If it is accepted that mesothelioma, for example, is caused by a single fibre of asbestos entering the lung, then *Fairchild* becomes a case of indeterminate causes. This is because each of the negligent defendants was equally likely to have exposed the claimants to the single asbestos fibre that caused the disease. By contrast, *McGhee*, on whose decision the decision in *Fairchild* rests, would not be a case of indeterminate cause, as the dust all came from the same place, albeit some was 'innocent' and some was 'guilty' dust.

In cases from other jurisdictions raising the issue of the inability to prove which of two negligent defendants actually caused the harm, courts have found another novel way to circumvent the 'but for' test. In the US case of *Summers* v *Tice* [1948] and the similar Canadian case of *Cook* v *Lewis* [1951], the court shifted the burden of proof in this type of situation. In both cases the issue was which of two negligent hunters had fired the shot that hit the claimant (and hence which should be held liable). Both had fired their guns at approximately the same moment. Evidence could show only that the bullet fired came from one of their two guns—therefore, if the 'but for' test was applied, the claimant could never win, as on the balance of probabilities neither

---

32. It should be noted that *Sidaway* was decided at a time when medical paternalism was rife, whereas *Chester* came at a time when patient rights were more carefully considered (following the implementation of the Human Rights Act 1998) and, even though the case was not based on human rights submissions, Carole Chester's human rights certainly seem to have been championed.

defendant would be more than 50 per cent likely to have fired the offending shot. Shifting the burden of proof in this situation meant that the court asked the defendant to prove that he was *not* responsible—if neither could do this then, the court held, they should both pay (each was jointly and severally liable). However, in *Fairchild*, the House of Lords, which discussed the 'two hunters' scenario, explicitly rejected the idea of reversing the burden of proof, deeming it artificial, as proof was the problem in the first place (Lord Hutton at [110]).

A close example to the 'two hunters' scenario can be seen in *Fitzgerald v Lane* [1987]. In this case, a pedestrian crossing a road was hit first by one negligent driver and then almost immediately by another, rendering him tetraplegic. It was not possible to establish which of the two impacts had actually caused the tetraplegia (and it may well have been a combination of both) and applying the 'but for' test would therefore have rendered each of the negligent drivers equally (50:50) responsible but, crucially, not liable for the harm. The Court of Appeal, using the 'material increase in risk' idea from *McGhee*, found each of the defendants liable.[33]

 Pause for reflection

In another US case, *Sindell v Abbot Laboratories* [1980], the problem of indeterminate causes was resolved in a different way. In this case, five pharmaceutical companies were all held liable for supplying a drug that caused vaginal cancer in women, even though, because the cancer developed a long time after the drugs had been taken, it could not be established by any of the claimants which company had supplied the particular drug that caused them to suffer harm. Any of the five companies could have been responsible, as the problem was in the design of the drug itself, rather than a manufacturing error. Had the 'but for' test been applied, none of the companies would have had to pay any compensation. The court surmounted this problem by adapting the rule from *Summers v Tice* and apportioning liability on the basis of each defendant's market share. Therefore, *all* the companies were liable (and so all had to pay), but the court also decided that the *amount* each should pay should be based on that company's share of the market.

Do you think this is a justifiable decision? Is apportioning the damages to be paid in this way more appropriate when the harm is caused by a product (rather than employers), particularly when all companies posed an equal risk of causing vaginal cancer?

9.2.2.4 Loss of chance

There has been an interesting and different response to the idea that while we know and can identify an increase in the *risk* of something happening, we cannot always say the same for the actual cause. These are sometimes referred to as 'loss of chance' cases.

---

33. It may also be notable that this case was decided before **Wilsher** reached the House of Lords, as noted by Lord Bingham in **Fairchild** at [28].

> ### *Hotson* v *East Berkshire Health Authority* [1987] HL
>
> Following an accident while climbing a tree, a boy fell to the ground and injured his hip. In hospital, the doctors who saw him were negligent in their diagnosis and failed to notice that vascular necrosis (a condition where blood vessels die) had developed and the boy was sent home without adequate treatment. Five days later he returned to hospital and the condition of his hip was correctly diagnosed, though by this time there was nothing that could be done about it. This meant that he would inevitably suffer paralysis. Expert medical evidence showed that had the diagnosis been made correctly at the time the boy first came to hospital, there would have been a 25 per cent chance that the condition could have been prevented. However, by the time he came back five days later, there was no chance that he could be cured.
>
> Applying the 'but for' test, it could not be shown, therefore, on the balance of probabilities, that the boy would have avoided the condition if there had been no negligence on the part of the doctors: there was a 75 per cent chance that he would have developed the condition even if he had been properly diagnosed initially. The House of Lords applied this test and, therefore, his claim failed.

Hotson, like *Barnett*, perfectly illustrates exactly what is needed for a claimant to pass the 'but for' test and be successful in proving factual causation: more than 50 per cent likelihood that the defendant's negligent actions caused the damage. However, notwithstanding the fact that the final outcome of *Hotson* can be seen as a straightforward application of the classic 'but for' test, the case raises further interesting issues. Both the court of first instance and the Court of Appeal accepted an alternative argument (or an alternative definition of the *harm* suffered)[34] that the claimant *could* have established that he had '*lost a chance*'—the 25 per cent chance of not having the condition—and that this harm was definitely caused (on the balance of probabilities) by the negligence in question. Because of this, they had awarded him 25 per cent of the total damages he would have received had he been successful in his initial claim. This 'lost chance' argument was rejected by the House of Lords.[35]

While this 'lost chance' idea was a novel approach, it was not one without a basis in law (damages for lost chance are, in some circumstances, available in economic loss claims and also in contract law). However, the idea clearly did not attract the House of Lords who returned to thinking about causation mechanistically rather than probabilistically. The question, they said, was whether Hotson had been 'doomed' when he came to the hospital in the first place, in a similar way that the claimant in *Barnett* had been. There was a 75 per cent likelihood that this was the case and that the negligent treatment therefore made no difference and, translating actual percentages into legal certainties, this meant that he had *no chance* of recovery.

---

34. So in this sense, lost chance is the reverse corollary of 'material increase in risk'.

35. Applying *Hotson*, Judy's claim in the scenarios outlined at the beginning of the chapter would also fail.

Pause for reflection

Is it right that if a claimant can show a 51 per cent likelihood that negligence caused their harm it will be treated as a legal certainty that it did (and 100 per cent of the damages will be recoverable), whereas if you can show only a 49 per cent likelihood that the negligence caused the harm it will be treated as a legal certainty that it did not (and no damages will be recoverable)? This is known as the 'all or nothing' rule and would seem fairer if we were talking about certainties, rather than probabilities.

It is not, however, clear from reading the House of Lords' decision in *Hotson* whether the law lords meant to rule out permanently the possibility of 'lost chance' claims in medical/personal injury cases. Interestingly, there have been a number of cases post-*Hotson* recognising the idea of a 'lost chance' when the claim has been one for economic loss (see, for example, *Allied Maples Group* v *Simmons and Simmons* [1995] and *Dixon* v *Clement Jones* [2004]), so clearly the type of loss is one that is still recognised within the law of negligence. The loss of chance issue, in relation to medical negligence, was revisited in *Gregg* v *Scott* [2005].

Gregg v *Scott* [2005] HL

The claimant went to the doctor complaining about a lump under his left arm, which the doctor failed to accurately diagnose as cancerous. As a result of this failure, the lump grew and the cancer treatment that the claimant eventually received was delayed by nine months, and his chance of survival decreased.

Medical evidence showed that 17 in every 100 people who developed the same kind of cancer could be cured by prompt treatment (defined as within one year of the tumour appearing) and that a further 25 in every 100 people would be cured even with a delay of one year. The other 58 people would be incurable, no matter when the cancer was diagnosed or treated. Working with these figures, the claimant alleged that he had started with a 42 per cent chance of being cured, had his treatment not been delayed, but that this had decreased to 25 per cent because of the delay that occurred.

A 3:2 split House of Lords rejected his claim, with the majority stating that the claimant needed to show that the doctor's negligence made it more likely than not (over 50 per cent more likely) that he could not be cured. Since, at the outset, he was 58 per cent likely to die anyway, he could not pass this test. Therefore, it could not be shown that 'but for' the doctor's negligent diagnosis he could not be cured.

In the alternative, the claimant argued that he had effectively lost a 17 per cent chance of survival (the difference between 42 per cent and 25 per cent). However, this claim was also rejected, with the majority of the House of Lords holding that loss of chance could not form the basis of a medical negligence claim.

The 'lost chance' argument in *Gregg* differs from that in *Hotson* in an important way—in *Hotson* there was an either/or situation: when he reached hospital the first time, the court viewed that either it was too late to do something about his hip, or it was not. In *Gregg*, the situation was different: even when the claimant first went to the doctor the chances of survival were against him and, on balance, he was 58 per cent likely to die from the cancer rather than survive. What the delay in diagnosis did was to *reduce* his *chance of survival*, not eradicate it, thus raising what is, arguably, the straightforward issue of whether someone can recover for a lost chance that can actually be calculated.[36]

> **Counterpoint**
>
> Lord Nicholls, in the opening paragraph of his powerful dissenting opinion in *Gregg*, described the issue as follows:
>
> > This appeal raises a question which has divided courts and commentators throughout the common law world. The division derives essentially from different perceptions of what constitutes injustice in a common type of medical negligence case. Some believe a remedy is essential and that a principled ground for providing an appropriate remedy can be found. Others are not persuaded. I am in the former camp. (at [1])
>
> Arguably, this passage sums up most of the law on factual causation—or at least those cases where an unorthodox approach has been taken or departure from the 'but for' test has been suggested. It seems like in some cases, notably employment and industrial cases, more of the judiciary is willing to recognise the 'injustice' that might stem from a rigid mathematical approach to causation than they are in medical negligence cases. Lord Nicholls goes on to describe the idea that a patient can only recover damages if his original chance of recovery had been more than 50 per cent is not only 'irrational and indefensible' (at [3]) but makes the duty of care a doctor owes their patients to take reasonable care 'hollow' (at [4]). We would agree.
>
> Baroness Hale (who was in the majority in *Gregg*), commented on the loss of chance argument, pointing out that if it could be concluded that a doctor's negligence had affected a claimant's chances to some calculable extent, then we would have 'a "heads you lose everything, tails I win something" situation', operating in favour of the claimant (at [224]). We suggest this is better than a 'heads I win something, tails I win nothing' situation, operating wholly in favour of the defendant, particularly when it is shown (or admitted) that the defendant is negligent.[37] The policy arguments that point in favour of a claimant-favouring
>
>

36. On an alternative view, the 'loss' that the claimant identified in *Gregg* is essentially fictional. On this view it is inaccurate to say that the claimant lost a chance—either the claimant was one of the 42 people out of 100 who would have survived with immediate treatment, or he was one of the 58 who would not. As one of the former group, the claimant had a 100 per cent chance of survival, if in the latter they had a 0 per cent chance. The difficulty is that we cannot know which group the claimant fell into so we are thrown back onto the statistical probability (58:42) that he fell within the latter class. Importantly, just because 42 out of 100 people survive in such a situation, it does not mean that *each one of those people* had a 42 per cent chance of survival; rather 42 of them had a 100 per cent chance of survival and 58 had a 0 per cent chance.

37. However, again, an alternative view should be noted. This suggests that if loss of chance claims were recognised, this would potentially change the outcome of almost every negligence claim. As discussed above, as things stand, if a claimant can establish on the balance of probabilities that the defendant's negligence caused him a loss, they recover all of their losses. If a claimant cannot prove

→

system stem from the underlying aims of the tort system itself, not least the desire to compensate those who have suffered harm due to the wrongs of another, but also in the more 'practical' aspects such as making people (in this example, doctors) act more *carefully* than they might otherwise do, meaning that the number of *future* potential claimants is reduced. However, when the defendant has *not* wronged the claimant, as may be the case, it would be unjust to make them pay. Crudely, as the law stands, it could be argued that the 'chance' of the claimant making a financial gain (or avoiding an economic loss) is valued more highly than the chance of the claimant not suffering a physical harm or even death.

Furthermore, the type of calculation that the court is being asked to make in a loss of chance claim is not one that is wholly unknown to them (and not only because lost chance is recognised in other types of claim, outside medical negligence or other personal injury). When damages for an 'ordinary' personal injury are calculated, reductions and increases in the amount to be awarded can be based on the 'chance' of something happening in the future.[38] Arguably, it would not be difficult to extend the principle.

After *Gregg* it seems that it will be extremely difficult for any claim to be based on lost chance when the issue is personal injury or medical negligence, although opinions differ as to whether the decision in *Gregg* rules out this type of claim in its entirety or merely restricts it to as yet undefined situations (Lord Phillips and, possibly, Baroness Hale refused to rule out lost chance claims in other contexts). Perhaps such a situation might fall factually somewhere between *Hotson* and *Gregg* or be an extension of the facts in *Gregg* where the lost chance claimed for has literally been lost.

 Pause for reflection

Do you think that the fact that Gregg was still alive at the time the House of Lords issued its decision in the case counted against him? If he had literally lost the chance of survival (by dying), might the decision have gone the other way? On this issue, look at the speech of Lord Phillips, who was in the majority, but seems to indicate that he might have ruled the other way (thus making the outcome 3:2 in favour of the claimant), had Gregg actually died.

this on the balance of probabilities he recovers nothing. However, very rarely are we 100 per cent sure that the claimant would have been harmed even without the breach, so almost every claimant could argue that they lost some chance of escaping unharmed. Moreover, where negligence claims succeed, we are rarely 100 per cent certain that the harm would not have been suffered but for the breach, because the question is necessarily hypothetical. Would acceptance of the loss of a chance argument entail that such claimants' damages be reduced to reflect the fact that there was a chance that the harm would have been suffered anyway? The loss of a chance approach appears to involve a shift away from the all or nothing approach we currently have. If so, cases like *Hotson*, *Wilsher* and even *Fairchild* (where 100 per cent of the loss was recoverable despite the uncertainties) would have to be overruled, unless we could say that, *in some situations*, the all or nothing approach applies, *whereas in others*, the lost chance approach does. This is something, it is suggested, which would be difficult to do without arbitrariness and inconsistency, though Lord Nicholls in his dissent sought to do just this.

38. This is simply a question of apportionment. See e.g. *Rothwell* v *Chemical and Insulating Co Ltd* [2007].

9.2.2.5 Uncertain actions

So far we have looked at cases where it has been difficult to show what has actually happened in the past, thus making the application of the 'but for' test problematic. A different problematic situation as regards this test has arisen in circumstances when either the claim being made relates to something that has not been done, but should have been (an omission), or—more precisely—when we cannot be quite *sure* what would or should have been done in a given situation.

In *Bolitho* v *City and Hackney Health Authority* [1998], it was alleged that a hospital consultant was negligent in failing to respond promptly to her pager, as a result of which the claimant's child died.[39] In seeking to establish a causal link between the doctor's failure to attend and the child's death, the question for the House of Lords was what the consultant *would* have done if she had responded to the call. The consultant argued that had she responded to her pager message and attended the child, she would not in fact have intubated the child. Medical evidence showed that this was the only course of action that could have saved the child at that time. So viewed, on the balance of probabilities, the child would have died whether she had responded or not. However, this was not the way the House of Lords chose to approach the case. Rather, they held that it had to be established whether the doctor's failure to intubate would have been negligent (applying the test from **Bolam v Friern Hospital Management Committee** [1957]). If it was, legal causation was *also* established because it could be said that what the doctor *should* have done, but negligently did not do, was the likely cause of the child's death.[40]

9.2.3 **Multiple sufficient causes**

We have looked above at the problems encountered where a claim involves potential multiple defendants who each *could have* caused the harm complained of, but cannot be proven to have done so, according to the 'but for' test. A similar but different problem arises where there is more than one defendant, each of whom *does* pass the 'but for' test, but where one of their actions comes later than that of the other. Or, the later action may be non-tortious, but still capable of giving rise to harm. Here, instead of indeterminate causes, we have what is known as multiple sufficient causes; the question is whether the action of the second party (negligent or otherwise) absolves the original tortfeasor from blame. Put another way, the question is whether the original defendant, who is clearly liable for *some* harm, should *remain* liable after the unrelated actions of another party.

Baker v Willoughby [1970] HL

The claimant suffered injury to his leg as a result of a car accident negligently caused by the defendant. The resulting pain and stiffness meant that he had to find alternative employment. Later, while working in a scrap-metal yard, but before the first case went

➡

---

39. *Bolitho* is discussed in more detail in Chapter 8, pp 206–207.
40. See also *Gouldsmith* v *Mid-Staffordshire General Hospitals Trust* [2007] and *Ganz* v *Childs & Others* [2011].

→

to trial, the man was shot in the same leg by criminals trying to rob the scrap-metal business. His leg was later amputated. The question for the House of Lords was whether the negligent driver should pay compensation for the effect of his negligence on the claimant's leg for the rest of the claimant's life, or whether his liability for this ended at the point of the second tortious event (the shooting). The defendant in the case argued that the act of the robbers in shooting the man in the leg 'obliterated' the effect of the injury caused by him. This argument had been accepted by the Court of Appeal, who awarded the claimant damages to compensate for the leg injury up until the time the later injury occurred. It was not in dispute that the criminals who shot the claimant would have been liable for the additional extent of the injury they caused to the leg, but these men had never been found, so could not be sued.

The House of Lords felt that this might lead to a gap in damages. If the original defendant was liable for the original injury only to the point in time that a later, more serious injury, caused by another party, occurred, and that other party (if able to be sued) was only liable for the *additional* harm caused, then there would be no compensation awarded for the continuing effects of the first injury. On this basis, they said that the original defendant's negligence continued to operate even after the additional harm caused by the gun shot.[41]

By way of contrast, what is the position of the court when the later event is either non-tortious or even naturally occurring? In such a situation, no one would have any liability for the additional harm caused by the later event.

Jobling v *Associated Dairies Ltd* [1982] HL

As a result of a workplace injury, the claimant suffered damage to his back which subsequently reduced his earning capacity. Before the trial against his employer, the man contracted an unrelated back disease which rendered him completely incapable of any work. As in *Baker*, the question for the House of Lords was whether the defendant should continue to be liable for the original injury and the loss of earnings associated with it past the point where the later (and greater) harm was suffered.

The House of Lords refused this claim. They relied on the fact that when assessing damages, account could be taken of the ordinary 'vicissitudes of life' (hardships) that a person might be expected to encounter, and that damages were usually reduced accordingly to take these into account. This meant that Jobling could only be compensated up until the point that he contracted the disease, as it could be said that this would have happened anyway.

The decision in *Jobling* means that the case can be seen as one where the later 'sufficient cause' of the harm complained of has overtaken or *superseded* the original cause

---

41. One tenuous way of putting this is that the decision could be justified on the ground that the claimant would not have been working in the scrap-metal yard (and so would not have been shot) had it not been for the negligence of the first defendant. For a more concrete exposition of this idea (though rejected), see *Gray* v *Thames Trains* [2009], where *Baker* was doubted.

(or 'obliterated' it, as was argued in **Baker**). When this happens, the defendant will be liable only for the damages relating to the extent of the injury they caused, up until the time of the superseding event. The point is that the superseding event, such as the disease in **Jobling**, would have happened anyway, whether the claimant had been previously injured or not and, as in this case, damages after that point in time are rendered irrelevant.

While **Jobling** did not explicitly overrule **Baker**, it could possibly be said that **Baker** is now a case 'confined to its facts' and it is therefore possible that if a similar situation arose today, the later event, even if tortious, would supersede the first (though see Lord Brown in *Gray* v *Thames Trains* [2009] at [96]–[97]). The question as to whether or not **Baker** 'survives' **Jobling** may in part be answered by *Murrell* v *Healy* [2001]. In this case, the claimant was injured in a car accident, for which he received £58,500 compensation from the other driver in an out-of-court settlement. Later in the same year, he was involved in another accident, and the question for the court was whether the defendant should have to pay a reduced sum of damages to make allowance for the fact that the claimant had already been compensated for *some* injury. The Court of Appeal held that the defendant should compensate Murrell only for any additional damage caused by the accident (the reverse of **Baker**, where the second tortfeasors were unable to be sued) and that if the first defendant's liability was unaffected by the second tort, the second defendant cannot be liable for any of the original losses. Murrell also developed joint problems in his legs which were unattributable to either of the accidents—following **Jobling** and the 'vicissitudes of life' idea, the damages he had been awarded were then reduced.[42]

 Pause for reflection

It should be noted that the question whether something is a supervening cause is very similar to the question whether the actions of a later tortfeasor (or otherwise) breaks the chain of causation back to the original defendant (thereby absolving them from liability in entirety). Where the line is drawn between these two issues is very hard to define, and people have different opinions—where do you think it is? Is *Murrell* a case where the chain of causation would have broken, but the claimant had been lucky enough to have already settled out of court with the first defendant?

9.3 Legal causation

When one or more factors, including the defendant's negligence, *are* found to be necessary conditions of the claimant's harm (factual causation), a claimant still has to determine the 'real' or 'operative' cause in law (legal causation). This involves two distinct tests, the first asking whether the harm was too remote a consequence of the defendant's negligence, and the second asking whether any subsequent event could be said to have broken the chain of causation that leads back to the defendant's negligent

42. In *Performance Cars* v *Abraham* [1962] the same idea is used in a case concerning property damage.

act. Each of these tests represents a value judgement on how far we think a defendant's liability should extend—that is, regarding the final question about to whom responsibility for harm is appropriately allocated. In this section we will deal with each of these tests in turn.

9.3.1 Remoteness

When a court asks whether a harm was too 'remote' a consequence of the defendant's negligence (breach of duty), what is essentially being asked is whether the consequences of the negligent action were so far removed from it as to have been *unforeseeable* by the defendant (judged by the standard of the 'reasonable person') at the time the action occurred. Put another way, the defendant may argue that the consequences of their action were *not* foreseeable—that is, that they were too remote. If this is the case then cause in law is not established and the claimant's case can go no further. The formulation of the remoteness test means that whether something is too remote is judged in light of what was known at the time the breach occurred; that is, with foresight, and not with the benefit of hindsight.

Overseas Tankship (UK) v Morts Dock and Engineering Co (The Wagon Mound) No 1 [1961] PC

The defendants were responsible for a ship that had been loading in Sydney Harbour, Australia. Due to the negligence of one of the crew, some furnace oil leaked into the water and formed a thin film over its surface. This spread to a neighbouring wharf owned by the claimants, where welders were working repairing another ship. Some days later, sparks from the welding managed to ignite the oil and the resulting fire caused serious damage to the wharf and other ships surrounding it.

At first instance, the judge found that damage caused by the oil itself (for example, to the slipway of the wharf) was reasonably foreseeable but, because evidence showed that it is difficult to ignite furnace oil spread thinly on water, damage to the claimant's property caused *by fire* would *not* have been foreseeable to a reasonable person (at the time the oil was spilt). The Privy Council agreed, finding that a reasonable person could not have foreseen fire damage as a possible consequence of the negligent act.[43]

Prior to the Privy Council's decision in **The Wagon Mound (No 1)**, a defendant was liable for *all* the direct physical consequences of their negligent act (*Re Polemis and Furness, Withy & Co Ltd* [1921]). What this meant was that defendants would be liable for any consequences of their breach of duty, as long as they were directly the result of the breach, whether or not these could have been foreseen, even if the consequences

---

43. By the time of **The Wagon Mound (No 2)**, evidence showed that though it was *unlikely*, it was quite *possible* for oil spread thinly on the surface of water to be ignited if a certain temperature was reached, such as if a welder's spark fell onto something floating in the oily water and smouldered for a while (as had, in fact, happened in this situation). Therefore, the issue in that case was not about foreseeability but whether, given that the damage *could* now be considered foreseeable, a reasonable person would have taken steps to prevent it—a breach issue.

may have been substantially different from those a reasonable person might expect, and even if the consequences ended up being far more serious than could have been anticipated. The decision in **The Wagon Mound (No 1)** substantially narrowed the *Re Polemis* test (indeed, the Privy Council stated that *Re Polemis* was no longer good law), establishing a far more defendant-friendly test. Following **The Wagon Mound (No 1)**, the question to be asked in order to establish whether the claimant's harm is too remote, is this: 'Was the *kind* of damage suffered by the claimant reasonably foreseeable at the time the breach occurred?' This test is still the primary test for remoteness of damage in negligence—and indeed extends further into other torts.[44] The decision in **The Wagon Mound (No 2)** did not change the nature of this test—it is simply that on the new evidence presented to the court by this time, the Privy Council could conclude that even a thin film of oil on water would ignite—although the risk of damage by fire was small, it still existed.

It should be noted here that the way the remoteness test has been formulated means that only the *type* of damage needs to have been foreseeable, not the *extent*. So, for example, as long as *some* physical damage was a foreseeable consequence of the breach, the *amount* of physical damage suffered need not be. Take a simple example of driving a car. It is clear to any reasonable person that if a car is driven negligently, physical injury to other road users (including other drivers, passengers, cyclists, pedestrians and so on) would be foreseeable, as would property damage to any other vehicle. So, it does not matter in law that, even with a small amount of carelessness (for example, a momentary lapse of concentration), a pedestrian is seriously injured or even killed. The equation is:

NEGLIGENT DRIVING = RISK OF PHYSICAL INJURY = LIABLE FOR ALL FORESEEABLE (PHYSICAL) CONSEQUENCES

Similarly, if a negligent driver hits another person's vehicle, it is evident that damage to the vehicle itself would be foreseeable, as would be damage to the contents of the vehicle. It would not matter what the contents of the vehicle are—so if a truck was transporting cheap beans or expensive designer clothing, the negligent driver would be liable for the full costs of whatever was damaged.

While this distinction (type versus extent of damage) appears relatively straightforward, it has not always proved to be so. For example, in *Doughty* v *Turner Manufacturing Co* [1964], the claimant, a factory worker, suffered serious burns when an asbestos lid was knocked into a vat of hot liquid, causing a chemical reaction that made the liquid boil up over the edge of the vat. The specific chemical reaction was not foreseeable to the reasonable person—but the claimant contended that as it would be foreseeable that the lid falling in would cause some liquid to splash out, and that the likely result of this would be that the claimant would be burnt, the *type of injury* he had suffered *was* foreseeable. However, the court disagreed with this interpretation, holding that an eruption of boiling liquid was different from being splashed by liquid.

Another case, however, appears to tell a different story. In *Hughes* v *Lord Advocate* [1963], an 8-year-old boy fell down a manhole in the street which had been left open by Post Office employees earlier that day. Upon finishing work, the men had covered

---

44. See, for example, Chapter 18, p 535. *Steele*, however, says that **The Wagon Mound (No 1)** test is 'beginning to show its age' (p 186).

the hole with a canvas tent and surrounded this with paraffin lamps to alert to the danger. The boy had picked up one of the lamps and taken it into the tent. While playing, he knocked the lamp over into the manhole and this caused an explosion of paraffin vapour and the boy fell into the hole and was badly burnt. The defendants claimed that they could not have foreseen that the boy would enter the tent with the lamp and be burnt by a subsequent explosion. The House of Lords disagreed. Finding the defendants liable, they held that it was reasonably foreseeable that the *type* of damage would be burns, therefore the exact means by which the burns occurred did not matter (see also *Jolley* v *Sutton London Borough Council* [2000]).

 Pause for reflection

How can the difference between the two previous cases be explained? Do you think the fact that both of the cases were decided in the two years immediately after *The Wagon Mound (No 1)*, which created a 'new' test, could have anything to do with it? Perhaps the judges were simply struggling to implement the new test. Or, perhaps for policy reasons, the court was simply more sympathetic towards a child?

As well as in *Doughty* v *Turner,* in the years following the reformulation of the remoteness test in the **Wagon Mound (No 1)**, there were still inconsistencies in attempts to convince a court that physical damage suffered was too remote to be attributed to the defendant. For example, in *Tremain* v *Pike* [1969], a defendant negligently allowed his farm to become infested with rats. The claimant, a farm worker, contracted Weil's disease[45] as a result of being exposed to rats' urine. Even though it is clearly arguable that physical injury from rats is foreseeable, the claimant lost his case because the court held that while injury from rat bites would be foreseeable, Weil's disease was not. However, in *Vacwell Engineering Co Ltd* v *BDH Chemicals Ltd* [1971], it was held that because a small chemical explosion might be foreseeable, all damage caused by a large explosion that occurred when ampoules of chemicals were being washed in water was foreseeable even though no one could have predicted this happening.

 Pause for reflection

It seems unlikely today that a court would follow the 'version' of the foreseeability test seen in *Doughty* v *Turner. Lunney & Oliphant* suggest that the 'modern trend', at least in relation to personal injuries, seems to be to interpret the *type* of injury in a broad sense (see, for example, *Smith* v *Leech Brain* [1962], discussed below), so the extent of the harm or the exact way in which it was caused poses no problems to claimants (p 275). This may also explain the decision to include psychiatric harm with physical injury under the more generous heading of 'personal injury' in **Page v Smith** [1996] and *Simmons* v *British Steel plc* [2004].

---

45. Weil's disease is an acute human form of Leptospirosis, also known as canicola fever, haemorrhagic jaundice, infectious jaundice, mud fever, spirochetal jaundice, swamp fever, swineherd's disease, caver's flu or sewerman's flu, and is a bacterial infection resulting from exposure to the *Leptospira interrogans* bacterium, often found in contaminated water.

9.3.1.1 The 'egg shell skull' rule

We have seen that the remoteness test is used to determine whether the type of damage suffered is foreseeable, not the extent. Therefore, once the type of harm is judged foreseeable, the defendant will be held liable for all the damage caused, even where the extent itself was not. Because of this, a rule has been developed to protect even those claimants who suffer what may be called 'extreme' damage because they already have some kind of susceptibility or 'weakness'.

The 'egg shell skull' rule, as it has become known, is basically a principle that states that a defendant will be liable for the full extent of the harm they caused, even if the person harmed suffered more harm than might be expected, due to an existing weakness or frailty. The maxim can be expressed as 'the defendant must take the victim as they find them'. The classic example of this principle comes from the case *Smith* v *Leech Brain & Co Ltd* [1962]. In this case, because of the defendant's negligence, the claimant was burnt on the lip. The claimant had a pre-cancerous skin condition, which became cancerous as a result of the burn, and he eventually died. The defendant was held liable for the full consequences of his negligence (that is, all the physical damage (*type*), so this included the cancer (*extent*)). The court held that as long as physical injury had been foreseeable, it did not matter what the extent of this was, or that the claimant was already more susceptible to a greater level of harm.

In *Lagden* v *O'Connor* [2003] it was confirmed that the 'egg shell skull' principle also applies to economic harms. This, if a claimant suffers heightened economic loss as a result of an already weak economic circumstance, a defendant will be liable for the full extent of the loss.

9.3.2 **Intervening acts**

Even if the defendant 'causes' an accident by setting off a sequence or chain of events, a later event or situation might be held to be the 'real' cause of the eventuating harm. In such circumstances, the chain of causation (which began with the defendant's negligence) is said to be 'broken'. The result of this is that the defendant is not held liable for the claimant's harm. The later event is often called a *novus actus interveniens* (literally, a new intervening act).

This is the second aspect to establishing cause in law (the first being whether the harm was too remote). It will already be a familiar idea to those who have studied criminal law. However, as we have already indicated, there is a very fine line between 'supervening' events (as seen in *Jobling* and which go to questions of cause in *fact*) and later 'intervening' acts (which involve questions relating to cause in *law*).

9.3.2.1 Later negligent acts

One question is what *kind* of later act is required in order for the chain of causation to be broken. It is clear that subsequent deliberately wrongful acts (crimes, for example) will be sufficient (*Weld-Blundell* v *Stephens* [1920]).[46] Beyond this, the question

---

46. This obviously has links to the situations in which a *duty* in respect of the acts of a third party can arise (see Chapter 4, but contrast *Topp* v *London Country Bus (South West) Ltd* [1993], p 88).

remains whether a later act has itself to be *negligent* in order to break the chain of causation. Whether what happens subsequently is foreseeable is also relevant—if it is something that is clearly likely to happen as a result of the defendant's negligence then it is unlikely this will break the chain. This was plainly expressed by Lord Reid in **Home Office v Dorset Yacht Co** [1970], who said that a subsequent negligent act of a third party: 'must have been something very likely to happen if it is not to be regarded as a *novus actus interveniens* breaking the chain of causation. I do not think a mere foreseeable possibility should be sufficient' (at 1030).

In *Rouse v Squires* [1973], for example, a lorry driver negligently caused his lorry to jack-knife and block part of a motorway. A car subsequently drove into the rear of the lorry. A second lorry driver stopped to assist, pulling over some distance in front of the accident. A third lorry driver stopped before the accident scene, leaving his headlights on for illumination. The driver of a fourth lorry was less careful and did not see the accident scene until he was almost upon it. He skidded into the back of the third lorry, killing its driver. The question for the court was which negligent lorry driver caused the death. At first instance, the trial judge held the fourth lorry driver wholly responsible as his negligent driving had broken the chain of causation in relation to the original negligent lorry driver. However, the Court of Appeal found that the chain of causation had not been broken. *Both* drivers were responsible and damages were apportioned between them.

Knightley v *Johns* [1982] CA

A serious traffic accident in a one-way tunnel was caused by the defendant's negligent driving and the police were called to the scene. Having forgotten to stop traffic entering the other end of the tunnel, the police officer in charge sent two officers on motorcycles, one of whom was the claimant, against the direction of the oncoming traffic to go back and close the tunnel. Both the instruction and driving against the flow of traffic were expressly contrary to police standing orders, but nevertheless the two officers complied with the instruction. Near the entrance to the tunnel, the claimant suffered injury when he was hit by a car being driven into it.

At first instance, the judge found that neither the officer's instruction nor the claimant had been negligent and that their actions did not break the chain of causation back to the original defendant, who would therefore be liable for the claimant's injuries in full. However, on appeal, the Court of Appeal found that the police officer giving the instruction *had* been negligent and that his negligence was sufficient to break the chain of causation between the defendant car driver's original negligence and the claimant's injuries. As a result, no claim could succeed against the defendant.

Where there is more than one party who can be said to be responsible for causing harm, it is unusual for the courts to find only one of them legally responsible. The Civil Liability (Contribution) Act 1978 means that the court can easily apportion damages between the parties responsible (or leave them to do this for themselves). Because of this, it may be less likely for a court to find that a later negligent act breaks the chain of causation back to the original defendant.

Thus, in *Wright* v *Lodge* [1993],[47] the first defendant's Mini broke down on a dual carriageway. While the driver was trying to restart the car, it was hit by a lorry being driven negligently over the speed limit, injuring a passenger in the car as a result. The lorry also crossed the central reservation, tipped on its side and collided with oncoming vehicles on the other side of the carriageway, injuring two drivers, one fatally. The injured parties sued the driver of the lorry, who joined (using the Civil Liability (Contribution) Act 1978) the driver of the Mini as a co-defendant. The first defendant was found to have been negligent in not pushing the car to the hard shoulder, and was ordered to pay 10 per cent of their passenger's damages. However, with respect to the injuries to the other claimants, the lorry driver was found to have broken the chain of causation and, as a result, was held wholly responsible for the compensation that had to be paid to them.[48]

9.3.2.2 Acts of the claimant

Can the claimant's own negligence break the chain of causation? It is rare for this to be the case, because generally if a claimant negligently contributes to their own injuries, this can be dealt with via the defence of contributory negligence (see Chapter 10). Since 1945 this has been only a 'partial' defence, meaning that the claimant's contribution to their own harm can be assessed as a proportion and their damages reduced accordingly. However, there may still be occasions where the claimant's own actions after the original negligence of the defendant are considered *so* careless that they should remove any share of the responsibility from the original defendant. An example of this can be seen in *McKew* v *Holland and Hannen and Cubitts (Scotland) Ltd* [1969]. In this case, McKew suffered a leg injury at work due to his employer's negligence, which resulted in stiffness and impaired mobility. Subsequently, he went to inspect a flat in the course of his work, which could only be accessed by descending a steep staircase without a handrail. As he was about to go down the stairs, his leg buckled and to avoid falling down the stairs and landing on his head, he threw himself forwards, breaking his ankle. McKew claimed that the defendant should be liable for this damage, as it was an extension of the original injury. However, the House of Lords rejected his claim. The claimant had negligently thrown himself down the stairs and, in so doing, had broken the chain of causation. The defendant was not, therefore, liable for his broken ankle.

McKew can be contrasted with *Wieland* v *Cyril Lord Carpets* [1969] where, as a result of the defendant's negligence, the claimant had to wear a neck brace. This restricted her ability to use her bifocal glasses properly with the result that she fell down some stairs, while being escorted by her son, and injured her ankle. The court found that she had been as careful as she could have been and therefore her actions could not break the chain of causation and her ankle injury was also caused by the defendant's negligence.

---

47. Contrast to *Rouse* v *Squires* [1973], above.

48. Consider this in relation to Pauline's claim against David. Did the police break the chain of causation? Compare *Knightley* v *Johns* [1982], *Rouse* v *Squires* [1973] and *Wright* v *Lodge* [1993]. Also see *Robinson* v *Post Office* [1974].

Pause for reflection

Do you think the difference between the two cases described above can be attributed to the amount of care the claimants took for themselves after they had sustained their original injury? Was it not reasonable for McKew to choose to fall in the way he did rather than risk suffering a different type of injury? What do you think the situation would have been if McKew's injured leg had buckled while actually on his way down the stairs? See *Spencer* v *Wincanton Holdings Ltd* [2009].

Perhaps surprisingly, a claimant's own actions in committing suicide while imprisoned (*Kirkham* v *Chief Constable of Greater Manchester Police* [1990]) or while being held in police custody (**Reeves** v **Commissioner of Police for the Metropolis** [2000]) has been found not to break the chain of causation back to the defendant. While this might seem surprising, as suicide is a deliberate act, the reasoning of the courts was that because the police had a duty of care to protect the specific claimant from suicide (in *Kirkham* by passing on the information that the prisoner was depressed and may become a suicide risk), the claimant doing exactly what may be expected of them should not negate that duty. In **Reeves**, however, the damages awarded were reduced for the contributory negligence of the claimant.

In *Corr* v *IBC Vehicles Ltd* [2008], a similar question arose. A man was seriously injured and almost killed in an accident at work. The accident and injuries led to his suffering clinical depression, and he later committed suicide. Here, his employers (the defendants) did not, as in **Reeves** and *Kirkham*, owe him a specific duty of care to prevent suicide. Instead, the question was whether the suicide had been caused by the original breach of duty (to keep employees reasonably safe) or whether the claimant's deliberate action had broken the chain of causation. The House of Lords found that the chain of causation was not broken, Lord Bingham in particular being swayed by the idea that the suicide was not a free and voluntary choice *because* of the effect of the accident on the mind of the claimant (at [16]). In contrast, the House of Lords found in *Gray* v *Thames Trains* [2009], that a later *criminal* act committed by the claimant, who had sustained both physical and psychiatric injuries in a train crash negligently caused by the defendants, did break the chain of causation.

9.4 **Conclusion**

After a claimant establishes that a duty of care is owed to them in respect of the harm they suffered, and that this duty has been breached by the defendant, the next 'hurdle' is establishing **causation**. In negligence, this has two parts: **cause 'in fact'** and **cause 'in law'**.

To establish cause in fact, the claimant must show, on the balance of probabilities (that is, more than 50 per cent likely), that the defendant's breach caused their harm. This is often expressed as a 'but for' test: Can the claimant establish that 'but for' the defendant's negligent act, they would not have suffered the harm? There are many flaws with this test. In particular, its inflexibility can often cause unjust outcomes, particularly when there are multiple potential causes of the harm. As a result, the courts have devised exceptions to the 'but for' test, which they use in specific types of exceptional case, usually where the outcome that would be generated by the 'but for' test is deemed to be unsatisfactory in some way. However, it should be remembered that the principal exceptions to the 'but for' test created here do not and cannot apply in all cases. To a very large extent they are limited to the type of case in which the decision was first made (for example, the material contribution tests seem only to apply—so far—in industrial cases, but do not apply in medical negligence cases; and the 'lost chance' idea seems limited to claims for economic loss, having been ruled out—for the moment at least—in medical claims).

The second part of causation is cause in law. There are two parts to this (though it may be that only one of them is relevant/arguable in a particular case scenario). Whichever way round the tests for cause in law are carried out, they encompass a remoteness test (which involves establishing whether the damage that occurred was foreseeable to the defendant at the time of the negligence). It is the *type* of harm (for example, personal injury) that must be foreseeable, not its *extent*. The last part of the test is to ask whether any intervening acts (acts that occurred after the defendant's breach) broke the chain of causation. If this is found to be the case, the defendant will not be liable.

✳ End-of-chapter questions

After reading the chapter carefully, try answering the questions below. If you would like to know what we think visit the Online Resource Centre (www.oxfordtextbooks.co.uk/orc/horsey2e/).

1. Is there a coherent way of explaining the difference between supervening and intervening acts?

2. Does the remoteness test lose some of its impact or validity with the incorporation of the 'egg shell skull' rule?

3. What policy reasons can you identify that have affected the courts in asbestos-related injury cases? Are they consistent?

4. To what extent do the rules on factual and legal causation help to achieve the general aims of tort law?

5. Consider the problem question at the start of this chapter. Now having read about the topic, how would you advise Gavin? If you need some pointers in thinking about how to answer this question, turn to the Appendix (p 589) where each problem is annotated with issues and cases to consider. Next, try to write your own answer and finally, log on to our Online Resource Centre (www.oxfordtextbooks.co.uk/orc/horsey2e/) to check your ideas against our suggested outline answer.

✱ Further reading

Reading on causation is often quite difficult, and many articles focus solely on one or two cases. Reading these—and case notes—is good to gain a detailed understanding of some of the more difficult or controversial cases. An excellent place to start your general reading is with Jane Stapleton's article (though this is a little out of date).

Laleng, Per 'Causal Responsibility for Uncertainty and Risk in Toxic Torts' (2010) 18(2) *Tort Law Review* 102

Laleng, Per '*Sienkiewicz* v *Greif (UK) Ltd* and *Willmore Knowsley Metropolitan Borough Council:* a material contribution to uncertainty?' (2011) *Modern Law Review*

Lee, James 'Causation in Negligence: Another Fine Mess' (2008) 24 *Professional Negligence* 194

Morgan, Jonathan 'Lost Causes in the House of Lords: *Fairchild v Glenhaven Funeral Services*' (2003) 66 *Modern Law Review* 277

Smith, LJ 'Causation: The Search for Principle' (2009) 2 *Journal of Personal Injury Law* 101

Stapleton, Jane 'Cause in Fact and the Scope of Liability for Consequences' (2003) 119 *Law Quarterly Review* 388

Steele, Jenny 'Breach of Duty Causing Harm? Recent Encounters between Negligence and Risk' (2007) 60 *Current Legal Problems* 296

10

Defences to negligence

Problem question

Read this problem question carefully, and keep it in mind while you are working through the chapter that follows. At the end of the chapter, you will be able to apply what you have learnt to the problem question and advise the relevant parties.

Ben, Graeme and Andy are old school friends. Every year they go camping together in Snowdonia National Park. After they arrive on the Friday night, they decide to go to the pub where Ben and Graeme spend several hours reminiscing and by the time they leave they are both over the legal driving limit. Andy has not been drinking. On their way back to the campsite they pass a farm and notice a tractor with its keys in the ignition. Graeme gets in and starts the engine. Ben and Andy quickly jump in beside him. None of them wears a seat belt. At first, Graeme drives slowly around the farmyard but when Ben says 'Is that the best you can do?' he decides to go 'off-road' and drives it into a field. Unfortunately, on the rough ground he loses control of the tractor and it overturns. Ben and Andy are thrown out onto the field. Ben is seriously injured. Though Andy escapes with only minor physical injuries, he later develops post traumatic stress disorder (PTSD) as a result of the incident. One day while walking home from work Andy 'snaps' lashing out at an innocent passer-by and causing them serious injury. Though it is recognised that his actions were as a result of his PSTD, he is jailed for six months and loses his job.

10.1 **Introduction**

Consider the following examples:

→ A cycle-courier is knocked down and seriously injured as she swerves to avoid a pedestrian crossing the road. She is not wearing a cycle helmet.

→ A footballer is seriously injured by a late, high tackle in the closing minutes of a crucial cup tie.

→ A would-be burglar is shot by a homeowner as he tries to prise open a down-stairs window.

→ A driving instructor suffers a serious knee injury when the student, to whom she is giving driving lessons, crashes into a lamp post.

In all these scenarios, even if all the other elements of a claim in negligence—that is duty, breach and causation—have been met, the defendant may still be able to deny liability by raising a defence. In so doing, the defendant is in essence saying that although they did carelessly injure the claimant there is nonetheless a good reason why the law should not hold them responsible. The defendant might, for example, argue that the claimant was (at least in part) to blame for their injuries or had accepted the risk of them occurring. Alternatively, they may suggest that an award of damages would be inappropriate on the basis that the claimant was injured while they were engaged in an illegal, or inherently risky, activity. Where a defendant is able to suc-cessfully raise a defence, it may work to defeat the claim entirely or merely reduce the amount of damages payable.

This chapter considers three key defences in the tort of negligence: **consent**, **con-tributory negligence** and **illegality**. While contributory *negligence* (as the name sug-gests) is (generally) confined to claims in negligence,[1] consent and illegality are general defences and, as such, are applicable throughout tort law.[2]

10.2 **Consent**

The defence of consent is based on the common sense notion that 'one who has invited or assented to an act being done towards him cannot, when he suffers it, complain of it as a wrong' (Lord Herschell, *Smith* v *Baker* [1891] at 360).[3] This idea is encapsulated in, and often referred to using, the Latin maxim *volenti non fit injuria* (literally: 'no wrong will be done to the willing'), usually abbreviated to *volenti*. Consent is a complete

---

1. This includes the special liability regimes considered in Part II. The scope of the defence is wide but not unlimited. For an example of its application in a non-negligence context see e.g. *Murphy* v *Culhane* [1977] and further Chapter 14).

2. There are other defences that are peculiar to specific torts. These are discussed in the appropriate chapters.

3. In this case the House of Lords rejected the application of *volenti* in relation to injuries suffered by an employee at work as result of his employers not warning him of the moment of a reoccurring danger (even though he was aware of the general risk of the danger occurring). See further Chapter 12.

defence; where it is made out it will defeat the claim and no damages will be payable. However, within this there are two different ways in which the defence can arise.

First, the defence applies where the claimant consents to the specific harm caused by the defendant and (sometimes) where they have consented to the risk of that harm. For instance, if I agree to you hurting me or damaging my property—say I invite you to punch me in the stomach or to tear up my textbook—you will have a defence to any tort claim I may bring against you. Similarly, if I willingly put myself into a dangerous situation—for instance, I agree to be taken for a ride on a pedalo with a 'driver' who is clearly drunk—my claim for any injuries I then suffer may well be defeated on the basis that I voluntarily undertook the risk of such injuries. In the context of negligence claims this involves consenting to not simply the risk of harm but the risk of being harmed by the defendant's negligence.[4]

Secondly, the defence will apply where the claimant consents (or, at least, is *to be treated as* consenting) to the defendant excluding their liability for any injuries they may cause (though here the defence may be restricted by the provisions of the Unfair Contract Terms Act 1977). This version of the defence is best exemplified in cases of occupiers' liability.[5] As we shall see, occupiers owe a duty of care to those they allow onto their premises. However, an occupier who is keen to avoid liability may put up a notice saying that visitors 'enter at their own risk' or, more straightforwardly, that they 'exclude liability for any injuries visitors may suffer on the premises'. If a visitor sees such a notice and enters the premises nonetheless—or indeed even if they do not see it but the occupier is held to have taken 'reasonable steps' to bring it to the visitor's attention—their claim for any injuries they then suffer will be defeated (see Occupiers' Liability Act 1957, s 2(1)).[6]

Although both forms of the defence are based on the consent of the claimant, the difference between them is that in each case the claimant is consenting to something different. In the first case, the claimant is consenting to the specific factual harms which they suffer and/or the risks to which they are exposed—for example a punch in the stomach or a pedalo capsizing. By contrast, in the second case, the claimant's consent is not to any particular factual harm or danger but rather to the defendant's exclusion or waiver of liability. Here the claimant is effectively saying not 'I accept that what I am doing is dangerous' but rather 'I accept that I cannot sue you if I end up injured'.

This difference between the two versions of the defence is reflected in how the defence is proved. You can only (meaningfully) consent to something if you know about it (though, as we shall see, the defence of consent requires something more than just knowledge). However, because the two versions of the defence involve consent to different things, each requires a different type of knowledge. With the first version whereby the claimant consents to the specific factual harm caused or the risk run, the defendant must show that the claimant did indeed consent to the harm which in turn

---

4. Evidently this doesn't happen very often. It is not the same as 'consenting' to the risk of being injured, for example by a kick in a football match or sustaining injury in any other 'risky' activity. See further Lord Diplock in *Wooldridge* v *Sumner* [1963] at 69–70 and **Morris v Murray** [1991] which is a very good example of just how far someone has to go for the courts to consider that the claimant consented to the risk of being harmed by another's negligence.

5. See Chapter 11.

6. Unless the premises are business premises, in which case the occupier cannot exclude liability for negligently caused personal injury or death (Unfair Contract Terms Act 1977, s 2(1)).

requires that they were aware of the risk of that injury. By contrast, the second version of the defence can be made out even where the claimant has no idea that they are in a dangerous situation and has not given any thought at all to the possibility of their being injured. Rather, since the defence is based on their consent to the defendant excluding liability, the question is whether they knew (or should have known) that the defendant was indeed intending to exclude liability for injuries the claimant may suffer.

Because of this, although described by Buckley LJ in *White v Blackmore* [1972] as 'somewhat analogous' (at 668), the two versions of the defence do not always run together. In this case, the claimant's husband was fatally injured while watching a motor race. At the time of his injury, the claimant's husband was standing with his family behind the spectator's ropes someway from the track. A car's wheel became tangled up in the safety rope which set in motion a chain of events which culminated in him being thrown into the air. The Court of Appeal held that, because the victim did not have full knowledge of the factual risks he was running, the first version of the defence could not succeed: 'It might not have been at all obvious to the deceased that he was standing in a particularly dangerous place when the accident occurred. Accepting this I do not think it can be said...that the deceased had full knowledge of the risk he was running' (at 668). However, the court held that the second version of the defence was available, since the defendants had taken reasonable steps to inform the victim that they were seeking to exclude liability. The various warnings were 'sufficient to exclude any duty of care on the part of the organisers...towards the deceased, the defendants were not guilty of negligence and consequently they do not need the shield of the doctrine of *volenti*' (at 668).

We shall look at the second version of the defence in greater detail in Chapter 11, when we deal with occupiers' liability. For now we shall focus on the first version of the defence.

10.2.1 **Voluntary assumption of risk/*volenti non fit injuria***

In order for the defence to be established the defendant must show that the claimant voluntarily took the risk of, or agreed to, the harm that materialised. While cases where the claimant has consented to the tortious action—for example a battery by agreeing to surgery or to give blood[7]—are (usually) relatively straightforward, those where the agreement is to the *risk* of harm are more tricky.[8] In such cases it is necessary to show that the claimant at the material time:

(1) knew the nature and extent of the risk of harm; and

(2) voluntarily agreed to it (***Morris v Murray* [1991]** at 18).

The test is a subjective one; it is not enough that a reasonable person might have been aware of the risk—the particular claimant must know and, importantly, agree to it. It is well established that awareness or knowledge of the risk is not enough: 'A com-

---

7. See Chapter 14, pp 397–400.

8. A note on terminology: typically the case law refers to 'consent' in the context of intentional torts and '*volenti*' or voluntary assumption of risk in relation to negligence, though, as *Rogers* notes, nothing turns on this distinction (p 1132).

plete knowledge of the danger is in any event necessary, but such knowledge does not necessarily import consent' (***Dann v Hamilton*** [1939] at 515).

Dann v Hamilton [1939] KBD

In this case, the claimant was injured in a car accident. It was clear that the accident was the result of the negligent driving of the defendant, Hamilton, who had been drinking. Dann brought a claim for damages against the driver's estate (he had been killed outright at the scene) who raised the defence of voluntary assumption of risk. The court found that the following exchange had taken place when another passenger was leaving the car the claimant was travelling in: 'You two [referring to the claimant and her mother, who was also in the car] have more pluck than I have' to which the claimant answered 'You should be like me. If anything is going to happen, it will happen' (at 514). Nevertheless Asquith J, rejecting the defence of *volenti*, held that, despite the fact that the claimant was aware that the defendant had been drinking and that this would materially reduce his ability to drive safely, she had not consented to, or absolved him from liability for, any negligence on his part that might cause her harm. Simply knowing the risk is not enough; the claimant must accept it.

IMPORTANT NOTE: The application of voluntary assumption of risk in relation to passengers in road traffic accidents is now excluded by the Road Traffic Act 1988, section 149.

While it is clear that the claimant must be shown to have consented to (rather than simply having been aware of) the risk of injury, what is less clear is what exactly this requires. Lord Denning MR in ***Nettleship v Weston*** [1971] took a very formalistic approach: 'knowledge of the risk of injury is not enough. Nor is a willingness to take the risk of injury. Nothing will suffice short of an agreement to waive a claim for negligence' (at 701). This view was approved by the House of Lords in ***Reeves v Commissioner of Police for the Metropolis*** [2000]. However, other cases appear to be less demanding.

Morris v Murray [1991] CA

After spending an afternoon drinking, during which Murray, the defendant, had consumed the equivalent of over half a bottle of whisky, he and the claimant decided to take Murray's light airplane for a spin. The claimant, Morris, drove to the airfield and helped to prepare the plane for take-off. Shortly after take-off the plane crashed, killing Murray and seriously injuring the claimant. The defendant's estate met Morris's claim for compensation with the defence that he had either voluntarily assumed the risk of injury or was contributorily negligent.

The Court of Appeal held that Morris had voluntarily assumed the risk of injury. He was not so drunk as to be unable to appreciate the extent and the nature of the risks involved and had willingly embarked upon the flight knowing that Murray was so drunk that he was very likely to be negligent.[9]

---

9. The latter requirement may mean that a claimant who is completely drunk is better protected than someone who is sober or only slightly tipsy. However, providing the claimant is still able to be aware of risk, it makes no difference if the alcohol makes them more likely to take the risk or, indeed, to give the risk no thought at all.

Pause for reflection

In *Morris* v *Murray* Fox LJ described the facts of the case as 'a drunken escapade, heavily fraught with danger' (at 12) and that 'the wild irresponsibility of the venture is such that the law should not intervene to award damages and should leave the loss where it falls' (at 17). More recently, May LJ noted that '[a]dults who chose to engage in physical activities which obviously give rise to a degree of unavoidable risk may find that they have no means of recompense if the risk materialises so that they are injured' (*Poppleton* v *Trustees of the Portsmouth Youth Activities Committee* [2008] at [1]).[10]

This reflects what *Cane* describes as an increasing emphasis on self-reliance and 'personal responsibility' by the courts (p 81). Even if we accept that the courts are right to stress that individuals must take responsibility for their own actions, and that the law of torts should limit the protection it offers to those who have little regard for their own safety, should the law leave those who are injured when acting irresponsibly without *any* legal claim? Would a better solution be to use the partial defence of contributory negligence, since this is designed to deal with just this problem and allows the court to reduce a claimant's damages in line with their own fault while not depriving them of all compensation?

Morris shares a number of parallels with **Dann**. In both cases, the claimant agreed to take a ride in a vehicle being driven by a drunk defendant, with full knowledge of the risks this involved. In both cases, the vehicle crashed, the driver was killed and the claimant badly injured. Yet in **Dann** the claim succeeded, while in **Morris** the defence of *volenti* was made out. Though the Court of Appeal in **Morris** sought to distinguish **Dann** on the basis that there the claimant was a reluctant passenger who felt unable to extricate herself from the drunken drive, this does not seem to have been the basis for the court's rejection of the defence in that case.

More fundamentally, **Morris** brings out the difficulty in identifying what is meant by consent. It is clear that the claimant knew that he was taking a great risk but, as cases such as **Dann** and **Nettleship** stress, knowledge of—or willingness to take—a risk is not the same as consent. But if something more is needed, what is it? Certainly the claimant in **Morris** did not *want* to be injured, though he did willingly engage in a course of conduct which might lead to that result. It is hard to resist the conclusion that, sometimes—where the risk run is particularly great or the activities of the claimant particularly irresponsible—the courts do treat knowledge as tantamount to consent.

 Counterpoint

In order to establish a defence based on the claimant's voluntary assumption of the risk, the claimant needs to have done more than simply put themselves in a dangerous situation. As

→

10. Although this case was decided on the grounds of duty of care rather than *volenti*, the issues it raises are on point. The claimant was badly injured and rendered tetraplegic after falling awkwardly from a climbing wall. Allowing the appeal, the Court of Appeal held that in light of the inherent and obvious risks in the activity which the claimant had voluntarily undertaken, the climbing centre was under no duty to prevent the claimant from undertaking said risks, nor to train to supervise him while he did so.

→

Lord Halsbury LC pointed out in *Smith* v *Baker & Sons* [1891], anyone crossing a London street knows that a substantial percentage of drivers are negligent. If a man crosses deliberately, with that knowledge, and is negligently run down, he is certainly not consenting to the risk of injury, and so without a remedy (at 337). Similarly, it might be argued that a young woman (or indeed young man) walking home alone late at night knows that they run a greater risk of being attacked than if they take a taxi.[11] However, no one would argue that they have voluntarily assumed the risk of any injury they may suffer.

This seems straightforward enough. But things become less clear if we compare these examples with *Morris*. As we have seen, there the claimant knowingly and willingly engaged in an inherently dangerous activity. When he was then injured, the court held that he had voluntarily assumed that risk. Yet the same appears also to be true in the above examples. The man who crosses the road knows there is the risk of being run over but crosses the road anyway. The woman knows there is a danger of being attacked but walks home late at night nonetheless. Of course, neither *wants* to be injured, but nor did the claimant in *Morris*.

One possible distinction between these cases lies in the likelihood of the risk eventuating. So, the chances of the plane crashing in *Morris* were greater than the likelihood of being run over crossing the road or of being attacked late at night. But should this be enough? It is unlikely that the woman's claim would be defeated by her voluntary decision to walk home however great the likelihood of her being attacked. Perhaps what distinguishes them is an element of culpability. The claimant in *Morris* was factually and morally responsible for his injury. Whereas few would argue that a man crossing a road or a woman walking home alone late at night are responsible for their injuries.

A claimant may consent to some harms or risks and not others. So, while Morris may have consented to the very great risk of injury that was likely to follow from embarking on a flight with a drunken pilot, if Murray had instead had a sudden and uncontrollable suicidal urge to crash the plane, it seems clear that Morris's consent to the drunken adventure would not have provided a defence (*Slater* v *Clay Cross Ltd* [1956]). Consent only goes so far. Similar issues arise in relation to consent in the context of sporting events. Here, though the potential claimant is not courting injury—in fact they wish to avoid it—they know it might happen. The courts have held that, by willingly engaging in such activities, the claimant voluntarily assumes the risks inherent in the relevant sport. It is unlikely, therefore, that consent would be seen as extending to injuries or risks which are not part and parcel of the game. So, while a footballer would be regarded as consenting to being tackled, even fouled, and any injuries so caused, their consent would not extend to serious foul play, such as a deliberate stamp or, perhaps, a dangerous high and late tackle (*Condon* v *Basi* [1985]).[12]

11. Let us assume that, like the claimant in *Morris* **v** *Murray*, they could easily have avoided the risk by returning home earlier or taking a taxi.

12. The same applies to spectators (*Wooldridge* v *Sumner* [1963]) though in such cases it is more likely that the claim will fail on the grounds that the conduct was not, in the circumstances of the case, negligent; discussed further in Chapter 8.

10.3 **Illegality**

The defence of illegality denies recovery to certain claimants injured while committing unlawful activities. Like *volenti*, it is a complete defence. It is typically seen to invoke a special rule of public policy. Lord Hoffmann in *Gray* v *Thames Trains* [2009] identified two formulations of the illegality defence. At its most narrow, the defence ensures that a claimant cannot recover in civil law for the consequences of a criminal sanction imposed as a result of one's own unlawful act (at [29]). If the law imposes a harm or loss (e.g. imprisonment or a fine) on someone as punishment for their wrongdoing, they cannot seek compensation for that loss by bringing an action in tort against a defendant they claim caused them to commit the wrong. Its wider formulation rests on the principle that a claimant ought not to be able to recover damages for losses they suffer while engaged in criminal activity: *ex turpi causa non oritur actio* (literally: no action may be founded on an illegal act). While the former is justified on the grounds of consistency, the latter rests on the view that 'it is offensive to public notions of the fair distribution of resources that a claimant should be compensated (usually out of public funds) for the consequences of his own criminal conduct' (at [51]).[13] As we shall see, the public notions of fairness can be a tricky thing to predict—especially when it comes to 'compensating criminals'.

Gray v *Thames Trains* [2009] HL

The claimant developed PTSD after being involved in the Labroke Grove rail crash, which killed 31 people and injured over 500 others, caused by the defendant's negligence. Two years later, under the effects of this condition, he stabbed and killed a pedestrian in a 'road-rage' incident. Gray was convicted of manslaughter on the grounds of diminished responsibility and sentenced to be indefinitely detained in hospital under the Mental Health Act 1983. Gray sued the defendants for, amongst other things, loss of earnings both before and during his detention as well as general damages for his detention, conviction and feelings of guilt and remorse and for the damage to his reputation. He also sought an indemnity against any claims that might be brought by the relatives of the pedestrian.

The House of Lords rejected his claim. An award of damages would set the civil law against the criminal law. Lord Rodger cited with approval the Law Commission's view in 2001 that 'it would be quite inconsistent to imprison or detain someone on the grounds that he was responsible for a serious offence and then to compensate him for the detention' (at [66]).[14] Gray's counter-argument that his earning potential had already been diminished by the defendant's negligence before his criminal act and that they remained responsible for this continuing partial loss also fell foul of the consistency principle, as well as being rejected by analogy with *Jobling* v *Associated Diaries Ltd* [1982].[15]

---

13. Though the defence is sometimes said to extend to *immoral* conduct, the Law Commission Consultation Paper *The Illegality Defence in Tort* (No 160, 2001) found just one example of the successful application of the defence in this context (*Hegarty* v *Shine* (1878), which would not be decided in the same way today (at [1.14]).

14. *The Illegality Defence in Tort* (2001), [4.100].

15. *Jobling* is discussed further in Chapter 9, pp 245–246.

Counterpoint

As Lord Brown notes, the facts of *Gray* and *Jobling* are not directly analogous. While the harm suffered by the claimant in the latter was superseded by a wholly unconnected disabling illness (the so-called 'vicissitudes principle'), there was no doubt in *Gray* that the manslaughter and detention were factually caused by the defendant's negligence: 'But for [their] negligence there would have been no manslaughter and no detention. That here is a given' (at [96]). Though *Baker* v *Willoughby* [1970] allows for some modification of the 'vicissitudes principle' in order to occasion justice, despite his sympathy for the 'tragedy' suffered by the claimant (at [89]), Lord Brown ultimately rejects this argument: 'Whilst recognising that…the tortfeasor benefits from criminality which in one sense he himself has contributed to bringing about, the opposite conclusion would result in the claimant being able to ignore a vicissitude for which he for his part has been held responsible (if only for a diminished extent)' (at [101]). Do you agree?

Gray leaves open what the position would be if the claimant had been found to be legally irresponsible by reason of insanity but is still indefinitely detained. It is not clear whether *ex turpi causa* would apply in such circumstances (see Lord Phillips at [15] and Lord Rodgers at [83]). What do you think a court would decide?

The existence of the defence of illegality does not, however, mean that one can *never* recover in tort for injuries suffered against a backdrop of criminality. If the illegal act of the claimant is trivial or simply forms the background to the defendant's tort, then it is unlikely to bar the claim. So, for example, if someone negligently damages your car while it is parked on double yellow lines, a court will not hold that your claim for damages is defeated on the basis that you were parked illegally. Your illegality is both trifling and in no meaningful way contributes to the damage you suffered. However if, to use Lord Asquith's example in *National Coal Board* v *England* [1954]:

> A and B are proceeding to the premises which they intend burglariously to enter, and before they enter them, B picks A's pocket and steals his watch, I cannot prevail on myself to believe that A could not sue in tort…The theft is totally unconnected with the burglary. (at 429)

 Pause for reflection

Bingham LJ noted in *Saunders* v *Edwards* [1987] that it is not for the court to 'draw up its skirts and refuse all assistance to the [claimant], no matter how serious his loss' (at 1134). It is a matter of judgement. The courts have to negotiate a tricky balance between not lending their aid to a party who is seeking to pursue an action which stems from a criminal activity and not wishing to create a class of legal outcasts. Think about where the courts drew the line in *Gray* and in the cases that follow—do you agree with the decisions they have made? Would you have drawn the line differently? If so, think about *why* this is and whether your preference would have been possible within the constraints of the defence.

> ### *Pitts v Hunt* [1991] CA
>
> The claimant and defendant were teenagers who had spent the evening drinking together. By the time they set off home on Hunt's motorcycle, Hunt was over twice the legal alcohol limit. Although Pitts knew that Hunt was under age, drunk, uninsured and unlicensed, he rode pillion and encouraged Hunt to drive recklessly and deliberately frighten the other road users. There was an accident. Hunt was killed outright and Pitts was seriously injured.
>
> The Court of Appeal refused Pitts' claim against Hunt's representatives on the basis of illegality.[16] In so doing, each of the three judges adopted a different line of reasoning. Dillon LJ relied directly on the principle of *ex turpi causa* to deny his claim—his injury was caused directly by, rather than being incidental to, the illegal act he was undertaking. Balcombe LJ based his decision on the inability (though it appears to be an unwillingness) of the court to set a standard of care owed by those jointly engaged in a criminal act as to do so would involve the courts in examining the detail of criminal activity. Finally, Beldam LJ relied on the simple, yet controversial, notion that to allow Pitts to recover would be an affront to the public conscience.[17]

Though a definitive justification for the illegality defence remains elusive—Lord Hoffmann in *Gray* commented that 'The maxim *ex turpi causa* expresses not so much a principle as a policy...based...on a group of reasons, which vary in different situations' (at [30])—there are a number of contenders including: consistency,[18] deterrence, a wish not to condone (or assist) wrongdoers and public opinion, typified by the apparent belief that 'bad men (or women) should get less'.[19] As the Law Commission notes the 'law would be clearer, more transparent and easier to understand if judges discussed these policy considerations openly in relation to the facts of the case before them'.[20] The House of Lords' decisions in *Gray* and *Stone & Rolls Ltd* v *Moore Stephens* [2009] appear to be a step in this direction.

Restricting claims on the basis of illegality might be more appropriate in cases where only the claimant is acting criminally (as opposed to cases like ***Pitts* v *Hunt*** where the claimant and defendant are involved in a *joint* criminal enterprise). In *Clunis* v *Camden & Islington Health Authority* [1998], for example, the claimant killed a man at Finsbury Park underground station for which he was convicted of manslaughter on the grounds of diminished responsibility. The claimant had a long history of mental illness and seriously violent behaviour but had been discharged from hospital to be cared for within the community. He argued that the Health Authority had been negligent in

---

16. *Volenti* was barred by what is now the Road Traffic Act 1988, s 149 and contributory negligence would have only reduced his damages by, at most, 50 per cent.

17. *Lunney & Oliphant* note that were the facts of ***Pitts*** to arise today it is likely that following the ECJ case of *Candolin* v *Pohjola* [2005], which limits the applicability of defences that deprive the claimant of the benefit of a compulsory motor insurance policy (at [29]), that the illegality defence would be restricted (p 330).

18. See further *Griffin* v *Hacker Young & Co* [2010].

19. It should be noted that the House of Lords in *Tinsley* v *Milligan* [1994] and *Stone & Rolls Ltd* v *Moore Stephens* [2009] rejected the notion of public conscience as a basis of the illegality defence. This was approved by the Law Commission *The Illegality Defence: A Consultative Report* (No 189, 2009), [7.45]–[7.51].

20. Law Commission *The Illegality Defence* (Law Com No 320, 2010), [3.10].

their assessment of his condition and that, as a result, he had not been prevented from committing the attack. His claim was rejected by the Court of Appeal on the ground of illegality—his claim arose directly out of a criminal offence he himself had committed. In *Vellino* v *Chief Constable of the Greater Manchester Police* [2001] the majority of the Court of Appeal rejected the claim of a man who suffered severe injuries after jumping from a second-floor window while trying to escape arrest. Assuming the police to have been negligent, recovery was precluded because the injury was the direct consequence of his own unlawful act:

> it is common ground that the policy of law is not to permit one criminal to recover damages from a fellow criminal who fails to take care of him whilst they are both engaged in a criminal enterprise. The reason for that rule is not the law's tenderness towards the criminal defendant but the law's unwillingness to afford a criminal [claimant] a remedy in such circumstances. I see no reason why that unwillingness should be any less because a defendant is a policeman and not engaged in any crime. (at [25])

In *Gray*, Lord Hoffmann suggested that the basis of the defence was best seen as a matter of causation: 'Can one say that, although the damage would not have happened but for the tortious conduct of the defendant, it was caused by the criminal act of the claimant'—as in *Vellino*—'Or is the position that although the damage would not have happened without the criminal act of the claimant, it was caused by the tortious act of the defendant' (at [54])—as was the case, in ***Revill* v *Newbery*** [1996] in which a burglar, who was shot by the owner of the property he was attempting to burgle, was able to recover for his injuries.

Revill v *Newbery* [1996] CA

The claimant, a burglar, was shot by the defendant as he attempted to gain access to his shed. Newbery, who was 76, had been concerned about the spate of burglaries in the area and had resolved to wait in the shed with a shotgun to defend his property. The Court of Appeal rejected the defendant's attempt to raise the defence of illegality. Although an occupier might use reasonable force to defend his property, to shoot indiscriminately at (assumed) burglars in an attempt to warn them off was 'out of all proportion to the threat involved' (Neill LJ at 571). The claimant was, however, found to be contributorily negligent in light of which his award of damages was reduced by two-thirds.[21]

Given the difficulties in relation to its application and justification, it is unsurprising that academics, members of the judiciary and the Law Commission have at times recommended the overhaul or even abolition of the defence of illegality and the use of contributory negligence and/or *volenti* in its place.[22] However, in light of the public

---

21. Think again about the burglar in the scenarios at the start of the chapter. Following ***Revill* v *Newbery*** the homeowner will be unable to rely on the defence of illegality; however, it is highly likely that the claimant's damages will be significantly reduced to reflect the extent to which they are contributorily negligent.

22. Though in its most recent report, in light of the shift in cases like ***Gray***, the Law Commission *did not* recommend legislative reform of the illegality defence as it applies to claims in tort (at [3.41]).

outcry over cases such as ***Revill v Newbery*** (where the trial judge eventually wrote to a national newspaper to explain his decision),[23] this seems unlikely. This is regrettable. As Sedley LJ noted in *Vellino v Chief Constable of Greater Manchester Police*:

> [T]he public conscience, an elusive thing, as often as not turns out to be an echo-chamber inhabited by journalists and public moralists. To allow judicial policy to be dictated by it would be as inappropriate as to let judges dictate editorial policy. It is not difficult, for example, to visualise how some sections of the media would choose to report a decision along the lines which I have proposed. The Law Commission's [2001] scholarly and constructive working paper has so far been reported under the headline 'Law paves way for thugs to sue victims' (*Daily Express*, June 30, 2001) and has earned the Law Commission the soubriquet 'Enemy of the people' (Sunday Times, July 1, 2001). In a free society such comment is perfectly permissible and its influence on public opinion no doubt considerably greater than that of a judgment or a Law Commission Paper. (at [60])

 Pause for reflection

In light of Sedley LJ's comment that 'since the passing of the Law Reform (Contributory Negligence) Act 1945 the power to apportion liability...has afforded a far more appropriate tool for doing justice than the blunt instrument of turpitude [illegality]' (*Vellino v Chief Constable of Greater Manchester Police* at [55]), *Weir* suggests that 'just as tortious negligence is taking over from the other torts, so contributory negligence is trying to eclipse the complete defences [illegality and voluntary assumption of risk]' (p 131). Would this be a bad thing?

10.4 **Contributory negligence**

Contributory negligence is a defence that operates not to defeat the claimant's claim entirely but rather to reduce the damages the defendant must pay. It is a partial defence. It will be raised by a defendant where the claimant has failed to take reasonable steps for their own safety and this failure has contributed to the injury the claimant has then suffered.[24] The Law Reform (Contributory Negligence) Act 1945 section 1(1) states that a court can reduce the claimant's damages by whatever amount seems just according to their share in responsibility for the damage.[25]

---

23. Richard Ford 'Judge tells why Shotgun Pensioner had to Pay' *The Times* 6 December 1994.

24. For instance, the driving instructor in the scenarios at the start of this chapter may be found contributorily negligent if they fail adequately to supervise the learner driver (for an example of this, see further ***Nettleship v Weston*** discussed at length in Chapter 8, pp 200–203).

25. Where the defence is raised successfully it will mean that both the claimant and the defendant are responsible, at least in part, for the claimant's losses and accordingly those losses are split between them. This is similar to, but should not be confused with, the situation where there is more than one *defendant* liable for the claimant's losses (so-called joint tortfeasors) where the law also splits losses between those responsible for causing them under the Civil Liability (Contribution) Act 1978 (see further Chapter 19, pp 564–566).

> **Law Reform (Contributory Negligence) Act 1945**
>
> Where any person suffers damage as the result partly of his own fault and partly of the fault of any other person or persons, a claim in respect of that damage shall not be defeated by reasons of the fault of the person suffering the damage, but the damages recoverable in respect thereof shall be reduced to such an extent as the court thinks it is just and equitable having regard to the claimant's share in the responsibility for the damage. (s 1(1))
>
> 'Fault' is defined in section 4 of the Act as 'negligence, breach of statutory duty or other act or omission which gives rise to a liability in tort'.[26] The same section also establishes that damage includes loss of life, personal injury, economic loss and property damage.

In order for the defence to be raised, three questions need to be addressed:

(1) Did the claimant fail to exercise reasonable care for their own safety?

(2) Did this failure contribute to the claimant's damage? and

(3) By what extent should the claimant's damages be reduced?

10.4.1 Did the claimant fail to exercise reasonable care for their own safety?

When determining whether the claimant has taken reasonable care for their own safety we apply an objective standard. In other words, we ask what a reasonable person in the claimant's position would have done to avoid being hurt.[27] This standard will vary according to the circumstances; it is clear that 'the law certainly does not require the claimant to proceed on his way like a timorous fugitive constantly looking over his shoulder for threats from others' (*Rogers* p 371).

> **Jones v Livox Quarries Ltd [1952] CA**
>
> The claimant was riding on the back of a traxcavator (a slow-moving tracked vehicle) at work, contrary to company regulations, when a dumper truck crashed into the back of it seriously injuring the claimant. He sued his employer, claiming that the driver of the dumper truck was negligent in falling to keep a proper look-out. In response, the defendants argued that the claimant had caused or contributed to his own injuries by his own carelessness in riding on the back of the truck.
>
> →

26. There is some evidence to suggest that the Law Reform (Contributory Negligence) Act 1945 may be applicable in cases involving intentional harm (*Murphy v Culhane* [1977]; **Reeves v Commissioner of Police of the Metropolis** [2000]). However this was doubted by Lord Rodger in *Standard Chartered Bank v Pakistan National Shipping Corp (No 2)* [2003] at [43]–[45].

27. Though the law does make some allowances for children (see discussion in Chapter 8, pp 203–204).

The Court of Appeal agreed: 'A person is guilty of contributory negligence if he ought reasonably to have foreseen that, if he did not act as a reasonable prudent man, he might be hurt himself; and in his reckonings he must take into account the possibility of others being careless' (Denning LJ at 615). The claimant's award of damages was reduced by 20 per cent.

 Pause for reflection

While at first sight contributory negligence appears to be a useful mirror image of negligence, which allows for the reduction of damages where the claimant is also 'at fault', the practical effects of a finding of contributory negligence are, *Cane* argues, somewhat less satisfying:

> To find a defendant guilty of negligence shifts the loss away from the claimant and typically spreads it by means of insurance...A finding of contributory negligence usually has precisely the opposite effect, which is to leave part or all of the loss on the claimant, who will typically be without insurance. Thus, reduction of damages for contributory negligence falls much more heavily on the claimant than liability for negligence bears on the defendant. (p 56)

This may be behind the courts' willingness to make allowances for the personal characteristics and qualities of the claimant—for example, their age—when making findings of contributory negligence. This is particularly important given that children and the elderly are disproportionately represented among pedestrians seriously injured or killed in road traffic accidents (*Cane* p 56).

In *Armsden* v *Kent Police* [2009] a police officer was responding to an emergency call when he collided with a car pulling out on to the A road from a minor junction, killing the driver. He was driving at 100 mph on a rural A road, with his blue lights flashing but no siren. Though the trial judge found that the police officer was the sole cause of the accident, on appeal the court held that the woman driving the car was *also* negligent in failing to notice the flashing blue lights and that the police officer was entitled to assume that she would not emerge from the junction without continuing to look for oncoming traffic. Nevertheless, the police officer's negligence in driving at excess speed, exacerbated by his failure to sound his siren, meant that he was 40 per cent responsible for the accident.[28]

Claims for contributory negligence do not just involve accidents. In *St George* v *Home Office* [2008] the claimant was injured falling from a top bunk while in prison as a result of an epileptic seizure brought on by drug and alcohol withdrawal. He suffered

---

28. For further examples of the types of situations in which the claimant has been found to have failed to exercise reasonable care for their own safety see *Heaton* v *Herzog* [2008], *Osei-Antwi* v *South East London & Kent Bus Co* [2010] (cf *Ahanonu* v *South East London and Kent Bus Co Ltd* [2008]).

severe brain damage leaving him permanently disabled. The Court of Appeal held that though the claimant was 'at fault' within the meaning of section 1(1) of the 1945 Act in becoming so addicted, and though 'but for' his addiction he would not have fallen from the bunk, his addiction was too remote in time and place to allow his injury to be properly regarded as a potent cause of the injury as required by the Act. As such, the claimant could not be considered contributorily negligent.

The issue of contributory negligence in the context of suicide was considered by the House of Lords in *Corr v IBC Vehicles Ltd* [2008] where the House of Lords held that an employee's suicide (following a horrific accident at work) was reasonably foreseeable.[29] Lords Bingham and Walker clearly stated that as the claimant was in no way to blame for his death there was to be no reduction for contributory negligence. However, the majority were of the view that the employee's action could amount to contributory negligence, though the defence had not, in the case at hand, been properly argued. Lord Scott even went so far as to suggest a reduction of 20 per cent—a comment that has since been described as 'distasteful and insupportable'.[30]

10.4.2 Did this failure contribute to the claimant's damage?

The claimant's own carelessness will provide a defence only where it made some contribution *to the injuries they suffered*. Though usually this will mean that the claimant contributed in some way to the accident which caused their injury, it also includes cases such as where the claimant's failure to wear a seat belt has contributed to their injury. It is important to note that in all successful cases of contributory negligence there will be more than one cause of the claimant's injuries—that is, both the claimant and defendant will have contributed to the accident (if the defendant's breach of duty was not a 'but for' cause of the injury then any claim would fail even before we get to the question of defences).[31] Equally, if the claimant is careless but that carelessness did not have any bearing *on their injury* then there will be no defence (their negligence is not contributory).

Even where the claimant's carelessness was a 'but for' cause of their own injuries the defence will not be available if the injuries they suffered arose from some risk or danger of which they were not aware and against which they could not have been expected to take precautions. For example, in **Jones v Livox Quarries Ltd**, Denning LJ considered what the position of the claimant would have been had he been negligently shot while riding on the back of the truck. In this case, he suggested, the claimant would not be contributorily negligent even though he was partly to blame—after all, had he not been acting unreasonably by riding on the back of the truck he would have been elsewhere when the shot was fired. In this example, we might say that the claimant's actions merely provide the setting or the circumstances in which the injuries were suffered,

29. Discussed further in Chapter 5, p 96.
30. Janet O'Sullivan 'Employer Liability for Injured Employee's Suicide' (2008) *Cambridge Law Journal* 241 at 243.
31. See Chapter 9, pp 224–226.

rather than being a cause of them; his loss—being shot—would have had nothing to do with why it was unreasonable to travel on the back of the truck (at 616).

10.4.3 By what extent should the claimant's damages be reduced?

When deciding by how much to reduce the award of damages to the claimant, the courts look to the *comparative blameworthiness* of the parties. If the parties are equally to blame the damages will be reduced by 50 per cent; if the defendant is twice as blameworthy as the claimant they will be reduced by 33 per cent, and so on.[32]

In *Young* v *Kent County Council* [2005], for example, a 12-year-old boy who was seriously injured after falling through a roof while attempting to retrieve his football was considered by the court to be 'as much to blame as the defendants' (at [34]). His damages were reduced by 50 per cent to reflect this. Similarly in *Badger* v *Ministry of Defence* [2005], the claimant's damages were reduced by 20 per cent to reflect the extent to which his failure to give up smoking had made a material contribution to his lung cancer (which was also caused by the defendants negligently exposing him to asbestos).[33]

Froom v Butcher [1976] CA

The claimant suffered head and chest injuries and a broken finger when his car was negligently hit by the defendant. The claimant was not wearing a seat belt because he did not like them and he had at one time seen an accident where the driver would have been trapped if he had been wearing one. At the time, there was no statute requiring people to wear seat belts.

Nevertheless, the Court of Appeal held that he was contributorily negligent in respect of the injuries he would have avoided if he had worn a seat belt. His damages were reduced by 20 per cent (as had been previously agreed by the parties).

The Court of Appeal went on to lay down guidelines in relation to the appropriate reduction in damages for failing to wear a seat belt (see Table 10.1).[34] These have subsequently been applied in relation to a claimant's failure to wear a motorbike helmet in *Capps* v *Miller* [1989] and in relation to cycle helmets in *Smith* v *Finch* [2009].[35]

---

32. The wording of the Act may be thought to suggest that the claimant can never be 100 per cent contributorily negligent. This was certainly the view of the Court of Appeal in *Pitts* v *Hunt* [1991]. The lowest allocation of responsibility has been 5 per cent. Most cases tend to be in a range of 25–75 per cent either way (*Rogers* p 379).

33. The fact that a claimant smokes (or has made similar lifestyle choices) will not amount to contributory negligence where, for example, the defendant's negligence relates to a failure to treat, or take into account, their condition or where these choices were made long before the defendant's negligence (*St George* v *Home Office* [2008]; *Calvert* v *William Hill Credit Ltd* [2008]).

34. This test was recently reaffirmed in *Stanton* v *Collinson* [2010].

35. It is likely therefore that the cycle-courier at the example at the start of the chapter will be found to be contributorily negligent.

Table 10.1 Reduction in damages payable for failure to wear a seat belt or appropriate crash helmet on a motorbike

Level of injury	Reduction
Prevented completely	25%
Less severe	15%
No difference	0%

Damages will be reduced by up to one-third in cases of injury to a passenger where the driver is drunk, unless the passenger engages in conduct that affects the driver's performance, for example by encouraging them to speed (*Stinton* v *Stinton* [1995]).

 Pause for reflection

It is clear from the judgment in *Froom* v *Butcher* that the claimant was reluctant to wear a seat belt and dubious of the safety benefits in so doing. At the time, wearing seat belts was not compulsory and, in the face of considerable parliamentary opposition, the government had to fall back on its Highway Code to 'strongly advise' motorists to fit and wear seat belts. This meant that although wearing seat belts remained, in principle, optional, the failure to wear one could be brought as evidence in civil proceedings. By finding the claimant in *Froom* v *Butcher* contributorily negligent, the Court of Appeal relied on the deterrent effects of tort law to fill this 'legislative gap'.[36] Motorists who may be willing to risk more serious injury by not wearing a seat belt were not, it seemed, as willing to risk a proportion of their award of compensation should the worse happen and began to buckle up (*Harlow* p 38). It remains to be seen whether the High Court's decision in *Smith* v *Finch* will have a similar effect in relation to cycle helmets.

10.5 Conclusion

Even if all the other elements of a claim in negligence have been met, the defendant may still be able to deny liability in whole or in part through raising a defence. This chapter has considered the application of three defences—**voluntary assumption of risk (*volenti*))**, **illegality** and **contributory negligence**. Although the latter is (usually) confined to negligence, the others apply generally throughout tort. In order to establish **voluntary assumption of risk** the defendant must show that the claimant consented to (rather than simply being aware of) the full extent and nature of the risk. As such it works to encourage the claimant to take personal responsibility for their actions, particularly when they are involved in inherently risky activities. **Illegality** operates to defeat a claim where the action arises out of an illegal activity. Its extent and the rationale as a defence have been subject to considerable scrutiny by the

---

36. It is now compulsory to wear a seat belt (Road Traffic Act 1988, ss 14 and 15).

judiciary, academics and the Law Commission alike; however, in essence, its existence is a matter of public policy. Finally, we looked at **contributory negligence**. This is the most common and successful defence in negligence. Unlike the other defences considered in this chapter, which exonerate the defendant from having to pay anything, contributory negligence *reduces* the damages of a claimant whose failure to exercise reasonable care for their own safety has contributed to their injury. It has been placed on a statutory footing through the Law Reform (Contributory Negligence) Act 1945.

✱ End-of-chapter questions

After reading the chapter carefully, try answering the questions below. If you would like to know what we think visit the Online Resource Centre (www.oxfordtextbooks.co.uk/orc/horsey2e/).

1. Outline each of the three defences discussed above. What do you think are their strengths and weaknesses?

2. The defence of illegality 'expresses not so much a principle as a policy. Furthermore, that policy is not based upon a single justification but on a group of reasons, which vary in different situations' (Lord Hoffmann, *Gray* v *Thames Trains Ltd* [2009] at [30]). Discuss with reference to relevant case law.

3. Consider again the problem question at the start of this chapter. Now having read about defences, what would be your advice to Ben and Andy—do you think they are likely to recover compensation in respect of their injuries from Graeme? (You should assume that, in the absence of applicable defences, they would have a good claim in negligence.) If you need some pointers in thinking about how to answer this question, turn to the Appendix (p 589) where the problem is annotated with issues and cases for you to consider. Next, try to write your own answer and finally, log on to our Online Resource Centre (www.oxfordtextbooks. co.uk/orc/horsey2e/) to check your ideas against our suggested outline answer.

✱ Further reading

There is limited reading specifically on defences, however, those listed below are a good place to start.

Davies, Paul 'The Illegality Defence: Turning Back the Clock' (2010) *Conveyancer* 282

Glofcheski, Rick 'Plaintiff's Illegality as a Bar to Recovery of Personal Injury Damage' (2006) *Legal Studies* 23

Jaffey, AJE 'Volenti Non Fit Injuria' (1985) *Cambridge Law Journal* 87

Law Commission *The Illegality Defence* (Law Com No 320, 2010), [3.2]–[3.41]

Lunney, Mark 'Personal Responsibility and the "New" Volenti' (2005) 13 *Tort Law Review* 76

Tan, Carol 'Volenti Non Fit Injuria: An Alternative Framework' [1995] *Tort Law Review* 208

Special liability regimes*

* The grouping of occupiers', employers' and product liabilities under this heading is *Lunney &*
Oliphant's, see Ch 11 in *Tort Law: Text and Materials* (4th edn, OUP, 2010). Ours differs only in so
far as breach of statutory duty and vicarious liability are discussed in the chapter on employers'
liability and we do not discuss the Euro-torts.

Introduction to Part II

1. Though much of tort law is based on general principles of common law, there are a number of situations where the legislature has intervened to introduce statutory rules. Typically, their purpose is to mitigate the harshness and inadequacies of the common law, though other factors have also played a part—in the case of product liability, for example, statutory intervention was necessary in order to implement a European Community Directive. In this Part we look at three 'special liability' regimes relating to occupiers, employers and defective products.

2. We begin, in Chapter 11, with **occupiers' liability**. An occupier may be liable where a person who comes onto their land is injured in or by unsafe premises if the occupier has not taken reasonable care to ensure that they, and those entering on them, are safe.

3. In such cases the common law has been superseded by the Occupiers' Liability Acts of 1957 and 1984. Before this, a complex system of common law rules governed this area of law, whereby the scope of the duty owed by the occupier depended on the circumstances in which the claimant came onto the premises. It continues to be important to define at the outset the category of visitor who has been injured: the Occupiers' Liability Act 1957 covers the safety of lawful visitors, whereas the Occupiers' Liability Act 1984 covers unlawful visitors (typically trespassers).

4. Although the Acts define the circumstances in which a duty of care will be owed (and tell us something as to its extent, as well as matters relating to its discharge and limitation), questions of breach and causation still need to be established by reference to the ordinary principles of negligence.

5. We then turn to **employers' liability**. This takes three distinct, yet overlapping, forms. First, an employer owes a **non-delegable duty of care** to their employees to ensure that they are reasonably safe when at work. This works to ensure that an employer remains responsible for key tasks even when their obligations have been delegated to another.

6. An employer may also be liable in the tort of **breach of statutory duty**. Unlike the statutory duties contained in the Occupiers' Liability Acts 1957 and 1984 or the Consumer Protection Act 1987 where liability arises directly according to the provisions of the statute itself, in a civil action in the tort of breach of statutory duty, liability arises **indirectly** where a statute imposes a duty (typically relating to criminal liability) but does not identify a civil remedy in the event of its breach. The tort is a combination of statute and the tort of negligence; the duty is defined by statute, while the action lies in the common law.

7. In the final section of Chapter 12, we look at the principle of **vicarious liability**, a form of secondary liability through which employers may, in certain circumstances, be liable for the torts of their employees (even though the employer themselves may be entirely blameless). This depends on the level of connection between the employee's tortious activity and what they are employed to do. As such, the imposition of vicarious liability is one of the most important exceptions to the general approach of the common law whereby liability for any wrongdoing is imposed on, and only on, the wrongdoer(s).

8. Finally, in Chapter 13, we turn to the special liability regime related to those injured by defective products. As with occupiers' liability, **product liability** is primarily governed by statute

(Part 1 of the Consumer Protection Act 1987). However, whilst in the context of occupiers' liability Parliament intervened in order to remedy the perceived failings of the common law, here they did so in response to a European Community Directive which required near-uniform product liability legislation across EU member states.

9. Unlike the Occupiers' Liability Acts 1957 and 1984, the Consumer Protection Act 1987 has not replaced the common law. A claimant can still bring a claim in relation to defective products in the tort of negligence (or any other tort); in fact, although such claims will generally be more difficult to establish than under the Consumer Protection Act (which creates a form of strict liability), they remain necessary given problematic statutory limitations in relation to certain types of claims.

11

Occupiers' liability

Problem question

Read this problem question carefully, and keep it in mind while you are working through the chapter that follows. At the end of the chapter, you will be able to apply what you have learnt to the problem question and advise the relevant parties.

'Camden Cool', an after school youth club run by the local authority, is holding an open day to raise funds for the club. One of the main attractions is a large bouncy castle supplied, erected and supervised by Elsinore Castles, a small local company. Joseph and Harry are the first to try it out. They both suffer minor cuts and bruises when the castle breaks free from its moorings and lifts into the air. It later turns out that it had not been appropriately tethered to the ground. Unfortunately, despite assuring Charlie, the club's youth worker, when he phoned to book the castle, that they had the necessary documentation, Elsinore's public liability insurance had expired two months before the accident.

In the chaos that follows, Esme, Phoebe's sister, wanders off alone. She is too young to be a member of the club and so doesn't know her way around the buildings. She is seriously injured when she falls down a flight of stairs after going through a door marked 'Private: No Unauthorised Entry'.

Meanwhile Frank and Freddy (who are members of the club) have sneaked off to play football. After a particularly poor shot at goal their ball lands on a flat roof. Although they know the roof is 'out of bounds', as everyone is busy at the open day, they decide to climb onto the roof to retrieve it. As they do so one of the skylights breaks. Freddy falls through the roof hitting his head hard, causing him to lose his hearing.

11.1 **Introduction**

Consider the following examples:

→ While on a picnic with some friends, a student dives into a lake to cool off. Unfortunately, he misjudges his dive into the shallow water and, as a result, hits his head on the lake bed and breaks his neck.

→ A shopper slips on some spilt milk in the dairy aisle of his local supermarket injuring his back and ruining his new suede jacket. The warning sign had been moved by another shopper to get to the food on the shelves.

→ A dinner guest trips over a child's toy left at the top of a flight of stairs and tumbles to the bottom, twisting her ankle.

→ On his way home from a night out, a student trips over an uneven paving stone on the driveway leading to his halls of residence.

Occupiers' liability deals with the risks posed, and harms caused, by dangerous places and buildings. In such cases, like those described above, the occupier of those premises—broadly understood to include not only buildings but also driveways, fire escapes and so on—may be liable if they have not taken reasonable care to ensure that those entering on to the premises are safe. What makes these claims distinctive is that the general principles of negligence (whereby if a breach of duty has caused injury liability will usually follow) have been incorporated into, and modified by, statute in the form of the Occupiers' Liability Acts 1957 and 1984.

This statutory intervention was considered necessary because of the harshness and complexity of the common law rules, whereby the scope of the duty owed by the occupier varied depending on the circumstances in which the claimant came on to the premises. Those who were on the premises by virtue of a contract (such as a plumber coming to fix a leaking tap) were owed a higher standard of care than so-called 'invitees' (for instance, a shopper), or friends the occupier had invited round for dinner, who were simply 'licensees'. They all fared better, however, than 'uninvited' persons or trespassers who were (until *British Railways Board* v *Herrington* [1972]) owed no positive duty of care at all; occupiers were simply under an obligation not to *deliberately* or recklessly cause trespassers harm (*Edwards* v *Railway Executive* [1952]).[1]

 Pause for reflection

Despite the Occupiers' Liability Act 1957 and, more particularly, its companion—the Occupiers' Liability Act 1984—Richard Buckley argues that the imposition of liability on occupiers remains 'an aspiration rather than an accurate statement of contemporary law' (2006, p 215). Recently, this traditional reluctance to impose liability—usually relating to a desire to leave landowners alone to enjoy their land as they wish—has been given a

→

---

1. See further p 296.

→
contemporary twist. The imposition of liability has been framed as an attack on the liberties of both individuals who choose to engage in dangerous pastimes at their own risk *and* people generally who wish to enjoy the countryside and other public spaces. Consider, for example, the following extract from the speech of Lord Hobhouse in *Tomlinson* v *Congleton Borough Council* [2004] in which he mirrors the concerns of many about the effects of 'an unrestrained culture of blame and compensation':

> [I]t is not, and should never be, the policy of the law to require the protection of the foolhardy or reckless few to deprive, or interfere with, the enjoyment by the remainder of society of the liberties and amenities to which they are rightly entitled. Does the law require that all trees be cut down because some youths may climb them and fall? Does the law require the coastline and other beauty spots to be lined with warning notices? Does the law require that attractive waterside picnic spots be destroyed because of a few foolhardy individuals who choose to ignore warning notices and indulge in activities dangerous only to themselves? The answer to all these questions is, of course, no. (at [81])

Do you agree with Lord Hobhouse? Think again about the purposes of tort law, contrasting the idea of corrective justice and its focus on individual responsibility and fault with the concerns of providing compensation and distributing losses across the community.[2]

It remains important to define at the outset the category of person who has been injured as the Occupiers' Liability Acts of 1957 and 1984, despite many similarities, crucially have different remits:

- Occupiers' Liability Act 1957 ('the 1957 Act')—covers lawful visitors (including invitees and licensees at common law and contractual visitors) (ss 1(2), 5).
- Occupiers' Liability Act 1984 ('the 1984 Act')—covers unlawful visitors (typically trespassers) (s 1(1)(a)).

Finally, there is one further point to make here. Although the Acts define the circumstances in which a duty of care will be owed and tell us something as to its extent, as well as matters relating to its discharge and limitation, when determining whether the duty has been breached and whether this breach caused the claimant loss we revert back to the ordinary principles of negligence.

11.2 **The Occupiers' Liability Act 1957**[3]

The 1957 Act provides that an occupier owes a duty of care to visitors in respect of dangers posed by the state of the premises or by things done or omitted to be done on them (s 1(1)). In line with its objective to simplify the common law, the 1957 Act abolishes

2. See further Jane Stapleton 'Tort, Insurance and Ideology' (1995) 58 *Modern Law Review* 820 and Morgan 2004.
3. Readers may find it helpful to refer to the annotated version of the 1957 Act (pp 293–295).

the various categories of visitor (and hence the varying duties owed to contractors, licensees and (implied) invitees) and provides that *all* lawful entrants should be owed the same common duty of care in respect of personal injury and property damage suffered on the premises (s 2(1)). The Act applies only to injuries suffered on the occupier's premises; if the injury is suffered outside the premises then there can be no claim on the basis of occupiers' liability, though a claim may lie under the ordinary principles of negligence, in the tort of nuisance (if there is an unreasonable interference with land) or under the rule in *Rylands* v *Fletcher* [1868] (if the damage is caused by the escape of a dangerous thing).[4]

11.2.1 **When is a duty owed?**

As stated above, under the 1957 Act a common duty of care is owed by an *occupier* to all *lawful visitors* who suffer injury on their *premises* (s 1(1)). It also states that occupiers and visitors are the same as those who would be treated as such at common law (s 1(2)). In order to establish when a duty of care is owed it is important to look to both the 1957 Act and the case law for answers to the following questions:

- Who is an occupier?
- Who is a lawful visitor?
- What are premises?

11.2.1.1 Occupiers: 'Occupation or control of premises'

The duty imposed by the 1957 Act is owed by those in occupation of premises.[5] Occupation is different from ownership; an occupier need not be the owner of the premises and nor is the owner necessarily the occupier. Neither is it simply a matter of who is physically present on the premises. Rather, the occupier is the person who has, or is able to exercise, a sufficient degree of control over the premises (s 1(2)).[6] Importantly, there may be more than one occupier at any given time. For example, a landlord and tenant may, depending on the circumstances, both be considered occupiers for the purpose of the 1957 Act.

Wheat v *Lacon & Co Ltd* [1966] HL

The defendants, Lacon & Co brewery, had let their pub to Mr Richardson to manage under a service agreement. They had also given Mr Richardson and his wife permission (on an informal basis) to live on the first floor of the pub and to rent out the other rooms to paying guests. The claimant's husband, Mr Wheat, was fatally injured after falling down a flight of poorly lit stairs while staying at the pub. The light bulb at the top of the stairs had been removed, which meant that Mr Wheat was unable to know when he reached the last

→

---

4. Discussed in Chapters 2–10, 17, and 18 respectively.
5. Section 1(2)(a) of the 1984 Act defines an occupier in the same way as the 1957 Act.
6. This explains why landlords are not (usually) liable under the 1957 Act (although they may be liable under the Defective Premises Act 1972, discussed further below).

→

step and was unable to see that the handrail finished three steps short of the end of the staircase.

The question for the court was whether the brewery (who owned the pub) was an occupier for the purposes of a claim under the 1957 Act (a claim in the tort of negligence against the landlord and his wife had failed).

The House of Lords held that *both* the brewery and Mr and Mrs Richardson were occupiers for the purposes of the 1957 Act and, as such, owed a common duty of care to the claimant (and other lawful visitors). The brewery, by simply granting a concession to allow Mr and Mrs Richardson to occupy the first floor, had not relinquished complete control of the premises: 'In order to be an "occupier" it is not necessary for a person to have entire control over the premises. He need not have exclusive occupation. Suffice that he has some degree of control. He may share the control with others' (Lord Denning at 578).

However, on the facts, neither party had fallen below the standard of care required of them. The fact that the stairs had a short handrail did not, in itself, make the stairs unreasonably hazardous and nor were they responsible for the actions of the stranger who had plunged the stairs into darkness by removing the light bulb, shortly before Mr Wheat attempted to walk down them.

Wheat v *Lacon* shows that an occupier need not have actual physical possession of the premises. Indeed one may be an 'occupier' for the purposes of the 1957 (and 1984) Acts despite never having resided in or physically occupied the premises. For instance, in *Harris* v *Birkenhead Corporation* [1975], as part of a slum clearance programme, a tenant was served a compulsory purchase order, which stated that the council would enter and take possession of the property a fortnight after the notice was served. The tenant moved out. Three months later the corporation had still not secured the property (by bricking it up), despite knowing that vacant properties in the area were often vandalised. As a result, vandals had broken down the front door and caused considerable damage inside the property, including removing the glass from a second floor window. The claimant (a 4-year-old girl), who entered the property through the damaged door, fell out of the window suffering severe brain damage. The Court of Appeal held that even though the corporation had never even been to the premises, they were nevertheless the occupiers as soon as the previous tenant had left. They had control over the property and, though they did not exercise it, the ability *and duty* to secure it.

Liability under the Defective Premises Act 1972[7]

Typically, a landlord who has leased out premises will not have retained sufficient control to be treated as an occupier for the purposes of the 1957 and 1984 Acts. In such situations, a tenant who suffers an injury as a result of a defect in the premises they are renting will

→

7. The Defective Premises Act 1972 is also discussed in relation to negligence liability for economic loss in Chapter 7, p 180. See also JR Spencer 'The Defective Premises Act 1972—Defective Law and Defective Law Reform' (1975) 34(1) *Cambridge Law Journal* 48.

> →
>
> have no claim under the 1957 Act; there is no 'occupier' (other than themselves) to sue. Nor does the common law offer much protection in such circumstances (*Cavalier* v *Pope* [1906]; *Bottomley* v *Bannister* [1932]).
>
> This gap is addressed by section 4 of the Defective Premises Act 1972. Where a lease imposes on the landlord an obligation in respect of the maintenance and repair of the property, the landlord will be held to owe a duty of care to all those who might reasonably be expected to be affected by any defects in the state of the premises, so long as (a) the landlord knows or ought to have known of the relevant defect and (b) the defect is one which the landlord should have remedied by virtue of the obligation to repair imposed by the lease. The important point to note here is that the duty is owed not only to the tenant, but also to others who may foreseeably be affected by defects, such as partners and other family members (s 4(1)).

11.2.1.2 Visitors: by invitation or permission only

An occupier owes a duty under the 1957 Act only to those they have invited or have (or are treated as having) given permission to enter or use the premises (s 1(2)).[8] The key question is then: Did the claimant have express, or implied, permission to be on the premises?

Such permission is rarely unlimited. As Lord Justice Scrutton notes: 'When you invite a person into your house to use the staircase, you do not invite him to slide down the banisters' (*The Carlgarth* [1927] at 110).[9] By limiting the extent of the permission they give to a visitor, an occupier can restrict the duty they owe to them (s 2(1)). For example, they might place restrictions on the time a visitor can spend on their premises (for example, opening hours), the purposes for which they can use it, or limit their permission to particular parts of the property. If a visitor goes beyond what they have been invited or given permission to do at that point, and to that extent, they will cease to be treated as a visitor and so will fall outside the provisions of the Occupiers' Liability Act 1957.[10] A person may be at the same time a visitor for some purposes and not for others depending on the scope of the permission granted by the occupier (compare, for example, **Darby** v **National Trust** [2001] and **Tomlinson**).

The occupier may change the terms of their permission and even revoke it entirely while the visitor is on the premises, changing the status of the 'visitor'. However, to be effective, this must be done in a way that is obvious to the visitor. A rather extreme example of this is provided by *Snook* v *Mannion* [1982] where a motorist told the policeman who had followed him up his driveway in order to breathalyse him to 'fuck off'. The court held that these words—which were taken to refer to the policeman's presence as well as his attempts to breathalyse the motorist—were not sufficient to revoke

---

8. This duty also extends to the lawful visitor's property (s 1(3)(b)).

9. This is largely a matter of common sense. Consider again the dinner guest who fell down the stairs. They will remain a lawful visitor (and the occupier liable) as long as their presence on the stairs was reasonable (see further *Gould* v *McAuliffe* [1941]).

10. Although in these circumstances the 1984 Act will apply.

the licence usually implied to allow people to use a driveway to approach the house on legitimate business. Notices merely stating 'keep out' or 'private' may also not be sufficient.

11.2.1.3 Premises: including 'any fixed or moveable structure'

Under the 1957 Act the definition of premises extends to 'any fixed or movable structure, including any vessel, vehicle or aircraft' (s 1(3)).[11] Clearly this broad interpretation of premises not only includes buildings, driveways, fire escapes and other real property but also encompasses less permanent structures like scaffolding, a derelict boat left on a council estate (*Jolley* v *Sutton London Borough Council* [2000]) and even a temporary 'splat wall'[12] (*Gwilliam* v *West Hertfordshire Hospital NHS Trust* [2002]).

11.2.2 **What is the duty owed?**

Under the 1957 Act, an occupier owes a positive duty to act to take 'such care as in all the circumstances of the case is reasonable to see that *the visitor* will be reasonably safe in using the premises for the purposes for which he is invited' (s 2(2)) (emphasis added).

The first point to note is that there is an ambiguity arising from the Act's formulation of the duty owed by an occupier. Section 1(1) speaks of 'dangers due to the state of the premises *or to things done, or omitted to be done on them*'. This has led to debate as to whether the Act imposes an 'activity' duty (that is, in respect of injuries caused by some activity which is taking place on the premises) or whether it is limited to an 'occupancy' duty (relating only to injuries caused by the static condition of the premises themselves) as apparently provided for under section 1(2).[13] Despite the wording of section 1(1), the 1957 Act applies *only* to dangers posed, and harms caused, by the condition of the premises (though, of course, the premises may be rendered dangerous by virtue of some activity that has taken place on them) (see Lord Goff in *Ferguson* v *Welsh* [1987] approved in *Fairchild* v *Glenhaven Funeral Services* [2002] (CA) at [113]–[155]).[14] The Act has no application where a claimant is injured by virtue of something that is happening on the defendant's premises. In *Bottomley* v *Todmorden Cricket Club* [2003], for example, the claimant was injured when helping to set up a firework display by filling a mortar tube with gunpowder. As his injuries arose from activities conducted on the defendant's land rather than due to the state

---

11. Section 1(2) of the 1984 Act defines a premises in the same way as the 1957 Act.

12. A Velcro wall which people attempt to stick themselves to by jumping off a trampoline.

13. The distinction between so-called 'occupancy' and 'activity' duties, developed by the courts as a way of avoiding the harshness of the common law, pre-dates the Occupiers' Liability Acts. While liability in relation to the former depended on the status of the visitor, the ordinary rules of negligence applied to the latter.

14. However the case law is not consistent on this. As *Lunney & Oliphant* point out, in *Tomlinson* s 1(1) was interpreted by Lords Hoffmann and Hobhouse to include activities 'conducted by the occupiers, or by others with his consent, that create a risk to persons on the premises (e.g., if shooting is taking place on the premises or speedboats are allowed to go into an area where swimmers are present' (p 566). Issues relating to occupiers' liability were not considered by the House of Lords in *Fairchild* (discussed in detail in Chapter 9, pp 230–232).

of the land itself, his claim under the Act failed (though, as in *Fairchild*, he was successful under the ordinary principles of negligence). This, Buckley argues, is the better view: 'All activities which take place do so *somewhere*, and the law relating to occupiers' liability would be extraordinarily wide if it were expanded to include all the activities which a defendant happens to carry out on his land' (2006, p 208). In any case, there is likely to be little difference, if any, between the duty owed under the 1957 Act and that under the ordinary principles of negligence (Brooke LJ, *Bottomley* at [42]).[15]

An occupier may, in certain circumstances, also be liable to a visitor for the harm caused by another visitor. In *Cunningham v Reading Football Club Ltd* [1992] a policeman was able to recover under the 1957 Act for his injuries suffered as a result of being hit by a concrete missile thrown by football hooligans. Although the actions of the hooligans (described by one witness as 'the worse they had seen at any football ground in Britain' at 144) might seem more akin to an activity (and, as such, to fall outside the scope of the 1957 Act), the court held that the defendants had breached their duty as occupiers under the 1957 Act. The premises were in a particularly dilapidated state and this allowed the hooligans to break off bits of concrete with their feet to use as missiles. Therefore the claimant's injuries could be attributed to the state of the premises and hence the defendant's breach of their occupancy duty.

11.2.3 Discharging the duty

Once the existence of a common duty of care has been established, it is necessary to consider whether the occupier has breached it. The issue of breach is determined by the same basic principles as in the common law of negligence (as reflected by the fact that some of the leading cases on breach are cases of occupiers' liability).[16] So, for instance, in determining what amounts to reasonable care, we take into account the likelihood and gravity of harm resulting from the state of the premises and the costs involved in rectifying any potential dangers. In particular, the 1957 Act requires courts to consider what is reasonable 'in all the circumstances of the case' (s 2(2)), including the degree of care expected from the visitor/claimant (s 2(3)). We looked at breach in detail in Chapter 8, and the cases discussed there are relevant here too. Here we shall draw attention only to a handful of issues which are either specific to occupiers' liability or are mentioned in the 1957 Act.

It is clear that the courts will take into account the resources of the occupier when considering what steps they might reasonably be expected to take to make their

---

15. It is worth noting here Smith LJ's remark in *Everett v Comojo (UK) Ltd (t/a The Metropolitan)* [2011] in which she suggests that the duty of care under the 1957 Act can inform the duty of care of an occupier at common law *even in situations where the potential liability does not relate to the condition of the premises*: 'It would be surprising if management could be liable to a guest who tripped over a worn carpet and yet escape liability for injuries inflicted by a fellow guest who was a foreseeable danger—for example in that he had previously been excluded on account of his violent behaviour and who on this occasion had been allowed in carrying an offensive weapon' (at [33]).

16. See, e.g. *Latimer v AEC Ltd* [1953].

premises safer.[17] The common duty of care is not owed 'in the abstract' but by particular defendants to particular claimants (*Lewis* v *Six Continents* [2005] at [24]).

Kiapasha (t/a Takeaway Supreme) v Laverton [2002] CA

The claimant broke her ankle after slipping over in the defendant's busy take-away after a night out. It had been raining earlier in the evening and the shop floor was wet and slippery. The shopkeeper had taken a number of precautions to prevent accidents: the shop floor had been re-laid using slip-resistant tiles; there was a doormat to limit the amount of water brought in on the feet of the customers (although this may have been kicked out of the way at the time of the accident); and a system for mopping up excess water, which usually took place six or seven times on a busy night.

The majority of the Court of Appeal held that the shopkeeper had done all that could reasonably be expected of him in his attempts to keep his shop floor dry:

> In some large businesses it may be reasonable to expect stringent precautions at the shop door, including mats large enough to absorb moisture from large numbers of customers who do not wipe their feet and/or a member of staff stationed near the door to mop up as required . . . The question is what was reasonable to expect of the defendant in the particular circumstances of the case and whether anything else would have made a difference. In my view, it would not . . . [I]n that particular shop, at that particular time, it was not reasonable to expect the shopkeeper to ensure that the mat was in place and to mop the floor often enough and efficiently enough to prevent its being wet, even significantly or considerably so. (Hale LJ at [19]–[23])[18]

Similarly, and again as with breach more generally, the occupier's duty to ensure that the visitor will be reasonably safe while on their premises does not mean that the visitor cannot be expected to take reasonable care for their own safety (s 2(3)). The 1957 Act makes particular reference to children and professionals.

11.2.3.1 Children

Children invited onto premises are owed a common duty of care like all other visitors. However, where the visitor is a child, more may be required of the occupier to ensure that they are kept *reasonably* safe. (It may be impossible to make the premises *completely* safe for children—especially when they run off from their parents (*Bourne Leisure Ltd* v *Marsden* [2009]).) In particular, the occupier must take into account that children will be less careful than adults (s 2(3)(a)). As such, occupiers will generally owe a higher

---

17. Thus, in relation to the examples posed at the beginning of the chapter, while an occupier might be reasonably expected to ensure that children's toys are tidied away before hosting a dinner party (this being fairly easily achieved), more information is needed (in relation to the resources of the occupier, extent of the unevenness, cost of repair and so on) before the same can be said in relation to the uneven paving stone at the student's halls of residence.

18. Consider again the spilt milk in a supermarket aisle in the examples at the beginning of the chapter—what additional information would the court need in order to decide whether the occupier was in breach of their duty (see further *Ward* v *Tesco Stores Ltd* [1976])?

standard of care to children than to older visitors (*Glasgow Corporation v Taylor* [1922]). In particular, a warning that might suffice to alert adults to dangers on the premises may be not be sufficient to warn children.

Jolley v Sutton London Borough Council [2000] HL

A boat had been abandoned for over two years on land owned by the defendant. Although it appeared sound it was in fact rotten. The claimant and his friend, aged 14 and 13, decided to fix it. The claimant was crushed, when the boat fell on him, suffering serious spinal injuries which left him paralysed. He brought an action against the council for damages under the Occupiers' Liability Act 1957. In holding the council liable, the House of Lords noted that the boat was likely to be a particular attraction—or an 'allurement'—to children. Therefore, though the boat was not likely to pose a danger to adults, who were more likely to steer clear of it, it was reasonably foreseeable that children may approach the boat. The council's duty of care as occupier accordingly required them to take steps to remove the dangers posed to those children who might be tempted to climb onto it.

It is worth stressing that the 'allurement' of the boat in *Jolley* was relevant to establishing the foreseeability of the children climbing onto the boat, and hence whether it was reasonable to have expected the council to have taken steps to ensure the boat was safe or to remove it. In other words, its relevance was to determining whether the defendant breached its duty to the claimant. Of course, this question only arises once we have established that the child claimant is indeed a visitor, that is has the occupier's permission to enter or use the premises, and so is owed a duty under the 1957 Act.

At one point, it seemed that the courts were willing to stretch the notion of permission in relation to children to ensure that they were treated as visitors.[19] However, now the Occupiers' Liability Act 1984 has extended the protection accorded to those injured when on another's premises without permission, there is far less need for the courts to stretch the notion of visitors when dealing with children. As such, the better view is that in determining both whether the claimant has permission to enter the defendant's premises and how far that permission extends—that is, determining whether a child is a visitor for the purposes of the 1957 Act—the same rules apply to adults and children alike: 'infancy as such is no more a status conferring rights, or a root of title imposing obligations on others to respect it, than infirmity or imbecility' (Lord Sumner, *Glasgow Corporation v Taylor* [1922] at 67).

It is usually argued that, in deciding whether the common duty of care has been breached, an occupier is entitled to assume that parents will take reasonable care of their children:

> ...the responsibility for the safety of little children must rest primarily on the parents; it is their duty to see that such children are not allowed to wander about by themselves, or at least to satisfy themselves that the places to which they do allow their children to go unaccompanied are safe for them to go to. It would not be socially desirable if parents were, as a matter of course, able to shift the burden of looking after their children from

---

19. As noted above, trespassers were afforded limited legal protection under the common law.

their own shoulders to those who happen to have accessible bits of land. (*Phipps* v
Rochester Corporation [1955] at 472)

In *Simkiss* v *Rhondda Borough Council* [1983], a child was seriously injured whilst playing with a friend on a steep bank. In the course of argument it became clear that the
child's father did not believe the bank to be dangerous. The Court of Appeal held that
it was not reasonable to hold the council to a higher standard of care than a reasonably prudent parent. Put bluntly, if the child's father did not consider the bank to be
dangerous, then why should the council? Moreover, even if the father *had* considered
the bank to be dangerous, the council was entitled to assume that the father would
warn his child of familiar and obvious dangers. The fact that he had not either meant
that he thought the bank was safe or was evidence of negligence on his part. However,
in *Perry* v *Butlins Holiday World (t/a Butlins Ltd)* [1997], the Court of Appeal found the
defendants had breached their duty of care in respect of injuries sustained by a 3-year-
old child who had fallen onto a low brick wall, seriously cutting his ear. In so doing,
they drew attention to the height of the wall (which made it more likely that a child
would fall on top of it rather than run into it), the inappropriateness of the material
used in its construction, the likelihood of the risk (the fact that children are more
likely to be at a holiday camp) and, of particular relevance here, the fact that children
were likely to be less closely supervised by their parents at such a holiday camp than
in other public places.

 Counterpoint

The decision in *Simkiss* appears somewhat harsh. Do you think it would have been
decided differently if the father had given a different answer to the question of whether
he considered the bank dangerous? It has been suggested that the state of the defendant's premises and the degree of care needed to make them safe ought to be assessed
objectively (*Markesinis & Deakin* p 354). In other words, why should the fact that the claimant's parents fail to give sufficient regard to their child's safety entitle occupiers to escape
liability for their own neglect? It is one thing to say that occupiers should not be expected to
make up for parents' shortcomings, quite another to hold them to a lower standard simply
because the child's parents would have done no better.

11.2.3.2 'Persons in the exercise of a calling'

While greater care must be taken in relation to children invited onto one's premises,
less is required of occupiers in respect of visitors who can be considered able to look
after themselves. In particular, skilled visitors are expected to guard against special
risks associated with their profession (s 2(3)(b)).

In *Roles* v *Nathan* [1963] two chimney sweeps died whilst trying to mend the chimney
of a coke-fired boiler. Though they had been warned repeatedly that the boiler room
was dangerous and were told to leave, they carried on working. The majority of the
Court of Appeal dismissed a claim under the 1957 Act by the chimney sweeps' widows
on two grounds: first a householder can reasonably expect a specialist to appreciate and
guard against dangers associated with their trade (s 2(3)); and secondly, the warning

had been sufficient to ensure that the sweeps were, in all the circumstances, 'reasonably safe' within the meaning of section 2(4). Accordingly, though Lord Denning MR held that the consequence of this was that no duty of care was owed to the sweeps, the better view is that, in the circumstances, 'the duty was discharged, at any rate in regard to the dangers that caused their deaths. If it had been a different danger, as for instance if the stairs leading to the cellar gave way, the occupier might no doubt be responsible, but not for these dangers which were special risks ordinarily incidental to their calling' (at 1123–4).[20]

11.2.3.3 Warnings

As we have seen above, an occupier may discharge their duty by giving a warning of the potential danger (s 2(4)(a)) or alternatively it may raise the defence of *volenti* or contributory negligence.[21] Warnings may be verbal, but can also be visual or written—for example a notice on the edge of a cliff, a barrier around a building site or a large yellow 'warning' sign on a shop floor. In all events a warning will be sufficient to discharge an occupier's duty to a particular visitor only if, in all the circumstances, it is enough to enable that visitor to be reasonably safe.[22] Lord Denning MR in *Roles* v *Nathan* [1963] uses this example:

> Supposing, for instance, that there was only one way of getting into and out of premises, and it was by a footbridge over a stream which was rotten and dangerous...[previously] the occupier could escape all liability to any visitor by putting up a notice: 'This bridge is dangerous', even though there was no other way by which the visitor could get in or out, and he had no option but to go over the bridge. In such a case, s 2(4)(a) [of the 1957 Act] makes it clear that the occupier would nowadays be liable. But if there were two footbridges, one of which was rotten, and the other safe a hundred yards away, the occupier could still escape liability, even today, by putting up a notice: 'Do not use this footbridge. It is dangerous. There is a safe one further upstream'. Such a warning is sufficient because it does enable the visitor to be reasonably safe. (at 1124)

By contrast, where the danger is obvious there is usually no need to give a warning. In *Staple* v *West Dorset District Council* [1995] the occupiers were under no duty to warn of the inherent dangers of a famous sea wall in Lyme Regis known as 'the Cobb', which is covered in seaweed and algae and obviously very slippery. Similarly, the failure to warn about one type of danger will not help the claimant if they subsequently suffer personal injury as a result of an unrelated danger (***Darby*** v ***National Trust*** [2001]).

Darby v _National Trust_ [2001] CA

The claimant's husband drowned while swimming in a pond at Hardwick Hall in Derbyshire owned by the National Trust. He was a competent swimmer, but the pond was murky, and

→

---

20. A similar claim against an occupier also failed in *General Cleaning Contractors* v *Christmas* [1953] (discussed in Chapter 13).

21. Discussed in Chapter 10.

22. Thus simply placing a warning sign in the supermarket aisle (in the example at the beginning of the chapter) may not be enough, in itself, to absolve the occupiers of liability.

as much as ten feet deep in places. Visitors often swam or paddled in the pond and the Trust did little to discourage this. There was a legible but inconspicuous notice near the car park, which—among other things—forbade bathing and boating. Wardens occasionally patrolled the ponds, and would discourage people from swimming in them, by warning of the dangers of catching Weil's disease from the water. The claimant argued that the Trust's failure to place 'No Swimming' notices around the pond (or to similarly warn of the risk of catching Weil's disease) amounted to a breach of their common duty of care under section 2 of the Occupiers' Liability Act 1957.

The Court of Appeal held that such notices would have told Mr Darby 'no more than he already knew' about the risks relating to swimming in open water and that the Trust's failure to warn about one type of danger (Weil's disease) could not help the claimant if they subsequently suffer personal injury as a result of an unrelated danger (drowning) (at [25]–[26]). There were no special or hidden dangers in relation to this particular pond and no duty on the part of the Trust to warn him of obvious dangers. The Trust had done all that was reasonable in the circumstances of the case to see that the claimant's husband was reasonably safe while using its premises:

> it cannot be the duty of the owner of every stretch of coastline to have notices warning of the dangers of swimming in the sea. If it were so, the coast would have to be littered with notices in places other than those where there are known to be special dangers which are not obvious. The same would apply to all inland lakes and reservoirs. (May LJ at [27])

11.2.3.4 Notices excluding liability

The presence of an effective warning notice will defeat a claim under the 1957 Act because it means that, in the circumstances, the defendant has taken reasonable care to ensure that visitors are safe on their premises. By issuing a warning the defendant has told visitors what they must do and not do to avoid being harmed, and has, in so doing, discharged the duty owed to the visitors. This should be distinguished from the situation under section 2(1) where, by a written notice or otherwise (for example, through an express term of a contract), an occupier seeks to restrict, exclude or otherwise modify their duty to a visitor. Unlike warning notices that seek to ensure that visitors are reasonably safe, thus satisfying the duty imposed on the occupier under the 1957 Act, such exclusions operate to prevent a duty from arising in the first place (or at least to limit its scope by setting out the conditions on which the claimant enters the premises).

Where the premises are occupied for business purposes, an occupier's ability to limit their liability is restricted by sections 2(1) and 2(2) of the Unfair Contract Terms Act 1977.[23] Such an occupier is unable to restrict liability for death or personal injury resulting from negligence; however, they are able to restrict their duty in relation to other damage where it is reasonable to do so. Of course, if the premises are in private

---

23. Section 1(1)(c) of the Unfair Contract Terms Act 1977 specifically refers to notices excluding or limiting liability under the 1957 Act.

use, the occupier is free to extend, restrict or otherwise modify their liability as much (or as little) as they choose.

11.2.3.5 Faulty execution of work

Where an accident is the result of a subcontractor's work on the premises, the occupier will not be liable if, in all the circumstances, they have acted reasonably in entrusting the work to an independent contractor and have taken steps (if any) as are reasonable to check that the contractor is competent and that the work has been properly done (s 2(4)(b)). Usually, the more technical the work, the more reasonable it will be to entrust it to an independent contractor (compare *Woodward* v *Mayor of Hastings* [1945] and *Haseldine* v *CA Daw & Sons Ltd* [1941]).

Of course, a claimant who is injured as a result of a subcontractor's faulty work may have a claim against that subcontractor under the ordinary principles of negligence. This raises an interesting related question as to when an occupier is under a duty to ensure that subcontractors who they entrust to do work on their premises are insured or otherwise have sufficient resources to meet any claims that may arise from their negligence?

Gwilliam v *West Hertfordshire Hospitals NHS Trust* [2002] CA

The 63-'year-old claimant was injured while using a 'splat wall' run by an independent contractor at a charity fun day organised by the defendant occupier, the NHS Trust. Her injuries were caused by the independent contractor's negligence. Unfortunately, the contractor's insurance policy had lapsed and so they were unable to meet her claim in full. The claimant sued the Trust for failing to ensure that the contractor was adequately insured.

The Court of Appeal denied her claim for the outstanding amount of damages. The majority of the court held, that though the Trust owed the claimant a duty to check that the contractor had adequate insurance (on the basis that this went to the competence of the contractor and so was relevant to the reasonableness of the occupier in choosing the particular contractor), on the facts the Trust had done enough (under s 2(4)(b) of the 1957 Act) to discharge their duty and so there was no breach. It would, the majority suggested, be unreasonable to require the occupier to go any further by, for example, checking the specific terms of the policy.

Sedley LJ strongly dissented on the existence of a duty (though all members of the court concurred in dismissing the appeal).[24] There was, he suggested, a big difference between a duty to protect visitors from physical injury and a duty to protect them from an inability to recover damages (at [56]).

The upshot of the decision in *Gwilliam* is that a defendant occupier may be liable to the victims of a third party's wrong, on the basis that they failed to ensure that the third party was in a position to meet any such liabilities. Yet, it is difficult to see why

---

24. He also disagreed with Lord Woolf CJ and Waller LJ on the issue of breach. If the Trust had owed a duty of care, given the ease with which the insurance certificate could have been checked (for example by being faxed or sent to the hospital), the Trust would have, on the facts of the case, breached their duty.

the simple fact that the third party's negligent work was conducted on the defendant's premises is sufficient reason for imposing on the defendant occupier a duty to see that victims of that third party's negligence are adequately compensated. ***Gwilliam*** appears to be grounded in a particular view of the functions of tort law: 'All three judges seem to agree that the overriding purpose of liability in tort law is to compensate loss by spreading it through an insurance pool, and therefore that a failure to bring this about by failing to carry insurance is itself, in principle at least, a wrongful act' (Morgan 2004, p 389). It is worth noting that in *Naylor* v *Payling* [2004] the Court of Appeal held that the owner of a nightclub had taken reasonable care to see that visitors to the club were safe and that, save in special circumstances, there was no general duty to take reasonable steps to ensure that an independent contractor was insured. More recently in *Glaister* v *Appleby-in-Westmoreland Town Council* [2009], the Court of Appeal affirmed Neuberger LJ's view of ***Gwilliam*** as 'a difficult case', stating a preference for the approach of Sedley LJ (at [54]). Rather than focusing on the loss-spreading benefits of insurance, the Court of Appeal in *Glaister* focused on the deterrent effect of such claims:

> I would reject the idea that those bodies, public or private, which try to encourage attendance at such events or undertake some responsibility in relation to them thereby expose themselves to legal liability for the negligence of other bodies participating in the event. I do not see the justice of it and I am concerned that the fear of it is likely to act as a deterrent to those…who freely give their time and energies to the encouragement of such events. If that were to happen, the result would be an impoverishment of our community life. (Toulson LJ at [48])

11.2.3.6 Defences

An occupier will have a defence where a visitor's injuries arise from 'risks willingly accepted as his by the visitor' (s 2(5)) (*volenti*) or where their own negligence has contributed to the injuries they have suffered (contributory negligence). These are not unique to occupiers' liability and are discussed further in Chapter 10.

11.3 The Occupiers' Liability Act 1957—annotated

Occupiers' Liability Act 1957

Preliminary

Puts the common law to one side; although see s 1(2) in relation to definitions of who is an occupier and visitor.

1.—(1) The rules enacted by the two next following sections shall have effect, in place of the rules of the common law, to regulate the duty which an occupier of premises owes to his visitors in respect of dangers due to the state of the premises or to things done or omitted to be done on them.

Definition of an occupier as someone who has control of the premises; see *Wheat* v *Lacon*.

(2) The rules so enacted shall regulate the nature of the duty imposed by law in consequence of a person's occupation or control of premises and of any invitation or permission he gives (or is to be treated as giving) to another to

See discussion on pp 285–286 relating to the distinction between so-called 'activity' duties and 'occupancy' duties.

→

enter or use the premises, but they shall not alter the rules of the common law as to the persons on whom a duty is so imposed or to whom it is owed; and accordingly for the purpose of the rules so enacted the persons who are to be treated as an occupier and as his visitors are the same (subject to subsection (4) of this section) as the persons who would at common law be treated as an occupier and as his invitees or licensees.

(3) The rules so enacted in relation to an occupier of premises and his visitors shall also apply, in like manner and to the like extent as the principles applicable at common law to an occupier of premises and his invitees or licensees would apply, to regulate—

(a) the obligations of a person occupying or having control over any fixed or moveable structure, including any vessel, vehicle or aircraft; and

(b) the obligations of a person occupying or having control over any premises or structure in respect of damage to property, including the property of persons who are not themselves his visitors.

(4) A person entering any premises in exercise of rights conferred by virtue of—

(a) section 2(1) of the Countryside and Rights of Way Act 2000, or

(b) an access agreement or order under the National Parks and Access to the Countryside Act 1949, is not, for the purposes of this Act, a visitor of the occupier of the premises.

Extent of occupier's ordinary duty

2.—(1) An occupier of premises owes the same duty, the "common duty of care", to all his visitors, except in so far as he is free to and does extend, restrict, modify or exclude his duty to any visitor or visitors by agreement or otherwise.

(2) The common duty of care is a duty to take such care as in all the circumstances of the case is reasonable to see that the visitor will be reasonably safe in using the premises for the purposes for which he is invited or permitted by the occupier to be there.

(3) The circumstances relevant for the present purpose include the degree of care, and of want of care, which would ordinarily be looked for in such a visitor, so that (for example) in proper cases—

(a) an occupier must be prepared for children to be less careful than adults; and

(b) an occupier may expect that a person, in the exercise of his calling, will appreciate and guard against any special risks ordinarily incident to it, so far as the occupier leaves him free to do so.

(4) In determining whether the occupier of premises has discharged the common duty of care to a visitor, regard is to be had to all the circumstances, so that (for example)—

→

Margin notes

Definition of a visitor as someone invited, or given permission to be, onto premises. Remember this permission can be revoked and/or restricted under s 2(1).

Very broad definition of premises.

Section 1 establishes when a duty is owed, this section establishes what duty is owed—i.e. its extent or scope.

e.g. the rules and regulations made and published under statutory authority—such as certain conditions in relation to rail travel—which are not 'agreed to' by the visitor.

Takes into account the fact that visitors ought to be responsible for their own safety, to an extent, and allows for the defence of contributory negligence.

See, e.g. *Jolley v Sutton.*

i.e. the standard of care necessary in order to discharge (or not breach) the duty.

The common law is incorporated into the Act—'licensees' and 'invitees' are combined into a single category 'lawful visitor'. Contractors are incorporated by s 5.

e.g. the shopper's suede jacket in the examples at the beginning of the chapter—even if it belonged to someone else.

See Occupiers' Liability Act 1984, s 1(6).

Note restrictions under ss 2(1) and 2(2) of the Unfair Contract Terms Act 1977 (UCTA) in relation to business premises.

It is the *visitor,* rather than the premises, which must be reasonably safe.

Definition of the common duty of care—effectively the common law duty in tort of negligence—see further Lord Denning's description of it in **Wheat v Lacon** as 'a particular instance of the general duty of care which each man owes to his "neighbour"' (at 578).

i.e. a professional, or skilled, visitor. See, e.g. *Roles v Nathan.*

This section is somewhat vague—it is likely that the courts will extend this beyond its strict reading and was applied 'by analogy' by the majority of the Court of Appeal in *Gwilliam*.

i.e. met the standard of care expected of them.

Defence of *volenti* (see further Chapter 10).

Establishes that 'contractual' entrants under the common law are visitors under the Act.

(a) where damage is caused to a visitor by a danger of which he had been warned by the occupier, the warning is not to be treated without more as absolving the occupier from liability, unless in all the circumstances it was enough to enable the visitor to be reasonably safe; and

(b) where damage is caused to a visitor by a danger due to the faulty execution of any work of construction, maintenance or repair by an independent contractor employed by the occupier, the occupier is not to be treated without more as answerable for the danger if in all the circumstances he had acted reasonably in entrusting the work to an independent contractor and had taken such steps (if any) as he reasonably ought in order to satisfy himself that the contractor was competent and that the work had been properly done.

(5) The common duty of care does not impose on an occupier any obligation to a visitor in respect of risks willingly accepted as his by the visitor (the question whether a risk was so accepted to be decided on the same principles as in other cases in which one person owes a duty of care to another).

(6) For the purposes of this section, persons who enter premises for any purpose in the exercise of a right conferred by law are to be treated as permitted by the occupier to be there for that purpose, whether they in fact have his permission or not.

…

Implied term in contracts

5.—(1) Where persons enter or use, or bring or send goods to, any premises in exercise of a right conferred by contract with a person occupying or having control of the premises, the duty he owes them in respect of dangers due to the state of the premises or to things done or omitted to be done on them, in so far as the duty depends on a term to be implied in the contract by reason of its conferring that right, shall be the common duty of care.

A warning does not automatically absolve an occupier from liability. It must enable the visitor to be reasonably safe in order to discharge the occupier's duty of care. Note also here the difference between a warning notice and a notice seeking to exclude or limit liability (s 2(1))—the former seeks to discharge an occupier's duty while the latter seeks to prevent it from arising in the first place.

e.g. the police entering with a warrant or employees of public utilities (gas and electricity) entering to read the meter enter the premises 'as of right' and as such are 'lawful visitors' even if the occupier may object to their presence.

11.4 **The Occupiers' Liability Act 1984**[25]

Under the 1984 Act, an occupier owes a duty (provided certain conditions are met (s 1(3)) to take reasonable care in all the circumstances to see that persons 'other than his visitors' do not suffer injury as a result of 'danger due to the state of the premises or to things done or omitted to be done on them' (s 1(1)). This negative category of non-visitors most obviously includes trespassers.[26]

25. Readers may find it helpful to refer to the annotated version of the 1984 Act (pp 302–304).
26. However, the term also applies to people exercising a private right of way and ramblers *lawfully* exercising a right of way by using a footpath across private land under s 2(1) of the Countryside and Rights of Way Act 2000 (s 1(4) of the Occupiers' Liability Act 1957). Those using public rights of way do not fall within the remit of either Act.

Pause for reflection

Imagine for a moment a 'trespasser'. Who do you have in mind? A burglar? A squatter? Someone sneaking a shortcut home across a neighbour's garden? A group of teenagers up to mischief on a building site? How about an elderly person who's gone onto the wrong property by mistake? Or a child fetching their football from a neighbour's roof? Or a person swimming in a lake in a country park?

Traditionally the law relating to trespassers has been very harsh. Trespassers went onto premises at their own risk and occupiers were simply under an obligation not to deliberately or recklessly cause them harm (*Addie & Sons (Collieries) v Dumbreck* [1929]). This was seen to be particularly harsh, especially in relation to young children. The turning point came in *British Railways Board v Herrington* [1972] where the courts introduced a 'duty to act humanely'. In this case, a child suffered severe burns while playing on an electrified railway track. Although the defendant knew that a gap in their fence was regularly used as a short cut and had seen children on the line they took no action. The House of Lords held that the claimant was able to recover; the British Railways Board knew of the risk of children playing near the railway tracks and in failing to take the necessary steps to repair the gap in the fence was in breach of its duty.[27]

The duty imposed on occupiers in *Herrington* clearly went beyond a duty not to intentionally or recklessly cause harm, but it was still lower than the duty set down 15 years earlier in the 1957 Act. The 1984 Act, coming almost 30 years after its predecessor, finally extended the same 'common duty of care' to trespassers—albeit in more limited circumstances.

Why do you think it took Parliament so long to pass the 1984 Act? Think about the policy reasons behind the harshness of the common law—the reluctance of the courts to interfere with a landowner's freedom to use and enjoy their property coupled with the understanding of a trespasser as a 'wrongdoer' deserving of their fate. This latter argument is particularly difficult to justify given that the term 'trespasser' covers a wide variety of cases like those listed at the start of this box.

Section 1(2) of the 1984 Act defines an occupier and premises in the same way as the 1957 Act. Similarly, as with the 1957 Act, the duty imposed on occupiers under the 1984 Act extends only to harm caused by the state of the premises rather than by the activities of those on the premises (*Keown v Coventry National Health NHS Trust* [2006][28]). So in **Revill v Newberry [1996]**, the occupier/defendant was not liable *under the 1984 Act* for shooting a young burglar who was attempting to steal from the defendant's garden shed. The claimant's injury arose as a result of the defendant's activity on the premises (lying in wait to shoot the claimant) rather than from the state of the premises themselves. The provisions of the 1984 Act were relevant

---

27. There is an interesting parallel here with land negligence cases such as **Sedleigh-Denfield v O'Callaghan**; *Goldman v Hargrave* and so on, discussed in Chapter 18, where awareness of a danger on one's land has resulted in liability if the landowner fails to do something about it.

28. In this case, the Court of Appeal held that the claimant's injuries were caused by his activity (in climbing up the underside of a fire escape) rather than the state of the premises (i.e. the fire escape itself).

only in so far as they assisted in determining the scope of the defendant's duty at common law.[29]

11.4.1 Establishing a duty

A crucial difference between the 1957 Act and the 1984 Act is that while an occupier will *always* owe a duty of care to a visitor; this is not true in relation to a non-visitor.

- **Occupiers' Liability Act 1957**—an occupier owes a 'common duty of care' to all visitors simply because they are visitors (s 2(1)).

In order for a duty to be owed under the 1984 Act three factors must be proved.

- **Occupiers' Liability Act 1984**—an occupier does not owe a duty of care to a non-visitor unless the following conditions, set out in section 1(3) of the 1984 Act, are met:
  (1) that the occupier is *aware* of the danger or has reasonable grounds to believe that it exists; and
  (2) the occupier *knows*, or has reasonable grounds to believe that someone is, or may come, in the vicinity of the danger (whether or not they have lawful authority to do so); and
  (3) the risk is one against which, in all the circumstances of the case, the occupier may *reasonably be expected* to offer some protection.

If the three conditions are satisfied the occupier will owe a duty of care in respect of any personal injury suffered by a non-visitor—unlike the 1957 Act, the 1984 Act does not extend to property damage (s 1(8)). One of the most important cases involving the 1984 Act in recent years is *Tomlinson v Congleton Borough Council* [2004].

Tomlinson v Congleton Borough Council [2004] HL

The claimant hit his head on the bottom of a lake (in a public park managed by the defendants) while attempting a shallow dive. He broke his neck and, apart from some small movement in his hands and arms, was paralysed from the neck down. Although boating and fishing were allowed, swimming was forbidden at the lake; prominent notices read: 'dangerous water: no swimming'. However these (along with the verbal warning from council-employed rangers) were frequently ignored by visitors to the country park and several accidents had already occurred. The council knew this and had planned, for a number of years, to plant vegetation on the 'beach' areas to prevent people from entering the water. They had not yet done this for financial reasons.

 The claimant sued the council on the grounds that they had breached their duty of care under the Occupiers' Liability Act 1984. The claimant's status as a lawful visitor to the

➡

---

29. The claimant's claim using the general common law principles of negligence was successful. This case was much discussed in the popular press—see e.g. Liz Searl 'Pensioner's Defence of his Property put him in the Dock' *Independent* 4 October 1995—and is considered further in Chapter 10, pp 266–267.

➡

park this status was limited to the time *before* he entered the lake. As he did not have the occupier's permission to enter the water (he had ignored the warning signs) he became a trespasser as soon as he did so.

The House of Lords (Lord Hutton *dubitante*) rejected the claim, overturning a majority Court of Appeal decision. The requirements for establishing a duty of care under section 1(3) of the 1984 Act had not been met. Though the defendants were aware of the danger and had reasonable grounds to believe that people were in the vicinity of it, the risk was not one that the occupier could be reasonably expected to offer protection:

> there was nothing about the mere at Brereton Heath which made it any more dangerous than any other ordinary stretch of open water in England... [Tomlinson] was a person of full capacity who voluntarily and without any pressure or inducement engaged in an activity which had inherent risk. The risk was that he might not execute his dive properly and so sustain injury. Likewise, a person who goes mountaineering incurs the risk that he might stumble or misjudge where to put his weight. In neither case can the risk be attributed to the state of the premises. (Lord Hoffmann at [26]–[27])

Nor did it make a difference that the council themselves had intended to take steps to reduce the danger by making it harder for people to gain access to the lake. Lord Hoffmann continued:

> it will be extremely rare for an occupier of land to be under a duty to prevent people from taking risks which are inherent in the activities they freely choose to undertake upon the land. If people want to climb mountains, go hang-gliding or swim or dive in ponds or lakes, that is their affair. Of course the landowner may for his own reasons wish to prohibit such activities. He may think that they are a danger or inconvenience to himself or others. Or he may take a paternalist view and prefer people not to undertake risky activities on his land. He is entitled to impose such conditions, as the Council did by prohibiting swimming. But the law does not require him to do so. (at [45])[30]

 Counterpoint

The House of Lords in *Tomlinson* affirmed the 'principle of individual responsibility' (Morgan 2004, p 401) and an understanding of tort law as a set of rules and principles of 'personal responsibility (and freedom) which concern how people may, ought or ought not behave in their dealings with others' (*Cane* p 24). Lord Hoffmann put it thus:

> the law does not provide such compensation simply on the basis that the injury was so disproportionately severe in relation to one's fault or even not one's own fault at all. Perhaps it should, but society might not be able to afford to compensate everyone on that principle, certainly at the level at which such compensation is now paid. The law provides compensation only when the injury is someone else's fault. (at [4])

➡

30. Readers may find it interesting to compare Lord Hoffmann's opinion in *Tomlinson*, with the majority of the Court of Appeal in *The Scout Association* v *Barnes* [2010] discussed in Chapter 8.

→

Of course, the inability of the claimant to establish fault means that he bears the entirety of the costs; his condition is no one's fault but his own.

The law lords' individualistic reasoning and focus in *Tomlinson* is also justifiable by reference to the 'social cost' of finding the council liable; the principles of distributive justice are used to limit rather than, as is more usual, to enable recovery:

> there is an important question of freedom at stake. It is unjust that the harmless recreation of responsible parents and children with buckets and spades on the beaches should be prohibited in order to comply with what is thought to be a legal duty to safeguard irresponsible visitors against dangers which are perfectly obvious. The fact that such people take no notice of warnings cannot create a duty to take other steps to protect them. (Lord Hoffmann at [46])

So viewed, the decision of the House of Lords was, perhaps, inevitable.[31]

Tomlinson provides an excellent example of the operation of the 1984 Act, and the difference between this Act and its 1957 counterpart. Under the 1957 Act, all the claimant needs to establish is that they were a lawful visitor to the defendant's premises. Once this is proved, the occupier will automatically owe the claimant a duty of care and attention shifts to the other stages of a claim: Was the duty breached? Did it cause the claimant loss? Are there any defences? Under the 1984 Act, however, establishing a duty is less straightforward, and more claims will be defeated at this stage. Before a duty will arise, three conditions must be met:

(a) the defendant must have reasonable grounds to believe that there exists a danger on their premises;

(b) they must know or have reasonable grounds to believe that someone is, or may come, in the vicinity of the danger; and

(c) it must be reasonable to expect the defendant to have offered some protection against that risk (s 1(3)).

Although the claimant in *Tomlinson* could establish the first and second of these, he could not prove the third, and so the House of Lords rejected his claim.[32]

31. It is worth noting, however, that the Court of Appeal in *Tomlinson* came to the opposite conclusion, that is that the council not only owed the claimant a duty of care but were in breach of this duty: 'Congleton Beach, as the place was also known, was as alluring to "macho" young men as other dangerous places were to young children. In my judgment the gravity of the risk of injury, the frequency with which those using the park came to be exposed to the risk, the failure of warning signs to curtail the extent to which the risk was being run, indeed the very fact that the attractiveness of the beach and the lake acted as a magnet to draw so many into the cooling waters, all that leads me to the conclusion that the occupiers were reasonably to be expected to offer some protection against the risks of entering the water. It follows that in my judgment the defendants were under a duty to the [claimant] ... The authorities were inviting public use of this amenity knowing that the water was a siren call strong enough to turn stout men's minds. In my judgment the posting of notices, shown to be ineffective, was not enough to discharge the duty' (Ward LJ at [29], [31]). Although the Court of Appeal agreed with the trial judge's decision that the claimant's damages should be reduced by two-thirds to reflect the extent to which he was contributory negligent.

32. Consider again the student injured when diving into a lake in the examples at the beginning of the chapter. What additional information would you need in order to advise them as to the potential outcome of their claim?

Pause for reflection

In *Tomlinson* the claim was rejected on the basis that no duty was owed to the claimant. This is because a duty will not arise under the 1984 Act unless the risk is one against which the occupier may reasonably be expected to offer some protection. In the circumstances, the House of Lords held that the council should not be expected to take steps to protect people from the obvious risks of diving into shallow water. As Lord Hoffmann noted, however, the same result would in substance have been reached had the claimant been classed as a lawful visitor and his case had been dealt with under the 1957 Act. The only difference would have been that the claim would have failed not at the duty stage (since the 1957 Act automatically imposes a duty to all visitors) but at the breach stage (since, as the House of Lords held, it was not reasonable to expect the council to take any steps to make the premises safer).

As such, although the two Acts will often lead to the same results, they will often do so for slightly different reasons. Cases that would fail on the basis that there was no breach under the 1957 Act will often be dismissed under the 1984 Act on the ground that no duty arose in the first place. This reflects an important but subtle difference in emphasis between the two Acts. As Lord Hoffmann stated: 'Parliament has made it clear that in the case of a lawful visitor, one starts from the assumption that there is a duty whereas in the case of a trespasser one starts from the assumption that there is none' (at [38]).

If, as Lord Hoffmann suggests, the end result is (or at least can be) the same, why then do you think Parliament has created this difference in the operation of the two Acts? Think again about the distinction between visitors and non-visitors and the policy reasons for limiting liability in respect of trespassers.

11.4.1.1 Awareness of (or reasonable grounds to believe in the existence of) danger

In order for an occupier to owe a non-visitor a duty of care, they must be aware of the danger, or have reasonable grounds to believe that it exists (s 1(3)(a)). While the first part of this ground is subjective—it requires the occupier to *know* about the danger—the second part is (at least partly) objective—it asks whether the occupier *reasonably ought* to know about it.

> **Rhind v Astbury Water Park Ltd [2004] CA**
>
> The claimant suffered serious injuries after he hit his head on a fibre-glass container diving into Astbury Mere in Cheshire to retrieve his football. The container was not visible from the surface; it was lying on the bed of the Mere, covered in silt. As there were clear notices near the Mere saying: 'Private Property: Strictly No Swimming Allowed' the claimant was a non-visitor (trespasser) and so the question for the Court of Appeal was whether the defendants owed a duty of care under the Occupiers' Liability Act 1984.
>
> Denying the claimant's claim, the court held that the defendants had no knowledge, nor were there reasonable grounds for them to believe, that the container was hidden beneath the surface of the Mere and that, as a result, no duty was owed.

11.4.1.2 Knowledge of (or reasonable grounds to believe in) the presence of a non-visitor in the vicinity of danger

The occupier must also be aware, or have reasonable grounds to believe, that a non-visitor is in the vicinity of the danger (s 1(3)(b)). When we say that a person has reasonable grounds to believe that something is true, this means that, from the knowledge they do in fact have, they should have worked out or discovered something else. So, for instance, you may have reasonable grounds to believe that a problem question on occupiers' liability will appear on this year's exam paper if such a question has been included in every paper in the past ten years. From your knowledge of fact A—the contents of the past exam papers—you have reason to infer fact B—that such a question will appear in this year's paper. Accordingly, before we can say that an occupier had reasonable grounds to believe that a non-visitor is, or may arrive, in the vicinity of the danger on his premises, he must have actual knowledge of such 'background' or 'primary' facts as would support such an inference. This was confirmed in *Swain* v *Puri* [1996].

So, for example, if I know that people are playing football next to my field and that, in the past, people have come onto my field to fetch their ball, I have reasonable grounds to believe (that is, I should have figured out) that they may do so again. However, if I had no knowledge that people had ever played football there or had gone onto the field to fetch their balls, *even if I should have known this*, I cannot be said to have reasonable grounds to believe they may do this in the future. To this extent, those who know less are less likely to be held liable, even though complete ignorance may be no less culpable than partial ignorance.

The other point to note is that the defendant must know, or have reasonable grounds to believe, that the claimant (or someone like them) is in the vicinity of the danger *at the time the claimant was injured*. So it is not in itself enough to show that the defendant knew that the claimant had been on the premises previously, or even that they were likely to do so again. This *may* provide grounds for a reasonable belief that the claimant was in the vicinity of the danger at the time of the accident but this will depend on the circumstances. For example, in *Donoghue* v *Folkestone Properties Ltd* [2003], the claimant's claim in respect of injuries he suffered while diving into the defendant's harbour was denied because, although the defendant was aware that people swam in the harbour during summer, they were not, and could not reasonably have been expected to be, aware that this would happen during a midwinter night, when the claimant was injured.

11.4.1.3 Reasonable expectation of protection against the risk

Finally, the risk must be such that in all the circumstances of the case the defendant may be reasonably expected to offer some protection from it (s 1(3)(c)). As we have seen, this is where the claim failed in **Tomlinson**. In determining whether it is reasonable to expect the occupier to offer protection, the courts must engage upon a balancing exercise similar to that which they embark upon when determining whether a duty of care has been breached. This would include taking into account the costs of requiring the occupier to take steps to make the premises safer. For example, in *Simonds* v *Isle of Wight Council* [2004] a 5-year-old boy fell off a swing breaking his arm. The swing was near to a playing field being used for a school sports day. It was argued that the school was under a responsibility to discourage the pupils from using the swings, for example by placing a cordon around them. This was rejected. One of the reasons the courts gave for this was that a likely consequence of finding the school liable was: 'that sports days and other simple pleasurable sporting events would not be held…Such events would become uninsurable or only insurable at prohibitive cost' (at [30]).

11.4.2 Discharging the duty

The occupier's duty, once it is established, is to 'take such care as is reasonable in all the circumstances of the case to see that the [non-visitor] does not suffer injury on the premises' (s 1(4)). It is likely that in determining what will amount to reasonable care the courts will take into account that under the 1984 Act the claimant will not have been invited (expressly or by implication) onto the premises. We may think that an occupier should not be expected to go as far to secure the safety of those they have *not* invited onto their land as they would in respect of those they have invited. As such it may be that the duty under the 1984 Act is not as exacting as the duty under the 1957 Act (*Donoghue* v *Folkestone Properties Ltd* (at [31]). Beyond this, and as with the 1957 Act, in assessing what amounts to reasonable care the courts will weigh up the same sorts of factors as in ordinary common law negligence claims including, for example, the resources of the defendant (cost of taking precautions) (*Ratcliff* v *McConnell* [1999]).

11.4.2.1 Warnings

It is possible for an occupier to discharge their duty under the 1984 Act by giving a warning or by discouraging people from entering the premises (for example, a locked gate) (s 1(5)). However, unlike under the 1957 Act, where the warning must be such as to enable the visitor in all the circumstances to be reasonably safe (s 1(4)(a)), under the 1984 Act all the occupier needs to do is to take reasonable steps to bring the danger to claimant's attention.

11.4.2.2 Risks willingly accepted by the non-visitor

As under the 1957 Act, no duty will be owed by the occupier in respect of risks willingly accepted by the non-visitor (s 1(6)). However, unlike the 1957 Act, under the 1984 Act, the defence of *volenti* is regarded as preventing a duty from arising rather than providing a defence once the other elements of the claim are made out. Thus in *Ratcliff* the Court of Appeal held that no duty was owed to a claimant who accepted the risk of serious injury from diving into water of an unknown depth when he climbed over a fence surrounding his college open-air swimming pool on his way home after a night out.

11.5 The Occupiers' Liability Act 1984—annotated

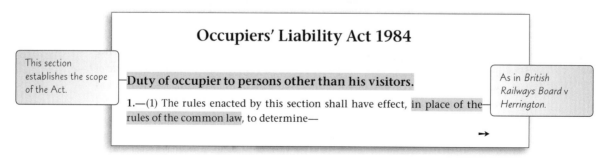

Occupiers' Liability Act 1984

This section establishes the scope of the Act.

Duty of occupier to persons other than his visitors.

1.—(1) The rules enacted by this section shall have effect, in place of the rules of the common law, to determine—

As in *British Railways Board* v *Herrington.*

An occupier's duty under the 1984 Act has to be established (s 1(3)) (cf s 2(1) of the Occupiers' Liability Act 1957).	(a) whether any duty is owed by a person as occupier of premises to persons other than his visitors in respect of any risk of their suffering injury on the premises by reason of any danger due to the state of the premises or to things done or omitted to be done on them; and

(a) whether any duty is owed by a person as occupier of premises to persons other than his visitors in respect of any risk of their suffering injury on the premises by reason of any danger due to the state of the premises or to things done or omitted to be done on them; and

Most obviously trespassers, but also includes ramblers by virtue of s 1(4) of the Occupiers' Liability Act 1957. Defined negatively—'non-visitors'.

(b) if so, what that duty is.

The 'content' of the duty.

(2) For the purposes of this section, the persons who are to be treated respectively as an occupier of any premises (which, for those purposes, include any fixed or movable structure) and as his visitors are—

Same wide definition of 'premises' as the Occupiers' Liability Act 1957 (s 1(3)).

(a) any person who owes in relation to the premises the duty referred to in section 2 of the Occupiers' Liability Act 1957 (the common duty of care), and

*As with the 1957 Act, the risk of injury must be due to the state of the premises rather than as a result of an activity on them (**Revill v Newberry**).*

(b) those who are his visitors for the purposes of that duty.

(3) An occupier of premises owes a duty to another (not being his visitor) in respect of any such risk as is referred to in subsection (1) above if—

Definition of an occupier.

(a) he is aware of the danger or has reasonable grounds to believe that it exists;

The requirements of this section must be met to establish the existence of a duty.

(b) he knows or has reasonable grounds to believe that the other is in the vicinity of the danger concerned or that he may come into the vicinity of the danger (in either case, whether the other has lawful authority for being in that vicinity or not); and

(c) the risk is one against which, in all the circumstances of the case, he may reasonably be expected to offer the other some protection.

(4) Where, by virtue of this section, an occupier of premises owes a duty to another in respect of such a risk, the duty is to take such care as is reasonable in all the circumstances of the case to see that he does not suffer injury on the premises by reason of the danger concerned.

This section establishes the content of the duty.

Warnings: simply has to be given (cf s 4(a) of Occupiers' Liability Act 1957).

(5) Any duty owed by virtue of this section in respect of a risk may, in an appropriate case, be discharged by taking such steps as are reasonable in all the circumstances of the case to give warning of the danger concerned or to discourage persons from incurring the risk.

Volenti operates under the 1984 Act to prevent a duty from arising (as opposed to being a defence).

(6) No duty is owed by virtue of this section to any person in respect of risks willingly accepted as his by that person (the question whether a risk was so accepted to be decided on the same principles as in other cases in which one person owes a duty of care to another).

(6A) At any time when the right conferred by section 2(1) of the Countryside and Rights of Way Act 2000 is exercisable in relation to land which is access land for the purposes of Part I of that Act, an occupier of the land owes (subject to subsection (6C) below) no duty by virtue of this section to any person in respect of

This section details certain circumstances where an occupier's duty is restricted in relation to ramblers.

(a) a risk resulting from the existence of any natural feature of the landscape, or any river, stream, ditch or pond whether or not a natural feature, or

→

→

(b) a risk of that person suffering injury when passing over, under or through any wall, fence or gate, except by proper use of the gate or of a stile.

(6B) For the purposes of subsection (6A) above, any plant, shrub or tree, of whatever origin, is to be regarded as a natural feature of the landscape.

(6C) Subsection (6A) does not prevent an occupier from owing a duty by virtue of this section in respect of any risk where the danger concerned is due to anything done by the occupier—

(a) with the intention of creating that risk, or

(b) being reckless as to whether that risk is created.

(7) No duty is owed by virtue of this section to persons using the highway, and this section does not affect any duty owed to such persons.

(8) Where a person owes a duty by virtue of this section, he does not, by reason of any breach of the duty, incur any liability in respect of any loss of or damage to property.

(9) In this section—

"highway" means any part of a highway other than a ferry or waterway;

"injury" means anything resulting in death or personal injury, including any disease and any impairment of physical or mental condition; and

"movable structure" includes any vessel, vehicle or aircraft.

[1A. Special considerations relating to access land.]

[In determining whether any, and if so what, duty is owed by virtue of section 1 by an occupier of land at any time when the right conferred by section 2(1) of the Countryside and Rights of Way Act 2000 is exercisable in relation to the land, regard is to be had, in particular, to—

(a) the fact that the existence of that right ought not to place an undue burden (whether financial or otherwise) on the occupier,

(b) the importance of maintaining the character of the countryside, including features of historic, traditional or archaeological interest, and

(c) any relevant guidance given under section 20 of that Act....]

Sidenotes:
- Incorporation of common law principle of 'common humanity' (*British Railways Board* v *Herrington*).
- An occupier does not owe a duty in relation to property damage (cf s 1(3)(b) Occupiers' Liability Act 1957).
- An occupier does not owe a duty to people using the highway (Highways Act 1980, s 1(8)).
- Details the extent of the duty owed to ramblers.

11.6 The Occupiers' Liability Acts 1957 and 1984—at a glance

Table 11.1 The Occupiers' Liability Acts 1957 and 1984—at a glance

	1957	1984
Type of damage (to claimant)	Property damage and personal injury (as old common law).	Personal injury only (ss 1(1)(a) and 1(4)). Property damage excluded (s 1(b)).

Table 11.1 *Continued*

	1957	1984
'Premises'	Wide definition: 'any fixed or moveable structure' including vehicles (s 1(3)).	As 1957 Act (s 1(2)).
'Occupier'	Person who would have been at common law (s 1(2); *Wheat v Lacon & Co Ltd*; *Harris* v *Birkenhead Corporation*).	As 1957 Act (s 1(2)(a)).
'Visitor'	All **lawful visitors** (s 1(2)) including invitees, licensees at common law and contractual visitors (s 5).	All **non-visitors** (usually trespassers) (s 1(1)(a)). Also **includes** ramblers (exercising a right under s 2(1) of the Countryside and Rights of Way Act 2000 (s 1(4) Occupiers' Liability Act 1957)). However, it **does not** cover people using the highway (s 1(7)) or people using other public rights of way (s 1A).
Duty	Occupier owes '**a common duty of care**' to all visitors simply by virtue of the fact that they are visitors (s 2(1)).	Occupier *only* owes a duty (defined in s 1(4)) if: 1. aware of danger (or has reasonable grounds to believe it exists); and 2. knows (or has reasonable grounds to believe) a non-visitor is (or may be) in vicinity of danger; and 3. the risk is one in all circumstances the occupier may be reasonably expected to protect against (s 1(3)).
Extent of the duty (or standard of care)	A duty to take **such care that the visitor is reasonably safe** while using the premises for the purposes for which they are invited (s 2(2)). It is the visitor, not premises, who must be reasonably safe; different standards of care apply for different visitors (s 2(3)).	A duty to '**take such care as is reasonable in all the circumstances of the case to see that the [non-visitor] does not suffer injury on the premises**' (s 1(4)).

Table 11.1 *Continued*

	1957	1984
Discharging duty (or breach)	As **ordinary principles of breach** (see Chapter 8). However, the occupier's duty to ensure that the visitor will be reasonably safe while on their premises does not mean that the visitor cannot be expected to take reasonable care for their own safety (s 2(3)). Standard of care may vary depending on the identity and expertise of the visitor, in particular: The standard of care expected will be higher in relation to **children**, who are 'less careful than adults' ((s 2(3)(a)); *Jolley* v *Sutton*). **Professional visitors** can be expected to 'appreciate and guard against special risks' (s 2(3)(b); *Roles* v *Nathan* [1963]). May be discharged by taking reasonable steps to give **warnings** must enable visitor to be 'reasonably safe' (s 2(4)(a); *Darby* v *National Trust*). Generally there will be no liability for harms caused where **independent contractors** have done faulty work on the premises as long as occupier has acted reasonably in entrusting the work to them (s 2(4)(b)).	As **ordinary principles of breach** (see Chapter 8). May be discharged by taking reasonable steps to give: a **warning** of the danger concerned (s 1(5)) (no requirement of reasonable safety); **discouragement** to persons from incurring the risk (s 1(5)).
Limitations and defences	Occupier can **extend, restrict, modify or exclude their duty** (so far as they are free to do so) **via a notice** or contract (s 2(1) (subject to UCTA, s 2)). No duty in relation to **risks** 'willingly accepted as his' by the visitor (s 2(5)). **Contributory negligence** (implied by s 2(3) although not mentioned in the statute used by courts).	No express provision—but probably as 1957 Act (s 2(1)). No duty in relation to **risks** 'willingly accepted as his' by the visitor (s 1(6); *Ratcliff* v *McConnell*). **Contributory negligence** (not mentioned in the statute but used by courts).

11.7 **Conclusion**

All injuries that do not happen at home or on the road must happen on someone else's property. In this chapter we have considered the circumstances in which an occupier may be liable for injuries sustained on their premises. Despite *Weir's* suggestion that accidents on private property have been marked out for special attention since 1866 when an employee of the gas company fell into an unfenced vat in a sugar factory (in *Indermaur* v *Dames* [1867], at 20), traditionally there has been a reluctance to allow such claims—usually relating to a desire to leave landowners alone to enjoy their land as they wish. This has recently been given a contemporary twist. The imposition of liability has been framed as an attack on the liberties of both the individual who chooses to engage in dangerous (but otherwise harmless) pastimes at his own risk *and* citizens as a whole to enjoy the countryside. This is particularly apparent in the leading case of *Tomlinson* where the House of Lords reasserted the importance of individual responsibility, fault and interpersonal justice as the foundations of tortious liability.

Nevertheless, an occupier will be liable if they have not taken reasonable care to ensure that those invited, and sometimes those not invited, onto their premises are reasonably safe. Occupiers' liability is a mixture of common law and statute; the law of negligence has been put into statutory form through a combination of two Acts—the Occupiers' Liability Acts 1957 and 1984 (*Markesinis & Deakin* p 341). Before this a complex system of common law rules governed this area of law whereby the scope of the duty owed by the occupier depended on the circumstances in which the claimant ended up on the premises. It continues to be important to define at the outset the category of person who has been injured. Under the 1957 Act an occupier owes a common duty of care to visitors to take as much care as is reasonable in all the circumstances to see that the visitor will be reasonably safe in using the premises for the purposes for which they were invited. Under the 1984 Act an occupier may owe a duty of care to non-visitors (typically trespassers) if they are aware that (or have reasonable grounds to believe) a danger exists and that a non-visitor is in its vicinity and the risk is such that it is reasonable for the occupier to be expected to offer protection from it. Although the Acts define the circumstances in which a duty of care will be owed (and tell us something as to its extent, as well as matters relating to its discharge and limitation), questions of breach and causation still need to be established by reference to the ordinary principles of negligence.

✳ **End-of-chapter questions**

After reading the chapter carefully, try answering the questions below. If you would like to know what we think visit the Online Resource Centre (www.oxfordtextbooks.co.uk/orc/horsey2e/).

1. What are the main similarities and differences between the Occupiers' Liability Act 1957 and the Occupiers' Liability Act 1984?

2. Do you think the House of Lords would have come to the same decision in *Tomlinson* if the claimant had been a 4-year-old child? Also, given the evidence before the House of Lords about 'macho male diving syndrome' what if he had been an 18-year-old woman?

3. Consider the problem question at the start of this chapter. Now having read about the topic what would be your advice to the various parties? If you need some pointers in thinking about how to answer this question, turn to the Appendix (p 589) where each problem is annotated with issues and cases to consider. Next, try to write your own answer and finally, log on to our Online Resource Centre (www.oxfordtextbooks.co.uk/orc/horsey2e/) to check your ideas against our suggested outline answer.

✳ Further reading

Much of the academic writing in this area concentrates on one or other of the two Acts. The best place to start your reading is with Buckley's 2006 article which looks at both Acts and so will give you an overview of the law with a comparative twist.

Buckley, Richard 'Occupiers' Liability in England and Canada' (2006) 35 *Common Law World Review* 197

Buckley, Richard 'The Occupiers' Liability Act 1984—Has *Herrington* Survived?' (1984) *Conveyancer* 413

Jones, Michael 'The Occupiers' Liability Act' (1984) *Modern Law Review* 713

Morgan, Jonathan 'Tort, Insurance and Incoherence' (2004) 67(3) *Modern Law Review* 384

Payne, Douglas 'The Occupiers' Liability Act' (1958) 21 *Modern Law Review* 359

Employers' liability

Problem question

Read this problem question carefully, and keep it in mind while you are working through the chapter that follows. At the end of the chapter, you will be able to apply what you have learnt to the problem question and advise the relevant parties.

Every Tuesday, Thursday and Friday evening there is a drop-in centre for young people between the ages of 11–16 at St Hilda's parish church. It is run by a team of youth workers employed by the Archdiocese of Durkenshire. Fred is youth counsellor at the centre. He is busy setting up the hall for the evening's activities when he slips on a puddle of greasy water from a leaking radiator. He had reported the leak to his supervisor, Father Cranky, over a week ago and it had still not been fixed.

Mrs Doogal works in the kitchen making snacks and drinks for the young people. She is using a food processor to make some cookies when a fragment of metal is thrown off by the machine and enters her eye. Another piece lands in the cookie dough unnoticed. Later on, Father Cranky eats a cookie whilst no one is looking. The shard of metal lacerates his tongue. The food processor had been serviced two weeks earlier in accordance with the provisions of the Kitchens Safety Act 2003 [a fictitious statute] which states that 'all moving parts on food-mixers must be maintained'.

Father Jack has special responsibility for outreach work in the centre. This means he is a well-known figure among the young people in the local area. Helen has been coming to the centre for a few weeks. Father Jack has been particularly welcoming. He often encourages her to stay late to help him tidy up and then gives her a lift home in his sports car. After one such occasion Helen, who is 12, complains that Father Jack has sexually assaulted her. A subsequent criminal investigation upholds her claim.

12.1 **Introduction**

Consider the following situations:

→ A factory worker is seriously injured when a piece of metal breaks off the machine he is using and hits him in the eye.

→ A window cleaner falls from her ladder. Her supervisor had not told her about the safety harness provided by her employers.

→ An employee working in a fast food restaurant accidentally slips on a pool of grease which has seeped from a poorly maintained deep-fat fryer, breaking his ankle.

→ A school teacher sexually assaults a pupil over several nights during a school trip.

→ An office worker is subjected to a sustained period of homophobic harassment and intimidation by his supervisor.

All these are cases in which tortious liability (on the part of employers, employees or both) might arise in the workplace. The common law and the various statutory provisions governing liability in the workplace impose a heavy burden on employers not only to ensure the safety of their workforce but also in relation to torts committed by their employees against others in the course of their employment.[1]

That an employer owes an employee a personal duty to take reasonable care to ensure their health and safety at work, competent work colleagues and so on at common law or according to statute is largely unremarkable. However, what is perhaps more surprising is that employers can be liable, even where they themselves are entirely blameless, if someone they employ commits a tort in the course of their employment. Take, for example, an overly aggressive bouncer who after his shift attacks a customer, rendering them paraplegic—it may be his victim also has a claim against the bouncer's employer using the mechanism of vicarious liability (*Mattis* v *Pollock (t/a Flamingos Nightclub)* [2003]). Accordingly, one of the principal issues we consider in this chapter is when vicarious liability can be established and the justifications for it. What about a policeman who wears his uniform while 'on the prowl' for vulnerable, young women (*N* v *Chief Constable of Merseyside Police* [2006]) or the warden of a children's home who sexually abuses his charges (***Lister* v *Hesley Hall Ltd** [2002])—should their employers also be liable for their actions?

In most cases, the victim will be able to bring a claim against both the employee *and* the employer. However, often an employee will not have the funds to be worth suing. Their employer, on the other hand, buttressed by compulsory employer's liability insurance, is a much more attractive prospect: their deep pockets are more likely to meet a substantial payout.

---

1. Though compensation claims against employers continue to fall, they comprise the second highest number of claims for personal injury. Nevertheless, in 2009–10 they made up just 9 per cent of the total number of claims registered with the Compensation Recovery Unit (CRU) (CRU performance statistics).

An employer's liability in tort typically arises in one of three ways:

(1) An employer owes a non-delegable common law duty of care to their employees and therefore may be personally liable for harm caused to their employees (***Wilsons & Clyde Coal Co Ltd v English* [1938]**).

(2) An employer may also be liable in the tort of breach of statutory duty which enables a claimant in certain circumstances to recover compensation for losses caused by the defendant's failure to comply with a statutory obligation.

(3) An employer may be also liable vicariously for injuries caused by their employees to others. That is, in certain circumstances, although the employer themselves may not be at fault, they may, nevertheless, be held liable (alongside the employee) for a tort committed by their employee in the course of their employment.

 Pause for reflection

Historically it was extremely difficult for employees to recover for injuries suffered at work. The 'unholy trinity' comprising the doctrine of common employment, which prevented an employee from suing their employer for injury negligently inflicted by a fellow employee (*Priestly* v *Fowler* [1837]), and the defences of contributory negligence (an absolute bar to recovery until the Law Reform (Contributory Negligence) Act 1945) and *volenti non fit injuria*,[2] effectively insulated employers from liability. Responsibility for safety in the workplace rested primarily with those least able to ensure it—the employees. The situation began to change towards the end of the nineteenth century as a combination of the growth in the power of trade unions, greater awareness of hazardous working conditions (particularly on the railways) and the increasing availability of employers' liability insurance encouraged the judiciary and the legislature to mitigate the harshness of these rules. By the mid-twentieth century all three obstacles had either been abolished or strictly confined.[3]

Today, however, employees are in a stronger position than many other accident victims and, as a result, workplace litigation (which includes actions for vicarious liability against employers) generates a high number of tort claims. The threat of adverse publicity and a desire to maintain labour/public relations means that many employers are likely to settle out of court and the Employer's Liability (Compulsory Insurance) Act 1969, which makes it compulsory for employers to insure against workplace accidents, means that employers are likely to be able to meet any award of damages.

As a result, someone injured at work (or by someone acting 'in the course of their employment') is more likely to be able to claim and, importantly, recover than someone who suffers the same injury outside the workplace. What are the justifications for this? Do you think this is fair?

Consider the following arguments: while employees often have limited control over the situations they find themselves in at work, employers are in a position to ensure that the

➡

2. See Chapter 10.

3. The doctrine of common employment was abolished by the Law Reform (Personal Injuries) Act 1948, s 1.

> →
>
> conditions they provide are safe; imposing liability on employers encourages them to improve working conditions (something they are uniquely able to do); and finally employers are (or at least should be) better informed about the various hazards of working for their particular company (for example, the machinery or chemicals they use), unlike an employee who may be inexperienced in the industry and may not be aware of the risks and, therefore, know how to take care.

12.2 An employer's personal non-delegable duty of care

An employer's personal duty of care, established in **Wilsons & Clyde Coal Co Ltd v English** requires an employer to see that reasonable care is taken for their employees' safety. Unusually, this duty is non-delegable in nature. This means that it is not enough for the employer themselves to take reasonable care to see that their employees are safe. Rather, their duty is to ensure that reasonable care *is* taken. This may not sound like much of a difference. However, its significance can be seen when we consider that in many businesses it is simply not feasible for the owner themselves to supervise all aspects of the day-to-day running of the business. In practice, all we can expect employers to do in such situations is to take reasonable care to ensure that the people they choose to delegate these jobs to are capable of doing so. However, by holding the employer's duty of care to be non-delegable the courts have held that an employer will nonetheless be held to have breached this duty if those they have entrusted with responsibility fail to exercise reasonable care in respect of the employees' safety. The employer cannot escape liability by showing that they themselves acted reasonably in delegating this task to the relevant person. In other words, as long as in the end reasonable care was not taken to see that the employee was reasonably safe when at work, the employer will be held to have breached his duty of care. It makes no difference that it was not the employer but rather the person to whom they had delegated this responsibility who had acted carelessly. So, though *factual* responsibility for employees' safety may (and often will have to) be delegated, *legal* responsibility cannot be.

> ### *Wilsons & Clyde Coal Co Ltd v English* [1938] HL
>
> A miner was crushed in a mining accident after haulage equipment was set in motion as he was travelling through the pit at the end of the day (contrary to recognised mining practice). He sued the mine owners on the basis that they had failed to provide a reasonably safe system of work. The defendants claimed they had discharged their duty by appointing (as required by statute) a competent and qualified manager to control the machinery.
>
> The House of Lords unanimously rejected the employer's argument. Finding them personally liable, Lord Wright said:
>
> > the [employer's] obligation is fulfilled by the exercise of due care and skill. But it is not fulfilled by entrusting its fulfilment to employees, even though selected with due
> >
> > →

→

care and skill. The obligation is threefold, the provision of a competent staff of men, adequate material, and a proper system and effective supervision. (at 78)

In other words, the defendant company had been put in breach of its duty by the failure of the manager to ensure the health and safety of the claimant.

 Pause for reflection

It might be asked why the claimant did not sue the defendants on the ground that they were vicariously liable for the actions of the manager. The answer lies in the doctrine of 'common employment', which, until its abolition in 1948, prevented an employee from suing their fellow employees for injuries they had negligently caused—and hence an employer could not be vicariously liable. An employee was deemed to have assumed the risk of negligence by their fellow employees (provided they had been selected with reasonable care by their employer) as one of the terms of their employment contract. Thus, as the miner had no claim against his manager, there could be no vicarious claim against the mine owner.

Where similar facts to *Wilsons & Clyde Coal Co* arise today, employees will argue that their employer is both personally *and* vicariously liable for the actions of their manager (see, for example, *McDermid* v *Nash Dredging & Reclamation Co Ltd* [1987], below).

An employer remains under a duty to ensure a safe system of work for an employee even when that employee is temporarily posted elsewhere.[4] In *McDermid* v *Nash Dredging & Reclamation Co Ltd* [1987] an 18-year-old deckhand was told by his employer, the defendant company, to work on a tug owned by the defendants' parent company. He suffered serious injuries to his leg, which had to be amputated, as a result of the captain of the tug's negligence. The issue was whether the deckhand's employer was liable for the captain's failure to operate a safe system of work. The House of Lords held that the defendants were liable on the basis that they retained personal responsibility for the deckhand's safety notwithstanding that he was working outside their usual workplace. That said, other parties to whom the employer has sent an employee to work can acquire similar duties toward the employee where they have 'assumed responsibility' for the employee's wellbeing (*Nelhams* v *Sandells Maintenance Ltd* [1996]).

In recent years, the courts have recognised that an employer's duty extends beyond ensuring an employee's physical safety to seeing that (at least in some cases) reasonable care is taken to prevent *psychiatric* injury, including workplace stress and suicide (*Corr* v *IBC Vehicles Ltd* [2008]). It may also extend to an employee's *economic* wellbeing—for example when writing a reference (***Spring* v *Guardian Assurance*** [1995], though

---

4. Although it is unlikely that this duty continues if an employee is sent to work abroad for a period of time; the employer's duty to ensure a safe system of work therefore only extends so far as the employer is able to control the employee's working environment (*Cook v Square D Ltd* [1992]).

cf *Reid* v *Rush & Tompkins Group* [1990]). However, the employer's duty of care does not extend to protection of an employee's property (*Deyong* v *Shenburn* [1946]).

Building on Lord Wright's statement in **Wilsons & Clyde Coal Co**, an employer's non-delegable duty is typically said to have four components, comprising the provision of:

- competent staff;
- adequate material;
- a proper system of working (including effective supervision);
- a safe workplace.

Although often considered separately for the sake of convenience or argument, they are, in fact, best regarded as manifestations of a single duty on the part of an employer to take reasonable care to ensure the safety of their workforce (*Wilson* v *Tyneside Cleaning Co* [1958]).

12.2.1 **Competent staff**

An employer owes their employees a duty not only to ensure that they employ competent colleagues, but also to properly supervise and train them in the use of equipment. This aspect of an employer's personal non-delegable duty is of less importance following the abolition of the doctrine of common employment; however, it may still be useful in circumstances where an employer is unlikely to be vicariously liable. In *Hudson* v *Ridge Manufacturing Co* [1957], for example, an employee was injured when a colleague, who had a reputation for being a practical joker, tripped him up. Although the joker had been officially reprimanded for his persistent horseplay by his employer, the court held that the employer was personally liable to the claimant. Given the seriousness of his conduct, they should have done more to deter the joker's behaviour and, in failing to do so, they had breached their duty of care.

An employer may also find themselves personally (as well as vicariously) liable[5] should they fail in relation to their duty not to expose their employees to bullying, victimisation or harassment by their fellow employees (**Waters** v **Commissioner of Police for the Metropolis** [2000]).[6]

> ### *Waters* v *Commissioner of Police for the Metropolis* [2000] HL
>
> The claimant suffered psychiatric injury as a result of a prolonged period of victimisation at work after she had made a complaint of sexual assault against a colleague (this claim was not pursued due to lack of evidence). She brought a claim against her employer on the ground that they had not taken reasonable care to prevent this bullying from taking place. The House of Lords, allowing the claimant's appeal against a striking-out claim held that where an employer knows, or should foresee, that an employee might suffer physical or psychiatric harm through the acts of fellow employees they will owe a duty of care to protect from such harm.

5. *Majrowski* v *Guy's and St Thomas' NHS Trust* [2006].
6. Discussed further in Chapter 6, p 152.

12.2.2 **Adequate material**

An employer has a duty to take reasonable care to provide all necessary equipment (including safety equipment), as well as instructions on how to use it and to maintain it in a reasonable condition.

Here the common law has been supplemented by the Employer's Liability (Defective Equipment) Act 1969. Section 1(1) establishes that if an employee is injured in the course of employment by a defect in equipment provided by their employer and the employee can prove that the defect was (wholly or partly) caused by the fault of a third party (usually the manufacturer) then the employer will be liable. Its purpose was to overcome the effects of *Davie* v *New Merton Board Mills Ltd* [1959]. In this case, an employee was blinded in one eye when a piece of metal chipped off the tool he was using. The tool had been negligently manufactured (causing it to become too hard for its purpose), although externally it appeared to be in good condition. Rejecting the claimant's claim for compensation from his employer, the House of Lords held that the employers had discharged their responsibility to provide proper tools by purchasing them from a reputable supplier. The practical effect of this decision was to leave the employee without compensation where the supplier or manufacturer could not be identified or was bankrupt.

 Counterpoint

Despite its wide scope (discussed further below), the Employer's Liability (Defective Equipment) Act 1969 does not completely remedy the problems posed by *Davie* v *New Merton Board Mills Ltd*. As well as establishing causation—that is, that the defect in the equipment caused the accident—the employee needs to prove 'fault' against the third party—that is, that on the balance of probabilities the defect was due to the fault of some other person (usually during its manufacture). This is not always easy.

Potential claimants may, however, be helped in this by the Consumer Protection Act 1987 as the definition of fault in the 1969 Act includes 'breach of statutory duty or other act or omission which gives rise to liability in tort'.[7]

Equipment, defined by section 1(3) of the 1969 Act as 'any plant and machinery, vehicle, aircraft or clothing', has (for the purposes of the Act) also been taken to include a ship provided by the employer for the purposes of employment (*Coltman* v *Bibby Tankers Ltd (The Derbyshire)* [1988]). In *Knowles* v *Liverpool City Council* [1993] the House of Lords extended this to include material used by the employee—in this case a paving stone which the claimant was laying and was injured by—holding that 'equipment' should include whatever the employee used for the purposes of the business.

However, an employer may be able to avoid liability in relation to a failure to provide safety equipment if they can establish that, even if such equipment had been provided, the employee would not have used it (**McWilliam v Sir William Arrol & Co Ltd [1962]**). The argument is one of causation: the employer is in clear breach of their duty, but as

---

7. See further Chapter 13. Consider again the factory worker injured by a faulty machine—what would be your advice to him?

the claimant would have suffered the same injury in any case, their failure to provide safe equipment cannot be said to have been a cause of the employee's injuries.

McWilliam v *Sir William Arrol & Co Ltd* [1962] HL

A steel erector fell to his death at work. He was not wearing a safety harness. His employers had failed (in breach of their statutory duty) to provide safety equipment. However, the House of Lords held that they were not liable for the claimant's death. The employers were able to provide strong evidence that the employee rarely, if ever, used a safety harness and so, even if one had been provided, it was reasonable to infer that he would not have worn it. As such, he would have suffered the same injury even if the employers had provided the necessary equipment.

12.2.3 **A proper system of working (including effective supervision)**

An employer has a duty to ensure a reasonably safe system of working and to give employees general safety instructions about their job. This includes the physical layout of the job, the sequence in which work is carried out and the provision, where appropriate, of warnings and notices. Thus, in *Pape* v *Cumbria County Council* [1992] a part-time cleaner who contracted dermatitis after working with various detergents and chemical cleaning products was able to recover as, although the defendants had provided rubber gloves, they did not warn her of the possibility of developing dermatitis, nor instruct her to wear them. It was not enough to simply provide the rubber gloves, the employer should also have taken reasonable steps to ensure that the safety equipment was properly understood and used by the claimant.

 Pause for reflection

It could be argued that *Pape* makes the employer liable for something which is the employee's responsibility: after all, do employees really need to be told when to use the safety equipment provided?

Why do you think the court came to this decision? It could be suggested that holding an employer liable in these circumstances will encourage safer working practices more generally. Do you agree?

The employer must not only ensure that there is a safe system of work, they must also take care to see that the system is implemented (*Mullaney* v *Chief Constable of West Midlands Police* [2001]). In so doing, they are expected to be aware that employees are often careless about taking safety precautions and that dangerous working practices can develop. In *General Cleaning Contractors* v *Christmas* [1953] a window cleaner was standing on the sill outside a first floor window when the window unexpectedly closed. The court held that the employer should have given clearer instructions to the window cleaner to ensure such accidents did not happen. By failing to do so they had failed to provide a safe system of work.[8]

The nature and extent of an employer's supervision was extended further in *Jebson v Ministry of Defence* [2000] to include effective supervision of soldiers on the way home from a night out. This case involved a group of soldiers who had gone for a night out. Anticipating that they would be worse for wear, the defendants—the soldiers' employer—sent a lorry to pick them up and bring them back to barracks. The claimant, who was very drunk, fell and injured himself as he attempted to climb onto the roof of the lorry as it journeyed home. In allowing his claim for compensation, the Court of Appeal held that, knowing the soldiers' drunken state, the defendants ought to have had a supervisor in the back of the lorry to ensure that none of them injured themselves.

12.2.4 **A safe place of work**

An employer must take reasonable care to provide a safe place of work. However, this does not mean that the employer must ensure that the workplace is completely safe.

Latimer v AEC Ltd [1953] HL

Heavy rainfall flooded the defendant's factory. The rain water mixed with oily liquid, which usually collected in channels in the floor. This meant that when the mixture was drained away the floor became very slippery. The defendants put down sawdust to remedy this. Although there was insufficient sawdust to cover the entire floor, the majority of the floor was covered. The claimant slipped on part of the untreated floor and broke his ankle.

The House of Lords held that the defendants were not liable. They had done everything that could reasonably be expected of them; the danger of injury to their employees was not such as to impose on the employer further costly and inconvenient measures, for example closing the factory until the floor had completely dried out.[9]

12.3 **Breach of statutory duty**

Although the expression 'breach of statutory duty' can be used to describe *any* breach of a tortious duty created by statute,[10] breach of statutory duty is also a tort in its

---

8. It is likely, therefore, that the employer of the window cleaner in the example posed at the beginning of the chapter will be liable—assuming, of course, that it can be established that she would have used the harness (***McWilliam v Sir William Arrol & Co Ltd***).

9. Are the facts of ***Latimer*** distinguishable from those of the example at the beginning of the chapter where the employee slips on a pool of grease in a fast food restaurant? The answer depends on whether efforts have been made to make the floor safe. As you are told that the machine is poorly maintained it is likely that the manager would have had an opportunity to put this right (unlike the sudden effects of the heavy rainfall in ***Latimer***).

10. See e.g. the Occupiers' Liability Act 1957 and Part 1 of the Consumer Protection Act 1987 which specifically create a duty actionable by an individual in private law (Chapters 11 and 13), as well as actions under s 7 of the Human Rights Act 1998 where a public authority is (or is likely to be) in breach of its duty in respect of a relevant Convention right.

own right.[11] As such it is separate to and conceptually distinct from the general common law principles of the tort of negligence. The tort of breach of statutory duty enables a claimant in certain circumstances to recover compensation for losses caused by a defendant's failure to comply with a statutory obligation. Historically, the tort played an important role in ensuring safety in the workplace by providing employees with an avenue for compensation that avoided the harshness of the doctrine of common employment and it continues to play a prominent role in this field. Typically, an employee who suffers an injury at work will bring a claim in both the tort of negligence and for breach of statutory duties (usually breach of health and safety regulations).

Unlike the statutory duties contained in the Occupiers' Liability Acts 1957 and 1984 or the Consumer Protection Act 1987 where liability arises directly according to the provisions of the statute, a civil action for the tort of breach of statutory duty liability arises *indirectly* where a statute imposes a duty (typically relating to criminal liability) but does not identify a civil remedy in the event of its breach. The tort is, therefore, a combination of common law and statute; the duty lies in the statute, the action in the common law:

> a claim for damages for breach of a statutory duty intended to protect a person in the position of the particular plaintiff is a specific common law right which is not to be confused in essence with a claim for negligence. The statutory right has its origin in the statute, but the particular remedy of an action for damages is given by the common law in order to make effective, for the benefit of the injured plaintiff, his right to performance by the defendant of the defendant's statutory duty. (Lord Wright, *London Passenger Transport Board* v *Upson* [1949] at 168)

In order to establish the tort of breach of statutory duty three specific questions (in addition to the usual requirements relating to causation and defences) need to be addressed:

(1) Does the statute give rise to a claim in tort law?

(2) Has the defendant breached their duty?

(3) Does the claimant's loss or injury fall within the scope of the duty?

Not every breach of a statutory duty gives rises to a claim in tort (**Lonrho Ltd v Shell Petroleum Co Ltd (No 2)** [1982]). Civil liability does not arise automatically. The first of these questions—that is, whether Parliament intended there to be a civil remedy—is often the most contentious.

12.3.1 **Does the statute give rise to a claim in tort law?**

Clearly, where a statute explicitly states whether a breach of its provisions gives rise to a remedy in tort as, for example, in the Health and Safety at Work Act 1974

---

11. Our consideration of breach of statutory duty within this chapter is, therefore, not unproblematic. However, given its continuing prominence in relation to an employer's potential liability in tort and that its development beyond the workplace, particularly in relation to statutory duties arising out of a 'scheme of social welfare' (Lord Browne-Wilkinson, *X* v *Bedfordshire County Council* [1995] at 731), has been much more restricted, it is worth looking at here. For a more detailed consideration of breach of statutory duty, see Keith Stanton *Breach of Statutory Duty in Tort* (2nd edn, Sweet & Maxwell, 1986).

(s 41(1)(a), (2)) or section 3 of the Protection from Harassment Act 1997, no problem arises. It is also clear that a breach of a public statutory duty does not always give rise to a claim; this will depend on the object and language of the particular statute (*Atkinson* v *Newcastle Waterworks Co* [1877]). Difficulties arise when the statute imposes a duty but is silent as to whether it intended there to be a civil action for its breach. Crucially, it does not follow that because Parliament has not included such a provision, no remedy exists. In such circumstances, the court must 'divine' the intention of Parliament.

 Pause for reflection

The process of establishing whether Parliament intended there to be a civil remedy in relation to a particular statute has been described by Glanville Williams as 'looking for what is not there'.[12] Lord Denning MR said something similar in *Ex parte Island Records Ltd* [1978]:

> The truth is that in many cases the legislature has left the point open . . . the dividing line between the pro-cases and the contra-cases is so blurred that you may as well toss a coin to decide it. (at 135)

Why do you think this is? Why might Parliament be unwilling to specify whether a civil remedy is available should a defendant breach a statutorily imposed duty? Think about who the defendants in an action for breach of statutory duty are likely to be. Although traditionally actions for breach of statutory duty were more likely to have been brought against individuals, usually employers, the tort is not limited in this way. A number of cases have been brought against public authorities (see, for example, *R* v *Deputy Governor of Parkhurst, ex p Hague* [1992]; *X (Minors)* v *Bedfordshire County Council* [1995]; *O'Rourke* v *Camden London Borough Council* [1997]). It may, therefore, be more politically astute to place responsibility for the absence of a civil law remedy following a public body's failure to perform its statutory duty at the feet of the judiciary rather than to explicitly state it in the statute itself.

Lonrho Ltd v *Shell Petroleum Co Ltd (No 2)* [1982] HL

Lonrho Ltd brought an action for breach of statutory duty in respect of heavy financial losses it had sustained (in contrast to its competitors) as a result of complying with sanctions imposed on the supply of oil following the unilateral declaration of independence by Southern Rhodesia (now the Republic of Zimbabwe) in 1965.

The House of Lords rejected the claim. In his leading opinion, Lord Diplock identified a number of factors that the courts should take into account when assessing whether breach of a statutory obligation should give rise to civil liability. Accepting the presumption in *Doe d. Bishop of Rochester* v *Bridges* [1824–34], that '[w]here an Act creates an obligation and enforces the performance in a specified manner we take it as a general rule that

→

12. 'The Effect of Penal Legislation in the Law of Tort' (1960) 23 *Modern Law Review* 233 at 244.

> ➙
>
> performance cannot be enforced in any other manner' (Lord Tenterden CJ at 859), Lord Diplock outlined two exceptions to this general rule: where the statutory duty is imposed for the protection of a limited class of people and where the statute creates a public right and a particular member of the public suffers 'special damage' (this second exception has not been developed) (at 185–6).
>
> Neither exception was applicable here: the sanctions, in the words of Fox LJ in the Court of Appeal, were not 'concerned with conferring rights either on individuals or the public at large. Their purpose was the destruction, by economic pressure, of the UDI regime in Southern Rhodesia; they were instruments of state policy on an international matter' (at 86).

In *X (Minors)* v *Bedfordshire County Council*,[13] Lord Browne-Wilkinson confirmed that although there is no general rule by which to determine whether a statute gives rise to civil liability, there are a number of 'indicators'. These include whether the duty was imposed for the protection of a limited class of the public; the provision of other remedies for its breach by the statute; the extent to which the statute's scope is limited and specific or general and administrative; as well as various, ubiquitous policy considerations (at 731–2).

An example may help here.

> ### *Groves* v *Lord Wimborne* [1898] CA
>
> Groves, a boy, worked in the defendant's iron works. He seriously injured his arm in the cog-wheels of a steam winch (his forearm was later amputated). The machinery had been left unfenced contrary to section 5 of the Factory and Workshop Act 1878, which imposed an absolute duty on the employer to ensure that certain dangerous machinery was fenced.
>
> The Court of Appeal allowed Groves' claim against his employer. The question for the court was whether the existence of alternative sanctions for breaching this duty (in the form of fines or penalties) prevented a claim for breach of statutory duty on the part of the claimant. The Court of Appeal recognised the existence of alternative means of enforcing the duty as a *factor* to be taken into account, however, it was, Lord Wright argued, 'by no means conclusive or the only matter to be taken into consideration' when determining whether an action will lie for non-performance of that duty (at 416). Other factors included whether the statute was passed for the benefit of the public at large or a particular class of people.

13. We looked at this case in relation to duty of care in the tort of negligence in Chapter 6. You can find the facts of the case in the case box on pp 136–137. As well as the claim in negligence, there was also a claim for breach of statutory duty. This also failed for the reasons discussed on p 322. It is possible given the considerable doubting of the negligence aspects of this decision in *Z* v *UK* [2001] and *D* v *East Berkshire* [2005] that the court's reasoning in relation to breach of statutory duty may also be reconsidered in future cases.

Pause for reflection

Consider the timing of the decision in *Groves*.

Since the early nineteenth century, the development of the railway system and increasing industrialisation had lead to a huge rise in the numbers of accidents and injuries, particularly in the workplace. Working conditions in many factories and quarries were extremely hazardous—hence the need for Acts of Parliament such as the Factory and Workshop Act 1878. The onus was very much on the *employee* to take responsibility for their own safety and, importantly, to bear the severe personal and financial consequences of any injuries suffered—a view encapsulated in the doctrine of common employment set down in *Priestly* v *Fowler* [1837].

However, toward the end of the century there were signs that societal attitudes were beginning to change. The Workmen's Compensation Act 1897 imposed, for the first time, liability on employers in relation to 'accidents arising out of and in the course of employment'. This change was also reflected in the courts. Just six years earlier, the House of Lords had sought to limit the scope of the defence of *volenti* or consent in a case involving an employee who was injured when a stone fell from an overhead crane. The court held that the employer could not escape liability by arguing that the employee had 'voluntarily accepted the risk' by virtue of the fact that the employee had continued to work there despite knowing of the danger of injury (*Smith* v *Charles Baker & Sons* [1891]).

In *Groves*, in 1898, the courts dealt another blow to the so-called 'unholy trinity'. At the time there was no other way the claimant could have obtained a remedy in tort (a claim in negligence would have been defeated by the doctrine of common employment). The statutory duty, however, was absolute and, importantly, imposed directly on the employer. The case was hugely important in establishing an oasis of protection for employees. Its approach reflected the mood of the time and was followed by the House of Lords in *Butler* v *Fife Coal Co Ltd* [1912] and, despite significant increases in health and safety protection in the workplace (notably the Health and Safety at Work Act 1974), it is still authority in respect of duties which predate, or fall outside the remit of, the 1974 Act (*George Ziemniak* v *ETPM Deep Sea Ltd* [2003]).

In *Cutler* v *Wandsworth Stadium* [1949] the courts considered another factor indicative of whether a civil claim may arise—who the statute is intended to benefit. In this case, the House of Lords held that the primary intention of the Betting and Lotteries Act 1934 (under which the claimant sought to claim) was to regulate ringside betting operations and that, while changes made under its regulation may benefit some bookmakers, this was not the intended purpose of the Act.

In *R* v *Deputy Governor of Parkhurst, ex p Hague* [1992],[14] a group of lawfully detained prisoners claimed their treatment in prison was in breach of Prison Rules 1964. Lord Jauncey rejected the prisoners' claim on the ground that the Rules were intended to ensure the management and smooth running of the prisons. In so doing, he appears

14. The claimants in this case also brought actions for false imprisonment. These were also unsuccessful (a change in prison conditions did not make the imprisonment unlawful) and are discussed further in Chapter 14, p 396.

to move away from the reasoning in *Groves* (where the question was whether the statute was intended to confer a *benefit* on the claimant) and focus on the provision of a *right of action*. This has significantly limited the scope of the tort of breach of statutory duty (especially in cases outside the field of health and safety)[15]: '[t]he fact that a particular provision was intended to protect certain individuals is not of itself sufficient to confer private law rights of action upon them, something more is required to show that the legislature intended such conferment' (Lord Jauncey at 170–1).

 Pause for reflection

The prisoners in *Ex parte Hague* were not, perhaps, overly sympathetic claimants—but what about the children in *X* v *Bedfordshire*? In this case, Lord Browne-Wilkinson goes even further and suggests that the starting point is a presumption *against* a right of civil liability unless this is clearly what Parliament intended. Thus, while the duties imported into the Children Act 1989 were clearly intended to benefit children in the position of the claim-ants, they were 'no more than public duties' and, as such, not intended to be enforced at civil law (at 748). Similarly, in *O'Rourke* v *Camden London Borough Council* [1998] the duty to provide temporary housing under the Housing Act 1985 was held to be enforceable only through judicial review.

Think back to what you learnt about the difficulty of establishing a duty of care in the tort of negligence against a public body. Do you think who the defendant is also makes a difference to these claims for breach of statutory duty? If so, is this problematic?

In July 2008, the Law Commission consulted on how best to achieve a clear, simple and just system of redress for individuals who have suffered loss as a result of seri-ously substandard administrative action. One of its suggestions was to abolish or sig-nificantly limit the ambit of breach of statutory duty as it applies to public bodies as it 'neither meets the requirements of aggrieved citizens or properly addresses the legiti-mate concerns of public bodies faced with seemingly ever expanding liability' (Law Commission *Administrative Redress: Public Bodies and the Citizen*, [4.34], [4.106]). Do you agree? Is a private law remedy in these cases an effective or justifiable use of public funds? Can these cases be distinguished from, say, cases against the NHS? Think about who ultimately pays the compensation—does this fit the distributive justice aims of tort law?

Fortunately, the restrictive approach of Lord Browne-Wilkinson in *X* v *Bedfordshire* in relation to 'social welfare' legislation appears not to have found favour in the field of health and safety (*George Ziemniak* v *ETPM Deep Sea Ltd*), although this case ought to be compared with the decision of a differently constituted Court of Appeal in *Todd* v *Adams* [2003] and the unfortunate decision in **Richardson v Pitt-Stanley** **[1995]**.

---

15. See further Lord Browne-Wilkinson in *X* v *Bedfordshire County Council* [1995] at 732.

> ### *Richardson v Pitt-Stanley* [1995] CA
>
> The claimant severely injured his right hand at work and successfully sued the company employing him in negligence and breach of statutory duty. Unfortunately, his employer company was uninsured (contrary to the Employers' Liability (Compulsory Insurance) Act 1969) and was unable to meet his claim.
>
> In response, the claimant sued the directors of the company personally for breach of their statutory duty under section 5 of the Employers' Liability (Compulsory Insurance) Act 1969. Somewhat surprisingly, the majority of the Court of Appeal held that there was no cause of action. The statute was not, in their view, *solely* intended for the benefit of those injured at work but rather was also intended to protect the insured against the effects of multiple and/or large claims: 'Although these consequences may not be so catastrophic as they are for a seriously injured employee who cannot enforce his judgment, they are likely to be serious, more widespread and more frequent' (Stuart-Smith LJ at 131).

12.3.2 Has the duty been breached and does the harm fall within the scope of the duty?

Once it is established that a statute allows for an action for breach of statutory duty, in order for a claim to succeed the claimant must also show that the duty has in fact been breached and that the harm suffered falls within the scope of the duty (as well as establishing causation and the inapplicability of any relevant defences). This is usually quite straightforward.

The scope and content of the duty will be defined by the statute. Although the duty may be strict (as in *Groves*), often it will be qualified, for instance by requiring 'reasonable care' to be taken or for the employer to do what is 'reasonably practicable'. Either way, once we know what the duty requires of the defendant, we shall know what constitutes a breach of that duty.

Additionally, the harm or damage suffered by the claimant must be of the type that the duty was intended to prevent. The leading case is *Gorris v Scott* [1874] which involved a cargo of sheep. The defendant shipowner was under a statutory duty to keep them securely penned when in transit in order to prevent the spread of disease. He did not do so—in breach of his duty—and as a result the sheep were swept overboard in bad weather. The claim for breach of statutory duty was unsuccessful. The duty was imposed in order to prevent disease, the damage in fact suffered was accordingly 'something totally apart from the object of the Act' (at 129–30).

Similarly, in *Vibixa v Komori UK Ltd* [2006], the Court of Appeal denied an employer's claim for property damage and economic loss under the Health and Safety at Work Act 1974. The purpose of the Act is to protect workers from injury at work. Thus, while it is likely that it will cover consequential property damage or economic loss on the part of an injured employee, these losses are not *per se* within the remit of the statute.

> ### *Fytche* v *Wincanton Logistics plc* [2004] HL
>
> Mr Fytche was employed by the defendant company to drive a milk tanker to collect milk from farms at night. One morning, after a particularly heavy snow shower, the tanker became stuck on an icy country road. Contrary to the company's standard procedures, the claimant attempted to dig the tanker out. It took three hours in sub-zero temperatures. Unfortunately, as a result, the claimant suffered frostbite in his little toe as a result of a leak in his right boot, provided under reg 4 of the Personal Protective Equipment at Work Regulations (PPE) 1992. The majority of the House of Lords held that there was no claim for breach of statutory duty in respect of the small hole in his boots (despite an obligation under reg 7(1) of the PPE 'to maintain equipment in good repair'). The boots had not been provided to protect his toes against frostbite (or similar weather risk), but rather to protect from impact injuries (from, for example, falling milk churns) and for which purpose they were still in good repair (at [15]). The employers were not, therefore, in breach of reg 7(1). Baroness Hale, in her dissenting opinion, saw things rather differently:
>
> > A boot with a hole, however small, which lets in water is not in good repair. The issue in this case...is who should bear the risk that the boots supplied for a particular reason turn out to have an incidental defect which causes the employee injury at work. I have no difficulty with the conclusion that the employer rather than the employee should bear that risk...I venture to suggest that a non-lawyer would find it odd indeed that Mr Fytche would have recovered damages if his employer had also thought the boots should protect against a weather risk but does not do so because his employer had a different risk in mind. (at [69]–[70])

12.4 Vicarious liability

Consider again the office worker subjected to a sustained period of homophobic bullying by his supervisor and the school pupil sexually assaulted by his teacher. There are a number of potential civil and criminal claims here: for example, the officer worker might bring a claim against his supervisor under the Protection from Harassment Act 1997.[16] Alternatively, he might sue his employer personally for breach of contract or in negligence for failing to provide a safe place of work (as discussed above). Similarly, alongside a criminal prosecution, the school pupil might bring a claim against his teacher in the tort of battery or against the local authority claiming they were negligent in their selection and control of their employee. In both cases there is also the possibility of a vicarious claim against the employers of the school teacher and supervisor.

Under the principle of vicarious liability an employer will be liable for wrongs committed by an employee in the course of their employment.[17] As a form of secondary

---

16. Chapter 14, pp 404–407.

17. Vicarious liability usually arises within an employment relationship; however, it can also arise outside this, e.g. where a partner of, say, a firm of solicitors commits a tort, the other partners may be vicariously liable (*Dubai Aluminium Co Ltd* v *Salaam* [2003]). Chief constables may also be vicariously liable for the torts of a police officer even though they are not technically employees (Police Act 1996, s 88(1)).

liability, it is not predicated on any wrongdoing of the employer—they may well be, and often are, entirely blameless.[18] Rather liability is imposed vicariously on the employer for the tortious actions of the employee who remains primarily liable (although typically they are not worth pursuing for financial reasons). The principle of vicarious liability is then at odds with the general approach of the common law and the principle of corrective justice whereby liability for any wrongdoing is imposed on, and only on, the wrongdoer(s). As it involves the imposition of strict, no-fault liability, it requires clear and principled justification.

Unfortunately, this is not forthcoming. The common suggestion is that vicarious liability is best understood as having developed not as a result of 'any very clear, logical or legal principle but from social convenience and rough justice' (*Imperial Chemical Industries Ltd* v *Shatwell* [1965] at 685). At its most basic it is a mechanism that ensures a just and practical remedy for harm, while seeking to deter future wrongdoing.[19] However, beyond this there is little agreement as to the policy objectives lying behind the imposition of vicarious liability. As Longmore LJ noted in **Maga v Birmingham Roman Catholic Archdiocese Trustees [2010]**:

> There is by no means universal agreement…Is it that the law should impose liability on someone who can pay rather than someone who cannot? Or is it to encourage employers to be even more vigilant than they would be pursuant to a duty of care? Or is it just a weapon of distributive justice? Academic writers disagree and the House of Lords in *Lister's* case did not give any definitive guidance to lower courts. (at [81])[20]

That said, and though these justifications (explored in more detail below) may, at times, pull in different directions, they are best taken together so that vicarious liability is applied where it is 'fair, just and convenient' (*Viasystems* v *Thermal Transfer* [2006] at [77]).

Possible justifications for vicarious liability

1. It is suggested that, as an employer derives an economic benefit from their employees' work, they should bear any related burdens: 'a person who employs others to advance his own economic interest should in fairness be placed under a corresponding liability for losses incurred in the course of the enterprise'.[21] Put another way, the employer should take the risk of harm occurring either because they gain a benefit from that risk or because of their role in creating it.

2. The victim of the wrongdoing should be able to seek compensation from a source better placed financially than the employee who actually committed the tort; that is, they

→

---

18. Although sometimes a claimant will claim that their employer is both directly (personally) and vicariously responsible for their injury (as in **Lister**), vicariously liability tends to be a simpler and more effective route for securing compensation given the broader and necessarily more open-ended definition of the employer's personal, non-delegable duty of care.

19. See e.g. Lord Nicholls in **Majrowski v Guy's and St Thomas' NHS Trust [2006]** at [9].

20. See further discussion in Giliker 2009, pp 35–6. Though compare Hughes LJ in *Catholic Care Welfare Society* v *Institute of the Brothers of Christian Schools* [2010] who stated: 'There is not much doubt about the principal rationale for this non-fault liability, which is loss distribution' (at [35]).

21. John Fleming *The Law of Torts* (9th edn, LBC Information Services, 1998), p 410.

→

should be able to recover from 'deeper pockets' of the employer who has 'a purse worth opening' (Williams 1956, p 232).

3. Vicarious liability is 'a loss-distribution device' whereby the financial loss arising from the wrongdoing can be spread more widely across the community through liability insurance and/or higher prices (*Lister* at [65]; *Catholic Care* at [35]).

4. Employers are in the best position to reduce the likelihood of workplace accidents, and indeed intentional wrongdoing by their employees through, for example, 'imaginative and efficient administration and supervision' (*Bazley* v *Curry* [1999] at [33]). The imposition of strict liability acts as an incentive encouraging employers not only to maintain standards of 'good practice' and to take care when making appointments but to explore ways of going beyond those set by the standard of the 'reasonable person'.

 Pause for reflection

As we have seen, courts and commentators tend to argue that vicarious liability can be justified, if at all, on the basis of a combination of various policy considerations: the desire to spread losses or shift them on to those best positioned to meet them, to encourage greater supervision of workers and so reduce future wrongdoing: a feeling (which perhaps does not stand up to close scrutiny) that employers should take the rough with the smooth and so bear the costs as well as enjoying the benefits of the employees' actions. All these provide reasons for requiring the employer to meet their employees' liabilities. The problem is that if we were really committed to furthering these particular policies, the law would look very different.

First, these policy considerations cannot explain the particular rules on vicarious liability that the courts have in fact developed. For example, as we will see, vicarious liability depends on the employee actually having committed a tort. But the concern to shift or spread losses applies irrespective of whether the employee acted wrongfully. So, if we were really motivated to impose liability because this would see the losses spread, we would have no reason for limiting vicarious liability to those cases where the employee has caused loss by committing a tort. Instead, we would make the employer liable wherever their employee causes others loss while doing their job. The same goes for the benefit and burden argument. By contrast, the argument that vicarious liability exists to encourage greater supervision by employers of their employees' conduct suggests that liability should be imposed on the employer only where this really would be likely to lead to greater supervision and so a reduction of future harms. Given that most cases of negligence arise from isolated and unpredictable acts of carelessness, which the employer could have done nothing to prevent, it is hard to argue that this policy supports the present practice of imposing vicarious liability in respect of *all* torts committed in the course of employment.

Secondly, these policy considerations extend beyond the employment context. For example, the argument that losses should be spread applies *wherever and however someone is injured* and so is not uniquely applicable when the injury is caused by an employee acting in the course of their employment. Again, if we *really* believed that the law of tort should be concerned with spreading losses, then we would have no reason for making liability in general dependent on a breach of duty or for having a general rule that liability

→

→

depends on the defendant having caused the relevant loss. If our motivation is to spread losses, it should be irrelevant whether the defendant acted carelessly or whether they were in any way responsible for the loss that was suffered. Instead we should impose liability on whomever we can find who carries insurance, since this is the best way of seeing the loss spread amongst society. That the law generally attaches liability only to those who actually caused the claimant's loss, and then, again as a general rule, only where their conduct has fallen below a particular standard, tells us that, at root, the law of torts is not designed to spread losses (though it may sometimes have this effect).

The same is true when we look at the other policies set out above. In each case, a real commitment to furthering these policies would lead not only to changes in the law of vicarious liability but a radically different law of tort—indeed, they would require us to view tort law as fundamentally misconceived. But if these policies cannot account for the law of tort *generally*, then we should be suspicious of any attempt to justify particular parts of tort law on this basis. We would be saying that, though generally these are not the policies which justify tort law as a whole, they do justify (some of) the rules of tort in the employment context. But why here and not elsewhere? We are left with a distinction that appears entirely arbitrary.

 Counterpoint

Of course, we should feel uncomfortable with the conclusion that an important and long-standing aspect of tort law is arbitrary and unprincipled. As such, lawyers have sought to find an explanation for vicarious liability which is consistent with the basic aims and structure of tort law generally. Perhaps the most important example of this is an argument recently made by Robert Stevens.[22]

His suggestion is that we should not view vicarious liability as an instrument for the law to impose on one person liability for torts committed by another. Rather it is just one particular example of the law on the attribution *of conduct*. What does this mean? The best example of this comes in relation to companies. Companies, as artificial legal constructs, can only 'act' (enter contracts, acquire property, commit torts) through other (natural) people. Accordingly the law needs a set of rules determining whose actions 'count' as the actions of the company; for instance, whose consent is needed for the company to enter into a contract. Stevens argues that we should understand the rules of vicarious liability in the same way. When the law holds an employer vicariously liable it is because the actions of the employee are attributed to the employer. The employee's actions are treated as the actions of the employer, and so torts committed by the employee are regarded as torts committed by the employer.

This suggests that, contrary to appearances, vicarious liability is not an exception to the general rule that the law of tort imposes liability only where the defendant has caused and is responsible for the loss suffered by the claimant. This is because, in the circumstances, the employer is indeed regarded as having caused and as being responsible for the injury suffered.

→

---

22. *Torts and Rights* (OUP, 2007), pp 257–74.

> →
>
> Unfortunately, this argument does not solve the problems posed by the law on vicarious liability. Even if we accept (and it is not clear why we should) that the law does indeed require, outside the context of companies, rules for the attribution of conduct, the question is why has the law chosen this set of rules rather than some other? Why should, in the context of employment, the actions of the employee be attributed to (and so regarded as the action of) the employer? This question is particularly important given that the effect of such rules is that the employer is held legally liable for losses which most of us would regard as caused by, and the responsibility of, someone else.
>
> This question just takes us back to where we started, needing a justification for the rules we have. Stevens's argument, if correct, tells us only what sort of rules these are: namely, rules of attribution. It does not tell us why we have or should embrace this particular set of rules. Unless we are content for the law to be and to appear arbitrary, these questions require an answer. As such, Stevens's argument ultimately fails to take us beyond the unpersuasive combination of policies set out above.

An employer will not be vicariously liable unless the following conditions are met:

- there must be an employer–employee relationship;
- the employee must have committed a tort; and
- the tort must be committed while the employee was acting in the course of employment.

12.4.1 **The employer–employee relationship**

In order for an employer to be held vicariously liable the tortious act must have been committed by one of their employees. However, identifying someone as an 'employee' is not as straightforward as one might expect—not everyone you pay to do work becomes your employee. So, for instance, if you hire a plumber to mend your toilet or take a taxi to drive you home, though these people are, in a sense, doing work for you, we would not, and the law does not, call them your employees. The problem is that though the notion of who is and is not an employer is clear at the extremes, things become more indistinct at the borders. Indeed, determining who is an employee has become more difficult in recent years given flexible working patterns and structures which have led to changes within the workplace with an increase in 'atypical' workers—for example, agency workers, homeworkers, part-time workers, the self-employed, 'regular' casual workers and so on—which 'depart radically from the standard employment relationship whereby an employee works regularly (that is, full-time) and consistently for his employer under a contract of employment' (McKendrick 1990, p 770).[23]

There is no single test of 'employment': 'no exhaustive list has been compiled and perhaps no exhaustive list can be compiled of the considerations which are relevant in determining that question, nor can strict rules be laid down as to the relative weight

---

23. Importantly, this does not mean an employer will never be liable for the torts of an independent contractor. In practice, the concept of an employer's non-delegable duty of care (discussed above) is used to overcome this distinction.

which the various considerations should carry in particular cases' (*Market Investigations Ltd* v *Social Security* [1969] at 184–5). While an agreement between the parties as to whether an individual is an employee is indicative, it is not definitive. An individual may not wish to call themselves an 'employee' (for tax or National Insurance evasion purposes, for example), but may nevertheless operate in every other way consistently with that expected of an employee (*Ferguson* v *Dawson* [1976]). Further, an individual's employment status is not fixed; employment status can be determined differently for different purposes—even purely for the purposes of a particular accident (*Viasystems*).

When seeking to establish whether someone is an employee, traditionally the courts look to the level of 'control' exercised by the employer (*Stephenson Jordan & Harrison Ltd* v *McDonall & Evans* [1952]). An example may help here.[24]

Ready Mixed Concrete Ltd v Ministry of Pensions and National Insurance [1968] QBD

The issue in this case was whether 'owner-drivers' used by Ready Mixed Concrete to deliver concrete were employees or independent contractors for National Insurance purposes. The facts pointed in both directions. On the one hand, the drivers were paid at fixed mileage rates and were expected to buy and maintain their own vehicles suggesting that, although they worked for the company, they did so as accessories, rather than an integrated part. Moreover, the contract clearly stated that the drivers were independent contractors. On the other hand, Ready Mixed Concrete exercised a high level of control—the drivers had to wear company uniforms and abide by company rules, and the vehicles (purchased through agreements with a financial organisation associated with the company) were painted in the company's colours and could not be used for any other business. The court held that the ownership of the vehicles, the fact that the owner-drivers had sufficient freedom in performance and, in particular, that they took the chance of profit and the risk of loss meant that they were independent contractors.

However, in a climate where employees are increasingly expected to show—and are rewarded to the extent to which they do show—initiative and exercise discretion, the control test reflects an outdated view of the workplace.[25] Take, for example, a consultant in a busy accident and emergency department. They are unlikely to take too kindly to being told how to treat their patients (although some restrictions will still be placed on them, for example, in relation to what drugs they can prescribe). More recently, the cases of *Viasystems* and **Hawley** v **Luminar Leisure Ltd** [2006] suggest that the courts are more likely to adopt a test which looks to the realities of the relationship between the parties rather than the form.

A further difficulty arises when an employee has been hired out to another company (**Mersey Docks and Harbour Board** v **Coggins & Griffith (Liverpool) Ltd** [1947]) or has

---

24. Though this case does not concern vicarious liability directly, the reasoning employed may nevertheless serve as a guide.
25. See e.g. the visionary comments of the Court of Appeal in *Cassidy* v *Ministry of Health* [1951].

more than one potential employer (*Viasystems*). Take, for example, an office 'temp'—are they an employee of the agency to which they belong (and which allocates the work) or the company which hires them for a particular period of time (and who tells them what to do)? Or maybe both?

Mersey Docks and Harbour Board v Coggins & Griffith (Liverpool) Ltd [1947] HL

Coggins & Griffith, a firm of stevedores, hired a crane and its operator from the harbour authority to assist in loading and unloading ship cargos. The contract stipulated that the crane driver was the stevedore's employee (although the harbour authority continued to pay his wages and retained power of dismissal). Unfortunately, the crane operator negligently injured another employee while loading a ship.

In finding the harbour authority vicariously liable for the crane operator's negligence, the House of Lords held that the agreement between the parties was not conclusive. Although at the time of the accident the stevedores were able to instruct the crane operator as to what to do (unlike the harbour authority), they had no control as to how he operated the crane. Moreover, the fact that the harbour authority continued to pay the operator's wages was a further indication that he was still their employee.

Usually the worker's permanent employer will remain liable for their actions and the heavy burden of showing that employment has transferred to the temporary employer rests on them. The courts will consider factors such as who pays the employee's wages and who has power of dismissal, alongside the usual tests of control and integration. A more recent example is the Court of Appeal decision in *Hawley* [2006].

Hawley v Luminar Leisure Ltd [2006] CA

A door steward, hired to keep order at the defendant's nightclub (Luminar), physically assaulted the claimant in the course of his employment, causing him permanent and serious brain damage. Luminar did not hire their door staff directly, but rather contracted with another company, ASE Security Services (which had since gone into liquidation), to provide appropriate staff. The question for the court was whether the door steward was the employee of the nightclub (for whom he worked on a day-to-day basis) or of ASE (with whom he and the nightclub contracted directly).

The Court of Appeal, framing the question as 'who was entitled and therefore obliged to control Mr Warren's [the door steward] act so as to prevent it?', held the owner of the nightclub vicariously liable: 'If anyone was going to prevent Mr Warren's behaving badly and this particular act, it was Luminar's manager. ASE's sole role seems to have been employing Mr Warren in the first place, providing him as a doorman at the club and paying his wages for as long as Luminar were happy to use his services' (at [84]). Moreover, he was clearly recognisable to others as Luminar's employee; his presence on the door, 'decked out' in the club's uniform had been a familiar sight for over two years (at [80]).

Pause for reflection

The decision in *Hawley* has been described as a rare instance where an employer was vicarious liable for the actions of a temporary employee. The Court of Appeal drew specific attention to the fact that the nightclub did not need to use the services of another company to employ door staff and that they did so partly to avoid aspects of employment law which they thought would limit their ability to manage the club (at [74]). Its refusal to allow this to prevent an employment relationship from being established between Luminar and the door steward reflects an increasing willingness by the courts to recognise the realities of the contemporary workplace. Ewan McKendrick argues that, in light of changing practices in the employment relationship and a rise in 'atypical' workers, a worker might be classified as an employee solely for the purpose of imposing vicarious liability on their employer so as not to undermine the compensatory and loss-distribution goals of the doctrine (1990, p 784). Do you agree? Think about whether companies should be able to utilise 'legal loopholes' in order to obtain all the benefits from an employment contract without incurring any of the risks. Who is likely to lose out in such arrangements?

But why should we choose *between* employers? Why not find *both* vicariously liable? Historically, it had been assumed that dual vicarious liability is not permitted: an employee 'is the servant of one or the other, but not the servant of one and the other; the law does not recognise several liability in two principals who are unconnected' (*Laugher v Pointer* [1826]). However, attitudes toward the possibility of liability of multiple parties have changed (see, for example, the Law Reform (Contributory Negligence) Act 1945 and Civil Liability (Contribution) Act 1978) and this view has now been rejected by the Court of Appeal in *Viasystems* which held that a person can have two separate employers at the same time providing they are compatible with each other (Rix LJ at [76]).

12.4.2 **A tortious act**

It is important to remember that an employee must have actually committed a tort for vicarious liability to arise. If the employee is not liable in tort, then there is nothing for their employer to be vicariously liable for.[26] Traditionally, the cases have tended to involve the tort of negligence (accidents in the workplace), however the cases also involved intentional torts (for example, battery (*Mattis* [2003])[27] or stealing (*Morris v CW Martin* [1966]; *Brink's Global Services Inc v Igrox Ltd* [2009])) and, more recently, the statutory tort of harassment (*Majrowski*).

Majrowski v Guy's and St Thomas' NHS Trust **[2006] HL**

Majrowski brought a claim against his employer in respect of harassing, bullying and intimidating treatment by his departmental supervisor under section 3 of the Protection from

➡

---

26. Although see Stevens 2007a.

27. Though cf the reasoning of the Privy Council in *Attorney General of the British Virgin Islands v Hartwell* [2004].

→

Harassment Act 1997.[28] He claimed that she had singled him out and was excessively critical about his work and time-keeping. He claimed this was fuelled by homophobia, since he was gay. An internal investigation (following a formal complaint from the claimant) established that harassment had occurred.

The question for the court was the whether the employers could be held vicariously liable for a statutory tort committed by an employee in the course of employment.

Finding for the claimant, the House of Lords held: 'it is difficult to see a coherent basis for confining the common law principle of vicarious liability to common law wrongs...the rationale also holds good for a wrong comprising a breach of statutory duty or prohibition which gives rise to civil liability, provided always the statute does not expressly or impliedly indicate otherwise' (at [10]). After all, Lord Nicholls continued: 'why should an employer have special dispensation in respect of the newly-created wrong and not be liable if an employee commits this wrong in the course of his employment? The contemporary rationale of employer's liability is as applicable to this new wrong as it is to common law torts' (at [27]).

 Pause for reflection

Lord Nicholls in *Majrowski* posed the following question:

> Take a case where an employee, in the course of their employment, harasses a non-employee, such as a customer of the employer. In such case the employer would be liable if his employee had assaulted the customer. Why should this not equally be so in respect of harassment? In principle, harassing arising from a dispute between two employees stands on the same footing. If, acting in the course of his employment, one employee assaults another, the employer is liable. Why should harassment be treated differently? (at [28])

Do you think harassment should be treated differently from physical assaults? Is there a danger of disgruntled employees, suffering from stress as a result of what is expected of them by their immediate superiors, deciding to bring fraudulent claims for harassment?

See Lord Nicholls' response to these fears (at [30]) and Baroness Hale's rather reluctant application of the principles of vicarious liability in her concurring opinion (at [64]–[74]).

More recently however, Maurice Kay LJ in the Court of Appeal expressed doubts over the number of workplace harassment cases:

> it is doubtful whether the legislature had the workplace in mind when passing an Act that was principally directed at 'stalking' and similar cases...I do not expect that many workplace cases will give rise to this liability. It is far more likely that, in the great majority of cases, the remedy for high-handed or discriminatory misconduct by or on behalf of an employer will be more fittingly in the Employment Tribunal. (*Veakins* v *Kier Islington* [2009] at [17])

---

28. See further Chapter 14, pp 404–407.

12.4.3 'In the course of employment'

An employer will be liable only for torts committed by an employee 'in the course of their employment'. Of course, this simply prompts another question: When exactly is an employee acting in the course of their employment? The case law provides us with limited guidance here: a nightclub bouncer who stabs a customer while on duty (*Mattis* [2003]) and a residential warden in a children's home who sexually abuses his charges (*Lister*) are acting in the course of their employment whereas the off-duty police man who wears his uniform while 'on the prowl' for vulnerable women (*N v Chief Constable of Merseyside Police* [2006]) or who abandons his post and 'in a jealous fit of rage' fires his police revolver in a bar injuring a tourist (*Attorney General of British Virgin Irelands v Hartwell* [2004]) are simply engaged in rather nasty acts of personal gratification or 'frolics of their own' (*Joel v Morrison* [1834]).

Traditionally when making these assessments, the courts relied on the so-called 'Salmond test' which asks whether the employee's act is 'a wrongful and unauthorised mode of doing some act authorised by the master'.[29] This test was rejected by the House of Lords in *Lister* in which the court made it clear that the relevant test is simply one of 'close connection'.

Lister v *Hesley Hall Ltd* [2002] HL

Mr and Mrs Grain were employed by Hesley Hall Ltd as the warden and housekeeper of a residential facility attached to a school, which specialised in teaching children with emotional and behavioural difficulties. Its purpose was to provide the children with a homely and caring setting—beyond and distinct from their school environment—in which to adjust to everyday living. The warden was responsible for the discipline and day-to-day running of the house; alongside managing the other staff, he also supervised the boys at bedtime and in the mornings, making sure they got to and from school, administering their pocket money and arranging their weekend leave and evening activities. Over the course of four years he systematically sexually abused a number of boys, including the claimants. Over 20 years later, he was sentenced to seven years imprisonment for multiple offences involving sexual abuse. Now in their 30s, three of the boys abused by the warden brought claims for personal injury against his employer on two grounds: first, that they were personally negligent in their care, selection and control of the warden (this was rejected at first instance and was not pursued further) and, secondly, that they were vicariously liable for the torts he had committed.

Despite recognising that 'sexual abuse is a particularly offensive and criminal act of personal gratification on the part of its perpetrator and therefore be easily described as the paradigm of those acts which an employee could not conceivably be employed to do' (at [53]), a unanimous House of Lords held the employers vicariously liable for the warden's

➡

---

29. JW Salmond *Law of Torts* (1907); now in the current edition of *Salmond & Heuston on the Law of Torts* (21st edn, Sweet & Maxwell, 1996), p 443. See e.g. the Court of Appeal decision in *Trotman v North Yorkshire County Council* [1999] in which the court refused to find the employers of a school teacher who sexually abused a pupil vicariously liable because the abuse was not an unauthorised mode of carrying out an authorised act. *Trotman* was overruled by the House of Lords in *Lister*.

actions. They did so by finding (with some ingenuity)[30] a test of 'close connection' within the traditional Salmond test (outlined above). Unfortunately, there are at least two versions of this test set down. Lord Steyn's formulation asked whether the warden's acts 'were so closely connected with his employment that it would be fair and just to hold the employers liable…the sexual abuse was inextricably interwoven with the carrying out by the warden of his duties' (at [28]). While Lord Hobhouse understood the employer's liability to be grounded in the assumed relationship between the employers and the claimants which imposes specific duties upon the employer in relation to the person they entrust with the performance of these duties (at [54]).

 Pause for reflection

It has been suggested that 'the facts in *Lister* shouted vicarious liability so loudly the outcome was obvious the moment the Lords freed themselves from the wooden reading of the Salmond test'.[31] Do you agree? Would your answer differ if the defendant was a non-profit organisation rather than a commercial enterprise? Think again about the justifications for the imposition of vicarious liability, particularly in relation to the allocation of risk. Is there a difference between a charity (which is not seeking to make a profit) and a company (which derives an economic benefit from their employee's work and is more easily able to spread the loss through liability insurance or higher prices) bearing the risk of an employee's deliberate wrongdoing?

Counterpoint

An employer may instruct their employee to take reasonable care or to avoid committing torts. If the employee nonetheless goes on to commit a tort, the employer could argue that, far from doing their job, the employee was doing the very thing they had been instructed not to do. However, it would clearly defeat the purpose of vicarious liability if the fact that such conduct was prohibited by the employer meant that the employee was to be regarded as acting outside the course of their employment. After all, few, if any, employers authorise the commission of torts by their employees.

The same applies when an employee ignores a specific direction given by their employer as to how to do, or not to do, their job. In *Rose* v *Plenty* [1976], for example, despite strict instructions to the contrary, a milkman allowed a boy to help him deliver the milk and to accompany him on his rounds. The milkman's employer was held vicariously liable for injuries the boy suffered when he fell from the milk float as a result of the milkman's negligent driving.

Indeed, following *Lister*, it seems the employer can do very little to avoid responsibility for the intentional wrongdoings of his employee: 'it is no answer to say that the employee

30. See further Giliker 2002, p 272.
31. Bruce Feldthusen 'Vicarious Liability for Sexual Abuse' (2001) 9(3) *Tort Law Review* 173 at 177.

→

was guilty of intentional wrongdoing, or that his act was not merely tortious but criminal, or that he was acting exclusively for his own benefit, or that he was acting contrary to express instructions, or that his conduct was the very negation of his employer's duty' (Lord Millett at [79]).

Do you think this is fair on employers? On one hand, one could argue that it is fair because the employer has a responsibility (and is in a strong position to be able) to ensure that employees act properly. However, on the other hand, an employer could do all they could reasonably be expected to do and yet still be vicariously liable should their employee commit a tortious act in the course of their employment—can this be justified? (Think again about the justifications for the imposition of vicarious liability listed on pp 325–326.)

The 'close connection' test in *Lister* is both practically and theoretically problematic. It is easier to state than apply. As Paula Giliker (2002) notes it simply prompts further question: how closely connected to their employment do the employee's actions need to be?

This 'close connection' test focuses attention in the right direction. But it affords no guidance on the type or degree of connection which will normally be regarded as sufficiently close to prompt the legal conclusion that the risk of the wrongful act occurring, and any loss flowing from the wrongful act, should fall on the firm or employer rather than the third party who was wronged. (Lord Nicholls, *Dubai* at [25])

Little wonder that the case law continues to provide illustrations on either side of the line. Compare, for example, the following cases involving off-duty policemen.

In *Weir* v *Chief Constable of Merseyside Police* [2003] a policeman, helping his girlfriend to move house, was acting in his capacity as a police constable (albeit very badly) when he assaulted a young man he found rummaging through his girlfriend's things, threw him down the stairs at the block of flats and locked him in the police van he had borrowed to help her move. Key here was that he had identified himself to the young man as a police officer and told him he was taking him to the police station while putting him in the van. By contrast, in *N* v *Chief Constable of Merseyside Police* [2006] a police officer who raped and indecently assaulted a severely intoxicated young woman, and who made a video film and created computer stills of the assault, was not found to be acting in the course of his employment. Although wearing his uniform and communications radio and displaying his warrant card, provided him with an opportunity to commit the acts, this did not establish a close connection between those acts and his employment. Thus, though the *Lister* decision may have achieved a just result for the claimants, it does so at the expense of practical and theoretical uncertainty, particularly in relation to the distinction between an employer's primary or non-delegable duties and vicarious liability.[32] Claire McIvor agrees, describing the close connection test as 'policy-driven analysis...loosely founded on

32. See e.g. Giliker 2009, pp 42–8; Robert Stevens 'Non-delegable Duties and Vicarious Liability' and John Murphy 'Juridical Foundations of Common Law Non-delegable Duties' both in Jason Neyers, Erika Chamberlain and Stephen Pitel *Emerging Issues in Tort Law* (Hart Publishing, 2007).

a theory of enterprise risk, and ostensibly guided by notions of justice and fairness' (2006, p 268). In the same vein, Po Jen Yap has suggested that 'the close-connection test in itself merely provides the court with a formula to confirm its result, rather than reach one in the first place'.[33]

 Counterpoint

It may be that cases such as *Lister* would be better dealt with through the imposition of a non-delegable duty of care on the defendant. This has the advantage of recognising the particular social need—that is increasing the protection of vulnerable parties in institutional care—without getting distracted by the various policy rationales of vicarious liability. However, as Giliker notes, existing precedent imposing vicarious liability for intentional torts and a reluctance to extend existing non-delegable duties means that such a development is unlikely (2009, p 44).

> The real obstacle in this context, however, is in fact the *nature* of liability sought to be imposed . . . the non-delegable duty proposed would be to ensure that no harm is suffered by a victim due to the negligent or intentional actions of the person to whom the duty is delegated . . . It is one thing for an employer to accept responsibility for its employees' . . . negligent failure to operate a safe system of work, but quite another to take responsibility for deliberate and criminal actions in the workplace. (2009, p 46)

Nevertheless, this has not stopped the courts appearing to frame questions of vicarious liability in terms of a non-delegable duty of care. In *Catholic Care Welfare Society* v *Institute of the Brothers of Christian Schools* [2010] a large number of pupils claimed to have been physically or sexually abused by staff at the school they attended. The staff had been supplied by the Institute of Brothers of the Christian Schools (also known as the De La Salle Institute), though they were employed by the managers of the school itself. The Court of Appeal held that though the Institute controlled the lives of the staff, who clearly considered that they were carrying out its work, the Institute did not have a sufficient interest in the running of or teaching at the school to ground the imposition of vicarious liability (at [88]): 'the Institute had not undertaken a duty of caring for the pupils at St William's and then delegated or entrusted it to the brother-teachers' (at [57]). But on this formulation the issue is one of the breach of an assumed duty, not the imposition of liability for the wrongs of another.

The Court of Appeal returned to the scope of 'close connection' test in *Gravil* v *Redruth Rugby Football Club* [2008], in which a rugby club was held vicariously liable for a punch thrown by one of its players (causing serious injury to a player in the opposing team) during a second division rugby union match and, more recently, in **Maga** v **Birmingham Roman Catholic Archdiocese Trustees [2010]**.

---

33. Po Jen Yap 'Enlisting Close Connections: A Matter of Course for Vicarious Liability' (2008) 28(2) *Legal Studies* 197 at 200.

> ### *Maga* v *Birmingham Roman Catholic Archdiocese Trustees* [2010] CA
>
> The claimant had been sexually abused by a priest as a young boy in the 1970s. The claimant was not a Roman Catholic, but had been befriended by the priest who employed him to do odd jobs around the church and presbytery.
>
> After holding that the claim was not time-barred under section 28(1) of the Limitation Act 1980 (the claimant suffered from a learning difficulty and so was not capable of conducting the litigation), the Court of Appeal went on to consider whether the defendants were vicariously liable. The main issue was whether the priest had abused the claimant in the 'course of his employment'. Though acknowledging that the claim was weaker than that in *Lister*, the court unanimously held that abuse had occurred in the course of the priest's employment. There was a sufficiently close connection between the priest's employment at the Church and his abuse of the claimant to make it fair, just and reasonable to make his employers vicariously liable (at [44]). In particular, Lord Neuberger MR noted that the priest, known as 'Father Chris' was in a position analogous to that of a parent or carer. He had special responsibility for youth work at the church and he was able to develop his relationship with the claimant through activities taking place at the church, allowing him to 'draw the claimant further into his sexually abusive orbit by ostensibly respectable means connected with his employment' (at [48]). Moreover, abuse was a known (however undesired) risk of the priest's employment.

The Court of Appeal in *Maga* provided little by way of clarity as to the application of the close connection test. Both formulations of the test in *Lister* (as well as the risk-based and policy-informed formulation of the Canadian Supreme Court in *Bazley*), were discussed and applied, with no acknowledgement of the tension between them. Moreover, the extension of the priest's employment to include his interactions with non-believers (the defendants acknowledged that, were the claimant an altar-boy, the abuse would clearly fall within the course of the priest's employment), suggests that religious organisations are more likely to face hefty compensation payouts if they do not prevent sexual abuse by their clergy.

> ### Pause for reflection
>
> In light of the uncertainty, and drawing on existing case law, Paula Giliker has suggested a two-stage test for ascertaining the existence of a 'close connection' between the employee's action and their employment when considering whether to impose vicarious liability for intentional torts. First, the employee must have been entrusted (expressly or implicitly) with a protective or fiduciary duty to be exercised at the employee's discretion and, secondly, the act must take place as part of their purported exercise of this discretion (2009, pp 50, 53–4). Of course, the second aspect of this test simply prompts a further question as to when an employee's action falls within the exercise of their discretion and, though most do, not every case fits within Giliker's framework.[34] However, in contrast to the lack of direction
>
> ➡

---

34. See e.g. *Bernard* v *Attorney General of Jamaica* [2005] and *Mattis*.

→

from the higher courts, it does have the benefit of providing some guidance as to when the close connection test is satisfied and, in turn, when vicarious liability might be imposed.

An alternative approach is that suggested by Bruce Feldthusen. He argues for a single stage test in cases where the activity of the employer has materially increased the risk of the employee's tort against the person to whom they owe a protective or fiduciary duty on deterrence and loss distribution grounds.[35] Which test do you prefer?

12.5 Conclusion

In this chapter we have considered ways in which an employer may be liable in tort for injury suffered by one of their employees and, more controversially, for the torts of their employees. An employer owes a personal non-delegable duty of care to their employees to ensure a safe workplace for their employees. This sees that the employer remains responsible for key tasks even when the performance of them has been delegated to another. The duty arises from the direct nature of the relationship between the claimant and the defendant—the conduct of the delegated employee is used to establish breach.

An employer may also be liable in the distinct tort of breach of a statutory duty. This enables a claimant in certain circumstances to recover compensation for losses caused by the defendant's failure to comply with a statutory obligation. However, not every breach of a statutory duty gives rise to a claim in tort. Parliament must have intended for liability to arise. Although its existence as a separate tort is largely the result of a historical need in the late nineteenth century to eschew the harshness of the common law in relation to employer's liability, it need not be (although it largely appears to be so at present) confined to workplace-related legislation.

Finally, an employer may also be liable vicariously for injuries caused by their employees to another (even in circumstances where they are entirely blameless). In such cases, the employee is also personally liable for the harm caused. An employer will be vicariously liable only if there is an employer–employee relationship; the employee has committed a tort; and the tort is committed while the employee is acting in the course of their employment. The principle of vicarious liability is exceptional in that it imposes liability on the employer *without fault* on the part of the employer (where the employer is at fault, they will also be personally liable) and as such requires adequate justification. The closest we may come to a sound justification looks not to the employer's deep pockets, but to their ability to spread the loss through, for example, liability insurance or higher prices.

✳ End-of-chapter questions

After reading the chapter carefully, try answering the questions below. If you would like to know what we think visit the Online Resource Centre (www.oxfordtextbooks.co.uk/orc/horsey2e/).

35. Above, n 31.

1. Critically evaluate the development of the common law duty of employers to their employees.

2. How is the tort of breach of statutory duty established?

3. In what circumstances will an employer be liable for the actions of an employee? How far, if at all, should this extend to cover things that the employee has been expressly forbidden by the employer to do?

4. Consider the problem question at the start of this chapter. Now having read about the topic what would be your advice to the various parties? If you need some pointers in thinking about how to answer this question, turn to the Appendix (p 589) where each problem is annotated with issues and cases to consider. Next, try to write your own answer and finally, log on to our Online Resource Centre (www.oxfordtextbooks.co.uk/orc/horsey2e/) to compare your answer against our suggested outline answer.

✳ Further reading

The best place to start your further reading here is with Paula Giliker's 2009 article which considers the decision in *Lister* and its subsequent application.

Atiyah, Patrick *Vicarious Liability in the Law of Tort* (Butterworths, 1967)

Giliker, Paula 'Rough Justice in an Unjust World' (2002) 65 *Modern Law Review* 269

Giliker, Paula 'Making the Right Connection: Vicarious Liability and Institutional Responsibility' (2009) 17 *Torts Law Journal* 35

Giliker, Paula 'Lister Revisited: Vicarious Liability, Distributive Justice and Course of Employment' (2010) *Law Quarterly Review* 521

McIvor, Claire 'The Use and Abuse of the Doctrine of Vicarious Liability' (2006) 35 *Common Law World Review* 268

McKendrick, Ewan 'Vicarious Liability and Independent Contractors—A Re-Examination' (1990) 53 *Modern Law Review* 770

Stanton, Keith 'New Forms of the Tort of Breach of Statutory Duty' (2004) 120 *Law Quarterly Review* 324

Stevens, Robert 'Vicarious Liability or Vicarious Actions' (2007a) 123 *Law Quarterly Review* 30

Weekes, Robert 'Vicarious Liability for Violent Employees' (2004) 63(1) *Cambridge Law Journal* 53

Williams, Glanville 'Vicarious Liability: Tort of the Master or Tort of the Servant?' (1956) 72 *Law Quarterly Review* 522

13

Product liability

Problem question

Read this problem question carefully, and keep it in mind while you are working through the chapter that follows. At the end of the chapter, you will be able to apply what you have learnt to the problem question and advise the relevant parties.

After many years of research, Rack and Horse Pharmaceuticals (RHP) develop a drug to treat breast cancer. After only 18 months of clinical trials, it receives a licence and goes on the market in the UK in March 2010. Although the drug itself is completely pure, it is known that in less than 0.5 per cent of patients (those who carry a particular gene) it can produce an undesirable side-effect known as Tort Syndrome. This side-effect is not widely publicised as both RHP and the government are keen to encourage widespread uptake of the drug in relevant groups of women.

In 2015, 20 claimants who were given the drug between 2010 and 2013 and who have contracted Tort Syndrome begin an action against RHP alleging both negligence and liability under the Consumer Protection Act 1987. RHP argues that it is not liable because up until 2013, there was no genetic test that could determine which individuals carried the gene in question.

The claimants bring evidence to show there was an article in an Outer Mongolian scientific journal, published both in hard copy and on the Internet in 2011, which suggested a test to determine whether individual women carried the specific gene for the reaction to the drug that causes Tort Syndrome. Had RHP conducted clinical trials for longer, the company would have been able to identify the characteristics of the women likely to react badly to the drug and to issue appropriate warnings and advice.

13.1 **Introduction**

Consider the following examples:

→ Stuart buys an MP3 player from a local electrical store. He later finds out that it does not work, because a small but crucial component is missing.

→ Chris buys an MP3 player from a local electrical store. He later tries to connect it to his computer but the wiring is faulty; he receives a small electric shock.

→ Theresa receives an MP3 player for her birthday. She later finds out that it does not work, because a small but crucial component is missing.

→ Alison buys a car for her mother. Two weeks later, one of the tyres explodes while she is driving, causing the car to swerve into her garden wall, which will cost £500 to rebuild. The car costs £1,000 to repair.

→ Rosie buys a car for her mother. After a year, the two front tyres need replacing. Two weeks later, one of these tyres explodes while she is driving, causing the car to swerve into her garden wall, which will cost £500 to rebuild. The car costs £1,000 to repair.

→ Zoe takes a drug to stop her head aching, but later finds out that she has a stomach ulcer caused by an unusual reaction to the drug.

At first sight, it might seem odd that we are considering product liability in a book on tort law, when most of us are more accustomed on a day-to-day basis to dealing with 'products' and the consequences of their defects via contract law. However, ***Donoghue v Stevenson*** [1932], the foundational case for all modern claims in negligence, *is* itself a case about a defective product (contaminated ginger beer) that harmed the end user (gastroenteritis).

Liability for defective products can, therefore, also be found in negligence, though the picture is, as we shall see, more complicated than might be expected. Much depends on what type of defect is being claimed for. It is more appropriate to sue in contract for some harms caused by defects in products and in negligence for others. In basic terms, this depends on whether the claimant takes their case against the retailer (contract) or the manufacturer (negligence) of the item. Often, if it is possible, a claim in contract might be recommended, as 'strict liability' (that is, liability without fault) is imposed by statute on retailers in respect of the quality of the goods that they sell. When claiming in negligence against a manufacturer, the usual hurdles of duty, breach and causation must be surmounted.

Because an understanding of liability for defective products in contract is an important part of the overall picture regarding defective products in law, this chapter will start by briefly looking, without too much complex detail, at the liabilities that may arise in contract. We will then look at manufacturers' liability in negligence and the problems claimants may encounter when trying to sue. This will lead us to a later legal development relating to product liability—the Consumer Protection Act 1987—which was passed to ensure better protection of consumers from defective goods by making *producers* strictly liable for harms caused by the products they market.

13.2 **Defective products—claims in contract**

When there is a defect in a bought product, the purchaser has the unequivocal right to take a claim for breach of contract against the retailer. Stuart, in the example above, would be able to claim for his broken MP3 player in this way. Contractual remedies are generally sought in relation to goods that are simply of poor quality (that is, 'defective'). This can include the cost of replacing or repairing the goods, although they are also available, subject to the restrictions of the doctrine of privity of contract,[1] where the defect in the goods causes consequential loss, such as personal injury (as in the scenario with Chris) or property damage.

The rights held by purchasers are what are commonly referred to as your 'statutory rights'. Primarily, these come from the Sale of Goods Act (SGA) 1979 and related legislation and regulations. Section 14 SGA implies terms regulating the quality and fitness of goods into all contracts of sale[2] as follows:

Sale of Goods Act 1979

14(2) Where the seller sells goods in the course of a business, there is an implied term that the goods supplied under the contract are of satisfactory quality.

14(2A) For the purposes of this Act, goods are of satisfactory quality if they meet the standard that a reasonable person would regard as satisfactory, taking account of any description of the goods, the price (if relevant) and all the other relevant circumstances.

14(2B) For the purposes of this Act, the quality of goods includes their state and condition and the following (among others) are in appropriate cases aspects of the quality of goods—

(a) fitness for all the purposes for which goods of the kind in question are commonly supplied,

(b) appearance and finish,

(c) freedom from minor defects,

(d) safety, and

(e) durability.

So, it can be seen that a breach of contract will occur if goods are not 'of satisfactory quality' according to the definitions in section 14. The missing component and faulty wiring mean that Stuart and Chris' MP3 players are clearly not of satisfactory quality. Some of the things taken into account when determining whether there has been a breach of contract are the safety of the item, its freedom from minor defects and its

---

1. The privity doctrine is explained further at p 345. In relation to the scenarios outlined above, it would prevent Theresa claiming against the retailer, even though she suffered the same harm as Stuart (who will be able to claim), as she did not purchase the MP3 player herself.
2. Where the seller sells goods in the course of a business. This excludes private sales, where the risk to the purchaser is defined by the maxim *caveat emptor*—'let the buyer beware'.

'fitness for purpose'. This is an idea mirroring section 14(3), which implies a further term into sale contracts (where the seller sells in the course of a business) that goods should be 'fit for the purpose'[3] they were supplied for, if this purpose has been made known (expressly or by implication) to the seller. Further implied terms from the SGA relate to sale by sample or description (it is an implied term that goods will correspond with the sample (s 15) or the description (s 13) of them).

We can see, therefore, that consumers are protected to a considerable extent if the goods they purchase are not of satisfactory quality. Furthermore, these 'statutory rights' cannot be limited or excluded in consumer contracts (see the Unfair Contract Terms Act 1977, s 6(2)). What this means in practice is that if goods are sold in the course of a business, and they turn out to be unsatisfactory in the sense that they are defective in some way, the customer has the unqualified right to a remedy. What this remedy consists of *may* depend on who the customer is: that is, whether they are a consumer or not. Section 14(6) SGA tells us that the implied terms from section 14(2) and (3) are 'conditions'. In contract law, what this means is that the non-breaching party (the customer) has the right to bring the contract to an end, or 'terminate' it. In the sense of sale of goods, this means the customer has a choice:

- they can keep the goods in question but demand that they be fixed;
- they can give the goods back and receive their money back; or
- they can give the goods back and receive alternative goods.

This can otherwise be expressed by saying that the customer has the right to the 'three Rs': Repair; Refund; or Replacement.

Non-consumers[4] are treated differently. Section 15A SGA modifies the remedies available for breach of these conditions in non-consumer cases as follows:

Sale of Goods Act 1979

15A(1) Where in the case of a contract of sale—

(a) the buyer would, apart form this subsection, have the right to reject goods by reason of a breach on the part of the seller of a term implied by section 13, 14 or 15 above, but

(b) the breach is so slight that it would be unreasonable for him to reject them, then, if the buyer does not deal as consumer, the breach is not to be treated as a breach of condition but may be treated as a breach of warranty.

Consumers are therefore given greater legal protection in contracts than non-consumers, who, if a breach is only 'slight', or has minor consequences, will not be able

---

3. 'Fit' here means the goods should be both appropriate for the purpose made known and able to do what was expected of them.

4. For our purposes, a non-consumer would be someone purchasing the goods in the course of a business, or for purposes related to their business, as opposed to someone doing so for private use and/or consumption. This definition is refined by *Stevenson* v *Rogers* [1999] where the Court of Appeal found that a fisherman who sold his boat was selling it in the course of a business, on the basis that it is not the nature of the goods that defines it, but the transaction.

to access the same remedies to which a consumer would be entitled. By implication, however slight the breach in a consumer contract, the consumer retains the right to any of the remedies outlined above.

 Pause for reflection

In the latter half of the twentieth century, there was a visible increase in consumer protection through various contract law statutes, including the modified provisions within the SGA (and the corresponding Supply of Goods and Services Act 1982) as well as the Unfair Contract Terms Act 1977 and, at the highest point of consumer protectionism, the Unfair Terms in Consumer Contracts Regulations 1999. John Adams and Roger Brownsword have indicated that the *courts* have also moved towards a more 'consumer-welfarist' approach.[5] Do you think it is fair that consumers should enjoy better rights under the law of sale of goods than non-consumers? Why? Take into account the fact that consumers are generally in a weaker bargaining position than non-consumers and may be more likely to incur greater harm (personal or financial) by defective products. But should these rules apply only when a 'real' harm has been suffered? The statutory provisions apply to any goods deemed not to be of satisfactory quality (including those with 'minor defects') so we are not talking simply about *harmful* goods here; in fact, the only harm that may be incurred as a result of purchasing goods with a minor defect is to the consumer's pocket.

The only time a consumer loses the right to reject the goods is when it can be deemed that the goods have been 'accepted'. According to section 35 SGA, this occurs either when the buyer intimates this to the seller, or when, after delivery, the buyer 'does any act in relation to [the goods] which is inconsistent with the ownership of the seller'. So, for example, if a consumer buys a car, then after it is delivered fits a new sound system into it and then drives it to Scotland and back, it is likely that this would be deemed inconsistent with the seller retaining 'ownership' of the car. Put another way, the buyer is clearly intimating that they own the car because of what they are doing with it.

Section 35 also states that where goods have not previously been examined by the buyer, the law will not deem him to have accepted the goods until there has been a 'reasonable opportunity of examining them' for the purpose of determining whether they are of satisfactory quality. Encompassed in this is the idea that goods will be deemed to have been accepted after lapse of a 'reasonable time' if the buyer is silent. Clearly, what is 'reasonable' on both these counts will depend on the nature of the goods (that is, delivery of the weekly grocery shopping will take less time to inspect than delivery of more complex items). While all this may already seem eminently protective of all buyers, particularly consumers, still more protection for consumers is added by the SGA. Indeed, Part 5A of the Act[6] is entitled 'Additional rights of the buyer in consumer cases'. This Part contains, within sections 48A–F, further rights in relation to the acceptance or rejection of goods by consumers, the remedies

---

5. See John N Adams and Roger Brownsword *Understanding Contract Law* (5th edn, Sweet & Maxwell, 2007), especially Ch 8.

6. The whole of Part 5A is a later insertion by the Sale and Supply of Goods to Consumers Regulations 2002, SI 2002/3045.

that they are entitled to and, not least, the fact (from s 48A(3)) that the consumer retains the right to their remedies for breach of the statutory rights outlined above for six months after the date of delivery of the goods. What this means is that if a fault or defect appears in an item bought by a consumer *any time within six months from delivery*, the consumer can terminate the contract and avail themselves of the appropriate remedy.

13.2.1 **The limits of contractual protection**

All this considered (and the above discussion was merely scratching the surface),[7] it appears that consumers are very well protected by contract law. Why, then, is an additional layer of protection present in tort? One answer is that, in terms of product liability more generally, contract law has some serious limitations. Clearly, to take advantage of contract law, there needs to be a contract in the first place, containing terms stipulating that the goods sold should be non-defective. As we have seen, this is unproblematic when the seller operates in the course of a business, but will not be in private sales (where neither party deals in the course of business) unless an express term is created. That said, as those with any prior knowledge of contract law will know, there may be the potential for a claim in misrepresentation in a private sale depending on what was and was not said by the seller before entering the contract. Furthermore, in non-consumer contracts at least, it is possible for the retailer to exclude or otherwise restrict their liability for any harm caused by a defect in a product they have sold by using a term of the contract to do so. Such exclusions or limitations have, however, been ruled out in consumer contracts.[8]

In addition, some people may not want to make claims against a retailer if the defective or inferior quality of the product in question was clearly not the retailer's *fault*. While many would have no qualms about returning sub-standard goods to many large retail chains or High Street stores—and while these retailers would be obliged to provide a remedy unless it could be deemed that the goods had been 'accepted'— what about smaller retailers/sellers? Evidently, the retailer in question would also have bought the goods from someone and so would also have a contract either with the manufacturer or, if not, a chain of contracts will exist eventually leading back to the manufacturer, however this seems a relatively inefficient way of making manufacturers ultimately liable for defects in the products that they produce.

Furthermore, contract law is greatly limited by the fact that it may not be a party to the contract who was harmed by a defect in the goods. If so, the party who suffered the harm has no claim (nor does the purchaser as they had suffered no loss).[9] This is, in very basic terms, the essence of the doctrine of privity of contract, which operated as a substantial bar to product-related claims for many years. According to the doctrine, only a party to a contract can sue or be sued under it—so if a retailer sells a defective product to someone that causes harm to someone else, the person harmed

---

7. For a more detailed account, see Colin Scott and Julia Black *Cranston's Consumers and the Law* (3rd edn, Butterworths, 2000).

8. By the Unfair Contract Terms Act (UCTA) 1977, s 6(2) and also, it would seem, by reg 5(1) of and Schedule 2 to the Unfair Terms in Consumer Contracts Regulations (UTCCR) 1999, SI 1999/2083.

9. This was the position of the claimant in **Donoghue v Stevenson** [1932].

has no way of suing the retailer for breach of contract. To some extent, the harshness of this doctrine has been ameliorated by developments in case law and, more recently, by legislation. The Contracts (Rights of Third Parties) Act 1999 makes it possible for a third party to sue under a contract in some circumstances, namely if 'the contract expressly provides that he may' (s 1(1)(a)) or if 'the term purports to confer a benefit on him' (s 1(1)(b)). To take advantage of either of these provisions, the party concerned (the third party) must be either 'expressly identified in the contract by name, as a member of a class or as answering to a particular description' (s 1(3)). Therefore, if I entered a contract stipulating that the product I was buying was for 'my mother', technically she will have been expressly identified and could therefore sue. Or, if I bought items for 'my children' they would be identified as members of a particular class (or fitting a particular description).

 Counterpoint

How helpful does the Contract (Rights of Third Parties) Act 1999 sound to people who suffer injury or harm from a defective product that they did not buy? While some people may be able to avail themselves of these provisions, how often when you buy something, even if for someone else, do you include a term in the contract that identifies that person or expressly states that he or she can enforce the contract? This generally does not happen in a retail context or, even where it does, there is often no proof that a person bought something for someone else (this factor may be contributing to the rise of the 'gift receipt' that more and more retailers appear to be offering).

Generally, it would seem that contracts of a larger scale than mere consumer retail transactions were in mind when these provisions were drafted—perhaps because by then other mechanisms existed to protect consumers and others against manufacturing defects, as we shall see in the next sections.

Overall, then, it seems that contract law protects some people better than others. Those *not* party to the contract under which a defective product was sold are left with only limited protection. The limitations of contractual claims in relation to defective products are illustrated in Table 13.1.

Table 13.1 Disadvantages to claims in contract

Problem	Solution?
There must be an express or implied term that the product should not be defective in order to be able to claim	In all contracts of sale where a seller sells goods in the course of a business, an implied term will exist regarding the 'satisfactory quality' of the goods, as well as implied terms about sale by sample or description where relevant (SGA, ss 13, 14, 15). This does not, however, cover private sales

Table 13.1 *Continued*

Problem	Solution?
A seller can sometimes exclude or limit their liability for breach	Such exclusions or limitations of liability in relation to products are subject to the UCTA and the UTCCR—exclusions and limitations are not allowed in consumer contracts (UCTA, s 6) and/or would be deemed 'unfair' (and so ineffective) under UTCCR, reg 5
Although a chain of contracts may go all the way back to the manufacturer, claims for breach of contract can only be made against the retailer	Claims in negligence or under the Consumer Protection Act 1987 may be made against the manufacturer of defective products (see below) where a recognised harm has occurred
Privity of contract means that only the person who entered the contract (i.e. the party who actually bought the product from the party who sold it) can sue	The doctrine of privity used to be fairly absolute (though see *Shanklin Pier* v *Detel Products Ltd* [1951]) but its harshness was lessened to a certain extent by the enactment of the Contracts (Rights of Third Parties) Act 1999, as well as developments in the law of negligence which allowed claims to be taken against manufacturers (see below) and the enactment of the Consumer Protection Act 1987 (see p 354)

13.3 **Defective products—claims in negligence**

As mentioned above, at its most narrow interpretation, *Donoghue* was a case about a defective product. Thus, it not only laid down the foundations of the tort of negligence as a whole but also for claims in negligence to be taken directly against the manufacturers of defective products.[10]

Donoghue is a landmark case. Before *Donoghue*, a person injured (either personally or through damage to their property) by defective goods had limited grounds for recovery. If they had a contract with the retailer of the goods then they may have had a claim for breach of contract and (subject to the various rules governing this type of claim) compensation could be awarded for both the cost of replacing the product itself *and* of putting right any damage to person or property caused by the product. However, in the tort of negligence, though someone in the position of Mrs Donoghue could be compensated for their illness and distress, the cost of the *product itself* would have been regarded as a pure economic loss and, as such, would not be recoverable.[11] The claimant would have received only compensation (in contract rather than tort law) covering the cost of the ginger beer itself if she had paid for it. If, as was the case in *Donoghue*

10. The facts of *Donoghue* are set out on p 31.
11. Chapter 7.

itself, she had no contract with the seller, she would be limited to a claim in negligence against the manufacturer.

Prior to 1932, a manufacturer could be liable only in relation to products if the product itself was classed as 'dangerous' or was manufactured to be dangerous, in which case a warning had to be given. However, the distinction between 'dangerous' and 'not-dangerous' was not always helpful. In *Donoghue*, the House of Lords overturned the distinction and also discarded what it termed the 'privity of contract fallacy', holding that there should be no reason why the same facts should not give one person a right in contract and another person a simultaneous right to sue in negligence. The court drew no distinction between the type or nature of the product—but it seems logical that this would be a factor to take into account when assessing the *standard* of care to which the manufacturer should be held and whether that has been breached. That is, it seems common sense to say that manufacturers of inherently dangerous products ought to be even more careful.

 Pause for reflection

The law lords in *Donoghue* were split 3:2 in favour of the claimant. Two of them dissented, mainly because of concerns about opening the 'floodgates' to claims (a similar argument is often seen in negligence cases today, where the court is being asked to expand the types of situations or relationships in which negligence might be claimed). Within the majority opinions, Lord MacMillan took a more pragmatic approach to the finding of liability than Lord Atkin's broad 'neighbour' principle— favouring a more cautious case-by-case approach (similar to that used now in novel types of claim following *Caparo* v *Dickman* [1990]).

Interestingly, three years prior to *Donoghue* a very similar case on the facts had been dismissed. In *Mullen* v *AG Barr* [1929] it was alleged that a bottle of ginger beer contained a decomposing mouse but, as there was no authority or precedent for the type of claim being made (ginger beer not being 'dangerous' in and of itself), the case failed. The same lawyers represented Mrs Donoghue—and were clearly very persistent—so it is them we need to thank for the law as it stands today!

Generally, the wide scope of the tort of negligence (and negligence in relation to product liability) is these days taken for granted and the impact and importance of the *Donoghue* decision itself is not really seen amongst all the later developments, limitations and rules. Consider how negligence might look if the claimant in *Donoghue* v *Stevenson* had failed or if Lord MacMillan's approach had been favoured over Lord Atkin's.

13.3.1 The scope of liability under *Donoghue*

As *Donoghue* is a negligence case, liability has to be assessed by looking at the various factors—duty, breach and causation—that a claimant has to establish when making any claim in the tort of negligence. As these have all been discussed in far greater detail in part one of the book, we will concentrate here on the more pertinent issues regarding product liability.

13.3.1.1 Duty of care

The duty owed is the ordinary common law duty of care—based on the presumed intention to supply the goods to the ultimate consumer in the same state they left the production line. The duty extends beyond the manufacturer/consumer relationship to include, for example, packers, machine operators, and distributors. Similarly, the 'ultimate consumer' not only covers the 'end-purchaser' of the product concerned, but includes also the ultimate user (as in *Donoghue*) and any person coming into contact with the product. In *Stennett* v *Hancock & Peters* [1939], for example, the manufacturer's duty of care extended to a pedestrian who was hit by a wheel of a lorry when it fell off.

The duty may also extend *beyond* the product itself to include, for example, containers, packaging or instructions (*Watson* v *Buckley, Osborne, Garrett & Co Ltd* [1940]). In *Donoghue*, Lord Atkin defined the type of products that the duty covers as 'articles of common household use, where everyone, including the manufacturer, knows the articles will be used by persons other than the ultimate purchaser' (at 46). Clearly, however, given the example of *Stennett*, above, the definition of 'products' must extend beyond 'household items' and could, logically, include *any* product where the definition of 'consumer' is taken in its broadest sense.

Despite the range of relationships covered and a broad understanding of what a product is, it should be noted that the principles *preventing* a duty of care from arising in the wider law of negligence also apply here. Damage to (or a defect in) the product itself, for which the only claim is the cost of replacement, is regarded as a pure economic loss, for which no duty can arise (**Murphy v Brentwood District Council** [1990]).[12] A claimant can therefore recover damages for anything the defective product causes injury *to*, but not for any injury to the product itself. The remedy in tort would seem, in this respect, to be less useful than that in contract.

 Pause for reflection

Is there a good reason for regarding the cost of replacing the item itself as pure economic loss, thereby preventing a remedy? Does it seem fair that if you bought the item for yourself, you would be able to claim this cost against the retailer (in contract), but if you were given the product as a gift, you could not obtain a replacement? While it might be thought that the person who bought the present could always bring a claim on your behalf (as would be the position of Alison in the examples at the beginning of this chapter), in reality they cannot as they will have not suffered any harm.

Before we leave 'duty' some mention should be made of the 'complex structure' theory.[13] Under this theory, component parts of a product are (sometimes) seen as a separate product entirely.[14] Therefore, if the component part is the defective 'product',

---

12. Chapter 7.

13. This theory is also discussed in Chapter 7 in relation to **Murphy v Brentwood DC** [1990] (p 180).

14. Although this has now been ruled out for buildings in the sense that foundations cannot be regarded as a separate component of a building.

and it causes damage to the rest of the product or another part of it, this can be classed as consequential damage and not pure economic loss (though the cost of the defective component itself would be pure economic loss). Consider how this relates to Alison and Rosie's situations outlined above. If the tyre exploded soon after the car had been purchased, then it is likely that the courts would view this as a defective *car* and therefore Alison's mother would have no claim (she did not buy the car herself so cannot claim against the retailer) for the cost of fixing the car, although she would be able to claim for the cost of rebuilding her wall. However, if the *replacement* tyre exploded, this could be considered to be one component of a 'complex structure' (the car) and subsequently any damage to the car, as well as the wall, would be consequential loss. All that Rosie's mother would be unable to claim would be the cost of replacing the tyre.

 Pause for reflection

Do you think that a manufacturer's duty should extend to taking steps to recall any defective products that have already gone into circulation?

In the American case of *Grimshaw* v *Ford Motor Co* [1981], Ford was alleged to have discovered a defect in the Ford Pinto which sometimes caused the cars to explode if they were hit by another car from behind. However, the company calculated that it would be cheaper to pay compensation to anyone injured in such an explosion than it would be to recall all the cars in circulation and repair the defect. If there had been a duty to recall the cars once the defect was known then Ford would have been in breach for not doing so. At trial, Ford was ordered to pay punitive damages in excess of $125 million, though this was reduced to $3.5 million on appeal (plus compensatory damages of just under $3 million).[15] This case is illustrative of many of the problems associated with using private law remedies in relation to product liability. The fact that you can be sued is meant to have a deterrent effect, changing the behaviour of producers. Yet, it seems, producers (particularly large-scale producers) are more likely to weigh up the risks and benefits to their profits and their shareholders than they are to consider 'wasting' time and money by rectifying defects in their products (even where these are dangerous enough to pose a risk to life, as in the *Ford* case). In this sense, it seems that stronger *public law* regulation might be a better deterrent for producers.

13.3.1.2 Breach and causation

Breach of duty of care was considered in Chapter 8. The question here is: Has the defendant manufacturer exercised reasonable care when making the product? This is to be assessed on a case-by-case basis.

Breach does not normally create any problems for the courts as it can often be inferred from the presence of the defect. That is, it is often assumed that any defect can only exist because there was some negligence during the manufacturing process—how else could a snail come to be in a sealed bottle of ginger beer, for example? The burden is placed on the manufacturer to rebut the presumption of carelessness with evidence. This principle can clearly be seen in operation in **Grant v Australian Knitting Mills Ltd [1936]**.

---

15. For explanation of different types of damages, see Chapter 19.

> ### *Grant v Australian Knitting Mills Ltd* [1936] PC
>
> Mr Grant purchased some woollen underpants and, after wearing them, suffered from a painful skin condition. This was caused by a reaction to sulphites present in the wool, left over as part of the manufacturing process. The claimant could not prove negligence on the part of the manufacturer and the manufacturer claimed that there had been no carelessness during the manufacturing process, and that they had taken reasonable care to ensure that chemicals used in the process did not remain in the wool.
>
> The court found that there could be no other explanation for the sulphites in the wool than that one of the employees had, at some point during the manufacture of the underpants, been careless, and the manufacturers were therefore held liable.

The principle to be taken from this case is that defects in a product that are present when the product reaches the end user can be inferred to have been caused by the manufacturer's carelessness, unless the manufacturer did not intend the product to reach the end user in the same condition it left the factory. So, following **Grant**, it should be easy to establish a breach of duty, as it appears that courts will often be willing to infer carelessness unless there is evidence to the contrary. This inference is not always made, however. In *Evans* v *Triplex Glass Co Ltd* [1936], for example, it was held that a claim against the manufacturer of windscreen safety glass could not succeed on the basis that the court believed that the fault was more likely to lie with the fitters of the glass than its manufacturer.

Once breach is established, it has to be decided whether the breach actually caused the harm complained of. The tests for causation in fact and in law are the same in product liability as for any other area of negligence.[16] In a sense, however, the duty requirement that the item must not have been subject to intermediate examination between leaving the manufacturer and reaching the end user can also be viewed as a breach/causation question. To find the defendant liable, a court must satisfy itself that they were responsible for the defect and that it was not due to the fault of someone else further down the chain of supply. If someone else—for example a distribution company who inspected the goods before they were supplied to retailers—could be said to be responsible for the defect, this will 'break the chain' of causation back to the manufacturer.

In **Grant**, the defendants argued that the goods may have been tampered with after leaving the factory and the fact that this might have happened (there was no real way of proving whether it had) should enable the manufacturer to escape liability. They argued that because the garments had been wrapped in paper packets and could be sold separately, there was a possibility that they had been interfered with. The court dismissed this argument, finding that interference was a question of fact (that is, evidence must be shown to prove that there was actually interference, otherwise the presumption will be that there was none). However, the decision in *Evans* v *Triplex Glass Co Ltd* [1936] (decided in the same year) tells us that if there is a 'reasonable possibility' or a probability of interference with the product, this will be enough to exonerate the manufacturer from liability.

16. Chapter 9.

The question of inspection may be a difficult one, especially if a party in the supply chain had the *opportunity* to inspect the goods but did not take it. There is no general obligation on intermediate parties (or, indeed, the end consumer) to exhaustively examine goods that pass through their control and so a manufacturer will remain liable unless they have a genuine or specific reason to believe that the goods will be inspected by another party before they leave the supply chain. This, of course, prompts another question: When *can* a manufacturer reasonably expect another party to examine the goods? While in *Andrews* v *Hopkinson* [1957] a second-hand car salesman had the opportunity to check cars and was held liable for failing to do so for any obvious faults (although a full and exhaustive inspection was not required), in *Hurley* v *Dyke* [1979] a seller of a defective second-hand car avoided liability as he had informed the buyer that it was 'as seen and with all its faults' (the warning moved the duty onto the buyer to inspect the car for himself).

13.3.2 The limits of negligence liability

So far we have considered the position under ***Donoghue*** in relation to manufacturing defects. However, a product can be also defective because of the way it was *designed*. It is in these circumstances that we begin to see the limits of a claim in negligence. This is problematic. Design defects by their very nature are likely to affect greater numbers of end-users—possibly even every consumer of a product—and are also likely to be difficult to discover by examination of the product either before it leaves the supply chain or by the ultimate consumer. In short, design defects are more serious and increase the possibility of harm to the end-users of a product.

However, it is also more difficult for a person to bring a negligence claim in relation to a design defect. While duty is relatively easy to establish, it will be difficult to show that there was carelessness in designing a product, that is, that the designers fell below—or breached—the standard of care expected of them. In relation to causation, the claimant must show two things: first, that the design defect *can* cause harm and, secondly, that the design defect *was* the actual or material cause of the specific harm being claimed for. This is a high threshold. For example, a claimant may be able to show that a particular drug, because of a design flaw, can cause cancer. However, it will be very difficult for them to prove, on the balance of probabilities, that taking the drug cased *their particular cancer*, particularly as other factors such as environment, genetics and lifestyle may also all be relevant.[17]

The particular difficulties associated with design defects became very apparent in the 1960s with the Thalidomide tragedy.

The Thalidomide tragedy

Thalidomide is a drug that was initially sold from the mid-1950s to 1961 in many countries worldwide and under many different product names. It was primarily prescribed →

17. So Zoe, in the scenarios above, may have difficulties establishing that the drug was the cause of her stomach ulcer.

→

to pregnant women, to help combat morning sickness and in order to help them sleep. However, it later transpired that Thalidomide is a potent teratogen, which means that it can cause severe birth defects if it is taken during pregnancy. The drug had been inadequately tested before being put on the market and approximately 10,000 children were born with birth defects after their mothers took it while pregnant. These defects include phocomelia, which is characterised by the shortness of the long bones in the arms or legs and therefore often severely shortened limbs. In 1962, in reaction to the tragedy, the US Congress enacted laws requiring tests for safety during pregnancy before any drug can receive approval for sale in America and numerous other countries enacted similar legislation. Thalidomide was not prescribed or sold for decades. However, perhaps surprisingly, it was never withdrawn completely from the medical marketplace and is used today to treat a number of conditions, including leprosy and several types of cancer.

The Thalidomide tragedy is a perfect example of a design defect. Nothing in the *manufacturing* process had gone wrong, causing a particular batch of the drug to produce negative side effects in those for whom it had been prescribed. Instead, part of the *design* process had been faulty. The parents of some of the children affected by Thalidomide brought legal actions in negligence against the various producers of the drug. The legal outcomes of their claims are unknown as they were settled before coming to court, however it is clear that although the manufacturers owed those affected a duty of care as the ultimate consumers, because the consequences of the drug were not foreseeable by a reasonable manufacturer at the time it was circulated, it would have been very difficult for them to show that the manufacturer had breached this duty by failing to take reasonable care in the design process. It would have also been difficult to establish causation—the birth defect could have been caused by a number of different things.[18]

What the Thalidomide tragedy did highlight was the need for change. While the common law was in a fairly satisfactory position in relation to manufacturing defects, where courts were willing to infer negligence (**Grant**) and generally had a fairly 'flexible' approach to liability, the Thalidomide cases showed what problems claimants might face if trying to claim for harms caused by a *design* defect. This led to demands for legal reform and, in particular (perhaps because it was 'fashionable' at the time), a call for strict liability to be placed on manufacturers of defective products.

Strict liability is liability without fault. What it would mean for manufacturers to be strictly liable for defective products is that even if they did nothing wrong in the manufacturing or design process (that is, there was nothing that could technically be called a 'breach'), they would have to compensate someone who suffered harm caused by a defect in their product. The main reasons suggested for this were:

• First, the manufacturer created the product and therefore created the hazard or harm. Since this was done in the pursuit of profit, it would be reasonable for them to accept liability for any harms actually caused by the product.

---

18. For a discussion of the difficulties posed by multiple potential causes, see pp 226–237.

- Secondly, the manufacturer would be in the best position to insure against the risks of any such hazards or harms (and the price of such insurance can be reflected in the product price and therefore distributed amongst all end-users of a product).

- Thirdly, imposing strict liability on manufacturers would provide them with an incentive to take all possible safety precautions during the design and manufacturing processes.

In light of increasing pressure worldwide in favour of strict liability, the European Community issued a Directive in 1985[19] requiring member states to change and harmonise their laws on product liability. In the UK, this took the form of Part 1 of the Consumer Protection Act 1987.[20]

13.4 Defective products—claims under Part 1 of the Consumer Protection Act 1987

Section 1(1) of the Consumer Protection Act (CPA) 1987 stipulates that:

> This Part shall have effect for the purpose of making such provision as is necessary in order to comply with the product liability Directive and shall be construed accordingly.

Thus, it may be that it is the terms of the Directive itself that should be followed, rather than the terms of the Act, as the CPA must be construed in line with the original meaning intended by the Directive—a point to which we shall later return.

The CPA makes the manufacturer of a product (and others dealing with it along the supply chain) liable *without proof of fault* (strictly liable) for personal injury and some property damage caused wholly or in part by a defect in the product concerned. This is a step forward from, and a contrast to, the tort of negligence, where fault must be proved. In so doing, strict liability as (supposedly) provided by the CPA should provide an easier route to redress.

Manufacturers are granted a number of specific defences under the CPA. These defences are problematic. The imposition of strict liability is considerably less strict if the defendant is able to defend a claim. One of the defences in particular has caused considerable controversy, as we shall see later in this section.

Essentially, establishing liability under the CPA requires a series of questions to be asked. The Act defines concepts such as 'product' and 'defect' and it is within these confines that claims must proceed.

13.4.1 Bringing a claim

Unfortunately, the CPA does not clearly set out who can sue and who can be sued.[21] Reading between the lines, it appears that anyone who suffers damage covered by the

---

19. Directive 85/374.
20. Brought into force 1 March 1988.
21. You may find it helpful to read this section alongside the annotated version of the CPA (pp 368–371) or the CPA 'at a glance' table on p 372.

Act as a result of a defective product can bring a claim (ss 2(1) and 5(1)). The definitions in section 1(2) and a further outlining of who potential defendants might be in section 2(2)(a)–(c) suggest that manufacturers and producers of goods can be sued, as well as 'own-branders' (companies who put their name to a product made for them by someone else) and importers into the European Union. Similarly, *suppliers* of goods can be sued if the conditions in section 2(3) are met. The purpose of the Act is to increase the protection of consumers (in the spirit intended by those advocating strict liability for defective products) by ensuring that *someone* within the European Union can be found liable in relation to defective products. This is underlined in section 2(5) which states that if more than one of the potential defendants can be liable for the same damage then they will be jointly liable.

To make a claim, the claimant needs to have suffered the right 'kind' of damage. This is defined in section 5 as death or personal injury, or property damage with a value of more than £275 (s 5(4)). Thus, small (in a monetary sense) claims for property damage are excluded (perhaps to limit the number and ensure the 'seriousness' of claims) although there is no upper limit to the total amount of damages that may be claimed (despite an option to limit this when implementing the Directive). Pure economic loss is also specifically excluded by section 5(2), which means that, as in the tort of negligence, the cost of *replacing* a defective product is not recoverable.

 Pause for reflection

Does a figure of £275 as the minimum claimable limit for property damage seem (a) quite arbitrary and (b) relatively low? Consider what you can buy for £275 these days and what could have been bought for that sum in 1987 when the CPA was passed. Should this figure be increased?

'Products' are defined in section 1(2) and include 'any goods or electricity and…a product which is comprised in another product, whether by virtue of being a component part or raw material or otherwise'. 'Goods' are further defined (s 45) to include 'substances, growing crops and things comprised in land by virtue of being attached to it, and any ship, aircraft or vehicle'. This definition is quite broad and possibly encompasses things that, as a consumer, one might not ordinarily have considered.[22]

The key aspect of the CPA is its coverage of 'defective' products—so the definition of defect is one that needs detailed analysis. It is here that most of the case law under the CPA can be found: the courts have found themselves tasked, on occasion, with ruling on whether or not a certain product is 'defective' for the purposes of the Act.

---

22. The original definition did not include agricultural produce or game, unless this had been subjected to an industrial process (e.g. in a meat-packing factory). EU member states were free to include or exclude this produce under the 1985 Directive. However, a further EU Directive made inclusion compulsory after the BSE crisis—agricultural produce has therefore been included within the definition of 'product' under the CPA since 2000.

13.4.2 **What is a 'defect'?**

Defects in products for the purposes of the CPA are defined in section 3. As a defendant is liable for any damage (of the right kind) caused wholly or in part by a 'defective product', this definition has become a key part of the Act. Section 3 defines a defect as follows:

> there is a defect in a product for the purposes of this Part if the safety of the product is not such as persons generally are entitled to expect . . .

Therefore, it seems that the standard (regarding what is and what is not defective) is set by 'persons generally'—not, for example, by manufacturers, consumers or any other specific group or individual. But the way the definition is phrased does mean that the perspectives of those groups or individuals has to be taken into account when considering what 'persons generally' might think. This seems, therefore, like a rather weak and circular definition. Indeed, *Lunney & Oliphant* suggest that the concept of 'defectiveness' is an unclear one, especially where this is governed by ideas of social acceptability (p 604).

 Counterpoint

If the CPA really is about **consumer protection**, it seems odd that the expectations of manufacturers and others with vested interests should be taken into account when deciding whether a product is 'defective'. Manufacturers will base their considerations on a cost/benefit analysis—for example, to them, a product will be 'defective' only if the magnitude of the danger it poses and the cost of preventing any harm occurring outweighs the product's utility—this risk/utility analysis is more familiar to us from the tort of negligence and in particular an assessment of the standard of care and whether a defendant has fallen below it. This, therefore, implies *fault*—and the CPA is meant to bring no-fault (strict) liability.

On the other hand, it is questionable whether strict liability is desirable in this area at all. Manufacturers have to absorb the costs and risks of development in other ways and, unless clearly negligent in the way they make a path to market (for example if a pharmaceutical company did not undertake any testing to determine whether a drug it was producing had any harmful side effects), it can seem unreasonable that they also have to pay for harms suffered by people using their products. Consumers generally welcome choice, innovation and competition (more products on the market; prices are kept down by competition; etc), so is imposing strict liability on producers allowing consumers the best of both worlds? Perhaps it is arguable that consumers should take more responsibility for themselves when it comes to injuries suffered in this context (see **Abouzaid v Mothercare (UK) Ltd** [2000] and *Pollard* v *Tesco Stores Ltd* [2006] as just two examples of cases where it might well be argued that had more care been taken by the consumer, the risk would not have materialised).

The CPA's definition of 'defect' allows products into the market that are potentially dangerous—but not defective. As the concept of a defect is linked to 'safety' and about what it is reasonable to expect this means that certain items that are inherently dangerous cannot be classed as defective. For example, a cut throat razor or a serrated bread knife will not be 'defective' products, as people are 'generally entitled to expect' that razors and knives will be sharp.

Pause for reflection

Where does this leave products such as cigarettes and alcohol? Are these as safe as 'persons generally are entitled to expect'? If so, what makes them this 'safe'? It could be argued that the damaging effects of cigarettes and alcohol are well publicised. For example, the potential consequences of smoking are already clearly pointed out on the packaging, and a recent government campaign has highlighted that people who consume alcohol should take into account how many 'units' of alcohol they consume, with products now being labelled to allow consumers to find this information easily. It is very unlikely that policy-makers would think it wise or practical to take tobacco and alcohol out of circulation (consider the 'Prohibition' experiment in the United States during the 1920s and 30s, which drove the supply of alcohol underground and created a criminal sub-culture). There are cultural issues with regulating an existing product which has been found to be dangerous long after release, as opposed to regulating the safety of a new product coming onto the market. So, while it might be said that tobacco and alcohol are not as 'safe' as other products, public expectations in relation to these substances clearly differ greatly from those in relation to others.

The question when deciding whether a product is defective for the purposes of the CPA is: What *are* 'persons generally entitled to expect'? This is an objective standard and can be difficult to assess, although section 3(2)(a)–(c) sets out guidelines as to what factors may be taken into account when considering the safety/defectiveness of a particular product, including:

- the manner in which, and purposes for which, the product has been marketed;
- the 'get-up' (packaging);
- use of marks (for example the 'Kite Mark');
- instructions or warnings accompanying the product when sold;
- what might reasonably be expected to be done with the product; and
- the time at which the product was supplied.

Counterpoint

The issue of defectiveness or non-defectiveness seems to be one of a common sense interpretation of the safety of a product, according to how and why it is marketed, how it is packaged, what people (consumers) are meant to do with it (and what they are not) and, importantly, any warnings accompanying the product when it is sold. From this it can be assumed that an adequate warning would be enough to make an otherwise defective (that

→

is, unsafe) product non-defective. This, too, does not sound like strict liability in any real sense. Either a product is unsafe or it is not—should giving a warning be enough to remove liability? Put another way, if there is a product which would be deemed unsafe if no warning came with it, are we saying the manufacturer is *at fault* for not supplying an adequate warning, and should therefore be liable? Conversely, if a warning is included, is there no fault and therefore no liability?

As the definition of defect is the key point of the CPA, the issue of whether a product is defective has unsurprisingly been the focus of most of the cases that have arisen under the Act. The question of whether adequate warnings were given (thus rendering a product 'safe') has also arisen in the case law generated by the CPA, of which there is surprisingly little. For example, in *Worsley* v *Tambrands Ltd* [2000], a woman complained that a tampon she had been using was defective when she suffered toxic shock syndrome after using it. She claimed that while it was known that the risk of this syndrome appearing was greater with misuse of the product, she had used it according to the instructions. As the evidence showed that she had read the comprehensive instructions, including the warnings given about the product, the court held that the tampon had not been defective as 'people generally' (in this case, women using the product) should know, as it was stated in the instructions and warnings, that a small risk of toxic shock syndrome was present even with ordinary use. Similarly, in *Richardson* v *LRC Products Ltd* [2001], the question for the court was whether a condom, from which the whole tip had sheared off during use (that is, it had more than just split or punctured during sex), was defective. The claimants were claiming for the costs associated with pregnancy and birth of an unwanted child. Again, because it was considered to be well known that condoms are not 100 per cent effective, due to the warnings to this effect that always accompany them (including on the outer packaging), the condom was not found to be defective.

⏩ Counterpoint

Richardson may be viewed outside the ambit of product liability as a case where a claim for 'wrongful birth' was being made. In other cases of this type (such as when a sterilisation operation has been performed negligently), the House of Lords is adamant in its view that this is not a compensable harm.[23] While they are prepared to award damages for the pain and suffering associated with the 'physical harm' of pregnancy and birth caused by negligence, damages for 'wrongful birth' are generally unavailable. This is largely due to policy reasons: either the harm suffered is not viewed as a legal harm, or the harm (the cost of raising an unwanted child) has been deliberately classified as 'pure economic loss' (see *McFarlane* v *Tayside Health Board* [2000]—discussed at p 183). Given the date of

---

23. Since *Rees* v *Darlington Area Health Authority* [2004] a 'conventional' award of £15,000 for loss of autonomy may now be awarded in such cases, though this in no way compensates for the financial losses caused by the negligence.

Richardson, it may well be assumed that this decision also had the weight of the public policy arguments from the wrongful birth negligence cases behind it, even though the same harm was caused in a different way.

In *Bogle and others* v *McDonald's Restaurants Ltd* [2002], customers of McDonald's fast food restaurants sued the company (in negligence as well as under the CPA) for scalding caused by hot coffee. The product—that is, the coffee—was 'defective' in two ways: first, the temperature at which it was served was too high and, secondly, the lids on the cups in which it was served came off too easily. The High Court dismissed the claims, holding that 'persons generally' would know that hot coffee could cause scalding if spilt and that care needs to be taken with hot drinks to avoid spillages. Because people want hot coffee, they have to suffer the 'inevitable' risk that comes with it. Field J said that:

> if McDonald's were going to avoid the risk of injury by a deep thickness burn they would have had to have served tea and coffee at between 55C and 60C. But tea ought to be brewed with boiling water if it is to give its best flavour and coffee ought to be brewed at between 85C and 95C. Further, people generally like to allow a hot drink to cool to the temperature they prefer. Accordingly, I have no doubt that tea and coffee served at between 55C and 60C would not have been acceptable to McDonald's customers. Indeed, on the evidence, I find that the public want to be able to buy tea and coffee served hot, that is to say at a temperature of at least 65C, even though they know (as I think they must be taken to do…) that there is a risk of a scalding injury if the drink is spilled. (at [33])

Put another way, the decision says that because customers in McDonald's want hot coffee, customers (who were usually adults and teenagers) should generally expect the coffee to be hot and should guard against spillages themselves. On the issue of the lids, the court found that the lids needed to come off easily to allow customers to put sugar and milk in their drinks; the fact the lids came off easily if the cups were knocked over did not make them defective. The test used here seems to be one of 'legitimate consumer expectation' and can probably be linked back to the use of the words *'entitled* to expect' in section 3 of the CPA—that what persons generally are 'entitled' to expect may well be different from what an individual claimant or claimants did in fact expect (that is, some people may have higher standards, but they may not be 'entitled' to these standards under the CPA).

 Pause for reflection

Bogle may be compared to the infamous American case of *Liebeck* v *McDonald's Restaurants* [1994], which is often used as an example of the US 'compensation culture'. The case became a flashpoint in the American debate over tort reform after a jury awarded nearly $3 million to a woman who burned herself with hot coffee bought from

→

➜

McDonald's.[24] Stella Liebeck, a 79-year-old woman, bought a cup of coffee from the drive-through window of her local McDonald's restaurant. She was sitting in the passenger seat of her grandson's car, which he had parked to allow Mrs Liebeck to add cream and sugar to her coffee. She placed the coffee cup between her knees and pulled the lid towards her to remove it, spilling the entire cup of coffee on her lap and burning herself in the process. Her award was reduced to $640,000 by the trial judge, though the case was later settled out of court for an unknown amount (thought to be less than $600,000) before an appeal was decided.

Do you think the *Bogle* case is evidence of there being a 'compensation culture' in the UK? Or do you think the claimants had a legitimate claim? Some often unreported information (or facts that are conveniently forgotten by those arguing that a compensation culture exists) about the *Liebeck* case is that the coffee, which had been absorbed by Mrs Liebeck's clothing, was then held against her skin as she sat in the puddle of hot liquid for over 90 seconds, scalding her thighs, buttocks and groin. She was taken to hospital, where doctors determined that she had suffered third-degree burns on six per cent of her skin and lesser burns over 16 per cent. She remained in the hospital for eight days while she underwent skin grafting, which was then followed by two years of further treatment. During the trial, the court heard that that McDonald's required its franchises to serve coffee at 180–190°F (82–88°C). At that temperature, it was said that the coffee could cause a third-degree burn in between two and seven seconds. Other evidence showed that from 1982 to 1992 the company had received more than 700 reports of people burned by its coffee, to varying degrees of severity, and had previously settled claims arising from scalding injuries for more than $500,000.

Mrs Liebeck had not intended this outcome: initially, she sought to settle with McDonald's for $20,000 to cover her medical costs, which were $11,000, but the company offered only $800. When McDonald's refused to raise its offer, she took her claim against them, alleging 'gross negligence' for selling 'unreasonably dangerous' and 'defectively manufactured' coffee. McDonald's then refused her lawyer's offer to settle for $90,000. Just before the trial, a mediator suggested a settlement of $225,000, but McDonald's again refused. In part, it can be said that all the refusals on the part of McDonald's were part of the reason for the high award of damages from the court. Another often-ignored fact is that the trial judge found Mrs Liebeck to be 20 per cent contributorily negligent.[25]

---

24. It should be noted here that one of the major differences—and possibly a contributing factor to the commonly held perception that in the US you can sue for anything—between the American and UK tort systems is the presence of a jury on tort cases. Typically, jurors tend to feel more sympathy to claimants (and antipathy to defendants) and this may be particularly true where cases are taken against large corporations. Jurors also 'decide' damages awards, and in the US there is far more scope for non-compensatory damages (e.g. punitive or aggravated damages) than in the UK (see Chapter 19). In a 1998 case against Philip Morris tobacco (one of the world's largest producers of cigarettes), a jury awarded $81m to the widow and children of a man who had smoked the company's Marlboro cigarettes for 40 years (since before the time the tobacco companies acknowledged the dangers of smoking). The family had sued for $100m but the award was reduced as the court found the man 50 per cent responsible for the harm he suffered. Less than two months later, in another claim against Philip Morris, another jury awarded $51.5m to a cigarette smoker with terminal lung cancer (though this was later appealed).

25. Chapter 10.

'Consumer expectation' was also relevant in *Pollard* v *Tesco Stores Ltd* [2006]. There, the Court of Appeal found that the child-resistant top of a bottle of dishwasher detergent was not defective, despite the fact that in this case, it had been opened by a child. The bottle top did not conform to the relevant British Design Standard, but even so, the claim was dismissed on the grounds that consumers would not generally know what the relevant design standard was; all they would expect would be that a 'child-proof' cap was harder for a child to remove than a normal cap. As this was still the case, the product was not defective.

 Pause for reflection

Does the outcome of the *Tesco* case seem like 'strict liability' to you? Would you think a bottle of chemicals from which a child could remove the supposedly child-proof cap fits the definition of a 'defective' product under section 3 of the CPA? We would argue that this certainly does not seem like strict liability. Furthermore, it seems as though the expectation of the manufacturers (who would or ought to know the relevant design standard), rather than of the public, was taken into consideration in this case. The CPA, it should be remembered, specifies that the relevant expectations should be those that 'persons generally' (including manufacturers) are 'entitled to expect' when determining whether or not a product is defective (s 3). Does the outcome of this case now mean that consumers are not entitled to expect that 'child-proof' caps on dangerous substances are, in fact, child-proof?

Despite there being only a limited number of cases concerning the meaning of 'defect' for the purposes of applying liability under the CPA and, more to the point, that manufacturers (as can be seen in the cases discussed) seem quite easily to be able to avoid their products being classed as defective, there have been some successful claims.

Abouzaid v Mothercare (UK) Ltd [2000] CA

The claimant, a 12-year-old boy, was injured when trying to do up a clasp on the strap used to affix a 'cosytoes' (a detachable cover that envelops a baby's torso and legs) to a pushchair. While the elastic on the strap was stretched, he let the strap go and it recoiled, hitting him in the eye and causing injury to the retina and leaving him with impaired sight.

The court held the defendants liable under the CPA because the product (the cosytoes) was defective. The court found that the manufacturer could have done more to prevent accidents of this type occurring, such as by using a different method to fasten the product to a pushchair, or by providing a warning. Because it was so easy to avoid the danger, and the manufacturer had not taken adequate steps to do so, the product was defective and Mothercare were liable for the harm it caused. Put another way, the ease with which the risk of injury could have been avoided was taken into account when determining liability.

In *Abouzaid* the Court of Appeal found that the relevant test was that the product must be judged against the expectations of persons generally in all the circumstances of the case—that is, whether the product had the level of safety which the general public would expect of such a product at the time the injury occurred. As the public would not expect injury to be able to be caused by something as generally innocuous as a cosytoes, this particular product *could* be deemed unsafe, and therefore defective, because it had unexpectedly caused injury.

 Pause for reflection

Compare the decision (in particular the reasoning) in **Abouzaid** with *Tesco*. Are the two decisions consistent in the way they have determined what a defective product is (or is not)? Which do you think is the better decision and why? One difference between the two cases is that a cosytoes will obviously come into close proximity with children, due to its very nature, whereas it might be expected that a cleaning chemical would be kept in a safe place away from children by responsible parents as an additional safeguard, despite it supposedly being child-proof. However, overall the decision in **Abouzaid** does seem to be more logical and 'in tune' with what the expectations of 'persons generally' might be.

A and others v National Blood Authority [2001] QBD

The claimants contracted Hepatitis C, a liver disease, after being supplied with contaminated blood during blood transfusions. The people who donated the blood had been infected with the Hepatitis C virus but, at the time they donated, there was no way of testing samples for the virus. At the time of the transfusions the medical profession was aware that Hepatitis C existed and that it could be transmitted by a blood transfusion, but there was still no way of testing the blood. Thus, it was known that some blood provided for transfusions *could* be contaminated with Hepatitis C, but no way of telling *which* blood this was. The public were not warned of this small risk.

The court had to decide whether the contaminated blood was defective for the purposes of establishing liability under the CPA. The defendants argued that the blood could not be deemed to have been defective because the public was only 'entitled' to expect the product to be as safe as it could be if reasonable precautions had been taken when handling it and in this particular instance there was nothing more that the blood authority could have done to make the product safer. In short, they argued that the risk was unavoidable and this fact had to be considered when the court looked at 'all the circumstances' that must be taken into account (under s 3(2) CPA). However, the claimants argued that to take such things into account would let 'questions of fault back in by the back door' (at 316).

The defendant's argument was roundly rejected by Burton J, who found the blood to be defective. He held that the question of avoidability or otherwise was not a circumstance that had to be taken into account as section 3(2) could be interpreted to mean 'all *relevant* circumstances': what the producer could or could not have done, therefore, was not a *relevant* consideration when looking at strict liability (although it would be in negligence).[26] He defined the infected blood as a 'non-standard' product—one that does not perform as

➡

---

26. It should be noted that this determination may not have survived the Court of Appeal or the then House of Lords had this case gone further.

> the producer of the product intends—adding that where there is a harmful characteristic in a non-standard product, a decision that the product is defective would be 'straight-forward'. The primary question would be whether the public accepted the non-standard nature of the product—that is, whether it could be said that the risk of some blood being affected was one that had been accepted by the general public. On this point, he found that the public was entitled to expect blood that was 100 per cent safe and therefore the blood authority should be held liable.

According to this case, as long as the product concerned is 'non-standard', and the public would not accept this 'non-standard' nature, the defendant will be liable. This is true irrespective of whether the 'non-standard' product could have been made standard (the only option being to withdraw the product from circulation), or whether the wholesale withdrawal of the product would have significant disadvantages to society. The decision in *A* v *National Blood Authority* has proved to be controversial and many argue that it was wrongly decided. However, if the point of the CPA was to achieve strict liability for 'defective' products that cause harm, then one might consider that this was in fact a correct decision, albeit that it does not necessarily seem to be *fair* that the blood authority were held liable, as there was literally nothing they could have done at the time to have made the blood safe. Strict liability is, however, not meant to be 'fair', it is meant to be strict, and the desirability of the outcome (compensation for the harm suffered by the claimants) is supposedly what justifies this. However, the decision does seem somewhat inconsistent with the majority of the other claims taken under the Act and it might be questioned why this is—was the judge, perhaps, swayed by the number of potential claimants?

Burton J, giving the decision in *A*, paid very close attention to the meaning of 'defect' under the CPA. Because the Act itself says that it must be interpreted in line with the EC Directive that created it, he used the definitional terms of the Directive rather than the provisions of the Act. In so doing he provided a three-stage test when determining under Article 6 of the Directive (and therefore presumably s 3 of the CPA) whether a product is defective:

(1) What harmful characteristic in the product caused the injury?

(2) Was the product 'standard' or 'non-standard'?

(3) What are the consumer's legitimate expectations as to the product?

From the way the test is constructed, it will be harder to establish that there is a defect in a 'standard' product than a 'non-standard' one. This would be similar to arguing that the problem came at the design stage rather than the manufacturing stage.[27] However, even with a non-standard product, the legitimate expectations of consumers must be considered, so being non-standard clearly does not equate to being 'defective' in and of itself (see *Richardson* v *LRC Products* [2001]). What consumers are entitled to expect will depend on whether any risk associated with the product is public knowledge and, crucially, whether this risk is thought to be socially acceptable in

---

27. A similar point has been made by *Markesinis & Deakin* p 714 and *Lunney & Oliphant* p 603.

a general sense. Infected blood, according to Burton J, clearly was not socially accept-able in any sense.

13.4.3 **Causation and limitations**

After establishing a defect, to establish liability under the CPA a claimant must still show that the defect caused the damage. The ordinary principles of legal causation apply.[28] Therefore, at the point of determining causation, when the claim is against a the manu-facturer of a medical product (for example a drug) in particular, the claimant would seem to be no better off than under the common law, particularly if there were multiple potential causes of the harm, especially given that the idea of 'materially increasing the risk of harm' in this type of case seems to have been ruled out in **Wilsher v Essex Area Health Authority [1988]**.[29] This point was clearly illustrated in *XYZ* v *Schering Health Care Ltd* [2002], where Mackay J concluded that because the evidence suggesting a causal connection between the third-generation oral contraceptive pill and cardio-vascular problems was contradictory and insufficient, the case would be doomed to fail on causa-tion, so there was no need to decide whether and how the CPA would apply.

Furthermore, there are time limitations placed on claims that can be brought under the CPA. A claimant must bring the claim within three years of the harm being suf-fered (also taking into account the situations where the claimant only discovers later that harm has been suffered—the three years run from this time, not from when the harm was literally caused). While this is quite generous, another limitation period exists, giving claimants only ten years to claim from the time the particular product was put into circulation.[30] This is to take into account consumer expectations—argu-ably if a product has (successfully) been on the market for ten years, it is not defective. What these limitations mean in practice, however, is that if a product has been on the market for nine years and 11 months, and then the claimant is harmed by a defect in the product, a claim must be taken almost immediately in order not to run out of time. If injury occurred a month later, no claim will be possible.

As long as an action is initiated within the ten-year period it can be decided. In *Horne-Roberts* v *SmithKline Beecham* [2001] the Court of Appeal ruled that this was the case even where proceedings had been mistakenly initiated against the *wrong* producer. The correct producer was later allowed to be substituted in the action even though the ten-year period had by then expired. In 2008, the House of Lords referred this issue to the European Court of Justice (ECJ), asking for clear guidance on the position where a claimant mistakenly names the wrong producer in an action commenced within the limitation period.[31] The ECJ ruled that certain circumstances would permit substitu-tion of a producer after the expiry of the time limit, despite the fact this limit was strict. These included those where the party sued is a wholly owned subsidiary of the producer, and 'the putting into circulation of the product' had in fact been determined by that

---

28. Chapter 9.
29. For a full discussion of the development and treatment of the concept of 'material increase of risk', see pp 229–230.
30. Limitation Act 1980, s 11A(3).
31. *O'Byrne* v *Aventis Pasteur SA* [2008]. The ECJ had already once provided guidance on the matter, in *O'Byrne* v *Aventis Pasteur MSD Ltd* [2006], though evidently this was not clear.

producer.[32] Upon the case's return (now to the Supreme Court), it was unanimously found that domestic law did not allow a producer to be substituted as the defendant in place of a wholly owned subsidiary, unless the parent company had actually determined when the supplier put the product in circulation. On the facts, this had not happened and the appeal was unsuccessful—the claimant was out of time.[33]

13.4.4 **Defences**

The availability of defences appears to allow the manufacturer to say 'it was not my fault'. Strict liability, by definition, ought not to be in any way fault-based.[34] While the presence of explicit defences in the CPA is controversial, it may be argued that liability under the Act should be strict, but not absolute.

However, of the six defences built into the CPA in section 4,[35] one defence in particular has proved especially contentious. Under section 4(1)(e) a manufacturer or other party who finds themselves liable under the Act can claim:

> [t]hat the state of scientific and technical knowledge at the relevant time was not such that a producer of products of the same description as the product in question might be expected to have discovered the defect if it had existed in his products while they were under his control.

This has become known as the 'development risks defence'. It covers circumstances where some time after the product was produced scientific or technical knowledge renders it 'defective'. Put another way, if a discovery is made after the product is put into circulation by the manufacturer, meaning that the product would now be regarded as defective, the manufacturer escapes liability (on that occasion only, as any time after the first time the defect would be known). Under the CPA, therefore, the Thalidomide claimants are unlikely to have been better off, despite this tragedy and other pharmaceutical harms being key factors leading to the movement to strict liability. That said, as Ross Cranston has pointed out, the large pharmaceutical companies operating from the UK are the biggest beneficiaries of the inclusion of the (optional) defence. In fact, the UK government was one of the most vocal when it came to implementing the Directive and was very much in favour of not using the derogation provision that would have allowed the defence to be excluded.

 Pause for reflection

Does the development risks defence sound, in essence, like a crude version of the *Bolam* test in negligence which applies to professionals when determining whether they have

---

32. *Aventis Pasteur v O'Byrne* [2009].
33. *O'Byrne v Aventis Pasteur SA* [2010].
34. Compare the Vaccine Damage Payments Act 1979, under which a statutory sum is awarded to people who become severely disabled as a result of vaccination against certain diseases, without proof of fault. The one-off lump sum payment increased from £100,000 to £120,000 in July 2007, having previously increased from £40,000 to £100,000 in 2000.
35. Contributory negligence is also available though not listed in s 4.

→

fallen below the standard of care expected of them? In that test, if the professional con-cerned can show that they acted in the same way as others from a respectable body of professional opinion would have done, they will not be in breach of their duty of care. This makes it harder to find professionals liable in negligence.[36] The development risks defence, as it is phrased in section 4(1)(e), appears to give manufacturers the ability to say that 'other manufacturers would not have been able to spot the defect, given the state of scientific and technical knowledge'. Do you think this is what it means? Is this a subjective or an objective test?

Commission of the European Communities v *United Kingdom (EC* v *UK)* [1997] ECJ

The CPA was meant to implement the terms of the EC Directive. The European Commission was concerned that the terminology of section 4(1)(e) of the CPA (the 'development risks defence') deviated from the wording of the defence under Article 7 of the Directive, creat-ing what could be called a subjective test, as it focused on the conduct and abilities of the 'reasonable manufacturer'. Article 7(1)(e) was worded differently and required an objective assessment of the state of scientific and technical knowledge at the time the product was put into circulation. It said that the defence would apply when:

[t]he state of scientific and technical knowledge at the time when the producer put the product into circulation was not such as to enable the existence of the defect to be discovered.

In *EC* v *UK*, the European Court of Justice said that the relevant test was to ask whether the information (that would make the product defective) was 'accessible' to the producer of the product concerned at the relevant time.

Relying on 'accessibility' of knowledge means that even if someone in the world might know the product is unsafe (because this is shown by later scientific or technical discover-ies) the *producer* might not necessarily be able to know this. This, however, appears to be a subjective rather than objective assessment. The ECJ suggested that this meant, for exam-ple, if a scientific discovery was made in a remote part of Manchuria (a region of China), and written up only in an obscure Manchurian journal (or not at all), then this informa-tion will not be 'accessible' to all producers. However, if a discovery is made in France, even if this was written up in French and published in a French journal, the information would be likely to be deemed to be accessible to the majority of manufacturers (particu-larly European manufacturers covered by the Directive). In short, accessible information means that risks become foreseeable, and therefore the defence will not apply.

In *A*, the defendant blood authority also contested the claim against them on the basis that even if a defect in the product could be established, they could avail them-selves of the development risks defence. Burton J, however, ruled that the defence was not applicable, as the general risk that the blood was contaminated with the virus was known (albeit unavoidable, as this knowledge did not extend to being able to find out

36. See Chapter 8, p 205.

whether a particular bag of blood was defective). This decision means that the defence could only be used the very first time a risk becomes known. The blood authority knew the risk existed, so the defence could no longer apply.

Pause for reflection

Do you think the National Blood Authority should have been found liable, especially given that it is obliged under statute to provide blood and could not at the time screen for the presence of the Hepatitis C virus in blood samples?

13.4.5 **Overall effect of the Consumer Protection Act 1987**

There have been very few cases taken under the CPA. While this might be in part due to the high costs of litigation, it might be argued that the Act has had a more silent effect in that the notion that manufacturers can be found to be strictly liable for harm caused by their products, even without negligence, may encourage more out of court settlements or have encouraged manufacturers to actually make their products safer. It might have been thought that the effect of the decision in *A*, where strict liability appeared to be taken to its strictest point, that more claims would be brought by consumers, as the decision is incredibly consumer-friendly. However, this does not appear to have happened and more recent cases tend to suggest that there is little benefit to bringing a claim under the Act rather than a claim in negligence. Considerations of 'fault' seem to have crept in to the CPA, particularly in the sense of what a defect can be said to be, despite Burton J's attempts in *A* not to 'dilute' the effect of the CPA.

Counterpoint

It also appears that the development risks defence may actually undermine the aims of the CPA. Arguably, what the defence does is to switch the burden of proof to producers to show that when they designed the product that has caused harm, they took the care expected of an expert/manufacturer at that time. In this respect, although strict liability in general and the CPA in particular were meant to make things easier for claimants in terms of *design* defects (remember that at common law the duty is clear and the courts are often willing to infer that a manufacturer was in breach (*Grant*),[37] meaning that it is relatively easy to sue for defects caused by the *manufacturing* process), it does not seem to have improved much at all. Claimants in the Thalidomide cases, for example, would have been no better off than they were in taking their claims in negligence. This, combined with the small number of cases actually taken under the CPA (and the even smaller number of successful claims), seems to suggest that it has been largely ineffective in achieving its supposed aims.[38]

→

37. It seems that this is also a possibility under the CPA: see *Ide* v *ATB Sales* [2008].

38. Though of course it may have a 'hidden' effect in encouraging either out of court settlements or swift(er) recall of defective products by manufacturers. See e.g. 'Hundreds Burnt by Toxic Sofas to Share £20 million Compensation' *The Times* 27 April 2010; 'Pushchair Maker Maclaren Agrees Compensation' BBC 6 May 2010.

➡️

Manufacturers have argued throughout the history of the implementation of the CPA that strict liability would, for example, hinder innovation and the placement of new, better and more cost-effective products onto the market. Strict liability, in their eyes, leads to increased costs, which in turn must be passed on to consumers. In turn, this leads to the question of whether private law mechanisms (that is, suing) are an appropriate response to defects in products at all, and whether increased public law regulation would better benefit society. In relation to strict liability for products the argument is whether we feel it is better that manufacturers/producers should bear the costs of unknown risks (through insurance?) or whether consumers, through product choice, would be better equipped to make decisions based on the level of risk they are prepared to accept. Forcing producers to compensate through a strict liability regime forces product prices up (as producers bear all, or most of the risk). In any case, imposing new or additional burdens on producers in the current economic climate would seem very unlikely.

However, the inhibition of innovation and design does not seem to have occurred in the 20+ years since the CPA came into force—perhaps again suggesting that the Act itself is not as 'strict' as it could have been in imposing liability on manufacturers and that the behaviour of producers is unlikely to have been significantly altered by the presence of the Act.

13.5 Part 1 of the Consumer Protection Act 1987—annotated

The Consumer Protection Act 1987

Part 1

1.—(1) This Part shall have effect for the purpose of making such provision as is necessary in order to comply with the product liability Directive and shall be construed accordingly.

> It is this EC Directive (85/374/EEC) that the UK had to implement, and did so by passing Part 1 of the CPA 1987—see the definition in s 1(2).

(2) In this Part, except in so far as the context otherwise requires—

["agricultural produce" means any produce of the soil, of stock-farming or of fisheries;]

> Anything in square brackets means this is a section inserted by later legislation or regulations.

"dependant" and "relative" have the same meaning as they have in, respectively, the Fatal Accidents Act 1976 [See Chapter 19.] and the Damages (Scotland) Act 1976;

"producer", in relation to a product, means—

> 'Producers' are those that can be held liable under the Act—as the rest of this section reveals (see emboldened text), the concept of who a producer is has been quite broadly defined.

(a) the **person who manufactured it**;

(b) in the case of a substance which has not been manufactured but has been won or abstracted, **the person who won or abstracted it**;

(c) in the case of a product which has not been manufactured, won or abstracted but essential characteristics of which are attributable to an

➡️

industrial or **other process having been carried out** (for example, in relation to agricultural produce), **the person who carried out that process;**

> "product" means any goods or electricity and (subject to subsection (3) below) includes a product which is comprised in another product, whether by virtue of being a component part or raw material or otherwise; and
>
> "the product liability Directive" means the Directive of the Council of the European Communities, dated 25th July 1985, (No. 85/374/EEC) on the approximation of the laws, regulations and administrative provisions of the member States concerning liability for defective products.

(3) For the purposes of this Part a person who supplies any product in which products are comprised, whether by virtue of being component parts or raw materials or otherwise, shall not be treated by reason only of his supply of that product as supplying any of the products so comprised.

2.—(1) Subject to the following provisions of this Part, where any damage is caused wholly or partly by a defect in a product, every person to whom subsection (2) below applies shall be liable for the damage.

(2) This subsection applies to—

(a) the producer of the product;

(b) any person who, by putting his name on the product or using a trade mark or other distinguishing mark in relation to the product, has held himself out to be the producer of the product;

(c) any person who has imported the product into a member State from a place outside the member States in order, in the course of any business of his, to supply it to another.

(3) Subject as aforesaid, where any damage is caused wholly or partly by a defect in a product, any person who supplied the product (whether to the person who suffered the damage, to the producer of any product in which the product in question is comprised or to any other person) shall be liable for the damage if—

(a) the person who suffered the damage requests the supplier to identify one or more of the persons (whether still in existence or not) to whom subsection (2) above applies in relation to the product;

(b) that request is made within a reasonable period after the damage occurs and at a time when it is not reasonably practicable for the person making the request to identify all those persons; and

(c) the supplier fails, within a reasonable period after receiving the request, either to comply with the request or to identify the person who supplied the product to him.

...

(5) Where two or more persons are liable by virtue of this Part for the same damage, their liability shall be joint and several.

(6) This section shall be without prejudice to any liability arising otherwise than by virtue of this Part.

Margin notes:

Definition of 'products' for the purposes of the Act—see also s 45. The case **A v National Blood Authority** says that blood received in transfusions is also a 'product' covered by the Act.

This is what makes a defendant liable—if they produce a product that has a defect which causes harm.

See definition of 'producer', above (s 1).

Importers can also be construed as producers, meaning that there will always be someone in the EU who can be sued.

This means that 'own-branders' can be construed as producers, even if they did not actually make the product but someone else made it for them—e.g. Co-op's own-brand cornflakes.

This section provides that even suppliers (retailers) can be liable in certain (limited) circumstances.

For an explanation of this term, see the chapter on damages, Chapter 19.

People are generally entitled to expect what is 'socially accepted' as a risk that comes with the product—see, e.g. *Richardson* v *LRC Products*; *Bogle* v *McDonald's* and contrast *A* v ***National Blood Authority***.

3.—(1) Subject to the following provisions of this section, there is a defect in a product for the purposes of this Part if the safety of the product is not such as persons generally are entitled to expect; and for those purposes "safety", in relation to a product, shall include safety with respect to products comprised in that product and safety in the context of risks of damage to property, as well as in the context of risks of death or personal injury.

Definition of 'defect'—the key part of the Act and what most of the case law pertains to.

(2) In determining for the purposes of subsection (1) above what persons generally are entitled to expect in relation to a product all the circumstances shall be taken into account, including—

Later (controversially) re-defined by Burton J in *A* v ***National Blood Authority*** as 'all the relevant circumstances', excluding consideration of whether reasonable care was taken by the manufacturer.

e.g. the packaging.

(a) the manner in which, and purposes for which, the product has been marketed, its get-up, the use of any mark in relation to the product and any instructions for, or warnings with respect to, doing or refraining from doing anything with or in relation to the product;

Instructions or warnings with a product can render it 'safe' and therefore not defective—see, e.g. *Worsley* v *Tambrands*.

(b) what might reasonably be expected to be done with or in relation to the product; and

(c) the time when the product was supplied by its producer to another;

and nothing in this section shall require a defect to be inferred from the fact alone that the safety of a product which is supplied after that time is greater than the safety of the product in question.

e.g. industry standard marks such as the 'Kite Mark'.

It is controversial that any defences are built into the Act—but the liability is 'strict', not 'absolute'.

4.—(1) In any civil proceedings by virtue of this Part against any person ("the person proceeded against") in respect of a defect in a product it shall be a defence for him to show—

(a) that the defect is attributable to compliance with any requirement imposed by or under any enactment or with any Community obligation; or

The 'development risks' or 'state of the art' defence. This is the most controversial of all the defences and the wording used in the CPA was challenged by the European Commission in *EC* v *UK*. They alleged that the CPA definition allowed a subjective interpretation of what a 'reasonable producer' could have been expected to know at the time, when the standard set by the Directive was meant to be objective. In that case it was deemed that all 'accessible' information or knowledge had to be taken into account.

(b) that the person proceeded against did not at any time supply the product to another; or

(c) that the following conditions are satisfied, that is to say—
(i) that the only supply of the product to another by the person proceeded against was otherwise than in the course of a business of that person's; and
(ii) that section 2(2) above does not apply to that person or applies to him by virtue only of things done otherwise than with a view to profit; or

(d) that the defect did not exist in the product at the relevant time; or

(e) that the state of scientific and technical knowledge at the relevant time was not such that a producer of products of the same description as the product in question might be expected to have discovered the defect if it had existed in his products while they were under his control; or

(f) that the defect—
(i) constituted a defect in a product ("the subsequent product") in which the product in question had been comprised; and
(ii) was wholly attributable to the design of the subsequent product or to compliance by the producer of the product in question with instructions given by the producer of the subsequent product.

...

5.—(1) Subject to the following provisions of this section, in this Part "damage" means death or personal injury or any loss of or damage to any property (including land).

(2) A person shall not be liable under section 2 above in respect of any defect in a product for the loss of or any damage to the product itself or for the loss of or any damage to the whole or any part of any product which has been supplied with the product in question comprised in it.

(3) A person shall not be liable under section 2 above for any loss of or damage to any property which, at the time it is lost or damaged, is not—

(a) of a description of property ordinarily intended for private use, occupation or consumption; and

(b) intended by the person suffering the loss or damage mainly for his own private use, occupation or consumption.

(4) No damages shall be awarded to any person by virtue of this Part in respect of any loss of or damage to any property if the amount which would fall to be so awarded to that person, apart from this subsection and any liability for interest, does not exceed £275.

(5) In determining for the purposes of this Part who has suffered any loss of or damage to property and when any such loss or damage occurred, the loss or damage shall be regarded as having occurred at the earliest time at which a person with an interest in the property had knowledge of the material facts about the loss or damage.

(6) For the purposes of subsection (5) above the material facts about any loss of or damage to any property are such facts about the loss or damage as would lead a reasonable person with an interest in the property to consider the loss or damage sufficiently serious to justify his instituting proceedings for damages against a defendant who did not dispute liability and was able to satisfy a judgment.

(7) For the purposes of subsection (5) above a person's knowledge includes knowledge which he might reasonably have been expected to acquire—

(a) from facts observable or ascertainable by him; or

(b) from facts ascertainable by him with the help of appropriate expert advice which it is reasonable for him to seek;

but a person shall not be taken by virtue of this subsection to have knowledge of a fact ascertainable by him only with the help of expert advice unless he has failed to take all reasonable steps to obtain (and, where appropriate, to act on) that advice.

(8) Subsections (5) to (7) above shall not extend to Scotland.

…

This would be pure economic loss in negligence and is also irretrievable under the Act.

Definition of 'damage'—i.e. what harms can be claimed for under the CPA. It is surprising, perhaps, that this definition comes so late.

To take a claim for property damage, the loss must amount to more than £275. This means small claims are excluded under the Act.

13.6 Claiming under Part 1 of the Consumer Protection Act 1987—at a glance

Table 13.2 Claiming under Part 1 of the Consumer Protection Act 1987—at a glance

Issue	Relevant sections	Explanation
Who can sue?	Sections 2(1) and 5(1)	A person who 'suffers damage as a result of a defective product' (see definitions of 'damage' and 'defect')
Who can be sued?	Sections 1(2) and 5(2)	Manufacturers, producers, 'own-branders' and importers into the EU Some suppliers can also be sued
What damage can be claimed for?	Section 5(1) See also sections 5(2) and 5(4)	Death, personal injury and property damage Pure economic loss excluded and property damage must exceed £275
What is a 'product'?	Section 1(2) See also section 45	Goods and electricity, component parts and raw materials 'Goods' includes substances, growing crops, things on land and any ship, aircraft or vehicle
What is a 'defect'?	Section 3(1) See also section 3(2) (a)–(c)	A defect exists when 'the safety of a product is not such that persons generally are entitled to expect' Packaging, normal use, instructions and warnings may be taken into account
Are any defences appropriate?	Section 4(1)(a)–(f)	There are six defences available under the Act Contributory negligence is also applicable

13.7 Conclusion

In this chapter we have looked at three ways in which liability for defective products is regulated in private law. Although perhaps somewhat out of place in a textbook on tort, we started by looking at some provisions of **contract law**, which provide a backdrop to the development of the law of negligence in this area. Under the SGA, purchasers are guaranteed a number of rights against the retailer when goods that they buy do not live up to the standard of 'satisfactory quality' as required by section 14(2) of the statute. These rights are more generous for consumers than they are for non-consumers, reflecting a more general trend in modern contract law toward consumer protectionism. However, we also saw that despite reform to the doctrine of privity of contract, many end-users of products would be unable to take contractual claims in relation to faulty or defective products. There are two main reasons for this. First, end-users who did not purchase the product (and thereby enter a contract with the retailer) cannot often sue retailers and avail themselves of the provisions of the SGA, despite the changes to the doctrine of privity. Secondly, under contract it is impossible to directly sue the manufacturer, which in many cases will be the preferred option. Thus the law of contract has its limitations in terms of consumer protection.

We then considered the way the tort of **negligence** has been used by claimants who suffer damage as a result of a defective product. As in all negligence claims, the hurdles of establishing duty, breach and causation must be overcome. While the first two are not difficult (as **Donoghue v Stevenson** gives the duty and a breach is often inferred on the facts), causation issues can often stand in the way of a successful claim. This is particularly true when considering design defects and it was recognition of these limitations in negligence that led in part to calls for strict liability in this area.

Strict liability (where the producer of a product is held liable without the need to show fault) for defective products was meant to have been put into place by the introduction of Part 1 of the CPA. However, the definition of defect is a weak one, being based on what 'persons generally are entitled to expect' and much of the case law has been devoted to finding that products are *not* defective. Furthermore, the inclusion of defences in the Act, particularly the 'development risks defence' seems to suggest that liability is still somewhat subjective and contains elements of fault, thus not making it totally strict. However, whether strict liability is actually desirable is still a matter of debate.

✱ End-of-chapter questions

After reading the chapter carefully, try answering the questions below. If you would like to know what we think visit the Online Resource Centre (www.oxfordtextbooks.co.uk/orc/horsey2e/).

1. What are the advantages and disadvantages of having a system of strict liability in relation to defective products? Does strict liability make more sense when the harm suffered is personal injury?

2. Who should bear the risks and costs associated with innovation and increased consumer choice?

3. Do the provisions of Part 1 of the Consumer Protection Act 1987 achieve their aims?

4. Consider the problem question at the start of this chapter. Now having read about the topic, what would be your advice to the claimants? If you need some pointers in thinking about how to answer this question, turn to the Appendix (p 589) where each problem is annotated with issues and cases to consider. Next, try to write your own answer and, finally, log on to our Online Resource Centre (www.oxfordtextbooks.co.uk/orc/horsey2e/) to check your ideas against our suggested outline answer.

✳ Further reading

Further reading on this subject is often centred on critiques of the Consumer Protection Act 1987 and in particular the development risks defence. *Cranston's Consumers and the Law* is a good starting point for a general overview of the way consumers are dealt with and protected by law, as well as a good introduction to many of the critiques of the current law and the philosophies behind it.

Department of Trade and Industry *Guide to the Consumer Protection Act 1987*

Fairgrieve, Duncan and Geraint Howells 'General Product Safety—A Revolution Through Reform?' (2006) 69 *Modern Law Review* 59

Gerling, Andrea 'A Matter of Degree: How a Jury Decided That a Coffee Spill is Worth $2.9 Million' *Wall Street Journal* 1 September 1994

Giliker, Paula 'Strict Liability for Defective Goods: The Ongoing Debate' (2003) *Business Law Review* 87

Howells, Geraint and Mark Mildred 'Infected Blood: Defect and Discoverability: A First Exposition of the EC Product Liability Directive' (2002) 65 *Modern Law Review* 95

Newdick, Christopher 'The Development Risks Defence of the Consumer Protection Act 1987' (1988) 47 *Cambridge Law Journal* 455

Scott, Colin and Julia Black *Cranston's Consumers and the Law* (3rd edn, Butterworths, 2000)

PART III

The personal torts

Introduction to Part III

1. In this Part we look at specific torts which protect an individual's interest in some aspect of their person—specifically their personal integrity, reputation and privacy.

2. We begin, in Chapter 14, by looking at the torts comprising trespass to the person—**battery, assault** and **false imprisonment**. Each seeks to protect an individual against an infringement of their personal integrity, that is against the infliction, or fearing the infliction, of unlawful force (battery and assault) and the unlawful restriction of a person's freedom of movement (false imprisonment).

3. The three trespass to the person torts have the same characteristics: the defendant must have intended both the *conduct* itself and (usually) *consequences* of their action (though they need not have intended to harm or hurt the claimant); the defendant's action must cause direct and immediate harm; and they are actionable *per se*, that is, without proof of loss. These characteristics distinguish these torts from the tort of negligence: while trespass to the person compensates the claimant in relation to direct and intentional harm (for example, being deliberately hit), negligence compensates the claimant for that which is unintentional or indirect (that is, accidental injury).

4. We then go on to consider **the rule in** *Wilkinson* v *Downton,* which provides a remedy for physical and psychiatric/emotional harm deliberately caused by a false statement (as opposed to physical impact or fear of such) and the **Protection from Harassment Act 1997** which imposes both civil and criminal liability for harassing conduct. Though the 1997 Act was originally introduced as a response to stalking, it is of general and (potentially) wide application as seen in its increasing use in cases of workplace harassment as a way of avoiding restrictions placed on occupational stress claims in *Hatton* v *Sutherland* [2003].[1]

5. Defamation, discussed in Chapter 15, is perhaps one of the most familiar torts and certainly one of the most glamorous (although increasingly it may have to share this honour with the new 'tort' of privacy). The law of defamation enables an individual (or, more controversially, a company) to prevent the publication of, or recover damages for, public statements which make, or are likely to make, people think less of them. As such it is unsurprising that many of the cases involve people in the public eye—celebrities, TV personalities, politicians and so on—and/or multinational corporations who are not only more aware of, but certainly have a greater interest in, their reputations. However, none of this should detract from the central question at the heart of the law of defamation: when should an individual's interest in what people think of them trump or silence the freedom of others to be able to say what they know, or think they know, about them?

6. A defamatory statement can take two forms: it can either be spoken (**slander**) or written (**libel**). Only a false statement can be defamatory. However a claimant need not be able to prove that is it false to bring (and win) a claim—it is up to the defendant to prove that the statement is true (justification) in order to avoid liability. Other defences include honest comment (on a matter of public interest) and privilege (where the statement is made in the performance of a duty).

---

1. See Chapter 5, pp 119–121.

Remedies include a 'gagging order' (an interim injunction) to prevent publication, a permanent injunction to prevent further publication and damages (which, unusually, can include exemplary damages).

7. Finally, Chapter 16 considers the nascent 'tort' of **invasion of privacy**. This area of law is highly topical and somewhat contentious. As with **defamation**, the development of an action to protect an individual's **privacy** involves delicately balancing media freedom and the public's 'right to know' against an individual's (often, but not always, someone in the public eye) right to a private and family life free from *unwanted* intrusion.

8. An individual's ability to protect their **privacy** in the UK is a little haphazard. Although a number of legal mechanisms offer some protection of privacy interests (for example, **trespass to the person**, private nuisance and breach of confidence), none of them protect privacy *per se* and all have quite substantial limitations. The Article 8 'right' to privacy is incorporated into UK law through the Human Rights Act 1998, but this does not create a freestanding action. There is no general 'tort' of privacy. This was confirmed by the House of Lords in *Campbell* v *MGN* [2004] where the House of Lords refused to recognise a new cause of action on the basis of section 6 of the Human Rights Act. They did, however, recognise that existing causes of action may require amending with the goal of protecting a claimant's privacy in mind. As a result, changes particularly in the action for breach of confidence (an action for unjustified publication of private information) may mean that such a tort now exists—'in all but name'.

14

Trespass to the person

Problem question

Read this problem question carefully, and keep it in mind while you are working through the chapter that follows. At the end of the chapter, you will be able to apply what you have learnt to the problem question and advise the relevant parties.

Dave, Arthur, Lucy and Ellie are sitting in the students' union bar discussing their outfits for the forthcoming 'Law Society Spring Ball'.

Mike, Lucy's ex-boyfriend, walks by and says quietly to Dave, 'I'll get you! No one steals my girl and gets away with it'. Although Dave is not particularly upset by this, he decides to teach Mike a lesson. When no one is looking, he deliberately trips Mike up. Mike falls over but is not hurt. He quickly jumps up and runs after Dave. Mike hits Dave and pushes him away and Dave falls awkwardly and hits his head. As Lucy rushes to get a doctor, Mike corners her and whispers, 'I miss you, let's try again'. She pushes him away.

Meanwhile Arthur and Ellie have sneaked into the bar's storeroom for some time alone. On seeing this, Mike locks the storeroom door. It remains locked until Stuart, the bar man, comes on duty some time later and unlocks it.

Later that evening, Mike calls Helen, Dave's pregnant ex-girlfriend, who lives some distance away, and tells her Dave has been badly hurt. She takes the news very badly. Mike then calls Lucy's mobile; as she is still at the hospital with Dave she does not answer it. By the time she checks her phone she has 12 missed calls.

14.1 **Introduction**

Consider the following examples:

→ An infatuated student makes multiple phone calls to a classmate's mobile suggesting that they meet up.

→ A man is shopping with his 3-year-old daughter in the toy department of a large department store. They are both locked in when the store closes for the evening.

→ A woman enters a lift with a male colleague at work. He sidles up to her, standing very close (but not touching) and whispers 'sweet nothings' in her ear. They are alone in the lift.

→ A doctor delivers a healthy child after performing a Caesarean section on the mother without her consent.

All of these cases involve a possible infringement of an individual's personal integrity. As such the harm lies not in whether the defendant's actions have caused physical damage but rather in the violation of the claimant's right to be free from unjustifiable interference. Trespass to the person is made up of three torts: battery, assault and false imprisonment. These were defined by Goff LJ in *Collins* v *Wilcock* [1984] (at 1177) as laid out in Table 14.1.

Table 14.1 The trespass to the person torts

The trespass to the person torts		
Assault	Battery	False imprisonment
'an act which causes another person to apprehend the infliction of immediate, unlawful force on his person'	'the actual infliction of unlawful force on another person'	'the unlawful imposition of constraint on another's freedom of movement from a particular place'

In addition to these three torts, this chapter also considers the rule in *Wilkinson* v *Downton* [1897]. While assault and battery provide a remedy for those in fear of, or who experience, immediate infliction of unlawful physical force, the rule in *Wilkinson* v *Downton* provides a remedy for those who suffer *psychiatric* injury or emotional harm as a result of another's intentional conduct (often confusingly referred to as 'indirect' harm). Though the House of Lords' decision in **Wainwright v Home Office [2004]** and the enactment of the Protection from Harassment Act 1997 have limited its scope, the rule continues to offer the possibility of recovery for harm suffered in circumstances not covered by the trespass torts, the 1997 Act or the tort of negligence.

Pause for reflection

The torts which comprise trespass to the person obviously have close connections with the criminal law and, in particular, the offences found in the Offences Against the Person Act 1861. Cases involving sulphuric acid being blown out of washroom hand dryers, threats of violence at a parish council meeting, a car deliberately running over a policeman's foot, or where a spurned lover's inability to let go turns into severe and disturbing harassment all amount to criminal offences. Why then does the law also recognise a civil action in these, and other, cases? And, why would the victim wish to bring a claim?

Think again about the purposes of tort law outlined in the introduction to the book.[1] Although some people may be motivated by a desire for financial compensation, a tort action may also be used to highlight a refusal of the Director of Public Prosecutions (DPP) to bring a criminal prosecution or following an unsuccessful prosecution (see *Ashley* v *Chief Constable of Sussex Police* [2008][2]). Many of the cases in this area of tort highlight abuses of, and discrepancies in, power—for example between men and women, police officer and suspect, doctor and patient. As the burden of proof is lower in the civil courts, the claimant may succeed (subject to any statutory restrictions) in proving their case on the balance of probabilities where the prosecution has failed in a criminal court to prove the allegations beyond reasonable doubt.

Consider, in particular, rape and other forms of sexual assault. As we shall see, these are also likely to be actionable using the trespass to the person torts.[3] Given the very low number of criminal convictions for rape, the civil law might be invoked here to strategic effect (see e.g. *Lawson* v *Glaves-Smith* [2006]). Do you think this would be a good idea? Think about the purpose of civil, as opposed to criminal, law.

Conventionally, the trespass to the person torts are described as having the same characteristics:

- they must be committed intentionally;
- they must cause direct and immediate 'harm';[4] and
- they are actionable *per se*, that is, without proof of loss.

These characteristics are said to distinguish the trespass to the person torts from the tort of negligence. Put simply, trespass compensates the claimant in relation to direct and

---

1. Chapter 1, pp 9–18.

2. On this case and point see further Nicholas McBride 'Trespass to the Person: The Effect of Mistakes and Alternative Remedies on Liability' (2008) *Cambridge Law Journal* 461.

3. See e.g. the claims for sexual abuse in childhood in *AB and Others v Nugent Care Society; GR v Wirral Metropolitan Borough Council* [2009] discussed in Nicola Godden 'Sexual Abuse and Claims in Tort: Limitation Periods After *A v Hoare (and Other Appeals)* [2008] and *AB and Others v Nugent Care Society; GR v Wirral MBC* [2009]' (2010) 18(2) *Feminist Legal Studies* 179.

4. We note here that the reference to 'harm' is misleading. The torts of trespass to the person are actionable *per se*, and so the claimant need not show that they have suffered any loss for their claim to succeed. As such, the claimant need not have suffered any bodily or psychiatric harm. Rather, the only 'harm' that need be proved is that the claimant was unlawfully touched, apprehended an immediate unlawful touching or was physically restrained (as the case may be).

intentional harm (for example, being deliberately hit), while negligence compensates the claimant for unintentional or indirect harm (that is, accidental injury).

It is worth noting at the outset that the term 'intention' is ambiguous. It can describe two different aspects of a person's conduct. First, we can speak of intentional *conduct*, that is, willed, voluntary action. The contrast here is with conduct which was out of the defendant's control—for example, a spasm or when they are physically manipulated by someone else. Secondly, and more commonly, the language of intention is used in connection with the *consequences* of one's willed actions—for example to touch or hurt someone or to score a goal. In this sense, intention requires a particular state of mind or attitude in respect of the result of one's conduct. Typically, one intends a particular consequence when one's purpose is to bring that consequence about through one's actions. The contrast here is with recklessness or negligence which involve, at most, an awareness of the risk that one's conduct will bring a particular result without intending to cause such a result.

It is clear that the torts we are concerned with in this chapter require intention in the first sense. A defendant will not be liable if they were not in control of their actions at the relevant time. It is less clear if intention in the second sense is needed—that is whether the defendant need intend the specific consequences of their actions (e.g., unlawful touching, or the claimant's fear of such touching, in the case of battery and assault respectively) or whether it is enough that the defendant was simply careless as to the possibility of the result occurring.

At one point it seemed that trespass could be committed negligently (*Fowler* v *Lanning* [1959]). However, the Court of Appeal decision in *Letang* v *Cooper* [1965] marked a change in direction. In this case, the claimant (wishing to avoid restrictions imposed by the Law Reform (Limitation of Actions, etc) Act 1954, s 2(1)) sued in trespass for injury caused by the defendant negligently driving his car over her legs as she sunbathed in the hotel car park.[5] In denying her claim, Lord Denning MR proposed that a clear line be drawn between trespass and negligence: trespass requires that the defendant intended to touch the claimant; by contrast 'when the injury is not inflicted intentionally but negligently, I would say that the only cause of action is in negligence and not trespass' (at 240).

This position was endorsed by the Court of Appeal in **Iqbal v Prison Officers Association** [2009]. The court held that 'it is well established that all forms of trespass require an intentional act. An act of negligence will not suffice' (Smith LJ at [71]).[6] However, Smith LJ went on to hold that intention here also includes subjective recklessness, that is where the defendant *foresees* that their actions would have the relevant consequences (the application of force in battery, the deprivation of the claimant's liberty in false imprisonment) and goes ahead with those actions nonetheless (at [73]). So, the person who throws a stone in a crowded area not intending (that is, setting out)

5. The Act stated that personal injury actions for 'negligence, nuisance or breach of duty' must be brought within three years while other tort actions were barred after six years.

6. In any case the discussion as to whether trespass can be committed negligently may be thought somewhat academic. After all, even if a defendant who negligently touches a claimant cannot be sued in trespass, so long as the claimant has suffered harm they will be able to sue for damages in the tort of negligence. And if the claimant has not suffered any harm then a claim in trespass would be largely useless since no more than nominal damages would be awarded.

to hit anyone *but knowing it is likely that someone may be hit*, will be liable in the tort of battery.

Pause for reflection

The decision in *Iqbal* does much to clarify the mental element needed for the trespass to the person torts. However, there are still some problems with how the Court of Appeal dealt with the issue. First, the use of the phrase 'intentional act' is unhelpful and potentially misleading. As we saw above, intention can be used in two senses: to describe action which is voluntary (rather than involuntary) or to describe a person's attitude to certain consequences of their action (that their purpose was to bring about those consequences). So if A locks the door to a room, not knowing that B is inside, A's locking of the door is intentional (in the first sense), even though A has no intention (in the second sense) to lock B in.

Because of this, saying there must be an 'intentional act' is ambiguous. Now we know from *Iqbal* that A does not falsely imprison B unless he intends to lock B in (or is aware that by locking the door he may lock B in but does this anyway). But then we would be better off making clear that what needs to be intended is *the imprisonment*—that is A needs to lock the door with the objective of locking B in (or at least knowing that by locking the door this is likely to happen). Similarly, in battery what needs to be intended is not (simply) the defendant's physical conduct—such as throwing a stone—but *the application of force*— the stone hitting someone.

The other point to make concerns the Court of Appeal's holding that subjective recklessness is a sufficient mental element for the trespass to the person torts. This aligns the law of torts with the criminal law offences of assault and battery, where it has long been clear that subjective recklessness is sufficient mens rea (*R v Venna* [1976]). Again, however, the courts could make this point more clearly. In *Iqbal*, Smith LJ stated that 'in the criminal law a reckless disregard of the consequences is taken as sufficient to satisfy the requirement of intention', before holding that the same should go for the law of torts (at [73]). Not only does this misdescribe the criminal law, where the courts have repeatedly stressed the difference between intention and recklessness, but it is clear that there is a difference between trying to hit someone and doing something which one knows may hit someone. As such, the clearer formulation would be to say that trespass requires intention *or* recklessness, rather than pretending that recklessness is a type of intention.

14.2 **Battery**

A battery is the application of unlawful force to another person: typically A stabs B; X shoots Y; Dave punches Mike. As a trespass tort, battery is actionable *per se*; there is no need to show that the defendant did in fact cause the claimant actual harm by touching them, let alone that they intended (or were reckless as to causing) any harm. Given that the essence of the wrong in the tort of battery is the impermissibility of bodily contact, any unwanted contact—anything from a pat on the back to an unwanted kiss to a violent blow to the head—can amount to a battery. Similarly, the fact that the contact was the result of a practical joke or similar is irrelevant: 'an unwanted kiss may be a battery although the defendant's intention may be most amiable' (*R* v *Chief Constable of Devon and Cornwall, ex p Central Electricity Generating Board* [1982] at 471). Put simply, any touching—as long as it is unlawful—is a battery.

Fortunately, this somewhat broad prohibition of unwanted conduct is subject to qualifications. In order to establish an actionable battery, force exceeding 'physical contact which is generally acceptable in the ordinary conduct of daily life' must be applied by immediate and direct means to another individual (*Collins* v *Wilcock* at 1177). In short, a battery requires:

(1) the application of force (the touching or contact) must be intentional (or reckless);

(2) the force must be direct and immediate; and

(3) the contact must be unlawful but need not be 'hostile'.

14.2.1 **Intention**

The torts of trespass are typically said to require intention on the part of the defendant. However, as we have seen, references to intention are ambiguous as the word 'intention' can be used in different ways. So, the voluntary throwing of a stone is an *intentional act*, whether or not the thrower *intends to hit* anyone. What is clear is that there needs to be more than an intentional throwing. There is no battery unless the stone thrower intends to hit someone with the stone (or at least is aware the stone might hit someone and throws it nonetheless). More generally we can say that the mental element necessary for the tort of battery is either:

(a) an *intention* (ie setting out) to apply force to another person; or

(b) *recklessness* as to (i.e. foreseeing the likelihood of) one's actions causing the application of force to another person.

Of course, there will be no battery unless the defendant acts voluntarily. So, no battery is committed if Lucy trips over and stumbles into Dave. However, if Mike pushes Lucy into Dave, Mike has committed a battery (*Gibbon* v *Pepper* [1695]).

There are two further points to make. First, if the defendant intends to make contact with A but instead touches B, the tort of battery will be committed against B. So, if Dave while trying to hit Mike hits Ellie instead she has a claim in battery against Dave by virtue of the rule of 'transferred intent' (*Livingstone* v *Ministry of Defence* [1984]). Secondly, the defendant will be liable to compensate the claimant for any harm he suffered as a result of the unlawful touching even if the defendant did not intend to cause any harm (or indeed even if the possibility of causing harm never crossed their mind). In *Williams* v *Humphrey* [1975], the defendant pushed the claimant into a swimming pool causing him to fall awkwardly and break his ankle. The defendant argued that he did not intend to hurt the claimant, but this did not matter. He had clearly intended to touch the claimant and there is no further requirement of intending any injury that follows. Similarly, a doctor who performs a medical operation without the claimant's consent will commit a battery even though their intention is to help rather than harm the claimant (as we shall see consent acts as a defence to battery).

A battery is also committed even if the original action by the defendant was involuntary, if they later have the chance but fail to put a stop to the battery. In *Fagan* v *Metropolitan Police Commissioner* [1969], Fagan accidentally drove his car on to a police constable's foot. To the police constable's understandable consternation, he deliberately left it there for a period of time, injuring the police constable's left big toe. Fagan was found guilty of criminal assault. Applying the reasoning of the majority of the Court of Appeal by analogy to the law of tort it seems that although Fagan's initial—unintentional—action of stopping his car on the police constable's foot did not amount to a tort, once he had knowledge of his car's position the offence was complete. By deliberately failing to move until the police officer had shouted 'Get off my foot' several times, he committed a battery.

14.2.2 **Direct and immediate force**

Historically, a basic requirement of any trespass action is that the unlawful touching must be the direct and immediate result of the defendant's actions. Traditionally, a distinction has been drawn between a person who is hit as a log is thrown onto the road and the claim of the person who subsequently trips over the log. While the claim of the former lies in battery, the latter's claim is restricted to the tort of negligence (*Reynolds* v *Clarke* [1725]). However, the courts have interpreted 'directness' extremely flexibly, and, in practice, this distinction is unlikely to be problematic. In *Scott* v *Shepherd* [1773], the defendant was found liable for battery after he had thrown a lit squib (firework) into a market place, despite the fact that it had been thrown on by two stallholders to protect themselves and their wares before it had eventually exploded in the claimant's face.

In *DPP* v *K* [1990] the defendant, a schoolboy aged 15, poured sulphuric acid into the upturned nozzle of a hand-drying machine. Another pupil later used the dryer with the result that the acid was blown onto his face, leaving a permanent scar. Though the fact that the case was subsequently held to be wrongly decided in criminal law,[7] it remains interesting in relation to tort law, as it seems to have been assumed that the contact was a direct (as opposed to a consequential) result of the defendant's act. The shortness of time between the act and the contact meant that the contact was sufficiently direct to satisfy the requirement of battery. If this is correct, it is likely that a person who trips over a log left in the road (assuming it happened relatively quickly after the log was thrown and the necessary intention could be established) would have a claim in trespass.

14.2.3 **Unlawful (though not necessarily hostile) touching**

Applied literally, battery covers all forms of contact—Ellie would commit a battery simply by tapping Lucy on her shoulder to get her attention. It would clearly be nonsense if a battery was committed in such circumstances. Nevertheless, whilst some limitation on the scope of battery is common sense, the courts have experienced difficulties in finding a theoretical basis as to where to draw the line between a battery and ordinary social contact.

7. See *R* v *Spatt* [1990].

An early, somewhat narrow, attempt to distinguish lawful from unlawful touching was made by Lord Holt CJ in *Cole* v *Turner* [1704], who stated that 'the least touching of another in anger is a battery'. This was interpreted by the Court of Appeal in *Wilson* v *Pringle* [1987] to mean that in order for a battery to be committed there must be some 'hostile' intent. In this case, a 13-year-old boy suffered serious injury to his hip when a fellow pupil pulled his school bag off his shoulder in an act of horseplay. The Court of Appeal, allowing the defendant unconditional leave to defend the action, held that liability depended on whether the pupil's actions had been 'hostile' as opposed to a schoolboy prank:

> Hostility cannot be equated with ill-will or malevolence. It cannot be governed by the obvious intention shown in acts like punching, stabbing or shooting. It cannot be solely governed by an expressed intention, although that may be strong evidence. But the element of hostility, in the sense in which it is now to be considered, must be a question of fact for the tribunal of fact. It may be imported from the circumstances. (Croom-Johnson LJ at 253)

This is not particularly helpful. All it does is restate the question that needs to be answered: What is hostile intent? In *Wilson* v *Pringle*, the Court of Appeal equates 'hostility' with 'acting unlawfully' (at 253). On this view, hostile intent appears here to mean 'little more than that the defendant has interfered in a way to which the claimant might object' (*Rogers* p 107). But what is 'hostile' to one person may seem quite the opposite to another. When does an over-enthusiastic slap on the back become hostile? As Lord Goff notes, is a surgeon's mistaken but non-hostile amputation of a patient's leg therefore not a battery?

A better approach is that of Goff LJ in the earlier case *Collins* v *Wilcock* [1984], who stated that touching will only amount to a battery where it does not fall within the category of physical contacts 'generally acceptable in the ordinary conduct of daily life' (at 1177). What is considered generally acceptable will depend on the context. So, while you wouldn't expect to be nudged while in the queue at the Post Office, being jostled at the bar in a busy nightclub is the sort of thing about which people cannot reasonably complain and is likely to be considered generally acceptable. Though of course being 'goosed' (that is, having your bottom pinched) while waiting at the bar would cross the line and be a clear battery.

Although this approach was criticised as 'impractical' in *Wilson* v *Pringle* (at 252), Lord Goff restated his views in the House of Lords case of *Re F (Mental Patient: Sterilization)* [1990] where he explicitly rejected the 'hostility' requirement:

> it has recently been said that the touching must be 'hostile' to have that effect . . . I respectfully doubt whether that is correct. A prank that gets out of hand; an over-friendly slap on the back; surgical treatment by a surgeon who mistakenly thinks that the patient consented to it—all these things may transcend the bounds of lawfulness, without being characterised as hostile. (at 73)

 Pause for reflection

Ultimately, Goff LJ's notion of generally acceptable touching falls foul of the same definitional difficulties as Croom-Johnson LJ's in *Wilson* v *Pringle*: what constitutes contact

➡

→

'generally acceptable in the ordinary conduct of human life' is just as problematic as what can be considered hostile. Consider, for example, the over-familiar work colleague who greets everyone—male and female—with a 'friendly' pat on their bottom—does this constitute acceptable or unacceptable behaviour?

Conaghan & Mansell have argued that Goff LJ's notion of 'generally acceptable conduct' is open to feminist charges of bias, as male perceptions of acceptable conduct are hidden under a guise of neutrality, thereby precluding the recognition of women's experiences and their divergence from those of men: 'what men may see as a compliment, women often experience as an insult; what men offer as a gesture of intimacy and friendship, women may perceive as an invasion of privacy' (pp 164–5). A woman who pursues a battery claim in circumstances that involve 'minor' touching, a wolf-whistle or similar, *Conaghan & Mansell* suggest, is likely to be regarded as petty or vindictive: 'her sense of insult and embarrassment discounted as an "over-reaction", precisely because the original act is perceived as benign' (p 166). Do you agree?

14.3 Assault

Consider again the following example: a woman enters a lift with a male colleague at work. He sidles up to her, standing very close (but not touching) and whispers 'sweet nothings' in her ear. They are alone in the lift. Clearly, there is no battery—but could the man's actions constitute an assault (*Conaghan & Mansell* p 170)?

Defined by Goff LJ in *Collins* v *Wilcock* as 'an act which causes another person to apprehend the infliction of immediate, unlawful force on his person' (at 1177), assault protects the claimant who fears or apprehends a battery. Unlike battery, the wrong of assault lies not in any physical invasion or contact, but in the *anticipation* of such a bodily invasion or contact. The tort of assault is committed where the defendant's actions cause the claimant to reasonably apprehend the direct and immediate infliction of force upon their person. Typically assault and battery will occur together; the immediate anticipation of a battery (an assault) will almost always be followed by a battery—unless, for example, the assailant changes their mind, misses their target or a third party intervenes.

Thus, if Mike points a gun at Dave he has committed an assault. It makes no difference whether the gun is loaded—Dave does not know and has every reason to apprehend a battery (*R* v *St George* [1840]). Only when Mike shoots the gun and hits Dave has he committed a battery. And, of course, if his aim is poor and he misses, only an assault has been committed. Not every threat will give rise to liability. If Mike says to Dave, 'I'm going to shoot you dead' but Dave knows that Mike has to go home to get his gun first it is unlikely that this will amount to an assault. Similarly, if Mike shoots Dave in his sleep he has committed only a battery, not an assault.

In order for there to be an actionable assault:

(1) the defendant must intend or be reckless as to the claimant's apprehending of the application of unlawful force;

(2) the claimant must reasonably apprehend immediate unlawful force being applied to them; and

(3) the threat must be of the application of immediate and direct force.

14.3.1 **Intention**

Once again the requirement of intention is a little misleading. Not only must the defendant have acted voluntarily, he must also intend to cause the claimant to apprehend having immediate unlawful force applied to them, or be subjectively reckless as to the possibility that their actions will cause the claimant to apprehend the application of such force.

14.3.2 **Reasonable apprehension of unlawful touching**

For there to be an assault the claimant must reasonably anticipate or expect the application of unlawful force or, in other words, the infliction of a battery. Thus, if Arthur creeps up behind Mike and strikes him he has committed a battery, but not an assault. It is only an assault if Mike knew Arthur was about to hit him. Conversely, if Mike ducks, and so avoids Arthur's blow, Arthur will have committed an assault but no battery.

> ***Stephens v Myers* [1830] Assizes**
>
> The claimant was acting as Chair at a parish council meeting sitting at the head of the table. The defendant was also at the table with about six or seven people between him and the claimant. Following a decision to ask the defendant to leave the meeting, the defendant threatened the Chair with violence saying he would rather throw the claimant out of his chair than leave the room. He then advanced toward the Chair with a clenched fist. Fortunately, his approach was stopped by the timely intervention of the churchwarden. The defendant was held liable for assault. Though the jury clearly thought the Chair was somewhat timid; its award of one shilling was trivial even in the 1830s.

The test of reasonable apprehension is an objective one. It is irrelevant whether the particular claimant was actually in fear or could have defended themselves successfully.

14.3.3 **Immediate and direct threat**

An assault requires that a claimant reasonably apprehends the infliction of immediate and direct force. If they know that the defendant is not in a position to do this then there can be no assault: 'It is not every threat, when there is no actual violence, that constitutes an assault, there must, in all cases, be the means of carrying that threat into effect' (***Stephens v Myers* [1830]**). This was confirmed in ***Thomas v National Union of Miners (South Wales Area)* [1986]** and more recently by the Court of Appeal in *Mbasogo v Logo Ltd* [2006].

> ***Thomas v National Union of Miners (South Wales Area)* [1986] HC**
>
> During the 1984–5 miners' strike, a group of working miners (strike-breakers) sought an interlocutory injunction against the National Union of Mineworkers to prevent its members
> ➡

> (striking miners) from verbally abusing and harassing them as they went to work. Each day a crowd of some 50–70 picketers gathered at the colliery gates as the working miners entered the workplace in vehicles surrounded by a police guard.
>
> Dismissing their claim, Scott J held that the strike-breakers were unable to categorise the actions as an assault: 'the working miners are in vehicles and the pickets are held back from the vehicles, I do not understand how even the most violent of threats or gestures could be said to constitute an assault' (at 62). The working miners were effectively protected by the police and, as a result, the requirements of immediacy and directness were not met.

However, this is not to say that there can never be an assault where the defendant lacks the immediate means to put it into effect. A bank robber who points a gun at the cashier and threatens to shoot unless his demands are met commits an assault—whether or not the gun is loaded—so long as the cashier reasonably believed that the gun was loaded and hence that the threat would be carried out.

Traditionally, the requirement of directness meant that threatening words needed to be accompanied by a physically intimidating gesture: 'No words or singing are equivalent to an assault' (*R v Meade and Belt* [1823]). However, it has long been recognised that a threatening gesture can be negated by words which suggest that an assault is *not* imminent. Thus in *Tuberville v Savage* [1669], for example, the defendant placed his hand on his sword and stated, 'If it were not assize time[8] I would not take such language from you.' As it *was* assize time, the defendant was in fact stating that he *did not intend* to strike the claimant and so there was no assault. The key point remains whether the claimant reasonably apprehended the infliction of immediate and direct force. As *Lunney & Oliphant* note: 'One wonders whether the [claimant] confronted by a man obviously angry and drawing a sword, would really be calmed by the addition of the words spoken by the defendant' (p 57). Circumstances in which the defendant's words negate their threatening gestures are distinguishable from conditional threats where the claimant is merely given an option by the defendant to avoid violence. This is clearly an assault. It is no excuse for the highwayman to claim that his victims had a viable alternative option when he said, 'Stand and deliver, your money or your life'.

'Highwaymen aside', the reason for judicial emphasis on gestures rather than words, *Conaghan & Mansell* suggest, lies in a concern to 'distinguish a mere insult (for which there is generally no legal remedy) from a serious and immediate threat' (p 170); in other words, to balance the conflicting interests of freedom of speech and public order. It follows, they continue, 'that the harasser who makes obscene remarks, "amorous" proposals or embarrassing or intimate comments has traditionally not been significantly inhibited by the tort of assault from doing so. There is, after all, no harm in asking' (*Conaghan & Mansell* p 170).

However, the House of Lords' decision in **R v Ireland** [1998] ended any doubt over whether mere words could amount to an assault. Its reasoning applies to tort, despite the fact it is a criminal law case.

---

8. That is, the time when judges from the King's Bench were visiting.

R v Ireland [1998] HL

Three women had been subjected to a lengthy period of harassment by the defendant, including repeated silent telephone calls, generally at night. The women suffered psychiatric illness as a result.

Lord Steyn in the House of Lords rejected the proposition that an assault could never be committed by words alone: 'A thing said is also a thing done. There is no reason why something said should be incapable of causing apprehension of immediate personal violence, e.g. a man accosting a woman in a dark alley saying "come with me or I will stab you"' (at 162).

Liability, therefore, depends on whether the claimant in the circumstances reasonably believed that the oral threat could be carried out in the sufficiently near future to qualify as an immediate threat of personal violence. On the facts, the court was prepared to accept that silence would be capable of giving rise to such fears:

> Just as it is not true to say that every blow which is struck is an assault...so also it is not true to say that mere words or gestures can never constitute an assault. It all depends on the circumstances...The words and gestures must be seen in their whole context. (Lord Hope at 166)

 Pause for reflection

Whilst the old saying goes 'sticks and stones may break my bones, but words will never hurt me', this seems to require an unduly high level of courage by the recipient of the verbal threats. As Lord Steyn notes at the beginning of his opinion:

> it is easy to understand the terrifying effect of a campaign of telephone calls at night by a silent caller to a woman living on her own. It would be natural for the victim to regard the calls as menacing. What may heighten her fear is that she will not know what the caller may do next. The spectre of the caller arriving at her doorstep bent on inflicting personal violence on her may come to dominate her thinking. After all, as a matter of common sense, what else would she be terrified about? (at 152)

Do you agree? Would it make a difference if the calls had been made to the claimants' mobile phones? Or by text? Or via Twitter? While the caller may not know the claimant's precise location, it is unlikely that this would have a significant (any?) impact on their state of mind. Nonetheless, in such a case it is likely that the claimant would find it harder to establish an assault—the caller's inability (subject to any evidence to the contrary) to pinpoint their exact location (which, of course, could still be in their own home) may make their fear of *imminent* and direct force less reasonable.[9]

---

9. Consider again the phone calls made by the student in the examples at the beginning of the chapter— *R v Ireland* suggests that, if sufficiently serious, they could amount to an assault. There may also be a claim under the Protection from Harassment Act—see pp 404–407.

As we shall see, a claimant who is the victim of harassing conduct but which doesn't amount to an assault may nonetheless still have a claim under the rule in *Wilkinson* v *Downton* or under the Protection from Harassment Act 1997.

14.4 **False imprisonment**

The tort of false imprisonment sits alongside battery and assault as the third in the family of torts comprising trespass to the person. Goff LJ in *Collins* v *Wilcock* [1984] defines false imprisonment as involving the 'unlawful imposition of constraint on another's freedom of movement from a particular place' (at 1177). This tort is concerned with the claimant's right to freedom of movement. As such, a *complete* restriction of this freedom, unless it is expressly or impliedly authorised by law, is necessary to render the defendant liable. To this end, 'false' means simply wrongful and 'imprisonment' extends to any actions that deprive the claimant of their freedom of movement. As with the other trespass torts, there is no false imprisonment where the claimant consents and, while there is no need to show force, a claimant must not be taken to be consenting simply because they do not resist.

In order for there to be an actionable claim for false imprisonment:

(1) the defendant must intend or be reckless as to the restriction of the claimant's freedom of movement;

(2) there must be a complete restriction of the claimant's freedom of movement; and

(3) it must be done without lawful authorisation.

14.4.1 **Intention**

As Smith LJ held in *Iqbal*, false imprisonment, like the other trespass torts, requires an intentional act. However, as we have seen this requirement is a little misleading. To give an example used by Smith LJ:

> If a security guard in an office block locks the door to the claimant's room believing the claimant has gone home for the night and not realising that he is in fact still inside the room, he has committed a deliberate act. However, he did not intend to confine the claimant. He may well be guilty of negligence because he did not check whether the room was empty but he would not be guilty of the intentional tort of false imprisonment. (at [72])

In this example, the fact that the locking of the door was intentional is not enough. The defendant must intend thereby to confine the claimant to that room. However, it is also clear from *Iqbal* that subjective recklessness will also suffice, so that there will be liability even where the defendant doesn't set out to imprison the claimant but he is nonetheless aware that this is a likely consequence of his actions. So if in the above example the defendant locked the door suspecting (and not caring) that the claimant may still be inside then, though he doesn't strictly *intend* to imprison him, he is nonetheless liable for false imprisonment.[10]

While the defendant needs to intend or be reckless as to the claimant's imprisonment, it is not necessary for the defendant to have intended to imprison them *unlawfully*. So, in *R v Governor of Brockhill Prison, ex p Evans (No 2)* [2001], the claimant was lawfully imprisoned for various criminal offences. However, the prison governor was held to have miscalculated her release date with the consequence that she was held for longer than she should have been. Her claim for false imprisonment was successful, even though the governor clearly did not intend to hold the claimant for any longer than the lawful duration.

14.4.2 **A complete restriction of movement**

There must be a complete restriction of the claimant's freedom of movement; the conditions for the tort are not satisfied if the claimant is able to move in another direction (***Bird* v *Jones*** [1845]) or if there are reasonable means of escape (though if the claimant is reasonably unaware of the means of escape, their detention is likely to amount to false imprisonment). Likewise, intimidation or emotional pressure designed to induce a person to remain in a particular place are unlikely to constitute false imprisonment (although it may amount to an assault if the person fears a physical attack to stop them leaving). However, if the claimant's freedom of movement is completely restricted it does not matter how long this restriction lasts. This means that acts which are 'primarily' batteries may also involve false imprisonment—thus, if A rapes B, B will have a claim for both battery and false imprisonment (and possibly assault) (*Rogers* p 119).

Bird v *Jones* [1845] QB

The defendant's employer had cut off part of the public footway on Hammersmith Bridge in London, without due permission, for seating to view a regatta on the river. Although this prevented the claimant using the footway, his freedom of movement was not completely restrained as he was able to turn back the way he had come.

The defendants were not liable for false imprisonment as they had not imposed a complete restriction on the claimant's freedom of movement: 'imprisonment is . . . a total restraint of the liberty of the person . . . and not a partial obstruction of his will, whatever inconvenience it may bring on him' (at 742).

It is a matter of contention whether a reasonable means of escape exists when the defendant imposes conditions on the manner in which the visitor leaves his/her

---

10. This is different to a situation where the defendant entirely innocently locks the claimant in a room (for which there will likely be no liability) and where a defendant ought to have known that there was someone in the room (in which case there will be a claim in negligence). In other words, the law distinguishes between the situation where you lock the door knowing that someone *is* inside (trespass), where you lock the door knowing that someone *might* be inside (which we tend to call (subjective) recklessness—but which will still meet the intention requirements of the tort) and the situation where you lock the door not thinking that someone might be inside but when you *ought* to have known this (negligence).

premises. There is authority suggesting that, provided the conditions are reasonable, the defendant is not liable if they refuse to allow the claimant to leave until these conditions are satisfied (*Robinson* v *Balmain New Ferry Co Ltd* [1910]). In this case the claimant had paid a penny to enter a wharf in order to catch a ferry but then changed his mind. He tried to leave the way he came. It was considered reasonable for the defendants to charge him another penny to leave.[11]

 Pause for reflection

Consider the following examples: a man has been deliberately locked in a room on the top floor of a seven-story building. The window is unlocked and there is a rope near it long enough for him to climb down safely—is this a reasonable means of escape to defeat a claim in the tort of false imprisonment? Would your answer change if the rope reached only as far as the first floor?

This was taken further by the House of Lords' decision in *Herd* v *Weardale Steel, Coke and Coal Co Ltd* [1915]. This case involved a miner who had descended into the pit at 9.30 am and who was due to remain until 4 pm. At 11 am, he refused to do certain work, on the basis that it was dangerous and demanded to be taken to the surface before the end of his shift. His employer initially refused. He was later brought to the surface at 1.30 pm although the lift had been available to carry men to the surface from 1.10 pm—so he was detained in the mine against his will for 20 minutes. The House of Lords held that the employer was not liable for false imprisonment—the miner had voluntarily entered the mine under a contract of employment and was deemed to have impliedly consented that he would not be brought to the surface until the end of the shift. In fact, the Court of Appeal went so far as to suggest the only claim would be that of the employer against the employee for breach of contract.

 Counterpoint

Paula Giliker and Silas Beckwith suggest that it is difficult to see *Herd* as anything other than a harsh ruling in favour of an employer's rights over his employee's. It is scarcely legitimate to suggest that imprisonment is a reasonable response to the employee's breach of contract.[12] However, the case is typically viewed as one involving an omission: following Herd's request to leave, the employers did not do anything to positively restrain him; they simply failed to provide him with a route out. As such, there could be no action for false imprisonment. Trespass is concerned with immediate and direct actions, not omissions— the employers had simply failed to do something they were not obliged to do.

---

11. See further Mark Lunney's interesting discussion of the historical and commercial context of this controversial case, including an explanation for the misprinting of the claimant's name—as Robinson rather than *Robertson*—in the authorised report of the Privy Council (2009).
12. *Tort* (Sweet & Maxwell, 2008), p 353.

That false imprisonment cannot generally be committed by an omission, was recently affirmed by the Court of Appeal in *Iqbal v Prison Officers Association* [2009].

Iqbal v Prison Officers Association [2009] CA

The claimant was a prisoner who was normally allowed out of his cell for six hours a day for work and recreation. The defendant trade union, the Prison Officers Association (POA), called an unlawful strike, as a result of which hardly any of the prison officers at the claimant's prison turned up for work on the relevant day. The prison governor decided that, given that there were not sufficient prison officers working, prisoners should remain in their cells for the entire day. The claimant brought a claim against the POA for false imprisonment for the period that he would usually be allowed out of his cell. (There was no claim against the prison governor ([21].)[13]

The Court of Appeal rejected the claim. The majority saw the central question as whether the prison officers could be held liable for an omission: their failure to release the claimant from his cell (both sides agreed that if the prison officers were liable then so too was the POA). They held that an omission could ground liability only if the defendants were under a positive duty to act *in relation to the claimant*. Since, in their view, there was no such duty—the prison officers' duty to release the claimant from his cell was a contractual duty owed to the prison governor and not the claimant—there could be no claim.

> At least as a general principle, defendants are not to be held liable in tort for the results of their inaction, in the absence of a specific duty to act, a duty which would normally arise out of the particular relationship between the claimant and the defendant. Such a hard and fast distinction between action and inaction may seem arbitrary to some people, but it is not unprincipled, and, while it may lead to apparent injustice in particular cases, it does help to ensure a degree of clarity and certainty in the law. (Lord Neuberger MR at [21])

Sullivan LJ dissented in *Iqbal* on the grounds that the prison officers association's action in calling the strike could not be sensibly considered a 'mere omission' as opposed to a positive act (at [94]). As such, the claimant's right not to be further restrained by the prison officers' unauthorised action was infringed.

 Pause for reflection

The extent to which the 'apparent injustice' in *Herd* and *Iqbal* is outweighed by the need to ensure clarity and certainty in the law will depend on one's views of the different interests of the parties. As Sullivan LJ notes, the prison governor's response to the strike was 'entirely predictable' (at [102]). In any industrial dispute resulting in strike action, third parties—here

→

---

13. Following *Ex p Hague* (see p 396), it is well established that a prisoner has no 'residual liberty' whilst lawfully detained in a prison: 'a prisoner cannot maintain an action for false imprisonment against the governor even if he is deprived of any limited degree of freedom which he usually enjoys under the prison regime. His detention anywhere within the prison is lawful' (*Iqbal* at [62]).

> →
>
> the prisoners—will often bear the brunt of the disruption. In the context of a prison this is likely to be felt through the loss of the measure of liberty afforded to the prisoners by the governor as part of the prison regime. However, he continued:
>
> > in so far as there is a conflict between the prisoners' right not to be deprived of that liberty by persons, including prison officers, acting otherwise than in accordance with the prison governor's authority, and the right of prison officers (absent any statutory prohibition) to strike, the former right must take precedence over the latter. While the right to strike is important, the right not to be falsely imprisoned is of fundamental importance. (at [103])
>
> Do you agree?

Despite earlier authorities to the contrary (*Herring* v *Boyle* [1834]), it is not necessary to show that the claimant knew of their imprisonment. The point here is simply that the tort protects the claimant's freedom of movement. Moreover, as proof of damage is not required, it is not necessary that the claimant has suffered from the knowledge of his/her false imprisonment:

> it appears to me that a person could be imprisoned without his knowing it. I think a person can be imprisoned while he is asleep, while he is in a state of drunkenness, while he is unconscious, and while he is a lunatic…Of course the damages might be diminished and would be affected by the question whether he was conscious of it or not. (Atkin, LJ, *Meering* v *Grahame-White Aviation* [1920] at 53–4)

This was confirmed *obiter* by the House of Lords in *Murray* v *Ministry of Defence* [1988] (in this case the claimant knew her freedom of movement was restricted): 'the law attaches supreme importance to the liberty of the individual and if he suffers a wrongful interference with that liberty it should remain actionable even without proof of special damage' (at 529). However, a person who is unaware of their imprisonment is likely to receive only nominal damages (see Smith LJ, *Iqbal* at [83]).[14]

This continues to be the position despite the House of Lords' decision in *R* v *Bournewood Mental Health Trust (ex p L)* [1999], in which it was held that there must be actual rather than potential restraint on the claimant's liberty. In this case a mentally ill patient was voluntarily held in an unlocked hospital ward. The staff at the hospital agreed that should he try to leave he would be detained compulsorily under the Mental Health Act 1983. This is indeed what then happened. A bare majority of the House of Lords dismissed his claim for false imprisonment in relation to the period prior to his compulsory detention. That the defendants were prepared to imprison the claimant was not the same as actually imprisoning him. The suggestion, then, is that there was no imprisonment until the defendant was sectioned. This might seem somewhat

---

14. Thus if the father and daughter, in the example at the start of this chapter, were found by the security guard before they realised they were imprisoned, their damages for false imprisonment (assuming the other elements of the tort can be established) would be reduced accordingly.

implausible; as Lord Steyn noted in dissent, the idea that the claimant could go free seems something of a 'fairy tale' (at 475).[15]

This decision appears at odds with that in *Meering*. In both cases the imprisonment consisted in the certainty that total restraint would have been enforced had the claimants tried to leave, even though neither had the knowledge that this would happen. Given the ECtHR's decision and that the circumstances in which a mentally ill patient can be detained has been clarified by the Mental Capacity Act 2005, is unlikely that the majority's decision in *Bournewood* will be followed in future.

14.4.3 **Without legal authorisation**

The essence of false imprisonment is the restraint of a person without lawful justification.[16] The tort of false imprisonment has a strong constitutional element. In particular, where the defendant is a public authority (under the Human Rights Act (HRA) 1998), a claim for false imprisonment may coexist with one in respect of Article 5 of the European Convention on Human Rights (ECHR).[17] A recent example of this is *Austin & Other* v *Commissioner of Police of the Metropolis* [2009]). This case was brought in response to a police cordon set up on Oxford Street, London on 1 May 2001, restricting the movement of some 3,000 people. The police had imposed the cordon after a large number of demonstrators—so-called 'May Day' protesters—some of whom were violent, had converged at Oxford Circus. The claimant was caught within the cordon and was prevented from leaving for several hours. She brought claims for false imprisonment and a breach of her right to liberty under Article 5. The House of Lords held that there had been no infringement of the claimant's Article 5 right. The police's actions in seeking to ensure crowd control had been resorted to in good faith, were proportionate and were not enforced any longer than was reasonably necessary (at [37]).[18]

In most cases of false imprisonment the person whose movement is restrained would otherwise be free to go wherever they please, however a difficult problem is posed by the question of whether a person who is lawfully imprisoned can ever complain of false imprisonment in relation to acts subsequent to his lawful imprisonment. In *R* v *Deputy Governor of Parkhurst Prison, ex p Hague* [1992] the House of Lords held that Hague, a category A prisoner, was unable to establish a claim for false imprisonment in relation to his continued segregation following a prison transfer (in breach of the Prison Rules) as to do so would be to confuse the fact of confinement with the conditions of confinement; the tort of false imprisonment is confined to the former. This decision is surprising. One might expect a breach of the Prison Rules to negate the prison governor's statutory authority. It is likely that the court was mindful of a desire to limit claims from disgruntled prisoners for technical breaches of the Rules. It

15. The judges in the European Court of Human Rights (ECtHR) agreed with Lord Steyn, unanimously holding that there had been a violation of the claimant's Art 5 rights (*HL* v *UK* [2004] at [91]).

16. Lawful authorisation is also sometimes referred to as a defence to false imprisonment.

17. Right to liberty and security.

18. The claim for false imprisonment was rejected by the Court of Appeal and was not considered by the House of Lords. The claimant accepted that if the House of Lords found that there was no infringement of her rights under Art 5 then her claim for false imprisonment must also fail, as her containment within the cordon would be in the lawful exercise of police powers (at [11]).

may be that there are other avenues to compensation in such a case: for example, an action for breach of statutory duty, negligence, misfeasance in public office (*Karagozlu v Commissioner of Police for the Metropolis* [2006]) or under the HRA. It is clear that if a prisoner is 'imprisoned' by another prisoner within the confines of the prison (or by a prison officer acting in bad faith) they will be able to bring an action for false imprisonment (*Ex p Hague* at 164). Similarly, as we have seen, a prisoner who is detained once their sentence has expired is likely to be successful in a claim for false imprisonment, the defence of lawful authority having expired (*R v Governor of Brockhill Prison, ex p Evans (No 2)*).

Things are slightly more complicated in relation to cases where a police officer 'detains' a person (without arresting them) on the basis of a 'reasonable suspicion' which might justify the detention. While generally trespass to the person is concerned with unlawfulness not unreasonable conduct, in such cases the burden of proof is on the claimant to show that the defendant's exercise of discretion is unreasonable (*Chief Constable of Thames Valley Police v Earl Gideon Foster Hepburn* [2002]; *Brooks v Commissioner of Police for the Metropolis* [2005]).

14.5 Defences

In this section we consider a number of defences that typically arise in this context—consent, necessity and self-defence. However, students should note that the defences discussed in Chapter 10 may also be applicable to the trespass torts.

14.5.1 Consent

Consent is the most important 'defence' in this area of law.[19] There is no battery when the claimant consents to the direct and immediate application of force by the defendant. If Ellie consents to being kissed by Arthur, she cannot later sue him for a battery; his kiss is not unlawful. Similarly, there will be no false imprisonment or assault if you ask to be tied up and threatened, say as part of a role-play.

Issues relating to consent arise often in the context of medical treatment.[20] A doctor does not commit a battery when operating on or treating a patient if the patient has validly consented to the treatment. Of course, this simply prompts a second question: when is a patient's content valid? In *Chatterton v Gerson* [1981], the claimant underwent an operation to reduce the severe pain she was experiencing from a post-operative scar in her right groin. Unfortunately, following the operation she lost the sensation in her right leg, had only temporary alleviation of the pain and could only move about with a stick. She

19. Consent can also be understood as one of the definitional elements of the trespass torts so that a battery is intended, direct and non-consensual contact. However, unlike these other elements the onus is on the *defendant* to establish the presence of consent and as such it is better to regard consent as a defence (although see *Freeman v Home Office (No 2)* [1984]). Consent is also considered as a defence to negligence claims in Chapter 10, pp 257–261.

20. For examples of consent in other trespass contexts see *R v Lincoln* [1990] concerning 'rough and tumble' on the football pitch and *R v Williams* [1923] in which a singing teacher was found guilty of raping a naïve claimant who had consented to his actions on the basis of his false assertion that his conduct would improve her singing voice.

claimed that her consent to the operation was not valid as she hadn't been fully informed of the risks. The court held that as she understood the 'general nature of the operation' her consent was 'real': 'once the patient was informed in broad terms of the nature of the procedure which is intended, and gives her consent, that consent is real, and the cause of the action on which to base a claim for failure to go into risks and implications is negligence, not trespass' (at 443).[21] However, this is not to suggest that trespass has no role to play in a medical context. Bristow J continued: 'if by some accident...a boy was admitted to hospital for a tonsillectomy and due to an administrative error was circumcised instead, trespass would be the appropriate cause of action against the doctor' (at 432).

But what about refusal of consent? If an individual is able to consent to what would otherwise be a battery, surely it follows that there is a corresponding ability to refuse consent to such actions? Consider again the following example: a doctor delivers a healthy child after performing a Caesarean section on the mother without her consent. Does she have an action against the doctor in battery?

The law is clear that an individual has an absolute right to the inviolability of their body:

> an adult patient who...suffers from no mental incapacity has an absolute right to choose whether to consent to medical treatment, to refuse it, or to choose one rather than another of the treatments being offered. This right of choice is not limited to decisions which others might regard as sensible. (Lord Donaldson MR, *Re T (Adult: Refusal of Treatment)* [1993] at 102)

A competent adult may therefore withhold their consent to any treatment (including the provision of food if provided by an intravenous tube or similar) even if said treatment is in their best interests, or necessary to save their life—or, somewhat more controversially, the life of their unborn child (*Re MB (Caesarean Section)* [1997] at 533). This common law position—and the test of capacity more broadly—has been enshrined in statute (for those over 16) in the Mental Capacity Act 2005.[22]

Mental Capacity Act 2005

Section 1
(2) A person must be assumed to have capacity unless it is established that he lacks capacity.
(3) A person is not to be treated as unable to make a decision unless all practicable steps to help him to do so have been taken without success.
(4) A person is not to be treated as unable to make a decision merely because he makes an unwise decision.
(5) An act done, or decision made, under this Act for or on behalf of a person who lacks capacity must be done, or made, in his best interests.

→

---

21. In this sense there is no requirement that consent need be 'informed' (*Sidaway* v *Bethlem Royal Hospital* [1985] (although cf **Chester v Afshar** [2005] discussed in Chapter 9, pp 237–238).
22. In *Re MM (An Adult)* [2007] Munby J held that there is 'no relevant distinction between the test in s 3(1) of the Act and the pre-existing common law' (at [74]).

(6) Before the act is done, or the decision is made, regard must be had to whether the purpose for which it is needed can be as effectively achieved in a way that is less restrictive of the person's rights and freedom of action.

A doctor can only treat a patient *in the absence of consent* where a patient is unable to consent, that is, they *lack the capacity* to make such a decision themselves. It is useful here to adopt Shaun Pattinson's explanation of the 2005 Act as setting out a two-stage test in sections 2 and 3 for determining capacity.[23] A patient will only be considered to lack capacity if both stages of the test are met. First, the patient must be suffering from an 'impairment of, or a disturbance in the functioning of, the mind or brain', which means they are unable to make a decision for themselves (s 2). This may be temporary or long term, and caused by a number of factors including mental illness, brain injury or alcohol or drug abuse. Secondly, the patient will be considered unable to make a decision if the doctor reasonably believes and takes reasonable steps to ensure (s 5) that the patient is unable:

(a) to understand the information relevant to the decision;

(b) to retain that information;

(c) to use or weigh that information as part of the process of making the decision; or

(d) to communicate his decision (whether by talking, using sign language or any other means) (s 3(1)).

Where this test is satisfied, a doctor will not incur liability so long as they reasonably believe that the treatment or procedure is in the patient's 'best interests' (s 5). By contrast, a patient who *is able*, for example, to understand the information relevant to the decision, has the capacity to make decisions about how they are to be treated and to give—and withhold—their consent. A doctor who operates or treats a competent patient who refuses their consent in relation to the relevant procedure will commit a battery.

 Counterpoint

The 2005 Act, like the common law, places considerable emphasis on the doctor's belief in the patient's capacity. Despite judicial rhetoric upholding an individual's right to self-determination, in cases where medical treatment is necessary to save the life of a woman and her unborn child, the case law suggests that the former's refusal to consent to medical intervention is less likely to be considered valid.[24] *Re MB* is a case in point. In this case, the claimant consented to a Caesarean section but withheld consent in relation to an

23. Shaun Pattinson *Medical Law and Ethics* (2nd edn, Sweet & Maxwell, 2009), pp 151–3 and generally Ch 5.

24. Celia Wells 'On the Outside Looking In: Perspectives on Enforced Caesareans' in Sally Sheldon and Michael Thomson (eds) *Feminist Perspectives on Health Care Law* (Cavendish Publishing, 1998), p 237.

→

accompanying medical procedure. She was found to be suffering from an impairment or disturbance of mental functioning rendering her unable to make a decision whether to consent to, or refuse, treatment (due to a fear of needles). Of course, the reality of the situation was that if the doctors had not intervened, the claimant *and her child* would have died.

An individual's right to make bad decisions is recognised in both common and statute law—how far do you think this should extend to those decisions which would negatively impact on the life of the foetus? In *St George's Healthcare NHS Trust* v *S* [1999] it was held that when deciding whether a Caesarean section performed against the wishes of a competent woman constitutes an actionable battery, the interests of the foetus do not weigh against the woman's autonomy. Do you agree?

14.5.2 **Necessity**

Previously in medical situations where a claimant is unable to consent a defendant might rely on the limited common law defence of necessity. This solved a practical problem experienced by emergency services and other medical professionals where an unconscious patient is incapable of consenting to necessary medical treatment. On this basis where a patient is unconscious but otherwise competent, and not known to object to the treatment, doctors may intervene in the best interests of the patient (*Re F; F* v *West Berkshire Health Authority* [1990]). It was also used in cases of permanent incapacity, for example where the patient is in a coma or mentally ill (e.g. *Airedale NHS Trust* v *Bland* [1993]).

Again, the common law in relation to this has been codified by the Mental Capacity Act 2005. As noted above, a medical professional will not incur liability for treating a patient who is temporarily or permanently incapacitated, so long as before doing so they take reasonable steps to establish, and reasonably believe, that the patient lacks capacity and the treatment or procedure is in the patient's 'best interests' (s 5). Where the patient's lack of capacity is only temporary—due to shock or anger or as a result of an accident—the medical professional may treat the patient in accordance with their best interests, though they should also take into account when the person is likely to regain capacity in relation to the matter in question and, if possible, wait until the patient has regained capacity before continuing with further treatment (s 4).

Though necessity is most often used where the claimant is unable to consent, it also applies in other situations (see, for example, the extended discussion in *Re A (Conjoined Twins)* [2001]) and in relation to other trespass to the person torts—for example false imprisonment (*Bournewood; Austin & Other* v *Commissioner of Police of the Metropolis* [2008] (CA)[25]).

14.5.3 **Self-defence**

The defendant may be able to argue that they acted in self-defence.[26] However, unlike the defendant in criminal proceedings who simply needs an honest belief (even if that

---

25. Note: the House of Lords did not discuss the application of the defence of necessity.

26. There is some evidence to suggest that the defence of contributory negligence may be raised in cases involving intentional harm (*Murphy* v *Culhane* [1977]; **Reeves** v **Commissioner of Police**

belief is unreasonable) that they were about to be attacked, the tort defendant's belief must be not only honest but also *reasonable* (*Ashley* v *Chief Constable of West Sussex Police* [2008]). Moreover, it has long been established that the defendant's actions must be proportionate to the force (to be) exerted against them. Thus, in *Cockcroft* v *Smith* [1705], the claimant's act of running with his finger extended towards the defendant's eyes did not justify the defendant's action of biting off part of the offending finger. Similarly, in *Lane* v *Holloway* [1968] the defendant's severe blow to the claimant's eye was out of proportion to the claimant's punch to his shoulder. *Lane* v *Holloway* is also authority for the proposition that provocation is not a valid defence in these cases.

Lane v *Holloway* can be contrasted with the decision in *Cross* v *Kirkby* [2000]. Here a farmer, who had been struck by a hunt saboteur with a baseball bat, wrestled the bat from him and struck a single blow to the head which caused the claimant serious injuries. In finding self-defence the Court of Appeal took into account the anguish of the moment in assessing whether this was an excessive or disproportionate response to the threat posed and held that the law did not require the defendant to measure the violence to be deployed with mathematical precision.

 Pause for reflection

Views will differ on what is or is not reasonable self-defence. Consider again the woman alone in a lift with a male colleague who begins to whisper 'sweet nothings' in her ear. Suppose the woman takes matters into her own hands and knees the man in the groin— will he have a claim for battery against her? Or is her conduct excusable on the grounds of self-defence? Is it a reasonable exercise of force? After all the words whispered to her were not threatening violence as such—there may have been insufficient indication that the words would be followed by any immediate unlawful force—and, even if they were, is the harm or injury of, for example, a stolen kiss comparable with that of a knee in the groin? Surely she used disproportionate force? Didn't she?

14.6 Intentional infliction of emotional or physical harm

So far this chapter has considered the three torts which comprise trespass to the person: battery, assault and false imprisonment. All these involve actual or potential physical infringements of the claimant's person: touching them, restricting their movement and so on. However, it is possible to cause another harm without physically interfering (or threatening to physically interfere) with them or their movements. In such cases, the trespass to the person torts offer no protection. Some of this ground is covered by the tort of negligence (though a claimant is only able to recover for emotional distress

of the Metropolis [2000]). However this was doubted by Lord Rodger in *Standard Chartered Bank* v *Pakistan National Shipping Corp (No 2)* [2003] who suggested that contributory negligence was not applicable in cases of intentional wrongdoing (at [43]–[45]).

if it amounts to a recognisable psychiatric illness), while the rest may be covered by the rule in *Wilkinson* v *Downton* and the Protection from Harassment Act 1997.

14.6.1 **The rule in *Wilkinson* v *Downton***

In *Wilkinson* v *Downton* [1897] the defendant falsely told the claimant that her husband had been involved in an accident in which he had been seriously injured. The defendant later claimed that he had intended it as a practical joke. Unfortunately for him it was misjudged. The claimant took the news very badly; the sudden and violent shock to her nervous system produced severe physical and psychological reactions. Wright J held that the defendant had 'wilfully done an act calculated to cause physical harm to the female [claimant]—that is to say, infringe her right to personal safety, and thereby in fact caused physical harm to her. That proposition, without more appears to me to state a good cause of action, there being no justification alleged for the act' (at 57).

This novel cause of action was approved by the Court of Appeal in *Janvier* v *Sweeney* [1919]. In this case a private detective pretended to be a police officer (in order to obtain some letters that were suspected of being forgeries) and threatened the claimant with arrest for corresponding with a German spy. The claimant was able to recover for her psychiatric illness suffered as a result.

Unlike the trespass to the person torts which are actionable *per se*, success under the rule in *Wilkinson* v *Downton* depends on the claimant being able to show that they have been harmed by the defendant's conduct. The question is whether the defendant needs to have *intended* to cause that harm. In *Wilkinson* v *Downton* itself, despite Wright J's reference to the defendant's action being 'wilfully done' and 'calculated to' cause harm it seems clear that the defendant did not set out to harm the claimant but only to play a practical joke. This suggests that the defendant need not intend to harm the claimant in order to be held liable under the rule, and that negligence or carelessness will suffice.[27] This question was addressed by the House of Lords in **Wainwright v Home Office** [2004].

> #### *Wainwright v Home Office* [2004] HL
>
> The claimants, Mrs Wainwright and her son, Alan, were subjected to 'sloppy' strip searches by prison officers while visiting a family member in Leeds prison. The searches were not conducted according to the Prison Rules 1964 and had been a humiliating and distressing experience for both claimants. The claimants sought, in part, to rely on the rule in *Wilkinson* v *Downton* to ground a claim for their anxiety and distress.
>
> The House of Lords unanimously rejected this claim.[28] Lord Hoffmann held that liability would require, at the very least, the defendants to have acted without caring whether they
>
>

---

27. See further Denise Réaume 'The Role of Intention in the Tort in *Wilkinson v Downton*' in Jason Neyers, Erika Chamberlain and Stephen Pitel *Emerging Issues in Tort Law* (Hart Publishing, 2007), p 533.

28. The House of Lords also dismissed the claimants' appeal in relation to Art 8 (right to private and family life). The privacy aspects of this case are discussed further in Chapter 16, p 451. A battery claim in relation to Alan, allowed in the Court of Appeal, was not appealed.

→

caused harm (recklessly). This was not established on the facts of the case; he accepted the trial judge's finding that the 'deviations from the procedure laid down for strip-searches were . . . not intended to increase the humiliation necessarily involved but merely sloppiness' (at [45]). He went on to suggest that *even if the necessary intention had been established in this case* not all intentionally caused psychiatric harm should give rise to liability under the rule.

> Even on the basis of a genuine intention to cause distress, I would wish . . . to reserve my opinion on whether compensation should be recoverable. In institutions and workplaces all over the country, people constantly do and say things with the intention of causing distress and humiliation to others. This shows lack of consideration and appalling manners but I am not sure that the right way to deal with it is always by litigation . . . The requirement of a course of conduct [in the Protection from Harassment Act 1997] shows that Parliament was conscious that it might not be in the public interest to allow the law to be set in motion for one boorish incident. It may be that any development of the common law should show similar caution. In my opinion, therefore, the claimants can build nothing on *Wilkinson* v *Downton*. It does not provide a remedy for distress which does not amount to recognised psychiatric injury and so far as there may be a tort of intention under which such damage is recoverable, the necessary intention was not established. (at [46]–[47])[29]

Pause for reflection

Wilkinson v *Downton* appears to be a case of negligent infliction of psychiatric injury. As Lord Hoffmann pointed out in *Wainwright*, the rule in *Wilkinson* v *Downton* was established in order to circumvent the decision in *Victorian Railways Commissioners* v *Coultas* [1888], which *prevented* recovery in relation to psychiatric harm in the tort of negligence. As we now have rules providing for claims in respect of negligently caused psychiatric harm , he argued the rule in *Wilkinson* v *Downton* should have 'no leading role in the modern law of tort'. As such, we may be better off letting the tort identified in *Wilkinson* v *Downton* 'disappear beneath the surface of the law of negligence' (at [40]–[41]). Do you agree?

The decision in **Wainwright** leaves the status of the rule in *Wilkinson* v *Downton* in some doubt. Where physical or psychiatric harm is inflicted negligently, we should leave this to be dealt with by the tort of negligence. *If* there is to be scope for an independent tort, then it seems it must be reserved for cases where *psychiatric* harm amounting to a recognised psychiatric illness (rather than mere discomfort or distress) is intentionally (or recklessly) inflicted (*Mbasogo* v *Logo Ltd* [2006]).[30]

29. The claimants were successful in the ECtHR where the court unanimously held that there had been a breach of their Art 8 and 13 rights (*Wainwright* v *UK* [2007]).

30. It has been suggested that *Wilkinson* v *Downton* has been given a new lease of life in the first instance decision of *C* v *D* [2006] (Réaume, above; Alan McKenna 'Torts: *Wilkinson* v *Downton*: A Final Curtain Call for an Old Favourite? *C* v *D* [2006] EWHC 166' (2007) 41(1) *Law Teacher* 102 at 105). In this case, a school pupil suffered psychiatric injury as a result of a sustained period of

Counterpoint

While Lord Hoffmann's suggestion that it is not in the public interest to allow the law from being 'set in motion for one boorish incident' (at [46]), *Wainwright* effectively destroys any future potential of the rule in *Wilkinson* v *Downton* to provide a legal remedy for intentionally caused anxiety or distress (which falls short of a recognised psychiatric illness).[31] Jonathan Morgan has argued that the decision reflects a continuing judicial reluctance to recognise the significance of distress as an actionable harm:

> it is characterised respectively as a flowing from a failure of etiquette, or from the good natured fun of traditional rites of initiation...Such a dismissive attitude to mental distress is perhaps a little surprising, when the facts of *Wainwright* itself provide a glaring example of degrading behaviour, by a public authority at that. A rule that only 'serious' distress is actionable would better meet concerns of a flood of trivial claims, while allowing recovery in cases of truly humiliating conduct.[32]

Another reason for the court's unwillingness to develop the rule in *Wilkinson* v *Downton* is the existence of an alternative remedy through the Protection from Harassment Act 1997, which enables a claimant to recover damages for '(among other things) any anxiety caused by the harassment' (s 3). It is to that Act that we now turn.

14.6.2 **The Protection from Harassment Act 1997**

The Protection from Harassment Act was a response to increasing public concern about harassment and, in particular, stalking. Its enactment attracted considerable media and celebrity attention, most notably from Princess Diana. More recently, the actress Sienna Miller was apparently awarded £53,000 in damages under the Act against the owner of a photographic agency for the harassing conduct of its photographers.[33]

---

sexual abuse by his headmaster. Though incidents involving physical contact were clearly batteries, on another occasion the defendant pulled down the boy's trousers and stared at his genitals. This invasion of his personal integrity, though not calculated to cause harm, the judge held, had caused the claimant to suffer from a mental abnormality (amounting to more than mere distress) (at [96]). The defendant's recklessness as to the possibility of harm was sufficient to ground the claim (at [99]). However, there is one further caveat to this case. Though the decision was not itself appealed, the Court of Appeal in a largely unrelated case—though also involving sexual abuse—took the somewhat unusual step of adding a footnote about *C* v *D* in which it suggested that 'it seems preferable for the law to develop along conventional modern lines rather than through recourse to this obscure tort, whose jurisprudential basis remains unclear' (*A* v *Hoare* [2006] (CA) at [136]). (The Court of Appeal decision was overturned on unrelated grounds; though *C* v *D* was cited in argument it was not considered by the House of Lords.) The rule in *Wilkinson* v *Downton* is certainly down, it remains to be seen whether it is—finally—out.

31. This is in marked contrast to the creativity of the courts in Australia and Canada (Réaume, above).

32. Jonathan Morgan 'Privacy Torts: Out with the Old, Out with the New' (2004) 120 *Law Quarterly Review* 393 at 395.

33. David Brown, 'Sienna Miller Wins £50,000 Payout from Paparazzi' *The Times* 22 November 2008.

The Act introduces a civil remedy for harassment (s 3) as well as a criminal offence of harassment (s 2).[34] In line with its principal purpose to prevent and protect rather than compensate, the Act provides for the imposition of an injunction, alongside damages and criminal sanctions for non-compliance (s 3). The key provision, in section 1(1), states that 'a person must not pursue a course of conduct (a) which amounts to harassment of another, and (b) which he knows, or ought to know, amounts to harassment of the other'.[35] The Act leaves the definition of harassment deliberately wide. Merely annoying or aggravating matters of everyday life will not amount to harassment. It may include 'alarming the person or causing the person distress' (s 7(2)), though conduct can still amount to harassment even where no distress or alarm are caused. It must however be of a level that is 'oppressive and unacceptable':

> Courts are well able to separate the wheat from the chaff at an early stage of the proceedings...Where...the quality of the conduct said to constitute harassment is being examined, courts will have in mind that irritations, annoyances, even a measure of upset, arise at times in everybody's day-to-day dealings with other people. Courts are well able to recognise the boundary between conduct which is unattractive, even unreasonable, and conduct which is oppressive and unacceptable. To cross the boundary from the regrettable to the unacceptable the gravity of the misconduct must be of an order which would sustain criminal liability under section 2. (Lord Nicholls, *Majrowski* [2007] (CA) at [30])

The conduct must also take place on 'at least two occasions' (s 7(3)).[36] The incidents must be similar in type and in context: 'the fewer incidents there are and the further in time they are apart, the less likely it will be that they can properly be treated as constituting a course of conduct' (Elias LJ, *James* v *DPP* [2009] at [11]).[37]

---

34. On the relationship between the criminal and civil aspects of the 1997 Act see Emily Finch 'Stalking the Perfect Stalking Law: An Evaluation of the Efficacy of the Protection from Harassment Act 1997' (2002) *Criminal Law Review* 703.

35. Section 1A (added by Serious Organised Crime and Police Act 2005) extends the remit of the 1997 Act to include a course of conduct directed at *two or more people* which the harasser knows or ought to know amounts to harassment *and* by which 'he intends to persuade any person (whether or not one of those mentioned (in s 1A(a)) (i) not to do something that he is entitled or required to do, or (ii) to do something that he is not under any obligation to do (s 1A(c)). In such circumstances, a course of conduct is defined as 'conduct on at least one occasion in relation to each of those persons' (s 7(3)(b)).

36. The Act does not, therefore, cover one-off incidents, such as the practical joke in *Wilkinson* v *Downton*, however serious. Though a victim who fears that a single incident of harassing conduct *might* in the future *become* a course of conduct may be able to claim under s 3(1) which provides a remedy for the 'apprehension' of a breach of s 1.

37. The Act is concerned with courses of conduct rather than individual instances of harassment. However, as Rix LJ recently noted in a case involving a series of letters from a firm of solicitors containing allegations against the personal and professional integrity of an assistant solicitor previously employed by them, it is not necessary for those two occasions to amount individually to harassment: 'Take the typical case of stalking, or of malicious phone calls. When a defendant, D, walks past a claimant C's door, or calls C's telephone but puts the phone down without speaking, the single act by itself is neutral, or may be. But if that act is repeated on a number of occasions, the course of conduct may well amount to harassment. That conclusion can only be arrived at by looking at the individual acts complained of as a whole...So it is with a course of communications such as letters. A first letter, by itself, may appear innocent and may even cause no alarm, or at most a slight unease. However, in the light of subsequent letters, that first letter may be seen as part of a campaign of harassment' (*Iqbal* v *Dean Manson Solicitors* [2011] at [45]).

The defendant need not intend to 'harass' or cause the claimant anxiety; liability is based on actual or constructive knowledge that their conduct amounts to harassment, that is whether the defendant *ought* to have known that their conduct amounts to harassment. The focus here is on the 'reasonable harasser': 'the person whose course of conduct is in question ought to know that it amounts to harassment of another if a reasonable person in the possession of the same information would think the course of conduct amounted to harassment of the other' (s 1(2)). This, Joanne Conaghan argues, 'assumes a degree of consensus [as to what constitutes harassing behaviour] which may not exist'.[38] Despite the view of the Court of Appeal in *Thomas* v *News Group Newspapers Ltd* [2001] that 'harassment is…a word which has a meaning that is generally understood' (at [30]), this may not always be the case. Opinions may differ on when, for example, a journalist's investigations in seeking to secure a 'scoop' amount to stalking or when an ex-lover's attempts to win a partner back become threatening (Conaghan 1999, p 207). Moreover, Conaghan continues, the 'adoption of the "reasonable harasser" perspective' fails to directly engage with the effect of the harasser's conduct on the *claimant* and 'inevitably incorporates a gender dimension into the standard applied, certainly where the conduct in question has a sexual dimension' (pp 207–8).

The Act excludes certain conduct from the remit of harassment. These defences are listed in section 1(3) and include activity for the purpose of detecting or preventing crime and that which is 'in the particular circumstances…reasonable' (s 1(3)(c)). The latter exception of 'reasonable harassment' is the most contentious. The Act gives no indication as to when this might be, although it is thought to address the activities of 'journalists, salespeople, religious activists, debt collectors and others carrying out legitimate activities'.[39]

Despite its initial focus on stalking, the Act has an extremely wide remit. It has been used in response to the publication of victimising newspaper articles (*Thomas* v *News Group Newspapers Ltd*); unjustified bills and threats of legal action (*Ferguson* v *British Gas* [2009]), bullying in the workplace (**Majrowski** and *Veakins* v *Kier Islington Ltd* [2009]) and intimidating public demonstrations, particularly in relation to animal rights campaign groups and anti-hunt campaigners (*Daiichi UK Ltd* v *Stop Huntington Animal Cruelty* [2004]).

 Pause for reflection

Maurice Kay LJ in *Veakins* v *Kier Islington Ltd* [2009] drew attention to the increasing use of the 1997 Act in the context of workplace harassment in order, he suggested, to avoid the more restrictive requirements to succeed in a negligence action following *Hatton* v *Sutherland* [2002].[40] Though there is nothing in the language of the Act to prevent its appli-

---

38. 1999, pp 207–8. Think again about the infatuated student in the examples at the start of the chapter—at what point do you think their phone calls will constitute harassment?

39. Equal Opportunities Review (1997), p 32, in *Conaghan & Mansell* p 186.

40. Keith Patten notes that a claim under the Act has three advantages over a claim in negligence: (1) no foreseeability requirement; (2) an ability to sue for 'anxiety' in absence of recognised psychiatric illness and (3) a longer limitation period (2010).

> →
>
> cation in this context, it was doubtful, he suggested, that this is what the legislature had in mind when enacting the provisions:
>
> > It should not be thought from this unusually one-sided case that stress at work will often give rise to liability for harassment. I have found the conduct in this case to be 'oppressive and unacceptable' but I have done so in circumstances where I have also described it as 'extraordinary'. I do not expect that many workplace cases will give rise to this liability. It is far more likely that, in the great majority of cases, the remedy for high-handed or discriminatory misconduct by or on behalf of an employer will be more fittingly in the Employment Tribunal. (at [17])[41]
>
> Similarly, Conaghan suggests that 'the idea that persistent criticism at work should be viewed and treated in the same way as stalking threatens the credibility and legitimacy of the Act' (p 210). Do you agree? It may be that it was not passed with cases such as this in mind, but should that matter? What role do you think the Act should play in such cases?

14.7 **Conclusion**

In this chapter we have consider the torts which comprise trespass to the person—battery, assault and false imprisonment. These torts protect an individual against an infringement of their personal integrity through the infliction (or the fear of the infliction) of unlawful force (battery and assault) or the unlawful restriction of their freedom of movement (false imprisonment). The three torts have the same characteristics: they must be committed intentionally; they must cause direct and immediate harm; and they are actionable *per se*, that is, without proof of loss. These characteristics distinguish the trespass to the person torts from the tort of negligence: while trespass compensates the claimant in relation to direct and intentional harm (for example, being deliberately hit), negligence compensates the claimant for unintentional or indirect harm (that is, accidental injury).

Finally, we considered the rule in *Wilkinson* v *Downton*, which provides a remedy for physical and psychiatric harm 'intentionally' caused by a false statement (as opposed to physical impact or fear of such) and the Protection from Harassment Act 1997 which imposes civil and criminal liability for harassment. The Act is deliberately vague as to what harassing conduct might entail though it is clear that the course of conduct complained of must be 'oppressive and unacceptable'.

---

41. Readers may find it helpful to compare the reasoning and decisions in two recent cases in this context: *Rayment* v *Ministry of Defence* [2010] (where an employer's failure, among other things, to remove pornographic photographs from the claimant's workplace was oppressive, unacceptable and amounted to harassment) and *Dowson* v *Chief Constable of Northumbria* [2010] (where a detective chief inspector's conduct though unacceptable and occasionally insensitive, belittling and overbearing, did not amount to harassment (at [277]–[278]).

✳ End-of-chapter questions

After reading the chapter carefully, try answering the questions below. If you would like to know what we think visit the Online Resource Centre (www.oxfordtextbooks.co.uk/orc/horsey2e/).

1. Does the common law, supplemented by the Protection from Harassment Act 1997, adequately protect people from intentionally committed harms and harassment?

2. To what extent, if any, is there a gendered dimension to the trespass to the person torts and the Protection from Harassment Act 1997?

3. Consider the problem question at the start of this chapter. Now having read about the topic what would be your advice to the various parties? If you need some pointers in thinking about how to answer this question, turn to the Appendix (p 589) where the problem is annotated with issues and cases to consider. Next, try to write your own answer and, finally, log on to our Online Resource Centre (www.oxfordtextbooks.co.uk/orc/horsey2e/) to compare your ideas against our suggested outline answer.

✳ Further reading

Much of the academic writing in this area pre-date the decision in *Wainwright*, nevertheless they continue to offer an insightful and relevant critique of the law in this area.

Conaghan, Joanne 'Enhancing Civil Remedies for (Sexual) Harassment: s 3 of the Protection from Harassment Act 1997' (1999) 7 *Feminist Legal Studies* 203

Lunney, Mark 'Practical Joking and its Penalty: *Wilkinson v Downton* in Context' (2002) 10(3) *Tort Law Review* 168

Lunney, Mark 'False Imprisonment, Fare Dodging and Federation—Mr Robertson's Evening Out' (2009) 31 *Sydney Law Review* 537

Patten, Keith 'Defining Harassment' (2010) 160 *New Law Journal* 331

Trindale, FA 'Intentional Torts: Some Thoughts on Assault and Battery' (1982) 2 *Oxford Journal of Legal Studies* 211

15

Defamation

Problem question

Read this problem question carefully, and keep it in mind while you are working through the chapter that follows. At the end of the chapter, you will be able to apply what you have learnt to the problem question and advise the relevant parties.

In the Hood, a weekly fashion and TV magazine, is famous for its celebrity 'scoops'. This week's issue includes the following stories:

'TV CHEF IN JUNK FOOD SHAME!'—a two-page story about a TV chef, who prides himself on his healthy recipes, has been spotted buying reconstituted meat in his local supermarket. In fact, he was accompanied by a film crew and was buying it for the new series of his show. The article does not mention this.

'EXPLOITED FOR THE SAKE OF FASHION'—a four-page feature in which claims are made about *Rack and Horse Design*, a discount clothing company. The article suggests that the company is:

- exploiting its shop workers in the UK by paying below-minimum wages;
- destroying the environment through its continued use of highly toxic dyes;
- forcing workers in the developing world to work in 'inhumane and degrading' conditions.

'BOOZED-UP, WASHED-UP, KICKED OUT'—a photo spread (accompanied by brief captions) of 'celebrities' appearing worse for wear after a night out. Underneath the headline—but in much smaller print—there is an explanation that these are staged photos using celebrity lookalikes.

15.1 **Introduction**

Consider the following examples:

→ A national newspaper suggests that a well-known celebrity couple are 'bad parents' to their three children.

→ A newly married TV presenter is revealed live on-air by her co-presenter as having had an affair with her dance partner while filming a TV show.

→ A TV 'self-help' guru is accused of plagiarism.

→ The CEO of a multinational company is 'exposed' as engaging in sadomasochistic sexual activities with allegedly fascist overtones.

→ A presenter on BBC Radio 5's *Test Match Special* accuses an England cricketer of fixing matches in return for significant sums of money.

In each of these cases there may be a potential claim in the tort of defamation. In contrast with, say, the torts of trespass to the person and (sometimes) negligence, which protect an individual's bodily or physical integrity, defamation protects a person's reputation. The law of defamation enables an individual (or, more controversially, a company) to prevent the publication of, or recover damages for, public statements which make, or are likely to make, people think less of them. As such unsurprisingly many of the cases involve people in the public eye—celebrities, TV personalities, politicians and so on—and/or multinational corporations who are inevitably not only more aware of, but certainly have a greater interest in, what other people think of them.[1] That said, defamation is not a tort exclusively for the rich and famous; we all have an interest in our reputation being maintained. The principles of defamation are applicable to everyone—although the high costs of bringing a claim, combined with the absence of legal aid to support such claims have, at least until recently, effectively meant that its universality is more theoretical than real.

In the tort of defamation reputation is pitted against freedom of expression. At its heart lies the question as to when an individual's interest in what people think of them should trump or silence the freedom of others to be able to say what they know, or think they know, about them. In fact, freedom of expression is considered so important that (in contrast with one's interest in one's reputation) it is protected under the European Convention on Human Rights (ECHR) and the Human Rights Act (HRA) 1998. However, as they both also make clear, one's right to freedom of expression is not unlimited. In other words, individuals do not have complete freedom to say whatever they like, whenever they like. Article 10(2) provides that an individual's ability to exercise this right can be restricted in the interests of a democratic society including 'for the protection of the rights and freedoms of others'. Accordingly, one of the

---

1. In 2009–10, the number of defamation cases rose by 6 per cent largely due to an increase in the number of celebrities bringing claims which almost trebled in the same period. The same report noted that just three of the 83 cases were brought by international claimants (Claire Ruckin 'New Figures Highlight Minimal Impact of Libel Tourism on Defamation Cases' *The Lawyer* 1 September 2010); see also James Hand 'The Compensation Culture: Cliché or Cause for Concern?' (2010) 37(4) *Journal of Law and Society* 569 at 584–7.

fundamental questions that the tort of defamation has to resolve is where to strike the balance between the right to freedom of expression and an individual's desire to protect their reputation.

However, it is argued, the courts continue to strike this balance 'in quite the wrong way...Reputation itself is not a protected right under the Convention, but it is certainly a protected right under English law' (*Weir* p 175). Supporters of this view point to instances where the rules of defamation have silenced free expression to disastrous effect. Companies, such as McDonald's and individuals, for example Robert Maxwell,[2] have used the threat of defamation claims to suppress criticism and free speech in order to try to prevent bad publicity. This should not be surprising. Subject to a few clarifications, the tort of defamation essentially allows an individual or company to sue another who says *anything* that might make a third party think less of the claimant. Moreover, they can do so without having to show that what was said is untrue, that it caused them harm or that the speaker was unreasonable or at fault.

 Pause for reflection

The tort of defamation, therefore, provides an individual or company with relatively heavy-duty tools with which to protect their reputation against another's fundamental right to free speech and expression. The protection of a person's reputation provided by defamation law is directly comparable with that provided in relation to someone's liberty, person and property in their possession by the tort of trespass. However, does an individual's reputation really require *as much protection* as their bodily integrity?

Weir continues '[T]he protection may be thought to be all the odder in that the only kinds of harm apt to result from being badmouthed are emotional upset and financial loss, neither of which is very readily redressed in the law even where the defendant's negligence has been demonstrated' (p 176).

Do you agree? Think again about the purposes of tort law (discussed in Chapter 1, pp 9–18).

The 'McLibel' litigation: a case study

The 'McLibel' trial has the dubious honour of being the longest trial in the history of UK libel law (it lasted 313 days).[3] The case, which ultimately went to the European Court of Human Rights (ECtHR), exposes a number of flaws in the process of bringing (and/or fighting) a case in defamation, which you should think about as you continue your reading. These

→

2. A BBC News profile suggests that 'Many people cowered from criticising [Robert Maxwell, Chairman of Mirror Group Newspapers (MGN)], not least because of his readiness to confront his critics in the libel courts' ('Robert Maxwell: A Profile' 29 March 2001).
3. Much has been written about the 'McLibel' trial—one of the best places to start is the official 'McLibel' website—www.mcspotlight.org—which includes transcripts of all 313 days of the trial (!).

➔

include issues relating to the lack of public funding for defamation cases, weaknesses in the defence of truth or justification, the strategic importance of a 'judge-only' trial and concerns that defamation law in the UK does not adequately protect freedom of speech or expression. In particular, the case epitomises the suggestion that large companies (who would not be able to sue in, for example, the US)[4] are able (and indeed prefer) to issue defamation proceedings that have a 'chilling effect' on free speech, as TV companies and newspapers err on the side of caution by not publishing criticism so as to avoid expensive litigation battles.

McDonald's—a multinational fast food chain—is (opponents of McDonald's argue) a company in point. Over the years McDonald's have sued (or threatened to sue) various UK newspapers (including *The Guardian*—over reports of poor working conditions in McDonald's restaurants in the UK), TV channels (including the BBC, for a BBC2 programme *Nature* commenting on the destruction of the rainforest in Central and South America; and Channel 4), other companies (for example Veggies Ltd, a vegan food cooperative based in Nottingham) and individuals (including the singer Morrissey). And, then in 1990, McDonald's turned its attention to Helen Steel and Dave Morris—a gardener and former postman from London.

The McLibel case concerned a factsheet written by 'London Greenpeace' (a group which was founded in the 1970s, predating and distinct from the more famous Greenpeace) entitled 'What's Wrong with McDonald's? Everything that you don't want to know.' It stated that McDonald's exploited children through advertising, promoted an unhealthy diet, exploited its workforce and was responsible for environmental damage and the ill treatment of animals. The factsheet was widely distributed—often outside McDonald's restaurants. In the late 1980s, McDonald's engaged a number of private investigators to infiltrate 'London Greenpeace' so that it could find out who was responsible for producing and distributing the factsheets. In 1990, McDonald's served writs on five people from 'London Greenpeace', including Morris and Steel.

The pre-trial process, including drafting the defence to each of the 18 points in the statement of claim, took 18 months. McDonald's applied for, and won, a trial by judge only. McDonald's argued that the trial would be too complicated for a jury to follow. However, given that the defendants were representing themselves, this seems somewhat disingenuous. An alternative explanation that it was afraid that a jury may be more sympathetic to the defendants appears more plausible.

Refusing attempts to settle, which would have involved Steel and Morris agreeing to refrain from criticising McDonald's in public, the case went to trial.

➔

4. This also relates to the issue of so-called 'libel tourism' whereby companies and individuals from outside England and Wales choose to bring proceedings in England and Wales in order to sue someone outside England and Wales so as to take advantage of our generous defamation laws. Indeed some US states have introduced laws to prevent 'unreasonable' rulings made in UK courts infringing on their own freedom of speech. (See discussion in Ministry of Justice *Report of the Libel Working Group* (2010), pp 4–16.) The Coalition Government's Draft Defamation Bill seeks to address the issue through a provision which ensures that a court will not accept jurisdiction unless satisfied that England and Wales is clearly the most appropriate jurisdiction to bring the claim (Ministry of Justice, 'Draft Defamation Bill' CP3/11). See Online Resource Centre for updates.

→

At first instance Mr Justice Bell held that Morris and Steel had not brought sufficient evidence to prove their allegations in relation to their claims that McDonald's contributed to the destruction of the rainforests or starvation in the developing world, that its food caused heart disease and cancer or that it exploited its workers. Importantly, this does not mean that the judge thought that the allegations were untrue, rather that Morris and Steel had failed to show that they were true (as required by the defence of justification). However, the judge did rule in the defendant's favour in relation to their claims that McDonald's advertising exploited children; that it falsely advertised its food as nutritious and so risked the health of its regular long-term customers; that it was 'culpably responsible for cruelty to animals'; and that it was strongly 'antipathetic to unions and pays its workers low wages'.

McDonald's was awarded £60,000, half the money it had claimed. The defendants refused to pay. McDonald's did not pursue this—presumably wishing to avoid further negative publicity—and the defendants were leafleting outside McDonald's two days after the judgment.

Morris and Steel appealed. They argued that the oppressive nature of UK defamation law allowed companies to stifle criticism because it could be so expensive and time consuming to fight them and, moreover, that following the decision in *Derbyshire County Council* v *Times Newspapers* [1993], which prevented county councils from bringing claims for this very reason, companies similarly ought not to be able to sue. The Court of Appeal rejected this on the basis that it was a matter for Parliament to decide; however, it did make further rulings in relation to the negative impact of McDonald's food on their customers' nutrition, reducing McDonald's damages by £20,000.

Morris and Steel appealed to the ECtHR (leave to appeal to the House of Lords was refused) on the grounds that the defamation proceedings brought against them had breached their Article 6 (right to fair trial) and Article 10 (freedom of expression) rights (*Morris and Steel* v *UK* [2005]). They argued that the refusal of legal aid rendered the proceedings unfair—that, had they been granted legal aid, they would have had the resources to prove that at least some of the charges against them were unjustified—and also that the trial process and outcome amounted to a disproportionate interference with their right to freedom of expression.

The ECtHR held that there had been breaches of both Articles 6 and 10 of the Convention. The Court held that whether the provision of legal aid was necessary for a fair hearing depended on the facts and circumstances of each case and in this case it was significant that Steel and Morris had chosen not to commence defamation proceedings but had acted in defence of their right to freedom of expression. Moreover, the disparity between the respective levels of assistance enjoyed by Morris and Steel (who had had to rely on pro-bono representation alone) and the legal might of McDonald's was such that unfairness was inevitable. The Court agreed with the defendants that, had they had the benefit of proper representation, they would have succeeded on a number of the issues. The Court also held that the restrictions placed on the defendants' freedom of expression were not such as were 'necessary in a democratic society' (Art 10(2)). Although protecting the commercial interests of companies competed with the public interest in open debate, it was essential to provide for procedural fairness and equality of arms. In this case, the UK had failed to strike the right balance.

→

➡

Responding to the Court's judgment, Keir Starmer QC (who represented Steel and Morris at the ECtHR) hailed it as a 'turning point' in libel law:

Until now, only the rich and famous have been able to defend themselves against libel writs. Now ordinary people can participate much more effectively in public debate without having to fear that they will be bankrupted for doing so. This case is a milestone for free speech.[5]

15.2 The torts of defamation: libel and slander

The tort of defamation comes in two forms: libel and slander. A distinction is drawn at common law between libel (a defamatory statement in permanent form, typically writing, but also including, for example, 'a statue, a caricature, an effigy, chalk marks on a wall, signs, or pictures' (**Monson v Tussauds Ltd [1894]** at 692)) and slander (that is, statements that are temporary or transitory, usually speech but also mimicry, gestures and sign language). Libel is seen as potentially having graver consequences for an individual's reputation and is therefore treated more seriously than slander.[6]

The key practical difference between the torts is that libel is actionable *per se* (that is, without the claimant having to prove that they suffered any harm or damage as a result of the defendant's statement). Though since *Jameel v Dow Jones & Co* [2005]), the claimant has to establish a 'real and substantial' wrong; trivial claims are likely to be thrown out as an abuse of process.[7] In contrast, an action for slander (usually) requires 'special damage'; the claimant needs to show that they were *actually* harmed by the defamatory statement, for example by losing money as a result of being shunned by business clients. Loss of association with friends or family is not enough. Moreover, the special damage must not be too remote—that is, it must be such damage as 'might fairly and reasonably have been anticipated and feared' on the facts of the case (*Lynch v Knight* [1861] at 600).

 Counterpoint

The distinction between the torts of libel and slander has been criticised as an unnecessarily historical relic ripe for reform.[8] Given the confusion that sometimes surrounds the classification of a defamatory statement and that a major justification for the requirement of establishing 'special damage' in the cases of slander—that this is needed to prevent

➡

5. Doughty Street Chambers (Press Release) 'McLibel Case Wins in Strasbourg: A Turning Point in English Libel Law' 15 February 2005.

6. Criminal libel was abolished in England and Wales in November 2009 through the enactment of the Coroners and Justice Act; it remains an offence in Scotland.

7. At the time of writing, the Draft Defamation Bill includes a measure that would put this on a statutory footing, although it stops short of aligning libel with slander (Ministry of Justice, 'Draft Defamation Bill' CP3/11). See the Online Resource Centre for updates.

8. See e.g. Faulks Committee *Report of the Committee on Defamation* (Cmnd 5909, 1975), [91]; JM Kaye 'Libel or Slander: Two Torts or One' (1972) 91 *Law Quarterly Review* 524.

→

frivolous claims—is increasingly dealt with by the high costs of bringing a claim, the distinction is largely redundant. Moreover, it has been abandoned (either formally or in practice—for example by making all slander actionable *per se*) in a number of overseas jurisdictions including New Zealand and some Australian states and Canadian provinces.

There are two further points to note. First, not all spoken insults are slander. Some 'speech' is treated as libel—for example defamatory song lyrics are libellous, despite the fact they are spoken. As noted above, the test is one of 'permanence' rather than form.[9]

> ### *Youssoupoff v Metro-Goldwyn-Mayer Pictures Ltd* [1934] CA
>
> The claimant was a Russian princess who was portrayed in the soundtrack accompanying the film *Rasputin, the Mad Monk* as having been raped or seduced by Rasputin. At the time the case was brought, the 'Talkies'—films with sound—were a recent invention. The question was whether the defamation in the film was 'slander' or 'libel'. The Court of Appeal held that as the soundtrack was synchronised with the film it was in a permanent—and therefore potentially libellous—form.
>
> Another interesting aspect of this case is the court's attitude to the allegation that the claimant had been raped. One might think that such an allegation would make right-thinking members of the public feel sympathy for the claimant, rather than lowering their opinion of her, nevertheless the Court of Appeal acknowledged her concern that she could be shunned and upheld her claim in defamation.

Ultimately, the questions of classification are largely a matter of common sense. Clearly, there are borderline cases—for instance, an insult written in sand on a beach. However, such cases arise more often in the imagination of tort textbook writers than in the courtroom.

Secondly, there are four (largely dated) exceptions to the need to prove special damage for an action in slander—that is, where the allegation is such that damage is presumed and so need not be proved by the claimant. These are where the statement imputes (1) criminal conduct (*Webb* v *Beavan* [1883]); (2) that the claimant has a contagious disease (*Bloodworth* v *Gray* [1844]); (3) incompetence in business dealings (as clarified by s 2 of the Defamation Act 1952); and (4) a lack of chastity in a *woman* (Slander of Women Act 1891, s 1).[10]

15.3 **Judge *and* jury**

One unusual feature of the tort of defamation is that, unless the courts think that the case is likely to involve lengthy examination of documents or scientific investigations, cases

---

9. Though some non-permanent forms of publication are treated as libel by virtue of various statutory provisions—such as radio and television (Broadcasting Act 1990, s 166) and public theatre performances (Theatres Act 1968, s 4).

10. The consultation paper published alongside the Draft Defamation Bill in March 2011 includes the recommendation that the Slander of Women Act 1891 be repealed in the proposed Repeals Bill (Ministry of Justice, 'Draft Defamation Bill' CP3/11). See the Online Resource Centre for updates.

can be heard by a judge *and* a jury (Supreme Court Act 1981, s 69 and County Courts Act 1984 s 66; *Gregson* v *Channel Four Television Corp* [2002]). In such cases, while the judge decides whether the statement is capable of bearing a particular meaning and whether that meaning *could*, in law, be defamatory (*Capital and Counties Bank Ltd* v *Henty* [1888]), the jury determines whether the statement *is*, in fact, defamatory. The jury also decides whether a defence has been made out (although the judge rules on what constitutes a matter of public interest in relation to the defence of honest comment and whether the publication is covered by qualified privilege) and the level of damages.

The right to trial by jury in defamation cases has been criticised as a major cause of delays and high costs in defamation cases.[11] Though the recent Ministry of Justice Libel Working Group could not come to a consensus on whether it would be appropriate to dispense with juries entirely,[12] what is clear however is that fewer cases are now heard by juries.[13] Section 8 of the Defamation Act 1996 allows a judge to dismiss a claim 'if it appears that it has no realistic prospect of success and there is no reason for it to be tried' or where there is no (or no realistic) defence. The 'fast track route' also allows the judge to award 'summary relief'—a declaration that the statement was false and defamatory, a correction and apology, and an award of up to £10,000 damages (s 9 of the 1996 Act).[14]

15.4 Establishing a claim in defamation

In order to establish a claim in the tort of defamation (whether libel or slander), four questions need to be addressed:

(1) Is the statement defamatory?

(2) Does it refer to the claimant?

(3) Has it been published?

(4) Do any defences apply?

We shall take each question in turn. However, before we do so, there is one further point to address: who can bring a claim in defamation.

15.4.1 Who can sue?

A defamation claim can be brought by any living human being. Whatever other reasons there may be for adhering to the old adage not to speak ill of the dead, fear of a

---

11. Faulks Committee *Report of the Committee on Defamation* (Cmnd 5909, 1975), p 490. This is particularly so in relation to setting the level of damages to be awarded, which in comparison to personal injury claims appear to be very high. In **John v MGN Ltd [1997]**, e.g. where the claimant's award of general damages was reduced from £75,000 to £25,000, Lord Bingham MR described the jury as being 'sheep loosed on an unfenced common, with no shepherd' (at 608).

12. Above, pp 34–5.

13. Rupert Jackson *Review of Civil Litigation Costs: Final Report* (2009), pp 328–9.

14. At the time of writing, the Coalition Government was consulting on the possible reform of the summary disposal procedure (Ministry of Justice, 'Draft Defamation Bill' CP3/11). See the ORC for updates.

defamation claim is not one of them—an action does not survive the death of either party (Law Reform (Miscellaneous Provisions) Act 1934, s 1(1)). We may also note here that, unlike when Morris and Steel started their defence against McDonald's, conditional fee arrangements now make it more realistic for an 'ordinary' person to bring a claim in defamation.[15]

More controversially, companies are also able to bring a defamation claim (*South Hetton Coal Co* v *North-Eastern News Association Ltd* [1894]). After all, it is argued, they too have a reputation to protect. This may be true. However, it is not immediately obvious why it needs quite *as much* protection as the reputation of any individual. In light of this, the Faulks Committee recommended that companies should not be able to sue unless they had suffered, or were likely to suffer, financial loss. However, this has not been implemented. Moreover, in **Jameel v Wall Street Journal Europe** [2007], the majority of the House of Lords rejected the argument of the defendant newspaper that to allow the company to bring an action in defamation, *without* proof of damage, was an undue restriction of freedom of speech, contrary to Article 10 ECHR. Lord Bingham continued:

> the good name of a company, as that of an individual, is a thing of value. A damaging libel may lower its standing in the eyes of the public and even its own staff and make people less ready to deal with it, less willing and less proud to work from it . . . I find nothing repugnant in the notion that this is a value which the law should protect. (at [26])

He did add, however, that where the company has suffered no financial loss, damages should be kept within modest bounds (at [27]).

Others go even further and argue that companies should not be able to bring defamation claims *at all*. Allowing them to do so, it is suggested, ignores the power of big business and can have a 'chilling effect' upon potential critics and challengers.[16] Moreover, it may be argued that some limit on companies' ability to claim in defamation would be in line with the decision in **Derbyshire County Council v Times Newspapers Ltd** [1993]. In this case, the House of Lords recognised that restricting an individual's ability to openly criticise national and local government would be contrary to the democratic process and would 'place an undesirable fetter on freedom of speech' (at 549).

Derbyshire County Council v *Times Newspapers Ltd* [1993] HL

Derbyshire County Council sued *The Times* newspaper over two articles which had questioned the propriety of its financial dealings. However, before the case could proceed, the

→

---

15. Conditional fees (sometimes called 'no win, no fee' arrangements) vary according to the result of the case. The argument that conditional fee arrangements (and, in particular, the ability of solicitors to increase their costs by 100 per cent) put newspapers at a disadvantage was rejected by the House of Lords in **Campbell v Mirror Group Newspapers (costs)** [2005] who ruled that conditional fee arrangements were consistent with Art 10.

16. Though the Coalition Government is of the view that the other measures included in the Draft Defamation Bill limiting the ability of *all* parties (including corporations) with greater resources to manipulate defamation proceedings (such as the introduction of new procedures and restrictions on costs) render specific restrictions on the ability of corporations to bring actions in defamation unnecessary, views on this are invited in the consultation paper accompanying the Draft Bill (Ministry of Justice, 'Draft Defamation Bill' CP3/11). See the Online Resource Centre for updates.

> →
>
> court had first to decide whether the county council was able bring an action. The House of Lords unanimously held that the county council was unable to sue in defamation:
>
> > It is of the highest public importance that a democratically elected governmental body, or indeed any governmental body, should be open to uninhibited public criticism. The threat of a civil action for defamation must inevitably have an inhibiting effect on freedom of speech. (Lord Keith at 547)

The reasoning in **Derbyshire** was applied to political parties in *Goldsmith* v *Bhoyrul* [1997]. However, crucially, these decisions do not prevent individual politicians from bringing defamation claims (although they may regret it!). Indeed, on the facts of **Derbyshire** itself, the council leader, Bookbinder, was able to bring a claim for damages (*Bookbinder* v *Tebbit* [1989]). An argument can be made that this ability to bring, or threaten to bring, defamation proceedings has the same 'chilling effect' on political debate and commentary and that, at least in relation to comments about their performance as MPs, this should similarly be restricted.

15.5 **A defamatory statement**

A statement will be considered defamatory if it is likely to make others think less of the person referred to. That is to say, the words or statement must tend to 'lower the claimant in the estimation of right-thinking members of society in general' causing them to be shunned or avoided (*Sim* v *Stretch* [1936] at 1240). There is, however, no need for the statement *actually* to have provoked such feelings. If, for example, the defendant says defamatory things about the claimant to their best friend, it does not matter whether the friend actually believes it; the claimant has still been defamed.

Of course, this definition of defamation simply prompts another question: Who are 'right-thinking members of society'? The answer is the ubiquitous reasonable person—here the reasonable reader, viewer or listener—described by Lord Reid in *Lewis* v *Daily Telegraph* [1964] as someone who is fair-minded, who is not avid for scandal, nor overly suspicious nor unduly naïve, nor bound to select one defamatory meaning when non-defamatory meanings are possible (at 260). Put another way, a right-thinking member of society is neither so open-minded that they will never think any worse of an individual nor so closed-minded that even the most trivial accusation is a shocking assault on an individual's reputation.

At present, the words must be such as to lower a person's reputation in the eyes of people *generally* rather than in relation to a particular group or class of people (*Tolley* v *JS Fry & Sons Ltd* [1931]). However, it has been argued that, as society becomes more diverse, this may need rethinking: 'the reputation of a person within his own racial or religious community may be damaged by a statement which would not be regarded as damaging by society at large' (Keene LJ in *Arab News Network* v *Jihad Al Khazen* [2001] at [30]).

In fact, this requirement is not as restrictive as it might first appear. In many cases, where a statement suggests that the claimant has broken or ignored the beliefs or practices of a particular group to which they belong, underpinning the statement is an implication of hypocrisy or disloyalty which is actionable in its own right, even if the ordinary person is indifferent to the claims made in the original statement. For example, to suggest that someone places the occasional bet is not in itself defamatory, however to suggest this of a local vicar who has campaigned voraciously against a new mega-bingo hall may be. The point here is not whether people generally think badly of occasional gamblers, but rather the implication of double-standards which could have a significant negative impact on an individual's reputation.[17]

Sometimes, the law's view of what counts as defamatory takes a rather rose-tinted view of human nature. For example, it is not defamatory to say that someone has reported criminal activity to the police. This is despite the fact that many people do indeed think that this is (or may be) bad form (**Byrne v Deane [1937]**). However, an additional comment that they had behaved dishonourably in so doing might be defamatory.

Byrne v *Deane* [1937] CA

A notice was placed on a golf club notice board implying that the claimant, a Mr Byrne, had told the police about illegal gambling machines in the club. It stated: 'he who gave the game away, may he byrnn in hell and rue the day' (the word 'byrnn' had been blacked out and replaced with the word 'burn'). Rejecting the claimant's claim, the Court of Appeal held that right thinking people would not view it as defamatory to suggest that someone had reported criminal activity:

> I have assigned to myself no other criterion than what a good and worthy subject of the King would think of some person of whom it had been said that he had put the law in motion against wrongdoers, in considering that a good and worthy subject would not consider such an allegation in itself to be defamatory. (Slesser LJ at 833)

What is considered to be defamatory will change over time. So, for example, society is generally more accepting of homosexuality than it was 50 years ago and so it is unlikely that simply referring to someone as 'gay' will be defamatory (*Quilty* v *Windsor* [1999]). Though, again, where there is a suggestion that the individual concerned has been hypocritical—for example that they been covertly engaging in extra-marital affairs while speaking openly about the importance of 'family values' and such like—it is more likely to be seen as defamatory.

 Counterpoint

Pursuing a libel claim can prove to be a double-edged sword. In 1992, Jason Donovan, an actor and singer, sued *The Face* magazine over claims that he was gay. The defamatory statement was not, Donovan argued, being called 'gay', but rather the implication of

→

---

17. In the same way, the suggestion that an individual buys processed unhealthy frozen food is not, in and of itself, defamatory (it is unlikely to detrimentally affect what people generally think of an individual). However, the implication of dishonesty which underpins the same statement in relation to a TV chef, who has publicly campaigned for healthy eating, will give rise to an action in defamation.

→

hypocrisy in the suggestion that he was lying to his fans about his sexuality. Unfortunately, despite the niceties of this distinction his actions were seen by many as homophobic. Despite winning his case, he ultimately lost much more than he gained—in trying to protect his reputation, he succeeded in destroying it. A last minute agreement to take less than the £200,000 he was awarded (in order to prevent the magazine from closing down) and an apology was not enough to prevent the loss of a huge proportion of his fan base.

In many ways, the tort of defamation itself treads a similarly thin line. There are certain things which in the eyes of most 'right-minded people' will not lower their estimation of an individual. Being gay, for example, or having been raped or having a serious contagious illness or disease and so on will (or should) not make people generally think badly of the person involved. Nevertheless, there are some people (however much we might wish otherwise) who *will* think less of the claimant in light of such allegations. The claimant—and then the law—is faced with a problem. While such allegations *should not* be considered damaging, and in the minds of *right-thinking* people *are not*, sadly they often are. Not all people are right-minded. Given this, statements which should not negatively impact on people's views of the claimant will nonetheless do so, sometimes seriously. The dilemma here is that if we take the requirement that the statement must lower the claimant's standing in the eyes of right-minded people seriously there will be situations where a claimant's reputation *is* unfairly damaged but for which the law provides no remedy. However, if the law is to recognise a claim in these circumstances then the law risks lending its support to the view that being gay, having been raped, suffering from a serious contagious illness and the like are negative attributes.

In deciding whether a right-thinking person could view the statement as defamatory, the courts will look at the statements in context. It is not enough for the claimant to point to a particular sentence or paragraph in isolation from the piece as a whole. In *Charleston* v *News Group Newspapers Ltd* [1995] the House of Lords held that the defendants were not liable in defamation for an article featuring degrading, faked photographs of the claimant as the accompanying text made it clear that the photographs were not real.

Charleston v *News Group Newspapers Ltd* [1995] HL

The claimants, Anne Charleston and Ian Smith, played Madge and Harold Bishop in the TV programme *Neighbours*. Under the headline 'Strewth! What's Harold up to with our Madge?', the *News of the World* had superimposed the actors' heads onto the bodies of a man and woman in pornographic poses. The claimants argued that, although the text of the article made it clear that the claimants had not been engaged in such activities and that the photos were not real, the average *News of the World* reader would not read the substance of the article and would therefore be left with the impression that they had done so.

The House of Lords disagreed. Although the photographs and headline taken alone were defamatory, together with the text they could not be so classified. The decision as to

→

whether the material was capable of being defamatory must be determined according to the meaning an ordinary, reasonable, fair-minded reader would understand from it, rather than on its effect on a sub-group of limited readers who looked only at pictures and headlines. However, Lord Nicholls did warn that if the explanatory text was tucked away where the reader was unlikely to find it, the courts were likely to take a different view (at 74).

 Pause for reflection

The decision in *Charleston* was heavily criticised by Kirby J in *Chakravarti* v *Advertiser Newspapers Ltd* [1998] as 'ignor[ing] the realities of the way in which ordinary people receive, and are intended to receive, communications of this kind. It ignores changes in media technology and presentation' (at [134]).

Do you agree? Think about the last time you read a newspaper—did you read to the end of every article? Do you think the case might be decided differently today following the increased availability of newspapers online?

Just as a statement may be defamatory even if the hearer does not believe it, it is no excuse for the defendant to say that they did not intend the words to be defamatory (although intention may be relevant to possible defences and may reduce the award of damages). The tort of defamation protects an individual's reputation, and a statement can damage an individual's reputation, even where it turns out that the defendant did not mean what they said.

However, a defendant may argue that the words were 'mere abuse', uttered in rage and not intended to be taken seriously. Mere abuse is not (usually) defamatory. The line between mere abuse and a defamatory statement is a fine one.

Berkoff v *Burchill* [1996] CA

Stephen Berkoff, an actor and film director, sued Julie Burchill, a well-known journalist, for libel over two comments made about him in her column in the *Sunday Times*. In the first she referred to him as 'hideously ugly' and on the second occasion, a review of a production of Frankenstein, she compared Berkoff to Frankenstein's monster: 'It's a very new look for the creature—no bolts in the neck or flat-top hairdo—and I think it works; it's a lot like Stephen Berkoff, only marginally better looking'. The defendants argued that the essence of the tort of defamation was damage to reputation not hurt feelings or annoyance and that while the statement may have caused the latter it had not caused the former.

This was rejected by the majority of the Court of Appeal. Holding that the word 'reputation' is to be interpreted '...in the broad sense as comprehending all aspects of a person's standing in the community' (at 151), Neill LJ went on to hold that the words 'hideously ugly' could be defamatory 'even though they neither impute disgraceful conduct to the [claimant] nor any lack of skill or efficiency in the conduct of his trade or business or professional activity, if they hold him up to contempt, scorn, or ridicule or tend to exclude him from society' (at 146).

Counterpoint

We would suggest the better view in this case is offered by Millett LJ's dissent, in which he pointed out that Burchill's words were an attack on Berkoff's *appearance* rather than reputation. Burchill had simply made a cheap joke at Berkoff's expense: 'it is [he argued] one thing to ridicule a man; it is another to expose him to ridicule...people must be able to poke fun at each other without fear of litigation' (at 153).

15.5.1 Innuendo

The tort of defamation is not confined to openly defamatory statements. This makes sense—were the law otherwise it would be possible to frame an attack on an individual's reputation indirectly, in the knowledge that they would be unable to do anything about it. The detrimental impact on a person's reputation is the same whether one says 'there was a miscarriage of justice when he was cleared of murder' as it is to say outright 'he is a murderer' (*Lewis* v *Daily Telegraph* [1964] at 258). These implied or veiled attacks on someone's reputation are generally called innuendo. Traditionally there are said to be two types of innuendo, although the line between them may, at times, be difficult to draw:

- false or popular innuendo—where the reader needs to simply read between the lines to uncover the true meaning of the defamatory statement;
- true or legal innuendo—where the defamatory nature of the statement is not apparent on its face but depends on facts or circumstances known to those to whom the statement is published.

Put simply, innuendo is the mechanism through which the courts are able to attribute to a statement its *legal* meaning. It typically arises in relation to statements that do not appear defamatory, but which, because of background knowledge or information, nevertheless make people think worse of the claimant. The test for the judge in deciding whether the ascribed meaning is capable of being defamatory remains an objective one: What view would right-thinking people knowing the additional information make of the statement? And it remains for the jury to decide whether it is, in fact, defamatory. Some examples may help here.

Monson v *Tussauds Ltd* [1894] CA

The claimant had been tried for murder in Scotland and released on a verdict of 'Not Proven'. The defendants placed a waxwork of the claimant with a gun in a room adjoining the 'Chamber of Horrors'. The Court of Appeal held that the scene was capable of being defamatory.

Another example of false or popular innuendo is *Lewis* v *Daily Telegraph* [1964]. The *Daily Telegraph* reported that the company (of which Lewis was the chairman) was being investigated by the Fraud Squad. It included reference to the claimant's name as chairman. After the investigation the company was absolved of all wrongdoing. The claimant sued in defamation. The statement that the claimant was chairman of a company being investigated by the Fraud Squad was (possibly) defamatory. But in itself this couldn't ground liability as it was true. The claimant therefore maintained that ordinary readers would also 'read between the lines' and assume that the company's affairs had been conducted dishonestly. This was rejected by the majority of the House of Lords: '[w]hat the ordinary man, not avid for scandal, would read into the words complained of must be a matter of impression. I can only say that I do not think that he would infer guilt of fraud merely because an inquiry is on foot' (Lord Reid at 260). Indeed, were it otherwise it would be impossible to report any criminal investigation.

Legal or true innuendo relies on some additional information known only to those to whom the statement is published. So, for example, the statement that the claimant 'is no Florence Nightingale' might imply to the ordinary reader that the claimant lacks compassion—as Florence Nightingale is well known for her compassion. Whereas to say that the claimant was seen having an intimate dinner with her dance partner is not in itself defamatory, it becomes so only in relation to people who know that she is recently married, to whom it might carry the implication that she is having an affair. In *Tolley* v *JS Fry and Sons Ltd* [1931], the claimant was a leading amateur golfer. Without his knowledge or consent, the defendants issued an advert for Fry's Chocolate showing him playing golf with a packet of their chocolate protruding from his pocket. Tolley brought an action for libel alleging that the advert suggested that that he had agreed to, and benefited from, its publication, undermining his amateur status. The House of Lords agreed.

15.6 Does the statement refer to the claimant?

The second element in establishing a claim in defamation is that the defamatory statement must refer to the claimant. The question to be asked is this: Would a reasonable person understand the statement as referring to the claimant? Where the claimant is named—including by a nickname, initials or even job title (for example, 'Home Secretary')—there is usually no difficulty. However, the more obscure the reference, the more need there is for a 'peg or pointer' in the statement itself or to be provided by the context in which the statement was made that identifies the claimant. In such cases, the test is whether the hypothetical reasonable reader, having knowledge of the circumstances, would believe that the article was referring to the claimant (*Morgan* v *Odhams Press Ltd* [1971]).

If the claimant is not clearly identified in the statement, and so where one would need to know certain additional background information to connect the claimant to the statement made by the defendant, the claimant must show that the statement was indeed published to people who knew such additional information—people who could have made the connection between the statement and the claimant. Otherwise, all we have is a statement which *could* have been defamatory of the claimant if addressed to the right people, but which, in the end, was not. By contrast, where the statement clearly identifies the claimant—that is, where a reasonable reader would have understood the article as referring to the claimant—the claimant need not show that anyone who knew them actually read or heard the statement (although if they are able to show this it may increase the amount of damages awarded).

What about statements that unintentionally refer to the claimant? For instance, certain names are common, and so a statement referring to, say, Dave Smith, may refer to any potential number of individuals who share that name. Can the author be liable in defamation, even where they did not intend their statement to refer to the claimant, and indeed intended it to identify someone else? The short answer is yes. The tort of defamation is not concerned with whether the defendant intended to harm an individual's reputation, but rather whether their words are capable of causing this outcome. Thus, a defendant may be liable even when they intended their statement as a piece of fiction (***Hulton & Co v Jones* [1910]**).

Hulton & Co v *Jones* [1910] HL

The defendants published a fictional account of a motor festival in Dieppe featuring 'Artemus Jones', a church warden from Peckham. The claimant was a barrister also called Artemus Jones. He was unknown to the author of the story and his editor (although he had once worked for the newspaper). He was not a church warden nor did he live in Peckham. He had not attended the motor festival in Dieppe. Nevertheless, he sued in libel, claiming that a number of his friends had read the story and believed it to refer to him. The House of Lords agreed. There was sufficient evidence to suggest that a jury could reasonably conclude that a reasonable person would believe that the reference was to the claimant.

Similarly, in *Newstead v London Express Newspaper Ltd* [1940], the defendant newspaper published an account of the trial for bigamy of 'Harold Newstead, a thirty year old Camberwell man'. Unfortunately for the newspaper, this description was true of more than one man. Another Harold Newstead, a non-bigamist who also lived in Camberwell and who was about the same age as the newspaper's Harold Newstead, successfully sued for libel. Although recognising the considerable burden their decision would place on newspapers, the Court of Appeal held that it was not unreasonable, given the significant consequences for the 'wrong' man, to expect the party who publishes such statements to make sure they identify the person so closely that little or no confusion arises.

In *O'Shea* v *MGN Ltd* [2001] the *Sunday Mirror* ran an advertisement for an adult internet service featuring a model who closely resembled the claimant. O'Shea sued in libel claiming that people who did not realise that the model in the advert was not in fact her would conclude that she had consented to appear on a highly pornographic website. Rejecting her claim, Morland J held that although the image was, at common law, defamatory to hold the newspaper liable in defamation would be contrary to Article 10 of the ECHR. Distinguishing *Hulton* and *Newstead* as cases where the claimant could have more easily been identified, it would impose an 'impossible burden on a publisher if he were required to check if the true picture of someone resembled someone else who because of the context of the picture was defamed' (at [43]).

Pause for reflection

O'Shea appears to create a distinction between unintentional defamation in photographs and unintentional defamation in writing, with only the latter being actionable. Is this distinction sustainable? Morland J's point is that it would be virtually impossible for defendants to ensure that the individuals in photos they publish could not be wrongly identified—after all most, if not all, of us look more or less like someone else. By contrast, when writing, there is more scope for ensuring that the correct person is identified, simply by including more information. So while there may be any number of people named Dave Smith, there are likely to be fewer who live in, say, Oadby, Leicester, and even fewer aged 24 and so on. In the end, by providing enough information, it will be possible to ensure that no mis-identification can occur.

However, this may be an unrealistic demand to make of publishers. Though we *could* demand that every time someone is named in a newspaper article, sufficient information is included to ensure that nobody else will be wrongly identified, this would also appear to impose a significant burden on publishers, and one which jars with the demands of newspaper and television reporting. This is, of course, the point that was made and rejected in *Newstead*, where the court reasserted that liability in defamation was strict and that it was no defence that the defendant acted reasonably and never intended to identify the claimant.

But then it seems to be precisely this argument that is accepted by the court in *O'Shea*. The fact that *O'Shea* concerned pictures and *Newstead* words, allowed Morland J to distinguish the decision and rule in *Newstead*. However, in substance both cases seem to raise the same basic question: Should a publisher who acts entirely reasonably and innocently, not intending their statement or story to identify the claimant, be held liable in defamation? It may be that mis-identification is more likely to occur where pictures are used, but, as cases such as *Newstead* show, the same problems can arise with words.

As such, to treat *O'Shea* as an exception to the general rule of strict liability, which applies to visual images only, may not be a satisfactory solution. If so, which way should the law go? Should we view *O'Shea* as wrongly decided or, alternatively, should the reasoning be extended to cases such as **Hulton** and *Newstead*? Think again about the balance the courts need to strike between the right to freedom of expression and an individual's desire to protect their reputation.

15.6.1 **References to a group or class**

Where the defamatory statement refers to a class or group of people, there is no liability unless the class or group is so small that the claimant can establish that the statement must apply to every member of the class or, alternatively, that the statement refers to them directly: 'In order to be actionable the defamatory words must be understood to be published of and concerning the [claimant]' (Lord Atkin, **Knuppfer v London Express Newspaper Ltd [1944]** at [121]). So, for example, the statement that 'all MPs are liars' is not actionable; while a statement suggesting that 'all the candidates for London Mayor are corrupt'—there were only ten contenders—may be.

> **_Knuppfer v London Express Newspaper Ltd_ [1944] HL**
>
> During the Second World War the defendant newspaper referred to the 'quisling activities'[18] of the Young Russian political party, Mlado Russ (or Young Russia). As there were only 24 British members of the party, the claimant, a Russian resident in London, argued that, as head of the British branch of the party, British readers would assume that the remarks referred to him.
>
> This was rejected by the House of Lords. The article referred only to the party's activities in France and the US. Since there were several thousand international members, there was no evidence that the claimant had been singled out: 'No doubt it is true to say that a class cannot be defamed as a class, nor can an individual be defamed by a general reference to the class to which he belongs' (Lord Porter at 124).

15.7 'Publication'

The third element of a claim in defamation is the requirement that the defamatory statement be 'published'. The term 'publication' can be misleading. The requirement is better understood as a need for 'communication'—the defamatory statement must be communicated to a third party. A private conversation or letter exchanged between the defendant and the claimant—however insulting or hurtful it may be to the claimant—cannot give rise to a claim in defamation (although the claimant may have an action under the Protection from Harassment Act 1997[19]). The wrong remedied by the tort of defamation is injury to an individual's reputation—what *others* think of them—so if nobody but the claimant hears what the defendant says there is no risk of this sort of harm.

As we have already seen, publication need not involve written or recorded images; anything said within someone else's earshot is clearly 'published'. All that is required is that the statement is intelligible and that it must reach a third party. As such, there will be no publication, and so no defamation, where, for example, a broken microphone prevents people from hearing the defamatory statement or the statement is spoken in a language that the audience does not understand. One important exception to the general rule is that there can be no publication between husband and wife. In other words, statements exchanged between married partners are not regarded as being published. This is on the basis that this might lead to 'disastrous results to social life' (*Wennhak v Morgan* [1888] at 639). There is good sense in allowing *all* partners to be able to communicate as they wish without fear of legal consequences, it is undesirable for the courts to inquire into the details of what couples talk about behind closed doors.

What about where the publication is unintentional—in other words, where the defendant did not intend anyone to read/hear what they wrote/said? Here the test is one of reasonable foreseeability. If it was reasonably foreseeable that a third party would see/hear the statement the defendant will be liable (***Theaker v Richardson*** [1962]).

---

18. Meaning they were colluding or sympathising with Hitler and the Nazi Party.
19. See further Chapter 14, pp 404–407.

> ### *Theaker* v *Richardson* [1962] CA
>
> The defendant wrote to the claimant accusing her of shoplifting, being 'a very dirty whore' and 'a lying low-down brothel-keeping whore and thief'. He put it in an envelope on which he typed the claimant's name and address and put it through her letter-box. Her husband opened it, thinking it was an election address. The claimant sued for libel. Allowing her claim and awarding her £500 damages, the jury found that it was reasonably foreseeable that someone other than the claimant might open the envelope.

The decision in **Theaker** v **Richardson** can be contrasted with that in *Huth* v *Huth* [1915], where a man sent his wife a letter which was defamatory of both his wife and their children. It was opened and read by the butler. The children sued (at the time, a wife was prohibited in law from suing her husband). The Court of Appeal held it was not foreseeable that a butler would open his employer's mail: 'it is no part of a butler's duties to open letters…addressed to his master or mistress' (Lord Reading CJ at 38).

Publication can be avoided by marking the mail 'private and confidential'. Messages on the back of postcards sent through the post are, understandably, always treated as published. Similarly, open documents on a desk (in both paper and electronic form) are at risk of publication to any visitors or cleaning staff who happen upon them. Finally, an author who dictates a document to their secretary has, in so doing, 'published' any defamatory statement contained therein (*Osborn* v *Thomas Boulter & Son* [1930]). Any confusion as to whether the secretary (re)published the material when returning it to the author is met by the defence of innocent dissemination (Defamation Act 1996, s 1).

15.7.1 **Distributors**

A distinction is drawn between those who publish and republish defamatory material—authors, editors, publishers and so on—and mechanical distributors—those who simply disseminate the material (usually booksellers, libraries, newsagents). While liability in relation to the former is strict, the latter, assuming they act 'innocently', will have a defence to any defamation claim. The common law defence of innocent dissemination, sometimes called 'innocent publication' applies where the defendant did not know that the material was defamatory, so long as their failure to know that a particular work was libellous was not due to their negligence (*Vizetelly* v *Mudie's Select Library* [1900]).

The common law defence has since been supplemented by the Defamation Act 1996. Section 1 of the Act provides that it is a defence to show that the defendant:

(a) is not the author, editor or publisher of the statement complained of;

(b) took reasonable care in relation to its publication; and

(c) did not know, or had no reason to believe, that what he did caused and contributed to the publication of a defamatory statement.

The Act extends the defence to 'mechanical distributors' who previously fell outside the common law defence to include printers (who were often sued, presumably because they were worth more than the original author) and to broadcasters of live programmes where they have no effective control over the person making the statement (s 1(3)(d)). The latter claim is comparatively rare. Most potentially defamatory programmes are either pre-recorded or, in order to meet the requirement of reasonable care (s 1(c)), shown 'as live' where transmission is slightly delayed. Finally, the Act extends to operators of a communications system such as an internet service provider (ISP) where the quantity of material means that it may have limited awareness of what is being added to the system. However, where an ISP receives notification of a defamatory statement, it will be liable for further republication if it fails to remove it promptly (*Godfrey* v *Demon Internet Ltd* [1999]).[20]

15.7.2 **Republication**

Every time a defamatory statement is published a new cause of action arises against each successive publisher (*Duke of Brunswick* v *Harmer* [1849]). It is no defence to say that you are simply repeating what someone else has said. Thus, a magazine article is 'published' on numerous occasions before it even hits the newsagent's shelves—the author, editor, printer and owner are all treated as 'publishers'.[21]

The general rule is that a defendant is not liable for another person's voluntary republication of the original publication unless (a) they have authorised the repetition or intended that the statement be repeated (for example, by speaking at a press conference); or (b) the person who repeated the statement was under a legal or moral duty to do so; or (c) the republication is, on the facts, reasonably foreseeable (*Slipper* v *BBC* [1991]).

The claimant in *Slipper* v *BBC* was a police officer who had been involved in attempts to bring Ronnie Briggs, one of the Great Train Robbers, back to the UK from Brazil. He claimed that a film called *The Great Paper Chase*, published by the BBC, portrayed him as an 'incompetent buffoon' and that this, and the press reviews which referred to it (for which he argued the BBC were responsible), were defamatory. The Court of Appeal (refusing to strike out the claim) held that where the repetition of the libel is a natural and probable consequence of the original publication, the original publisher will remain liable. However, this rule was doubted in *McManus* v *Beckham* [2002].

McManus v *Beckham* [2002] CA

Victoria Beckham was alleged to have said to others in a memorabilia shop that a signed photograph of her husband, David, was a forgery. Her defamatory statement was repeated extensively by the press. The *Daily Mirror* published the story both in print and on their

➡

---

20. The law 'as usual', suggests *Weir*, 'looks for some analogue in the pre-technical age' (p 180). Here it is with **Byrne** v **Deane** where the golf club's failure to remove the anonymous statement from the club notice board within a reasonable time amounted to publication.

21. The Government consulted on the so-called 'multiple publication rule' during 2009 (Ministry of Justice *Defamation and the Internet: The Multiple Publication Rule* CP20/09) and measures to alter this rule were included in the Coalition Government's Draft Defamation Bill published in March 2011 (Ministry of Justice, 'Draft Defamation Bill' CP3/11). Please see the Online Resource Centre for updates.

→

website under the headline 'Posh goes stropping—Beck's "Forgery Fury"' as did the *News of the World*: 'Posh has another boob job'. The defendant sued Victoria Beckham in respect of the original publication (her statement in the shop), but also sought to recover damages caused by that original publication when part or all of the allegation had been repeated in the media.

The Court of Appeal held that the simple test of reasonable foresight suggested in *Slipper* imposed an unfair burden on the defendant. Liability, they argued, should be imposed only where the defendant is aware that what they say or do will be reported, or where they should have appreciated a risk of this happening, *and* that the repetition of the defamatory statement (in whole or in part) would increase the damage caused to the claimant. Nevertheless, they refused to strike out that part of the claim and the matter was referred back to trial.

Ultimately, the case was settled out of court. Victoria Beckham gave the claimant £55,000 for hurt and damage caused, together with a set of official merchandise signed by David.

15.8 **Defences**

Not all defamatory statements will result in an award of damages. There are a number of specific defences to defamation that seek to maintain a balance between an individual's freedom of expression and a person's ability to protect their reputation.

The defences fall, broadly, into two categories, reflecting different forms of statement. Statements of *fact* are covered by the defences of justification and privilege while *opinion* are subject to the defence of honest comment. In addition, the defendant may, in certain circumstances, choose to apologise (usually accompanied by some form of compensation)—known as an offer of amends—rather than fight the action through the courts.[22] We shall look at each of these in turn.[23]

15.8.1 **Justification or truth**

Not all defamatory statements are untrue. Calling a thief a thief may damage his reputation but this is hardly something the thief can complain about. Unsurprisingly, therefore, the truth of a defamatory statement is a defence to a claim in defamation: 'the law will not permit a man to recover damages in respect of an injury to a character which he does not or ought not possess' (*McPherson* v *Daniels* [1829] at 272).[24] For example, a married TV presenter who *is* having an affair with her dance partner will not be able

22. Also where the claimant has consented (either expressly or impliedly) to the publication of the defamatory material, this will be a defence (*Cookson* v *Harewood* [1932]).

23. Readers should note that at the time of writing, the Coalition Government had introduced a Draft Defamation Bill which included measures to put a number of the common law defences on a statutory footing (Ministry of Justice, 'Draft Defamation Bill' CP3/11). Please see the Online Resource Centre for updates.

24. The Rehabilitation of Offenders Act 1974, s 8 provides a single statutory exception to this. When referring to a spent conviction, the defendant both must show that it is true and an absence of malice in publishing the information (s 8(5)).

to sue in the tort of defamation where this is reported or alleged in the press. Nor will the author exposed for plagiarism, however much embarrassment and damage to their reputation the revelation may cause.[25] (However, where this information is considered 'confidential' or private, the first person to reveal it may be liable in the emerging tort of invasion of privacy (***Douglas* v *Hello! Ltd* [2001]).[26]

What may be more surprising is that the burden of proof here is on the defendant to show that the statement is true. In other words, a claimant bringing a claim in defamation only has to show that the statement was defamatory—he does not also have to show that the defamatory statement was untrue. As such, even *false* defamatory statements are actionable in the tort of defamation.[27] This poses a problem for defendants not simply because of the difficulty in proving that the allegation is true (the defendant may not be able to access the necessary evidence, a journalist may be unwilling to reveal their sources and so on), but also because defending defamation claims is an expensive business.

Conversely this also means that a successful claimant in a defamation case *never* leaves court completely vindicated. They may have been awarded substantial damages, but they have not proved that the statement was false—it is simply that the defendant has been unable to produce sufficient evidence to prove the truth of the allegation. Moreover, a prolonged court case may increase the injury to the claimant's reputation and aggravate the jury, which may—should the defence not be established—be reflected in the damages awarded. Pursuing an action in defamation for a true statement (on the assumption that the defendant will be unable to prove its truth) is often a dangerous ploy—as Oscar Wilde, Jonathan Aitken, Neil Hamilton, Jeffrey Archer, Bruce Grobbelaar and others have learnt to their cost (*Weir* p 183).

In order for the defence of justification to succeed, the statement must be shown to be 'true in substance and fact' (*Sutherland* v *Stopes* [1925]). However, where there are two or more distinct charges, section 5 of the Defamation Act 1952 provides that the 'defence of justification shall not fail by reason only that the truth of not every charge is proven if the words not proven to be true do not materially injure the [claimant's] reputation, having regard to the truth of the remaining charges'. That is, the defence of justification will not fail simply because the defendant cannot show that *every* allegation is true—especially when those not proven are relatively insignificant in light of the other proven charges. In *Alexander* v *North Eastern Railway Co* [1865], for example, the defendants published a notice at all its stations that the claimant had been charged with travelling without a ticket and had been punished with a fine of £9 1s 10d or 3 weeks' imprisonment. In fact, the claimant had been sentenced only to 14 days in prison, after defaulting on his fine and costs. He argued that the defendant's exaggeration made his offence appear worse than it actually was. His claim was denied. The defence of justification had been made out.

25. BBC News 'Media Doctors Admits to Plagiarism' 16 June 2008. Although, of course, if the statement is untrue, the damages awarded may be extensive (see BBC News 'GMTV Host Garraway wins Damages' 10 April 2008).

26. See further Chapter 16.

27. A challenge to this in the Court of Appeal in *Jameel* v *Wall Street Journal* [2005] as contrary to Arts 6 and 10 of the ECHR was dismissed for having come too late in the proceedings. However, the point remains open—*Steel and Morris* v *UK* [2005] provides some support for the view that it may, in exceptional circumstances, be a breach of Art 10.

However, it is also true, in the words of Brooke LJ that 'It is no defence to a charge that 'you called me A' to say 'Yes, but I also called you B on the same occasion, and that was true' (*Cruise (and Kidman)* v *Express Newspapers* [1999] at 954). The defendant cannot defend themselves simply by establishing the truth of a wholly unconnected claim which also happens to be included in the article. However, where the claims are necessarily connected to each other, the claimant cannot choose which one to object to—the article will be put before the jury, which will decide whether the statement is defamatory in the context of the article as a whole.

That said, the 'sting' of a defamatory statement is not always clear (***Grobbelaar* v *News Group Newspapers Ltd** [2002]).

Grobbelaar v *News Group Newspapers Ltd* [2002] HL

Bruce Grobbelaar was a footballer who at the time played for Southampton. He was covertly videoed by the *Sun* confessing to having fixed matches in the past and took £2,000 offered by the informant to fix future matches. The *Sun* reported this under the headline 'Grobbelaar took bribes to fix games'. Grobbelaar started proceedings for defamation but was subsequently arrested. The criminal case was eventually dropped after he was acquitted of conspiracy as the jury could not agree as to whether he had taken bribes to throw (lose) matches. In the civil court, Grobbelaar was awarded £85,000 in damages. However, the verdict was subsequently overturned as perverse by the Court of Appeal.

In the House of Lords, the point at issue was whether the 'sting' of the defamation in this case was the allegation that the claimant had simply conspired to throw matches or whether he had actually gone on to throw matches. The defendants argued that it was the former, and that this could be shown to be true by their video evidence of the defendant discussing throwing a match. Grobbelaar, however, argued that the sting was that he had actually thrown a particular match. This, he argued, could not be proved to be true. There was a video of the match and he called expert evidence from other professional goalkeepers who testified that he appeared to be making a genuine attempt to stop the goals he had conceded.

The House of Lords allowed Grobbelaar's appeal, holding that in the defence of justification it is for the jury to decide, on the facts, the sting of the defamatory comment. The jury's decision, therefore, that the sting related to the allegation that the claimant threw a particular match (which had not been shown to be true by the defendants) was not perverse and should not be overturned. The law lords did, however, reduce his damages to £1 in light of the fact that Grobbelaar had been proven to be corrupt.[28]

15.8.2 Privilege

The defence of privilege allows people to speak and, crucially, publish without fear of defamation proceedings in circumstances where it is important that people are able

---

28. Consider again the BBC Radio 5 presenter's comment in the examples at the beginning of the chapter. His statement is clearly defamatory. The only issue therefore (as in *Grobbelaar*) is whether the defence of justification can be made out. This depends on how the specific allegations are interpreted—the problem that the defendant faced in *Grobbelaar* was that they could prove that he took the money but not that he threw the matches and hence the defamatory statements *that he threw matches* could not be justified.

to speak freely. In such situations—described as 'privileged'—freedom of expression takes priority over an individual's right to protect their reputation. The term 'privilege' may be misleading; the defence might better be understood as providing 'immunity' from actions for defamation (*Rogers* p 617).

The defence of privilege comes in two forms: absolute and qualified. Absolute privilege covers situations where it is crucial that people are able to speak with complete freedom. In such circumstances, it is not possible to bring a claim in defamation, however outrageous or false the statement and however malicious the speaker. In contrast, qualified privilege only protects the maker of a defamatory statement who speaks honestly and without malice. Here it falls to the claimant to prove malice (the existence of which is a question for the jury), once the privilege has been established (a question for the judge).

15.8.2.1 Absolute privilege

There are five circumstances where the defence of absolute privilege operates to ensure that no action can be taken against a person who makes a defamatory statement.

(1) Statements in Parliament.

(2) Reports, papers, votes and proceedings ordered to be published by either House of Parliament.

(3) Judicial proceedings.

(4) Reports of Court Proceedings in the UK.

(5) Communications between certain officers of state.

Prior to the Defamation Act 1996, no statement in Parliament could ever lead to liability in court: 'the freedom of speech and debate or proceedings in Parliament ought not to be impeached or questioned in any court or place out of Parliament' (Bill of Rights [1688]). This meant that anything said in either House (statements made outside the House are not privileged)—however ludicrous or false—was absolutely privileged and, as such, could not give rise to a claim in defamation. However, section 13 of the Defamation Act 1996 now allows MPs to waive their right to parliamentary privilege to allow them to sue (or be sued) in situations when discussion of statements made in Parliament would be inevitable (*Hamilton* v *Al Fayed* [2001]).

 Counterpoint

Section 13 of the Defamation Act 1996 was passed in response to then Conservative MP Neil Hamilton's defamation action against *The Guardian* over its allegations that he had received cash for asking questions in Parliament. The courts had stayed Hamilton's action on the grounds that the newspaper would not be able to defend itself because it would have to address what had happened in Parliament. (Neil Hamilton later withdrew his claim.)

The section has been highly criticised for working only one way.[29] While MPs can waive their privilege, the section gives no corresponding right to the opponent to demand

➡

---

29. See, e.g. Kevin Williams '"Only Flattery is Safe": Political Speech and the Defamation Act 1996' (1997) *Modern Law Review* 388.

> →
> that parliamentary privilege be removed. Indeed, it may be that the *absolute* privilege of parliamentary proceedings is itself problematic. While some argue that parliamentary democracy rests on the unlimited freedom of MPs to say what they wish—others question the extent to which this should include a corresponding privilege knowingly to lie.

Judicial proceedings are also privileged. Witnesses and jury members—as well as lawyers and judges—cannot be sued for statements said in court or made in the investigation or preparation of the case (*Taylor* v *Director of the Serious Fraud Office* [1999]). Communications between solicitor and client about the case at hand are similarly protected, as are fair and accurate contemporaneous reports of the proceedings (Defamation Act 1996, s 14). Finally, certain communications between some officers of state (usually understood as only extending to Ministers) are absolutely privileged to ensure their 'freedom of action' in matters of state (*Chatterton* v *Secretary of State for India* [1895]). The *absolute* nature of the privilege here is, again, somewhat problematic. Arguments that a person will be better able to fulfil their duties free from the fear of being sued are equally applicable to other public officials and, indeed, private individuals. Absolute privilege—which deprives an individual of an action in relation to all defamatory statements however maliciously spoken—should, it is argued, cover only circumstances in which unrestricted freedom of speech and expression is so important that this restriction on an individual's ability to protect their reputation is absolutely justified (*Merricks* v *Nott-Bower* [1965]).

15.8.2.2 Qualified privilege

Qualified privilege is much wider in scope than absolute privilege. It is often relied on by the media as it seeks to protect the publisher of a statement where it is in the public interest that the statement be published notwithstanding the fact that it cannot be proven to be true. Central to this is the conduct of the publisher. The defence only applies in situations where the statement is made without malice. A defendant acts maliciously, in this context, if they use 'the occasion...for an indirect or wrong motive' (*Clarke* v *Molyneux* [1877])—for instance, the statement is made with the intension of damaging the claimant's reputation—or where the defendant does not believe that the statement is true, or makes the statement without caring whether it is true or not. However, where the defendant honestly believes in the truth of the statement they are entitled to the protection of qualified privilege however unreasonable or prejudiced the defendant was in coming to the conclusion that the statement was true. As Lord Diplock put it in *Horrocks* v *Lowe* [1975]:

> In ordinary life it is rare indeed for people to form their beliefs by a process of logical deduction from facts ascertained by a rigorous search for all available evidence and a judicious assessment of its probative value. In greater or in less degree according to their temperaments, their training, their intelligence, they are swayed by prejudice, rely on intuition instead of reasoning, leap to conclusions on inadequate evidence and fail to recognise the cogency of material which might cast doubt on the validity of the conclusions they reach. But despite the imperfection of the mental process by which the belief is arrived at it may still be 'honest', that is, a positive belief that the conclusions they have reached are true. The law demands no more. (at 150)

Unlike absolute privilege, it is not possible to compile a definitive list of circumstances in which the defence of qualified privileged will arise. However, we do know that current examples are not exhaustive:

> The established categories are no more than applications, in particular circumstances, of the underlying principle of public policy. The underlying principle is conventionally stated in words to the effect that there must exist between the maker of the statement and the recipient some duty or interest in the making of the communication. . . . The requirement that both the maker of the statement and the recipient must have an interest or duty draws attention to the need to have regard to the position of both parties when deciding whether an occasion is privileged. But this should not be allowed to obscure the rationale of the underlying public interest on which privilege is founded. The essence of this defence lies in the law's recognition of the need, in the public interest, for a particular recipient to receive frank and uninhibited communication of particular information from a particular source. That is the end the law is concerned to attain. The protection afforded to the maker of the statement is the means by which the law seeks to achieve that end. Thus the court has to assess whether, in the public interest, the publication should be protected in the absence of malice. (Lord Nicholls, *Reynolds* at 194)

As suggested in this extract, the issue of qualified privilege was traditionally said to turn on the relationship between the giver and recipient of the relevant information:

> a privileged occasion is . . . an occasion where the person who makes a communication has an interest or a duty, legal, social, or moral, to make it to the person to whom it is made, and the person to whom it is so made has a corresponding interest or duty to receive it. This reciprocity is essential. (Lord Atkinson, *Adam* v *Ward* [1917] at 334)

However, **Reynolds** suggests that the key focus should be what *interest* there is in the recipient receiving the relevant information. And here the question is not whether the recipient would be 'interested' in receiving the information—we might be interested in hearing all sorts of idle and frivolous gossip. Rather, it is whether the public interest in the recipient receiving such information is sufficiently strong that the law should protect the maker of the statement even if his information is wrong, so long as he does not act maliciously.

A clear example of communications covered by qualified privilege is the provision of a reference concerning a prospective employee to his potential employer. Here there is a clear public interest in the employer hearing the honest views of the referee as to the qualities and failings of the prospective employee. Of course, what this means is that, even if the reference turns out to be inaccurate, the subject of that reference will have no claim in defamation so long as the referee has acted without malice. This meant that traditionally claimants who lost out on jobs because of inaccurate and bad references could obtain no remedy in law, unless they could show that the referee had acted dishonestly. However, their position has been improved—and the protection afforded by the defence of qualified privilege undercut—by recent developments in the tort of negligence.

In **Spring v Guardian Assurance** [1995] the claimant was unable to set up his own business after his previous employer negligently provided a highly damaging reference about him. Unable to prove malice, the claimant contentiously got round the application of the defence of qualified privilege by successfully arguing in the House of Lords that the *Hedley Byrne* principle in relation to negligent misstatements should be extended:[30]

> I can see no good reason why the duty to exercise due skill and care which rests upon the employer should be negatived because, if the [claimant] were instead to bring an action for damage to his reputation, he would be met by the defence of qualified privilege which could only be defeated by malice. (Lord Goff at 324)[31]

An example of the limits of qualified privilege is provided by *Watt* v *Longsdon* [1930]. The defendant, a company director, received information suggesting that the claimant, who was employed overseas, was acting immorally and dishonestly and, in particular, that he was misbehaving with other women. Without waiting for the information to be verified, the defendant informed the chairman of the company and the employee's wife. The information was not true and the claimant sued. The Court of Appeal held that although the defendant's communication of the information to the chairman of the company was privileged (there was a common interest in the affairs of company), this privilege did not attach to his telling the employee's wife. While she may have been 'interested' in knowing what her husband was getting up to, the company director was under no duty to tell her—which is to say that the public interest in wives learning whether their husbands are misbehaving (at least not from their husbands' employers) is not sufficiently great as to merit the protection of qualified privilege.

In **Reynolds**, the leading case on qualified privilege, the House of Lords considered whether media reporting should be protected by a new category of qualified privilege relating to political information. Once again the court was being asked to balance an individual's ability to protect their reputation and the media's Article 10 right to freedom of expression. The importance of the role of the press in a democracy in relation to informing the public of the potential impact of laws and other regulations on their everyday lives is explicitly recognised in section 12(4) of the HRA.

Reynolds v *Times Newspapers* [2001] HL

Libel proceedings were brought against the *Sunday Times* for an article suggesting that Albert Reynolds, the former Prime Minister of the Republic of Ireland had misled the Irish Parliament. The article made no attempt to put his side of the story. Reynolds sued in defamation and *The Times* argued that it was protected by qualified privilege.

In the House of Lords, *The Times'* main argument was that the common law should recognise a separate category of qualified privilege for 'political information' covering all reporting of such matters, except where motivated by malice. This was unanimously rejected by the court, and the majority went on to hold that *The Times'* application should be dismissed. It would be wrong, they argued, to single out political debate from other

➡

---

30. See further Chapter 7, pp 175–177.
31. It should be noted, however, that Lord Keith dissented on exactly this point. He argued that to impose negligence liability in such cases would allow the claimant to effectively subvert the defence of qualified privilege and lead to the same consequences that the defence is said to guard against.

→

matters of public importance. The existing protection provided by the defences of privilege and honest comment was adequate when dealing with matters of public interest.

The appeal failed. Though there was a public interest in the reasons for the claimant's resignation, it was not established that the public interest in the particular story published by the defendants, given how it was presented, was such to attract the protection of qualified privilege. As Lord Hobhouse put it, '[t]he publisher must show that the publication was in the public interest and he does not do this by merely showing that the subject matter was of public interest' (at 239).

However, *Reynolds* nonetheless marks a shift in the law of defamation in favour of media freedom. In particular, Lord Nicholls set down a 'responsible journalism' test in which he listed ten (non-exhaustive) factors to be taken into account when determining whether publication of the relevant information is in the public interest and hence whether the defence of qualified privilege will be available. He held that, when balancing the competing interests of an individual in protecting their reputation against freedom of expression, the court should take into account the following factors:

> 1. The seriousness of the allegation. The more serious the charge, the more the public is misinformed and the individual harmed, if the allegation is not true. 2. The nature of the information, and the extent to which the subject matter is a matter of public concern. 3. The source of the information. Some informants have no direct knowledge of the events. Some have their own axes to grind, or are being paid for their stories. 4. The steps taken to verify the information. 5. The status of the information. The allegation may have already been the subject of an investigation which commands respect. 6. The urgency of the matter. News is often a perishable commodity. 7. Whether comment was sought from the plaintiff. He may have information others do not possess or have not disclosed. An approach to the plaintiff will not always be necessary. 8. Whether the article contained the gist of the plaintiff's side of the story. 9. The tone of the article. A newspaper can raise queries or call for an investigation. It need not adopt allegations as statements of fact. 10. The circumstances of the publication, including the timing...

> The weight to be given to these and any other relevant factors will vary from case to case...In general, a newspaper's unwillingness to disclose the identity of its sources should not weigh against it. Further, it should always be remembered that journalists act without the benefit of the clear light of hindsight. Matters which are obvious in retrospect may have been far from clear in the heat of the moment. Above all, the court should have particular regard to the importance of freedom of expression. The press discharges vital functions as a bloodhound as well as a watchdog. The court should be slow to conclude that a publication was not in the public interest and, therefore, the public had no right to know, especially when the information is in the field of political discussion. Any lingering doubts should be resolved in favour of publication. (at 205)

Nevertheless, some have criticised the test in ***Reynolds*** for doing 'little to foster an editor's "confidence" in publishing any given story', which is the point of privilege (*Steele* p 792). This can be seen from the number of cases seeking to clarify the ***Reynolds*** test, most recently *Jameel*, where the House of Lords, considering the 'public interest' aspect of *Reynolds* privilege, suggested that the defence was being applied too cautiously by the lower courts.

Jameel v *Wall Street Journal Europe* [2007] HL

The claimants brought an action in libel in response to a newspaper article suggesting that the bank accounts of a number of businessmen and companies, including the claimants' trading group, were being monitored on the suspicion that they were being used to channel funds to terrorist organisations. The lower courts rejected the newspaper's defence of qualified privilege because it had failed to delay publication of the claimants' names long enough to give them time to comment on the article. The House of Lords, however, allowed the newspaper's appeal, holding that the decision of the lower courts was contrary to the 'liberalising intention' of the *Reynolds* test, which should be applied in a flexible and practical manner.

The court identified three questions to be addressed when considering the defence of qualified privilege in relation to the media. First, is the subject of the article containing the defamatory statement a matter of the public interest? Second, if so, was it justifiable to include the specific defamatory statement of which the claimant is complaining? In answering this second question, it should be noted that 'the more serious the allegation, the more important it is that it should make a real contribution to the public interest element in the article'. However,

> allowance must be made for editorial judgment. If the article as a whole is in the public interest, opinions may reasonably differ over which details are needed to convey the general message. The fact that the judge, with the advantage of leisure and hindsight, might have made a different editorial decision should not destroy the defence. That would make the publication of articles which are, ex hypothesi, in the public interest, too risky and would discourage investigative reporting. (Lord Hoffmann at [51])

Third, if the statement was justifiable in light of the public interest in the subject to which the article is directed were the steps taken to gather the information responsible and fair: that is, did the publication meet the standards of responsible journalism? It is in answering this question that the ten factors identified by Lord Nicholls in *Reynolds* are relevant. However, these were not intended and so should not be treated as ten tests or hurdles which must be overcome before the defence can succeed. On the facts of the case, the defence was established. As Baroness Hale noted: 'We need more such serious journalism in this country and our defamation law should encourage rather than discourage it' (at [150]).

 Pause for reflection

In *Jameel* [2007], Lord Hoffmann endorsed the view first put forward by the Court of Appeal in *Loutchansky* v *Times Newspapers Ltd* [2002] (at 806) that '*Reynolds* privilege' is 'a different jurisprudential creature from the traditional form of privilege from which it sprang'. As such, he considered that '[i]t might more appropriately be called the *Reynolds* public interest defence rather than privilege' (at 46).

→

→

The traditional forms of privilege attach to the *occasion* in which the statement is made. These are occasions marked out by a reciprocity of duty (on the part of the maker of the statement) and interest (on the part of its recipient); such as statements made in court, the provision of references and so on. The privilege then attaches to any statements made on such occasions, unless in turn that privilege was abused by demonstrating malice on the part of the defendant. As such, there is, as Lord Hoffmann described it, a 'two-stage process' (at [50]): first, we ask if the statement was made on a privileged occasion; and, second, if so, we ask whether that privilege is defeated by the defendant's malice.

By contrast, the defence outlined in *Reynolds* works differently. Here what is privileged is not the *occasion* on which the statement is made but the *material* that is communicated. And whether this material is privileged depends not simply on the occasion on which the statement is made, but also the contents of the statement and the conduct of the parties in publishing this material in that form. Accordingly, there is no need for a separate inquiry into the possibility of the privilege being removed on the basis of the defendant's malice since 'the propriety of the conduct of the defendant is built into the conditions under which the material is privileged' (at [46]).

Compare, however, the views of Lord Scott who (at [135]), while agreeing with the substance of this analysis, preferred to see *Reynolds* as an application or 'expression' of traditional privilege.

As well as being a common law defence, certain aspects of qualified privilege have been clarified by the Defamation Act 1996. The publication of any 'report' or other statement detailed in Schedule 1 to the Act will be protected by qualified privilege (s 15). These include fair and accurate *non-contemporaneous* reports of court proceedings anywhere in the world (contemporaneous reports are covered by absolute privilege); details of parliamentary proceedings that are not already absolutely privileged; public proceedings of an overseas legislature, court, public inquiry or international organisation anywhere in the world; and, finally, fair and accurate copies or extracts from an official register or court notice.

15.8.3 Honest comment

The defence of honest comment (labelled until recently *fair* comment) provides that there will be a complete defence if the defamatory statement is an honest comment on a matter of public interest. Unlike qualified privilege, the defence of honest comment is not limited to a particular group of people or to statements made on particular occasions—anyone can, and should be able to, comment on a matter of public interest. Although the defence does not require an individual's opinion to be balanced or fair, it must be based on true facts, honestly held and made without malice.

In order to establish this defence, the defamatory statement must be:

- a comment or opinion (rather than a statement of fact);
- on a matter of public interest;
- honestly held.

15.8.3.1 Opinion not fact

There is a fine line between a comment *on* facts as opposed to a statement *of* fact and to suggest that comment is restricted to statements of opinion risks oversimplification. A basic rule of thumb is that facts are simply descriptive, whereas comments and opinions are evaluative. So to say, for example, that McFly's new album contains 11 songs is a statement of fact; to say that it is their best yet is obviously a statement of opinion. The veracity of statements of fact is not dependent on the perspectives and values of the person who makes the statement: there is in such cases *a fact of the matter*, and this is the case even if people disagree over what this is. By contrast, opinions are *necessarily* dependent on an individual's values and preferences.

Though sound in principle, drawing this distinction in practice can be difficult. Indeed the courts have on occasion suggested that the same statement could be either a statement of fact or a statement of opinion depending on the context. A famous example of this was given by Ferguson J in the New South Wales case of *Myerson* v *Smith's Weekly* [1923]: 'To say that a man's conduct was dishonourable is not comment, it is a statement of fact. To say that he did certain specific things and that his conduct was dishonourable is a statement of fact coupled with a comment.' As noted by the Supreme Court in *Joseph* v *Spiller* [2010], this cannot be right.

To say that a man's conduct was dishonourable is not a simple statement of fact. It is a comment coupled with an allegation of unspecified conduct upon which the comment is based. A defamatory comment about a person will almost always be based, either expressly or inferentially, on conduct on the part of that person (Lord Phillips PSC at [5]).

So, while comments that do not identify the conduct on which they are based have sometimes been treated as if they were statements of fact, the better view is that they remain statements of opinion. What is undisputed, however, is that the defence of fair comment will not succeed in such cases. Instead the only defence open to the defendant is justification, which requires that they prove the existence of facts which justify the comment.

Nonetheless, a recent Court of Appeal case highlights the difficulties of distinguishing fact and opinion.

British Chiropractic Association v Singh [2010] CA

The defendant published a newspaper article containing the following:

> The British Chiropractic Association claims that their members can treat children with colic, sleeping and feeding problems, frequent ear infections, asthma and prolonged crying, even though there is not a jot of evidence. This organisation is the respectable face of the chiropractic profession and yet it happily promotes bogus treatments.

The claimant sued for libel and the defendant sought to rely on the defence of fair comment. The question for the court was whether these were assertions of fact (in which case the defence would not be available) or statements of opinion. The trial judge, Eady J, held that they were statements of fact, but the Court of Appeal allowed the defendant's appeal.

→

Though the words 'not a jot of evidence' may be thought to involve a question of fact—either such evidence exists or it does not—the court said the words should be read as meaning there is 'no worthwhile or reliable evidence'. And whether evidence not only exists but is *worthwhile* is a value judgement, and so a matter of opinion. The claim that the treatments were 'bogus' was to be understood in the same light.

 Pause for reflection

Some of the cases have been prepared to treat *inferences of fact* as amounting to comment for the purposes of fair comment, so long as the facts from which the inference is drawn are identified and true. An inference of fact is a statement of fact which is drawn (inferred) from other factual material. So one might infer from the fact that a married TV presenter has a private dinner with her dance partner a further fact: that they are having an affair. *British Chiropractic Association v Singh* appears to endorse this view, at least in so far as we are concerned with scientific or medical matters where the question of what inferences (of fact) can be drawn from the available evidence is contested.

The Supreme Court in *Joseph v Spiller* noted that one possible reform of the defence of honest comment would be to extend it to inferences of fact. However, Lord Phillips PSC was unconvinced by the merits of such a reform.

> Some decisions have gone further and treated allegations of verifiable fact as comment…It is questionable whether this is satisfactory. Prejudiced commentators can draw honest inferences of fact, such as that a man charged with fraud is guilty of fraud. Should the defence of fair comment apply to such inferences? Allegations of fact can be far more damaging, even if plainly based on inference, than comments on true facts. (at [114])

Is it correct to say that allegations of fact will typically be taken more seriously and hence will cause more damage than comments and statements of opinion? Can we maintain the line between statements (including inferences) of fact and statements of opinion without severely limiting individuals' freedom to challenge (potentially) bogus scientific claims?

The defence of honest comment will be available only where the statement is one of opinion rather than fact *and* the facts on which that opinion is based are sufficiently identified. The question then is what amounts to sufficient identification.

The original cases of honest comment concerned reviews of literary works and plays. In such circumstances it was clear to the reader what material the opinion was directed to and so, so long as the comment was not motivated by malice, the defence would be made out. As Lord Phillips PSC held in *Joseph v Spiller*, 'where adverse comment is made generally or generically on matters that are in the public domain I do not consider that it is a prerequisite of the defence of fair comment that the readers should be in a position to evaluate the comment for themselves' (at [98]).

Things became more difficult when the defence was extended to other matters, in particular the conduct of individuals. Here the courts required that the defendant do more to make clear the factual basis for their comments and criticisms. For example, in *Telnikoff* v *Matusevich* [1991], the defendant wrote a letter published in the *Daily Telegraph* attacking an earlier article, published in the same paper and written by the claimant, as racist and anti-Semitic. The House of Lords held that the defendant could not rely on portions of the original article which had not been quoted in his letter in support of a defence of fair comment. However, the most recent authority suggests that the courts are relaxing this requirement.

Joseph v *Spiller* [2010] SC

The claimants were musicians who had entered into a contract with the defendant booking agency. The contract included a 're-engagement clause', which provided that if the claimants were to perform at a venue for a second time within a 12-month period, this second booking was to be arranged through the defendant. The defendant wrote to the claimants complaining that they had breached this clause by arranging a second booking directly with the venue. In their reply by email, the claimants wrote, 'your contract…holds no water in legal terms'. The defendant then posted a notice on their website stating that they would no longer accept bookings for the claimants as 'following a breach of contract' they had advised that 'the terms and conditions of "contracts hold no water in legal terms"'.

In response to the claimants' defamation claim, the defendant pleaded fair comment. The claimants applied to have this defence struck out, *inter alia*, on the basis that the facts to which the comments were directed were not identified with sufficient particularity in the notice on their website, since the details of the alleged breach of contract were not specified. The application succeeded at first instance and in the Court of Appeal, but the defendant's appeal was successful before the Supreme Court.

Giving the leading opinion, Lord Phillips PSC held that for the defence to be available,

> the comment [need not] identify the matters on which it is based with sufficient particularity to enable the reader to judge for himself whether it was well founded. The comment must, however, identify at least in general terms what it is that has led the commentator to make the comment, so that the reader can understand what the comment is about and the commentator can, if challenged, explain by giving particulars of the subject matter of his comment why he expressed the views that he did. A fair balance must be struck between allowing a critic the freedom to express himself as he will and requiring him to identify to his readers why it is that he is making the criticism. (at [104])

More generally, he noted the need for the defence of fair—or, as the Supreme Court preferred, honest—comment to develop to fit modern modes of communication.

> Today the internet has made it possible for the man in the street to make public comment about others in a manner that did not exist when the principles of the law of fair comment were developed, and millions take advantage of that opportunity. Where the comments that they make are derogatory it will often be impossible for other readers to evaluate them without detailed information about the facts that have given rise to the comments. Frequently these will not be set out. If [the defendant were required to provide sufficient facts as to enable a reader to judge if the comments are well founded] the defence of fair comment will be robbed of much if its efficacy. (at [99])

➙

> ➡
>
> Lord Walker JSC echoed these sentiments:
>
> The creation of a common base of information shared by those who watch television and use the internet has had an effect which can hardly be overstated. Millions now talk, and thousands comment in electronically transmitted words, about recent events of which they have learned from television or the internet. Many of the events and the comments on them are no doubt trivial and ephemeral but from time to time (as the present appeal shows) libel law has to engage with them. The test for identifying the factual basis of honest comment must be flexible enough to allow for this type of case, in which a passing reference to the previous night's celebrity show would be regarded by most of the public, and may sometimes have to be regarded by the law, as a sufficient factual basis. (at [131])

Finally, except for where the statement relied on was made by a person on a privileged occasion, the facts commented on must be true. A commentator cannot simply make up facts upon which to comment. However, the defence of honest comment no longer fails if the truth of one or more of the statements relied upon is not proven. Section 6 of the Defamation Act 1952 provides that 'a defence of fair comment shall not fail by reason only that the truth of every allegation of fact is not proved if the expression of opinion is fair comment having regard to such of the facts alleged or referred to in the words complained of as are proved'.

15.8.3.2 'Of public interest'

The comment must be on a matter of public interest. However, it is clear that 'public interest' is understood very broadly here. Lord Denning MR in *London Artists Ltd* v *Littler* [1969] defined this as anything 'such as to affect the people at large, so that they may be legitimately interested in, or concerned at, what is going on' (at 391). So this covers not only important political matters such as the conduct of government or the judiciary, but also extends to reviews of films, books, music and the like. It also covers the contractual dispute between the parties in *Joseph* v *Spiller*. Indeed the Supreme Court in *Joseph* was invited by counsel for the defendant to redraw the defence of honest comment so as to remove the requirement that the comments pertain to a matter of public interest. And, though the Supreme Court did not take this step, the remarks of Lord Walker JSC quoted above, concerning comments directed to 'the previous night's celebrity show', suggest that few matters in the public domain will fall outside the public interest.

15.8.3.3 Honest

As has been noted already, the defence we now call honest comment used to be labelled *fair* comment. As Lord Nicholls has said in *Reynolds*:

> the time has come to recognise that in this context the epithet 'fair' is now meaningless and misleading. Comment must be relevant to the facts to which it is addressed. It cannot be used as a cloak for mere invective. But the basis of our public life is that the crank, the enthusiast, may say what he honestly thinks as much as the reasonable person who sits on a jury. The true test is whether the opinion, however exaggerated, obstinate or prejudiced, was honestly held by the person expressing it. (at 193)

This shift from fair to honest comment was finally confirmed by the Supreme Court in *Joseph* v *Spiller*.

Moreover, the defendant does not need to prove their honesty. Honesty will be presumed and it is for the claimant to attempt to disprove this. In substance the defendant's honesty is determined by asking whether the comment was 'one which could have been made by an honest person, however prejudiced he might be, and however exaggerated or obstinate his views' (Lord Nicholls in *Tse Wei Chun* v *Cheng* [2001] at [20]).

Traditionally the defence of fair comment—like the defence of qualified privilege—was defeated by malice on the part of the defendant. Here too, however, it appears that the requirement may now simply reduce to one of honesty. In *Tse Wei Chun* v *Cheng* [2001] Lord Nicholls took the view that malice in the context of honest comment is not established simply by showing that the defendant was motivated by spite or ill-will when making his comments. Instead the question is simply whether he honestly believed his comments were justified. Whether this narrow conception of malice, excluding the defendant's motives and inquiring only into their honesty, is correct is less clear. Though the matter did not arise for decision in *Joseph* v *Spiller*, the Supreme Court noted but did not endorse Lord Nicholls's narrowing of the malice rule.

15.9 **Offer of amends**

Where the defamatory statement is unintentional—for example where the defendant knows that the statement refers to the claimant but honestly and reasonably believes that it is true or where (as in cases of mistaken identity described above) the defendant never intends to refer to the claimant—the defendant can choose to make an offer of amends under section 2 of the Defamation Act 1996. An offer of amends is not strictly a defence, aimed at showing that the defamatory statement was justified or excusable. Rather, it provides an opportunity for defendants to acknowledge they were wrong and to prevent the claim from going any further.

Timing is crucial here. The offer must be made before the service of a defence to the claim; that is, the defendant must choose whether they are going to fight the defamation action or admit they were wrong. If the defendant's offer is accepted, the action stops and damages are agreed by the parties. If damages cannot be agreed, a court sits without a jury to decide. If the offer is not accepted, the defendant can use the fact that the offer was made in their defence (unless the claimant is able to show that the defendant *knew* that the comments referred to the claimant and were false and defamatory).

Under section 2 of the Defamation Act 1996, the defendant must:

- admit that they were wrong;
- offer in writing to make a suitable correction and apology;
- publish the correction and apology in a manner that is reasonable and practicable in the circumstances;
- pay the claimant such compensation (if any) and such costs as may be agreed or determined to be payable.

There are many examples of an offer of amends in practice—see, for example, the *Daily Express* and *Daily Star*'s front-page apology to the parents of Madeleine McCann for suggestions that they had in some way contributed to her death and Kathleen Turner's apology to Nicolas Cage over allegations made in her autobiography (which was extracted in the *Daily Mail*).[32]

15.10 Remedies: damages and injunctions

An award of damages is the primary remedy in defamation. The amount of damages awarded in defamation cases often appears out of proportion with those awarded for personal injuries. This is partly because an action in defamation is one of the few times in tort law where a compensatory award (for loss of reputation) may be supplemented by aggravated or exemplary damages. Moreover, while the purpose of personal injury damages is primarily compensatory, damages for defamation (as well as being compensatory in respect of material losses caused by the defamatory statement) incorporate the additional purposes of vindication (repairing and re-establishing the claimant's reputation), punishment and deterrence. However, the latter purpose is not particularly effective. It is far from uncommon for defendants, typically newspapers, to publish a story that they either know or suspect or are careless as to whether it is true, because the profit (and publicity) gained from publication will outweigh any financial penalties (*John v MGN Ltd* [1997]).

Unusually, in defamation the award of damages is decided by the jury (although it is never left to a jury to decide whether exemplary damages should be awarded, or their amount). The apparent discrepancy between awards for injury to a person's reputation and, say, physical injury, has led some (usually accompanied by more general arguments for the abolition of jury trials in defamation) to question whether the award of damages might be better left *solely* in the hands of the judge (as in personal injury claims). The argument goes that this would ensure greater consistency which, in turn, would make it more likely that the parties would settle out of court (in line with general principles of civil litigation). However, this solution was rejected by the Law Commission, in its report on damages for non-pecuniary loss, who instead adopted a 'wait and see' strategy following the enactment of the Defamation Act 1996 and the HRA.[33]

In the meantime, section 8 of the Courts and Legal Services Act 1990 allows the Court of Appeal to substitute its own figure of damages for that of the jury without the need for a retrial. In *Rantzen v Mirror Group Newspapers (1986) Ltd* [1994]), *The Mirror* newspaper had accused the television presenter Esther Rantzen, who founded ChildLine, of knowingly protecting a person guilty of sexual abuse. Setting aside the jury's award of £250,000, the Court of Appeal (responding to freedom of expression arguments) substituted the figure of £110,000. The court went on to suggest awards of damages should relate to the ordinary values of life and that the question to be asked

---

32. BBC News 'McCanns Welcome Papers' Apology' 19 March 2008; BBC News 'Turner Apologises for Cage Libel' 4 April 2008.

33. Law Commission *Damages for Personal Injury: Non-pecuniary Loss* (Law Com No 257, 1999), [4.23].

in cases where there are large awards of damages is whether 'a reasonable jury [could] have thought that their award was necessary to compensate the plaintiff and to re-establish his reputation?' (Neill LJ at 692).

Since the Court of Appeal's decision in *John* v *MGN*, judges have been able to inform juries of the level of damages in personal injury cases as a way of trying to guide their decision and prevent disproportionate libel awards. This, is it hoped, will make the assessment of damages in defamation cases 'more rational and so more acceptable to public opinion' (at 616).

John v *MGN Ltd* [1997] CA

The Mirror published a story about Elton John suggesting that he had an eating disorder and had been seen at a party in California chewing food and then disposing of it in his nap-kin. The story was untrue. However, the Court of Appeal reduced the exemplary damages awarded by the jury (in light of the fact that the newspaper had not even checked if he was at the party) from £275,000 to £50,000. He was also awarded £75,000 in compensatory damages which were reduced to £25,000. Sir Thomas Bingham MR warned that:

> principle requires that an award of exemplary damages should never exceed the mini-mum sum necessary to meet the public purpose underlying such damages, that of punishing the defendant, showing that tort does not pay and deterring others. (at 619)

 Pause for reflection

Bingham MR acknowledged in *John* v *MGN* that:

> there can be no precise correlation between loss of a limb, or of sight, or quadriple-gia, and damage to reputation. But if these personal injuries respectively command conventional awards of, at most, about £52,000, £90,000 and £125,000 for pain and suffering and loss of amenity . . . juries may properly be asked to consider whether the injury to his reputation of which the plaintiff complains should fairly justify any greater compensation. (at 614)[34]

How helpful is it *really* to compare awards of damages in personal injury cases and those in defamation?[35]

An award of damages is often accompanied by a final injunction prohibiting further publication of the defamatory material. An injunction is an immediate court order preventing someone from taking certain steps, and a defendant who fails to comply with it can be imprisoned for contempt of court. An injunction can be obtained in a matter of days or, in extremely urgent cases, a matter of hours. The award of an injunction after a statement has been accepted by the courts as defamatory is relatively

---

34. See also Sedley LJ's powerful dissent in *Kiam* v *MGN* [2002] at [66]–[69].
35. See further discussion of damages more generally in Chapter 19.

uncontroversial. More problematic are so-called 'gagging orders' or interim injunctions which seek to prevent publication until a full trial. Traditionally the courts have been reluctant to grant such orders and they will only do so where the defendant has no realistic chance of succeeding in a defence (*Bonnard* v *Perryman* [1891]).

15.11 **Reform**

As we have seen there have been a number of important developments in the law of defamation in the last few years, coming both from the courts (in cases such as **Reynolds** and **Joseph v Spiller**) and from Parliament (the Defamation Act 1996). However, even with these developments, the question of further reform looms large over the law of defamation. In March 2011, the Coalition Government published its Draft Defamation Bill and accompanying Consultation Paper.[36]

The measures contained in the Draft Bill include the 'new' statutory defences of responsible publication on matters of public interest, truth (replacing the common law defence of justification) and honest opinion (replacing the common law defence of honest comment) as well as extending the circumstances in which the absolute and qualified privilege are available. The Draft Bill also includes measures to address the issues of so-called 'libel tourism', by only allowing claims to proceed if the court is satisfied that, of all the places where the defamatory statement has been published, England and Wales is clearly the most appropriate place to bring the claim, and multiple publication by restricting claims against the same publisher for the same material to within one year of the original publication of the material to the public or section of the public. Finally, it removes the presumption in favour of a jury trial and introduces a requirement that a statement must have caused, or be likely to cause, substantial harm to the reputation of the claimant in order for it to be defamatory (though this is simply the common law position established in *Jameel* v *Dow Jones & Co* [2005]).

While the stated purpose of these proposals is to 'create libel laws that will be a foundation for free speech, instead of an international embarrassment',[37] in fact the Draft Defamation Bill does little beyond restating the existing law.[38] It remains to be seen whether this will be enough to ensure that these proposals—unlike others before them—make their way onto the statute books. And, if it does so, it maybe that it is welcomed most strongly, not by those calling for libel reform, but by the lawyers who

---

36. Ministry of Justice 'Draft Defamation Bill (Consultation Paper CP3/11)'. The consultation closes in June 2011. Make sure to check the Online Resource Centre for updates. Alongside the measures included in the Draft Bill, the Coalition Government is also consulting on a number of related issues. These include whether there should be greater protection for Internet Service Providers (ISPs) and others, and the necessity of further measures to address the 'inequality of arms' between parties in defamation proceedings such as through the introduction of a new court procedure to resolve key preliminary issues as early as possible so that cases are decided more quickly and with less expense and/or the imposition of restrictions on the ability of corporations to bring actions in defamation.

37. Nick Clegg 'We Will End the Libel Farce' *The Guardian* 15 March 2011.

38. Joshua Rosenberg 'The Libel Reforms are a Step in the Right Direction—But do they Go Far Enough? *The Guardian* 15 March 2011.

will spend their time (and their client's money) arguing over the extent to which the new statute does—*or does not*—change the common law.[39]

15.12 Conclusion

In this chapter we have looked at the tort of defamation. Defamation protects an individual's or a company's reputation by allowing them to prevent the publication of, or recover damages for, public statements which make, or are likely to make, people think less of them. In so doing, the courts seek to decide whether an individual's interest in what people think of them should trump the freedom of others to be able to say what they know, or think they know, about them (Art 10). While everyone has a reputation to protect, high costs and a lack of public funding mean that most defamation claims are brought by celebrities and politicians (usually) against newspapers.

In order to bring a claim, the statement must be defamatory (as opposed to simply insulting), it must refer to the claimant and must be published. The defendant can however defeat a claim in defamation by showing that the statement they made was, though defamatory, true. Other defences apply to honest comments on matters in the public interest and to statements which are privileged. Where the defamation is unintentional, the defendant can also offer to make 'amends' under section 2 of the Defamation Act 1996.

However, the distress caused to the victim of a libel may result as much from the intrusion into their private life which accompanies publication as from the hurt to their feelings caused by the untrue statements. It is unsurprising, therefore, that the nascent tort of invasion of privacy (discussed in the next chapter) has developed (at least in part) by analogy with, and to fill the gaps of, the defamation torts.

✳ End-of-chapter questions

After reading the chapter carefully, try answering the questions below. If you would like to know what we think visit the Online Resource Centre (www.oxfordtextbooks.co.uk/orc/horsey2e/).

1. Who can and who cannot sue in defamation? Explain the reasons for this.

2. To what extent, if at all, does the so-called *Reynolds* defence ensure responsible journalism?

3. What is the difference between fact and opinion? Is this distinction maintained by the Court of Appeal in *British Chiropractic Association v Singh*?

4. Consider the problem question at the start of this chapter—now having read about the topic what would be your advice to the editor of *In the Hood*? If you need some pointers in thinking about how to answer this question, turn to the Appendix (p 589) where each

---

39. Dominic Crossley 'Libel Reform? Defamation is the Least of our Problems' *The Guardian* 16 March 2011.

problem is annotated with issues and cases to consider. Next, try to write your own answer and finally, log on to our Online Resource Centre (www.oxfordtextbooks.co.uk/orc/horsey2e/) and check your ideas against our suggested outline answer.

✱ Further reading

The best place to start your reading is with Carol Harlow's chapter. It is also worth taking a look at the BBC news clips on the Online Resource Centre.

Barendt, Eric 'Libel and Freedom of Speech in English Law' [1993] *Public Law* 449

Descheemaeker, Eric 'Veritas non est defamatio? Truth as a Defence in the Law of Defamation' (2011) *Legal Studies* 1

Dunlop, Rory 'Article 10, the Reynolds Test and the Rule in the Duke of Brunswick's Case—the Decision in *Times Newspapers Ltd v United Kingdom*' (2006) *European Human Rights Law Review* 327

Gibbons, Thomas 'Defamation Reconsidered' (1996) 16(4) *Oxford Journal of Legal Studies* 587

Haplin, Andrew 'Law, Libel and the English Court of Appeal' (1996) *Tort Law Review* 139

Harlow, Carol *Understanding Tort Law* (Sweet & Maxwell, 2005), Ch 7

McNamara, Lawrence *Reputation and Defamation* (OUP, 2007)

Mullis, Alastair and Andrew Scott 'Something Rotten in the State of English Libel Law? A Rejoinder to the Clamour for Reform of Defamation' (2009) *Communications Law* 173

Invasion of privacy

Problem question

Read this problem question carefully, and keep it in mind while you are working through the chapter that follows. At the end of the chapter, you will be able to apply what you have learnt to the problem question and advise the relevant parties.

Elizabeth is the fiancée of a Premiership footballer, Alessandro Talentti. She is 28 years old, beautiful and glamorous. She has always been happy to be photographed with Alessandro at awards evenings, film premieres, and charity events and also while out with her girlfriends shopping or lunching, or with other footballers' wives and girlfriends watching football matches.

Recently, as she has started to organise her wedding, which she wants to be an intimate and private affair, Elizabeth has found the media attention intrusive and has had several arguments with photographers wanting to take her picture whilst out shopping or in small, quiet restaurants. One photographer, Chris, is particularly persistent and takes photographs when she is leaving a hospital after visiting her mother who is very ill. He also photographed her (using a long-range lens) going in to a small London bridal boutique when she was shopping for bridesmaids' dresses with her young sister and niece.

On the wedding day—the press having been successfully excluded from the venue—one of the caterers secretly takes some pictures of the ceremony and the reception, at which there were many famous guests. He then sold these pictures to *Peachy!*, a well-known celebrity glossy magazine; the pictures are published in the following week's issue as an 'exclusive'.

16.1 **Introduction**

Consider the following examples:

→ Karen, a famous pop singer, is photographed entering a treatment centre for anorexics and the pictures are published in a tabloid newspaper.

→ Dave, a well-known fashion model, is filmed on CCTV kissing a girl in a restaurant—pictures from the film are published in a tabloid newspaper.

→ Long-range photographs are taken of Molly, a television newsreader, swimming in a pool on holiday in a private resort. These are published in a tabloid newspaper.

→ Nancy, a British actress, marries a Hollywood actor. They agreed to sell their wedding photos to *Look and See!* magazine but secret photos of the ceremony are published in *Look Here!* magazine.

→ Eric, a teenager, is caught on CCTV vandalising a shop front. Images of him are published in a local newspaper and put on the local TV news.

In each of these examples the 'privacy' of the parties has, in some way, been invaded. Although the UK does not have a specific privacy tort, the law offers some protection of privacy interests through various torts and statutory mechanisms. Trespass (to the person and to land), private nuisance, malicious falsehood and defamation are all torts that overlap to some extent with aspects of an individual's privacy interests. Further protection of these interests can be found in equity (breach of confidence) and copyright laws, as well as the Protection from Harassment Act 1997 and the Data Protection Act 1998.

However, none of these legal mechanisms protect an individual's privacy *per se* and all of them are limited in the protection they can offer. For example, despite the protectionist in-road made in *Khorasandjian* v *Bush* [1993], since **Hunter v Canary Wharf [1997]** an individual requires a proprietary interest in land to claim in private nuisance.[1] Similarly, for recovery under the 1997 Act, there must be a 'course of conduct' that amounts to harassment.[2]

Article 8 of the European Convention on Human Rights (ECHR) tells us that all citizens have 'the right to respect for...private and family life...home and...correspondence'. As we shall see, this Article, alongside the passage of the Human Rights Act (HRA) 1998, has helped the law regarding privacy protection develop in ways so that it might be said a 'tort of invasion of privacy' exists 'in all but name'. However, the impact of Article 8's protection of privacy is somewhat curtailed by a competing and equally important Convention right: the right to freedom of expression (Art 10). Much of the most recent case law focuses on the interplay between these rights.

Many (but not all) of the claims made regarding violations of privacy interests are made by 'celebrities'—who (usually but not always) allege that it is the media that has intruded into their private world. For this reason, 'privacy' has become somewhat contentious. When asking whether someone should have had the right to remain private

---

1. Chapter 17, 495–496.
2. Chapter 14, p 405.

in a particular situation, regard is often had to their fame or notoriety. Some people think that because celebrities 'court fame' to one extent or another, they should accept inevitable media intrusion into their lives. However, it should be remembered that 'celebrity' cases help to set the precedents used in cases that apply for everyone and, while many of us will not suffer from an invasion of privacy by the media, there are other ways our privacy can be invaded (see, for example, **Wainwright v Home Office [2004]**; *Peck v UK* **[2003]**) and clearly non-celebrities may also be affected by media intrusion (see, for example, *Venables v News Group Newspapers* [2001]; *X (a woman formerly known as Mary Bell) v SO* [2003]).

This chapter will begin by considering why there is no free-standing tort of invasion of privacy, before looking at another judicial mechanism recently adapted to protect claimants' privacy: breach of confidence—a legal concept that straddles tort and equity and deals with 'secrets'. The next part of the chapter will ask whether developments in the law protecting privacy have begun to threaten the media's freedom of expression and therefore the general public's 'right' to know information about celebrities, including royalty and politicians.

16.2 **A tort of invasion of privacy?**

In the House of Lords' decision in **Wainwright v Home Office** [2004], Lord Hoffmann stated that English law neither contains nor needs to create a specific privacy tort. He also indicated that English law has been unwilling and might even be *unable* to create such a tort (at [18]). Similarly, Baroness Hale has stated that 'our law cannot, even if it wanted to, develop a general tort of invasion of privacy' (**Campbell v Mirror Group Newspapers [2004]** at [133]). While this seems constitutionally inaccurate, as clearly Parliament could create a tort of privacy should it want to, Baroness Hale's comment (particularly when read alongside Lord Hoffmann's) can be deconstructed. Clearly she is referring to the common law, not Parliament. First, she says that English law does not *want* to create such a tort. Secondly, her use of the word 'cannot' is inaccurate—this would be better replaced with either 'should not' or 'will not'.

Both the judiciary and Parliament have a history of reluctance when it comes to the creation of a tort protecting privacy. Many possible reasons have been suggested for this, including a lack of precedent, lack of a suitable definition of privacy,[3] as well as concerns about frivolous claims, the appropriate remedy (and whether any remedy could be effective, especially after the event) and the impact of placing restraints on freedom of expression.

 Counterpoint

In our view, none of these reasons are convincing. Lack of precedent does not prevent Parliament enacting legislation nor, in other areas, has it stopped the courts 'creating law'

→

3. *Markesinis & Deakin* p 820.

➡️

in the past (even if they do not or will not acknowledge that this is what has been done—see, for example, the rule in *Wilkinson* v *Downton* [1897] or the action under **Rylands v Fletcher** [1868]). Defining 'privacy' may be problematic, but such problems are clearly not insurmountable. The Younger Committee described privacy—as far back as 1972—as 'privacy of information, that is the right to determine for oneself how and to what extent information about oneself is communicated to others'.[4] This subjective interpretation seems to fit well with the majority of the case law we discuss in this section—perhaps indicating that defining privacy is either not as problematic as is assumed or that a definition is relatively unimportant.

The concern about frivolous claims is one that surfaces each time a new harm is potentially identified in tort. Yet the 'floodgates' that the judiciary seem so concerned to avoid opening do not seem to have opened elsewhere (in Germany, for example, where the right to privacy is more broadly protected) and, given the personal and financial cost of bringing any legal claim, particularly as Legal Aid would not be available, it is unlikely that many people would bring so-called frivolous issues before a court. If the courts are concerned merely that there will be *more* claims, this is a different issue—but an increased number of claims may simply reflect an increased number of invasions of privacy, in which case, this should be no barrier to making a claim and should also be an indicator that those who are continuously infringing on individuals' personal and private lives (for example, the press) ought to be reined in by other means than by private law actions.

Remedies for privacy violations are more problematic. Most claimants will want to prevent information reaching, or the withdrawal of information from, the public sphere. Often it will be too late to do this (for example in the form of an injunction prohibiting publication of certain information). However, this difficulty is not used as a reason to *deny* a remedy in other areas: for personal injuries caused by negligence there is no remedy that can give a claimant back a lost limb, yet the 'appropriateness' of the remedy, which has to be monetary, does not prevent claims from being actionable.

Concerns about infringements on the right to freedom of expression are more valid. It is right in a democratic society that people, including the media, are free to form and speak their opinions. However, again (and as the case law discussed later in this chapter shows) the problem is not insurmountable. None of the reasons so far given are qualitatively good reasons for bluntly refusing to create a tort of invasion of privacy.

The reality is that Parliament is reluctant to create an overarching tort of privacy within the current legislative framework and this reluctance has been a major obstacle for English law in developing the tort. This legislative reluctance can be illustrated with a short review of Committee Reports and bills presented to Parliament and parliamentary opinion thereafter.

In the 1960s three Bills were presented before Parliament directly relating to privacy; two of which expressly provided for an actionable right for citizens to claim that their privacy had been infringed. Each of the bills failed. Lord Mancroft's Bill (1961) was withdrawn due to lack of governmental support; Mr Alexander Lyon's Bill (1967)

4. *Report of the Committee on Privacy,* Chairman: Kenneth Younger (Cmnd 5012, 1972), p 10.

was rejected for being too limited; and Mr Brian Walden's Bill (1969) was rejected for encroaching too far into freedom of expression.[5]

Soon after, the Younger Committee presented its *Report on Privacy*.[6] This concluded by stating that there was 'no need to extend the law of privacy further'. The principle objection related to defining 'privacy', but it was also thought that sufficient remedies for intrusion of one's privacy already existed, and self-regulation of media outlets was preferred. Similar views were subsequently advocated by the McGregor Commission in 1977.[7] These reports were followed by two bills presented within the 1988–9 parliamentary sessions—again, both failed.[8]

In 1990, the Calcutt Committee reviewed the question of privacy, again rejecting a tort of privacy in favour of self-regulation through the Press Complaints Commission.[9] The Committee found that even after reviewing the laws of France, Germany and the US, a satisfactory definition of privacy could not be found. A final statement of the Calcutt Committee expressing the government's view was presented in 1995. Once again self-regulation was seen as best and no intention was expressed to introduce a tort of privacy.[10] In fact, this view appears to be becoming even further entrenched. Although in 2004 the House of Commons Culture Media and Sport Committee advocated a specific right of privacy,[11] more recently it has acknowledged that:

> To draft a law defining a right to privacy which is both specific in its guidance but also flexible enough to apply fairly to each case which would be tested against it could be almost impossible. Many people would not want to seek redress through the law, for reasons of cost and risk. In any case, we are not persuaded that there is significant public support for a privacy law.[12]

16.2.1 How do we protect privacy?

As noted above, one of the key problems in protecting privacy interests has been the lack of a coherent definition of what privacy is, despite various attempts over time to define it. One reason for a lack of a suitable common definition is that the notion of privacy might be different for different people. It has variously been described as 'the right to be let alone',[13] to be free from an 'unwanted gaze' or 'unauthorised interference with a person's seclusion of himself'[14] or to have unfettered control of information about or images of oneself.

---

5. The complete text of each of the three Bills is available in the appendix of the Younger Report.

6. Cmnd 5012, July 1972.

7. *(Third) Royal Commission on the Press*, McGregor Commission (Cmnd 6810, July 1977).

8. Bill on Protection of Privacy and Right of Reply introduced by John Browne MP and Tony Worthington MP.

9. *Committee on Privacy and Related Matters Report of the Committee on Privacy and Related Matters*, Chairman: David Calcutt (Cm 1102, June 1990).

10. *Privacy and Media Intrusion* (Cm 2918, July 1995).

11. This was rejected by the government at the time (Privacy and Media Intrusion: Replies to the Committee's fifth report 2002–2003, First Special Report HC 213, February 2004).

12. Culture, Media and Sport Committee 'Self Regulation of the Press' Seventh Report of Session 2006–2007 (July 2007) High Court 375, [53].

13. Thomas Cooley *Cooley on Torts* (2nd edn, 1888), p 29.

14. Percy H Winfield 'Privacy' (1931) 47 *Law Quarterly Review* 23.

Other nations have well-established privacy protections, suggesting that workable definitions are possible. However, these protections vary in their severity and, consequently, such variation may be one of the factors making a universal definition so hard to find. In France, for example, invasion of privacy is a crime and therefore people, including 'celebrities' are able to keep their private lives very private indeed. German law offers lesser protection but still privacy forms part of the Constitution written after the Second World War and protects information about citizens' personal and private lives from becoming public. The notion of what is to be considered private has been developed by the courts over time in a flexible way and many claimants have been able to satisfactorily resolve their claims. In the United States, the protected interest seems to be freedom of speech, at the expense of privacy. The second restatement of the US Constitution favours the freedom of the press and the courts have been reluctant to second-guess what editors think is appropriate.

As early as 1931, Percy H Winfield said that he hoped the House of Lords would develop a new area of tort specifically to protect privacy. However, 60 years later, the common law still had no defined privacy protection, as is clearly illustrated in *Kaye* v *Robertson and Sport Newspapers Ltd* [1991].

> ### *Kaye* v *Robertson and Sport Newspapers Ltd* [1991] CA
>
> Gordon Kaye, who was at the time a well-known TV personality, suffered extensive brain injuries when a billboard collapsed onto his car. While recovering in hospital an editor and photographer from the *Sunday Sport* tabloid newspaper managed to gain entry to his room, take photographs of him lying semi-conscious in bed and conduct an 'interview'. The nature of his injuries left Kaye with no memory of this interview occurring. The newspaper marketed the interview and photographs as a 'scoop'. Kaye's agent tried to obtain an injunction against the newspaper to prevent the pictures and story being published, alleging these were an invasion of his privacy. As there was no specific tort to this effect, he had to try various other existing torts; these included defamation, passing off, malicious falsehood and trespass to the person.
>
> All but the malicious falsehood claim failed. This meant only that the newspaper had to remove any references that said Kaye had consented to be interviewed or photographed—the photos themselves were still published. The Court of Appeal recognised that it was a clear invasion of privacy to be photographed in one's hospital bed, particularly when it was not in one's power to prevent this, however there was nothing more that could be done. English tort law had created various 'boxes' of liability which, if a claim does not fit, will leave no redress:
>
>> If ever a person has a right to be let alone by strangers with no public interest to pursue, it must surely be when he lies in hospital recovering from brain surgery and in no more than partial command of his faculties. It is this invasion of his privacy which underlies the [claimant's] complaint. Yet it alone, however gross, does not entitle him to relief in English law. (Bingham LJ at 70)

In *Kaye*, the Court of Appeal recognised the need for the creation of a tort of invasion of privacy but deferred responsibility for this to Parliament: 'The facts of the present case are a graphic illustration of the desirability of Parliament considering whether and in what circumstances statutory provision can be made to protect the privacy of individuals' (Glidewell LJ at 66).

This judicial reluctance to 'create' a common law tort of privacy is reflected throughout the case law. In *Malone* v *Metropolitan Police Commissioner (No 2)* [1979], for example, a case concerning telephone tapping, Sir Robert Megarry VC emphasised that the courts should not 'legislate' where a new right has not yet been created. He stated that 'where Parliament has abstained from legislating on a point that is plainly suitable for legislation, it is indeed difficult for the court to lay down new rules of common law or equity that will carry out the Crown's treaty obligations' (at 373, referring to the state's obligations under the ECHR). This desire to refrain from judicial intervention in favour of legislative action was also acknowledged in **Wainwright**, where Lord Hoffmann (with whom the other law lords all agreed) expressly acknowledged what was said in previous judgments, explicitly agreeing with Sir Robert Megarry VC in *Malone* and rejecting any 'broad brush approach' of the common law (at [33]).

It seems, however, that despite this lack of common law protection of privacy interests, the legislature is unlikely to respond. As was indicated above, it favours self-regulation and giving more authority to the Press Complaints Commission (PCC), an independent organisation monitoring British newspapers' and magazines' adherence to ethical guidelines. The government does not want to be seen to be curbing the important, and protected, right to freedom of expression. This view is supported by the Culture, Media and Sport Select Committee which, in its report *Self-regulation of the Press*, concluded that there had been significant progress in terms of ensuring the correct balance between protecting privacy and the right to publish—so much so that any statutory regulation would, in its view, 'represent a very dangerous interference with the freedom of the press. We continue to believe that statutory regulation of the press is a hallmark of authoritarianism and risks undermining democracy' (at [54]).

The PCC operates an Editors' Code of Practice which addresses accuracy of reporting (clause 1) and invasions of privacy (clause 3), and includes, for example, guidance restricting the use of long-range lenses.[15] Other aspects of the Code that touch on privacy relate to people in grief, children and people in hospital. Clause 3 of the Code of Practice is currently laid out as follows:

'3 *Privacy

Everyone is entitled to respect for his or her private and family life, home, health and correspondence, including digital communications.[16]

Editors will be expected to justify intrusions into any individual's private life without consent. Account will be taken of the complainant's own public disclosures of information.

It is unacceptable to photograph individuals in a private place without their consent.

Note—Private places are public or private property where there is a reasonable expectation of privacy.'

---

15. The most recent version of the Code was ratified by the PCC in January 2011.

16. This obviously has implications for the long-running *News of the World* phone hacking scandal. See e.g. 'Long Way to Run for Andy Coulson Phone-hacking Story' BBC 21 January 2011.

The asterisk above denotes a section of the Code which, according to the PCC itself, can be derogated from if it is in 'the public interest to do so'. This is defined as follows at the end of the Code:

'THE PUBLIC INTEREST'

There may be exceptions to the clauses marked * where they can be demonstrated to be in the public interest.

1. The public interest includes, but is not confined to:
   i) Detecting or exposing crime or serious impropriety.
   ii) Protecting public health and safety.
   iii) Preventing the public from being misled by an action or statement of an individual or organisation.
2. There is a public interest in freedom of expression itself.
3. Whenever the public interest is invoked, the PCC will require editors to demonstrate fully that they reasonably believed that publication, or journalistic activity undertaken with a view to publication, would be in the public interest.
4. The PCC will consider the extent to which material is already in the public domain, or will become so.
5. In cases involving children under 16, editors must demonstrate an exceptional public interest to over-ride the normally paramount interest of the child.

The PCC markets itself as 'fast, free and fair'—and its main advantage is that it will generally be much quicker to achieve adjudication via the PCC than it would usually be through the court system. People who think their privacy has been violated (for example by the publication of a photograph taken in a private place, or of confidential information) can complain to the PCC, which—after considering the allegation against the 'justifications' for intruding on someone's private life—can obtain a retraction and an apology, but cannot provide any further remedies such as damages.[17]

 Pause for reflection

Sara Cox, the radio DJ and TV presenter, complained to the PCC after a tabloid newspaper published long-range photographs of her sunbathing topless on a private beach on her honeymoon. She complained that the photographs were taken when she was in a place

→

17. e.g. a complaint by Dannii Minogue against two newspapers, for publishing the fact that she was pregnant before she had announced it, was upheld (28 January 2010). In contrast, a complaint made by Patricia Hewitt MP on behalf of her son, who was reported to have been arrested for possession of cocaine, was not upheld (6 November 2009). In October 2010, 497 complaints were made to the PCC. Of the two complaints that were adjudicated in this period, both were upheld, while 26 others were 'resolved' (PCC *Monthly Complaints Summary October 2010*).

where she had a reasonable expectation of privacy and were published in breach of her right to respect for her private life.

Following adjudication by the PCC, the editor of the newspaper published a prominent apology and wrote privately to Ms Cox, but she sued the newspaper anyway,[18] later settling out of court.

Why do you think Sara Cox took her case even after an apology was obtained? Once private photographs have been published, they cannot be retracted—is an apology enough? Do you think the fact that the newspaper settled out of court is an indication or an admission of wrongdoing?[19]

 Counterpoint

As the Sara Cox case illustrates, the PCC is somewhat 'toothless' and lacks the ability to provide an effective remedy. Furthermore, the board of the PCC is comprised mainly of representatives from the press, including editors of national newspapers—so to an extent it has a vested interest in what is and is not published and what newspapers can get away with in order to generate sales.

Ofcom, the independent regulator and competition authority for the UK communications industries—with responsibilities across television, radio, telecommunications and wireless communications services—has further powers in that it can issue fines and withdraw licences from repeat offenders. One of its principle duties, established under statute (Communications Act 2003), is to maintain 'adequate protection for audiences against unfairness or the infringement of privacy'. Still, however, it seems that this is not enough to prevent abuses of people's privacy interests, as it covers only limited aspects (such as radio and TV programmes).

It is apparent that existing 'boxes' of liability, such as those used in ***Kaye* v *Robertson***, as well as other methods of regulation such as the PCC and Ofcom, have limited effect when an individual claims that their right to privacy has been infringed. Seemingly for this reason, the courts have developed another route which has offered—and is currently offering—more protection of privacy: actions for breach of confidence.

16.3 **Breach of confidence**

Breach of confidence is an action that stems from equity and is designed to protect 'secrets' or confidential information. This primarily relates to business and commercial secrets, but in some instances can be used in relation to personal secrets. In all

---

18. *Sara Cox v MGN Ltd* [2003].
19. And would this be enough to satisfy Molly, in the scenario above?

cases it can be used only when a *duty* of confidentiality can be established. In *Coco v AN Clark (Engineers) Ltd* [1968], the duty was said to be breached when:

- there is information which has 'the necessary element of confidence about it';
- the defendant could be said to be obliged to keep the information confidential; and
- 'unauthorised use' of the information was made by the defendant.

As the action was primarily used to protect business secrets it would appear to have little application to the type of privacy cases we have so far been discussing. Conventionally, a pre-existing relationship was required to bring about the duty to maintain confidentiality. So, there would only be limited application in the context of personal secrets, for example in a relationship between husband and wife or between a party and someone taken into their confidence.

However, in *Attorney General* v *Guardian Newspapers Ltd (No 2)* [1990], a case that related to the publication of the controversial *Spycatcher* book, Lord Goff declared that a duty of confidentiality exists when:

> confidential information comes to the knowledge of a person... in circumstances where he *has notice or is held to have agreed* that the information is confidential with the effect that it would be just in all the circumstances that he should be precluded from disclosing the information to others. (at 281, emphasis added)

So viewed, a pre-existing relationship is not necessarily required. A duty not to disclose information will arise if a party gains knowledge of it and knows (or ought to know) that they would be expected to keep this information confidential, however it was obtained. This has far broader implications for the protection of privacy, particularly in relation to press intrusion into people's personal lives. This point is clearly illustrated in *Venables* v *News Group Newspapers* [2001] and *X (A woman formerly known as Mary Bell) v SO* [2003]. In *Venables* an injunction was imposed *contra mundum* (against the whole world) to prevent any disclosure of information that might reveal the identity or whereabouts of the killers (who had themselves been children at the time of the murder) of toddler Jamie Bulger. The justification for this was that another right was at issue—the right to life of the claimant—who may well suffer at the hands of members of the public if his identity was revealed (at 1069). Similarly, in *X*, an injunction was imposed to prevent the publication of information that might identify Mary Bell (who had also killed children when she was a child herself) and also her own, now adult, daughter.

 Pause for reflection

Following *Venables* and *X*, do you think that what might make information confidential depends on how much *harm* would be caused to the parties concerned if the information was leaked? As you read through the chapter, think how a harm-based analysis fits with other cases decided in favour of the claimants. Do you think this is an appropriate test? Photographs of holidays, weddings or even of someone's sexual activities in public being published without consent can be viewed as causing little or no real harm when compared to a risk to the right to life. But on the other hand, it depends what we consider 'harm' to be—if the harm is the invasion of privacy itself then are all of the claimants in these cases deserving?

The defence to a breach of confidence claim—as ever—is to show that disclosure of the information, though confidential in nature, is justified in the public interest. That is, the public interest in disclosure must be weighed against the interest of the claimant in maintaining confidentiality (*Attorney General* v *Guardian Newspapers Ltd* [1990]).[20]

In *Douglas, Zeta-Jones and Northern & Shell plc* v *Hello! Ltd* [2005] breach of confidence essentially became a privacy action in all but name.

Douglas, Zeta-Jones and Northern & Shell plc v Hello! Ltd [2005] CA

The celebrity couple Michael Douglas and Catherine Zeta-Jones were married in a New York hotel. They entered a £1 million contract with *OK!* magazine to publish exclusive photographs of the wedding and it was a term of the contract that the couple would have the final say regarding which photographs could be used. The wedding was otherwise private. Its location had not been made public, guests were asked not to bring cameras and it was an invitation-only event. However, despite the security provided by the couple, a freelance photographer managed to get into the wedding and take covert pictures, which he then sold to rival magazine *Hello!* The couple sought and failed to achieve an interim injunction to prevent *Hello!* publishing the pictures, relying in part on breach of confidence and the new 'privacy' law (which they argued had been created by the HRA). After the photographs had been published, the court awarded the couple £15,000 damages for interference with the remaining right of privacy they had after selling the photographic rights in the first place.

The court disagreed with the claimants' submission that the HRA had created a new action in law on the basis that existing law was enough to protect people's privacy interests. It found there had been a breach of confidence, relying on the *Coco* v *AN Clark* definition. It said that *Hello!* should clearly have realised that 'an obligation of confidence' existed in relation to the photographs (otherwise the photographer would not have had to obtain them secretly) and that there was no authority for their use, especially as it had been widely publicised that the wedding was to be a private event. The couple was awarded £14,500 damages. (*OK!* magazine was also awarded more than £1 million for lost profit; this award was overturned by the Court of Appeal but later restored by the House of Lords in 2007.)

Pause for reflection

If there were hundreds of people at the wedding anyway, and the wedding photographs were going to be sold to a publication that would be seen by millions, can it really be said

20. See further discussion of the public interest in the context of defamation (Chapter 15, p 442).

➡

that the wedding was a private affair? What made the unauthorised photographs an invasion of Michael Douglas and Catherine Zeta-Jones' privacy, when they had already contracted to share their wedding day with the world? Does this case fit with the 'harm' analysis mentioned earlier? If so, what was the harm? Some harm has clearly been caused here (to the claimants' happiness and pride). Moreover, the claimants would presumably feel saddened to know that covert photography had taken place on their wedding day by someone seeking to make a profit through the publication of unflattering photographs.

Do you agree with the decision in this case? If not, is this *because* the couple had entered a contract that was designed for them to have control over which information (photographs) stayed private and which were made public?

The court in **Douglas** found that it did not matter that there were so many people at the wedding as everyone there *knew* it was private. So understood, the photographs, because of the way the contract with *OK!* had been designed, were confidential information precisely *because* of their commercial value. Thus, in effect the Court of Appeal was simply applying the normal rules on breach of confidence. As in **Kaye** and other cases before it, the court made it clear that it was for Parliament to create an actual tort of invasion of privacy, not the judiciary, who could only work with existing laws. However, because of the nature of the case—and who brought it—it has been seen as establishing, even for people in the public eye, a (limited) right to privacy.

Douglas seems to have inspired a number of other claims. One such case was *A v B plc* [2003]. In this case, which involved the publication of newspaper stories about extra-marital affairs conducted by Premiership footballer Gary Flitcroft, ,the Court of Appeal held (reversing the decision of the lower court) that the information *could* be disclosed as, after the balance between maintaining confidentiality and the public interest in knowing the information had been weighed up (essentially the Article 8 v Article 10 balancing exercise), the court found that it was more important *in this case* that the public were made aware of what had happened.[21]

 Pause for reflection

The Court of Appeal in *A v B* found that it was in the public interest for information about the footballer's extra-marital affairs to be published in the newspaper concerned. The information had come to the newspapers directly from the woman concerned (that is, it was what is described as a 'kiss and tell' story and the woman had sold this to the paper).

Do you think it is really in the public interest for information like this to be published? If so, why? Does this reflect what the public interest is, or *what the public is interested in*? Is there a difference?[22]

21. In particular, the Court of Appeal seemed keen to stress that the protection afforded to information about sexual behaviour in 'transient relationships' should not be as great as that afforded to sexual relationships within a marriage (see e.g. Lord Woolf CJ at [11] and [43]).
22. Compare *Mosley v News Group Newspapers Ltd* [2008], p 471.

A similar claim was taken by TV presenter Jamie Theakston (*Theakston v MGN Ltd* [2002]) in an attempt to prevent publication of a story that he had visited a brothel, written by one of the prostitutes who worked there. His claimed failed. The information was already in the public domain and therefore did not have the necessary degree of confidentiality. With a different result, despite the fact that some knowledge of her actions must also have been in the public domain, supermodel Naomi Campbell tried to suppress details of her rehabilitation from drugs being published in a national newspaper.

Campbell v *Mirror Group Newspapers* (MGN) [2004] HL

The *Daily Mirror* published a number of stories referring to the fact that Naomi Campbell was seeking treatment for drug addiction. On one occasion it published a photograph showing the model leaving a Narcotics Anonymous meeting in London as well as details about what her treatment might entail. Having tried and failed to sue for invasion of privacy, Naomi Campbell framed her action as a claim for breach of confidence, on the grounds that details of her actual treatment and where this was taking place was clearly confidential information and that any 'reasonable person' would realise that this information had the necessary degree of confidentiality.

By a bare majority, the House of Lords upheld her claim—in part. Because she had previously denied having a drugs problem, despite acknowledging that many models did take drugs, the law lords held that the newspaper story detailing the fact that she did in fact use illegal drugs, and was attending Narcotics Anonymous for help in overcoming this problem, could be published, as this was correcting an inaccurate image she had portrayed of herself to the public. However, the law lords went on to hold that the details of her treatment as well as the photograph of her leaving the meeting could not be published. Medical information is always a confidential matter, and to publish the photograph may allow people to discover where her treatment was taking place. Both things, if published, could have negative effects on the treatment itself.

Campbell is significant. It has been described as the closest any court has come to 'recognising a tort of privacy—always under the name of breach of confidence'.[23] In so doing, their lordships took the opportunity to clarify the relationship between breach of confidence and privacy interests. Lord Nicholls (dissenting), while accepting that the nature of breach of confidence had changed once the requirement that there be a pre-existing relationship had been removed, maintained that 'there is no over-arching, all-embracing cause of action for "invasion of privacy"' (at [11]). However, he did acknowledge that recent developments in the law, particularly with regard to breach of confidence actions, had been prompted by the passage of the HRA and that because the duty of confidence now arose where 'a person receives information he knows or ought to know is fairly and reasonably to be regarded as confidential' this had in essence

---

23. *Markesinis & Deakin* p 841. Though note that, ironically perhaps, the ECtHR has recently ruled that the *Daily Mirror*'s right to freedom of expression was violated by having to pay the £1 million legal costs (partly lawyers' 'success fees') when it lost the original case (*MGN Ltd v UK* [2011]).

created a tort of 'misuse of private information' (at [14]).[24] Furthermore, the HRA, plus jurisprudence from the European Court of Human Rights (ECtHR), prompted him to say that 'the time has come to recognise that the values enshrined in Articles 8 and 10 are now part of the cause of action for breach of confidence' (at [17]). Thus, future cases would need to concentrate more on the balance of the claimant's right to private, home and family life (Article 8) and the defendant's right to freedom of expression (Article 10). This balance is explored more fully below.

In *Campbell*, a new two-stage test was defined by the House of Lords (replacing the test from *Coco* v *AN Clark*) to determine when a breach of confidence or 'misuse of private information' has occurred. The test is as follows:

(1) Did the claimant have a 'reasonable expectation of privacy' with regard to the information?

and, if so,

(2) Does the claimant's interest in maintaining their right to privacy outweigh the defendant's interest in freedom of expression (that is, the ability to publish the information)?

16.3.1 A 'reasonable expectation of privacy'

In *Campbell*, it was held that a reasonable expectation of privacy would arise when it was 'obvious' that the information being disclosed was private (see also e.g. *McKennitt* v *Ash* [2006]; *HRH Prince of Wales* v *Associated Newspapers Ltd* [2008]). Clearly, any detail relating to treatment for drug addiction would be private, even if the person being treated was well known. In relation to Naomi Campbell, while the majority of the law lords thought that information about treatment *was* obviously private, they did not think the same of the photograph, as this was taken on a public street.[25]

 Pause for reflection

Lord Nicholls (dissenting) argued that treatment for an addiction at Narcotics Anonymous followed a well-known pattern and as such the disclosure of information about this was no more significant than 'saying a person who has fractured a limb has his limb in plaster or that a person suffering from cancer is undergoing a course of chemotherapy' (at [26]).

Do you agree? Or does the fact that a drug addiction is connected with a person's mental wellbeing and is associated with judgements that can be made about their personality and private life, as well as their physical health, distinguish the two examples?

A secondary test was proposed for situations when it is not 'obvious' that information was meant to be private, and that was to ask whether disclosure of the information

---

24. This new tort has already found favour with some. See e.g. Nicholas McBride and Roderick Bagshaw *Tort Law* (3rd edn, Pearson Education, 2008), p 320.

25. Nor, it seems, is the identity of a secret blogger, particularly when the blog in question criticised the internal workings of the police force from an insider's point of view: see *Author of a Blog* v *Times Newspapers Ltd* [2009].

would cause offence to a 'person of ordinary sensibilities' if the information was about them.[26] This is, we would argue, a fairly bizarre subjective–objective test, as the courts have to put themselves into the minds of a 'person of ordinary sensibilities' who find themselves in the same situation as the claimant—often situations that are unlikely to happen to most 'ordinary people'. In this case, because on this secondary test it could be harmful to Naomi Campbell's treatment of and recovery from addiction to publish a photograph from which the location of her treatment could be identified, publication was prevented. In other words, because to publish a photograph which could enable people to find out where an obviously private medical treatment was taking place might cause offence to 'a person of ordinary sensibilities', she could establish a 'reasonable expectation of privacy' in relation to the photographs. As Baroness Hale noted, it would have been different if Naomi Campbell was merely 'going about her business in a private street' because:

> she makes a substantial part of her living out of being photographed looking stunning in designer clothing. Readers will obviously be interested to see how she looks if and when she pops out to the shops for a bottle of milk. (at [154])

 Pause for reflection

Look again at *Kaye*. If the same events happened today, would the case be decided differently? The images of him in hospital would have a 'reasonable expectation of privacy' attached (even more so than in *Campbell*, as photographs of a person in hospital, unable to give their consent, can easily be considered 'obviously' private) and it would be unlikely that the photographs of him would be in the public interest, even if there would be public interest in reporting the fact that he had been injured. The question is about where the line should be drawn about what information the public should be given about the private lives of others.

In *McKennitt* v *Ash* [2006], the 'reasonable expectation of privacy' test was used in relation to information shared between friends.

Loreena McKennitt v *Niema Ash* [2006] CA

Niema Ash, a former close friend of Canadian folk artist Loreena McKennitt, wrote a book detailing her time travelling on tour with her. The book included information about McKennitt's sexual relationships and health, her ongoing legal dispute with Ash and her

➡

---

26. This is similar to, yet different from, the formulation in the US *Second Restatement of Torts* and the Australian case of *Australian Broadcasting Commission* v *Lenah Game Meats* [2001]: that disclosure must be 'highly offensive to the reasonable person' in order to ground an action (Gleeson CJ at [42]). In *Campbell*, Lord Nicholls said that the phrase 'highly offensive' should not be relied on as it suggested a stricter test than 'reasonable expectation of privacy' and 'could be a recipe for confusion' (at [22]).

business partner over some property, and McKennitt's emotional response to the death of her fiancé. McKennitt sued, alleging breach of confidence.

The Court of Appeal found that McKennitt had a reasonable expectation of privacy in relation to the personal information she had shared with Ash during their friendship. In fact, Ash herself acknowledged this, as her book was prefaced with a comment saying that it contained information that would be known only because of the close nature of the two women's friendship. An injunction against further publication was granted and £5,000 damages were awarded.[27]

A 'reasonable expectation' of privacy will, therefore, generally be quite 'obvious'.[28] A decision that perhaps calls this into question is *Elizabeth Jagger* v *John Darling & Others* [2005]. Elizabeth Jagger (the daughter of Mick Jagger) obtained an injunction preventing the publication of and use of pictures and CCTV footage of her and Calum Best (the son of footballer George Best) engaged in 'sexual activities' just inside the front door of a nightclub. Mr Justice Bell found that she had a reasonable expectation of privacy as, although in a public space, she was unaware of being observed in any way, particularly by CCTV (at [13]).[29]

Once the legitimate expectation is established, the second part of the test is to determine whether the claimant's interest in maintaining their right to privacy outweigh the defendant's interest in freedom of expression (that is, the ability to publish the information)? In *Jagger*, Bell J said that he could see 'no legitimate public interest in further dissemination of the images which could serve only to humiliate the claimant for the prurient interests of others' (at [14]). However, as *Campbell* shows, usually in cases where a 'reasonable' expectation is less obvious, a further test is necessary, based on the 'person of ordinary sensibilities', in order to determine whether the claimant might be negatively affected in some way if the information was published.

▶◀ Counterpoint

Is the 'person of ordinary sensibilities' test, which applies when it is not obvious that there would be a reasonable expectation of privacy, basically the same as the second part of the test that applies when there *is* a legitimate expectation (from *Campbell*)? That is, are we saying that even when there is no *obviously* confidential nature to the information, the claimant's interest in (or right to) keeping the information private should be weighed against

27. The House of Lords refused leave to appeal, suggesting that they agreed fully with the Court of Appeal's reasoning.

28. Would this be the case for Karen, in the scenarios outlined at the beginning of this chapter? If so, would her right to privacy outweigh the newspaper's freedom of expression? Would this depend on anything she had said/done in relation to anorexia before?

29. Presumably, then, this action would be available for Dave in our scenario at the beginning of the chapter, as long as he was unaware that he was caught on camera. Arguably, the fact that he was in a restaurant (a different time of day, a different type of setting) could make a difference (though see *Mosley* v *NGN* [2008] where it was suggested that one's sexual activities are generally to be considered private information).

the defendant's interest in not doing so (see, for example, *A* v *B*; *Douglas*)? If so, could it be said that this is essentially only *one* test, but which has two different levels (in that it would be easier to find in favour of the claimant if the information was obviously meant to be private)?

Whichever test is used, essentially this becomes a battle between privacy and freedom of expression, and it is these concepts that must be balanced in order to determine outcomes. The following section will explore privacy in this context, as this is where the battleground now seems to be.

16.4 **Balancing privacy and freedom of expression**

Article 10(1) of the ECHR gives the right to freedom of expression. As with the Article 8(1) right to private and family life, home and correspondence, this is a qualified right, meaning that while it must be protected by the state, certain things (listed in Arts 10(2) and 8(2) respectively) are considered legitimate infringements on a person's exercise of that right. Among other things, Article 10(2) states that the right to freedom of expression may be curtailed in the public interest (for example, in the interests of national security) or where there are other, competing, individual rights at stake (for example, the right of people to protect their reputations or to prevent the disclosure of information given in confidence). So, at the outset, neither right is absolute. By definition, also, each right impinges on the other, particularly in the context of claims about invasion of privacy by the media. The media, as part of a democratic society, has a vital role to play in disseminating information. The question is how far the press can go—especially into someone's 'private' affairs—before they are deemed to have gone 'too far'.[30] In this sense of proportionality, freedom of expression needs to be balanced against the 'right' to a private life.

 Pause for reflection

What does the term 'private and family life' encompass? In the ECtHR case of *Niemietz* v *Germany* [1993] the Court said that it was neither 'possible nor necessary to' attempt an exhaustive definition of the notion of private life (at [29]). The Court added:

> However, it would be too restrictive to limit the notion to an 'inner circle' in which the individual may live his own personal life as he chooses and to exclude therefrom entirely the outside world not encompassed within that circle. Respect for private life must also comprise to a certain degree the right to establish and develop relationships with other human beings. (at [29])

Thus, it seems that one's 'inner circle', at least, may be protected, as well as—to a degree— one's relationships with others, but each case will be decided on its own facts.

---

30. This was essentially the question for the law lords in *Campbell*.

> ➡
>
> How far do you think one's private and family life extends? Is this the same for ordinary citizens and for celebrities? Clearly there is no right or wrong answer to this—people have their own perceptions about how far celebrities open themselves up to invasions of privacy. Indeed, as we have seen, the courts have struggled to define privacy in such situations. It is likely that there is a 'spectrum' of private information: ranging from the very private (an evening spent at home with one's young children, for example) to less private (such as a presentation given at one's workplace). But celebrity lifestyles make for difficult cases. For example, where on the spectrum would a celebrity's wedding sit if they had not undertaken the kind of measures Michael Douglas and Catherine Zeta-Jones had to try and keep it private?

Lord Hoffmann once described freedom of expression as 'the trump card that always wins' (*R v Central Independent Television plc* [1994] at 203). It appears highly unlikely that the statement is true today—if it was then. On the face of it at least the courts seem more inclined to protect privacy interests than they once were. Freedom of expression no longer immediately trumps privacy. This position is underscored by *Earl Spencer v UK* [1998] where, according to Lord Hoffmann, the UK satisfied the ECtHR that breach of confidence is capable of providing an adequate remedy where Article 8 has been violated.[31] In a fresh look at the balance of freedom of expression against privacy, in *Campbell*, he said that there is 'no question of automatic priority. Nor is there a presumption in favour of one rather than the other' (at [55]). In fact, by 2006, in **McKennitt**, it was acknowledged by Buxton LJ, with whom Latham and Longmore LJJ agreed, that both Article 8 and Article 10 ECHR are 'now the very content of the domestic tort that the English court must enforce' (at [11]).

16.4.1 The effect of the Human Rights Act 1998 and European case law

Lord Irvine (then the Lord Chancellor) said, during the parliamentary debates on the Human Rights Bill, that:

> the judges are pen-poised regardless of the incorporation of the Convention to develop a right of privacy to be protected by the common law … it will be a better law if the judges develop it after incorporation because they will have regards to Articles 8 and 10, giving Article 10 its due high value … I believe that the true view is that the courts will be able to adapt and develop the existing domestic principles in the laws of trespass, nuisance, copyright, confidence and the like to fashion a common law right to privacy.[32]

However, as *Lunney & Oliphant* point out, there has been very little 'express reliance' on the HRA—though its shadow operates in a background to many recent privacy cases.[33] This is perhaps *because* of the judicial development of the breach of confidence action.

---

31. Speaking in *Wainwright* at [32].
32. HL Debates, vol 583, col 784 (24 November 1997).
33. *Lunney & Oliphant* p 800.

Human Rights Act 1998, s 12(4)

The court must have particular regard to the importance of the Convention right to freedom of expression and, where the proceedings relate to material which the respondent claims, or which appears to the court, to be journalistic, literary or artistic material (or to conduct connected with such material), to—

(a) the extent to which—
> **(i)** the material has, or is about to, become available to the public; or
> **(ii)** it is, or would be, in the public interest for the material to be published;

(b) any relevant privacy code

Under section 12(4) HRA, the UK courts must therefore undertake a balancing exercise when considering the competing rights from Articles 8 and 10. Section 12 is, however, headed 'freedom of expression' and applies when 'a court is considering whether to grant any relief which, if granted, might affect the exercise of the Convention right to freedom of expression' (s 12(1)). Clearly, granting someone relief (a remedy) for infringement of their privacy (for example, by the press) may have an effect on freedom of expression. So it seems that section 12 in a way prioritises this freedom above any 'right' to privacy, merely by assigning it special status in the HRA.[34] Perhaps this does suggest that freedom of expression, while no longer 'the trump card that will always win', continues to be valued more than any so-called right to privacy.

Section 12(4) has been taken to mean that the courts must balance any 'privacy codes' against the objective of protecting freedom of expression. The PCC and Ofcom have their own privacy codes. In fact, though requiring a slight stretch of the imagination, Article 8(1) is itself akin to a privacy code. Lord Hoffmann clearly thought that freedom of expression was the paramount right, but it appears from later cases that the two rights (and the ability to derogate from them) are to be treated equally when deciding a case.

According to section 6(1) HRA it is 'unlawful for a public authority to act in a way which is incompatible with a Convention right'. Courts and tribunals are deemed 'public authorities' (s 6(3)), as is 'any person certain of whose functions are functions of a public nature', which may include organisations such as the PCC and Ofcom. Furthermore, section 7 HRA gives individual citizens the right to bring proceedings in a domestic court against any public authority that has acted in contravention of a Convention right. The situation that this leaves us with is that a citizen may claim in a domestic court that their right to private and family life, granted by Article 8(1) of the Convention, has been infringed by a public authority or other who falls within the definition in section 6. However, if the proceedings taken relate to 'journalistic, literary or artistic material' (that is, we are talking about information about someone's private life being published in some way, as most of the case law seems to deal with),[35]

---

34. It is notable, e.g., that freedom of expression and 'freedom of thought, conscience and religion' are the only Convention rights given this express treatment under the HRA—that is, only these rights are singled out as deserving special attention by the courts.

35. Exceptions include *Malone v Commissioner of Police for the Metropolis (No 2)* [1979], which concerned phone tapping by the police, and **Wainwright v Home Office** [2004], concerning an intimate strip search of visitors to a prison.

then section 12 comes into play, and the court must weigh up whether giving relief for the invasion of privacy would have an unjustifiable impact on the respondent's freedom of expression.

 Pause for reflection

Lord Hoffmann, interpreting the Convention and referring to jurisprudence of the ECtHR in *Wainwright*, found nothing to convince him that a general privacy principle was required. Instead, he said, domestic courts could provide an adequate remedy for an invasion of privacy made contrary to Article 8. In this context, he described sections 6 and 7 HRA as 'substantial gap fillers' (at [34]), suggesting that in conjunction with Article 8(1) the job of protecting the privacy of individual citizens can be done adequately and without the need to create a free-standing tort to protect privacy.

He concluded his speech saying that:

a finding that there was a breach of Article 8 will only demonstrate that there was a gap in the English remedies for invasion of privacy which has since been filled by sections 6 and 7 of the 1998 Act. It does not require that the courts should provide an alternative remedy which distorts the principles of the common law. (at [52])

Lord Hoffmann seems to suggest that invasion of privacy is a harm that has always been recognised—but that the law has not always provided adequate remedies when the harm has occurred, and it is this remedial gap that is filled by the HRA. Do you agree? Consider domestic case law decided since the coming into force of the Act—have the decisions become any easier for judges to make? Are they making the right decisions and providing the right remedies for the right claimants?

The most notable ECtHR decision in the context of privacy came in ***Von Hannover v Germany*** [2004]. This judgment was handed down a short time after the House of Lords' decision in ***Campbell***, and has become a key decision in determining how to balance the two competing rights.

Von Hannover v *Germany* [2004] ECtHR

Princess Caroline of Monaco went to the European Court of Human Rights alleging that media intrusions into her daily routine were infringing her rights under Article 8. Princess Caroline has celebrity status in much of Europe. Not only is she a princess and the presumptive heir to the throne of Monaco, she is also the eldest child of the late Prince Rainier III of Monaco and his wife, the late American film actress Grace Kelly. In particular she claimed that numerous paparazzi photographs of her undertaking daily activities, including some which showed her children, were an invasion of her right to private, home and family life. She had previously taken her claim in the German courts, but the rulings had gone against her on the ground that, as a public figure *par excellence*, she should expect members of the public to take an interest in her daily life.

➡

➡

The ECtHR upheld her claim, holding that the key issue when weighing up the rights under Articles 8 and 10 was to ask how far the information being published would be in the 'public interest', which the judges held was different from what the public might genuinely be interested in. They also distinguished between Princess Caroline's public functions and private life. Clearly, they said, when performing or attending a public function, there would be a legitimate public interest in pictures of her being published but, when going about her private life, she had a 'reasonable expectation' of privacy.

16.5 **Where do privacy claims stand today?**

Today, it seems our right to privacy is best protected by a breach of confidence claim underpinned by the Article 8 right to privacy and its competing consideration of freedom of expression. Assessing whether a claimant's right to privacy has been infringed will now always entail a careful balancing of these competing interests. Where celebrities are concerned, this exercise will continue to be difficult. In *Elton John* v *Associated Newspapers* [2006], Sir Elton John complained that a picture taken of him walking away from his car with his driver was an invasion of his privacy. The court found that the picture contained no obviously private information and was merely a snapshot of him going about his ordinary life, not doing anything in particular. However, in *Lord Browne of Madingley* v *Associated Newspapers Ltd* [2007], the law was further extended to include confidential business information within the protection zone of Article 8. Soon after, Michael Douglas and Catherine Zeta-Jones were granted damages, albeit minimal, for violation of their Article 8 rights when information of a commercially sensitive nature was distributed by a third party without authorisation (in ***Douglas v Hello!***). The Court of Appeal decision of ***Murray*** v ***Express Newspapers plc*** [2008], another case involving pictures of a celebrity's child, confirmed the ***Von Hannover*** approach.

Murray v *Express Newspapers plc* [2008] CA

JK Rowling, the author of the Harry Potter books, brought an action on behalf of her 18-month-old son David, after a long-lens photograph of him in his pushchair was published in 2004. Rowling (whose married name is Murray), sought damages for the infringement of David's right to privacy as well as an injunction to prevent further publication of similar pictures. Her case failed in the High Court. Mr Justice Patten said that the law did not provide for a 'press-free zone' (at [66]) for celebrities and their children in respect of everything that they do, adding that 'an area of routine activity which, when conducted in a public place, carries no guarantee of privacy'.

The Court of Appeal overturned the decision, finding that David had a legitimate expectation of privacy, even while in his pushchair on a public street.

Interestingly, Express Newspapers settled the claim out of court when it was still at the High Court—the action survived only against the picture agency that took and supplied the photographs to the newspaper. Giving the judgment of the Court of Appeal, Sir Anthony Clarke said:

> As we see it, the question whether there is a reasonable expectation of privacy is a broad one, which takes account of all the circumstances of the case. They include the attributes of the claimant, the nature of the activity in which the claimant was engaged, the place at which it was happening, the nature and purpose of the intrusion, the absence of consent and whether it was known or could be inferred, the effect on the claimant and the circumstances in which and the purposes for which the information came into the hands of the publisher. (at [36])

This interpretation allowed the Court of Appeal to go on to find that the High Court judge had not given enough consideration to the fact that the claimant was a child. This was a decisive factor. Sir Anthony Clarke found that:

> if a child of parents who are not in the public eye could reasonably expect not to have photographs of him published in the media, so too should the child of a famous parent. In our opinion, it is at least arguable that a child of 'ordinary' parents could reasonably expect that the press would not target him and publish photographs of him. The same is true of David, especially since on the alleged facts here the Photograph would not have been taken or published if he had not been the son of JK Rowling. (at [46])

Perhaps *Murray* tells us that there is a legitimate expectation of privacy if you are the (young) child of a famous person, because you cannot be said to have courted any kind of celebrity status. Whether the celebrity parents themselves are equally deserving of protection from being photographed going about their ordinary lives, is more debatable. Some people feel strongly about this, arguing that if you become a celebrity, you should expect what comes with the territory. This was recognised by the Court of Appeal in *Murray*, in comparing the difference between *Campbell* (a House of Lords' decision under which our courts are bound) and *Von Hannover* (an ECtHR decision that is influential, but not *binding* on domestic courts).[36] As the comments of Baroness Hale in *Campbell* tell us, many people are interested in what celebrities look like when they pop to the shops for a pint of milk. With regard to adults, it seems that only when to publish photographs or news stories might cause some harm that the question of protecting privacy seems to arise.[37]

 Pause for reflection

Although it seems that the courts will now protect someone's privacy if it would be more harmful not to do so, it might be argued that the harm is not what 'might happen' to the

➡

---

36. Note that in *Von Hannover* the ECtHR took a broader view of what falls into private life than the House of Lords did in *Campbell*. If there is a conflict between the two, domestic courts must follow *Campbell*.

37. Though see the successful claim in *Wood v Chief of Police for the Metropolis* [2009], where the Court of Appeal ruled that the taking and retention of photographs of the claimant (an arms trade protestor) by the police was a violation of his Art 8 right.

> ➡
>
> claimant if the photographs were printed, or the news story was run, but simply the very fact that this might happen. Hundreds of celebrities and well-known public figures are captured on camera every day, their photographs ending up in newspapers and glossy magazines. But not all of them take legal action—so is taking legal action *itself* the actual (first) indicator that harm has been suffered? In our view, it is hard to qualify harm objectively and therefore its subjective nature must be taken into account. Not to do so would suggest that some actions are taken for other, less 'valuable' reasons.

In *Mosley* v *News Group Newspapers Ltd* [2008], Max Mosley, the head of the International Automobile Federation (FIA), the governing body of world motorsport, won a privacy claim against the *News of the World* over the publication of an article about him taking part in a Nazi-style orgy.[38] Mosley, the son of the 1930s British Fascist leader Sir Oswald Mosley, had been filmed by the paper with five prostitutes in a basement flat in London. The *News of the World,* describing it as a 'sick Nazi orgy' and a 'truly grotesque and depraved' event, posted the film on its website alleging that Mosley had been assuming the role of a concentration camp commandant, saying: 'In public he rejects his father's evil past but secretly he plays Nazi sex games'. The website film was viewed by 3.5 million people. In court, Mosley admitted involvement in sadomasochistic sex, but denied the link to Nazism. Mr Justice Eady ruled that Mosley had a reasonable expectation of privacy in relation to his sexual activities, though unconventional, if they took place between consenting adults on private property (at [232]). He said that the authorities tend to show that 'people's sex lives are to be regarded as essentially their own business—provided at least that the participants are genuinely consenting adults and there is no question of exploiting the young or vulnerable' (at [100]). Given that the link to Nazism was not proved, Mr Justice Eady further concluded that there was:

> no public interest or other justification for the clandestine recording, for the publication of the resulting information and still photographs, or for the placing of the video extracts on the News of the World website—all of this on a massive scale. Of course, I accept that such behaviour is viewed by some people with distaste and moral disapproval, but in the light of modern rights-based jurisprudence that does not provide any justification for the intrusion on the personal privacy of the claimant. (at [233])

Notably, Mr Justice Eady stressed that this was not a 'landmark' decision (at [234]), but one that applied 'recently developed but established principles' to an unusual set of facts.[39] In late 2008 Mosley filed a claim to the ECtHR, asking it to uphold a right to

38. 'F1 Boss has Sick Nazi Orgy with 5 Hookers' *News of the World* 30 March 2008. Mosley sued for both aggravated (punitive) and compensatory damages (see Chapter 19, p 554) but was awarded only compensatory damages, plus costs. The award was £60,000, reported to be over three times higher than the previous highest privacy award (though note that the BBC reported that the same judge awarded Hugh Grant, Liz Hurley and Arun Nayar £58,000 in May 2008 in a privacy case concerning long-range photographs of them on a private Maldives beach (Mark Sweney 'Grant and Hurley Win Privacy Payout' *BBC News* 17 May 2008)).

39. Though the recognition of a 'reasonable expectation of privacy' in this case does *not* seem consistent with either *Theakston* v *MGN Ltd* [2002] (brothel visitation by single man) or *A* v *B Plc* [2003] (extra-marital affairs), particularly given that Max Mosley was married. Eady J may, however, have been referring to the 'recently developed' principle of the 'reasonable expectation of privacy'.

prior notification—that is, for newspapers etc to have to warn people in advance about potential privacy violations. His claim was rejected on 10 May 2011.[40] Thus it remains to be seen what the future holds for privacy claims and, in particular, whether Lord Nicholls was right, in *Campbell*, to call it a tort (at [14]).

One question left unresolved is that of 'iniquity'.[41] When the claimant has been doing something they shouldn't this may justify, in the name of freedom of expression, publication of information which may otherwise seem to be an invasion of privacy. *Mosley* shows that sexual activity is generally considered inherently private. Recent cases involving anonymity orders and so-called 'super-injunctions'[42]—in particular in relation to the sexual activities of celebrities—support the idea that 'public interest' will simply not be enough to warrant publication of such stories—or even the names of the individuals concerned: something more is required.

In *John Terry* v *Persons Unknown* [2010], this 'something more' may have been the public interest in exposing the iniquity of the claimant in having an affair with his team-mate's girlfriend, particularly when he was seen as a 'role model'.[43] In contrast, the Court of Appeal recently granted an anonymity order to 'a well known sportsman' (at [7]), though not an injunction protecting the disclosure of certain facts about his infidelities (*JIH* v *News Group Newspapers* [2011]).[44] Lord Neuberger, giving the judgment of the court, said:

> There is obvious force in the contention that the public interest would be better served by publication of the fact that the court has granted an injunction to an anonymous well known sportsman...than by being told it has granted an injunction to an identified person to restrain publication of unspecified information of an allegedly private nature. (at [33])

In *JIH* the Court of Appeal was apparently swayed that an injunction granting anonymity would better balance the claimant's and public's interests because information was already in the public domain relating to an earlier, similar story about the claimant. Lord Neuberger said that if his identity but not the information was disclosed, the public and the media would be able to work out easily what information the injunction was designed to protect, thus defeating its purpose—it would be a 'classic, if not very difficult, jigsaw exercise' (at [40]).

---

40. *Mosley* v *UK* [2011] (Application no 48009/08). See, in particular, para 119.

41. *Lunney & Oliphant* suggest this is something that perplexed the House of Lords in *Campbell*, as the claimant had misrepresented herself to the public (p 812).

42. Injunctions granting not only anonymity but also prohibiting publication of information about the very existence of legal proceedings.

43. This was perhaps compounded by the fact he was the captain of the England football team and the exposure of his wrongdoing came in the run-up to the 2010 World Cup. Similarly, in finding nothing to substantiate Terry's application for a super-injunction, the court appeared influenced by the claimant's desire (or that of his agent) to protect his commercial interests. See also Sam Jones 'John Terry Case Sparks Government Concern over Super-injunctions' *The Guardian* 31 January 2010.

44. The anonymity order was granted despite indications that some of the information about the claimant's affairs was already in the public domain. This seems contrary to some earlier cases, notably *Theakston* [2002].

Pause for reflection

Does the balance of rights have to come down to either anonymity plus details or names plus no details? Is this a logical advance?

Consider Lord Rodger's opinion in the earlier case of *In re Guardian News and Media Ltd* [2010]:[45] 'if newspapers can identify the people concerned they may be able to give a more vivid and compelling account which will stimulate discussion...Concealing identities simply casts a shadow over entire communities' (at [65]).

Concealing one or the other feature of a case may, however, be more favourable in the interests of 'open justice' than the granting of 'super-injunctions'. Surely allowing the press to publish *something* is preferable to restrictions on publishing *anything*?

In *CDE* v *MGN Ltd* [2010] Eady J extended anonymity orders further in a case brought by a married man who 'often appears on television' (at [4]) and his wife, seeking to protect their family from the revelation of a 'virtual' (i.e. via text message, email etc) affair he had briefly conducted with another woman (the second defendant in this case—who had been persuaded by a journalist to sell her story to the *Sunday Mirror*). The claimants in this case had always, it was found, 'guarded their private lives closely' and 'never sought publicity' (at [4]). They were granted anonymity, though this was *also* extended to several individuals not actually party to the case, including the couple's teenage children, the child of the second defendant *and* one of the journalists on the defendant newspaper, the second defendant's solicitor and 'publicity advisor'! Is this taking anonymity too far?

16.5.1 **Limits to the current protection**

As breach of confidence extends only to confidential information, it is clear that there will be some limitations on its effectiveness as a means for protecting privacy—although some of these weaknesses may be eradicated after its reformulation in *Campbell*.[46] The limits of the action are clearly shown in non-celebrity cases, for example *Wainwright* v *Home Office* and *Peck* v *UK*.

In *Wainwright*, the claimants sued the Home Office for invasion of their privacy (as well as under the torts in trespass to the person),[47] following a 'sloppily' performed strip search while visiting a family member in prison. The House of Lords took the opportunity to state categorically that there is no tort of invasion of privacy.[48] Rather, privacy was an interest that could, and should, only be protected by using other existing legal mechanisms. *Wainwright* failed because there was no question of there being any private information (or photographs) being disclosed: it did not fall into the same category of 'privacy' (or confidence) that had by then been recognised by the judiciary, even though what happened to Mrs Wainwright was a clear invasion of her privacy (in terms of personal autonomy) in the commonly-understood sense. It should be noted,

45. Note that this was a case in relation to the anonymity or otherwise of three brothers subject to freezing orders in connection with terrorism allegations.

46. And see *Mosley* v *News Group Newspapers*.

47. The facts and other claims in *Wainwright* are discussed further in Chapter 14, pp 402–403.

48. See, in particular, the speech of Lord Hoffmann at [31]–[35], with whom Lords Hope and Hutton agreed. Lord Hoffmann later reiterated the same point in *Campbell* at [43].

however, that if prison visitors were treated the same way today, an action would lie directly against the Home Office under the HRA—this was later confirmed by the ECtHR in *Wainwright* **v** *UK* **[2006]**, where violation of Articles 8 and 13 ECHR were found.

Peck v *UK* [2003] ECtHR

Peck was filmed on CCTV in a town centre trying to commit suicide with a knife. The police stopped and detained him under the Mental Health Act. He was later released. His claim arose after the CCTV footage of him was used by the local authority and passed to TV and newspapers to demonstrate the effectiveness of the CCTV system. Although his face was somewhat obscured when the images of him were published, people who knew him were clearly able to recognise him, and he alleged this infringed his right to privacy. He complained to the predecessor of Ofcom and to the local authority but his claims were dismissed. He then took his case to the ECtHR alleging breaches of his Article 8 and 13 rights.[49] The government relied on the fact that the information had lost any characteristic of confidentiality as it was already in the public domain—that is, Mr Peck's actions were committed in public.

The ECtHR found that Article 8 had been breached as, although his actions took place in a public place, showing him on TV and in newspapers was not the same as him being seen by passers-by. The relevant moment was judged to have been 'viewed to an extent which far exceeded any exposure to a passer-by or security observation' (at [53]). Consequently, as no remedy had been provided in UK law, there was also a breach of Article 13.[50]

Thus it appears that where breach of confidence is an inadequate means of providing a remedy for invasion of privacy, a human rights claim may still be fruitful. The developments in this area are 'excessively patchy, messy and unprincipled' but are ongoing—and certainly worth watching out for.[51] Indeed, in *Campbell*, Lord Nicholls acknowledged that this is 'a fast-developing area of the law' both in the UK and in other jurisdictions (at [11]).[52]

 Counterpoint

It is arguable that a gender issue exists in the developed domestic law relating to privacy. While it has become apparent that a perceived 'harm' will attract judicial protection under what can loosely be termed Article 8 principles—in that privacy appears to override

---

49. Article 13 guarantees the right to an effective remedy.

50. Would the same be the case for Eric, the teenager in the scenarios at the beginning of the chapter, caught on CCTV committing an act of vandalism? It is not clear that it was merely the fact that publication of the pictures or also the fact that his actions were *inherently* of a private nature that was decisive in that case.

51. *Markesinis & Deakin* p 831.

52. See the New Zealand Court of Appeal decision in *Hosking* v *Runting* [2004], for example.

→
freedom of expression when to invade the private sphere would or could cause 'harm' in some way (such as a set-back in drug rehabilitation or health (*Campbell*), right to life issues (*Venables; Peck*), breach of a contractual obligation (*Douglas*), concern for children (*Bell; Murray*)), these are all harms that the law might find it fairly easy to recognise and, as such, deem 'deserving' of protection.

But when the claimant's harm becomes less tangible, such as the mere 'distress' suffered by Mrs Wainwright, the sympathetic application of Article 8 by the domestic courts seems to greatly diminish. As with other areas of tort law, *who* is protected turns on what is understood as a 'harm':[53] 'Perceptions of harm then are closely linked to law, and legal recognition—in the form of a right to redress—is a key signifier that harm has been incurred'.[54] Moreover, judicial reluctance to widen the scope of the nascent privacy laws—to include privacy related harms such as those suffered by Mrs Wainwright—may well have gender implications, as restrictions are placed on recovery in relation to harms which (historically at least) tend to be associated with (although, of course, not exclusively suffered by) women (especially mothers).[55]

16.6 Conclusion

As we have seen in this chapter, there has been a long-standing reluctance on the part of both Parliament and the judiciary to create a specific tort of invasion of privacy. Early cases had to be moulded into legal actions that did not necessarily fit and, it seems, could offer little protection even when they did (*Kaye*). Largely, the problems stemmed from difficulty in defining (or unwillingness to define) what the right to protect one's privacy would actually encapsulate.

However, in more recent years there has been a judicial development of the (equitable) principle of breach of confidence, which has been successfully used in a number of high-profile privacy cases. Following cases such as *Campbell* and *Douglas*, it might be thought that this development has reached so far as to have created a tort of invasion of privacy in all but name. To establish breach of confidence, as reinterpreted in the case law on privacy, a claimant must establish that they had a legitimate expectation of privacy and that disclosure of the information about them was not in the public interest.

This brings into sharp focus (and in fact the development of the law was shaped by) human rights considerations. A right to private life is enshrined in the ECHR and now the HRA. However, rights must be balanced against competing rights and here the right to freedom of expression becomes important. That said, while this may once have 'trumped' any notion of a right to privacy, it is apparent from the most recent case law that neither right is paramount and, in fact, privacy might just about be coming to be seen as equally (or perhaps more, depending on the context) important.

53. Compare the decision in *Grieves v FT Everard & Sons* [2007] on the harm caused by the development of pleural plaques following negligent exposure to asbestos fibres (Chapter 5, p 102) or the birth of unwanted children after a doctor's negligent action or advice (Chapter 7, p 183).
54. Joanne Conaghan 'Law, Harm and Redress: A Feminist Perspective' (2002) 22(3) *Legal Studies* 319 at 322.
55. Joanne Conaghan 'Tort Law and Feminist Critique' (2003) *Current Legal Problems* 175 at 186.

✱ End-of-chapter questions

After reading the chapter carefully, try answering the questions below. If you would like to know what we think visit the Online Resource Centre (www.oxfordtextbooks.co.uk/orc/horsey2e/).

1. Why do you think the judiciary and various governments in the UK have been so reluctant to formulate a specific law relating to the invasion of privacy?

2. Look at the recent cases that revolve around invasions of privacy (for example, *Von Hannover*, *Douglas*, *Campbell*, *Murray*, *Mosley*). How many of the claimants in these cases really had a 'reasonable expectation of privacy' in respect of the information they did not want to be in the press? Can you define 'a reasonable expectation of privacy' any more easily than 'privacy'?

3. What harm(s) does the law find should be recognised as invasion of privacy? Is there any common element among the successful cases?

4. Consider the problem question at the start of this chapter—now having read about the topic what would be your advice to Elizabeth? If you need some pointers in thinking about how to answer this question, turn to the Appendix (p 589) where each problem is anno-tated with issues and cases to consider. Next, try to write your own answer and finally, log on to our Online Resource Centre (www.oxfordtextbooks.co.uk/orc/horsey2e/) and check your ideas against our suggested outline answer.

✱ Further reading

There has been a proliferation of articles written on the subject of privacy in recent years, many of which focus on a particular case or cases. A good place to start is with some of the general comment pieces, such as by Aplin, Delaney or McLean, or with Bennett's theoretical explorations of 'horizontal privacy' post-*Campbell*. Mr Justice Eady's speech is also enlightening. Unfortunately, as the law in this area is moving so fast, some of the writing, even the more recent articles, may need updating!

Aplin, Tanya 'The Development of the Action for Breach of Confidence in a post-HRA Era' (2007) *Intellectual Property Quarterly* 19

Bennett, Thomas 'Corrective Justice and Horizontal Privacy: A Leaf out of Wright J's Book' (2010) *The Journal Jurisprudence* 545

Bennett, Thomas 'Horizontality's New Horizons—Re-examining Horizontal Effect: Privacy, Defamation and the Human Rights Act: Part 1' (2010) 21(3) *Entertainment Law Review* 96

Bennett, Thomas 'Horizontality's New Horizons—Re-examining Horizontal Effect: Privacy, Defamation and the Human Rights Act: Part 2' (2010) 21(4) *Entertainment Law Review* 145

Delany, Murphy 'Towards Common Principles relating to the Protection of Privacy Rights? An Analysis of Recent Developments in England and France and before the European Court of Human Rights' (2007) 5 *European Human Rights Law Review* 568

Eady, Mr Justice *Speech at University of Hertfordshire* 10 November 2009 (available from Judiciary of England and Wales website)

McLean, Mackey 'Is there a Law of Privacy in the UK? A Consideration of Recent Legal Developments' (2007) 29(9) *European Intellectual Property Review* 389

Moreham, Nicole 'Privacy in Public Places' (2006) *Cambridge Law Journal* 606

Morgan, Jonathan 'Privacy in the House of Lords, Again' (2004) 120 *Law Quarterly Review* 563

Phillipson, Gavin 'Transforming Breach of Confidence? Towards a Common Law Right of Privacy under the Human Rights Act' (2003) 66(5) *Modern Law Review* 726

Pillans, Brian 'McKennitt v Ash: The Book of Secrets' (2007) 12(3) *Communications Law* 78–82

Schreiber, Arye 'Confidence, Crisis, Privacy Phobia: Why Invasion of Privacy should be Independently Recognised in English Law' (2006) 2 *Intellectual Property Quarterly* 160

The land torts

Introduction to Part IV

1. In this Part we consider the role of the 'land torts'—here the torts of trespass to land, private and public nuisance and the rule in *Rylands* v *Fletcher*—in the regulation of the use of land.

2. In Chapter 17, we look specifically at the torts of **trespass to land** and **nuisance**. **Trespass to land** is concerned with intentional and direct physical interferences with rights over property. Like trespass to the person (discussed in Chapter 14), it is actionable *per se* (without proof of harm).

3. The tort of **private nuisance** is concerned with *indirect* and unreasonable interferences with property interests and, as such, often involves less tangible harms. Unlike trespass to land, some harm must be shown. While private nuisance can be concerned with actual physical damage, it is more often used to deal with interferences with claimants' 'amenity' interests. That is, claims are usually based on the loss of enjoyment of land. Private nuisance seeks to regulate the relationship between neighbours, defining their mutual rights and obligations with respect to property use, and seeking to protect the claimant's ability to use and enjoy his/her land without unreasonable interference by the defendant. The governing concept is one of 'reasonable use of land' and, in deciding whether a defendant is a reasonable user, a 'matrix of factors' can be taken into account. Unlike negligence, the *conduct* of the defendant is not (usually) relevant. A defendant can take all manner of precautions yet still be an unreasonable land user.

4. Some elements of private nuisance have been affected by emerging human rights law. In particular, human rights issues have been raised in relation to the requirement that only those with a proprietary interest in the property alleged to be affected by a nuisance can sue, and in relation to violations of Article 8 of the European Convention on Human Rights with respect to the right to home, private and family life.

5. **Public nuisance** is primarily a crime, which may, in certain circumstances, also lead to a civil cause of action. Its role has largely been overtaken by statute and our purpose here is simply to provide a short overview. An individual can bring an action in public nuisance only where s/he has suffered particular harm arising from a nuisance that has materially affected the reasonable comfort and convenience of life of a sufficiently large number of citizens.

6. The 'tort' of *Rylands* v *Fletcher* is considered in Chapter 18. This is distinct from nuisance in that it involves the consequences of one-off 'escapes' of things on land (as opposed to an ongoing state of affairs) and it imposes 'strict liability' for these escapes. Essentially, this action has been shaped over time by three key cases: *Rylands* v *Fletcher* [1868], *Cambridge Water Co Ltd* v *Eastern Counties Leather plc* [1994] and *Transco* v *Stockport MBC* [2004]. The latter two decisions have placed important limitations on the application of the rule.

7. The development of the *Rylands* v *Fletcher* rule has led to an increased overlap with ideas from nuisance and, importantly, negligence. In fact, there is a category of cases—where a state of affairs is continued or adopted and where there is later an escape—that seemingly could now be defined in any of the three torts. In other jurisdictions, the rule has been completely swallowed up by negligence. Without doubt, this is a rule that is now very limited in scope and application—it perhaps has more historical interest than practical application in the twenty-first century.

17

Trespass to land and nuisance

Problem question

Read this problem question carefully, and keep it in mind while you are working through the chapter that follows. At the end of the chapter, you will be able to apply what you have learnt to the problem question and advise the relevant parties.

Lekan owns a large country estate in Buckhampton. He is keen to develop it as an environmentally friendly residential adventure centre catering for stressed-out city executives. To this end, he has constructed a network of ropes, ladders and bridges in the canopy of his woodland for them to come and 'Swing High' from tree to tree. Unfortunately, misplaced marketing has led to the majority of his customers being large, noisy groups of young people on stag and hen weekends. Lekan also provides facilities for paintballing and a quad-bike cross-country course. In line with his stated environmental policy, he has recently begun to use large volumes of seaweed, collected from nearby beaches, as fertiliser for his large organic vegetable patch. He has been encouraged to do so by his local council's recycling officer, who is keen to stop waste material going to landfill sites (driven by a need to comply with an EC Directive).

Lekan receives the following complaints:

(a) Sarah, who lives downwind of Lekan's estate, complains that the smell of the rotting seaweed makes her physically sick.

(b) Sandy, a 14 year old, lives on a neighbouring farm. He complains that the noise from the quad bikes is causing his guinea pigs to miscarry their young.

→

➜

(c) Jess who, when she walks her dogs, parks her car next to Lekan's boundary fence, complains that her car has, on a couple of occasions, been hit by stray paintballs.

(d) Ailsa complains that the 'Swing High' centre is 'lowering the tone of the neighbourhood' and that her back garden can be seen from the platforms in the trees.

17.1 Introduction

Consider the following examples:

➜ Christine does not like her neighbour's overhanging tree, as it causes too much shade to fall on her garden. As the neighbour refuses to cut it back, Christine retaliates by having frequent late-night garden parties through the summer months.

➜ Barry runs a relaxation and meditation centre and complains that the noise from the dance studio on the floor above him stops his customers relaxing properly.

➜ Juliet lives near an industrial estate which has grown in size since she moved there. She complains that the noise of lorries delivering goods at all hours of the day and night keeps her awake at night.

➜ Nico, who grows organic roses, complains that his roses are wilting due to toxic smoke being emitted from a nearby factory.

➜ Laura complains that rats, which have infested the compost heap in her neighbour's garden, keep coming onto her property.

➜ Antony's neighbour sweeps up leaves in his garden and piles them up near the adjoining fence. The pile of leaves topples over and touches the fence. Some leaves are carried over the fence by a strong gust of wind.

➜ Sarah has a dinner party. Upon going upstairs to get a cardigan, she finds one of the guests in her bedroom, looking in her wardrobe.

The scenarios above indicate situations where tort law might regulate the conduct of the land users involved. In this chapter we will be considering the part the torts of trespass and nuisance play in the regulation of the use of land. We will also begin to explore the possible contribution that these torts make, or could make, to the protection of the environment. Specifically, we will look in this chapter at trespass to land, private nuisance and public nuisance.[1] The subsequent chapter

---

1. It should be noted, however, that various statutory nuisances exist, e.g. under the Environmental Protection Act 1990, which therefore give a wider protection of interests in land than these chapters will indicate.

will look at what is known as the 'tort' or rule in **Rylands v Fletcher** [1868], which again may have some value in terms of environmental protection. All these torts are far older than the tort of negligence, which was not 'created' until the twentieth century. They are used to protect the claimant's ability to use and enjoy their land freely without unwanted and unwarranted interference by the defendant. This idea is distinct from negligence, which seeks only to protect the individual from harm (including harm to land) that is inflicted carelessly. Negligence is a *conduct*-based tort, but the land torts are primarily *consequence*-based (though there are some circumstances where the courts take the conduct of the defendant into consideration). Fault plays a very limited role; the land torts are not organised in the 'duty-breach-damage' formulation that we are familiar with from negligence and, as we shall see, nor has their exact relationship and/or overlap with the tort of negligence ever been properly established.

17.2 **Trespass to land**

Trespass to land, like trespass to the person (see Chapter 14) is concerned with *direct* harm and the tort's primary importance is the protection of property rights. As with trespass to the person, it is actionable *per se* (that is, without proof of damage). When we refer to harm in this context, we do not necessarily mean actual *damage* to the land concerned. The harm lies in the fact that land owned by one party has been unjustifiably interfered with by another. What constitutes unjust interference is a matter of debate. The most obvious interference is where someone enters someone else's land or property (or remains there) without permission, but there are other, less clear, interferences as we shall see.

When we refer to land in this context, we mean not only what would be commonly understood as land, but also things under it, built on it and even the airspace above it. To claim in trespass, the claimant must either own or otherwise be in possession of the land (by being a tenant, for example)—it is the fact of possession of the land in question that is the interest protected. The interference complained of must be direct—it must also be *physical*, in the sense that something must have happened. A commonly-used example is that of neighbouring home-owners and overhanging plants. If I had pruned a tree growing in my garden and threw the branches into your garden, I would be committing a trespass, as this would be a direct action with a physical consequence (the branches land in your garden). However, if you had a problem simply because I did *not* prune the branches, so much so that they grew out over your garden, this would be only an indirect and non-physical consequence of the action, so would not usually be a trespass (although it may be trespass into airspace or otherwise actionable in private nuisance—see below).

What is physical interference? This can be broken down into four categories, as in Table 17.1. As you will see from the examples given in the table, there are many more things that can be a trespass than you might have originally thought—and possibly you have done many of these things without thinking.

Table 17.1 Types of physical interference with land

Nature of the interference	Examples
Crossing a boundary on to land	Walking across a field or garden without permission Entering someone's house or other premises without permission Putting an arm through a window or door without permission Branches or signs overhanging someone else's property
Remaining on land	Not leaving property when asked to do so by the owner or occupier
Going beyond what is permitted while on someone's land	Dinner guests take a peek into the bedrooms without permission A shopper goes past a 'no entry' sign at the back of a supermarket
Putting or placing objects on someone's land	Deliberately throwing items from one property onto another Cattle straying from one person's land to another's Allowing an unrestrained dog to run across a private field Leaning a bicycle against the wall or window of someone's property

17.2.1 Intention

A key element of trespass is intention—the act that constitutes the trespass must be intentional. However, it is not the trespass that must be intended, but merely the direct action (for example, entry into a property) that resulted in it. Put another way, it does not matter that you did not deliberately trespass on someone else's property—if you voluntarily took yourself there it will be a trespass.[2] In *League Against Cruel Sports* v *Scott* [1985] hunting dogs strayed onto the claimant's land (areas of Exmoor where there were wild deer sanctuaries)—this amounted to a trespass.[3] Here, the court avoided the fact that there was clearly no actual intention to allow the dogs onto the land by saying that persistently and frequently holding hunts alongside the land, when there was no means of preventing the dogs from straying, could be seen as an implied intention

2. Note, however, that if your actions were *involuntary*—e.g. you were pushed onto the land by someone else—you would not have trespassed. What is considered to be a 'voluntary action' is not always straightforward. Here we can compare *Smith* v *Stone* [1647] with *Gilbert* v *Stone* [1647]: in *Smith*, a man who was carried onto the claimant's land was held not to have acted voluntarily, thus was not held liable in trespass. In *Gilbert*, a man entered another's premises under duress (he was being threatened), though this was still a trespass as the act of entering the land had been deliberate and intentional—even if not perhaps wholly 'voluntary'.

3. In fact it seems that this trespass was deliberately crafted by the claimants, see Chapter 1, p 18.

to trespass. Therefore, because it is the act that must be intentional, rather than the actual trespass, some trespasses can be committed accidentally, or make what would otherwise seem to be innocent use of land a trespass.

This is evident in the 'airspace' trespass cases. When does something entering the space above one's land amount to a trespass to land owned or occupied by the claimant? In *Laiqat* v *Majid* [2005], an extractor fan on the defendant's land was held to be a trespass as it protruded over the claimant's land by 75 centimetres at a height of 4.5 metres. Similarly, in *Kelsen* v *Imperial Tobacco Co* [1957], the defendant's advertisement sign that jutted out eight inches into the area above the claimant's shop was a trespass. In a less permanent sense, if the arm of a crane swings over airspace above one's property then this too can be a trespass (see *Anchor Brewhouse Developments Ltd* v *Berkley House (Docklands Developments) Ltd* [1987]).[4]

 Pause for reflection

How far up can a trespass occur in the airspace above someone's property? In *Lord Bernstein of Leigh* v *Skyviews & General Ltd* [1978], the claimant argued that a light aircraft flying above his property to take aerial photographs amounted to a trespass. His claim was rejected, as the activity being carried out by the defendant took place above the level of an ordinary user of land. The Civil Aviation Act 1982 (which had an earlier predecessor) specifically states that a trespass is not committed if an aircraft flies above property at a 'reasonable height' having regard to the prevailing conditions (s 76(1)).

While this distinction helps us to determine where a trespass might stop (how high up), it also poses further questions: Is flying (on) an aeroplane not an 'ordinary' activity in the twenty-first century? And, if not, why is the use of an industrial crane (*Anchor Brewhouse*) to be regarded as 'ordinary'? Do you think the cases are helpful? Or should there be another way of deciding whether something in the airspace above land is a trespass, such as whether it blocks out light? Think about *Laiqat* and *Kelsen* again—do these *really* seem like trespasses to you?

A recent case has considered trespass in the other direction: below the claimant's property.

Star Energy Weald Basin Limited and another (Respondents) v Bocardo SA (Appellant) [2010] SC

Bocardo (a company owned by former Harrods owner Mohamed al Fayed) owns the Oxsted Estate in Surrey, under which part of an oil field lies. Star Energy have a licence granted by the Crown allowing them to bore for and obtain petroleum from the oil field from neighbouring land vested in the Crown. Without acquiring a contractual licence from

➡

---

4. So might the overhanging branches that annoy Christine, in the scenario above, also be a trespass?

→

Bocardo to do so, Star Energy drilled three wells from the Crown land, which travelled diagonally downwards and entered the estate below ground level (at depths between about 800ft and 1,300ft) and ran through the estate for between about 250m and 700m. No material physical harm was done to the estate by the drilling and installation of the wells and there was no interference with Bocardo's use or enjoyment of its land. Bocardo also had no right to the petroleum. Nevertheless, when Bocardo became aware of the wells, it commenced an action in trespass.

The High Court held that the wells constituted an actionable trespass and this decision was affirmed by the Court of Appeal. The Supreme Court considered the issue of how far below the surface ownership rights extend. Lord Hope said:

> There must obviously be some stopping point, as one reaches the point at which physical features such as pressure and temperature render the concept of the strata belonging to anybody so absurd as to be not worth arguing about. But the wells that are at issue in this case, extending from about 800 feet to 2,800 feet below the surface, are far from being so deep as to reach the point of absurdity. Indeed the fact that the strata can be worked upon at those depths points to the opposite conclusion. (at [27])

Thus, Star Energy had trespassed on Bocardo's land. On a secondary issue relating to the appropriate measure of damages, the Supreme Court affirmed the Court of Appeal's decision that damages were only available for the amenity loss caused by the technical trespass. This sum was measured at £1,000.[5]

17.2.2 Defences

As we have indicated, a necessary ingredient of trespass is a lack of permission. This also means that permission (express or implied)—or a 'licence'—to enter or remain on land constitutes a valid defence, subject to the person with that permission (the licensee) not exceeding the boundaries of the permission (as, for example, the dinner guest looking in Sarah's wardrobe in the scenario above).[6] Licences to be on someone else's land can be revoked, although the manner in which this can be done often depends on what type of licence was initially granted—for example whether it was one given under a contract.

Legal justification is a valid defence to a claim in trespass (such as where the police are authorised by law to enter premises to carry out an arrest under the Police and Criminal Evidence Act 1984). However, exceeding the boundaries of such authority carries severe consequences and, if this happens, the trespass alleged is deemed to have begun at the moment the defendant entered the property (even though at that time, they had legal justification to be there). This is known as trespass *ab initio*, and is discussed further below.

5. The High Court had awarded Bocardo nine per cent of the proceeds from the field since 2000 (£621,180 plus interest), and the same percentage of future income. According to newspaper reports, al Fayed is to take the case to the ECtHR (see e.g. Paul Cheston 'Mohamed Al Fayed's Dream of Becoming an Oil Baron is Capped by Court' *London Evening Standard* 28 July 2010).

6. This has notable similarities with the duty owed under the Occupier's Liability Act 1957 to only those visitors that have been expressly invited or have been (or are treated as having been) given permission to enter or use the premises (s 1(2)) for a particular purpose: 'When you invite a person into your house to use the staircase, you do not invite him to slide down the banisters' (Scrutton LJ in *The Carlgarth* [1927] at 110). See Chapter 11, p 284.

Another defence to a claim in trespass to land is necessity.[7] What is meant by this is that the action claimed as trespass might be deemed a necessary one for the defendant to have done in order to protect either a public interest (such as to prevent floodwaters spreading by going on to someone else's land to lay sand bags)[8] or a private interest (e.g. to prevent the defendant themselves from personal injury or property damage). In *Esso Petroleum* v *Southport Corporation* [1956], the defence of necessity was successfully used by a ship's captain, who discharged oils into the sea, polluting the shoreline. While there was some debate about whether this action amounted to a trespass or to nuisance, it was found to have been a necessary action in order to prevent the ship breaking up at sea and endangering the lives of the crew.

➡️⬅️ Counterpoint

What is necessary in a given situation often depends on the viewpoint of the person being asked—the court may or may not agree with the viewpoint of the defendant, as necessity in many situations is subjective. In particular, it seems that for the necessity defence to be successful, a sufficient degree of 'peril' is required. In *Southwark London Borough Council* v *Williams* [1971], for example, squatters who had occupied a number of the council's empty properties claimed necessity as their defence. Lord Denning MR thought differently, saying that 'if homelessness were once admitted as a defence to trespass, no-one's house would be safe' (at 744). He relied on the 'floodgates' policy argument, saying that if the defence were used once it 'would open a door that no man could shut'. He also invoked a fear of lawlessness, stating that the:

> courts must, for the sake of law and order, take a firm stand. They must refuse to admit the plea of necessity to the hungry and the homeless; and trust that their distress will be relieved by the charitable and the good. (at 744)

Thus, he was arguing that there may be better means to address problems such as homelessness, rather than for the courts to be seen to condone squatting.

More recently, in *Monsanto plc* v *Tilly* [2000], a group of protesters went onto land belonging to Monsanto, a company famous for developing and growing genetically modified (GM) crops. The protesters, of whom the defendant was one, believed that GM crops have harmful effects on the environment and on society and, as part of their campaign, thought it *necessary* to enter land owned by Monsanto and uproot the crops, in order to protect both public and environmental health. Tilly's argument was rejected by the Court of Appeal—though it was recognised that there might be some occasions when the destruction of one crop might be necessary in order to save others. In this instance, the court felt that the crop destruction had, for the most part, been a symbolic gesture, designed to attract media attention, thus the necessity argument could not prevail. Furthermore, the fact that there is public law protection offered to 'the public interest' in relation to GM crops clearly influenced the court's decision—as in the squatters case, it was perceived that there were better ways to achieve the intended goals than to use trespass.

7. As it is in a trespass to the person claim, see Chapter 14, p 400.
8. In *Dewey* v *White* [1827] the necessity defence was allowed where firemen deliberately destroyed the claimant's chimney to prevent the spread of fire to neighbouring properties.

17.2.3 **Trespass *ab initio***

If a party was permitted to be on land by statute or common law (as opposed to by licence only), but commits a wrongful act while there (that is, 'oversteps the boundaries'), then their original entry onto the land becomes a trespass. Essentially, their authority to be there is cancelled retrospectively. This is a historical concept, first defined in *The Six Carpenters* [1610]. In that case, six carpenters went to an inn, where they ordered and paid for bread and wine. Later, they ordered more wine but refused to pay for it. The court held that a wrongful act committed after lawful entry onto someone's premises could make the original entry a trespass (however, the carpenters were not liable as they had not committed a wrongful act, only an omission). There is little distinction between the principle and the one that operates when a person is on someone else's premises under licence (such as a guest at a dinner party) but goes on to do something that they should not do (such as look in the bedroom wardrobes). However, a distinction is made in terms of remedy. While peeking in the wardrobes may turn someone into a trespasser, there is little harm that can be compensated, so any damages award is likely to be nominal (see below). By contrast, if the six carpenters had been found liable, the innkeeper could have recovered damages for the wine not paid for, as well as for the fact that a trespass had occurred.

In *Elias* v *Pasmore* [1934], police officers had legally entered a man's premises in order to arrest him. While there, they seized some items belonging to him—some of the items were seized lawfully but others were unlawfully seized. The court found that a trespass was committed only in respect of the unlawfully seized items; it did not render the original entry illegal. Thus, it seems that trespass *ab initio* will occur only where the later wrongful act contravenes the entire basis for the original entry. As the original basis of entry was to make an arrest, the court found that this purpose had not been disturbed by the wrongful act.

 Counterpoint

On the basis of the decision in *Pasmore*, it may seem that the doctrine of trespass *ab initio* has little muscle. It seems to us that a doctrine that can protect people against abuses of authority while on their land is a useful one, particularly given the limited scope that exists for suing organisations such as the police in negligence.[9]

In *Chic Fashions (West Wales) Ltd* v *Jones* [1967], the existence of the doctrine was criticised. The police searched the claimant's premises for stolen goods, and seized goods that they wrongly thought to have been stolen. While the wrongful seizure itself was held to be lawful (as the police warrant gave them the authority to remove any goods that they considered to have been stolen), Lord Denning MR (*obiter*) suggested that the trespass *ab initio* doctrine was antiquated and failed to recognise the simple fact that a lawful act should not be rendered unlawful by subsequent events (at 313, 317 and 320). However, he later went on to make use of the doctrine in *Cinnamond* v *British Airports Authority* [1980], finding taxi drivers who were unlawfully touting for business to have trespassed

→

---

9. See Chapter 6, pp 144–153.

from the moment they entered the airport premises. Perhaps this tells us that the decisions in *Pasmore* and *Chic Fashions* say more about the judicial attitude to claims against the police (in a similar vein to within the tort of negligence) than about the trespass *ab initio* doctrine itself.

17.2.4 Remedies

A claimant will usually ask for damages and/or an injunction in trespass. Damages compensate the claimant for the harm already suffered by them due to the direct interference with their property. An injunction may be used to prevent a continuing trespass.[10] However, other remedies may be used in appropriate situations, such as re-entry (when the rightful owner/occupier of land has been excluded from it). This 'self-help' remedy may be used only if 'reasonable force' is all that is required to assert the right to re-enter. In the opposite situation, where an owner or occupier of land has lost possession, an action for the recovery of land might be taken, allowing (if successful) the defendant to be ejected from the land. This is done by court order. Further, an action for mesne[11] profits may be taken to claim money from anyone who has wrongfully occupied the land and made a profit or saved expenditure in the process of doing so (such as a tenant who outstays the terms of their tenancy agreement and does not pay rent for the extended time spent in the property). It also covers the costs associated with putting right any deterioration to the fabric of the property as well as any (reasonable) costs associated with repossession.

17.3 Private nuisance

Whereas trespass is concerned with *direct* interferences to land, private nuisance is concerned with *indirect* and *unreasonable* interferences to land, including what might be called consequential interferences resulting from a direct action (*Southport Corporation v Esso Petroleum Co Ltd* [1954]). Private nuisance is located squarely within the relationship between neighbours; that is, the people living next door or upstairs rather than the kind of 'neighbour' relationship we consider in negligence (***Donoghue* v *Stevenson* [1932]**). In short, private nuisance regulates the relationship between neighbours, defining their mutual rights and obligations with respect to their land use. In this way, *Conaghan & Mansell* suggest, nuisance is often viewed as a 'minor' tort with minimal implications or impact beyond the cosy world of neighbourly squabbles or 'ordinary people' against industry (p 124). This means that references to its increasing role within the realm of environmental protection are to a large extent downplayed; they become a 'pale green' aside its traditional concerns.[12] So viewed, nuisance continues to be understood as defining the rights and obligations of individuals whose interests

10. Though interesting issues arise in the context of protestors, in the sense that preventing protests may amount to a violation of the right to freedom of expression given by Art 10 ECHR. See *Mayor of London* v *Hall* [2010].
11. Pronounced 'mean'.
12. *Conaghan & Mansell* Ch 6.

in the use and enjoyment of land conflict, by striking a fair and reasonable balance between them as it seeks to protect the claimant's ability to use and enjoy his/her land without unreasonable interference by the defendant.

 Counterpoint

Behind the usual accounts of private nuisance, which manage to give the tort the appearance of coherence, is a more nuanced picture of a tort that has developed piecemeal over time to protect particular interests of particular sections of society. It should not be thought that the ordering of nuisance into particular categories in a textbook serves to make the tort coherent. Dean Prosser articulates this well: 'there is perhaps no more impenetrable jungle in the entire law than that which surrounds the word nuisance' (*Markesinis & Deakin* p 509). Nuisance has also been described as a tort of 'mongrel origins',[13] uncertain and lacking definition or any coherent goals or purpose.[14]

Conaghan & Mansell argue that traditional accounts of nuisance conceal a more sinister subtext extending well beyond neighbours engaging in garden-fence disputes. There are many examples of this when the cases themselves—not just the principles the judgments leave behind—are deconstructed. Behind, for example, the 'seemingly innocuous conflict between a cricket club and a house owner who objected, reasonably, to the showering of cricket balls in her back garden' (*Miller* v *Jackson* [1977], below), appears the 'elusive and potentially dictatorial character of the Public Interest' (*Conaghan & Mansell* p 124). Similarly, 'hovering on the sidelines of a dispute between the occupant of a "good class residential street" and his next-door neighbours, who were engaged in an activity ... which allegedly threatened the values of property and the character of the street' (they ran a brothel (*Thompson-Schwab* v *Costaki* [1956])), is 'the dark and rather ominous shadow of Civilised Society' (p 124).

So viewed, nuisance tells stories of more than just un-neighbourly behaviour. In its tales of polluted shrubs and rivers and disrupted TV signals, its narratives of anti-social boat-racing, cricket and piano playing, it reveals its social, historical and ideological contexts. Its case law is at times also indicative of the struggle between the 'haves and have-nots', the cosy privileged classes of Belgravia and those living in the one-time slums of Bermondsey.[15] Our point is this: there is more going on in nuisance than neighbourly squabbles that can be resolved with a simple application of legal principles. Traditional expositions of nuisance—its textbook appearance—are not only an excellent example of the ability of judges and legal academics to rationalise and synthesise the irrational and fluid (*Conaghan & Mansell* p 125), but also can be seen to clothe, subdue, constrain and ultimately obscure its political underpinnings, history and environmental potential. It could be argued that nuisance has failed to achieve its potential to develop into a real environmental tort—perhaps because of the balancing acts undertaken and the 'privileging' of the already privileged.

---

13. FH Newark 'The Boundaries of Nuisance' (1949) 65 *Law Quarterly Review* 480.

14. Conor Gearty 'The Place of Private Nuisance in a Modern Law of Torts' (1989) 48 *Cambridge Law Journal* 214 at 215. Maria Lee also argues that the '"boundaries" of private nuisance remain somewhat "blurred"' (2003, p 298).

15. See **Sturges v Bridgman**, discussed at pp 510, 511.

17.3.1 **What is private nuisance?**

According to Percy H Winfield, private nuisance is 'any unlawful interference with a person's use or enjoyment of land or some right over it'.[16] It is primarily concerned with conflicts that arise over neighbours' respective uses of land and seeks to protect the claimant's use and enjoyment of land from an activity or state of affairs for which the defendant is responsible. Unlike trespass to land, it is concerned with *indirect* interferences (smells, noise, or vibrations, for example) and is actionable only on proof of some *damage* (including the subjective damage of 'amenity' interests as well as actual forms of (physical) damage).

Things that may be included in an action for private nuisance are:

- actual (physical) damage to land (for example, by flooding, noxious fumes or vibrations);
- interference with 'amenity' interests—the use and enjoyment of land (for example, by the creation of smells, dust or noise);
- encroachment (for example, by tree roots or overhanging branches).

Table 17.2 Basic differences between nuisance and trespass

	The legal harm	When actionable	Example
Trespass	Direct interference with land	Actionable *per se* (i.e. without proof of damage)	I dump some waste on your land. As well as, most likely, this being a breach of various waste offences, I have committed a trespass. I have directly interfered with your land and even if you tell me to move it and I do; that is, even if there is no continuing harm, I will still have committed the trespass. The most obvious example of a trespass is walking (without permission) across someone's land; this is also a direct interference.
Nuisance	Indirect interference with use and enjoyment of land	Actionable upon proof of damage (to the interest in the land)	Instead of dumping the waste on your land, I simply leave it on my land to go putrid. It begins to smell, and flies gather—possibly there are rats that may go onto your land. This would give rise to an action in nuisance, as an indirect harm arising on one person's land and spreading to another's (though compare *Gregory* v *Piper* [1829], a trespass case).[17]

16. Percy H Winfield 'Nuisance as a Tort' (1931) 4 *Cambridge Law Journal* 189 at 190. Note, however, that he prefaced this with the comment that 'nuisance' is not a term capable of exact definition.

17. Laura, in the scenarios outlined above, would seem only to have an action in private nuisance. Antony may have a trespass claim in respect of his neighbour's leaves touching his fence—though only a claim in nuisance (subject to the principles outlined below) in respect of the leaves that have blown over.

In seeking to protect ownership rights, nuisance encourages people to be good neighbours (though, as we shall see, this really extends only to those neighbours with a proprietary interest in land—mere 'users' of land are not necessarily protected). At the heart of nuisance is a balancing act—to use one's land so as not to harm the land-based interests of others.

Private nuisance came into its own during the Industrial Revolution when courts were faced with new and pressing problems arising out of the actions of extremely polluting industrial land use, which were not compatible with how neighbours wanted to use their parcels of land—or, more to the point, the cases arose because the actions were *defended* by the industrial polluters. One case that highlights well the problems that came with industrialisation is *St Helens Smelting Co* v *Tipping* [1865].

St Helens Smelting Co v Tipping [1865] HL

Poisonous vapours from the defendant's copper smelting works caused damage to trees and shrubs on Mr Tipping's 1,300 acre estate in Lancashire one and a half miles away, and a claim was made in nuisance. The defendant contended that, as almost the whole neighbourhood was devoted to copper smelting or similar manufacturing activities, he could continue his activities with impunity.

The House of Lords disagreed. Lord Westbury distinguished between nuisance that produces what he called 'material injury to property' or 'sensible injury to the value of the property' and that which merely leads to 'personal discomfort' (lost amenity). He held that the former category—'material damage to property'—can never arise from a reasonable use of property—that is, it will always amount to a nuisance.[18] The injury to the claimant's trees and shrubs gave rise to an action in nuisance irrespective of whether the pollution from the defendant's works was normal for the locality.

Lord Westbury's reasoning in *St Helens Smelting*, about the difference between damage to property and personal discomfort, later developed into the so-called 'locality' rule—which simply means that the locality in which the nuisance takes place will be taken into account where there is interference with amenity interests (that is, use and enjoyment of the land), but not where there is actual physical damage.

 Counterpoint

The consequence of this distinction is that physical damage is seen to be a graver form of injury than 'mere' discomfort or inconvenience. Or, put simply, that 'actual' damage to land is worse than damage to people's subjective interests in it. The courts are clearly more willing to find an actionable nuisance where there is physical damage to property; 'mere' personal discomfort is treated with more latitude, unless the intrusion is such that it

→

---

18. So it seems that Nico, in the scenarios outlined at the beginning of the chapter, will have a successful claim in nuisance, despite the argument that his use of land was 'sensitive'—see p 503.

→

'materially interferes with the ordinary comfort physically of human existence, not simply elegant or dainty modes or habits of living' (Knight-Bruce VC, *Walter* v *Selfe* [1851] at 852). On this basis, loss of a view from one's property is loss of 'elegant' living (amenity) and not interference with the ordinary comfort of human existence. There is no remedy in private nuisance against a neighbour whose new greenhouse blocks your beautiful uninterrupted view because 'the law does not give an action for such things of delight' (Wray CJ in *Bland* v *Moseley* [1587]). Whilst it might be easy to say that noxious fumes that destroy every plant in my garden should be actionable in nuisance, it is far more difficult to weigh up the complaints of a resident in an industrial area who says that lorries travelling to a factory nearby cause noise and dust which affect her subjective property interests (amenity), for example by making her unable to sleep at night and worsening her asthma.

This distinction is, however, perhaps easier to articulate in theory than in practice—there are definite grey areas between damage to amenity and damage to property. Moreover, what is the locality? It is the court that will make the judgment as to whether an area is, for example, an industrial or rural or commercial area. We must therefore be careful not to approach the locality rule in too narrow a way. This is not to suggest, however, that there are, in essence, two torts: one dealing with physical damage and the other with discomfort or inconvenience. In fact, the idea that two divergent torts had been created by *St Helens Smelting* was ruled out by the House of Lords in the more recent case of *Hunter* v *Canary Wharf Ltd* [1997]. Instead, the distinction between amenity interests and physical damage is best seen as a question of degree. Interference that results in physical damage is more likely to be regarded as unreasonable than a less tangible harm such as lost amenity (feeling sick, worsened asthma, inability to sleep and so on), which usually requires the courts to engage in a more intricate balancing exercise, taking into account a number of factors, before deciding whether an alleged interference is a nuisance.

The difference between physical damage and lost amenity retains a somewhat uneasy presence in modern nuisance law. It is not always easy to distinguish between 'sensible injury to property' and 'personal discomfort': surely if your land becomes uncomfortable to live on, then its value (to you) is similarly diminished? Both interference with amenity and damage to property can cause 'sensible injury to the value of property'. The House of Lords in *Hunter* v *Canary Wharf* affirmed that both material physical damage and loss of amenity amounted to interference with property interests. This would suggest that, in deciding whether conduct amounts to a nuisance, the same factors should be considered for each. If both are property interests, why should a lengthy exposure to horrible smells be treated differently from one that causes material damage to property?

As we have indicated, private nuisance, unlike negligence, is an uncertain tort—it is often difficult to say with certainty what will or will not be a nuisance. Compare, for example, driving while under the influence of alcohol—someone doing so will obviously be in breach of their duty of care and therefore driving negligently. Moreover, unlike the defined cases of negligence developed incrementally by the courts, in principle *anything* is capable of amounting to a nuisance, as long as there is an 'emanation'—something (for example a smell, smoke or noise) must move from one neighbour's land onto another's (***Hunter***; cf *Southport Corporation* v *Esso Petroleum Co Ltd* [1956]).[19]

That said, it seems self-evident that not *every* interference with a person's use and enjoyment of land can amount to private nuisance. For example, if one neighbour listened to pop music to relax at the end of the day and even if they sang along—no matter how badly—it would not matter that the other neighbour, who might prefer the resonance of classical music, did not like this. If they were able to complain and establish that pop music or singing was a nuisance either because any music is played or, perhaps more hurtfully, because it is what some would consider as being 'bad' music, people would be severely limited in what they could enjoy in their own homes. A neighbour would, in effect, be given the power to veto another neighbour's choice of activity. However, if listening to pop music extended to playing one song loudly on repeat between the hours of 2 am and 4 am every morning, then any neighbour would appear to have legitimate grounds for complaint—nuisance is about 'reasonable' use of land, but must have built into it some 'give and take'.

Although it is relatively straightforward to state that the tort of private nuisance protects only against *unlawful* interference, the question as to what constitutes unlawful interference is somewhat problematic. Interference is only deemed to be unlawful when a court considers it to be *substantial* and *unreasonable*. In the modern law of nuisance, unlawfulness is equated with unreasonableness. The question is this: Was there an *unreasonable interference* with the *claimant's* use and enjoyment of land or, put another way, was/is the *defendant* an *unreasonable user* of their land?

As Lord Wright said in ***Sedleigh-Denfield* v *O'Callaghan* [1940]**: 'a balance has to be maintained between the right of the occupier to do which he likes with his own, and the right of his neighbour not to be interfered with' (at 903). So, the test is one of the 'reasonable user': balancing the interests of the claimant to have quiet enjoyment of his land against the interests of the defendant to use their land as is legally permitted. It is a 'rule of give and take, live and let live' (Bramwell J, *Bamford* v *Turnley* [1862] at 32). As a result, the ordinary, or reasonable, use of your home, will not amount to a nuisance even if it includes playing pop music *reasonably*, and even if it discomforts your neighbour due to poor soundproofing or insulation (*Southwark Borough Council* v *Mills* [2001]). However, we are still left with the problem of how to define reasonable use of land. The case law built up on private nuisance over time can help us to determine this—it has created a 'matrix of factors' which can be weighed up to determine whether an activity on land is likely to be a nuisance.[20]

17.3.2 **Who can sue?**

To succeed in private nuisance a claimant must first establish that they have legal standing—that is, the right to sue. Nuisance is not the only place in tort law where standing is an issue and where what seem like potentially legitimate claims can fail

---

19. Although it should be noted that in *Laws* v *Florinplace* [1981] the movement of prostitutes into a local sex shop/cinema was held to be an actionable nuisance even though there was no 'emanation' as such.

20. See pp 498–508 for discussion of these factors.

even before they begin.[21] In relation to who has standing in private nuisance, *Malone v Laskey* [1907] set the initial boundaries. A woman was injured while using the toilet when its cistern fell on top of her. It had been dislodged by vibrations emanating from the electricity generator on the neighbouring defendant's property. Despite her injuries, the Court of Appeal held that she had no cause of action in nuisance against the defendants, because she had no proprietary interest in the premises—the house belonged to her husband's employer. She was 'merely present in the house'.

As the aim of private nuisance is to protect the claimant's use and enjoyment of land, it is perhaps obvious that the claimant must have an interest in the land that has been unreasonably interfered with. However, it is more difficult to establish exactly what link or interest the claimant must have. Does this mean an interest in land as defined by property law or simply a substantial link with the land?

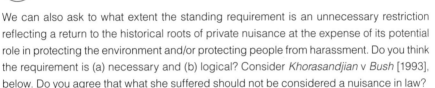

 Pause for reflection

We can also ask to what extent the standing requirement is an unnecessary restriction reflecting a return to the historical roots of private nuisance at the expense of its potential role in protecting the environment and/or protecting people from harassment. Do you think the requirement is (a) necessary and (b) logical? Consider *Khorasandjian* v *Bush* [1993], below. Do you agree that what she suffered should not be considered a nuisance in law?

This traditional view of nuisance—the 'interest in land' requirement—was challenged in *Khorasandjian* v *Bush* [1993]. Miss Khorasandjian had been subjected to a campaign of harassment by a former boyfriend.[22] She sought an injunction to prevent him 'harassing, pestering or communicating' with her, especially by means of persistent and unwanted telephone calls to her mother's home, where she lived. Like Mrs Malone, she had no proprietary interest: she merely lived in the house with her mother. Nevertheless, Dillon LJ in the Court of Appeal stated that 'the court has at times to reconsider an earlier decision in light of changed social conditions... If the wife of the owner is entitled to sue in respect of harassing telephone calls, then I do not see why that should not also apply to a child living at home with her parents' (at 735) and therefore allowed her to claim in private nuisance. This innovative approach to nuisance was subsequently followed by a differently constituted Court of Appeal in *Hunter* v *Canary Wharf Ltd* [1996]. Here, Pill LJ found that it was enough that the claimant could demonstrate a 'substantial link' with the property in question (the occupation of a property as a *home* was therefore sufficient to enable the occupier to sue in private nuisance). However, the House of Lords rejected this argument.

---

21. In a claim under the Consumer Protection Act 1987 in relation to a defective product that has caused consequential property damage, for example, a claimant must first establish that the *value* of that property damage exceeds £275 (see Chapter 13, p 355). Further, strictly speaking, in negligence a claimant can sue only if they have suffered a recognisable *harm* (**Grieves v FT Everard & Sons** [2007]; cf *Rees v Darlington Memorial Hospital NHS Trust* [2002]).

22. Of course, should the same facts arise today the claimant would be able to rely on the Protection from Harassment Act 1997; see further Chapter 14, p 404.

> ### *Hunter v Canary Wharf Ltd* [1997] HL
>
> A number of local residents, including homeowners, their families and other licensees, complained about the erection of the Canary Wharf tower in the London docklands development. The tower—which is nearly 250 metres high, over 50 metres square, and has a metallic surface—was found to interfere with the television reception of neighbouring homes. Two preliminary questions arose: first, could an actionable nuisance exist in respect of interference with television reception? Secondly, if this was possible, who of those affected could sue?
>
> The House of Lords held that interference with the television reception was not capable of amounting to a nuisance. There was no 'emanation' from the Canary Wharf tower which, according to Lord Hope at least, was thought to be a requirement of a nuisance claim. The tower was simply stopping something going onto the property of its neighbours. It was held, by analogy to cases that refused liability for blocking a view, that the defendants were free to build what they wanted to on their land subject to planning permissions and other restrictions such as easements. Hence, complaints could be made only at the planning stage and not by means of private nuisance.
>
> Although technically unnecessary to do so, when addressing the secondary question, the law lords reasserted the traditional view stated in *Malone*. Defining nuisance as a 'tort directed against the plaintiff's enjoyment of his rights over land' (at 688),[23] Lord Goff held that claims in nuisance can be brought only by claimants with an interest in land—that is, landowners, tenants, grantees of an easement or *profit à prendre*, or those with exclusive possession of the land.

The decision in **Hunter** means that a person cannot claim in private nuisance if they are merely a member of the landowner's family (as in *Khorasandjian*), a guest (long or short term), a lodger or an employee (including live-in employees, such as *au pairs*). Recognising that such people had a right to sue, the law lords suggested, would be to effect a fundamental change in the nature and scope of the tort and would give rise to a number of practical difficulties. They also believed that to extend nuisance in this way would transform it into a tort *to the person* and would render redundant what they viewed as sensible restrictions on the right to sue for personal injury in negligence, for example by allowing liability for mere discomfort without damage (lost amenity). Put simply, the House of Lords was keen to reinforce nuisance as a tort to land, not to people.

 Counterpoint

It is unclear the extent to which the House of Lords' decision in *Hunter* is compatible with Article 8(1) of the European Convention on Human Rights (ECHR) (as incorporated into domestic law by the Human Rights Act (HRA) 1998), which establishes that 'everyone has the right to respect for his private and family life, his home and his correspondence'. The 'interest in land' standing requirement might need to be reconsidered in light of the HRA in order to secure fuller protection of the right to respect for private and family life, and

➡

23. In reference to Newark, above.

possibly also the right not to be discriminated against (Art 14). As we see below, Article 8(1) has already been interpreted broadly by the European Court of Human Rights (ECtHR), permitting parties without rights in the home to sue.

In *Khatun* v *UK* [1998]—an appeal to the European Commission of Human Rights on part of the *Hunter* decision—it was found that the distinction made in *Hunter* between those with a proprietary interest in land and those without was not applicable for the purposes of Article 8(1) (although it was felt that the defendant's activities (building the tower) could be justified under Article 8(2) as pursuing a legitimate and important aim given the public interest importance in developing the once run-down Docklands area of London and the limited interference to the applicant's home). The decision in *Khatun* suggests that, should a suitable case arise, a court would be able to challenge the *Hunter* limitations. Indeed, to an extent this may already have happened.

McKenna v *British Aluminium Ltd* [2002] HC

Claims in private nuisance and in *Rylands* v *Fletcher* (see Chapter 18) were taken by over thirty children from a number of households alleging that emissions and noise from the defendant's neighbouring factory were an invasion of privacy and had caused them mental distress and physical harm. The defendants argued that following *Hunter* the claims should be struck out unless each of the claimants could point to a proprietary right—that is, show they had standing to take their claim.

In the High Court, Neuberger J rejected the defendant's argument and refused to strike out the claims, saying that:

> there is obviously a powerful case for saying that effect has not been properly given to Article 8(1) if a person with no interest in the home, but *who has lived in the house for some time* and had his enjoyment of the home interfered with, is at the mercy of the person who owns the home, as the only person who can bring proceedings. (at [53])

This was only a striking-out action. Neuberger J (now Lord Neuberger) thought that the claimants in *McKenna* had an arguable case that this restrictive aspect of the common law should be extended in the light of the HRA, so dismissed the defendant's application to strike out the claims as disclosing no cause of action.[24]

 Pause for reflection

The way the law currently stands—as identified by counsel for the claimants in *McKenna*—excludes one very large group in particular from ever being able to take a claim in private nuisance: children. Children are never likely to have the required proprietary interest in a property to be able to sue. Do you think this should be the case?

---

24. Also see *Dobson* v *Thames Water Utilities Ltd* [2009], discussed at pp 519–520.

17.3.3 **The concept of the 'reasonable user'**

As indicated above, private nuisance is a consequence-based tort, thus liability is not based on whether the defendant acted reasonably or whether they did all they could to prevent the nuisance occurring. Put another way, taking reasonable care does not prevent liability. Instead, the court has to consider a range or a 'matrix' of factors in order to say whether something is or is not a nuisance.

The factors that the court can take into account can be split into three categories:

(1) always considered (intensity—including duration, frequency and timing of the interference);

(2) sometimes considered, dependent on the *type* of claim (the nature of the locality); and

(3) sometimes considered, if *relevant* to the claim (sensitivity of the claimant; bad intention of the defendant).

As we will see, many of these factors are also important in relation to the question of remedies. We will look at each category in turn. Essentially, each of the (relevant) factors has to be weighed against the others. It is helpful to imagine a set of simple balancing scales (see Figures 17.1a and 17.1b)—then mentally place each factor onto the scales at the relevant point, working out in whose favour the scales will tip. If the scales tip towards the claimant then they will have a successful claim—if towards the defendant then the claim fails.

17.3.3.1 Factors that are always considered

The intensity of the interference
Unlike trespass to land where any interference to property can amount to a trespass, in private nuisance a threshold exists—everyone has to put up with some interference from their neighbours at some time or other (*Southwark London Borough Council* v *Mills* [2001]). However, interferences can become unreasonable when they occur frequently or for long periods of time, as the pop music example above indicates. The idea is best explained by Lawton LJ in *Kennaway* v *Thompson* [1981]:

> [N]early all of us living in these islands have to put up with a certain amount of annoyance from our neighbours. Those living in towns may be irritated by their neighbours' noisy radios or incompetent playing of musical instruments; and they in turn may be inconvenienced by the noise caused by our guests slamming car doors and chattering after a late party. Even in the country the lowing of a sick cow or the early morning crowing of a farmyard cock may interfere with sleep and comfort. *Intervention by injunction is only justified when the irritating noise causes inconvenience beyond what other occupiers in the neighbourhood can be expected to bear.* The question is whether the neighbour is using his property reasonably, having regard to the fact that he has a neighbour. The neighbour who is complaining must remember, too, that the other man can use his property in a reasonable way and there must be a measure of give and take, live and let live. (at 94, emphasis added)

If any interference could amount to a nuisance, the tort simply would not work. The interference needs to be substantial, in the sense that, for example, it goes on for a

Figure 17.1 A) Weighing up the factors in a private nuisance claim (1). B) Weighing up the factors in a private nuisance claim (2).

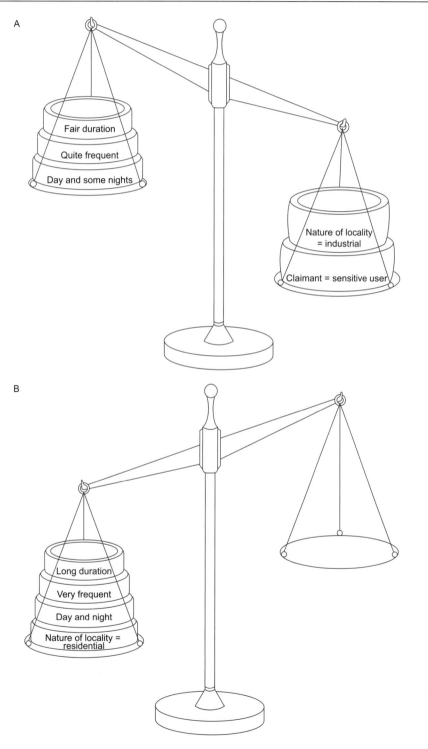

long time or takes place at an unreasonable time of day (or night). That said, while ordinary everyday living cannot be an unreasonable use of land, an action for physical damage to property, even if caused by a temporary or short-lived activity, is likely to succeed—though in such cases the court will award damages rather than an injunction (this makes sense: as the nuisance has finished, there is nothing on which to base injunctive relief). In *Crown River Cruises Ltd* v *Kimbolton Fireworks Ltd* [1996], a 15–20 minute firework display at the end of the fiftieth anniversary of the Battle of Britain celebrations was held to be a nuisance to a Thames boat owner whose boat suffered substantial fire damage.

17.3.3.2 A factor that is sometimes considered, dependent on the type of claim

The nature of the locality

The reasonableness of land use can depend on, alongside other considerations, the character or nature of the area it is in—its 'locality'. In assessing whether noise from a local factory causes a nuisance to local residents, courts will be more likely to find nuisance if the factory is in the middle of a residential area rather than an industrial one. Similarly, farmyard smells and noises are less likely to be a nuisance in an overwhelmingly rural area. However, as we have indicated above, following **St Helen's Smelting**, the 'locality principle' applies only in cases where the claimant has suffered lost amenity. It is not a relevant consideration where the claim is about material physical damage (for example, dead plants killed by poisonous fumes), which in law can never arise from a reasonable use of land.

A classic quote summing up what is meant when we say that the 'nature of the locality' must be taken into account is found in **Sturges** v **Bridgman** [1879], where Thesiger LJ said that 'what would be a nuisance is Belgrave Square would not necessarily be so in Bermondsey' (at 865). Clearly he meant that the character of the neighbourhood in question must be considered when determining whether a nuisance has or has not happened—put another way, people in some (poorer?) areas should be expected to put up with more than (affluent?) people in others.

⏩⏪ Counterpoint

The above quote supports the idea that nuisance is highly subjective and contextual. By this, we mean that for an activity to be a nuisance, someone must have complained about it—and this depends on their own subjective interpretation of the context in which the activity is taking place.

The effect of the locality rule is to accentuate and mirror inequalities that already exist within society. Those who live in what the court considers to be economically and socially poorer areas are expected to have to cope with more interference from others, more environmental pollution and so on. *Conaghan & Mansell* point out that, historically, the compromise 'distinction drawn in *St Helens Smelting Co v Tipping* [1865] between inflicting material damage to property and producing "sensible personal discomfort"', and the so-called locality rule, were of 'crucial significance in limiting the liability of industrialists for nuisance' (p 133). They point to an observation made by Cornish and Clark that in the 'period

→

immediately after 1865, it was almost impossible to sue for amenity damage (smells, noise, vibrations) if one lived in an industrial area'[25] and conclude that 'inevitably the distinction had a disproportionate class impact by protecting the primary interests of residential land-owners (in the physical integrity of their property) while denying any redress to those who simply wish to live in an environment free from the stench and clamour of industrial activity' (p 133). In short, it seems those who suffer most from the ravages of pollution are deemed to be the least worthy of protection.

And it seems that things have not moved very far in this respect. In *Baxter* v *Camden London Borough Council (No 2)* [2001], the tenant of the first-floor flat within an old converted terraced house complained of continuing noise from the flats above and below her to the council that had converted the property (with inadequate sound proofing) in 1975. Dismissing the claimant's appeal, Tuckey LJ in the Court of Appeal returned to a familiar concept, saying that 'occupiers of low cost, high density housing must be expected to tolerate higher levels of noise from their neighbours than others in more substantial and spacious premises' (at [10]).

The nature or character of a locality may change. For example, over a period of time the primary use of land may evolve from industrial to residential (or vice versa) or from green fields to commercial. Such evolution might be gradual or it may be faster and deliberately calculated to change the area, such as the current development of the east end of London in preparation for the 2012 Olympic Games. Therefore, when considering a claim, the courts have to consider the locality as it is, not how it once was. When there is deliberate development or quick, radical change to the nature of an area, it is likely that planning permission will have been sought and received. So, is it the granting of permission or the actions taken on the back of the permission, once granted, that change the nature of a locality?

Gillingham Borough Council v *Medway (Chatham) Dock Co Ltd* [1993] QBD

In 1982, a disused Royal Naval Dockyard in Chatham, Kent, was closed by the government. The area was subsequently divided into three parts, one of which was taken over by the Medway Ports Authority to be used as a 24-hour commercial port. Many residents complained about the level of traffic passing their properties, particularly throughout the evening and night. At one point it was recorded that a lorry was passing every 1.5 minutes in the early hours of the morning. The residents claimed of interrupted sleep and general disturbance to their manner of living—for example, few of them could ever open the windows at the front of the house because of the heavy volume of passing traffic. As a substantial group of residents was affected, the local council took an action in (public) nuisance on their behalf, asking for an injunction to prevent the movement of the lorries, particularly at night. The same council had granted the planning permission to the defendants

25. *Law and Society in England: 1750–1950* (Sweet & Maxwell, 1989), p 157.

> →
> allowing them to develop the port at the site of the old naval dockyard, even though it had been aware of the likely disturbance this would cause to local residents. When the planning application was made, local residents had been given a chance (as is usually the case) to voice their opinions.
>
> Buckley J held that the granting of planning permission had in this instance changed the nature of the locality, which was now wholly commercial in its character. Local residents therefore could not complain about the serious disruption caused to them by commercial operations.

The decision in *Gillingham* does not mean that every time planning permission is granted the nature of a locality will change. It is a question of fact to be decided in each case. In this respect, *Gillingham* should be contrasted with *Wheeler v JJ Saunders Ltd* [1996].

> ### *Wheeler v JJ Saunders Ltd* [1996] CA
>
> The defendant situated pig sties on his farm as near as possible to his neighbour's land in order to annoy the claimant, with whom he did not get on. Between the two neighbours a house, with outbuildings and an adjacent farm, were in common ownership. Wheeler bought the house and the outbuildings and was granted planning permission from the local council to convert the outbuildings into holiday cottages. The farm was let to the defendants, who also obtained planning permission, even though the claimants opposed this, to extend the capacity of their pig farm and build two new sheds, each capable of housing 400 pigs, with an opening for ventilation, a slatted floor and a channel to contain the pigs' excrement underneath it. One of them was situated only 11 metres from Wheeler's house. On occasion, strong smells emanated from the pig farm to the claimant's property, which affected them and also visitors to their holiday cottages. Wheeler claimed that the defendants were liable in nuisance in respect of the smells emanating from the pig farm. At first instance, an injunction was granted which prevented the defendants using their new sheds and £2,820 in general damages was awarded to the claimants.
>
> The Court of Appeal held that the smell emanating from the defendants' pig farm amounted to an actionable private nuisance. Although they agreed that statutory authority would be a defence, planning permission was not the same and so could not operate as a legitimate defence to a claim in nuisance. Following *Gillingham*, although planning permission could alter the nature of a locality, it had not done so in this instance—the nature of the locality remained the same, so the defendants remained liable.

In distinguishing the effect of the planning permission in *Gillingham*, the court found that this had been 'strategic' in nature—that is, it was a deliberate attempt to change the nature of the locality for the good of the community. In *Wheeler* the purpose of the planning permission was merely 'expansive'—it allowed an already existing pig farm to become bigger. This difference meant the planning permission to expand the pig farm adjacent to holiday accommodation did not change the *nature* of the entire locality and so did not prevent a nuisance being caused to the claimants by the smell emanating from the farm.[26] More recently, the Court of Appeal, in *Watson v Croft Promosport Ltd* [2009], ruled that despite planning permission being given for an activity (motor racing) on the basis that it was reasonable for the locality, an injunction could be granted to prevent that activity from continuing for more than 40 days per year.

17.3.3.3 Other factors that are sometimes considered, if relevant to the claim

The sensitivity of the claimant

To be a nuisance, a court must find that the defendant's use of land is potentially unreasonable to *anyone*. This implies that someone affected because of their own sensitivities (where an 'ordinary' person would not be so affected) will be unable to claim. For example, in *Heath v Mayor of Brighton* [1908], the vicar and trustees of a church sought to stop the noise emanating from the defendant's power station as the vicar complained that it disturbed his deliberations over his sermons but, as no one else appeared to be disturbed by the noise, an injunction was refused.

The idea is better explained by *Robinson v Kilvert* [1889]. The claimant rented premises from the defendant, which he used as a paper warehouse. The defendant then started a manufacturing business in the cellar of his building for which he needed the air to be both hot and dry. Heating the cellar to achieve this caused the temperature of the floor of the claimant's warehouse above to rise to 80° Fahrenheit. This, while it would not have damaged ordinary paper or caused anyone using the building any physical discomfort,[27] dried out the specialist brown paper that the claimant was storing (and, as the value of the paper was affected by its weight, it lost value). The claimant sought an injunction preventing the defendant (his landlord) from heating the cellar. The Court of Appeal rejected his claim, holding that 'a man who carries on an exceptionally delicate trade cannot complain because it is injured by his neighbour doing something lawful on his property, if it is something which would not injure anything but an exceptionally delicate trade' (Lopes LJ at 97). However, despite the fact that a claimant's sensitivity may sometimes render a claim in nuisance ineffective, it is clear that after an actionable nuisance *is* established, a claimant will receive damages for all of their losses even if these are the result of interference with what may be considered a sensitive use of land. In *McKinnon Industries Ltd v Walker* [1951], for example, the claimant was able to recover the cost of damage to his orchids (as well as lost profits on them), even though the defendant contended that orchid growing was a sensitive activity.[28]

---

26. Juliet is unlikely to be able to claim in private nuisance if the locality was already industrial when she moved there, even if the industrial operations have increased over time. However, as locality is only one factor to be taken into account, the outcome of her claim may depend on the intensity of the disturbance.

27. As noted by Cotton LJ at 94.

28. Barry, in the examples at the start of the chapter, may therefore have difficulty in taking his claim, unless he can show that the noise from the dance studio would also affect someone with a less delicate trade.

Counterpoint

It may often be difficult to determine what is 'unduly sensitive', particularly as this relates to the claimant's use of land and not to the claimant themselves. If the storage of a particular type of paper is unduly sensitive (*Robinson*), but the growing of orchids is not (*McKinnon*), would the idea of sensitivity extend, for example, to the supply of a signal to television viewers, which surely encompasses much of the population?

In *Bridlington Relay* v *Yorkshire Electricity Board* [1965], a company that provided a residential relay system of sound and television broadcasts, claimed in private nuisance alleging that its business would be affected by electromagnetic interference from two electricity pylons erected between 200 and 250 feet from its mast and wiring that passed, at its nearest point, 169 feet from the mast. Buckley J refused to allow the claim for an injunction, pointing to the sensitive nature of the business, saying that interference with facilities that were purely 'recreational' (such as television reception) was not actionable in nuisance.

As with many cases in private nuisance, *Bridlington Relay* may be a product of its time. Perhaps recognising this, Buckley J referred to the electrical interference not being actionable 'at present', meaning that as times change, so might the question about 'recreational' facilities. Indeed, the *Bridlington Relay* decision was ruled 'out of date' in the Canadian case of *Nor-Video Service* v *Ontario Hydro* [1978]. Despite the House of Lords' reluctance in *Hunter* to answer the question as to whether the case would be decided differently today, it is hoped this would be the case and that the ability to receive an adequate television signal (a 'recreational' activity enjoyed by the vast majority of people) would in fact now be regarded as an ordinary and natural use of land.

The position on 'abnormal sensitivity' has since moved on, in that it seems that today this must be considered alongside (or as part of) the issue of foreseeability.

Network Rail Infrastructure Ltd v Morris (t/a Soundstar Studio) [2004] CA

Network Rail appealed against an order to pay Mr Morris damages for nuisance caused by electromagnetic interference emitting from a signalling system, which had affected the sound of electric guitars in Morris's recording studio. They submitted that Morris's use of the studio was abnormally sensitive to the magnetic waves and was not protected by the law of nuisance as he was involved in an extraordinary commercial activity, rather than the ordinary use of equipment in an ordinary way. Additionally, Network Rail argued that it could not have reasonably foreseen the problem, taking into account the distance between the signalling system and the studio, where the magnetic field was much weaker. Morris contended that Network Rail should have foreseen the nuisance as it had inherited a report from British Rail which had detailed similar complaints from third parties who had musical rehearsal studios either in or near the affected area.

The Court of Appeal adopted a considered approach. Allowing the appeal, the judges felt that the modern law of tort had done away with some established detailed rules and

→

instead required a broad approach to be taken. To establish liability for private nuisance, the test was not that of foreseeability alone, but of foreseeability as an aspect of reasonableness. The concept of abnormal sensitivity was thought outmoded and, whether Morris's use of his studio was a special or sensitive use of premises was irrelevant. The correct test was whether it was *foreseeable* that specific damage would be caused to a specific claimant. However, even though the use of electronic equipment was a feature of modern day life in the ordinary use and enjoyment of property, it was not reasonable to expect Network Rail to foresee the interference caused based on a report which had been made several years prior to them taking over the maintenance of the rail track and which contained observations that were not specific enough to have reasonably expected them to have taken any preventative action.[29]

Unlike the tort of negligence, private nuisance is not supposed to be a tort based on the defendant's fault. The defendant can take as much care as possible, but if the way they use their land has the *effect* of causing nuisance to a neighbour then a claim will be established against them. Nuisance is (at least in theory) supposed to be consequence-based—so perhaps in this sense the concept of foreseeability is misplaced.

 Counterpoint

It does seem that over time some elements of the tort of private nuisance have changed, making it appear closer to negligence in terms of the factors that may be taken into account. The question is always whether what the law considers to be an unreasonable use of land on the part of the defendant also amounts to them being 'at fault' for the way they use their land. In the *Wagon Mound (No 2)*, which we have already looked at in the chapter on breach in negligence (p 214), Lord Reid pointed out that while the level of fault may not be such as to amount to a breach of duty in negligence, some level of fault is almost always necessary in nuisance (at 639). But what did he mean by 'fault'? As we will see, since the case of *Cambridge Water* v *Eastern Counties Leather plc* [1994] (discussed in the chapter on actions under *Rylands* v *Fletcher*), foreseeability in the *Wagon Mound* sense has become a consideration in the land torts as well as in negligence. As *Network Rail* indicates, this requirement has already become 'dominant' over some of the more traditional concerns in nuisance cases. An activity on land can be a nuisance only if it is reasonably foreseeable to the defendant that the activity might be a nuisance to someone else—so where does this leave fault?

Bad intention of the defendant

In assessing whether the defendant is a reasonable user of their land, their motive may be taken into account. This is really an issue only where actions by the defendant are undertaken in bad faith or with malice towards the claimant.

29. Would it be reasonably foreseeable to the owners of a dance studio that noise emanating from it could cause others nuisance?

Christie v Davey [1893] HC

Christie was a music teacher who occasionally worked from home. Her children also played musical instruments. The claimants had lived in their home for three years with no problems with their neighbours until, on 30 September 1892, the defendant wrote to Mr Christie saying:

> During this week we have been much disturbed by what I at first thought were the howlings of your dog, and, knowing from experience that this sort of thing could not be helped, I put up with the annoyance. But, the noise recurring at a comparatively early hour this morning, I find I have been quite mistaken, and that it is the frantic effort of some one trying to sing with piano accompaniment, and during the day we are treated by way of variety to dreadful scrapings on a violin, with accompaniments. If the accompaniments are intended to drown the vocal shrieks or teased catgut vibrations, I can assure you it is a failure, for they do not. I am at last compelled to complain, for I cannot carry on my profession with this constant thump, thump, scrape, scrape, and shriek, shriek, constantly in my ears. It may be a pleasure or source of profit to you, but to me and mine it is a confounded nuisance and pecuniary loss, and, if allowed to continue, it must most seriously affect our health and comfort. We cannot use the back part of our house without feeling great inconvenience through this constant playing, sometimes up to midnight and even beyond. Allow me to remind you of one fact, which must most surely have escaped you—that these houses are only semi-detached, so that you yourself may see how annoying it must be to your unfortunate next-door neighbour. If it is not discontinued I shall be compelled to take very serious notice of it. It may be fine sport to you, but it is almost death to yours truly. (at 317–18)

Taking offence at the letter, Christie did not reply. Instead of writing again, the defendant chose to show his annoyance by creating his own disturbances: he banged on the wall, clattered metal trays together, whistled and shouted each time he could hear music emanating from the claimant's house. In response to this, the claimant (Mrs Christie) sued in private nuisance—unsurprisingly her claim was met by a counter-claim from the defendant.

The claimant won an injunction against the defendant, but his counter-claim was not allowed. Giving judgment, North J commented that the defendant had acted 'only for the purpose of annoyance', adding 'in my opinion, it was not a legitimate use of the defendant's house' (at 327).

It can be seen from this case that—with reference to the scales analogy—both claims may have been equally weighted until the defendant's malicious motive was added to the equation. This firmly tipped the scales in favour of the claimant.[30]

---

30. So, Christine's bad intention in holding frequent late-night garden parties as retaliation for overhanging branches may amount to a nuisance and allow her neighbour to make a claim against *her*!

Pause for reflection

What do you think would have happened if, instead of writing the letter to Mr Christie, the defendant had taken an action in nuisance against the claimant and her family, alleging that the music they played was 'to me and mine...a confounded nuisance and [causes] pecuniary loss, and, if allowed to continue, it must most seriously affect our health and comfort. We cannot use the back part of our house without feeling great inconvenience through this constant playing, sometimes up to midnight and even beyond'? Do you think the outcome of this case was correct? Would the decision have bettered the relationship between the neighbouring families?

Having said that the defendant's bad intention tipped the balance in favour of the claimant in *Christie*, it does not do so in all cases where malicious behaviour is exhibited. In *Bradford Corporation* v *Pickles* [1895], the defendant deliberately drained his land with the intention of decreasing the supply of water to his neighbour, in the hope that this would force the neighbour to buy his land. However, the House of Lords rejected the claim for an injunction, refusing to take the defendant's alleged malice into account.

 Counterpoint

The *Bradford* decision is distinguishable from *Christie* in various ways. In *Bradford*, the claimant company had no *right* to receive the water supply and therefore no right had been interfered with on which legally to base the alleged nuisance. As the case involved so-called 'natural rights' (water rights) and it was already well-established law that a land owner has the absolute right to do as he wishes with water filtering through his land even if his behaviour appears to others to be utterly unreasonable, the motive of the defendant was 'irrelevant'. It should, however, be acknowledged that a *laissez-faire* attitude prevailed when this case was decided and a lenient approach was taken to people who wanted to better themselves—in fact this was seen as largely commendable. Pickles had done no more than try to get a good deal on the sale of his land—his behaviour was not malicious, but sensible. Perhaps what has caused this case to be included in textbook sections on malice or bad motive is the fact that the case speaks of Mr Pickles as being an unpleasant character—possibly, whether this was true or not, the claimants wanted to portray him as such to make his behaviour look all the more malicious and encourage the court to follow *Christie*.

Malice also appeared as an issue in *Hollywood Silver Fox Farm Ltd* v *Emmett* [1936]. Here, the defendant deliberately fired guns on his own land near its boundary with the claimant's fox farm, knowing this would cause the foxes distress and probably stop them breeding. An injunction was granted to stop him doing this, even though the claimant's use of the land for the specific purpose of breeding foxes could be said to be abnormally sensitive. Had noise been made by the defendant *without* malice (if, for example, noise was a natural consequence of his use of land), it seems the claim would have failed.

 Pause for reflection

Does taking malice into account, where relevant, seem to make private nuisance at least in part based on *conduct*? If the defendant's motives are to be taken into account, can it truly be said that private nuisance is a consequence-based tort?

17.3.4 **Defences to nuisance**

There are a number of defences which can be raised against an action in private nuisance. First, it is important to note that the general defences of *volenti non fit injuria* and contributory negligence (discussed in Chapter 10) also apply to nuisance. Additionally, there are defences specific to nuisance claims (including public nuisance, discussed below). The most important of these are dealt with below,[31] before we go on to consider some things that are *not* valid defences.

17.3.4.1 Statutory authority

If the defendant's activities are authorised by statute or, more specifically, if a statute provides that the defendant must use their land in a particular way, which then inevitably causes a nuisance to a neighbouring land user, then the defendant will have a total defence to nuisance claims (*Manchester Corporation v Farnworth* [1930]). So, even though a nuisance may be established on the facts, the claimant will have no remedy. In a sense, this is the idea of separation of powers in action—courts cannot challenge or undermine what Parliament has determined the situation should/will be. Convention suggests that Parliament will have considered what is best for the area and its occupants, including the various conflicting uses of land. Statute may also authorise whether, when and how much compensation is to be paid to those affected by the defendant's activities.

Statutory authority, then, is exactly that. The defendant has the authority, created by statute, to use their land in a particular way, with particular consequences. This must be distinguished from planning permission, which we discussed when looking at the nature of the locality in private nuisance claims (p 500). Planning permission, as we have said, can change the character of an area so much that a claim in nuisance simply will not be made out (*Gillingham*), meaning that there is no need to look at potential defences. This does *not* mean that the defendant's actions have been authorised by Parliament.

The effect of statutory authority is clearly illustrated in *Allen v Gulf Oil Refining Ltd* [1981]. The expansion of the Gulf Oil company in an area of Wales was expressly authorised by statute (the Gulf Oil Refinement Act 1965). The statute stipulated that an oil refinery should be built but was silent on the way the refinery should operate

---

31. Though it should be noted that other defences exist, such as 'inevitable accident', 'act of God', or an (unforeseeable) act of a stranger.

once in use. In a test case, local residents claimed in nuisance, alleging that noise and vibrations emanating from the refinery caused them unreasonable levels of disturbance and asking that its operations cease. The House of Lords thought the issue came down to statutory interpretation and considered whether the nuisance complained of was impliedly or expressly authorised by the statute. However, in so doing, it placed the burden of establishing this on the defendant, meaning that the test for the defence is a high one. A bare majority held that the operation of the refinery was implicitly authorised by the relevant statute, meaning that the nuisance caused by its operation was inevitable and therefore raising a full defence to the claim.

 Pause for reflection

It is interesting to note that the claimants in *Allen* would potentially have had a successful claim in negligence, had the nuisance created exceeded that which was authorised by the statute. That said, in order to be able to sue in negligence, each claimant would have needed to establish a tangible harm on which to found their claim. What do you think the 'harm' was here and could a claim in negligence be based on this?

While statutory authority remains an available defence to a claim in nuisance, it must now be considered alongside the HRA. Section 3(1) of the HRA requires legislation to be interpreted in a way that is compatible with people's fundamental rights under the ECHR. Clearly, in a nuisance claim, the most apparent of these rights is that from Article 8(1), which guarantees respect for one's private, home and family life. The inclusion of the word 'home' seems to suggest that nuisance-type claims suffered by 'ordinary' people may often have a human rights dimension to them. In the context of statutory authority, this means that courts will have to be careful in the way they interpret statutes giving a defence to a claim in nuisance, particularly when 'implying' an authorisation rather than it being expressly written. It should also be remembered that Article 8(2) allows derogation from the right where this satisfies a legitimate aim, is in accordance with the law and is *necessary* in a democratic society. While this does not necessarily provide an escape clause for the creators of nuisance under statute, the fact that Parliament (presumably operating for the good of democratic society) has authorised an activity suggests that individual claimants trying to rely on human rights arguments might face an uphill struggle.

Hatton v UK [2003] ECtHR

The claimant lived near Heathrow airport. In 1993, a new system for controlling night flights was introduced, relying on a 'noise quota' as opposed to a restriction on the number of flights that could come into or out of the airport. Hatton and other nearby residents claimed that the pattern of night flights from the airport was an unreasonable use of land in that there was too much noise, which caused lack of sleep and other symptoms, in violation of their right to respect for private, home and family life under Article 8(1). Although it was

➡

→

possible for the claimants to seek a judicial review of the operation of the night flights, they argued that they had not received (and could not receive) an effective remedy for this violation, in breach of Article 13.[32]

The lower chamber of the ECtHR agreed that there was a violation of Article 8(1) and that any derogation from this under Article 8(2) had to be proven, rather than assumed. Modest damages of around £4,000 were awarded.[33] However, on appeal by the UK government, the Grand Chamber overturned the finding on Article 8(1), based on the exceptions given in Article 8(2). In particular, the Grand Chamber noted that night flights would reasonably contribute to the economic wellbeing of the country and that affected residents could easily move from the area if they wished.[34] However, the finding on Article 13 was upheld, so the claimants received the compensation, because although the decision could be judicially reviewed, this could not provide the claimants with an effective remedy as the merits of the case could not be considered.

17.3.4.2 Twenty years' prescription

It is also a defence if an otherwise unreasonable user of land can show that they have been using their land in the way complained of for more than 20 years in which the claimant had been able to claim. Put simply, if you have put up with something for 20 years and then try to complain about it, you will not be able to. The clock starts ticking from the point at which the claimant becomes aware of the nuisance-causing activity.

Sturges v *Bridgman* [1879] CA

The defendant had operated as a confectioner for more than 20 years in premises that adjoined the garden of premises where a doctor had his practice. The confectioner used grinding equipment in the rear of his premises. The doctor built a consulting room in his garden and then found that noise and vibrations emanating from the confectioner's work interfered with his work. He sued the confectioner in nuisance asking for an injunction to prevent the grinding from continuing. The confectioner argued that this should not be granted on the grounds that (a) he had operated in the same way for such a long time and (b) the doctor, in building his consulting room where he did, had 'come to the nuisance'.

The doctor was granted the injunction even though the confectioner had operated in the same way from those premises for more than 20 years—and the doctor knew this and had

→

32. Under Civil Aviation Act 1982, s 76, private law claims in the domestic courts had not been possible.

33. Though it should be noted that the cost of compensating everyone similarly affected was estimated at approximately £2 billion.

34. Similar justifications had been used in a previous case relating to noise from Heathrow (generally, rather than specifically night flights) in *Powell and Rayner* v *UK* [1990]. In **Hatton**, a strong dissenting judgment thought this approach was too conservative, and argued that Convention rights should be interpreted in a way that would expand protection against environmental pollution.

> →
>
> made no prior complaints about it. The time ran only from the point that this began to be a nuisance, and this was after the consulting room had been built by the doctor. The court also viewed 'coming to the nuisance' as an ineffective defence, so this could not be relied upon by the confectioner.

This decision seems somewhat harsh. The doctor, knowing who his neighbour was, had built his consulting room right by the site of the activity that would—perhaps inevitably—become a nuisance to him. However, it has long been the case that 'coming to the nuisance' is not a defence, and the defence of 20 years' prescription did not apply in this case as, despite the fact that the claimant was seemingly aware of how his neighbour used his premises, he was able to argue that he became aware of the *nuisance* only once his surgery had been extended. Put another way, nuisance law protects people even if their actions (such as moving closer to a boundary fence) cause those of their neighbour to become a nuisance. This has increasingly become an issue as cities and towns expand, as residential areas are built ever closer to things such as tanneries, sewage works and factories that were once on the outskirts. Despite the fact that it might be argued that these people should have chosen better where they moved to, or researched the area more thoroughly, it is no defence for these industries to say they were there first.

A classic case in this respect is *Miller* v *Jackson* [1977]. The defendant cricket club had played cricket on its ground for more than 70 years when the land on one side of the ground was sold to developers who subsequently built a housing estate there. The claimants were the purchasers of one of the properties and claimed in nuisance alleging that cricket balls were frequently hit into their garden or house. The fence around the cricket ground had been raised when the houses were built in recognition of the fact that the club should do its best to retain any stray balls. A majority of the Court of Appeal (Lord Denning MR dissenting) reluctantly found that the cricket club's activities constituted an actionable nuisance. **Sturges** was affirmed as good law—the fact that the claimants had 'come to the nuisance' could not be used as a defence against them. What this means is that a claimant will always have the right to sue, even if it could be said that they are in some way to 'blame' for the fact that they have become so affected (for example, by moving to the nuisance). In so deciding, the majority of the Court of Appeal (Lord Denning MR dissenting) prioritised the personal right of claimants freely to enjoy their land, even where this may have negative effects on established enterprises or community interests. However, if an injunction was awarded, it would effectively enable people who had chosen to move into the houses overlooking the cricket ground to stop it from being played. In *Miller*, a different majority (Lord Denning MR and Cumming-Bruce LJ) refused to award an injunction, awarding damages instead, on the ground that the community interests outweighed the personal interests of the claimant.

 Counterpoint

The decision in *Miller*, particularly Lord Denning's judgment, warrants closer scrutiny, as it further illustrates the subjective nature of the tort of nuisance. While a textbook account of

→

private nuisance deals with concepts and tests which seem to exist in and of themselves and take on some kind of rational form, Lord Denning's judgment shows that, actually, a particular legal outcome is preferred which subsumes nuisance almost entirely within personal judicial preferences. Indeed, arguably the only significant constraint on the judges is the linguistic one that they must justify their decisions using the language of these concepts, tests and standards, rather than by reference to the subjective preferences that in fact underlie them. It is judges, for example, who decide what kind of inconvenience a claimant should have to tolerate. They do this by reference to what is required of the ordinary reasonable person (taking into account what they feel their expectations ought to be as a resident of the area in which they live—for example, Bermondsey or Belgrave Square). This, particularly when allied alongside the locality rule, has, and still does, operate as an excellent vehicle for judicial prejudices while at the same time disguising the essentially class-based nature of the exercise being carried out. The whole balancing exercise undertaken in the test of 'reasonableness' is a means by which judges can offer their intuitive sense of the justice of the case as a legal solution. Our fascination with learning the 'rules', principles and concepts has arguably, therefore, distracted us from what is really going on.

Conaghan & Mansell argue that textbook emphasis on the minority status of Lord Denning's judgment in *Miller* downplays its subversive aspects (p 138). After all, if he failed to persuade the rest of the Court of Appeal, why should we look at his judgment? The important point is that Denning 'felt free to deny liability', to fail to find an actionable nuisance, taking into account the nature of the locality and the value of the defendant's activity. As *Conaghan & Mansell* point out, however, 'at the same time, to impose liability as the majority held, emphasising the degree of inconvenience experienced by the plaintiffs in the enjoyment of their property (including the threat of physical danger) was also neither inappropriate nor incorrect. *Either outcome* could be considered consistent with legal doctrine. The difference between the majority and minority on the question of liability is explicable largely in terms of the weight attributable to the social value of cricket' (at p 138, emphasis added).

They continue:

For Lord Denning cricket is a game, which in the summertime 'is the delight of everyone'. It is a game where 'the young men play and the old men watch', a game which, in this instance, has gone on for 70 years on a green which until recently was adjoined by 'a field where cattle grazed'. This field has now become a housing estate occupied by, among others, the plaintiff, 'a newcomer who is no lover of cricket'. Lord Denning views the closure of the cricket club as a potentially disastrous calamity. The cricket ground might be replaced by 'more houses or a factory. The young men will turn to other things instead of cricket. The whole village will be much the poorer. And all this because of a newcomer who has just bought a house there next to the cricket ground' (p 341). In this passage, Denning is appealing to a quaint and charming picture of English country life. He conjures up images of green fields, sleepy sunny afternoons, the quiet sounds of a cricket match on a summer's day. His head is populated with old men, young men and grazing cattle. His characters are white, male and English. Threatening this bucolic vision of English men at play is a newcomer, the sort of person

➡

who lives on a housing estate, who does not appreciate the finer points of cricket, who might even be female and who brings in her wake the threat of social degeneration as young men are forced to abandon cricket and go work in factories. (pp 138–9)

The images presented by Lord Denning are deliberate. Their purpose is to persuade the court that there was *no nuisance* (rather than merely refusing the injunction, as the majority held). However, in so doing, Lord Denning MR's description of rural England borders on overstatement. As William Twining notes:

Lord Denning missed an important trick as an advocate. By innuendo (or confabulation) he suggests a romantic picture of rural life in the South of England—a nostalgic evocation of village cricket in Hampshire between the Wars, almost straight out of *England Their England*. But Lintz was a depressed mining village in the North of England, where cricket is a serious matter. Would not a picture of an impoverished community dependent on an activity that seriously engaged young males be a much stronger argument for saying that this was a reasonable use of land?[35]

While it may be said that public benefit or the 'utility' of the defendant's activity was once a factor that had some bearing on whether that activity would be regarded as a nuisance, these days the utility value (for example the overall benefit to society) of the defendant's use of their land is generally not taken into consideration (or not explicitly) when asking whether their use of land is unreasonable. That said—except, perhaps, for Lord Denning—it was never a factor that carried heavy weight (see, for example, *Adams* v *Ursell* [1913]). However, it does seem that utility value is still considered by courts when determining what *remedy* should be awarded to the claimant (see below). Claimants who ask for a cessation of the activity that is causing a nuisance to them are likely to want an injunction. As this is an equitable remedy the court has considerable discretion in deciding *whether* an injunction should be granted and, if so, to what *extent* the defendant's activities should be prevented. Where the defendant's activity has high social utility, an injunction is less likely to be awarded as the court will deem it appropriate that the activity should continue (see **Dennis v Ministry of Defence** [2003]).

17.4 Remedies and the human rights dimension

Although it makes sense for us to look at remedies for private nuisance here, it is important to note that the remedies we will detail can also be sought in relation to a claim in public nuisance and under the rule in **Rylands v Fletcher** (considered in Chapter 18).

There are two main remedies in nuisance: injunctions (which seek to prevent or stop a nuisance) and damages (compensation). In basic terms, the primary remedy for nuisance is an injunction. As we shall see, it is also possible for a claimant to recover under the HRA.

---

35. William Twining *Rethinking Evidence* (CUP, 2006), pp 303–5.

17.4.1 **Injunctions and abatement**

When a claimant seeks an injunction they are asking the court to prevent the part of the defendant's activity that amounts to a nuisance, rather than to prevent the activity from continuing in its entirety (though sometimes the two may be indistinct). As an injunction is an equitable remedy it is therefore discretionary. This means that a court can decide to award an injunction in whole or in part (for example, injunctive relief might be temporary or partial—that is, it may operate for a specific period of time or may restrict particular activities at certain times of the day). As seen in *Miller*, the courts are generally willing to award an injunction unless there are specific reasons that indicate damages should be viewed as being more suitable (*Shelfer* v *City of London Electric Lighting Co* [1894]; *Regan* v *Paul Properties Ltd* [2006]).[36]

In *Shelfer*, a pub landlord complained that vibrations and noise caused by the defendant were a nuisance and was granted an injunction, even though doing so would inevitably deprive many people in the London area of electricity. In this case, Smith LJ laid down four conditions that a court must take into account when deciding whether to grant damages *in lieu* (in the place of) of an injunction:

(1) The injury to the claimant's legal rights is small,

(2) And is one which is capable of being estimated in money,

(3) And is one which can be adequately compensated by a small money payment,

(4) And the case is one in which it would be oppressive to the defendant to grant an injunction (at 322–3).

Whilst this does not suggest that damages can never be awarded, the implication of the decision is that damages will (or should) be a 'rare' outcome. If a defendant has already been judged to be an unreasonable user of land, it hardly seems appropriate that the harm suffered by the claimant would be characterised as 'small' and 'adequately compensated' by money. It is the nature of the harm itself—particularly when a claim is made in respect of the amenity interest—that makes injunctions more appropriate. In *Shelfer*, the court was concerned to prevent defendants (who would often have more legal presence and strength than those who claimed against them) from 'buying the right' to commit a nuisance by paying damages to those affected.

As we have discussed above, the appropriateness of an injunction was examined by the Court of Appeal in *Miller* where the majority held that an injunction should not be granted, even though the activity of the cricket club was a nuisance. The decision to award damages *in lieu* was in part justified on the basis that village cricket was an activity that held much 'public interest'. This issue was raised again in **Kennaway v Thompson** [1981].

> ### *Kennaway v Thompson* [1981] CA
>
> The claimant complained that the noise caused by power boat racing in a lake close to her home was a nuisance. The defendants contended that she had chosen to build her
>
> ➡

---

36. See also Supreme Court Act 1981, s 50.

➡

house near the lake in the knowledge that some racing took place, thus she should not be entitled to an injunction.

In the Court of Appeal, Lawton LJ was critical of the judgment in *Miller* and found that the relevant authority was that found in *Shelfer* in light of which the claimant should be awarded an injunction *despite* the fact she may have been aware of the power boat racing or any public interest that might be involved in allowing the activity to continue. However, the court exercised its discretion and awarded only a partial injunction, requiring the racing organisers to adhere to a planned timetable of events.

Essentially, the partial injunction awarded in **Kennaway** was used to create a compromise between neighbouring users of land. As we highlighted earlier in this chapter, being reasonable neighbours requires some give and take—in such a situation the claimant might be expected to have to put up with *some* noise; the Court of Appeal was simply establishing how much was reasonable.[37]

Notwithstanding Smith LJ's guiding principles in *Shelfer*, and Lawton LJ's approval of these in **Kennaway**, what governs the award of an injunction (or, more specifically, whether damages will be awarded *in lieu*) remains open to question. More recent case law—as well as the enactment of the HRA—seems to indicate that a different approach to remedies may be required if the activity complained of is carried out by a public authority in the public interest. In such cases, even when an activity amounts to a nuisance, it may be felt that the public interest in the continuation of the activity outweighs the claimant's right to an injunction and that damages might be the more appropriate remedy.[38] This idea is explored further, below.

Abatement is a 'self-help' remedy. It involves the claimant taking it upon themselves to do something to stop the nuisance continuing. Clearly, this is a risky strategy as, by taking action in this way, one might become a trespasser. As such, it has limited application to most nuisances, though might apply in situations where the problem complained of is one of encroachment. That is where, for example, tree roots or branches from one property grow so that they encroach (intrude) into a neighbouring property. Often in such cases, instead of issuing nuisance proceedings, a potential claimant may avail themselves legitimately of the remedy, as long as they do no more than is necessary to abate the nuisance.[39]

17.4.2 **Damages**

Aside from where damages are awarded in lieu of an injunction, there are other nuisance claims where damages (perhaps *as well as* an injunction) may be considered appropriate. With the exception of trespass to land, the land torts become actionable

---

37. A similar exercise was undertaken in *Watson* v *Croft Promosport Ltd* [2009].

38. As in **Hatton v UK**, above.

39. Most recently confirmed in *Delaware Mansions Ltd* v *Westminster City Council* [2001]. In the scenarios outlined at the beginning of the chapter, Christine may have been able to trim back her neighbour's branches, as long as she did so reasonably. This may have removed her perceived need for retaliation.

only with proof of harm. The award of damages in each case is subject to the foresee-ability test set out in *The Wagon Mound (No 2)*, namely that the liability can arise only for damage of a type that can be reasonably foreseen (for example, personal injury, property damage and so on). As these are *land* torts, however, the question of if and when damages for *personal injury* should be awarded is a difficult and contentious one. Put simply, if the harm has to be categorised as a harm to the land (or an interest in it), then how can personal injury fall into that category?

In public nuisance, as we shall see, it is possible to make a claim for personal injury. However, in private nuisance (and under the rule in *Rylands v Fletcher*), it is techni-cally not possible to claim damages for personal injury: these are torts which protect the claimant's interest in land only. Because of this, damages for private nuisance are awarded only where the value of the land concerned (in sale or rent) has decreased, or for the affect a nuisance has on the claimant's use and enjoyment of the land (their 'amenity' interest). This was confirmed by the House of Lords in relation to private nuisance in *Hunter v Canary Wharf*.[40] One effect of damages being awarded for the injury to the land not the person is, therefore, that the sum awarded will not increase even if many people are affected on the same piece of land (*Hunter*).

However, 'personal injury' (for which the appropriate claim would be in negligence), is not the same thing as 'personal discomfort'. This is more properly thought of as *part of* a diminished enjoyment of the land in question (lost amenity), and damages for this *are* recoverable. In *Bone v Seale* [1975], for example, the claimant recovered damages for the personal discomfort they suffered as a result of the unpleasant smell emanat-ing from a neighbouring pig farm. While the monetary value of the claimant's land could not be shown to have decreased, the damages awarded reflected the claimant's lost enjoyment of the land that was being affected by the smell (this has to be the case, otherwise smell could never be a nuisance).

 Pause for reflection

Do you find this argument convincing? In claims of this type the law says that it is the *land* that suffers (because there are smells that come over it), not the *claimant* (who complains about the smell).[41] If it was truly the land that suffers, then it must follow that *all* neighbours would be equally affected. However, as people have different sensitivity to smells, not all would consider the same smell to be a nuisance—how can it be the land that is affected? Would the argument carry more or less weight if the people complaining were actually made physically sick by the smells? Would it be better simply to acknowledge that per-sonal injury *is* recoverable in nuisance?

Because of the nature of the harm (to land), economic losses such as lost profits can be recovered only where they are a consequence of the claimant's inability to use their land to make those profits. Put another way, economic loss consequential upon

---

40. Similarly, in *Transco v Stockport MBC* [2004], the House of Lords confirmed that this was the position in relation to claims under *Rylands v Fletcher*.

41. See Paula Giliker and Silas Beckwith *Tort* (3rd edn, Sweet & Maxwell, 2008), p 340.

damage to a proprietary interest may be recoverable, but 'pure' economic loss is not. For example, in *Andreae* v *Selfridge & Co Ltd* [1938] a hotel owner was able to receive damages for lost profits when her hotel suffered a drop in custom while the defendants carried out construction work nearby. It is far easier to claim for damage to property. Damages for this type of harm are readily recoverable and their quantification is straightforwardly assessed according to normal principles. In *Halsey* v *Esso Petroleum Co Ltd* [1961], damages were awarded for damage to clothes hung on a washing line in the claimant's garden.

 Pause for reflection

Does the fact that a claimant could recover damages for something as 'unimportant' as laundry seem surprising to you? Damage to any kind of property owned by the claimant is compensable—in practical terms this means that while a claimant would be unable to recover for their own broken leg, they would be able to recover damages for the broken leg of any animal on the land owned by them![42] Can this be a correct distinction?

That said, it seems that damage to property must be allowed, even though damages for personal injury remain unavailable. What would happen, Paula Giliker and Silas Beckwith ask, if a farmer complained that poisonous fumes which emanated from the defendant's factory subsequently ruined not only his crops but also caused some of his cattle to die? If he could recover only for damage to his land then the farmer would be awarded only damages for his crops (which would be treated as part of the land in question). Yet both of these are simply alternative means of farming one's land—so there would seem to be no reason why the law should protect one and not the other.[43]

17.4.3 **Under the Human Rights Act 1998**

There have been tensions within the ECtHR about human rights claims based on environmental issues that result in nuisance. The ECtHR has held that forms of environmental pollution nuisances may fall within the scope of the right to respect for the home and private life provided for in Article 8(1).[44] For example, in *Powell and Rayner* v *UK* [1990], a case about noise from Heathrow airport, the ECtHR held that the rights of Mr Rayner, who owned land just over a mile away from a major runway, were clearly at stake because of the noise levels (although it ultimately found that running the airport was a modern economic necessity which justified the violation under Art 8(2)).[45] In comparison, in *López Ostra* v *Spain* [1995], the claimant's Article 8 rights *were* found to have been violated by exceptionally severe pollution coming from a factory 12 metres

---

42. Newark, above, p 490.
43. *Tort* (3rd edn, Sweet & Maxwell, 2008), p 341.
44. The other main applicable right is Art 1 Protocol 1, the right to peaceful enjoyment of possessions.
45. As was the case in **Hatton v UK**, discussed above. See also *Khatun v UK* [1998].

away from her home. This was the first time that what might be termed an 'environ-mental' case had succeeded.[46]

Marcic v *Thames Water Utilities plc* [2003] HL

Mr Marcic sued in private nuisance and for a violation of his Article 8 rights following fre-quent sewage floods at his home. The sewage flooded his garden and lapped at his back step but never flooded his house. Thames, the sewerage undertaker, prioritised renova-tion work to combat internal flooding. The cause of the flooding was the overloading of the sewer network which, although originally adequate, by then had too many properties connected to it (under statute, new properties are given a right to discharge into the exist-ing sewerage network). Marcic asked for damages and a mandatory injunction compelling Thames to make improvements.

The Court of Appeal relied on the ECtHR decisions in *Powell and Rayner* and *S* v *France* [1990]—a case about interference with property from a nearby nuclear plant—finding that if a 'fair balance' was to be struck between claimants whose rights have been breached and the public interest, then even though states have a margin of appreciation, they must still compensate those whose rights are necessarily breached. In *S* v *France* the Commission said that: 'when a state is authorised to restrict rights or freedoms guaranteed by the Convention, the proportionality rule may well require it to ensure that these restric-tions do not oblige the person concerned to bear an unreasonable burden' (p 263). Thus, the Court of Appeal found in favour of Mr Marcic and awarded him compensation.[47]

However, the House of Lords rejected the nuisance action, holding that Thames had not acted unreasonably. The law lords stressed the particular position that Thames was in; that is, it was a company which funded improvements to, *inter alia*, the sewerage network under a formula derived from legislation (Water Industry Act 1991) and operated by the economic regulator for the water industry (Ofwat). This was the downfall for the human rights claim, because the law lords considered that Parliament had already provided a statutory remedy (enforcement orders), which Ofwat can serve on sewerage companies where it is felt that they should do more to protect the interests of their customers from things such as sewage flooding. So, the issue was whether this *statutory scheme* violated Mr Marcic's human rights: the law lords held that it struck the right balance between the different interests involved (for example, the interests of those affected by flooding and all customers who ultimately pay for systematic improvements through their bills). Lord Nicholls found that 'the malfunctioning of the statutory scheme on this occasion does not cast doubt on its overall fairness as a scheme' (at [53]). Essentially, Marcic lost because he had not asked Ofwat to make an enforcement order and instead took a private law action in the courts. That is, he had not established that there was the type of 'domestic irregularity' that seems to be required post-*Hatton*. Had Marcic's claim succeeded, it was estimated that the cost to Thames alone would have been in the region of £1 billion.

---

46. Though it can be noted that part of the reason for her success was that there had been 'domestic irregularity' in the sense that Mrs López Ostra had clearly been let down by a culpable failure on the part of the Spanish regulatory authorities. Thus, it seems that in comparable cases, such 'domestic irregularity' will need to be shown in order for there to be a successful claim.

47. Note that **Dennis** was decided after the Court of Appeal decision in **Marcic** but before the House of Lords' decision.

Pause for reflection

Lord Nicholls went on to say (echoing the Court of Appeal judgment) that 'the minority who suffer damage and disturbance as a consequence of the inadequacy of the sewerage system ought not to be required to bear an unreasonable burden' (at [45]), but did not expand on this. Lord Hope addressed this point, finding that by compensating those whose properties are flooded internally, offering a free clean-up service in the case of external flooding and bearing in mind Thames' obligation to allow domestic connections and the funding formula, a fair balance was struck.

Do you think the decision in *Marcic* protects sewerage companies at the expense of customers? Because a scheme for making enforcement orders under the Water Industry Act 1991 exists, water and sewerage companies—who often operate at considerable profit—will rarely have to compensate those who, like Mr Marcic, suffer because of their inaction. A second issue here is the extent to which public law controls are actually used by public regulators, for example the enforcement orders so relied on by the House of Lords in *Marcic*, had at the time *never been used* by Ofwat. Is a 'fair balance' between the competing interests really being struck here?

In *Dobson* v *Thames Water Utilities Ltd* [2008] the claimants were a large number of residents, some occupying properties as owners or lessees and some with no legal interest in the properties, who lived near a sewage treatment works operated by Thames. They complained that odours and mosquitoes from the sewage works caused a nuisance as a result of negligence by Thames. The case was therefore distinguishable from *Marcic* and Thames should be liable for damages for nuisance, negligence and under the HRA (based upon alleged breaches of Art 8 and Art 1 of Protocol 1 to the ECHR). Thames argued that complaints about odour or mosquitoes from the sewage works were complaints about a failure of its duty to 'effectually deal' with the contents of sewers at the sewage works under section 94 of the Water Industry Act 1991 and/or a failure properly to treat waste water received and discharged by the sewage works in accordance with the Urban Waste Water Treatment (England and Wales) Regulations 1994. Thames contended that, as such failures were enforceable under section 18 of the 1991 Act by Ofwat, following *Marcic*, no common law remedy or remedy under the HRA arose to enforce those duties toward an individual claimant. Ruling on preliminary issues in the High Court, Ramsey J agreed that the principle in *Marcic* would preclude the claimants from bringing a claim in nuisance, absent any negligence. However, where the allegation related to a nuisance *caused by* negligence, a claim would lie.[48] He said:

> Whilst the principle in *Marcic* precludes the claimants from bringing claims which require the court to embark on a process which is inconsistent and conflicts with the statutory process under the [1991 Act], it does not preclude the claimants from bringing a claim in

48. It is notable that Ofwat intervened in *Dobson,* submitting that it was reasonable to assume that their lordships in *Marcic* intended to preserve scope for claims to be brought arising out of allegations of negligence in the physical operation of sewers or sewerage treatment works. In *Marcic* Thames was not accused of having failed to operate its sewerage system properly. Ofwat also submitted that such allegations are unlikely to raise the issues of regulatory balancing and infrastructure investment which were the focus of the decision in *Marcic* (at [103]–[112]).

nuisance involving allegations of negligence where, as a matter of fact and degree, the exercise of adjudicating on that cause of action is not inconsistent and does not involve conflicts with the statutory process. (at [148])

Similarly, a claim under the HRA would be allowed to proceed. An appeal from *Dobson* questioned not the finding of 'negligent nuisance', but the appropriateness of the remedies available.[49] Two issues were considered in particular. The first was whether the child claimants in *Dobson* had received 'just satisfaction'.[50] Ramsey J had concluded that they had, in the damages that were awarded to their parents for the private nuisance to the *household* (at [209]). The Court of Appeal refused to say so as bluntly, instead preferring to be directed by comments from **Hunter** to the effect that the impact on all occupiers of the land in question may have been taken into account when assessing damages in nuisance. According to Waller LJ, the essential question was:

> whether it is *necessary* to award *damages* to another member of the household or whether the remedy of a declaration that Article 8 rights have been infringed suffices, alongside the award to the landowner, especially where no pecuniary loss has been suffered. (at [45], original emphasis)

This was an issue that would have to be readdressed by the judge at trial and accordingly the decision of Ramsey J was reversed on this point (at [46]).

The second issue on remedies was similar, questioning whether those (with proprietary interest in their homes) who *had* received damages for nuisance could claim *additional* damages under the HRA (i.e. for their own personal damages rather than damages to the 'land'). Unsurprisingly, given their comments above, the Court of Appeal found that this would be 'highly improbable, if not inconceivable' (at [50] and [52]).

The HRA does not provide for a new tort of 'breach of the Convention' which one individual can rely on against another. But, as we have seen, when deciding cases involving any human rights element, courts must consider whether a claimant receives 'just satisfaction' if their human rights have been violated. If domestic law does not provide a sufficient remedy then additional remedies may have to be given for such violations. There is no reason, however, why these must be remedies in tort law.

Further, despite what we have said in relation to **Miller**, above, the role played by the social or public interest in an activity has become part of the consideration of the appropriate remedies for a proven nuisance.[51] This overlaps with the impact of the HRA, as can be seen in **Dennis v Ministry of Defence [2003]**.

Dennis v Ministry of Defence [2003] HC

Dennis was the owner of Walton Hall, a property with a considerable estate near Stamford in Cambridgeshire, situated about two miles from RAF Wittering, a site owned by the Ministry

→

---

49. *Dobson* v *Thames Water Utilities Ltd* [2009].
50. HRA, s 8(3).
51. This was explicitly argued by the claimants in *Watson v Croft Promosport Ltd* [2009], though the Court of Appeal found that only in 'a marginal case where the damage to the claimant is minimal...consistent with the principles of *Shelfer*, the effect on the public of the grant of an injunction is properly to be taken into account' (Richards LJ at [51]).

→

of Defence (MOD) and used as an operational and training base for Harrier jump jets. The frequent noise (there were, on average, seventy occurrences each day) from the planes, which were often flown at low altitude, caused Dennis and his family disturbance. They argued that this caused diminution in the capital value of the property and that they had been unable to develop the commercial potential of the Hall, consequently losing profit. Dennis sought an injunction and damages or damages *in lieu* amounting to £10,000,000.

The MOD accepted that flying the aircraft caused noise and disturbance to the claimant but did not accept it was an actionable nuisance. It countered the claim with a number of arguments, including that the use of RAF Wittering for training pilots was an 'ordinary use' of land in the modern era and that the training exercises were undertaken for the public benefit. Furthermore, because Dennis had purchased Walton Hall after RAF Wittering was established, the claimants had 'come to the nuisance'. Similarly, the MOD argued that it had gained a prescriptive right to use the land for training Harrier pilots; and that the claimant's land was not capable of generating the commercial profit they had estimated.

The court refused to award an injunction and instead awarded Dennis damages of £950,000. This sum was meant to represent any loss of capital value, and reflect past and future loss of use and amenity in the land. Buckley J held that (1) the noise from the Harrier jets was highly intrusive, frightening, persistent and unpredictable and accordingly constituted a very serious interference with the claimant's enjoyment of their land; (2) the training of Harrier pilots could not be regarded as an 'ordinary use' of land even where the use was justifiable on other grounds. The level of noise and disturbance had increased considerably since the introduction of Harriers in 1969. The use was now so extreme that it could not be regarded as a feature of the area. In any event, even if such a use were to be considered 'ordinary', it had to be conducted in a manner which did not appear to maximise the disturbance to the claimant (whether such conduct was deliberate or not); (3) a public benefit might excuse an otherwise actionable nuisance provided no more damage was done than was reasonably necessary (following *Marcic*). A defence based upon public benefit should not, however, be allowed to succeed where a claim based upon the breach of human rights (in this case Art 8(1) ECHR) would succeed.

In essence, it can be seen that Buckley J tried to reach his decision by balancing the orthodox elements of nuisance with a rights-based approach. The 'public benefit' of training Harrier pilots was not considered when determining whether the training was a nuisance, but became relevant in determining the appropriate remedy. When public benefit was factored in, Buckley J awarded the claimant damages *in lieu* of an injunction. The effect of this is that the noise from the flights, which the court had *agreed* was a nuisance, was allowed to continue. The award of damages in ***Dennis*** goes far beyond any previous relaxation of the *Shelfer* requirements. In effect, it allowed the RAF to 'buy' the right to continue the nuisance, exactly the position that the court in *Shelfer* said should be avoided. So, while 'public benefit' (as defined by the court) cannot prevent something being a nuisance, it can have a significant impact on the remedy awarded, even where human rights are affected.[52]

52. In ***Dennis***, Buckley J held that because the award of loss of amenity was based on loss of enjoyment of the estate which envisaged enjoyment by a family as opposed to one individual, it

One further point to note regarding potential human rights claims in relation to nuisance actions is that Article 14 ECHR provides that other Convention rights must be enjoyed without discrimination. This might be thought to have the potential to affect the refusal of claims based on standing after *Hunter* (that is, who has standing to sue and who does not). However, in *Khatun* v *UK* [1998], the European Commission on Human Rights found no violation of Article 14 because everyone in the locality was treated in the same way, meaning there was no discrimination. Put another way, the rich and poor of the London Docklands area were treated alike. That said, Article 14 may affect the locality rule, as judging the reasonableness of a polluting activity (alleged nuisance) differently according to whether it interferes with a 'run down' or 'high class' location may well be discriminatory.[53]

17.5 **Public nuisance**

Public nuisance is primarily a crime, which in some circumstances, where the harm is suffered by a section of the community or the community as a whole, can also lead to a civil action, including where the harm is personal injury.[54] Although the courts frequently draw comparisons between private and public nuisance they are in reality very different and each seeks to protect very different interests;[55] we therefore do not spend much time discussing public nuisance here. Public nuisance is distinct from private nuisance in that its object is the recognition and protection of publicly held rights and not the protection of property rights. In this sense, claimants do not necessarily claim in respect of some harm done to their interest in land, but in respect of community-based activities. Essentially, whilst private nuisance seeks to protect private rights in land, public nuisance acts as a general measure of public protection.

An individual can bring an action in public nuisance only where s/he has suffered particular harm arising from a nuisance that has materially affected the reasonable comfort and convenience of life of a sufficiently large number of citizens. This is because the essential characteristic of public nuisance is the infringement of a *public* right, an interference with the interest of a community rather than an individual:

> [A]ny nuisance is 'public' which materially affects the reasonable comfort and conven-
> ience of life of a class of Her Majesty's subjects. The sphere of the nuisance may be

was not appropriate to award further sums to Mrs Dennis based on a violation of *her* human rights. In *Dobson*, Ramsey J said that this was 'a finding which depended on the facts and was not a finding that, as a matter of law, an award of damages in nuisance would provide just satisfaction to all those in the same household' (at [206]). Note how this contrasts with his opinion on child claimants, outlined above at p 520.

53. That said, the justification tests still have to be applied, as does the judicially constructed test of 'domestic irregularity', and the circumstances where amenity damage will be so excessive as to be a human rights violation will undoubtedly be rare.

54. In *Corby Group Litigation Claimants* v *Corby Borough Council* [2008] the Court of Appeal confirmed that *obiter* comments in *Hunter* and *Transco* had not impliedly reversed this principle and that the essence of the right protected by the tort of public nuisance is the right not to be adversely affected by an unlawful act or omission whose effect is to endanger the life or health of the public.

55. Recently reaffirmed by the Court of Appeal in *Corby Group Litigation* v *Corby District Council* [2009].

described generally as 'the neighbourhood'; but the question whether the local community within that sphere comprises a sufficient number of persons to constitute a class of the public is a question of fact in every case. It is not necessary...to prove that every member of the class has been injuriously affected; it is sufficient to show that a representative cross-section of the class has been so affected...(Romer LJ, *Attorney General v PYA Quarries Ltd* [1957] at 184)

In the same case, Denning LJ also refused to say how many people needed to be affected in order for a nuisance to be public. Instead, he described a public nuisance as being 'a nuisance which is so widespread in its range or so indiscriminate in its effect that it would not be reasonable to expect one person to take proceedings on his own responsibility to put a stop to it' (at 191).

A commonly used example of a public nuisance is an obstruction of the highway, but public nuisance is more than this. As *Conaghan & Mansell* point out, it has also 'been held to include quarry-blasting...an ill-organised pop festival, and engineering a hoax bomb scare' (pp 127–8, but see *R v Rimmington; R v Goldstein* [2005]). Most recently, in *Corby Group Litigation* v *Corby District Council* [2009], a local authority was liable in public nuisance for 'causing, allowing or permitting the dispersal of dangerous or noxious contaminants' from land reclamation sites, which had caused birth defects in many children in the area. The question as to what constitutes a 'class' of Her Majesty's subjects is a question of fact for the court. We know that it is not necessary to show that every member of that section of the community has been affected, as long as the nuisance can be shown to have affected a representative cross-section of that group of people.[56] That said, it is not enough for an individual who wants to claim to show merely that they are a member of the affected group—they must show that they have suffered 'special' or 'particular' damage in excess of that suffered by the public at large. This can include personal injury (unlike private nuisance), property damage and loss of custom, profit or business. In *Castle* v *St Augustine's Links* [1922], for example, a car driver on the road next to the defendant's golf course was struck by a golf ball hit from the thirteenth tee. Evidence showed that balls from the golf course frequently went over the highway and the court ruled that the positioning of the thirteenth tee amounted to a public nuisance. The class of persons affected were highway users and among them the claimant had suffered special damage. In *Tate & Lyle Industries Ltd* v *GLC* [1983], parts of the river bed of the Thames had silted up because of the erection of ferry terminals by the defendants. Large vessels were unable to access a jetty that had been built and the claimants incurred expense in carrying out their own dredging operations. Their claim in public nuisance was successful because the building of the ferry terminals had interfered with the public right of navigation enjoyed by all users of the river and special damage had been suffered by the claimant (the cost of the dredging). In *R v Rimmington; R v Goldstein* [2005], both cases concerning the sending of malicious items through the post, neither defendant was found guilty (these were criminal cases) of public nuisance. Rimmington sent 538 racially offensive items to people across the country. Goldstein had, as a joke, sent some salt through the post to a friend. When the envelope leaked in the sorting office, an anthrax scare ensued.

56. An example is *East Dorset District Council v Eaglebeam Ltd* [2006].

Neither incident, however, affected what their lordships thought to be a 'class' of Her Majesty's subjects in the required way, but only 'individuals' (Lord Rodger at [47]).

17.6 **Conclusion**

In this chapter we have started to look at the 'land torts'. These are distinct, in particular from negligence, in that they are supposedly based on establishing liability without fault. **Trespass to land** involves the direct and intentional act (it must be the act that is deliberate, not necessarily the trespass) of entering land upon which you have no permission (express or implied) to be. As a tort, it is actionable *per se*, in that no damage needs to have been caused—the (legal) harm is the trespass itself.

Private nuisance differs in that it governs the relationship only between neighbours, producing liability when one neighbour (in the literal sense) interferes with the rights of another to use and enjoy their land. As it is a tort to the land, not to the person who has rights over it, a proprietary interest in the land affected is required in order to be able to sue (**Hunter**). Essentially, the rules of nuisance require that there be a certain amount of give and take between neighbours—the tort is committed only when one becomes an 'unreasonable user' of land. What makes someone an unreasonable user of their land is the central question—it has to do with the nature of the locality or neighbourhood, and, in respect of the act complained of, its intensity, frequency or duration. A factor that may prevent a successful claim—even before defences are considered—is the 'sensitive' use of the claimant's land, though this now seems to be subsumed into the more familiar (from negligence) notion of foreseeability (**Network Rail**).

Public nuisance is different in its scope and application, not only because it is primarily a crime, but also because it seeks to recognise and protect publicly held rights rather than an individual's property rights. That said, many things that are public nuisances could also be a private nuisance if an individual's interest in land was affected.

What may impact most on nuisance law in the future is the development of rights-based claims, particularly with respect to Article 8(1) ECHR. Activities carried out in the 'public interest' (though potentially human rights violations) may, however, affect only the available remedy. Whereas an injunction would often seem more appropriate, as it stops the nuisance continuing (or limits it), damages may be awarded *in lieu* where the defendant can show that what is a nuisance to one person (or even many) has a broader benefit for society.

✽ End-of-chapter questions

After reading the chapter carefully, try answering the questions below. If you would like to know what we think visit the Online Resource Centre (www.oxfordtextbooks.co.uk/orc/horsey2e/).

1. What is the nature of the harm controlled by private nuisance?

2. In negligence, duty of care (and in some cases, the standard of care) is used as a means of restricting claims. Where are such limitations to be found in nuisance?

3. Do the land torts appropriately weigh the interests of the individual against those of wider society?

4. Do the land torts protect landowners' interests too much, or not enough?

5. How could the interests of the environment be protected using nuisance?

6. Consider the problem question at the start of this chapter—now having read about the topic what would be your advice to the claimants? If you need some pointers in thinking about how to answer this question, turn to the Appendix (p 589) where each problem is annotated with issues and cases to consider. Next, try to write your own answer and, finally, log on to our Online Resource Centre (www.oxfordtextbooks.co.uk/orc/horsey2e/) and check your ideas against our suggested outline answer.

✱ Further reading

The best place to start your reading is with Maria Lee's article as it shows not only how the tort of private nuisance is not based on constant and clearly definable principles but also on value judgements.

Campbell, David 'Of Coase and Corn: A (Sort of) Defence of Private Nuisance' (2000) 63 *Modern Law Review* 197

Lee, Maria 'What is Private Nuisance?' (2003) 119 *Law Quarterly Review* 298

Simpson, AW Brian, 'Victorian Judges and the Problem of Social Cost: Tipping v St Helen's Smelting Company (1895)' in *Leading Cases in the Common Law* (OUP, 1995), p 163

Wightman, John 'Nuisance—The Environmental Tort? *Hunter v Canary Wharf* in the House of Lords' (1998) 61(6) *Modern Law Review* 870

18

Actions under the rule of *Rylands* v *Fletcher*

Problem question

Read this problem question carefully, and keep it in mind while you are working through the chapter that follows. At the end of the chapter, you will be able to apply what you have learnt to the problem question and advise the relevant parties.

Grab-and-Buy supermarket owns land on which it has built a huge two-storey metal-framed car park for its customers. One day, after extremely stormy weather with strong winds and heavy rain, the top level of the car park buckles, some of the metal railing breaks free and falls onto the neighbouring premises, a petrol station owned by Low-Price-Pumps. The impact damages the pumps and injures one of Low-Price-Pumps' customers. Furthermore, water that had collected on the upper level of the car park due to an inadequate drainage system pours on to Low-Price-Pumps, flooding the forecourt of the petrol station, meaning that it has to close down for two days, causing £10,000 loss of profit.

Low-Price-Pumps spends £50,000 having the forecourt cleaned and making safe the pumps. Grab-and-Buy argues that damage to the pumps caused by high winds is something that Low-Price-Pumps could and should have insured against.

18.1 **Introduction**

Consider the following examples:

→ Townbury Council's outdoor swimming pool has to be shut down after an adjacent ornamental lake bursts its banks after heavy rainfall and lake water floods into the pool, making it unsafe.

→ Townbury's water supply is contaminated by a chemical which makes it unsafe to drink. The contamination is traced back to spillage of chemicals onto the floor of a factory belonging to Red Horse Paint Company. The chemicals concerned are no longer used in paint manufacture as they were banned by a European Directive in 1995.

→ A gas pipe owned by Racksco and supplying gas for domestic use is exposed after a tap is left on accidentally by an old lady living in a warden-assisted flat provided for her by Townbury Council. Over a period of time, water seeps from the premises to an embankment supporting the pipe, causing it to weaken and eventually crumble.

→ A large pile of wood and other materials is collected on land belonging to Townbury Fire Brigade, in preparation for its annual bonfire party on 5 November, to which all citizens of the town are invited. A group of youths is caught trying to set the pile of wood alight, and fire officers dampen the wood down until they are ready to light it themselves. However, wind transports some still smouldering pieces of wood to the neighbouring property, where they burn down a garden shed.

In the last chapter we considered the way in which trespass, private nuisance and, to a lesser extent, public nuisance protect a person's ability to exercise his/her rights to enjoy land without undue or unreasonable interference. In this chapter we will consider a particular cause of action, a variation on the nuisance theme—the rule from *Rylands* **v** *Fletcher* [1868]—which protects an occupier against interference due to an *isolated* escape from (as opposed to an *ongoing interference with*) neighbouring land. This action has been shaped over time by three key cases: *Rylands* **v** *Fletcher* from the 1860s, *Cambridge Water Co* **v** *Eastern Counties Leather plc* [1994] and *Transco* **v** *Stockport MBC* [2004].

The *Rylands* rule is therefore another legal method for regulating the use of land. It emerged out of the widespread impact on society from the Industrial Revolution, beginning in the eighteenth century, with the country becoming a changed place by the mid-nineteenth century—far less agricultural and much more industrial. With industry came increased risk of harm from things such as water, noxious chemicals and so on 'escaping' from factories, reservoirs and the like. *Rylands* was a direct legal response to some of these risks. It created so-called 'strict liability' for such escapes—that is, liability without fault.[1] This means that owners of factories, reservoirs and so on would be liable even if they had taken all reasonable care to ensure that an escape did not occur. As in

---

1. Readers will have previously encountered the idea of strict liability in relation to product liability in Chapter 13.

the previous chapter, in this chapter we will also look at the contribution the **Rylands** rule makes, or could make, to the protection of the environment—given its very nature it perhaps has a clearer role to play in this respect than nuisance. However, we will see not only that the rule has limited use in the modern day, but also that the strictness of liability under it appears to have become somewhat diluted over time.

18.2 **The rule in *Rylands* v *Fletcher***

The rule in **Rylands v Fletcher** holds that where there has been an escape of a dangerous thing in the course of a non-natural use of land, the occupier of that land is liable for the damage to another caused as a result of the escape, irrespective of whether they were at fault. However, a strict liability rule seems somewhat incongruous against the increasing incidence of fault-based considerations in modern nuisance cases.[2] That said, liability under the rule, while strict, is not absolute. There are defences to the action and, more recently, the courts have decided that the defendant is to be held liable only for the foreseeable consequences of escapes. In fact, until relatively recently, the rule was largely considered to be of little real significance and more a piece of interesting legal history—as we shall see, the action has been rarely used. Though the decision over 100 years later in **Cambridge Water Co v Eastern Counties Leather plc [1994]** reawakened interest (particularly academic), any enthusiastic revival of the rule might seem overly ambitious given that the **Cambridge Water** decision actually appears to further *limit* the scope of actions under **Rylands** and arguably, therefore, its usefulness. In **Transco v Stockport MBC [2004]**, Lord Hoffmann remarked that 'it is perhaps not surprising that counsel could not find a reported case since the Second World War in which anyone had succeeded in a claim under the rule' (at [39]). As we will see, this seems unlikely to change following **Transco**.

Rylands v Fletcher [1868] HL

The defendant was a mill owner who employed independent contractors to build a reservoir on his land to provide water for his mill. While constructing the reservoir, the contractors discovered some disused shafts from an old coal mine on the defendant's land, which they assumed had been blocked up. However, when the reservoir was filled, the water in it burst through the old shafts and flooded the claimant's operating mine. The claimant sought compensation from the mill owner for the damage caused.

While the independent contractors had clearly been negligent in failing to ensure that the mineshafts were properly blocked up, the claimant's action was against his neighbour (not the contractors), but he had not (and could not reasonably have) known of the existence of the shafts on his land and so could not be shown to be negligent (nor was he vicariously liable for the contractors' negligence). The court also doubted whether an isolated escape of something from one land to another (as opposed to an ongoing emanation) could found an action in nuisance. Nevertheless, the claim succeeded.

➞

---

2. See e.g. **Network Rail Infrastructure Ltd v Morris (t/a Soundstar Studio) [2004]**.

→

Although the case went right to the House of Lords, it was Blackburn J in the Court of Exchequer Chamber (*Fletcher* v *Rylands and another* [1866]) who has long been considered to have given the classic statement of principle, finding that:

the true rule of law is that the person who for his own purposes brings on his land and collects and keeps there anything likely to do mischief if it escapes, must keep it in at his peril, and, if he does not do so, is *prima facie* answerable for all the damage which is the natural consequence of its escape.

The House of Lords approved this principle (at 339–40), though Lord Cairns added the stipulation that the defendant must also be engaged in a 'non-natural' use of land (at 338).

In **Rylands,** the defendant was held strictly liable for all the damage caused by the escape of the water from the reservoir, even though he was not in any way to blame for the escape.[3] While this may not, at first glance, seem very 'fair', like many cases it is a product of its time. It was decided in a climate of rising social and political concern about the dangers of reservoirs and other processes of industrialisation at a time when another serious reservoir incident had recently occurred.[4] This may have persuaded the courts that strict liability in such circumstances was necessary in order to ensure 'social justice' in the sense of protecting people against the ravages of industrialisation.[5]

There are four requirements that must be established for the claimant to successfully sue under the rule. The first three come from **Rylands** itself; the first two being derived from Blackburn J's often-quoted statement in the Court of Exchequer and the third added by Lord Cairns in the House of Lords. The fourth requirement was not added until much later and comes from the leading opinion of Lord Goff in **Cambridge Water.**

(1) The defendant brings on his land for his own purposes something likely to do mischief...

(2) ...if it escapes...

(3) ...which represents a non-natural use of land...

(4) and which causes foreseeable damage of the relevant type.

We will look at each of the requirements in turn.

3. So, would the owner of the ornamental lake in the first scenario at the beginning of this chapter be liable to Townbury Council? The question will always be whether the requirements of a claim under **Rylands v Fletcher** have been met—have they?

4. With severe loss of life. See AW Brian Simpson 'Legal Liability for Bursting Reservoirs: The Historical Context of **Rylands v Fletcher'** (1984) 13 *Legal Studies* 209 at 219.

5. Though it is interesting to note that the reservoir bursting in **Rylands** was essentially an accident, albeit large-scale, which led to property damage only, yet convinced the courts to act to create a rule of strict liability. This stands in stark comparison to other 'large-scale' accidents and personal tragedies we have seen in the law of tort (e.g. the Hillsborough Stadium disaster, see further Chapter 5, pp 105–107), following which the courts have sought to *restrict* liability.

18.2.1 'The defendant brings on his land for his own purposes something likely to do mischief...'

This requires a voluntary act of bringing something on the land, and is perhaps the natural result of concern about industrial practices. Blackburn J justified his rule by explaining that it could deal with the effect of industry on those who had no control over it, saying:

> the person whose grass or corn is eaten down by the escaping cattle of his neighbour, or whose mine is flooded by the water from his neighbour's reservoir, or whose cellar is invaded by the filth of his neighbour's privy, or whose habitation is made unhealthy by the fumes and noisome vapours of his neighbour's alkali works, is damnified without any fault of his own. (at 280)

The interesting question, however, is what constitutes things that can be brought onto land that are 'likely to do mischief'—though it must be remembered that 'brought onto' in this sense probably means 'kept on'. It should also be noted that most of the things the cases have been concerned with would be perfectly harmless in and of themselves, if they were not allowed to escape. In *Rylands*, water (collected in large volume in one area) was obviously within the 'likely to do mischief' category and, since then, other cases have determined that electricity (*National Telephone Co v Baker* [1893]), gas (*Batchellor v Tunbridge Wells Gas Co* [1901]), noxious fumes (*West v Bristol Tramways Co* [1908]), and even a flagpole (*Shiffman v Order of St John* [1936]) or a part of a fairground ride (*Hale v Jennings* [1938]) also come within it. Put simply, the thing or substance brought onto land needs not to be ultra-hazardous, but it must be capable of causing damage—and therefore be dangerous—if it escapes.

This requirement seems to have been reinforced and made harder to satisfy by the House of Lords' decision in *Transco*.

Transco v Stockport Metropolitan Borough Council [2004] HL

The defendant was the owner of a block of flats built next to a disused railway embankment, which it also owned. A pipe carrying water to the flats from the water main leaked and a large quantity of water travelled through a crack in the ground and to the embankment, over time saturating it and causing it to collapse. There was no evidence that the leak was due to any carelessness on the part of the defendant. When the embankment collapsed it exposed and left unsupported a high-pressure gas pipeline owned by Transco (formerly part of British Gas), who had to act promptly in order to prevent the pipe fracturing. In doing so, they incurred costs of about £94,000.

The first question for the court was whether the defendant had 'brought something on to his land likely to do mischief'. In answering it, Lord Bingham said:

> I do not think that the mischief or danger test should be at all easily satisfied. It must be shown that the defendant has done something which he recognised, or judged by the standards appropriate at the relevant place and time, he ought reasonably to have recognised, as giving rise to an exceptionally high risk of danger or mischief if

→

> ↠
> there should be an escape however unlikely an escape may have been thought of.
> (at [10])
>
> This set a very high threshold, which the House of Lords found was not satisfied in *Transco*.
> In addition, Lord Scott stated that Transco's claim should fail because there had been
> no 'escape' from the defendant's land (see below)—the water from the leaking pipe had
> simply moved from one part of the defendant's land to another; it had not exited the land
> or gone over any boundary.

So, the test as to what is 'likely to do mischief if it escapes' is in fact quite strict. Only when it can be shown that the defendant recognised (or should have recognised) that an *exceptionally* high risk of danger arose if the thing or substance accumulated on their land was able to escape will there be any possibility of liability arising. This would not change even if the risk of an escape taking place was low.[6]

 Counterpoint

Essentially, the 'likely to do mischief' test has been transformed by the decision in *Transco* into a foreseeability test. A defendant will not now incur liability if they could not have foreseen an exceptionally high risk of danger should the thing or substance on their land escape. As we indicated in our discussion of private nuisance in the preceding chapter (pp 504–505), foreseeability, as a requirement in land torts (which are traditionally understood to being distinct from the tort of negligence and stemming from the trespass torts), seems rather misplaced—it hints at there being a requirement of fault. This is particularly troubling in relation to *Rylands* liability, which is supposed to be strict. So, it should not matter whether the defendant could or should have 'recognised' (foreseen) that a thing would give rise to an exceptionally high risk of danger if it escaped.

18.2.2 '...if it escapes...'

The rule in *Rylands* was established to deal with isolated escapes from land and therefore proof of an actual escape of a 'thing likely to do mischief' is vital to a claim. In *Read* v *Lyons* [1947], a munitions inspector was injured while visiting a munitions factory when an artillery shell exploded during the manufacturing process. As there was no indication that there had been any negligence by the manufacturers, the claimant brought an action in *Rylands* but the House of Lords rejected her claim. There had been no 'escape'—the shell had not left the defendant's premises. Crucially, the claimant was still on the property when she was injured: had she stepped over the threshold, she would have had a successful claim. The law lords held that an escape occurs

---

6. Have you now changed your mind about whether Townbury Council would be able to recover damages from the owner of the ornamental lake? Similarly, would Racksco have any claim since the *Transco* decision?

only when the substance or item causing damage actually moves from the defendant's premises to a place outside the defendant's occupation or control.

 Pause for reflection

Lord Macmillan held (*obiter*) in *Read* v *Lyons* that he was not prepared to allow personal injury claims under *Rylands*: He said that 'as the law now stands an allegation of negligence is in general essential to the relevancy of an action of reparation for personal injuries' (at 16–17).[7] Do you agree with this? Should liability be confined to property damage or do you think that when people keep 'dangerous' things or substances on their land which injure someone if they escape, they should pay compensation?

There has been some debate as to whether *intentionally* releasing something from one's land is capable of being viewed as an 'escape' and therefore falling within the ***Rylands*** sphere of liability. In *Rigby* v *Chief Constable of Northamptonshire* [1985], police officers, in an attempt to catch a criminal hiding in a shop, fired CS gas into the premises to 'flush' the man out. This resulted in a fire which damaged the shop. The court held that where direct harm had been caused by an intentional act, trespass would appear to be the correct action. However, in *Crown River Cruises Ltd* v *Kimbolton Fireworks Ltd* [1996], Potter J suggested that intentional releases (in this case fireworks) *could* be deemed to be 'escapes' if not deliberately aimed in the direction of the claimant or their property.

18.2.3 '...which represents a non-natural use of land...'

As we have seen, the third requirement that there be a 'non-natural' use of land was added by Lord Cairns in the House of Lords in ***Rylands***. This was his interpretation of the original formulation from Blackburn J in the lower court, who referred to the defendant bringing onto or accumulating on the property something 'which was not naturally there'. This means that the rule does not apply to things that are naturally to be found on a particular area of land and that subsequently escape, causing damage. However, what is naturally on land—or what is 'non-natural use'—has been subject to various interpretations over time.

On the one hand, it does seem to be clear that no liability can arise in respect of trees, shrubs or other plants that are naturally found on the defendant's land, even if some part of these 'escapes' onto the claimant's property (*Giles* v *Walker* [1890]). It might be different, however, if the trees or plants in question were *introduced* by the defendant. The classic definition of 'non-natural use' is found in *Rickards* v *Lothian* [1913]:

> It is not every use to which land is put that brings into play [the] principle. It must be some special use bringing with it increased danger to others, and must not merely be the ordinary use of land or such use as is proper for the general benefit of the community. (Lord Moulton at 280)

---

7. Note, however, the recent confirmation that personal injury claims can be made in *public* nuisance: *Corby Group Litigation* v *Corby Borough Council* [2008], discussed in Chapter 17, p 521.

In *Rickards*, a tap had been left on by an unknown party in the part of a building leased by the defendant. This caused a flood, which in turn damaged the claimant's goods stored on the floor below. Despite there being an escape, no liability was found as the defendant was found to have been using the premises in an ordinary way.

> ⏩⏪ **Counterpoint**
>
> 'Non-natural' use appears to have become 'non-ordinary' use—which is a much narrower definition, as many things that are not 'natural' on land will in fact be quite ordinary. Further, what is 'ordinary' will depend on the time, place and context of the use of the land in question. This definition begins to make the test look a little like negligence (or like the reasonable user test in nuisance) and has allowed the courts to decide that various industrial activities are in fact 'natural' uses of land. This not only goes against the strict liability origins of the rule but would seemingly water down any impact that the rule from *Rylands* could have on environmental protection.
>
> In *British Celanese* v *Hunt* [1969], strips of metal escaped from the factory where the defendants manufactured electrical components. These hit overhead power lines, subsequently causing a power failure to the claimant's factory. However, because the area in which both factories were sited was given over to an industrial estate, the defendants escaped liability under *Rylands* (although they were on other grounds found liable in both negligence and nuisance). The substance in question was certainly not 'naturally' on the land: it had been brought there by the defendant and had escaped, causing harm—but the use of the land was 'ordinary' in the context of industry, as well as being beneficial to the community (in the sense of providing a necessary commodity, creating employment, etc). Similarly, in *Read* v *Lyons*, the manufacture of artillery shells in wartime was found to be a natural use of land given the political/social context (although it should be noted that the *Read* decision was later doubted in *Transco*).
>
> So, what is an 'ordinary' use of land will inevitably change with time (for example, keeping a car was 'non-natural' in 1919, but would not be regarded as so today) and context. But having such a broadly interpretable rule allows the courts considerable flexibility when deciding whether to apply the rule in a new case. Overall, in our view, this had a negative effect on the use of the rule in *Rylands* as it means that a claimant is far less likely to succeed in any claim taken against general industrialised activity, which, of course, are the very activities likely to do the most damage (and the very activities from which the strict liability principle arose). There is no real explanation why the courts felt that this change of direction was necessary. Perhaps it was to limit the number of claims in a similar way to the duty of care in negligence, which may in turn be a consequence of changed emphasis in the law of tort and whose interests it is used to protect.

18.3 *Cambridge Water v Eastern Counties Leather plc*

The next case to substantially change the meaning of what is 'non-natural use' (or 'non-ordinary use') of land was *Cambridge Water Co Ltd* v *Eastern Counties Leather plc* [1994]. It should be noted that in the background to this case sit a number of common law decisions (such as *Ballard* v *Tomlinson* [1885]) which recognised that downstream landowners hold a 'natural right' to receive water in its 'natural quality and quantity'.[8]

Cambridge Water Co Ltd v *Eastern Counties Leather plc* [1994] HL

The defendants owned and operated a tannery and, in the process of degreasing leather pelts, used a particular chemical solvent—perchloroethene (PCE)—for many years, ceasing its use in 1976. In the tanning process, large quantities of the solvent had been spilled onto the concrete floor of the tannery. Over time, this seeped through the concrete and into the soil below, from where it 'travelled', eventually entering the water course and polluting a well situated 1.3 miles away and owned by the claimants for extracting drinking water for the city of Cambridge. The PCE pollution in the water was only discovered in 1983 when the water company became obliged to test for certain chemicals, including PCE as the result of the implementation of an EC Directive. Cambridge Water was forced to move its well, at a cost of more than £1 million, and sued the defendants for the costs associated with the pollution in negligence, nuisance and under the rule in *Rylands*.

By the time the case reached the House of Lords, the claims in negligence and nuisance had failed, largely because the harm that had occurred had been unforeseeable to the defendants. This left only the action under *Rylands*. Giving the leading opinion in the House of Lords, Lord Goff felt bound to say that 'the storage of substantial quantities of chemicals on industrial premises should be regarded as an almost classic case of non-natural use' (at 309), notwithstanding any benefit to the community that is served by the industry or the fact that this might be seen (especially in a tannery) to be an 'ordinary use' of the land in question. He also found that the PCE entering the water course could be viewed as an isolated escape, despite the fact it had happened over a period of time and was caused by many separate spillages. However, while this was the case, the claimants could not recover because the damage was too remote.

18.3.1 '…and which causes foreseeable damage of the relevant type'

Lord Goff's view on the 'escape' and the issue of 'non-natural' use of land appears to ride roughshod over the direction taken by the courts in the mid-twentieth century. While this may be thought of as a good thing, in that courts would subsequently be more able and therefore more likely to find that something was a 'non-natural' use of land (a triumph for environmentalists), the *reason* for the changed approach shows that this is not indeed the case. As we mentioned above, a *fourth* requirement to the **Rylands** test was added in **Cambridge Water**—what prevented the claimant's recovery of damages was the fact that the harm suffered was regarded as too remote. The requirement that the damage caused by the escape must be *foreseeable* had been added

8. Though note that the decision in *Ballard* was not about the reasonableness or otherwise of upstream use but was more a policy decision reflecting the fact that people downstream tend to suffer more from pollution.

to the test by Lord Goff and, in considering this, he held that it was not foreseeable to the skilled person that quantities of chemical seeping into the ground would cause damage to the claimant's water. Although some damage from the spillage of the PCE might be imagined, the damage to the claimant's well could not be, particularly given that the EC Directive had not been in force.

Lord Goff justified his findings by analogy to nuisance (which, as discussed in Chapter 17, also has a foreseeability requirement, pp 504–505) and by allusion to Blackburn J's original formulation of the *Rylands* test, in which he referred to 'anything *likely* to do mischief if it escapes'. In fact, it is said that as a student at Oxford Lord Goff had read and been very impressed by an article by FH Newark which argued against the separation of *Rylands* liability and private nuisance.[9] The facts in **Cambridge Water** provided him with an opportunity to put this into practice. He closed the gap between *Rylands* and nuisance in two ways. First, by equating non-natural use with reasonable use he established the rule as essentially being an application of nuisance to one-off escapes (a position later confirmed by the House of Lords in *Transco*). Secondly, he introduced the remoteness principle from *The Wagon Mound (No 1)* [1961].[10]

As we indicated above, the 'non-natural use' requirement had come to be interpreted so as to *limit* liability under *Rylands* where the courts felt it necessary or appropriate to do so. However, Lord Goff recognised that the addition of the foreseeability requirement would sufficiently limit the scope of liability, so there remained no need to do so with the 'ordinary use' test, which he relaxed.

 Pause for reflection

Why do you think the courts felt it necessary to try and keep liability under the rule in *Rylands* within what they believed to be reasonable bounds? If the objective of the rule was originally to protect claimants (or society as a whole) from the negative environmental and other effects of industrialisation, do such limitations seem appropriate? And for whose benefit were these limitations being put in place?

There has been some discussion as to how far the test of foreseeability goes and about what exactly must be foreseeable—the harm alone or also the escape in the first place? Lord Goff's opinion is not entirely clear on these points (perhaps a reflection of his priorities at the time), but the commonly held view is that it is not the *escape* that must be foreseeable, merely the *damage* resulting from the escape. As *Conaghan & Mansell* point out:

> authority for this position can be derived from the *Rylands* decision itself: Blackburn J's allusion, for example, to 'anything likely to do mischief' suggests that the defendant must reasonably recognise the dangerous nature of the substance under his control but, having done so, he 'must keep it at his peril', implying liability regardless of whether or not he could reasonably have foreseen and/or guarded against an escape. (p 144)

9. FH Newark 'The Boundaries of Nuisance' (1949) 65 *Law Quarterly Review* 480.
10. Chapter 8, p 247.

Therefore, the correct question is: *Once there has been an escape, is the damage suffered by the claimant of a type or kind that was a reasonably foreseeable consequence of such an escape?*[11]

Lord Goff also considered the ongoing position. There was still clearly PCE pollution affecting the particular well—once the testing of the water had included tests for PCE post-EC Directive, the problem was known. On this point, Cambridge Water argued that, even though the damage (pollution by PCE) may have been unforeseeable *when it was spilt*, it had clearly *become* foreseeable by the time the case reached the court, *and* the PCE was still escaping. Could the defendant therefore be liable for the *continuing* escapes? Lord Goff dismissed this argument, holding that because the defendants could not possibly have foreseen the fact that the well would become polluted at the date of the spillages, strict liability for the damage (which became foreseeable at a later date, but by which time nothing could be done to prevent the escapes continuing) should not be imposed upon them. The PCE had escaped beyond the defendant's control (even though it would have been possible—but expensive—to clean up the water).[12]

 Counterpoint

Before leaving the decision in *Cambridge Water* it is interesting to consider the following passage from *Conaghan & Mansell*:

> the interesting question is not whether *Cambridge Water* was correctly decided but rather *why* the Law Lords chose to decide the case as they did. To some extent, the result can be attributed to good housekeeping instincts—Lord Goff considered that the application of a foreseeability criterion to the determination of liability in *Rylands* would lead to 'a more coherent body of common law principles' (at 76)…More generally, however, it is instructive to consider the broader social and political context within which *Cambridge Water* was decided. [Eastern Counties Leather] is judicially perceived as a model company which excites the admiration of right-thinking people. Mann LJ notes that it is of 'high repute' locally, taking a proper 'pride in its history' as a business which was first incorporated in 1879 (at 56). Lord Goff commends the company's 'good standard of housekeeping' and its 'modern and spacious' accommodation (at 63). Into this idyllic scene of industrial industriousness comes a European regulation which, for no demonstrable health reason, renders water from the Sawston borehole no longer 'wholesome' and thereby threatens the whole future of this well-established business with a damages bill of almost £1,000,000. Anyone could be forgiven for thinking that this offends justice and common sense, particularly in circumstances where the alleged polluters couldn't possibly have known that their

→

---

11. Might it be argued, therefore, that Red Horse Paint Company, in the scenarios outlined at the beginning of the chapter *would*, unlike Eastern Counties Leather, be liable, as such pollution is foreseeable since *Cambridge Water* itself?

12. Note, then, that the decision goes against the environmental principle that the 'polluter should pay'.

→

activities would have such expensive consequences... However the effect of placing the cost of pollution on Cambridge Water is equally disquieting—they will inevitably recoup their loss through raised water rates, but in what sense is it more just to require the residents of Cambridge to foot the bill? (pp 146–7)

In economic and environmental terms, then, the decision in *Cambridge Water* favours industry over society (and distributive rather than corrective justice); the losses or costs are spread among the citizens who pay for their water. The question is whether this is a better solution than one requiring the polluter to pay. An environmental perspective may reflect an entirely different outcome—making the polluter pay is surely preferable to making society pay for both the environmental and social cost of industry. Lord Goff considered the environmental question—and whether this should be a policy consideration that weighed heavily against Eastern Counties Leather—but thought that the creation of mechanisms for protecting society from pollution was more properly the role of Parliament, not the judiciary through the development of one small rule in tort. Put simply, he believed that pollution should be regulated in public, not private, law.

It is also questionable just how much 'development' of the tort the imposition of liability on Eastern Counties Leather would involve. In *Rylands*, the defendant landowner could not possibly have foreseen that one potential consequence of his erection of a reservoir would be the flooding of his neighbour's mine. The point was that despite the unforeseeable nature of the harm, he should be held strictly liable for it happening, as by building the reservoir he had *assumed the risk* of all harms that might be caused by the water escaping, whether foreseeable to him or not. Why should this be any different when we are faced with a modern 'model company'?

 Pause for reflection

Do you think that the decision in *Cambridge Water* was correct? Could the case have been decided differently? Remember that the House of Lords found major disagreements on some points thought to be determinative by the Court of Appeal (which had found in favour of Cambridge Water). Does this mean the House of Lords is necessarily right and the Court of Appeal was necessarily wrong? You may like to take into consideration the fact that although PCE was not known to have any deleterious health consequences to humans, it had, by the time *Cambridge Water* was decided, been found to cause liver cancer in mice.

Also consider what the damages claim in *Cambridge Water* was *for*. The costs incurred related to the finding of a new site for a water borehole and the sinking of a new well. What this means is that the *old well was never cleaned up*. Should there have been an obligation on one of the parties to clean up the PCE from the old well? If so, which party, and why?

18.4 *Transco v Stockport MBC*

The latest word on *Rylands* comes from the House of Lords in *Transco*, which approved and expanded upon Lord Goff's opinion in *Cambridge Water*. Dealing with what could be considered to be 'non-natural use' of land, the House of Lords agreed with the

Court of Appeal in this case that the provision of a piped water supply from the mains to a block of flats was a totally natural use of land. The *Transco* decision will now make it even harder for claimants to establish a defendant's liability. Not only will the 'mischief test' be harder to satisfy, the 'non-natural use' test will also be. The House of Lords noted the link between these two concepts and all five law lords thought that a correct redefinition or re-interpretation of 'non-natural use' should require there to be some use that is extraordinary and unusual according to the standards of the day. Lord Bingham suggested the question should be whether the use of land was 'extraordinary and unusual' (at [11]); Lord Walker agreed, also adding the word 'special' to the requirement (at [106]). Piping water to a block of flats in an urban area clearly does not fit this definition, therefore there would have been no liability in *Transco* on this point either. In typical fashion, Lord Hoffmann reverted to economic analysis, suggesting that the role of insurance in cases of this type would also be relevant, saying that 'a useful guide in deciding whether the risk has been created by a 'non-natural' user of land is to ask whether the damage which eventuated was something against which the occupier could reasonably be expected to have insured himself against' (at [46]).

 Pause for reflection

Should it matter whether the party was—or is considered by the court to ought to have been—insured? The question, when it comes down to economic analysis, is about which party is better placed to bear the costs. If Transco had to bear the cost, it could then redistribute this cost by increasing the prices paid by all its customers. Similarly, if Stockport MBC had to pay, an increase in council tax for local residents would cover the cost. Similar points arise if we consider payment 'in advance', via the payment of insurance premiums. Do you think it should be councils who insure themselves against eventualities of this type, or the companies who provide the services (for example, gas), usually in the interests of making profit? Or, more accurately, should it be citizens in a particular area who bear the costs, or the customers of a profit-making enterprise?

Lord Hoffmann seems to suggest that if an occupier of land could have foreseen such an eventuality occurring, they should (a) have insurance and (b) the use of land would be classified as 'ordinary' so the *Rylands* test would not be satisfied. This puts the insurance burden firmly upon occupiers (potential claimants). Put simply, on this view a claimant cannot say that they thought that there might be a risk of harm occurring, but they chose not to insure, and then go to court seeking damages under the rule in *Rylands*. Lord Hoffmann's approach, however, was not favoured by the other law lords and was in fact explicitly rejected by Lord Hobhouse (at [60]).

18.5 **Standing and defences**

18.5.1 **Who can sue?**

Cambridge Water seemed to move the rule in *Rylands* closer to nuisance, with the addition of the foreseeability requirement. Indeed, this was Lord Goff's intention. Only a few years later, the House of Lords decision in the private nuisance case of **Hunter v Canary Wharf** [1997] made having a proprietary interest in land a prerequisite to a claim in nuisance. This meant that the question arose as to whether this would extend to those taking claims in **Rylands**. It is clear that others have successfully claimed under the rule in the past (*Perry* v *Kendrick's Transport Ltd* [1956]) but this was criticised in *Read* v *Lyons*. However, if the focus of both actions is the same, namely the protection of rights to and over land, as Lord Goff suggested, it would seem logical that the right to be able to take a claim would be the same for each. This position was confirmed by the House of Lords in **Transco**;[13] therefore only parties with ownership or exclusive possession of the land concerned can claim under **Rylands**.

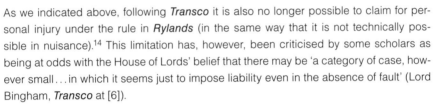

Counterpoint

As we indicated above, following *Transco* it is also no longer possible to claim for personal injury under the rule in *Rylands* (in the same way that it is not technically possible in nuisance).[14] This limitation has, however, been criticised by some scholars as being at odds with the House of Lords' belief that there may be 'a category of case, however small . . . in which it seems just to impose liability even in the absence of fault' (Lord Bingham, *Transco* at [6]).

Roderick Bagshaw argues that it is strange to limit the rule to damage to real property especially given that one of the reasons for the rule in the first place was as a response to a loss of life in a number of disasters. For example, Lord Walker in his speech refers to the Aberfan tragedy in which 144 people (including 116 school children) were killed when on 21 October 1966 thousands of tons of colliery waste from the Merthyr Vale Colliery slid down a mountain side above the village of Aberfan in south Wales, destroying 20 houses and the village school. To suggest (in the absence of negligence) there would only have been good reason to compensate the property owners and not for the deaths and personal injuries of those involved seems extraordinary. This, however, is the result of subsuming *Rylands* within nuisance.

It also appears that other losses are excluded from the rule, now it has been subsumed into private nuisance and (see further below) more closely aligned with negligence. In *D Pride & Partners (A Firm)* v *Institute for Animal Health* [2009],[15] for example, Tugendhat J excluded claims for pure economic loss from both nuisance and a claim in **Rylands**.

18.5.2 **Defences**

The initial defences available under the rule in **Rylands** come from Blackburn J's original judgment. He indicated that there should be three defences to liability. These are outlined in Table 18.1.

---

13. See e.g. Lord Hoffmann (at [46]), in the context of who is best placed to insure against property damage, Lord Hobhouse (at [52]) who indicates that 'other parts of the law of torts' cover personal injuries and, perhaps most conclusively, Lord Bingham (at [9]).

14. In the past personal injury claims had been included without question: *Hale* v *Jennings* [1938]; *Perry* v *Kendrick's Transport Ltd* [1956].

15. Discussed in Chapter 7, p 171.

Table 18.1 Defences to a claim under the rule in *Rylands* v *Fletcher*

Defences to a claim under the rule in *Rylands* v *Fletcher*	
Defence	Examples
Fault of the claimant or express or implied consent	*Ponting* v *Noakes* [1894] The claimant's horse died after it had reached over a fence and eaten poisonous leaves from a tree on the defendant's land. The defendant was not liable as the harm suffered was due to the horse's own intrusion.
Escape caused by the unforeseeable act of a stranger	*Box* v *Jubb* [1879] A reservoir overflowed onto the claimant's land, but this was the result of the actions of another neighbouring reservoir owner, over which the defendant had no control and of which he had no knowledge; the defendant was therefore not liable. *Rickards* v *Lothian* [1913] The claimant's premises were flooded due to a continuous overflow of water from a sink on the top floor of the building. This was caused by a tap being turned on full and the waste pipe plugged by the deliberate act of a third party. The defendant was not liable as he could not reasonably have known of the act so as to do anything to prevent the harm. *Perry* v *Kendricks Transport Ltd* [1956] A disused motor-coach in the defendant's car park was set on fire by young boys, causing injury to a 10 year old. However, it had not been left in such a condition by the defendant that it was reasonable to expect that children might meddle with it and cause the fire. The act of the third party must be *unforeseeable*. If the defendant should have foreseen the intervention, the defence will not be established. *Northwestern Utilities Ltd* v *London Guarantee Co* [1936] The claimant's hotel was destroyed by fire after a gas leak ignited. It was foreseeable that works undertaken by a third party near the defendant's gas mains might cause damage and require remedial work. It was therefore no defence to argue that the fire was caused by the acts of a third party.

Table 18.1 *Continued*

Defences to a claim under the rule in *Rylands* v *Fletcher*	
Defence	Examples
Escape caused by an 'act of God'	*Nichols* v *Marsland* [1876] The defendant had some ornamental pools on his land, which contained large quantities of water and which had been formed by damming up a stream that ran through his property. Due to extraordinarily high rainfall the banks of the pools broke and the escaping water destroyed four bridges on the claimant's land. The court ruled that the defendant should not be found liable for an extraordinary act of nature, which he could not have reasonably foreseen. *Greenock Corporation* v *Caledonian Railway* [1917] A concrete paddling pool for children had been constructed by the local authority in the bed of a stream, requiring an alteration of its natural course. An extraordinary level of rainfall caused the pool to overflow. Due to its construction, water which would have ordinarily flowed downstream flowed down a public street. The House of Lords held that such an event did **not** qualify as an 'act of God'.

Pause for reflection

The defendant will not be liable where an escape happens solely because of natural causes, in circumstances where no human foresight or prudence could reasonably recognise the possibility of such an occurrence and provide against it. However, it is arguable that advances of modern technology and science render this defence largely defunct. Do you think that exceptionally heavy rains or violent winds would be unforeseeable today? What kind of exceptional situations would now be considered (after *Greenock*) an 'act of God'?

Blackburn J's defences are not the only ones applicable to **Rylands** claims, others that we are more familiar with from nuisance can also arise. Statutory authority is the primary example and the approach to this is the same as is taken in nuisance.[16] Contributory negligence and *volenti non fit injuria* are also applicable to **Rylands** claims.[17] The fact that defences are available at all is somewhat controversial—they essentially suggest that an element of fault resides in an area of tort that is supposed to have created strict liability. This, in our opinion, weakens the action's potential use in environmental

16. Chapter 17, pp 508–509.

17. As was indicated in *Colour Quest* v *Total Downstream UK Plc* [2009]. *Steele* argues that 'consent' in this form must mean something closer to 'shared benefit' if it is to be consistent with the purpose of the rule (p 689). See further Chapter 10.

protection. The subsuming of the action into nuisance has also created doubt about its usefulness in the modern day and, as we shall see in the following section, it appears that to some extent any residual application of **Rylands** is edging closer and closer in some circumstances to a fault-based land tort.

18.6 The nuisance/*Rylands* v *Fletcher*/ negligence overlap

Lord Walker, in **Transco**, suggested that liability in nuisance (and presumably, therefore, the rule in **Rylands**) 'overlaps with (indeed, is a sort of condominium with) that of negligence' (at [96]). There are a series of cases that indicate this—that is, cases in which there is clearly fault on the part of the defendant, but where the harm has been caused to the claimant's interest in land and liability has been found in nuisance or **Rylands**.[18] These cases started within a category known as 'continuing or adopting a nuisance', and refer to those situations where a pre-existing nuisance (created usually by a third party) was allowed to continue by the defendant, sometimes resulting in the 'escape' of something from the defendant's land. Furthermore, in *Burnie Port Authority* v *General Jones Pty Ltd* [1994], the Australian High Court formally incorporated the **Rylands** rule into the tort of negligence. In **Cambridge Water** a foreseeability requirement—more familiar from negligence and considerations of fault or wrongdoing—was added to both claims in private nuisance and under **Rylands**. Lord Walker, in **Transco**, thought that the scope of the action had been restricted by developments in negligence (at [99]). Thus, it seems that questions must now be asked about the role of fault within these types of claim, particularly in those cases that seem, on their facts, to straddle private nuisance and **Rylands**.

Sedleigh-Denfield v *O'Callaghan* [1940] HL

A pipe on the defendants' land which served the purpose of draining a ditch had been constructed by the local authority without the defendants' knowledge. When the pipe was built, its end should have been covered with a grille or grate to stop debris blocking it and causing a flood. A grate had been provided but was put in the wrong place, where it served no useful purpose. The claimant's land was flooded on more than one occasion when the pipe became blocked by debris following heavy rainfall, causing damage, which the claimant sued for.

The House of Lords held the defendants (an order of monks) liable on the ground that they had 'continued or adopted' an existing nuisance. While it was clear that the nuisance itself—that is, the problem—had been *created* by the local authority in its negligent construction of the pipe, the defendant had done nothing to rectify the problem. Because at least one of the monks was found to have known about the existence of the pipe, and the fact that the problem would have been easy to rectify, it was held that the defendants had not taken reasonable steps to stop the nuisance continuing.

---

18. *Steele* states that **Rylands** 'provides a direct alternative to negligence in some circumstances', adding: 'In terms of long-term survival, that has been its problem' (p 679).

This case shows clearly what we mean by a claim 'straddling' the tort of private nuisance and an action under **Rylands**. The applicability of a particular action turns on what is categorised as the 'nuisance' or problem in the first place. If it is the pipe, then this is an ongoing situation (at least, the risk created would be) and would fall in the private nuisance category. However, if it is the flooding of the claimant's land then it could be viewed that the water, once *accumulated* behind the blockage in the pipe, had 'escaped', making this case sit squarely in **Rylands**. However, it also seems eminently possible that what we are talking about here is, in fact, negligence—the defendants did not act reasonably or failed to take reasonable steps to do something about the grate and the potential problem that the pipe could become blocked. This is clearly a fault-based consideration and shows how the three different tort actions overlap. Is what is actually being said that there is a *duty* to do something about a known and existing state of affairs, if it could pose a potential problem?[19] If so, this is clearly *breached* by not doing so, and is what *causes* the damage complained of, subject to any considerations of foreseeability. As Conor Gearty says, '[t]his was negligence pure and simple, confused by an ill-fitting and woolly disguise of nuisance' (p 237).

The harm in **Sedleigh-Denfield** originated from the actions of a third party, but the same effect is felt regarding situations caused by acts of nature. In *Goldman* v *Hargrave* [1967], a gum tree on the defendant's property was struck by lightning. The defendant took what turned out to be inadequate steps to alleviate the risk that the tree would catch fire. The tree continued to smoulder, eventually igniting, the fire travelling to the neighbouring property and causing damage. The Privy Council in this case followed the **Sedleigh-Denfield** principle and held the defendant liable for the damage, based on the fact that he had knowledge of the foreseeable danger.[20] Again, this seems both like an escape (of fire) and a fault-based consideration, aligning it more closely with negligence, and indeed the Privy Council treated it as such, though they refused to state whether the case could also come under nuisance.

18.6.1 **The 'measured duty of care'**

All the cases in this area seem to involve an escape of one sort or another and without the added limitations to the **Rylands** rule would seem to be almost classic examples of the type of harm that Blackburn J imagined would attract strict liability. In relation to them a new term of art has been coined: a 'measured duty of care' in nuisance, in which *positive* duties are owed by landowners to act to prevent damage to others.[21]

In *Leakey* v *National Trust* [1980], a portion of a large mound of earth on the defendant's ground collapsed (as exposure to weather conditions had weakened it over time), damaging two houses owned by the claimant which were situated at the bottom of the mound. As the defendants had long been aware of the effect of the weathering on the

19. In negligence this would be dealt with as a question of duty regarding the actions of a third party which then cause damage to the claimant—see, for example of a case with no real discernible difference, *Smith* v *Littlewoods*, Chapter 4, pp 89–90.

20. Thus it seems that Townbury Fire Brigade, in the scenarios outlined above, could also be liable.

21. *Steele* points out that the notion of 'duty' is alien to nuisance, but also that the analysis of these cases is not typical of negligence, either, due to their subjective rather than objective standard (p 620).

earth, they were found liable. Here, again, the Court of Appeal explicitly considered the relationship between nuisance and negligence in claims of this type, essentially coming to the point that the two actions were one and the same in these situations. We would add that given the 'type' of nuisance being considered, *Rylands* is subsumed in these claims as well, by virtue of the 'escapes' that cause the damage in all of them. The result of *Leakey* is that a claim can now be taken in nuisance or negligence, but cases since have tended to rely on nuisance, possibly because it is easier to do so than to go back to 'duty, breach, harm' formulations, given the precedents set. It is also perhaps arguable that where the only harm is to amenity interests, the claim must by its very nature be framed in nuisance and, therefore, all claims of this type might as well be.[22] However, at least where there is actual damage to property, the claims seem as though they would equally as easily succeed in negligence if framed in that way (see, for example, *Holbeck Hall Hotel Ltd* v *Scarborough Borough Council* [2000]; *Lippiatt* v *South Gloucestershire Council* [2000]; *Bybrook Barn Centre Ltd* v *Kent County Council* [2001]; *Delaware Mansions Ltd* v *Westminster City Council* [2002]), yet all are considered nuisance actions. Indeed, in the latter case cited, Lord Cooke went as far as to say that the nuisance/negligence distinction in these cases 'is treated as of no real significance' (at [333]). That said, a recent case indicates that the *scope* of the duty may be used to limit claims even in cases where a measured duty of care seems appropriate. In *Lambert and others* v *Barratt Homes Ltd and another* [2010], a local authority succeeded in its appeal against a finding that it should have prevented the flooding of the claimant's land from surface water that accumulated on its own land by constructing a catch pit and drainage system for the water at considerable cost. As the accumulation of the surface water had in fact been caused by Barratt (by blocking a drainage ditch and culvert on land adjacent to the local authority's)—and because Lambert could recover the entire cost of drainage work from Barratt in nuisance, the scope of the authority's 'measured duty' extended only to cooperation and to allowing others to facilitate the drainage of water from its land.

 Pause for reflection

Given the arguments made above, and the cases cited there, do you think there is any continuing role for the action in *Rylands*, or would it be better to do as the Australians have done and subsume the action into the tort of negligence?

18.7 Where does *Rylands* v *Fletcher* fit today?

In **Cambridge Water**, Lord Goff questioned whether the rule from **Rylands** was best seen as analytically distinct from nuisance or if they should be viewed as two parts of the same thing. Even though the **Rylands** rule had developed out of a desire to protect landowners from the risks of isolated escapes from industry and other risky activities, he held that 'it would . . . lead to a more coherent body of common law principles if the

---

22. Though as we have seen, to claim for personal injury, one would have to sue in negligence.

rule were to be regarded as essentially an extension of the law of nuisance to isolated escapes from land' (at 306). In **Transco**, the House of Lords confirmed that the rule from **Rylands** should be viewed as a sub-species of private nuisance. This, to a large extent, brought to an end a long period of uncertainty and academic speculation on the matter. In this case, their lordships also reviewed the scope, relevance and application of the rule in the modern day and provided guidance as to its future application.

In particular the House of Lords in **Transco**:

- rejected the suggestion that the rule should be absorbed into the tort of negligence as in Australia and Scotland;

- rejected the suggestion that the rule should be more generously applied, and confined it to 'exceptional' circumstances where the occupier has brought something onto his land which poses an 'exceptionally high risk' to neighbouring property should it escape and which amounts to an 'extraordinary and unusual use of land' given the place and time in which it occurs; *and*

- clarified that only those with rights to land could sue, bringing the action into line with private nuisance, following **Hunter**, and confirming that no claim for personal injury could be brought under it.

The decision in **Transco** limits the rule in **Rylands** to a role in the protection of interests in land (as in nuisance). In so doing it prevents it from taking on a broader role in ensuring that those who wish to indulge in ultra-hazardous (but socially beneficial) activities make appropriate provision for absorbing the inevitable costs of occasional catastrophes and environmental harms. In this respect, the function or purpose of this area of tort law as a regulatory system—if it ever had one—is lost.

It is clear that the rule in **Rylands** has been uneasy to rationalise throughout its existence, and particularly so in the modern day, where it seems largely unnecessary to hold on to it. It was judicially created in a context of industrialisation to deal with the perceived dangers caused by large-scale building of reservoirs for industry, making it seem like an exception to nuisance through its dealing with one-off events via the imposition of strict liability. However, by the mid-1990s, as **Cambridge Water** shows, its impact and potential as a tool for environmental protection was constrained— again, a product of the time, post-Thatcher, but still while the country was under Conservative government and business concerns were prioritised. Furthermore, many of the practices on which it may have had an impact had, by this time, already been regulated in other ways—reservoirs, for example, by then coming under the Reservoirs Act 1975. Sadly, things have not really improved following the reconsideration of the action by the House of Lords in **Transco**, as to all intents and purposes **Rylands** is now merely a sub-species of nuisance and, as we argued in the previous section, potentially more accurately viewed as a sub-species of negligence. As a result, its deliberate differences from nuisance, including the ability to recover for personal injury and 'wrongful' conduct—as well as most of its environmental potential—have either been lost or become (unintentional) inconsistencies. On these points, Bagshaw says that:

> [i]t is often asserted that 'hard cases make bad law', but *Transco* confirms that bad law is also easily made when a case is too straightforward. Perhaps it was because it was so clear to their Lordships that the claim should not succeed (the defendant's activity being too commonplace, insufficiently risky, there being no escape and the claimant's loss

being easily insurable) that they allowed inconsistencies and controversial propositions to stray into their speeches. But given that very few claims rely on the rule in *Rylands* v *Fletcher* and *Transco* did nothing to encourage greater use of the rule, the main effect of these imperfections will probably be to challenge law students and textbook writers. (p 392)

18.8 **Conclusion**

In this chapter we have looked at the rule from *Rylands* v *Fletcher*, a judicially created way of suing someone when something had escaped from their land and caused damage to you, their neighbour. This rule was created completely as a product of the time—there were societal concerns about the effects of mass industrialisation, including, as in the case itself, the building of artificial reservoirs.

Due to its place in history, the rule has been (and can be) used only in limited circumstances and the primary bulk of case law comes from the late nineteenth and early twentieth century. But it should be remembered that the tort of nuisance was already in existence before the rule in *Rylands* was created, and this would allow people to sue for uses of land that interfered with their own interests on a more frequent or ongoing basis. It should also be noted that the tort of negligence emerged as a separate entity in the early twentieth century, and many of the cases under the rule in *Rylands* could, in some ways, be construed as part of negligence. These days, it is only those situations where a completely accidental escape occurs that could be said to fall outside of the bounds of negligence.

The rule today is best understood through a trilogy of cases: *Rylands* v *Fletcher* itself, then *Cambridge Water* v *Eastern Counties Leather* in the mid-1990s, followed by *Transco* v *Stockport MBC* early this century. These decisions, all from the House of Lords, have in their own way shaped the way the rule can be used, either by adding new requirements (*Cambridge Water*), or redefining the way the existing requirements should be interpreted (*Transco*). That said, there is potential—subject to its now stringent requirements—to use the rule to help to protect the environment from one-off catastrophes, not in a preventative sense but perhaps with more regard to clean-up measures when things go wrong. Whether this was what was intended when the rule was created is debateable—it was more likely intended as a vehicle to compensate (wealthy) land*owners* than to protect the land itself.

The usefulness of the rule is certainly in question in the modern day—it appears from the decision in *Cambridge Water* and, also, the nuisance case of *Hunter* that its scope (particularly as a tool for environmentalists) has been severely restricted. The rule has moved closer to nuisance (and negligence), with all that that entails, including the need for foreseeability and for a proprietary interest in land in order to be able to take a claim. In other jurisdictions, the rule has been swallowed up by negligence. Without doubt, this is a rule that is now very limited in its scope and application—it would seem that it has more historical interest than practical application in the twenty-first century.

✳ End-of-chapter questions

After reading the chapter carefully, try answering the questions below. If you would like to know what we think, visit the Online Resource Centre (www.oxfordtextbooks.co.uk/orc/horsey2e/).

1. How could the action under *Rylands* v *Fletcher* be used to help to solve environmental problems?

2. Does the action under *Rylands* v *Fletcher* serve any useful purpose in the modern day?

3. Do you think the courts in this country should follow the Australian High Court and formally view the action under *Rylands* v *Fletcher* as a species of negligence?

4. Consider the problem question at the start of this chapter—now having read about the topic what would be your advice to Low-Price-Pumps? If you need some pointers in thinking about how to answer this question, turn to the Appendix (p 589) where each problem is annotated with issues and cases to consider. Next, try to write your own answer and, finally, log on to our Online Resource Centre (www.oxfordtextbooks.co.uk/orc/horsey2e/) and check your ideas against our suggested outline answer.

✳ Further reading

A good place to start your further reading is the chapter by AW Brian Simpson, which helps to contextualise the **Rylands v Fletcher** litigation. More up-to-date and insightful interpretations are provided in numerous other articles, particularly by Bagshaw and Nolan.

Amirthalingam, Kumaralingam '*Rylands* Lives' (2004) *Cambridge Law Journal* 273

Bagshaw, Roderick '*Rylands* Confined' (2004) 120 *Law Quarterly Review* 388

Gearty, Conor 'The Place of Private Nuisance in a Modern Law of Torts' (1989) *Cambridge Law Journal* 214

Lee, Maria 'Private Nuisance in the House of Lords: Back to Basics' (2004) 15 *King's College Law Journal* 417

Nolan, Donal 'The Distinctiveness of *Rylands v Fletcher*' (2005) 121 *Law Quarterly Review* 421

Simpson, AW Brian 'Bursting Reservoirs and Victorian Tort Law: *Rylands and Horrocks v Fletcher* (1868)' in *Leading Cases in the Common Law* (OUP, 1995), p 195

Wightman, John 'Liability for Landslips' (2000) 2(4) *Environmental Law Review* 285

Liability, damages and limitations

Introduction to Part V

1. In this Part of the book we look at various issues in relation to damages in tort law. In practice, damages dominate tort law, yet *liability* is the focus of most teaching.

2. We begin by looking at the principles that lie behind damages awards, finding that the primary object of the law is to compensate those who have been harmed by another's wrongdoing.

3. This is done by making an award that seeks to put the claimant into the position that they would have been in had the harm not occurred. Damages awards can encompass pecuniary (financial) and non-pecuniary losses, such as pain, suffering and loss of amenity. Special (quantifiable at the time of trial) and general damages (including future losses, not quantifiable at the time of trial) are awarded. These are calculated using multiplicands (the sum to be multiplied) and multipliers (the number of years the loss should be multiplied by). In the past, damages tended to be awarded as a lump sum. More recently there has been some movement towards structured damages settlements.

4. Multiple defendants can incur liability independently, jointly or severally. Either the court will apportion damages between them or one defendant can seek a contribution from another under the Civil Liability (Contribution) Act 1978.

5. We then look at limitation periods that exist in respect of all damages claims—not uncontroversially. Subsequently, we consider a number of further critiques that can (and have) been made of the damages system as well as some proposed alternative systems.

6. Finally, we come back to the idea of 'compensation culture', analysing whether, in fact, we do live in such a culture and, if so, what response would be appropriate. We also consider recent government proposals to the reform of the damages system.

19

Damages in tort

Problem question

Read this problem question carefully, and keep it in mind while you are working through the chapter that follows. At the end of the chapter, you will be asked to apply what you have learnt to the problem question and advise the relevant parties.

Emma is a 45-year-old London-based consultant paediatrician. Because of her increasingly high profile and the fact that she is held in high respect by her peers, she has in recent years also fronted a number of popular television series that delve into various aspects of children's medicine and medical treatments. In the last year alone, she was paid over £50,000 for this. She also does a lot of work, including fundraising, for various children's charities: last year she was sponsored to cycle the Great Wall of China and raised over £15,000. She enjoys time with her two teenage children (she is divorced from their father) and in particular loves weekends away with them sailing or waterskiing, although also enjoys sharing more simple activities with them, such as taking their dog for long walks in the park. She is an avid cook and attends a cookery class every Thursday evening, followed by a meal out with her friends.

Emma is seriously injured in a multiple car accident on the M25, for which she was in no way to blame. She is rendered paraplegic, is confined to a wheelchair and suffers constant pain. She has to give up her job, but continues to try and do some of the voluntary work for the charities she is involved with. She, along with her two children, has to move out of her three-storey house in north London and into a specially adapted ground-floor flat. Her boyfriend, Clive, who has a career in advertising, agrees to move in with her and

> →
>
> be her carer; he gives up his job. She loses interest in sex and is unable to carry on with the majority of her leisure pursuits.
>
> It is established that a combination of two other drivers' negligence caused the accident in which Emma was injured.

19.1 Introduction

Consider the following examples:

→ A pedestrian is knocked down and seriously injured by a speeding motorist.

→ An office worker suffers psychiatric injury after being subjected to a campaign of transphobic bullying by his supervisor.

→ An elderly resident catches her foot in a small hole on the village green left by a maypole, breaking her ankle.

→ A school fails to diagnose a student's dyslexia believing the student's poor performance is simply down to laziness. The student fails their GSCEs.

→ A house is burnt down as a result of an explosion at a nearby oil refinery.

→ A prisoner is kept in their cell for 24 hours after the prison guards walk out on an unofficial strike.

→ A group of ramblers take a short cut over a farmer's field without the farmer's permission.

→ A student collapses unconscious after an evening of heavy drinking. His housemates decide to lock him in the garden shed overnight while he sobers up.

→ A first-time buyer buys a house on the basis of an inaccurate survey. As a result the property is worth significantly less than they paid for it.

→ A professional footballer wants to stop a national newspaper from publishing allegations about his private life.

→ The lead singer of a Smiths tribute band is branded as a 'meat-eating wannabe who can't hold a note' on their former management's website.

As we explained in the introduction to this book, one of the primary functions of the tort system is to provide compensation for those 'wronged' by someone else. Despite the fact that the majority of tort textbooks (including this one) focus more on the principles of establishing *liability*, suing in tort is central to its operation, rather than secondary, as in contract law. This is often expressed by saying that in tort, the wrongs come first, and these define the right; whereas in contract, the rights come first and define the wrong.[1] In all the situations outlined above (many of which are largely based on cases you may now have come across) a legal wrong, for which the law provides a remedy, may have occurred. Damages (monetary compensation) are the primary remedy available in the tort of negligence, but the same is true of, for example, trespass (to land and to the person), defamation and claims against manufacturers for defective products.[2] Other torts attract damages less, due to the very nature of the harm(s) involved. In privacy claims, for example, claimants seeking to prevent publication of private information are more likely to ask for an injunction. The reason for this is that injunctions, in a sense, come *before* a harm and operate to prevent it from materialising (or at least to its worst potential). However, if private information has *already* been published, then the only thing that can be done—in terms of a remedy—is to seek compensation.[3] Once a harm has occurred, it is hard to imagine (particularly in the economic climate in which we live) how it can be rectified other than by the payment of money. In all the situations above, subject to a tort being established according to the rules set out elsewhere in this book, damages could therefore become payable.

This chapter focuses on damages: who gets them, who pays, how they are calculated and whether the system we have works well. The focus will, in the main, be on negligence claims. We will also return to some of the larger themes and ideas that have permeated previous chapters.

As we have noted above, far more emphasis is given in tort texts to the rules and principles governing the imposition of liability than to the rules governing damages awards. However, in a vast number of cases, liability is not contested—therefore there are considerably more cases in the *background* of tort, notwithstanding those successful (disputed) claims we have already encountered in earlier chapters, in which damages are awarded. This is the bread and butter of the civil lawyer in practice. As *Markesinis & Deakin* have pointed out:

> It is extraordinary how much attention is focused upon issues of liability as opposed to the quantum of damages. Practitioners are bemused by the pre-occupation of academics with the rules on fault: they are aware that liability is infrequently challenged by insurers—being raised as a preliminary issue in only about 20 per cent of their cases—whereas the amount of compensation is almost always open to some negotiation. (p 87)

Everything that follows should be considered in this context. Only four tort claims were dealt with by the House of Lords (later the Supreme Court) in 2009, compared with a total number of claims made in the same year (for personal injury) in the county court and Queen's Bench Division of the High Court of over 180,000.[4] In the county court, more than half of the claims were for less than £5,000. Many of the claims will

---

1. i.e. it is the contract that one enters into that defines one's rights in contract law and a wrong can occur only if those rights are breached. In tort, there must be a wrong (e.g. negligence) for the right to claim damages to accrue.

2. Other remedies, more appropriate to the particular torts they apply to, have been discussed in the relevant chapters.

3. See e.g. *Mosley* v *News Group Newspapers Ltd* [2008], discussed in Chapter 16 at pp 471–472.

4. Ministry of Justice, Annual Judicial and Court Statistics 2009 (published September 2010).

have been settled or dismissed before even proceeding to full trial, and more still are
settled after trial.

19.2 **What are damages for?**

While the primary focus of damages is compensatory, it should be noted that other
types of damages (other than those designed to compensate a claimant for the harm
they suffered) exist; though these are very limited in their scope. These 'non-compensatory damages' include:

- exemplary damages (where a high (or higher than usual) sum must be paid, in part
  as a 'punishment' or to set an example to other potential defendants when there
  has been 'outrageous' conduct);[5]

- aggravated damages (where a higher sum than is usual is awarded to a particular
  claimant in recognition of the fact that they have suffered to a higher degree than
  would be expected, as a result of the defendant's actions);[6]

- contemptuous damages (where a claimant receives a lesser sum than might be
  usual, in recognition that a legal wrong has been committed against them, but
  showing the court's displeasure that such a claim has been brought);[7] and

- nominal damages (where there has been a legal wrong committed but no actual
  (recognised) harm has been suffered by the claimant).

Many of these link directly back to some of the other functions of tort—deterrence,
retribution and so on.

Making a defendant pay (compensatory) damages can also often be seen as being
about more than simply compensating the claimant for the wrong that was done to
them. The fear of having to make large damages payouts may influence behaviour
and in this sense may have a deterrent effect among potential defendants. For example, once one employer pays compensation for having poor safety conditions in the
workplace, it can only be hoped that other (similar) employers will take note and
alter their safety conditions in a manner that both protects their employees from
suffering harm and avoids the necessity for them to have to pay out compensation
in the future. The idea is that people can learn from their mistakes, and the mistakes
of others.

In another sense, compensatory damages can operate as a type of retribution. Whatever the size of the award, successful claimants are more likely to feel
vindicated—that the law was on their side—than those who receive nothing. Put
another way, when someone is to blame for the harm you suffered, it is quite natural to want to 'make them pay'. Similarly, compensation payouts may be seen as an
acknowledgement of the wrong that was done—or even as an apology for it.

---

5. For a recent example in the context of false imprisonment, see *Muuse* v *Secretary of State for the
Home Department* [2010] at [71]–[77].

6. *Lunney & Oliphant* describe aggravated damages as occupying 'a murky middle ground between
normal compensatory damages and exemplary damages' (p 864).

7. See e.g. **Grobbelaar v News Group Newspapers** [2002].

Counterpoint

Though it can be said that tort claims are brought for a variety of (often inter-twining) reasons,[8] for most people, in most claims, monetary compensation is probably the ultimate aim. The reasons for this can be seen to stem from as far back as the Industrial Revolution, which inevitably increased the number of serious accidents suffered, particularly in the workplace. Similarly, the introduction of motorised transport clearly will have had an effect on the number of injuries people sustain. These things (among others) led, over time, to the gradual emergence of claims for damages for personal injury as the 'dominant' tort action.[9] The problem with this is that it leads to a perception of tort as being purely a vehicle for accident compensation, when that is not its sole function, nor the reason it was created. Primarily, tort was a system for righting wrongs (corrective justice), coupled with the notion of individual responsibility, in that people (wrongdoers) were held responsible for their harmful actions. If tort *is* (realistically?) primarily a mechanism for accident compensation (more akin to distributive justice), then it will necessarily be compared with other forms of accident compensation and, when this happens, we can see that tort performs incredibly badly. If the aim is to achieve compensation for as many people as deserve it, then the tort accident compensation system has a surprising number of flaws—which largely stem from the fact that the system is based on fault, blame and culpability.

Many questions are raised by having a tort system that is both fault-based and centred around the principle of compensation. This becomes particularly apparent when we look at who actually pays the majority of compensation that is awarded (insurers, employers, etc) and how the costs of compensation are then spread among other ('innocent') members of society. Moreover, while this question is not often asked, there may be perhaps other, better ways of ensuring that those who *need* money (for example, in order to pay healthcare costs, or because they are unable to live the way they did before they were harmed, including their earning potential) actually receive it and not merely those few who are able to find someone to (legally) blame for the harms they suffered. One of the problems with the tort system being based on *fault* is that other justifications for compensation are largely overlooked.

Furthermore, in most cases, the *degree* of fault is not considered—a worse act of negligence, for example, does not lead to higher awards of damages. In essence, there is a fixed sum given for a particular harm, or at least fixed parameters for calculating the sum, as long as it can be shown (in negligence at least) that this is someone else's fault (see further p 560).

The realities of what the tort system is about are often lost when trawling through textbooks, cases, actuarial tables (see below) and so on. Cases are brought on the basis of injury, loss and disability, but all these aspects are sanitised from the version we, as lawyers, see—we deal in legal principles, costs and awards, rather than stepping back and remembering who it is we are talking about, the injuries they have suffered and the disabilities (physical and societal) that they may face.

---

8. See Chapter 1.
9. Remember that negligence—the primary vehicle for personal injury claims—did not really 'emerge' until 1932.

> **Pause for reflection**
>
> Should it be the purpose of tort law to do anything *other* than attempt to compensate victims of harm? Is punishment or retribution more suited to the public law mechanisms of criminal law than a private law suit taken by an individual or individuals? Does making a defendant pay damages work as a deterrent from committing further wrongs? Consider the fact that many 'torts' committed (especially within negligence) are *accidental*—how can you deter someone from having another accident in the future? Should we punish someone because they did?
>
> Looking at it another way, even 'simple' accidents, such as those caused by a momentary lapse of concentration while at the wheel of a car, may be deterred by making the 'wrongdoer' pay compensation—the driver may be more likely to be more careful in future. Similar ideas may transpose further up the scale of carelessness—a factory owner who has had to pay once may be more likely to instil more carefully regulated working practices on his employees in future (thereby preventing further injuries occurring). But is this really what happens? Who actually pays in these situations (see, for example, the comments of Lord Denning in **Nettleship v Weston** [1971])?

Compensatory damages in tort are designed, as far as money can do so, to provide *restitutio in integrum*,[10] defined as:

> the sum of money which will put the party who has been injured, or who has suffered, in the same position he would have been in if he had not sustained the wrong for which he is now getting compensation or reparation. (Lord Blackburn, *Livingstone* v *Raywards Coal Co* [1880] at 39)

Therefore, damages are meant to put the claimant back (as far as money can do so) into their pre-tort position: the position they were in before any harm was done to them. This may include both general and special damages (see below) covering pecuniary (financial) and non-pecuniary (emotional, social, amenity and so on) losses. Losses are meant to be moved from one party to the other who is (usually) better able to bear the cost.

This principle contrasts with the way damages are awarded for breach of contract claims, where the aim is to put the claimant into the position they *expected to be in* if the contract was perfectly executed. While it is usually relatively easy to envision this (for example, a contract may have been entered into with expected profits already calculated), it is often quite difficult to imagine what money compensates for in tort. In a classic example of a negligent act, even a momentary lapse of consciousness on the part of a driver might lead to substantial injuries being suffered by a pedestrian. Say, for example, a pedestrian was hit by a car being driven negligently and was rendered permanently paraplegic as a result. How does money compensate for the loss of the ability to walk, run or dance? How can a monetary award put that person back to the position they were in before the tort occurred? Furthermore, if the same claimant also suffered depression as a result of their injuries, how could (and should) this be

---

10. Literally, from Latin, restoration to the original position.

compensated? These are the primary difficulties we face when looking at damages in a tort context—the calculation does not work according to how *deserving* someone is or even necessarily according to their *need*, but is based purely on what economic worth is put on a particular harm.

 Pause for reflection

Now that you have looked in more detail at the law(s) of tort(s) and, with an awareness that the financial implications are not comparable:

(1) Rank, on a scale of 1–10 (10 high), **how deserving** of compensation are those who suffer the following harms due to the wrong of another?

(2) **How much** do you think a claimant should be awarded for each the harms listed?

    (a) A broken leg.

    (b) A mental breakdown resulting from stress.

    (c) Trauma after witnessing the death of a child in an accident.

    (d) The burning down of a home.

    (e) The loss of a person's life savings.

    (f) The publication of intimate details in a national newspaper.

    (g) The birth of a child following a failed sterilisation.

    (h) Failure to recognise a child's special educational needs.

    (i) Disturbance by constant noise from a nearby factory.

Take time to consider why have you ranked the harms in the way you have, and why you have awarded more money to some of the claimants than others—what do the monetary sums reflect?

It should be recognised at the outset that the award of damages, even where there is clearly someone to blame, is subject to all the rules that we have discussed in the earlier sections of this book and which *limit liability*—and consequently—the *availability* of compensation. A claimant in negligence, for example, still has to overcome the technical hurdles of establishing a duty of care, breach of that duty and a harm caused by that breach which is not too remote a consequence of it. Only if this can be done does the law state that compensation is justified—and it should be remembered that these 'hurdles' are judicially created obstacles placed *in the way of* recovery. Exclusionary rules on duty, for example, are clearly used as devices to *control and limit* liability (that is, who pays) and keep it within what the courts insubstantially define as 'reasonable bounds'—claimants who are seriously harmed by clearly negligent actions on the part of a public body, for example, will find it hard to establish that a duty was owed to them.[11] Similarly, where the harm suffered is either 'purely' economic, or psychiatric, or was caused by an omission or the actions of a third party, a claimant who is unable to establish that a duty was owed will be unable to recover damages for their injury

11. See Chapter 6.

no matter how serious it is and *however clearly negligent the defendant was.*[12] Additional problems for claimants, as we have seen, come with establishing breach and causation in fact and law, notwithstanding the fact that the defendant may have a defence. Thus, from the outset, it should be clear that not all those who might *deserve* compensation, in the sense that they have been injured by the wrong of someone else, can receive it.

19.3 Calculating damages

19.3.1 Forms of damages payments

Damages in tort have been traditionally awarded on a 'one-shot, lump sum' basis. This means that the court has to assess, at the date of trial, the amount of compensation required by the claimant to meet their needs, considering investment returns, for the rest of their life and such an award was final.[13] Understandably, despite the attraction of a 'clean break' between claimant and defendant,[14] this method attracted much criticism, even the judiciary noting that 'there is really only one certainty: the future will prove the award to be either too high or too low' (Lord Scarman, *Lim Poh Choo v Camden & Islington Area Health Authority* [1980] at 183).

As we have explained, damages in tort are supposed to put the claimant, as far as money can do so, into their pre-tort position. This means that if, for example, someone becomes unable to work as a result of physical injuries caused by someone else's negligence, the compensation they receive will include a sum that reflects *what they would have earned* had they not been injured.[15] Similarly, with respect to expenses, where costs are incurred by the claimant *as a result of the injury*, the compensation awarded will include this as, without the tort occurring, money would not have been spent in that way.

Lump sum damages are calculated using 'multiplicands' and 'multipliers'.[16] A multiplicand is the sum that must be multiplied (for example, a sum of £20,000 lost earnings per year) and the multiplier is the number of years this needs to be multiplied by. However, there may be various multipliers applied to different multiplicands—for example, a person would only be expected to *work* until retirement, so this will help determine how many years any lost earnings should be multiplied by, but they would be expected to *live* longer than this, so medical costs incurred for the rest of someone's life would be multiplied by a greater number of years than their salary would be. That said, the calculations are not as simple as it might seem—working out the multiplier

12. See Chapters 4–5 and Chapter 7, above.
13. Awards were traditionally based on a high rate of return—4.5 per cent. It has more recently been realised that this is not realistic and changes have been made with the aim of protecting claimants against lower rates of return. How this has been done, and the effectiveness of such changes, is beyond the scope of this chapter.
14. A principle that might more commonly now be referred to as 'closure'.
15. For a fairly extreme example, consider *Collett v Smith* [2009]. In this case, an 18-year-old reserve player for Manchester United was injured by a negligent tackle and was awarded £4,577,323—£3,854,328 of this for future lost earnings.
16. 'Multiplicands' obviously still have a place in periodic payments (below)—it is the *method* of paying them that differs.

requires more than simply an assessment of how much longer a person had to work until they reached retirement age. The retirement age is 65, but the salary multiplier for a 40-year-old will not be as much as 25 years when there is a lump sum payment. Reduced multipliers are used for two main reasons: first, the fact that when payments are made in a lump sum, the fact that this sum is supposed to be invested means that to award the full number of years could *overcompensate* someone. Secondly, the court considers the 'vicissitudes of life'—the fact that illness, disease or other circumstances might have prevented that person working until retirement age.

For a 40-year-old woman expected to retire at 65 the multiplier is approximately 18 years! Based on a 2.5 per cent annual rate of return (interest), the maximum multiplier for a person aged about 20 and in good health is about 26.5 years, and that for a 50-year-old is about 12 years and so on. The figures are not plucked from thin air: the courts look at actuarial tables (compiled by a group including actuaries, lawyers and insurers), known as the 'Ogden Tables' to help them. In 1999, the use of these tables in assessing damages claims was formally approved by the House of Lords in *Wells* v *Wells*. Different tables exist depending on at what age retirement was expected, when a pension would have started to pay out and a person's life expectancy. The tables are different for males and females (to take into account differences in expected mortality, among other things).

In terms of particular injuries being suffered, guidelines issued by the Judicial Studies Board suggest 'prices' or a range of 'prices' that may be attached to various injuries when a judge is calculating the amount of damages to be awarded. For example, for the complete loss of sight in one eye, the award would currently be in the range of £32,250–36,000. For quadriplegia it would be £212,500–265,000. For 'severe' post traumatic stress disorder £40,000–66,000, and for a 'moderate' knee injury the award can be up to £17,500. More 'prices' from the judicial guidelines are shown in Figure 19.1.[17]

Pause for reflection

Do you find the awards that can be made for various injuries surprising (and it should be remembered that these will be injuries caused by someone else's negligence)? Are there any that you think are quite high, in relation to the injury itself or, conversely, any that do not seem to be enough? Who decides these figures and what are they based on? Should we consider injuries and losses in monetary terms?

Since 1982, 'provisional' damages awards have been allowed, for actions in which it is 'proved or admitted to be a chance' that the claimant's condition will seriously worsen in the future.[18] Damages awarded initially would be based on the claimant *not* suffering this extended harm, with the proviso that they were able to return to court if they

---

17. Figures are taken from the Judicial Studies Board *Guidelines for the Assessment of General Damages in Personal Injury Cases* (10th edn, OUP, 2010).

18. Administration of Justice Act 1982, s 6, inserting s 32A into the Senior Courts Act 1981.

Figure 19.1 Judicial guidelines for damages in personal injury cases

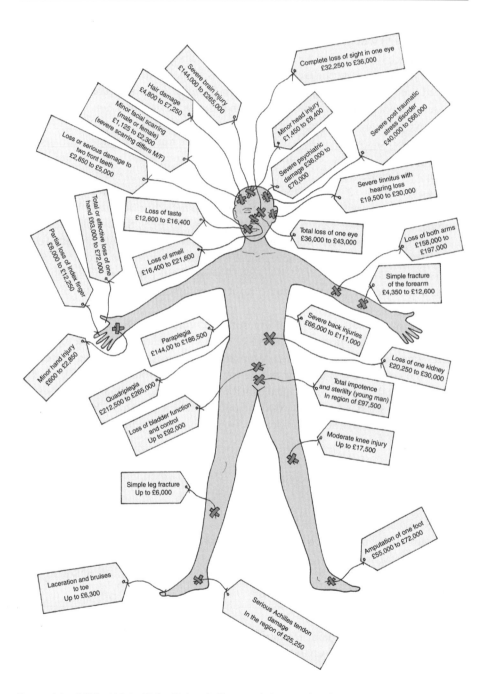

Complete loss of sight in one eye
£32,250 to £36,000

Severe brain injury
£144,000 to £265,000

Hair damage
£4,800 to £7,250

Minor head injury
£1,450 to £8,400

Severe post traumatic
stress disorder
£40,000 to £66,000

Minor facial scarring
(male or female)
£1,125 to £2,300
(severe scarring differs M/F)

Severe psychiatric
damage £36,000 to
£76,000

Loss or serious damage to
two front teeth
£2,850 to £5,000

Severe tinnitus with
hearing loss
£19,500 to £30,000

Total or effective loss of one
hand £63,000 to £72,000

Loss of taste
£12,600 to £16,400

Total loss of one eye
£36,000 to £43,000

Loss of both arms
£158,000 to
£197,000

Partial loss of index finger
£8,000 to £12,250

Loss of smell
£16,400 to £21,600

Simple fracture
of the forearm
£4,350 to £12,600

Minor hand injury
£500 to £2,850

Paraplegia
£144,00 to £186,500

Severe back injuries
£66,000 to £111,000

Loss of one kidney
£20,250 to £30,000

Quadriplegia
£212,500 to £265,000

Total impotence
and sterility (young man)
In region of £97,500

Loss of bladder function
and control
Up to £92,000

Moderate knee injury
Up to £17,500

Simple leg fracture
Up to £6,000

Amputation of one foot
£55,000 to £72,000

Laceration and bruises
to toe
Up to £6,300

Serious Achilles tendon
damage
In the region of £25,250

Source: Artwork © David Eaton/Oxford University Press; statistics reproduced with kind permission of Oxford University Press and the Judicial Studies Board. Taken from *Judicial Studies Board Guidelines for the Assessment of General Damages in Personal Injury cases* (10th edn, 2010)

did suffer it in the future.[19] Use of provisional damages was, however, rare. An alternative was 'structured settlement'. These were agreements under which a portion of the damages award was used to buy the claimant a life assurance policy, payable until their death or another agreed (earlier) date. The advantage was that doing so ensured a regular 'income' for the claimant, often on top of an initial (smaller) lump sum. However, structured settlements were based on agreement between the parties and the courts had no power to impose them, however sensible this may have seemed in the circumstances. The take-up rate was not high.

In 2002, the government consulted on the question of whether to give courts the power to award *compulsory* periodical payments, concluding that periodical payments 'better reflect the purpose of compensation' and 'place the risks associated with life expectancy and investment on defendants'.[20] Periodical Payment Orders (PPOs) were subsequently introduced by the Courts Act 2003.[21] Courts are now *required* to consider them in respect of future pecuniary loss derived from personal injury, and may now order that damages are wholly or partly to take the form of periodical payments based on the claimant's annual future needs, without the need for Ogden Table multipliers or discounts applied to take into account future life events.[22] Further, the courts have been given the power to vary PPOs where the claimant's condition seriously worsens—or considerably improves—at a later date, but only if it was specified at the time of the original order that it was to be variable.[23] PPOs are not without their critics and some commentators have indicated that even where PPOs would be more appropriate a lump sum will still be preferred by claimants in a number of cases.[24]

19.3.2 **Special and general damages**

Special damages are awarded for those costs that are readily quantifiable at the time of trial, such as the loss of earnings or pension already suffered by the claimant or the money already spent on care, medical treatments, special equipment (a wheelchair, for example), transport and household costs (including adaptations), plus interest accrued on these sums. Essentially, these will be pecuniary (financial) losses only.

General damages are those that cannot be quantified at the time of trial and are designed to compensate a claimant for the losses they suffer more generally arising from the harm they have incurred as a result of a tort being committed. These are generally more problematic, and include *future* pecuniary losses such as (*inter alia*) loss of net future earnings and future medical and social costs, as well as future costs, such as any special equipment that might be needed, transport and household costs (including adaptations). Importantly, general damages can also include sums for

---

19. Only *one* return is permitted and only for the injury/disease specified in the original claim.

20. Lord Chancellor's Department *Damages for Future Loss: Giving the Courts the Power to Order Periodical Payments for Future Loss and Care Costs in Personal Injury Cases* (Consultation paper, March 2002), [22].

21. Amending s 2 of the Damages Act 1996, though coming into force in April 2005.

22. For a concise explanation of how damages can be calculated in these awards, see Richard Lewis 'The Indexation of Periodical Payments of Damages in Tort: The Future Assured?' (2010) 30(3) *Legal Studies* 391, especially pp 395–6.

23. Damages (Variation of Periodical Payments) Order 2005, SI 2005/841.

24. See e.g. Richard Lewis 'The Politics and Economics of Tort Law: Judicially Imposed Periodical Payments of Damages' (2006) 69(3) *Modern Law Review* 418 and Lewis, note 22, at pp 406–7.

non-pecuniary losses, such as pain, suffering and lost amenity incurred as the result of personal injury.[25]

The cost of future care is recoverable, as long as it is necessary or reasonably incurred. It is not necessary for a carer to be a professional. If a partner or close relative, for example, gives up work to become a carer for an injured person, the law provides that they should be paid for doing so. In *Hunt* v *Severs* [1994], a woman injured in a motorcycle accident required long-term care. The claimant later married the defendant motorcyclist, and he became her carer. The House of Lords held that the claimant could claim the cost of a carer from the defendant and that this part of her damages award would be held in trust for the carer. Because of the specific situation in this case, however, the damages were not paid as their lordships found that public policy did not justify the payment of a damages award by the defendant simply for them to have to be given back to him. However, it should be noted that it would not have been the *defendant* who paid but his insurers, therefore the decision seems somewhat strange. Following *Hunt*, it would seem that claimants will be left worse off if the person who cares for them is also the defendant. Where this is not the case, a full sum for the cost of (past and future) care can be awarded.[26]

19.3.3 **Death and damages**

When a claimant dies, any claim that they might have had against a defendant survives them.[27] That is, their estate will be able to bring the claim and, if any damages become payable, they will be paid to the estate (thus can be passed on in inheritance terms, etc).[28]

Death is also dealt with under the Fatal Accidents Act 1976, which establishes a mechanism whereby dependants of the deceased can make a claim for *their* losses (for example, the loss of the main income into a household) and for bereavement.[29] Dependants, for the purposes of the Act, include the spouse or civil partner and children (under the age of 18) of the deceased as well as any *de facto* dependants.[30] Non-married partners are also included, provided that they had lived with the deceased 'as

---

25. Not without controversy, particularly when the claimant's condition is such that they will not know they have lost amenity (*Lim Poh Choo* v *Camden and Islington Area Health Authority* [1980]).

26. The Law Commission recommended in 1999 that this position (in respect of past but not future care costs) be legislatively reversed (Law Com No 262). In May 2007, a government consultation *The Law on Damages* proposed that the law be amended to make the claimant personally obliged to account for the money to the carer and that this should also apply to future care services 'gratuitously provided' (at [115]–[116]). A clause was included in the government's draft Civil Law Reform Bill (2009) to this effect. Following public consultation on the Bill, the government has decided not to proceed with it, as it would 'not contribute to the delivery of the government's priorities' (Ministry of Justice 'Civil Law Reform Bill: Response to Consultation', 10 January 2011).

27. Since the Law Reform (Miscellaneous Provisions) Act 1934 (s 1), with the exception of defamation claims and claims for bereavement under the Fatal Accidents Act 1976 (see below).

28. Further, s 1(4) of the Law Reform (Miscellaneous Provisions) Act 1934 provides that if the defendant dies and there was a time period before the *defendant's* death in which the claimant would have been able to claim damages (if, e.g., they were injured as a result of negligence then the defendant died before the claim came to court), the claim can still be brought against the defendant's estate.

29. Sections 1 and 1A respectively.

30. The full list is given in s 1(3).

husband or wife' for at least two years prior to their death.[31] However, it is only possible for a dependant to claim *if the deceased party would have been able to bring a claim had they lived*—that is, a proven tort must have been committed, without a suitable defence being available, and subject to limitation provisions (below).[32] Dependants can claim all financial losses incurred by them due to the death, such as the proportion of the deceased's earnings that would have been spent on them (ongoing or in the form of savings for the future, and including 'non-essentials' such as annual holidays). They can also claim the 'value' of the 'service' of the deceased—for example, if they were the main childcare provider, the value of the time of childcare could be claimed by the spouse or partner in order that the child was able to attend nursery or similar, meaning that the surviving spouse would not have to give up work, etc. Such losses are either assessed by the multiplier/multiplicand[33] method as before (though clearly involving even more complicated calculations) or by periodical payments.

In terms of claiming for bereavement itself the Act provides for damages of £11,800 to be paid,[34] a sum meant in some way to compensate for the 'other' (non-pecuniary) losses associated with a person's death. This sum cannot be claimed by children of the deceased, only by a spouse or partner or, if the deceased was a minor, the parents—there are more limitations here than for dependency claims. Notably, then, if a 19-year-old child was killed, no compensation for the parents' bereavement would be available and, in the reverse situation, children who lose a parent may receive compensation for the pecuniary losses they suffer, but not for the non-pecuniary bereavement and grief.

 Pause for reflection

Is the death of a loved one (caused by the 'fault' of somebody else) adequately compensated by £11,800? How can such an arbitrary line be drawn? Comparing some of the guidance figures for claimants who suffer personal injury, we can see that it is often much cheaper to kill your victim than it is to 'merely' injure them. Because the effects of many injuries last a lifetime, the compensation which can be awarded for them does too. Doesn't the effect of someone's death last a lifetime? Is this properly taken into account by the Fatal Accidents Act?

Patrick Atiyah, however, calls bereavement damages 'highly objectionable'.[35] His reasons are two-fold. First, the 'motives of relatives in seeking such awards may be questionable' and, more importantly, he contends, 'it seems arbitrary to select the death of a close relative as the criterion for paying what is still to many people a substantial sum of money . . . the relatives of a person who is very severely injured (but not killed) in an accident may well suffer much greater mental suffering than the relatives of someone who is killed'.

31. Section 1(3)(b).
32. Section 1(1).
33. Which would be the annual value of the dependency, net of deductions.
34. Up from £10,000 for all deaths before 1 January 2008, itself an increase from £7,500 in 2002.
35. Peter Cane *Atiyah's Accidents, Compensation and the Law* (7th edn, CUP, 2006), p 90.

> ➡
>
> Secondly, he argues that a statutory award fails to take into account the differences in the actual relationships covered—regardless of the actual closeness of the parties or, for example, the state of the deceased party's health. Do you agree? Compare the availability of damages for psychiatric harm suffered through witnessing a negligently caused accident and what has to be proved before one can bring a claim as a secondary victim.[36]

19.4 Independent, joint and several concurrent liabilities

It is, of course, possible that there is more than one wrongdoer in a single tort claim, in that there may be more than one party whose actions are partly or wholly the cause of the claimant's harm. When this occurs, the law has found it necessary to delineate which party or parties can be sued by an individual claimant, by establishing the categories of independent, joint and several and concurrent defendants.

Where two or more parties cause different harms to the claimant at different times (although there may be only minutes between them), who pays (and what for) is often a question of causation (that is, whether the latter defendant broke the chain of causation back to the harm caused by the original defendant). When we say that harms are different in this context, we might mean for example that they are different *types* of harm entirely (for example, personal and psychiatric injury) or that they are essentially the same *type* of harm but operate at different *levels* (for example, the difference between a leg injury suffered in a car accident followed by death after being treated at hospital). Each defendant in such circumstances is potentially liable independently of the other. In *Rahman v Arearose Ltd* [2000], a man was attacked in his workplace, a fast food restaurant—his employer was held vicariously liable for the violent attack, which left him needing hospital treatment. In hospital, he received negligent treatment to his right eye, leaving it blinded. He subsequently developed various psychiatric complaints, which his psychiatrist was able to attribute, to various extents, to the initial attack and to his loss of sight.[37] The Court of Appeal apportioned damages respectively between the employer and the health authority concerned—each defendant was clearly negligent and therefore liable to pay some compensation—the question was what proportion of the total damages each should pay.

However, there are instances where it can be said either that two parties being sued were acting with the same common goal and caused the same damage, or that the actions of two or more separate defendants happened independently but all contributed to the same harm (a common example is where a claimant suffers whiplash after their car is crashed into by two negligently driven cars at the same time). In such cases, the law has created mechanisms that make it easier for the claimant to receive the total

---

36. See Chapter 5, p 103.
37. Note, however, that the 'divisibility' of psychiatric harm has more recently been doubted in *Dickins v O2 Plc* [2008].

sum of damages that the law deems appropriate for the harm: the claimant may claim against one of the defendants for the whole of the damages.[38]

In the former example, where two or more defendants act with a commonly held goal, each is held jointly liable.[39] The claimant can then sue either both or all parties together for the entirety of the damage. A court will rule on the amount of damages to be paid and this can be recovered by the claimant from one, both or all of the defendants (but the whole sum can be recovered only once).[40] This mechanism (and legal fiction) ensures that the claimant can receive the whole sum, without having to locate multiple defendants. It also means, for example in the employer/employee situation, that there is someone joined to the action—and liable—who has sufficient funds to pay (and probably also insurance). The claimant may have other entirely practical reasons for suing one rather than the other, for example if both defendants were companies and one has become bankrupt.

In the second example, the liability would be several and concurrent (see *Fitzgerald* v *Lane* [1988]; *Vision Golf* v *Weightmans* [2005]). As with joint liability, the claimant can choose to sue either defendant for the entirety of the damages (although can recover only once). Again, this is a mechanism used to ensure that further barriers are not put in the way of the claimant receiving compensation. It is not as unfair as it might seem—whichever defendant pays is then able to seek a contribution to the damages paid out (via the Civil Liability (Contribution) Act 1978). That is, unless, as in the bankruptcy example, the co-defendant is unable to pay or, where the amount is disputed, a separate court action may ensue where the amount to be paid by each will be judicially apportioned. The benefit of this is that the claimant in the original action is not affected by any arguments that ensue between co-defendants, on whom the burden of apportionment of damages (and therefore 'blameworthiness'?) squarely falls.[41] Apportionment is based on each defendant's proportion of responsibility for the injury that occurred (and of course will be subject to a reduction if the claimant was also in part responsible (contributorily negligent) for their own harm, as in *Fitzgerald* v *Lane*).

Table 19.1 Multiple defendants: what type of liability?

Description	Example	Type of liability	Who pays what?
Two or more parties cause different harms to the claimant	A car is hit by one negligent driver, causing property damage, then later by another negligent driver, causing injury to the claimant	Independent	Each co-defendant pays for the actual harm they caused (but only one case needs to be brought to the court by the claimant)

38. And that defendant may later take proceedings against any other defendant who was equally liable, via the Civil Liability (Contribution) Act 1978. Section 2 states that apportionment shall be calculated to a degree that is 'just and equitable having regard to the extent of that person's responsibility for the damage in question'.

39. Joint liability also applies to employers and employees, where the employee commits the tort and the employer becomes liable for it via the principle of vicarious liability—see Chapter 12.

40. See e.g. ***Fairchild* v *Glenhaven Funeral Services*** [2002], discussed in Chapter 9, pp 230–231.

41. Though cf ***Barker* v *Corus*** [2006], discussed in Chapter 9, at pp 232–236.

Table 19.1 *Continued*

Description	Example	Type of liability	Who pays what?
Two parties being sued were acting with the same common goal and caused the same damage	An employee commits a tort in the course of his employment, for which the employer would be vicariously liable	Joint	Either party (or both) can be sued for the entirety of the damage
The actions of two or more separate defendants happened independently but contributed to the same harm	A claimant suffers whiplash after their car is crashed into by two negligently driven cars at the same time	Several concurrent[42]	Either party (or both) can be sued for the entirety of the damage. Where only one party is sued, they can recover an appropriate portion of the damages paid out via the Civil Liability (Contribution) Act 1978

19.5 **Time limitations on claims**

Section 2 of the Limitation Act 1980 provides that tort actions, including those for trespass to the person, must be brought within six years of the tort being committed, the main exception being for minors, where the time period runs from when they reach the age of 18. Sections 11–14 contain provisions, first introduced by the Limitation Act 1975, which make exceptions for actions for 'damages for negligence, nuisance or breach of duty', where the claim is in respect of personal injury. In these cases, the limitation period is *three* years from either the date when the cause of action accrued or the 'date of knowledge',[43] whichever is the later. Importantly, this applies in situations where a negligent act causes what is known as 'latent damage'—damage that only arises (or is recognised) later, not as an immediate consequence of the tort, though still a result of it—here the limitation period runs from the time that damage or harm begins to be suffered.

In *Stubbings* v *Webb* [1993], the question arose as to whether a claimant could claim in negligence for what were in fact *intentional* acts (trespass to the person, which technically involve no 'breach of duty'), where the harm suffered was latent. In this case, a woman claimed damages from her adopted father and step-brother for sexual abuse and rape, which had occurred between 16 and 28 years before, when

---

42. Note that in both joint and several concurrent liability, where an employer/employee or insurer/insuree are held liable, recovery of some of the costs from the actual wrongdoer (e.g. employee) is technically possible through the principle of 'subrogation'.

43. Defined in s 14.

she was a child. She sought to use the exception created under section 11 of the 1980 Act because although she clearly knew that she had been abused (and had not sued at the time, when she would have had an action in trespass), she did not realise until 1984 that she had suffered psychological injuries as a result of the abuse. Given the timing, hers was a novel claim, seeking to make use of the extended limitation period for latent damage caused by negligence. Put simply, she claimed that the abuse had been *negligent*, rather than framing it as an intentional tort, because the law would have prevented her claim in trespass, but it did not do so in negligence as the law had there dealt with the possibility that harm could be suffered later than when the tort itself was committed. Her claim was made one month away from the end of the extended limitation period under section 11, as she had become 'aware' of the psychological harm almost exactly three years previously. Not surprisingly, the defendants argued that she was statute-barred as hers was purely and simply a trespass claim, and was thus subject to a six-year limitation period which had long since expired.

In the Court of Appeal, the woman's claim was allowed. However, the House of Lords unanimously overturned the decision, turning to technical interpretation of the statute and the precise meaning of the words 'negligence, nuisance of breach of duty' used in section 11(1) and what the law lords perceived the intended meaning of Parliament to be. Lord Griffiths held that he could not construe the words 'breach of duty' as including deliberate acts and also that Parliament could not have intended the phrase to include abuse and rape. In discussing the difference between breach of duty and infringing rights—which is how he saw deliberate acts—he asked '[i]f I invite a lady to my house one would naturally think of a duty to take care that the house is safe but would one really be thinking of a duty not to rape her?' (at 508). Unsurprisingly, the case was decided in favour of the defendants: the woman was statute-barred from taking her claim. The unanimous decision meant that section 11 could not apply to a case of deliberate assault, including acts of sexual assault or abuse, and that actions for intentional trespass to the person are not actions for 'negligence, nuisance or breach of duty' within the meaning of section 11(1). Subsequently, the European Court of Human Rights agreed (in *Stubbings* v *UK* [1996]). However, this position has now been remedied by the House of Lords in *A* v *Hoare* [2008].

A v Hoare, X v Wandsworth LBC, H v Suffolk, CCC v Middlesbrough Council, Young v Catholic Care (Diocese of Leeds) [2008] HL

Hoare was a conjoined appeal in which a number of claimants sued a number of different institutional defendants, both private and public bodies (including local councils and a Catholic Church care organisation) and, in one case, a private individual. This was *A* v *Hoare* itself, where the claimant, who was raped by the defendant, had not sued him earlier (for it is rarely worth suing for compensation from someone without the means to pay it), but later decided to do so when she learnt that he had won £7 million on the lottery while in prison.

→

→

All the claimants were victims of sexual assaults and abuse of one sort or another and were seeking to frame their claims in negligence to avoid the problem of the limitation period outlined above. To avoid the obstacle of *Stubbings*, many of the cases against institutions alleged 'systemic abuse' so as to show that the organisation was *negligent* in allowing the abuse to continue, rather than that each individual act was negligent in itself. The lower courts in *Hoare* followed the precedent set in *Stubbings*, but the claimants appealed further, submitting that *Stubbings* was wrongly decided and that the House of Lords should overturn it.

Lord Hoffmann, giving the leading judgment, summarised the claimants' position:

> The general rule is that the period of limitation for an action in tort is six years from the date on which the cause of action accrues. This period derives from the Limitation Act 1623 and is now contained in section 2 of the 1980 Act. All the claimants started proceedings well after the six years had expired. It follows that, if section 2 applies, their claims are barred. But sections 11 to 14 contain provisions, first introduced by the Limitation Act 1975, which create a different regime for actions for 'damages for negligence, nuisance or breach of duty', where the damages are in respect of personal injuries. In such cases the limitation period is three years from either the date when the cause of action accrued or the 'date of knowledge' as defined in section 14, whichever is the later. In addition, section 33 gives the court a discretion to extend the period when it appears that it would be equitable to do so. The chief question in these appeals is whether the claimants come within section 2 or section 11. In the latter case, the claimants say either that the date of knowledge was less than three years before the commencement of proceedings or that the discretion under section 33 should be exercised in their favour. (at [1])

The House of Lords held that *Stubbings* had indeed been wrongly decided and, in respect of *A v Hoare*, allowed the woman's appeal, referring the case back to the High Court for assessment of whether the section 33 discretion could be exercised. In the other cases, the claims were either upheld (with the damages that the lower courts said they would have awarded if they had been able to) or referred back to see whether the section 33 discretion should be applied—the implication being that it would (see Lord Hoffmann at [49]), given the very nature of the injuries suffered.

Technically, the House of Lords can depart from precedent (that is, say that a previous case decided by them was wrongly decided) only when the decision in the former case can be thought to be 'impeding the proper development of the law or to have led to results which were unjust or contrary to public policy' (Lord Hoffmann at [20]). This is exactly what had happened in the law since *Stubbings* was decided and was the reason that the House of Lords felt they could overturn that decision. The development of the law relating to vicarious liability[44] weighed heavily on the law lords, as did decisions in cases that seemed to defy all logical principles and which could clearly be described as

---

44. Where it has been recognised that organisations or institutions may be vicariously liable for acts of sexual abuse committed by an employee during the course of their employment (see *Lister v Hesley Hall* [2002], discussed in Chapter 12, p 333).

'impeding the proper development of the law' or having an 'unjust' result. As Baroness Hale acknowledged:

> the abuse itself is the reason why so many victims do not come forward until years after the event. This presents a challenge to a legal system which resists stale claims. Six years, let alone three, from reaching the age of majority is not long enough . . . (at [54])

One such case was *KR v Bryn Alyn Community (Holdings) Ltd* [2003]. Here, the Court of Appeal said that the need to frame a claim in artificial ways (such as the 'systemic abuse' negligence claims in **Hoare**) when the real cause of complaint was deliberate sexual abuse for which the employer ought to be vicariously liable was causing 'arid and highly wasteful litigation turning on a distinction of no apparent principle or other merit' (Auld LJ at [100]). In *S v W (Child abuse: damages)* [1995], a girl sued her parents in respect of sexual abuse conducted by her father: her father was sued in trespass and her mother in negligence, for not preventing the abuse. As her action was brought nearly ten years after the last intentional act, the girl was statute-barred from taking the claim against her father but the claim against her mother fell under section 11 of the 1980 Act and also section 33, where a discretional extension to the limitation period could be granted. Put simply, the girl could sue her mother but not her father; the person who actually abused her and caused her harm. Sir Ralph Gibson, in the Court of Appeal, felt that such an outcome was both 'illogical and surprising' and said that the Law Commission should look into the situation. Subsequently, the Law Commission reviewed the law of limitation of actions and presented its findings to Parliament in 2001.[45] The report described the legal effects of *Stubbings* as 'anomalous', with particular reference to *S v W* (at [1.5]). Partly on this basis, the Law Commission recommended a uniform regime for personal injuries, whether a claim was taken in negligence or trespass (at [1.14]). No action on this had been taken by Parliament prior to the decision in **Hoare**.

 Counterpoint

As *Lunney & Oliphant* point out, the decision in *Stubbings* 'attracted few admirers' (p 49) and it was seemingly quite out of date with modern thinking about rape and abuse. The problem in such cases is that victims of child abuse often do not acknowledge or understand the harm they have suffered until much later and may not tell anyone or seek advice until later still. So, in terms of taking a claim, those abused as children may be in their twenties or thirties by the time they realise that they have suffered harm and/or that they want to do something about the harm they suffered. However, the law then stood in their way, as abusive behaviour is not negligent but intentional. This meant that claimants had to attempt to distort and bend the law in order to frame their claims in negligence, where they might have been able to take advantage of the exception created by sections 11 and 14 of the 1980 Act and the discretion available to judges under section 33. This made some arguments tenuous, as can be seen from the claims of 'systemic negligence' made in the

→

---

45. *Limitation of Actions* (Law Com No 270, 2001).

→

conjoined appeals in *Hoare* and, because it meant people who had suffered serious and deliberately inflicted harms would have no option but to do this to achieve justice, cast the law into disrepute in the process. The House of Lords did no more than acknowledge this in *Hoare*, but the decision can be seen as particularly significant as it removes the legal barrier faced by future claimants in similar situations; claimants who it must be remembered may already face serious and considerable personal problems in identifying and acknowledging the harm done to them—precisely the reason that the limitation period issue arises. In this sense, this is a good example of the judges adapting law where Parliament has failed to act on either previous judicial prompting or even advice from its own advisory body, the Law Commission.

The situation following the *Hoare* decision has been described as follows:

[A]s their Lordships observed, the situation as it stood was bringing the law into disrepute, both by forcing the distortion of legal arguments and failing to do justice to tort victims. Many difficulties remain for abuse victims seeking civil redress. And there are still issues to be debated about whether litigation is really the best way to address these kinds of social ills. However, at the individual level, the injustice wrought by the harshness of *Stubbings* appears for the time being to have been alleviated.[46]

The Limitation Act 1980 also provides that any action where contribution is sought between several concurrent defendants must usually be started within two years of the original date of settlement or award. A limitation period of three years exists in relation to the Fatal Accidents Act 1976; the time period runs from the date of death, not the date of the tort, if this came earlier. Claims under the Human Rights Act (HRA) 1998 are the most significantly limited—s 7(5)(a) states that they must be initiated before the end of one year after the act complained of took place.[47]

19.6 **The problem with damages**

Tomlinson v *Congleton Borough Council* [2004]

We previously looked at this case in the chapter on Occupiers' Liability, above (p 197). Tomlinson was a teenager who dived badly, against the rules, into the shallow part of a

---

46. Peter Cane and Joanne Conaghan *The New Oxford Companion to Law* (OUP, 2008), p 7. See also Nicola Godden, 'Sexual Abuse and Claims in Tort: Limitation Periods after *A v Hoare (and other appeals)* [2008] and *AB and others v Nugent Care Society; GR v Wirral MBC* [2009]' (2010) 18(2) *Feminist Legal Studies* 179; *Raggett* v *Society of Jesus Trust of 1929* [2010]. In different contexts, see *Whiston* v *London Strategic Health Authority (successor body in law for the Queen Charlotte's Maternity Hospital)* [2010] (an adult claiming in respect of brain injuries suffered at birth) and *B* v *Ministry of Defence* [2010] (injuries arising from nuclear testing in the 1950s).

47. Though this can be extended if the court thinks it 'equitable having regard to all the circumstances' (s 7(5)(b)).

→

lake, ending up tetraplegic (paralysis of all four limbs). As you will remember, he sued the local council (a public body), which had control of the lake and its surroundings. Had the case not been appealed to the House of Lords, Tomlinson would have received a large sum of money in damages, as the Court of Appeal believed his claim to be successful. Because of the ruling of the majority of the House of Lords, however, Tomlinson received *nothing*.

Such a case clearly illustrates the dilemma where two demands of 'justice' collide. On the one hand, it can be argued that Tomlinson should gain compensation in order to make his life more bearable (in terms of pain, suffering, quality of ongoing care, etc). On the other hand, the defendant has an equally valid claim that it should not be made to pay for things which were not caused by its own fault and, especially, when having to pay would put demands on a budget that would mean money could end up being diverted from public services and amenities.

The many reasons for claiming damages in tort can be highlighted here, though two in particular stand out:

(1) Corrective justice—justice can be seen to be about fairness and correcting the situation (by putting the claimant back into the position he would have been in had the accident not occurred) is one way of doing this. But in cases of death, or where there is injury to such a serious extent as that suffered by Tomlinson, this simply is not possible, although compensation can play a role in holding people accountable for their (negligent) actions.

(2) Compensation—as we have indicated above, an action in tort is often simply about getting the money required in order to live life to an acceptable standard. Given that Tomlinson could not be cured, what he wanted was enough money to be able to live comfortably and not to worry about the future. But the question also has to focus on who is being asked to pay, and whether they should—was the council really to *blame* in any way for Tomlinson's injuries? Often, the answer to the 'who pays?' question is that it will be insurance companies who pay (in ***Tomlinson*** the council would have had insurance)—in which case, should we be concerned about who was to blame?

There are many limitations to the system within which damages are awarded in tort. The primary reason for most of these is that *legal* fault (negligence) does not always equate with *moral* blame. If we say that a fault-based system is justified then it often does not seem fair that those who are truly to blame are not the ones who pay—the principles of vicarious liability and the increased prevalence of insurance, particularly compulsory insurance, shift the focus of the system to ask who *can* pay rather than who *should* pay, as a system truly based on fault (and the idea of corrective justice and individual responsibility) would do. Given that this is the case, perhaps we should ask whether fault and blame should necessarily be the framework around which we base how we award compensation. There are perhaps other ways to measure it, one of these being need. To ask who *needs* damages, however, is more closely aligned to asking who *can* pay; both are underpinned by ideas of collective rather than individual responsibility, and focus on the fact that the primary aim of tort is (or has become) compensation. It is only when need is separated from fault that any kind of equitable distribution of compensation can be envisaged—that is, if everyone who needed it (whether there was someone else to blame *or not*) received adequate compensation for the injuries they suffered, we truly would live in a fairer society.[48] Furthermore, it is not at all clear why judges should become the arbiters of who should get compensation, from whom, in what circumstances and how much.

To date, fault-based liability has been heavily undermined by the growth of the insurance industry and the expansion of the principle of vicarious liability. If the system was truly fault-based, it would be far easier to see the principles of retribution, deterrence, justice, etc playing a part in the tort system—but as it is not in fact the wrongdoer (legal *or* moral) who usually pays, it could be argued that all of these other aspects and functions of tort no longer hold true—compensation alone has become the true focus. In part, this must be what led to the claims that we now live in a 'compensation culture' (see panel in Introduction, pp 14–15). This is hardly surprising given that the legal system itself seems to focus on compensation rather than justice. We shall look more closely at the idea of a compensation culture below.

 Pause for reflection

Why do you think the emphasis of the tort system changed? There are various things that can be considered as factors in this. On the one hand there was the inevitable increase in accidents attributable to employers and other parties who made suitable targets for tort actions following the Industrial Revolution. Similarly, the rise of the car—and the rise of the tort of negligence itself—helped to contribute to the gradual emergence of a damages action for personal injury caused by negligence as the predominant action in tort. A growing number of car accidents (and, therefore, injuries) led to the passage of the Road Traffic Act 1930, which introduced compulsory liability insurance for motorists (the first example of this type of insurance in the UK), as well as the establishment of the Motor Insurers' Bureau in 1936. These were later followed by the Employers' Liability Act 1969, another compulsory insurance scheme meaning that employers would be *able* to pay, via insurance, when someone was injured in the course of their employment. In addition, the rise of the largely unjustified (except in the sense that someone would be able to pay) spectre of vicarious liability has helped to change the focus from ensuring that the defendant pays to ensuring that the claimant *gets paid.*

Moreover, when looking at whether the loss has actually been shifted from the innocent victim to the wrongdoer, we encounter further issues. We can ask again, with the principle of vicarious liability and the fact that the whole tort system operates under the shadow of the insurance industry, is loss-shifting really what is happening? Given that when, for example, employers, drivers, goods manufacturers or NHS trusts become liable, they are likely to be insured against the loss, the question may be asked as to who is actually bearing the costs of the wrongs committed. If manufacturers have to keep paying out, the price of consumables will rise, and society ends up paying for the harms incurred by individuals and therefore the risks associated with manufacturing. If employers (or their insurance

➡

---

48. See e.g. the Government Workers' Compensation Scheme, introduced in the late nineteenth century—a no-fault scheme; everyone injured was entitled to compensation.

➜

companies) end up paying for the torts of their employees, the price of insurance as a whole goes up, and society as a whole ends up paying. If a driver's insurance company pays damages following an accident, not only will the individual driver's insurance premiums rise, but so will the premiums paid by other drivers insured by the same company, or at least those within the same insurance bracket (based on age, gender, experience, etc). If an NHS trust pays out, not only could it be said that we are taking money away from an already stretched health service, thereby potentially depriving others of quality care, but it will be the taxpayers who ultimately pay. In all these examples (and more), there is no instance of the wrongdoer paying in any sense, thus it cannot truly be said that the tort system is a loss-shifting system. If anything, it operates as a system of loss-distribution, and society at large bears the costs of all harms and all risk.

While it may be said that suing regulates conduct by the deterrent effect of liability avoidance, and therefore has implications for society in the future, the fact that we have deviated from a moral towards a purely legal notion of blame has some potentially undesirable social consequences. A growth in litigation and what has been called 'litigation consciousness' perhaps inevitably brings with it an increase in the number of 'frivolous' claims being made. Society, and the organisations within it (including public bodies, employers, etc), in realising this, may adopt a 'safety' culture and defensive practices. Similarly, a blame culture may grow, where few accept that there can be such things as 'accidents' and even fewer are prepared to take risks—which may once have been seen as necessary and vital, for example in terms of innovation and improvement. On this issue, sociologist Frank Furedi argues that '[r]isk avoidance has become an important theme in political debate and social action'.[49] He highlights the precautionary approach seemingly adopted by today's society, which now sees 'risk' as a bad thing. As an example of the negative effect of this, in the context of tort/regulation and school trips, he says that:

> the tragic death of a child on a school outing invariably turns into a major national story about the risks involved in such activities. Such tragedies are usually followed by calls for tighter regulation of school outings. Another response is to seek someone to blame. Not surprisingly, many teachers have become reluctant to organise such events. (pp 7–8)

Responding to the *British Medical Journal's* 2001 declaration that it was to ban the word 'accident' from its pages, stating that 'most injuries and their precipitating events are predictable and preventable', Furedi argues that:

> cleansing the term accident from our cultural narrative inexorably leads to a relentless search for someone to blame. This is where the legal profession takes over and provides the injured with an obvious target for a compensation claim…Educating people to discover that what they thought was their fault can actually be blamed on someone else seems to be part of the project of purging the idea of an accident from the English language…Like the BMJ censors, [claims management companies] believe that behind every injury lurks an act of negligence. (p 11)

49. Frank Furedi *The Culture of Fear* (2nd edn, Continuum Press, 2002), p 2.

In terms of law, he contends that almost all accidents, with hindsight, can be reinterpreted so as to show that there was some 'culpable negligence' involved. Further, he argues that the implication of all this is a restrained society, identified by its lowered expectations and a 'dissipation of the human potential'[50]—something he describes as the creation of 'a society that celebrates victimhood'. Whether Furedi's interpretation goes too far into hyperbole remains to be seen—he is certainly correct in one respect: a move toward compensation rather than true fault does result in a different type of blame. Almost exclusively it seems that the ultimate goal of anyone seeking redress through the tort systems is achieving compensation, rather than a desire to initiate change, make public a wrong or force an apology. Tort as a system of accident compensation seems to be a view that is now widely shared. Indeed, *Making Amends*, a government report published in 2003, said that the system provides little incentive to report incidences of medical negligence or to learn from them.[51] Focusing on the immediate cause (the negligence of the doctor) rather than how things can more generally be improved (for example, in the Health Service as a whole) hinders the deterrent function of tort. The courts can also be seen, on occasion, to turn their focus to achieving compensation for claimants, rather than any other principles of justice, sometimes distorting the law in order to achieve this aim. An example of this is **Nettleship v Weston**, where it can clearly be argued that the young and, crucially, inexperienced driver was not at (moral) fault, yet the court held her to the standard of a competent driver in order that she would necessarily fall below the standard required of her (that is, she would be in breach) and the instructor could therefore be compensated through her insurance for her 'negligence').[52] Unusually, this is openly acknowledged in the judgment itself—perhaps due only to the typical candidness of Lord Denning.

 Pause for reflection

It is quite likely that the majority of those who suffer injury do want money—this is both necessary and enabling. However, as we discussed in the introduction, often claimants seek other things too: an explanation or apology, reassurances that some action will be taken to prevent the same harm happening to someone else in the future and so on.[53] The tort system, as it stands, seemingly fails to provide these things—do you think its focus should be changed? Do you think that tort (and private litigation through the courts) is the appropriate vehicle to address these issues in the first place or to initiate any necessary changes? If not, what is the alternative?

That tort should become a vehicle for accident compensation is not a view shared by everyone, and the tort system was not designed to function in this way—distributive

---

50. Furedi, above, p 13.

51. Sir Liam Donaldson, Chief Medical Officer *Making Amends: a consultation paper setting out proposals for reforming the approach to clinical negligence in the NHS* (2003), p 55.

52. Discussed in Chapter 8, p 200.

53. Note that the Compensation Act 2006, passed following an inquiry of the Constitutional Affairs Select Committee into 'compensation culture' and contingency fees, contains a provision to the effect that in claims for negligence or breach of statutory duty, an apology, offer of treatment or other redress shall not of itself amount to an admission of liability (s 2).

justice (for that surely is the end result, even if unintended, of an accident compensation system) simply was not part of the agenda. When compensation *is* based on fault in the way that it currently seems to be, all kinds of questions are raised about who gets it, and whether they are more deserving than anyone else suffering the same type of harms. A study of the system would also show that the tort system, when compared with other avenues of 'compensation' such as social security, is actually very generous, in terms of the sums awarded. One of the obvious reasons for this is the difference in the way compensation is paid—usually in a lump sum, rather than on a weekly or monthly basis, and not as dependent on an individual's financial circumstances (a person injured by the fault of someone else would still be able to claim from them even if they had large sums of money in savings, but many benefits are means-tested).

However, this 'generosity' of tort should not be misunderstood; only a select few (those that overcome all the 'hurdles') will get any compensation at all. In 1972 the Pearson Committee was established to survey all accident compensation in England and Wales. When it reported in 1978, it showed that only 6.5 per cent of people physically harmed in accidents actually received damages in tort. When we consider that accident victims (those who are potentially able to frame their claim in tort) make up only about 10 per cent of those disabled in society, the true figure of those who will receive damages for disabling injuries is closer to one per cent. This figure clearly stands in stark contrast to the 'compensation culture' claim that too much is being paid out!

Furthermore, our tort system, based as it is on the payment of damages where fault can be established, is expensive to operate and largely inefficient in doing what it is supposed to do well. This is not in itself a criticism of the decisions of any particular case or cases, or of government failure to amend the system in a particular way. Again, it is a case of the figures speaking for themselves. The Pearson Committee calculated that the cost to run the tort system (in the 1970s) amounted to 85 per cent of the sums paid out. Put simply, this means that for every pound paid in compensation, 85 pence had to be spent to achieve that result. Or, for every £10,000 paid out, £8,500 had to be put in. In comparison, the running costs of the New Zealand system discussed below are estimated at about seven per cent. To summarise, tort as accident compensation is expensive to run, compared with social security, for example, but relatively high awards of compensation can be achieved (compared to the sums paid by social security). The 6.5 per cent of accident victims who *do* achieve compensation through the tort system are therefore estimated to consume about 40 per cent of the total money actually paid out to all accident victims. Bearing in mind that some of those victims will get nothing, the tort system appears heavily skewed towards those who can successfully jump through hoops and it seems little wonder that it has been described as a 'damages lottery'.[54]

 Pause for reflection

Consider *Tomlinson* again. Why should his future have depended solely on the fact that (overall) five senior judges voted one way, and four voted the other? This shows that there is at least an element of doubt as to the correctness of the outcome of this case. But if he

➡

54. Patrick Atiyah *The Damages Lottery* (Hart, 1997).

➡

did deserve compensation, what does this say about the people with incapacities who are unable to gain a remedy? For example, what about people born with spinal defects, who cannot 'blame' anyone—are they more, less or equally deserving of compensation than John Tomlinson? Is litigation—taking a claim in private law through the courts—the appropriate mechanism in this kind of situation or, as a society, ought we to be doing more for *everyone* with a disability, no matter how it was caused?

On the other hand, consider the effect that this case might have had if the House of Lords had *not* reversed the Court of Appeal's decision. While tort law can be said to be useful in terms of its potential deterrent effects, this is positive only where the activity being deterred is wrongful or does not have social value—that is, the idea is not to deter socially valuable activities. In a similar vein, but not necessarily speaking about the tort system, Frank Furedi gives the example that 'some local councils are worried that children might get injured through conkering—the age old custom of playing with horse-chestnuts. Consequently, local councils have implemented the policy of "tree management"—cutting down trees—to make horse-chestnut trees less accessible to children'.[55] What would have been the practical effect of the Court of Appeal's decision in *Tomlinson* had it been allowed to stand—that is, what would the council have had to do?[56]

19.6.1 Alternative sources of compensation

A study of tort law, dominated as it tends to be by negligence and considerations of fault and blame, often means that the fact that compensation could be achieved in other ways is under-considered or even overlooked. Particularly where the harm concerned is personal injury or property damage, other mechanisms of compensation—or other types of compensation scheme—would perhaps better serve the needs of claimants. Despite the textbook perception, in reality, tort plays only a very minor role in compensating those who suffer these kinds of harms. The Pearson Committee's figure showing that only 6.5 per cent of people injured in accidents receive damages indicates that the bulk of 'compensation' for physical harms must be derived from other sources—or simply is not present at all (that is, some people must go uncompensated in entirety). These other sources might include payments from employers, insurance and other schemes (such as the Criminal Injuries Compensation Scheme or Motor Insurers' Bureau) and social security. What should be noted, however, is that claimants pursuing these alternatives are likely to receive less than they would in an award of damages. Because of the *restitutio in integrum* principle, tort damages seek to compensate victims for the whole of the harm they have suffered, including future losses and costs.

---

55. Furedi, above, p 4.

56. See also *Simonds* v *Isle of Wight Council* [2003]. Note, however, that s 1 of the Compensation Act 2006 requires courts considering the *standard* of care in a claim for negligence or breach of statutory duty to take into account whether requiring particular steps to be taken to meet the standard would prevent or impede a 'desirable activity' from taking place. This provision was designed to improve awareness of this aspect of the law and to help to ensure that 'normal' activities are not prevented because of a fear of litigation and excessively risk-averse behaviour and essentially enshrines the House of Lords' position in *Tomlinson* into statute. According to the explanatory notes to the Act, the provision was also designed to address the misperception that there is a compensation culture following the 2004 report of the Better Regulation Task Force (see p 583).

Counterpoint

Many accident victims who would in theory be able to bring a claim in tort do not do so, meaning that (a) even fewer people receive full compensation than ought to (if that is the principle we adhere to), and (b) more people rely on other systems such as social security, funded by the taxpayer, than ought to. While this may not be seen as a problem if one believes that society as a whole should be shouldering the costs of risk and injury, it is still worth considering why this may be—why do people who may have a potentially 'winnable' claim in tort, not take their claims, given that they will receive full compensation if they did win?

One of the problems here is built into the system itself—litigation is not only costly for most people (in that the claimant must be able to fund their action and risks losing two sets of costs if the claim fails)[57] but is also incredibly time-consuming. Some cases take years to come to court. Moreover, because the rules and hurdles of tort (especially negligence) have become so well established and familiar, there will be greater pressure from defendants and legal advisors acting for either party to settle out of court. Why risk losing everything (full compensation) if what you consider to be a fair (or almost fair) proportion of it is guaranteed? Furthermore, despite numerous claims to the contrary that suggest that there is evidence of a litigation explosion based on solicitors offering contingency fee arrangements and the existence of a 'compensation culture', it remains more difficult than would be expected, not only in terms of money, for lay-people to enter the legal system.[58]

The Pearson Committee made a number of other proposals for reforming the compensation system in England and Wales, the main one being that a 'mixed' system of tort and social security be retained, with greater emphasis being put on social security and more finesse in how the two systems worked alongside each other. Outside this, it was recommended, a separate scheme should exist for victims of road accidents, howsoever caused. Even the limited reforms proposed were, however, never adopted—perhaps one reason for this was simply due to bad timing—and the change of government in 1979. Under Mrs Thatcher, it was never likely that we would see an expansion of state-funded or collective schemes and far more likely that emphasis on individuals would be retained.[59] Now, it seems that the question is not what the tort system could be replaced with (or whether it should be replaced), but what improvements or reforms we can make to the existing system. Along with various procedural reforms which have taken place and, for example, the expansion of the use of conditional fees, some changes have clearly happened. Whether these changes can be viewed as positive is debateable and, indeed, the focus seems to have changed again, including judicially, now looking at how the availability of the tort system can be constricted. Perhaps this is a reaction to the fears of a developing 'compensation culture' and, in particular, to more and more claims being made against public bodies, especially post-HRA. With

57. Subject to the increased prevalence of conditional fees and after-the-event insurance schemes.

58. Note that claims management companies are now statutorily regulated under the Compensation Act 2006, Part II.

59. Similar things can be said about the latest government.

such constriction in mind, the question can again be asked whether the tort system is the right place for these issues to be addressed (injuries, disability, the responsibilities of public bodies, etc) and, if not, where they *should* be addressed, and who by?

19.6.1.1 'No-fault' liability and simple compensation schemes

The principle of 'no-fault' liability is a radical one and support for it is based on the fact that if the aim of the tort system is primarily to ensure that those harmed receive compensation, the current system is inefficient, expensive, arbitrary and inadequate. Put another way, creating liability without having to first find fault would enable more people to receive compensation for the injuries they suffered, whether or not they could legally attach blame to someone. Such a system would be more closely aligned with need than blame. Another likely benefit of a no-fault system is that it would be cheaper (and therefore also more cost-effective) to run. There is some precedent for the establishment of a system of this type. In New Zealand, a no-fault compensation scheme has been in operation since 1974 and tort actions have been significantly reduced. The costs of such a system are met by premiums paid by, for example, road users, industry and employers (and therefore inevitably passed on in some smaller way to individuals). While it is true to say that the scheme has since become more restrictive (rather than expanded, as may have been hoped) due to rising costs, it still remains cheaper than a fault-based system such as our own with the added benefit that more people can more easily access compensation.[60]

 Pause for reflection

What does the fact that we have chosen fault as the primary consideration in determining who gets compensation say about the society in which we live?

In the *Making Amends* consultation document, the government proposed reform of the approach to clinical negligence in the NHS. One proposal was that a no-fault scheme should be established in relation to certain ('lower value') types of clinical negligence, in response to rising payouts by the NHS. This was rejected, largely due to the cost of implementing such a scheme, though the report also identified that levels of compensation might be lower and that there would not necessarily be any deterrent or learning effects if such a scheme were to be put in place (pp 14–15).

A further recommendation in *Making Amends* was that 'an NHS Redress Scheme should be introduced to provide investigations when things go wrong; remedial treatment, rehabilitation and care when needed; explanations and apologies; and financial compensation in certain circumstances' (p 1). The idea was not only to be able to provide compensation more easily to those in need, but also to lessen the costs faced by the NHS when defending claims, in terms of both money and staff time, as well as to improve morale, restore public confidence in the NHS and prevent an increase in 'defensive practice' and

---

60. Though see Nicholas Mullany, who says the New Zealand system is 'not as expansive as many have assumed' ('Accidents and Actions for Damages to the Mind—Kiwi Style' (1999) 115 *Law Quarterly Review* 596).

litigation avoidance. The rationale for such changes was based on reported figures from the NHS Litigation Authority.[61] These showed that 60–70 per cent of medical negligence claims did not proceed beyond initial contact with a solicitor or disclosure of medical records; 30 per cent of claims formally pursued were abandoned by the claimant and 95 per cent reached out of court settlement. Further, the adversarial nature of the tort system, with the effects this could have on all concerned, was taken into account, as was the ineffectiveness and expense of continuing to operate the existing system.

The consultation resulted in the NHS Redress Act 2006, designed to provide a simpler system for achieving compensation, without recourse to court proceedings, in cases of 'lower value' medical negligence where the harm could have been avoided and if the adverse outcome was not the result of the natural progression of an illness. Section 3 of the Act also provides for full investigation of the incident which is alleged to have caused harm and of the harm that has resulted; provision of an explanation to the patient and of the action proposed to prevent future incidents; development and delivery of a package of care providing remedial treatment, therapy and arrangements for continuing care. In addition, payments for pain and suffering, out-of-pocket expenses and care or treatment which the NHS cannot supply are provided for. In theory this tallies with the responses given to a survey commissioned by the government before *Making Amends* was published, which asked respondents what they felt the most appropriate response from the NHS would be to negligently inflicted injuries. The responses are summarised in Table 19.2.

Table 19.2 Response considered most appropriate for negligently inflicted injuries

Response considered most appropriate to the event[62]		
Response	Frequency	Per cent
An apology or explanation	134	33.9
An inquiry into the causes	92	23.3
Disciplinary action	23	5.8
Financial compensation	44	11.1
Support in coping with the consequences	65	16.5
Don't know	11	2.8
Not stated	0	0
Other	89	22.5
Total	395	100

Source: © Crown Copyright (2006)

61. *NHS Redress Act 2006 Regulatory Impact Assessment*, p 3.
62. Above, p 4.

Overall, the government predicted that the NHS Redress Scheme will, in the context of 'lower value' medical negligence claims:

> provide a real alternative to litigation for the less severe cases, removing the lottery and risks of litigation, whilst reducing the general burden of unnecessary legal costs. It will provide a fair, equitable and appropriate response to people who have been harmed in the course of their health care. In this respect, the scheme will be consistent with wider Government policy on improving access to justice.[63]

In a similar vein, following a 2007 public consultation, in March 2010 the Ministry of Justice introduced proposals for a 'quick and simple compensation scheme for road traffic accidents', saying that this would 'apply to apply to road traffic accident personal injury claims valued between £1,000 and £10,000, which in the past have formed the vast majority of claims'.[64] The scheme came into effect for all personal injury claims arising from road traffic accidents from 30 April 2010.

19.6.1.2 First-party insurance

Given that we all accept risks (the risk of crossing a road, for example), as well as what has been said above about compensation through the tort system and how many people actually receive it, perhaps first-party insurance should play a role in ensuring that everyone can be paid the compensation they need when they are injured. If we insured *ourselves* against damage (some people already do, for example David Beckham's legs were reported to be insured for £100 million in 2006, with other examples reputed to include Mariah Carey's voice, Jennifer Lopez's body, Dolly Parton's chest, Michael Flatley's legs, etc) then we are each more or less guaranteed a payout that meets our needs when injury occurs.[65] More importantly, recovery of compensation would not be based on the requirement to show someone else's fault. Crucially, also, a high degree of personal autonomy, individual responsibility and choice would be recognised, for example in the types or sums of excess chosen (the amount you must pay yourself before the insurer starts paying), upper limits for claims or what types of harm are covered. Allowing people to make their own choices in this way would let individuals, to a large extent, set their own premiums and decide what they were willing to pay and what risks they were willing to accept by not paying for them. Individuals would assume the responsibility for their own misfortunes before they happened and there would be quick and easy payments for those who suffer injury, rather than having to sue someone *after* the event (if they could be found).

---

63. *NHS Redress Act 2006 Regulatory Impact Assessment*, p 5. Note: the National Health Service Redress (Amendment) Bill 2010, designed to 'facilitate faster resolution of claims and reduce costs' had its first reading in Parliament in October 2010. Its second reading is currently scheduled for 9 September 2011.

64. The Young Report described this as a 'model of how an effective system should work' and recommended extension of a similar system to low-value clinical negligence claims (p 22). It also said that raising the threshold of low-value car accident claims to £25,000 should be considered, as should the introduction of a 'good Samaritan clause' (see Chapter 4, p 77). In October 2010 the Road Traffic Accident (Personal Injury) (Amendment) Bill 2010–11, which would see the threshold raised to £25,000 for low-value claims, had its first reading in Parliament. Its second reading is scheduled for March 2011.

65. Though, of course, whether David Beckham would *need* £100 million if his legs are injured is doubtful.

There are further practical reasons for at least contemplating personal insurance plans as an alternative to compensation decided on and awarded by the courts. As we have seen in many of the chapters above, whether the judiciary are explicit about it or not insurance considerations play a large part in the development of the law and the success or otherwise of a number of claims (see, as just some of the many examples, Lord Hoffmann in *Transco*, Lord Denning in *Nettleship*, etc). How far insurance considerations have so far influenced the law is, however, disputed. Some argue that it should not matter to the courts whether parties are insured, as the primary focus should be on the claimant and compensating them if the 'rules' show that we should. But others, particularly members of the judiciary, have taken insurance to be a realistic consideration when deciding liability.

Patrick Atiyah is a strong advocate for first-party insurance rather than fault-based compensation gained through the court system. He points out that the decline of the welfare state, coupled with the recognition over time of new types of harm, alongside the inadequacies of the tort system mean that litigation on an individual basis is no longer the answer—if it ever was. He argues that because the majority of compensation can be said, in the long run, to be paid by insurance companies, we should recognise this and move towards first-party insurance. Wedded to this is the fact that insurance (via tort) currently does not cover certain kinds of injury or certain ways in which injuries were caused—a first-party insurance system would rectify this. He proposes such a scheme for road traffic accidents (replacing the current compulsory third-party insurance scheme) advocating that this would be relatively simple and cost-effective to implement, as well as fairer in terms of who pays in and out. Indeed, he goes further than this and recommends also that for all other accidents, injuries and disabilities, however they are caused, 'the action for damages for personal injuries should simply be abolished, and first-party insurance should be left to the free market' (p 189).

 Pause for reflection

Consider *Tomlinson* again. Had he known that he was the kind of person who liked to take risks and had the foresight to insure himself against any injuries he might suffer, there would have been no tort action and his insurance company *would have paid out*, probably without any argument. Does this show the potential value of first-party insurance?

 Counterpoint

The idea of first-party insurance sounds very good but suffers from the problem that all people are not equal—some could afford more cover than others (David Beckham again). Even though Atiyah contends that because the wealthy would pay more, as their premiums to protect their earnings or any valuable assets would be higher than those of the ordinary person, there is no real solution proposed for those at the opposite end of the scale. While he acknowledges that with third-party insurance schemes, the more highly paid are favoured and the lower paid, retired and unemployed may be discriminated against,

→

→

he does not acknowledge that this might apply to first-party insurance in the same way. If someone is poor, they may be tempted to pay lower premiums, thereby insuring themselves and their family for less. This is all very well when it comes to abstract notions of personal autonomy and individual responsibility: it would be their choice. But it has to be questioned, we think, how autonomous such a choice would be. Someone in this situation may insure themselves for less, because they believe they cannot afford more, yet be in more 'risky' employment. If first-party insurance was made compulsory (in a similar way to comprehensive motor insurance) then we agree that this would increase competition on the free market and prices may be kept down—but, as another thing to pay for each month, there are still going to be some people who would find themselves substantially worse off. Furthermore, it is undeniable that insurance companies would be the main beneficiaries of such a scheme and this casts further doubt on the value of such a scheme for the truly poor. Atiyah merely brushes over these issues in his concluding paragraph, saying that:

> the answer is that almost everybody will actually save more money by abolishing the present system than they will need to pay for their new first-party insurance. The poorest people, especially, will actually save on their motor insurance policies ... Of course some state social security safety net will still be needed for those not otherwise covered at all. (p 193)

Interestingly, Lord Justice Jackson, in his extensive review of civil litigation costs published in January 2010, recommended increasing the availability and use of 'Before the Event' insurance, encouraging people to take out legal expenses insurance, for example as part of their household insurance.[66] The whole report was designed to find ways in which to reduce the disproportionate cost of civil litigation, while at the same time maintaining access to justice. This is not the same as insuring oneself *against the losses caused by injuries* as first-party insurance would be, but is an example of a way claimants can take responsibility and protect themselves against the cost of litigation should this become necessary.

19.7 Debunking the compensation myth

The phrase 'compensation culture' is a pejorative term used to describe a society in which it is acceptable for anyone who has suffered personal injury to seek damages through litigation, even when the injury is minimal or the argument that the defendant was at fault is tenuous.[67] The term has been used in relation to the tort system in England and Wales, emerging particularly over the last decade or so, with the growth in conditional fee schemes and the increased pervasiveness of claims management companies. As Atiyah has pointed out, 'complaints are often heard that we are "going

---

66. Lord Justice Jackson *Review of Civil Litigation Costs: Final Report* (TSO, 2010), Ch 8. A government consultation, *Proposals for reform of civil litigation funding and costs in England and Wales*, seeking views on implementing Jackson's proposals, has recently closed (14 February 2011).

67. See panel in Introduction, p 14.

down the American road" without, very often, explaining what the American road is, or what is wrong with it'.[68]

Furedi has said that 'our litigious culture has helped foster a climate where adverse experience is readily blamed on someone else's negligence' (p 11) and that 'the corollary of this blame-game is a feeble sense of personal responsibility for one's predicament…that is why people who trip and fall on the pavement feel that they are entitled to sue their local authority for compensation' (pp 11–12). In **Tomlinson**, Lord Hobhouse said that the 'pursuit of an unrestrained culture of blame and compensation has many evil consequences' (at [81]). Similarly, the government seems to be fixated on the idea that we live in what has been described many times, as recently as 2010, as a 'compensation culture'.[69] Prime Minister David Cameron said that:

> A damaging compensation culture has arisen, as if people can absolve themselves from any personal responsibility for their own actions, with the spectre of lawyers only too willing to pounce with a claim for damages on the slightest pretext.[70]

But is this really the case? Are too many claims being made (particularly frivolous ones) and, more importantly, are these claims, if they *are* being taken, being won? In other words, are defendants paying out when they should not be?

In May 2004, the Better Regulation Task Force produced a report entitled *Better Routes to Redress* which showed that UK expenditure on tort claims was 0.6 per cent of GDP (in comparison with one per cent cited by the Institute of Actuaries in 2002). On a comparative analysis, this was found to be less than that spent by ten other industrialised countries and only Denmark was found to spend less (p 15).[71] Similarly, the report showed that the overall number of personal injury claims had declined (p 11) and, on these grounds it concluded that the existence of a compensation culture was more a self-perpetuating idea than reality. That is, many people believed there was such a culture, and therefore behaviours changed in reaction to this. In the first paragraph of its response to the report, the government said that it was:

> determined to scotch any suggestion of a developing 'compensation culture' where people believe that they can seek compensation for any misfortune that befalls them, even if no-one else is to blame. This misperception undermines personal responsibility and respect for the law and creates unnecessary burdens through an exaggerated fear of litigation.[72]

We can also debate whether seeking compensation for injuries—or encouraging people to do so—should necessarily be viewed negatively. While there may be some who try to 'play the system' there are, as should by now be apparent, many hurdles in place before a claimant can be successful and few people, as we outlined in a different

---

68. *The Damages Lottery*, p 2.

69. Lord Young *Common Sense, Common Safety* (Cabinet Office: 2010) described as a 'Whitehall-wide review of the operation of health and safety laws and the growth of the compensation culture' (see in particular p 19). The term had previously been used in another government consultation document: Department of Constitutional Affairs *The Law on Damages* (Consultation Paper CP 9/07, 4 May 2007), 'Introduction' p 10.

70. Young Report, 'Foreword by the Prime Minister', p 5.

71. The figure for the US was 1.9 per cent.

72. 'Tackling the "Compensation Culture": Government Response to the Better Regulation Task Force Report: "Better Routes to Redress"' (10 November 2004).

context above, actually receive tort damages. It may be true that increased awareness of rights encourages more people to take claims, and even that this results in more settlements out of court but, largely, any organisation, business, company, public body or other defendant who settles will have been advised to do so by their lawyers, either because it is cheaper to do so in terms of both finances and reputation or, crucially, because there is already existing precedent that suggests that the claimant might in fact have a case. None of these so-called frivolous claimants are able to evade the law. It should be remembered that, for example, in **Tomlinson**, a case often cited as an example of the 'have-a-go' culture and the types of frivolous claims that might be made, his injuries were incredibly severe and there was at least the *potential* that the council concerned had not done all it could to prevent such injuries occurring—as the Court of Appeal recognised.

The *Better Routes to Redress* report stated that 'the compensation culture is a myth; but the cost of this belief is very real' (p 3). The idea that we live in a compensation culture can in the main be shown to be a myth perpetuated by sensationalist media coverage of a small number of cases, which often do not go as far as reporting on the *outcome* of unusual claims being made (which may never reach court, let alone succeed—but *will* sell papers) or give any idea of the context in which the claim was taken. The 2010 Young Report tells us that 'the problem of the compensation culture prevalent in society today is…one of perception rather than reality',[73] and also went to some effort to explode the myths behind 'health and safety hysteria in the media'.[74]

Perhaps this is the problem we are actually faced with—the *idea* that a compensation culture exists has become so prevalent that its effects are felt in a multitude of ways, often with negative consequences. So, the question is: Do we need to tackle the perception in order to improve the system and, if so, how would we do so? The government's view is that much of the problem can be tackled by reforming access to justice:

> If there is one law that Parliament cannot repeal it is the law of unintended consequences, and it is the unintended consequences of well meaning legislation that are at the root of our problems today. The Access to Justice Act 1999 brought about three major changes in the compensation landscape. These were the introduction of conditional fee agreements (CFAs), the growth of after the event (ATE) insurance and the proliferation of claims management companies. The shift towards increased fears of litigation can be seen to have its roots in these changes. The 2006 report concluded that problems lay in the public's increased awareness that it was possible to sue without any financial risk. The changes encouraged the belief that claiming compensation for even the most minor of accidents is quick and easy, while at the same time incentivising lawyers to rack up high fees in the knowledge that they will be covered by the losing party.[75]

It can be argued that the effects of such a myth may be both positive (resulting in easier access to compensation for the majority of those affected by medical negligence, for

---

73. At p 19—seemingly contradicting the Prime Minister's statement in the foreword.
74. See Annex D, pp 49–50.
75. Young Report, p 19 and subsequent pages. See also the Jackson Report, which proposed a raft of changes to the ways costs are calculated and paid in civil claims. As mentioned above, the government has recently finished consulting on the implementation of Jackson's reports and it remains to be seen what changes will be made and—more importantly—what effect these will have.

example) or negative (in the sense of encouraging 'defensive' practices or the removal of services in order to avoid being faced with litigation). In 2004, the then government said that 'we need to take action: both to tackle practices that help spread the misperceptions and false expectations; and to improve the effectiveness and efficiency of the system for those who have a genuine claim to compensation'.[76] Part of this, as they saw it, was the tighter regulation of claims management companies, including what they could and could not do in terms of advertising and facilitating greater transparency in relation to the fees to be paid by the consumer. It seems that such a policy prevails with the latest government and we wait to see which of Lord Justice Jackson's proposals are implemented, and how. 'No win, no fee' seems an attractive proposition, but it must be remembered that such companies will tend to take on only the cases they are certain of winning and that a large proportion of any compensation won will be extracted in fees. Furthermore, companies who offer to take cases on a 'no win, no fee' basis may encourage the misleading belief that such cases are risk-free, when in fact the defendant's legal costs may end up being awarded against the claimant.

19.8 **The future of damages**

In 2007 the Department for Constitutional Affairs (now the Ministry of Justice) undertook a further consultation on damages. *The Law on Damages* consultation paper set out various issues relating to the way damages are awarded which had been raised in a series of reports published by the Law Commission and are seemingly still at issue, despite the provisions already implemented in the Compensation Act 2006. These issues included, *inter alia*, whether changes should be made to claims for wrongful death made under the Fatal Accidents Act; liability for psychiatric illness (for which a statutory solution was rejected); damages for medical, nursing and other expenses associated with personal injury; and aggravated, exemplary and restitutionary damages. The consultation document started by telling us that:

> The Government is committed to tackling perceptions of a compensation culture and to improving the compensation system for valid claims. It is taking forward a wide-ranging programme of work to:
>
> - stop a compensation culture from developing;
> - tackle perceptions that can lead to a disproportionate fear of litigation and risk averse behaviour;
> - find ways to discourage and resist bad claims; and
> - improve the system for those with a valid claim by providing fair compensation in a more timely, proportionate and cost-effective way.[77]

The Jackson Report appears to be the next response or articulation to some of these claims and concerns, added to by further considerations of risk and blame in the Young

---

76. Note 73 above, pp 2–3.
77. Department of Constitutional Affairs 'The Law on Damages' (Consultation Paper CP 9/07, issued 4 May 2007), 'Introduction' p 10.

Report. As far as we can tell, both the government and the judiciary are taking reform of some of the negative aspects of the damages system seriously—it may be that we are in for sweeping changes to the civil justice system in the years to come.

19.9 **Conclusion**

In this chapter, we have looked at how damages are awarded following tort claims. We started by looking at the principles lying behind damages awards, finding that the primary object of the law is to compensate those who have been harmed by another's wrongdoing. This is done by making an award that seeks to put the claimant into the position that they would have been in had the harm not occurred. Damages awards can encompass pecuniary (financial) and non-pecuniary losses. Future losses (those not quantifiable at the time of trial) are calculated using multiplicands (the sum to be multiplied) and multipliers (the number of years the loss should be multiplied by). In the main, damages are awarded as a lump sum.

Multiple defendants can incur liability independently, jointly or severally. Either a court will apportion damages between them or one defendant can seek a contribution from another. However, there are time limits placed on all damages claims—not uncontroversially. Many further critiques of the way damages can be and are awarded can be (and have been) made, not least those referring to the need to establish fault and blame in order to achieve compensation, and the fact that this means that many people go without. The tort system, viewed in this way, seems to benefit very few people and other ways of achieving fairer compensation for more people have been proposed.

✳ **End-of-chapter questions**

After reading the chapter carefully, try answering the questions below. If you would like to know what we think visit the Online Resource Centre (www.oxfordtextbooks.co.uk/orc/horsey2e/).

1. Should the focus of the tort system be based on fault, or on other considerations such as need, equality or deterrence?

2. Is it right that society as a whole largely shoulders the burden of higher compensation payouts, through principles of insurance, higher prices for goods and services, and tax?

3. Do we (as a society) blame and claim too much?

4. Is the tension between achieving justice for claimants and doing justice by defendants simply irreconcilable?

5. Should any time limitations be put on tort claims?

6. Should the tort system be more concerned with distributive than corrective justice?

7. Consider the problem question at the start of this chapter. Now having read about the topic, what compensation should Emma receive from the two negligent drivers? If you

need some pointers in thinking about how to answer this question, turn to the Appendix (p 589) where each problem is annotated with issues and cases to consider. Next, try to write your own answer and finally, log on to our Online Resource Centre (www.oxfordtext-books.co.uk/orc/horsey2e/) and check your ideas against our suggested outline answer.

✳ Further reading

The further reading outlined below is primarily related to critiques of the damages system. Many of the books, articles and other reading below have already been directly cited or mentioned in the text but, for reasons of space and conciseness, we have not been able to treat each of these in full. Therefore, we would recommend at least browsing through all listed here, to get a better picture of how the law on damages currently stands, as well as the critiques of the system.

Atiyah, Patrick *The Damages Lottery* (Hart Publishing, 1997)

British Medical Journal 'BMJ Bans "Accidents" ' (2001) 322 *BMJ* 1320 (2 June)

Cane, Peter *Atiyah's Accidents, Compensation and the Law* (7th edn, CUP, 2006)

Conaghan, Joanne 'Tort Litigation in the Context of Intra-familial Abuse' (1998) 61 *Modern Law Review* 132

Donaldson, Liam (Chief Medical Officer) *Making Amends: a consultation paper setting out proposals for reforming the approach to clinical negligence in the NHS* (HMSO, 2003)

Furedi, Frank *The Culture of Fear* (2nd edn, Continuum Press, 2002)

Hand, James 'The Compensation Culture: Cliché or Cause for Concern?' (2010) 37(4) *Journal of Law and Society* 569

House of Commons Constitutional Affairs Committee 'Compensation Culture', Third Report of Session 2005–06, vol I

Lewis, Richard, 'The Politics and Economics of Tort Law: Judicially Imposed Periodical Payments of Damages' (2006) 69(3) *Modern Law Review* 418

Lewis, Richard, Annette Morris and Ken Oliphant 'Tort Personal Injuries Claims Statistics: Is There a Compensation Culture in the United Kingdom?' (2006) 14 *Torts Law Journal* 158

Morris, Annette 'Spiralling or Stabilising? The Compensation Culture and our Propensity to Claim Damages for Personal Injury' (2007) 70(3) *Modern Law Review* 349

Oliphant, Ken 'Beyond Misadventure: Compensation for Medical Injuries in New Zealand' (2007) 15 *Medical Law Review* 357

Williams, Kevin 'State of Fear: Britain's Compensation Culture Reviewed' (2005) 25 *Legal Studies* 499

Appendix: annotated problem questions

The purpose of these annotations is not to give you the 'answers' but to suggest things you need to be thinking about when answering the problem questions at the beginning of each chapter. Sometimes the same issue will arise at different points in the question; where this happens we will only point it out once. As you become more familiar with answering tort problem questions you will begin to recognise the issues more easily. Remember, however, that although problem questions are usually on one or two issues, you need to make sure that you consider *all* aspects of the claims so that your answer is as detailed as possible. So, for example, in relation to a negligence problem question which primarily raises issues relating to 'breach', you should also address those relating to duty, causation and defences (even if only very briefly). More detailed outlines to the problem questions are available on the Online Resource Centre (www.oxfordtextbooks.co.uk/orc/horsey2e/). These are not model answers, but rather more detailed guidance which breaks the question down into more manageable pieces and points you in the right direction. To get the most out of the problem questions, you should try to draft an answer to them before looking online. The annotated answers in this appendix are all available to download from the Online Resource Centre.

Another thing to bear in mind is that most of the problem questions we have used in this book are based on quite complex fact situations and may each, therefore, raise a number of claims and legal issues. We have tried to 'contain' each question as far as possible within the context of the chapter in which it appears, but inevitably there will be some 'bleeding' between issues in the various chapters, and we have tried to highlight this in the annotations.

What markers of problem questions are primarily (but not necessarily exclusively) looking for is:

(1) An ability to sort out the facts (including those that are relevant from those that are not).

(2) An ability to identify (all) the possible claims—who makes them, who will the defendant(s) be and, importantly, *what* will they be for (e.g. personal injury or property damage).

(3) An ability to distinguish the unproblematic issues (to be dealt with very briefly) from the legally difficult ones (to be discussed and analysed in more detail).

(4) Intelligent *argument* on the difficult legal issues (often with acknowledgement that there is no 'answer' but merely arguments that can be put forward, some that might be stronger than others).

(5) Appropriate use of case law.

Omissions and third parties annotated problem question

Margaret, who is 75 years old, is doing her weekly supermarket shop on a busy Saturday afternoon when she begins to feel pains in her chest. It transpires she is having a heart attack and she collapses to the floor. Although the supermarket is crowded, no one comes to help her.

Brian, the store manager, puts a call out over the tannoy system asking if there is a doctor present, but otherwise offers no assistance. Hearing the announcement, Karen, a nurse, comes forward and tries to help Margaret, but fails to put her in the recovery position and she later dies.

Meanwhile, some youths see Margaret's car near the entrance to the supermarket. She has left it open with the keys in the ignition, as she did not want to spend time looking for a parking space. The youths drive off in the car, failing to stop at a pedestrian crossing, hitting Jill and her daughter Heather who were crossing the road. Both are injured, Heather seriously. One of the youths, Luke, who was not wearing a seat belt, also suffers a serious head injury.

At the outset it is important to note what claims will be made, by whom, for what and against whom. Here, we have M v B (and the supermarket vicariously?), M v K, J & H v M, L v M.

The question here is whether these are all 'callous bystanders' (Lord Nicholls, *Stovin v Wise*) or whether anyone owed M a duty to come to her aid.

Does the action B has taken mean that he has 'assumed responsibility' for M in any way? See *Barrett v MOD*.

This indicates negligence on M's part. Can she be sued even though she is dead? (See Chapter 19). Who would sue her? Or would this make her contributorily negligent (see Chapter 10).

This is definitely assumption of responsibility by K—is a duty then owed? If so, what is the *content* of the duty?

Here, L is another potential claimant. However, the question here is whether M should owe him a duty of care, even though he, as the third party, was (at least in part) responsible in some way for his own injuries. See also Chapter 9 on causation points (quite tricky here).

Does this mean that even if L can establish a claim against M he should be found contributorily negligent? See Chapter 10.

The alleged negligence (whether K fell below the standard of care expected) would have to be established. Failing to do something is an omission, which is why it is first important to establish whether K owed M a duty of care in respect of omissions.

So who would actually be taking this action, and what for? See Chapter 19.

Therefore, J and H have been harmed by the actions of the youths, who become the third party in relation to a claim against M. The question is whether M should be held to owe J and H a duty of care in respect of the actions taken by third parties as a result of her own negligence (leaving the car unlocked). Compare *Topp v London Country Bus*.

Psychiatric harm annotated problem question

Following months of speculation the legendary indie guitar band—*Blinking Idiot*—are about to embark on a reunion tour of the UK. They are performing a warm-up gig at a small intimate venue when a spotlight falls onto the stage causing a massive explosion killing the band members: Madeleine, Rob and Dave. Unfortunately, the lighting rig (onto which the spotlight was fitted) had been negligently maintained by Rack & Horse Lighting. The sight is particularly gruesome.

Hannah, Rob's wife, is watching the gig from the VIP area of the venue. She is physically unharmed, but later suffers nightmares and depression. This is particularly traumatic for her as she had previously suffered from depression, but had sought help and recovered.

Pete, Madeleine's brother, is listening to the live radio broadcast of the gig from his hotel room in Paris. He hears the explosion and thinks he can hear Madeleine screaming. He rushes to the airport, managing to catch a flight that is just leaving, and arrives at the hospital three hours after the accident. Unfortunately, Madeleine's body has not yet been moved to the morgue and is still covered in blood and grime from the explosion. He develops post-traumatic shock disorder.

Lucy has attended every *Blinking Idiot* gig in the UK and has travelled to a number of their overseas concerts. She is a founder member of their fan club and regularly contributes to their fan magazine. She always tries to stand as close as possible to the stage. Miraculously she was unhurt by the explosion but has since been overcome with grief.

Tim was one of the first on the scene. He is a trainee ambulance man and this was his first major incident. He rushes to the stage but quickly sees that there is little he can do. He spends the next two hours comforting distraught fans. He later suffers from recurring nightmares and panic attacks.

Stuart, one of the roadies, is overcome with feelings of guilt and depression. It was his job to fix the lighting and he feels the explosion was his fault. A subsequent investigation completely exonerates him.

Advise the parties.

Annotations:

Rack and Horse Lighting will be the defendants in all the claims.

Pete will need to satisfy the secondary victim criteria as set down in *Alcock*. The key issue here is proximity in time and space—could hearing Madeleine on the radio be akin to seeing her on TV? Given what the law lords said in *Alcock* about TV images, this is unlikely to be successful. He will also need to establish a close tie of love and affection with his sister. You should apply and distinguish *Alcock*, *McLoughlin* and *Galli-Atkinson*.

Tim is a rescuer. Following *White* he will need to establish that he meets either the primary or secondary victim requirements.

Stuart would be considered an involuntary participant as in *Dooley*. He may also be a primary victim depending on how close he is standing to the stage.

Although Lucy may be a primary victim (on the basis of *Page*), she has not suffered a recognisable psychiatric illness—mere grief is not recoverable.

Hannah is likely to be too far away to be a primary victim (although this depends on how far away the VIP area is—if it was near to the stage she could be in the zone of danger as in *Page*). If she is not a primary victim, she would therefore need to show that she meets the criteria set out in *Alcock*.

Note that her previous depression will not defeat her claim as a secondary victim if a person of 'ordinary phlegm and fortitude' would have suffered some sort of psychiatric harm. Assuming this is the case the egg-shell skull principle will allow her to recover for the full extent of her injury (even if it goes beyond what is reasonably foreseeable).

Public bodies annotated problem question

PC Plod and PC Bill both work for the Countyshire Constabulary. They are part of a team involved in investigating a high profile criminal case involving a bank robbery.

One night, PCs Plod and Bill are on patrol on the M7 motorway, when a car passes them at a fairly high speed. PC Plod, who is driving the patrol car, recognises the car as belonging to one of his neighbours, Mr Smith, with whom he has had a longstanding feud since Mr Smith had an affair with his wife. Determined to get his own back on Mr Smith, PC Plod, despite PC Bill's objection, decides to give chase. As the cars approach 110 mph, PC Plod loses control and the two cars collide. Mr Smith's car turns over several times before eventually coming to a stop. PC Bill is injured.

PC Plod calls an ambulance from the Countyshire Ambulance Service. This takes 30 minutes to arrive and, even then, because of staff shortages, the paramedic on board is an unqualified trainee. He examines Mr Smith and concludes that he is dead, so devotes his attention to a fairly minor leg wound suffered by PC Bill. Half an hour later a doctor arrives at the scene. When he examines Mr Smith he realises he is actually alive, but deeply unconscious. Despite the doctor's best efforts, Mr Smith dies on the way to hospital.

Meanwhile, the criminal gang under investigation take part in another bank robbery in a nearby town, during which a hostage is killed. Witnesses had called the police and been assured that they were on their way. In fact, the call had gone out to PC Plod, who had ignored it because he was more interested in chasing Mr Smith. Bruce, the husband of the hostage who died, believes the police could have done more to prevent her death. The owner of the bank also believes the police were negligent in failing to prevent more bank robberies in the area.

Advise the families of Mr Smith and the hostage as to any potential claims in negligence.

This is your starting point. Who are the people who will be suing? Who will the defendants be? What is the negligence alleged? Note there may be quite a number of different claims here.

You should note that it is often important to look out for 'red herrings' or facts that simply aren't relevant to the claims you are dealing with. Here, e.g., there is no question about whether this car was 'speeding' or whether the driver of the car was negligent, as the driver is not a defendant.

Note that the Chief Constable of Countyshire Constabulary may also be a defendant through the principle of vicarious liability, should either of the officers be found to have committed a tort.

This might be relevant to any defences raised by PC Plod.

This would seem to suggest negligence on PC Plod's part, indicating that he will be a defendant.

So there is (at least) a claim for personal injury stemming from the collision.

Again, this relates to any potential claim that may be taken against the ambulance service. Is it 'negligent' to have an unqualified trainee on board an ambulance? If so, this might be a claim against the ambulance service *directly*, for failing to provide an adequate service. However, you should be aware of the policy/operational distinctions that operate in these types of claims.

So, a claim here is likely to be made by the family of Mr Smith (e.g. either acting on behalf of his estate or even directly, if there are dependants—see Chapter 19). The allegation is that the unqualified paramedic was negligent in his assessment of Mr Smith, leading to the delay that subsequently may have caused his death (note there may be a factual causation issue here, see Chapter 9). This is still going to be a claim against a public body, however, because if found to be negligent, the ambulance service will be responsible for the tort of the paramedic through the principle of vicarious liability (see Chapter 12). The ambulance service may also be sued directly here, for sending an unqualified trainee (although breach would not be self-evident in them doing this). NOTE: this is therefore a different claim from the one made directly against the ambulance service (for arriving late), above.

The claim here is that the police were negligent in their efforts to prevent a crime. Can the police be sued in this respect? See e.g. *Hill* and *Smith v Chief Constable of Sussex Police*. Also see *Van Colle* in relation to a claim under the Human Rights Act—can this case be distinguished?

This raises similar issues to those in the claim above, although that was about personal injury (death) and this is about a financial loss. Does that make a difference here? Note, however, you are not asked to advise the owner of the bank.

This relates to any claim made against the ambulance service and the question here will be whether they had a duty to arrive promptly and, if they did, whether they have breached it by taking 30 minutes to arrive. See *Kent v Griffiths*. The breach issue might depend on exactly why they took so long and if this could be considered reasonable in the circumstances—see Chapter 6.

Economic loss annotated problem question

Rachael and Chris invest in a business after speaking to Amanda, a personal friend who is also an auditor. Amanda has prepared a financial report for the trustees of Read-Sing-Sign, a children's charity bookshop that is for sale. The report shows that the bookshop is doing well and makes a good annual profit. On the basis of the report, which Amanda showed them 'off the record', Rachael and Chris decided to buy the shop. Each of them pays £100,000. It later transpires that the audit was inaccurate as Amanda failed to include some unpaid debts in the figures and the shop is in fact worthless.

Meanwhile, Rachael, who was relying on a £70,000 inheritance from her grandfather in order to be able to pay for most of her share of the shop, is told by the solicitors dealing with her grandfather's will that it is invalid and the terms of his previous will, which left everything to a local cats' home, would have to be followed. This is because he failed to sign both copies of the latest version of the will. The solicitor's copy was filed without checking the signature was present.

Advise Rachael and Chris as to the likelihood of success of any claims in negligence that they may take.

It should be noted at the outset that there is generally no duty of care owed in respect of claims for pure economic loss and that their only potential route would be to rely on *Hedley Byrne* v *Heller* and any later derivations of this rule.

Would this invoke a relationship of 'trust and confidence'?

A has clearly been negligent in her preparation of the report. The question is whether she would owe R & C a duty of care in respect of the economic loss they have suffered. As indicated in the chapter, this depends on whether their claim can be said to fall within the exception to the general exclusionary rule created in *Hedley Byrne*.

This brings into question whether any reliance on the part of R & C would be 'reasonable'.

This is a negligent act—again, the question is whether the solicitors would owe a duty of care to Rachael. A duty of care would clearly be owed to the grandfather but he (and his estate) has suffered no loss. See *White* v *Jones*. Note, however, this is not a question of the negligent drafting of a will, but negligent administration. Would the outcome be any different?

Compare *Caparo*. Is this a similar situation?

This is, therefore, Rachael's loss.

Breach annotated problem question

Kate and Troy have spent the afternoon looking at wedding dresses. Before heading home they go to a new champagne bar to celebrate finding 'the one'. Troy offers Kate a lift home in his car, assuring Kate that he's alright to drive as he's 'probably only just over the drink-drive limit'. On the journey home Troy loses control of the car and crashes into a lamp post. Kate suffers minor cuts and bruises and is taken to hospital for a check up. At the hospital Kate contracts an infection in a cut to her right arm. The doctor on duty decides not to treat the infection with antibiotics immediately as he has recently read a report in a little-known medical journal which suggested that it is better to allow the body 'time to heal' following a trauma. Kate's right arm is partially paralysed.

Advise Kate.

Kate also has a claim against the doctor. You should compare and contrast the decisions in **Bolam** and **Bolitho** here in order to establish whether his actions are reasonable. The doctor's actions also raise issues relating to causation (Chapter 9).

Troy clearly owes Kate a duty of care, and has caused her injuries so the question you need to consider is whether Troy is acting as a reasonable driver?

You should also consider whether Kate was contributorily negligent when she got into the car with Troy (Chapter 10).

Causation annotated problem question

Stefaan and Gavin spend the evening drinking in the pub. Stefaan offers Gavin a lift home in his car, assuring Gavin that this will be fine as he is 'probably only just over the limit'. Driving home, Stefaan swerves to avoid a fox and crashes the car. The paramedics who arrive at the scene find that Gavin has broken his arm but otherwise only has minor cuts and bruises. Gavin is taken to hospital to be checked by a doctor.

At the hospital Gavin is seen by Cheryl, the doctor on duty. Cheryl disagrees with the paramedics' opinion and, deciding Gavin's arm is not broken but only sprained, puts it in a sling, without setting it in a cast. As she was so busy that evening, she decided not to bother sending him for an X-ray first. Gavin returns to hospital the following month with pain in his arm. It transpires that his arm *was* in fact broken and, because it was not set in the proper cast, the bones have fused together wrongly, resulting in a permanent disability. An expert witness says that there was a chance this might have happened anyway, even if Cheryl had not been negligent. Gavin has to have an operation to try and re-set the bones, but this will not improve his arm to the condition it was in before the accident.

A week later Gavin is knocked down by a speeding motorist who fails to stop and cannot be traced. His right arm is so badly injured that it has to be amputated.

Advise Gavin in relation to the claims in negligence he may bring.

Margin annotations:

Can we say that 'but for' S's negligence, G would not have suffered these injuries?

In doing so, the question is whether any of these actions fell below the standard of care expected by a doctor and, as such, will be guided by the **Bolam** and **Bolitho** tests.

This raises a question about what would have happened had she not acted negligently. See **Bolitho** for similar points.

There is no problem establishing duty here and it seems likely that breach is easily established.

Is this harm a foreseeable consequence of (a) a car accident and (b) negligent treatment for a broken arm? What has to be foreseeable (see **Wagon Mound No 1**)?

Whatever the outcome of G's claims, will any of the defendants be able to raise a defence? Should he have got into the car?

The question, in trying to establish factual causation, is 'how much chance'? If it was more than 50% likely that the permanent disability would have originated from the original break, then C is not the 'but for' cause of this harm (see **Barnett** and **Hotson**). However, unlike in these cases, there is a previous act of negligence: Does this mean that S will remain the 'but for' cause, even for these 'extended' injuries? What happens if it was less than 50% likely that this injury would have resulted from the original accident? Could C's actions (if negligent) break the chain of causation back to S?

How does this affect the claims to be made against (a) S and (b) C? The motorist cannot be sued as he is untraceable. See **Baker** and **Jobling**.

Defences annotated problem question

Ben, Graeme and Andy are old school friends. Every year they go camping together in Snowdonia National Park. After they arrive on the Friday night, they decide to go to the pub where Ben and Graeme spend several hours reminiscing and by the time they leave they are both over the legal driving limit. Andy has not been drinking. On their way back to the campsite they pass a farm and notice a tractor with its keys in the ignition. Graeme gets in and starts the engine. Ben and Andy quickly jump in beside him. Neither of them wears a seat belt. At first, Graeme drives slowly around the farmyard but when Ben says 'Is that the best you can do?' he decides to go 'off-road' and drives it into a field. Unfortunately, on the rough ground he loses control of the tractor and it overturns. Ben and Andy are thrown out onto the field. Ben is seriously injured. Though Andy escapes with only minor physical injuries, he later develops post-traumatic stress disorder (PTSD) as a result of the incident. One day while walking home from work Andy 'snaps' lashing out at an innocent passer-by and causing them serious injury. Though it is recognised that his actions were as a result of his PSTD, he is jailed for six months and loses his job.

Advise the parties (you should assume that, in the absence of applicable defences, Ben and Andy would have a good claim in negligence).

You need to address this point both in relation to *volenti* (is Ben too drunk to consent to the risk?) and contributory negligence (has Ben failed to exercise reasonable care?).

This is an important detail. It means the Road Traffic Act 1988 would not apply and so the defence of *volenti* is arguable.

Will Andy's claim against Graeme be defeated by the defence of illegality? You should consider the application of *Gray* here.

Can Ben's failure to wear a seat belt (together with his jumping in quickly alongside Graeme) be used to argue that he accepted the nature and extent of the risk he was exposed to? The cases to consider here are *Morris* v *Murray* and *Dann* v *Hamilton*—which one is close to the facts you have been given? What about Andy? As he *hadn't* been drinking, is *volenti* more likely to be made out?

Consider why this piece of information is included here—can Ben's active encouragement be used to argue that Ben and Graeme are engaging in a joint criminal enterprise (as in *Pitts* v *Hunt*)? It may also be helpful in arguments relating to contributory negligence.

You should consider each defence in turn. Remember when considering contributory negligence you should work through each of the three requirements: (1) failure to exercise reasonable care for his own safety; (2) whether his actions contributed to his damage; and (3) what would be a just and equitable reduction? Consider the guidelines in *Froom* v *Butcher*.

Occupiers' liability annotated problem question

Although usually an occupier will not be liable for the negligence of an independent contractor, the facts here are very similar to those in *Gwilliam*. In that case it was held that there was a duty to check that the independent contractors had appropriate liability insurance but, on the facts, it had not been breached. (Cf *Naylor* v *Payling* and *Glaister* v *Appleby-in-Westmoreland Town Council*.

'Camden Cool', an after school youth club run by the local authority, is holding an open day to raise funds for the club. One of the main attractions is a large bouncy castle supplied, erected and supervised by Elsinore Castles, a small local company. Joseph and Harry are the first to try it out. They both suffer minor cuts and bruises when the castle breaks free from its moorings and lifts into the air. It later turns out that it had not been appropriately tethered to the ground. Unfortunately despite assuring Charlie, the club's youth worker, when he phoned to book the castle that they had the necessary documentation, Elsinore's public liability insurance had expired two months before the accident.

In the chaos that follows, Esme, Phoebe's sister, wanders off alone. She is too young to be a member of the club and so doesn't know her way around the buildings. She is seriously injured when she falls down a flight of stairs after going through a door marked 'Private: No Unauthorised Entry'.

Meanwhile Frank and Freddy (who are members of the club) have sneaked off to play football. After a particularly poor shot at goal their ball lands on a flat roof. Although they know the roof is 'out of bounds', as everyone is busy at the open day, they decide to climb onto the roof to retrieve it. As they do so one of the skylights breaks. Freddy falls through the roof hitting his head hard, causing him to lose his hearing.

Advise the parties of any claims they may have under the Occupiers' Liability Acts 1957 and 1984.

It is likely that Joseph and Harry are visitors—however you need to establish why this is and not just assume it. This means an action will be brought against the local authority under the OLA 1957.

Here you are told that Frank and Freddy are members of the club and so should be treated as visitors under the 1957 Act—but an occupier can restrict their duty as has been done here (by making the roof 'out of bounds') and *Tomlinson* would suggest that when they are on the roof they are trespassers. You therefore need to assess whether the local authority owes them a duty of care by working through the subsections of s 1(3). Remember after doing so you also need to consider issues relating to breach and causation. Finally, it is likely that Freddy would be found to be contributory negligent (see Chapter 10, p 267 and, in particular, the case of *Young* v *Kent County Council* [2005]).

Note that here you need only to consider a claim under the OLAs. If neither of the Acts are applicable there may also be a claim in negligence—as this is harder to establish you should go to the OLAs first.

It is crucial to establish here whether Esme is a visitor or a non-visitor—the 1957 and 1984 Acts say different things about 'warnings'. If Esme is a trespasser (assuming a duty can be established) all the occupier needs to have done is to take 'reasonable steps' to bring the risk to her attention (the 1984 Act, unlike the 1957 Act, does not make special allowances for children). You should also consider the position if Esme is a visitor, and her position under the 1957 Act.

Employers' liability annotated problem question

All the claims will be brought against the Archdiocese—you should establish this at the outset.

Every Tuesday, Thursday and Friday evening there is a drop-in centre for young people between the ages of 11–16 at St Hilda's parish church. It is run by a team of youth workers employed by the Archdiocese of Durkenshire. Fred is youth counsellor at the centre. He is busy setting up the hall for the evening's activities when he slips on a puddle of greasy water from a leaking radiator. He had reported the leak to his supervisor, Father Cranky, over a week ago and it had still not been fixed.

Remember there are two potential claimants here—you should consider both as the situation will be slightly different in relation to each.

Mrs Doogal works in the kitchen making snacks and drinks for the young people. She is using a food processor to make some cookies when a fragment of metal is thrown off by the machine and enters her eye. Another piece lands in the cookie dough unnoticed. Later on, Father Cranky eats a cookie whilst no one is looking. The shard of metal lacerates his tongue. The food processor had been serviced two weeks earlier in accordance with the provisions of the Kitchens Safety Act 2003 which states that 'all moving parts on food-mixers must be maintained'.

Father Jack has special responsibility for outreach work in the centre. This means he is a well-known figure among the young people in the local area. Helen has been coming to the centre for a few weeks. Father Jack has been particularly welcoming. He often encourages her to stay late to help him tidy up and then gives her a lift home in his sports car. After one such occasion Helen, who is 12, complains that Father Jack has sexually assaulted her. A subsequent criminal investigation upholds her claim.

Advise the parties.

The reference to a fictitious statute suggests that the markers want you to consider whether there might be an action for breach of statutory duty. However, there may also be a breach of the Archdeacon's non-delegable duty of care.

The facts here are very similar to *Maga v Birmingham Roman Catholic Archdiocese Trustees*. You will need to work through the three conditions necessary for vicarious liability to be established: (1) an employee–employer relationship; (2) the employee must have committed a tort; and (3) this must have been committed while the employee was acting in the course of their employment).

a fictitious statute, however could there be a claim under the Employer's Liability (Defective Equipment) Act 1969 or for breach of statutory duty?

Perhaps a classic case of a non-delegable duty of care—Neil owes Roger a duty to ensure a safe system of working—see further *Latimer v AEC Ltd* [1953].

Product liability annotated problem question

After many years of research, Rack and Horse Pharmaceuticals (RHP) develop a drug to treat breast cancer. After only 18 months of clinical trials, it receives a licence and goes on the market in the UK in March 2010. Although the drug itself is completely pure, it is known that in less than 0.5 per cent of patients (those who carry a particular gene) it can produce an undesirable side-effect known as Tort Syndrome. This side-effect is not widely publicised as both RHP and the government are to encourage widespread uptake of the drug in the relevant groups of women.

In 2015, 20 claimants who were given the drug between 2010 and 2013 and who have contracted Tort Syndrome begin an action against RHP alleging both negligence and liability under the Consumer Protection Act 1987. RHP argues that it is not liable because up until 2013, there was no genetic test that could determine which individuals carried the gene in question.

The claimants bring evidence to show there was an article in an Outer Mongolian scientific journal, published both in hard copy and on the Internet in 2011, which suggested a test to determine whether individual women carried the specific gene for the reaction to the drug that causes Tort Syndrome. Had RHP conducted clinical trials for longer, the company would have been able to identify the characteristics of the women likely to react badly to the drug and to issue appropriate warnings and advice.

Advise the parties.

Annotations:

In a claim under the Consumer Protection Act, Rack and Horse Pharmaceuticals would be the 'producer' and should be identified as such, using the relevant section of the statute.

The drug is clearly a 'product' for the purposes of the Consumer Protection Act and should be identified as such, using the relevant section of the statute.

Under the Consumer Protection Act the test for liability is different and producers will be liable for any harm caused by defects in their products.

But is the reaction to the vaccine the only potential cause, or might there be multiple potential causes? If so, cause in fact might be difficult to establish (see Chapter 9).

The claimants here have suffered physical harm (and there may be some consequential losses).

This suggests negligence and so the claimants may wish to claim in the tort of negligence as well. They would need to establish liability using the normal principles of duty, breach and causation—could they?

Should this risk have been made public? Is it negligent not to have done so (this may be an alternative claim)?

Does this make the vaccine 'defective' for the purposes of the Consumer Protection Act (s 3)? Consider the case *A v National Blood Authority*.

The criteria is that such knowledge should be 'accessible'—is this? See *EC v UK*. Can RHP rely on the 'development risks defence'?

To succeed in a negligence claim the claimants must establish duty, breach and causation. There is no problem with duty (*Donoghue*), and possibly not breach—but causation is likely to prove tricky unless the drug is the only potential cause of Tort Syndrome.

Trespass to the person annotated problem question

Dave, Arthur, Lucy and Ellie are sitting in the students' union bar discussing their outfits for the forthcoming 'Law Society Spring Ball'.

Mike, Lucy's ex-boyfriend, walks by and says quietly to Dave, 'I'll get you! No one steals my girl and gets away with it.' Although Dave is not particularly upset by this, he decides to teach Mike a lesson. When no one is looking, he deliberately trips Mike up; Mike falls over but is not hurt. He quickly jumps up and runs after Dave. Mike hits Dave and pushes him away; Dave falls awkwardly and hits his head. As Lucy rushes to get a doctor, Mike corners her and whispers, 'I miss you, let's try again.' She pushes him away.

Meanwhile Arthur and Ellie have sneaked into the bar's store room for some time alone. On seeing this, Mike locks the store room door. It remains locked until Stuart, the bar man comes on duty some time later and unlocks it. (Later that evening, Mike calls Helen, Dave's pregnant ex-girlfriend, who lives some distance away, and tells her Dave has been badly hurt. She takes the news very badly. Mike then calls Lucy's mobile; as she is still at the hospital with Dave she does not answer it. By the time she checks her phone she has 12 missed calls.

Advise the parties.

It will be easier to answer this problem question chronologically by claim rather than by party.

You need to consider here whether Mike's whispered comment is an assault—also remember to address the point raised by the following sentence—it does not matter that Dave is not upset by Mike's threat (see *Stephens* v *Myers*).

Could Mike's comment be an assault? If so, is Lucy's action in pushing him away self-defence? If not, then Lucy's actions will amount to a battery.

Be careful here—the facts are not the same as *Wilkinson* v *Downton*. You would need to make an argument for it to apply in relation to *true* statements. If not, could there be a claim in negligence (for communication of shocking news) (see Chapter 5)?

A clear case of false imprisonment—as with the other torts you need to work through the elements of this tort emphasising that it makes no difference to the existence of the tort that they were unaware of their 'imprisonment' (although this will affect the amount of damages awarded)— remember to cite the appropriate case law.

The point to emphasise here is the one raised in *Williams* v *Humphrey*—i.e. that Mike will be liable for the full extent of Dave's injuries (even though he did not intend to hurt him to this extent). Also remember to address any relevant defences here.

Here you need to discuss whether Mike's actions amount to harassment under the Protection from Harassment Act 1997.

This will be a battery (and, possibly, if Mike noticed what Dave was doing an assault). You need to work through the requirements for each of these torts. Remember there is still an actionable battery even though Mike is not physically hurt, you need to say why this is.

Defamation annotated problem question

In the Hood, a weekly fashion and TV magazine, is famous for its celebrity 'scoops'. This week's issue includes the following stories:

'TV CHEF IN JUNK FOOD SHAME!'—a two-page story about a TV chef, who prides himself on his healthy recipes, who has been spotted buying reconstituted meat in his local supermarket. In fact, he was accompanied by a film crew and was buying them for the new series of his show. The article does not mention this.

> What is it that is defamatory here? Think about why the magazine does not mention why the chef is buying the reconstituted meat.

'EXPLOITED FOR THE SAKE OF FASHION'—a four-page feature in which claims are made about *Rack and Horse Design*, a discount clothing company. The article suggests that the company is:

- exploiting their shop workers in the UK by paying below minimum wages;
- destroying the environment through their continued use of highly toxic dyes;
- forcing workers in the developing world to work in 'inhumane and degrading' conditions.

> Will *In the Hood* have to establish the truth of all these claims in order to rely on the defence of justification? Could the defence of honest comment apply here?

'BOOZED-UP, WASHED-UP, KICKED OUT'—a photo spread (accompanied by brief captions) of 'celebrities' appearing worse for wear after a night out. Underneath the headline—but in much smaller print—there is an explanation that these are staged photos using celebrity lookalikes.

Advise *In the Hood*'s editor as to the magazine's potential liability in the tort of defamation.

> You should first consider whether each of the claims is capable of being defamatory before considering any applicable defences, if necessary.

> Compare
> ***Charleston* v *New Group Newspapers Ltd***—do you think the reasoning in this case is likely to be applied? Is *O'Shea* a closer analogy? If not, why not?

Privacy annotated problem question

Elizabeth is the fiancée of a Premiership footballer, Alessandro Talentti. She is 28 years old, beautiful and glamorous. She has always been happy to be photographed with Alessandro at awards evenings, film premieres, and charity events and also while out with her girlfriends shopping or lunching, or with other footballers' wives and girl-friends watching football matches.

Recently, as she has started to organise her wedding, which she wants to be an intimate and private affair, Elizabeth has found the media attention intrusive and has had several arguments with photographers wanting to take her picture whilst out shopping or in small, quiet restaurants. One photographer, Chris, is particularly persistent and takes photographs when she is leaving a hospital after visiting her mother who is very ill. He also photographed her (using a long-range lens) going in to a small London bridal boutique when she was out shopping for bridesmaids' dresses with her young sister and niece.

On the wedding day—the press having been successfully excluded from the venue—one of the caterers secretly takes some pictures of the wedding ceremony and the reception, at which there were many famous guests. He then sold these pictures to *Peachy*, a well-known celebrity glossy magazine; the pictures are published in the following week's issue as an 'exclusive'.

Advise Elizabeth as to any legal actions she might be able to pursue.

[Annotation] In the past E has not minded publicity—will this affect any of her claims?

[Annotation] Do her wishes add anything to her claims?

[Annotation] Is the fact that she has made public her desire for her wedding to stay private relevant? See *Murray v Express Newspapers*.

[Annotation] Is this comparable with *Campbell*? Does it make her claim stronger that another person is involved? Does E have a 'reasonable expectation of privacy' in this situation? If a court has to weigh up the right to privacy (Art 8 ECHR) to the right to freedom of expression (Art 10 ECHR), who do you think will win here?

[Annotation] Following *Douglas v Hello!* would this be actionable? Is there a difference in this case in that there was no existing arrangement to sell pictures to another magazine? If so, would that go in E's favour or against her?

[Annotation] Would this fall foul of the Press Complaints Commission Code of Practice? If so, would any remedy the PCC could provide be acceptable?

[Annotation] Does the fact that there are children being photographed help her claim? See *Murray v Express Newspapers*. Does E have a 'reasonable expectation of privacy' in this situation? If a court has to weigh up the right to privacy (Art 8 ECHR) to the right to freedom of expression (Art 10 ECHR), who do you think will win here?

[Annotation] Is there any 'harm' done by these pictures? Compare e.g. *Campbell v MGN*. Does E have a 'reasonable expectation of privacy' in this situation? If a court has to weigh up the right to privacy (Art 8 ECHR) to the right to freedom of expression (Art 10 ECHR), who do you think will win here? See also *Mosley v News Group Newspapers*.

[Annotation] Does this suggest that it is a 'private' wedding? Leading to the couple having a legitimate or 'reasonable expectation of privacy' with all relating to it?

Trespass to land and private nuisance annotated problem question

Lekan owns a large country estate in Buckhampton. He is keen to develop it as an environmentally friendly residential adventure centre catering for stressed-out city executives. To this end, he has constructed a network of ropes, ladders and bridges in the canopy of his woodland for them to come and 'Swing High' from tree to tree. Unfortunately, misplaced marketing has lead to the majority of his customers being large, noisy groups of young people on stag and hen weekends. Lekan also provides facilities for paintballing and a quad-bike cross-country course. In line with his stated environmental policy, he has recently begun to use large volumes of seaweed, collected from nearby beaches, as fertiliser for his large organic vegetable patch. He has been encouraged to do so by his local council's recycling officer, who is keen to stop waste material going to landfill sites (driven by a need to comply with an EC Directive).

Lekan receives the following complaints:

(a) Sarah, who lives downwind of Lekan's estate, complains that the smell of the rotting seaweed makes her physically sick.

(b) Sandy, a 14 year old, lives on a neighbouring farm. He complains that the noise from the quad bikes is causing his guinea pigs to miscarry their young.

(c) Jess who, when she walks her dogs, parks her car next to Lekan's boundary fence, complains that her car has, on a couple of occasions, been hit by stray paintballs.

(d) Ailsa complains that the 'Swing High' centre is 'lowering the tone of the neighbourhood' and that her back garden can be seen from the platforms in the trees.

Lekan, the 'creator' of the alleged nuisances, will be the defendant.

The first question, following **Hunter**, would be to ask whether Sarah has 'standing' to sue.

Sarah is complaining that the smell of the seaweed is a nuisance. What remedy would she require? Might the 'nature of the locality' affect her claim?

Will Jess be able to claim? Does she have standing?

Would a child of this age have 'standing'?

The alleged nuisance.

Can this be construed in any way as a harm to the land affected? Is Sandy 'abnormally sensitive' in his use of land? Or would the harm be 'foreseeable' (**Network Rail**).

What kind of claim is this? Is it one based on human rights? Or is it trespass?

Is this a nuisance claim? Possibly public nuisance if this affects 'a class of Her Majesty's subjects'.

Is this trespass? If so, the standing issue may not be a problem—but her car is not 'land', nor is she on her own land.

Physical sickness cannot be claimed in private nuisance—although it might be part of 'lost amenity'. Is there a potential claim in public nuisance? What would she have to show? Does she have a human rights-based claim?

Rylands v Fletcher annotated problem question

Grab-and-Buy supermarket owns land on which it has built a huge two-storey metal-framed car park for its customers. One day, after extremely stormy weather with strong winds and heavy rain, the top level of the car park buckles, some of the metal railing breaks free and falls onto the neighbouring premises, a petrol station owned by Low-Price-Pumps. The impact damages the pumps and injures one of Low-Price-Pumps' customers. Furthermore, water that had collected on the upper level of the car park due to an inadequate drainage system pours onto Low-Price-Pumps, flooding the forecourt of the petrol station, meaning that it has to close down for two days, causing £10,000 loss of profit.

Low-Price-Pumps spends £50,000 having the forecourt cleaned and making safe the pumps. Grab-and-Buy argues that damage to the pumps caused by high winds is something that Low-Price-Pumps could and should have insured against.

Advise the parties.

In the *Rylands v Fletcher* claim for the property damage suffered by LPP, LPP would need to establish liability using the 4 criteria, as modified by *Transco*:
(1) The defendant brings on his land for his own purposes something likely to do mischief ...
(2) ...if it escapes ...
(3) ...which represents a non-natural use of land ...
(4) ...and which causes foreseeable damage of the relevant type.
Note that since *Transco* the substance brought or accumulated on land must bring with it an 'exceptional' danger.

Does this suggest an alternative action in negligence?

If there is a possibility that liability can be established, can GAB use the stormy weather as a defence?

LPP's first claim is for property damage.

Do these harms meet the foreseeability requirement from *Cambridge Water*?

Would the customer be able to sue for their personal injuries under *Rylands v Fletcher*? If not, is there any other route they could take? Negligence is usually the best chance for personal injury claims but is there any evidence of negligence on the part of GAB here? The claimant would need to establish duty, breach and causation—would there be a problem doing so? Alternatively, if LPP have to pay the customer compensation, would it be able to claim this from GAB in its *Rylands v Fletcher* claim?

Is this a relevant argument? See discussion of the role of insurance in *Transco*.

LPP is the claimant here. The first question to ask is whether they have standing to take a claim (as *Transco* confirmed that this is a requirement in *Rylands v Fletcher* claims) as it is in nuisance (following *Hunter*).

These are the losses LPP will be claiming (possibly in addition to a claim representing the cost of compensating their customer for personal injury).

Damages annotated problem question

Emma is a 45-year-old London-based consultant paediatrician. Because of her increasingly high profile and the fact that she is held in high respect by her peers, she has in recent years also fronted a number of popular television series that delve into various aspects of children's medicine and medical treatments. In the last year alone, she was paid over £50,000 for this. She also does a lot of work, including fundraising, for various children's charities: last year she was sponsored to cycle the Great Wall of China and raised over £15,000. She enjoys time with her two teenage children (she is divorced from their father) and in particular loves weekends away with them sailing or waterskiing, although also enjoys sharing more simple activities with them, such as taking their dog for long walks in the park. She is an avid cook, and attends a cookery class every Thursday evening, followed by a meal out with her friends.

Emma is seriously injured in a multiple car accident on the M25, for which she was in no way to blame. She is rendered paraplegic, is confined to a wheelchair and suffers constant pain. She has to give up her job, but continues to try and do some of the voluntary work for the charities she is involved with. She, along with her two children, has to move out of her three-storey house in north London and into a specially adapted ground-floor flat. Her boyfriend, Clive, who has a career in advertising, agrees to move in with her and be her carer; he gives up his job. She loses interest in sex and is unable to carry on with the majority of her leisure pursuits.

It is established that a combination of two other drivers' negligence caused the accident in which Emma was injured.

Advise the parties.

These are all physical activities that E may not now be able to enjoy. While she can still spend time with her children, the non-pecuniary losses here will have to be compensated.

Can she still do this? If not, it adds to her non-pecuniary loss.

This also goes to her non-pecuniary losses.

We are not told what her precise salary is, so the multiplicand figure here (as we know that she has to give up her job) will largely be guesswork. However, it is fairly safe to say that a consultant paediatrician working in London will be on quite a high salary! Remember that the multiplicand will also take into account future prospects of promotion etc. What would the multiplier be on her lost earnings?

How does liability split between them? See e.g. *Fitzgerald v Lane*.

Is this anything that is claimable by E? Or not a loss that she has suffered? Does it merely add to her non-pecuniary losses? Could *she* continue to fundraise in other ways?

Would E be able to claim damages for the cost of care provided by him? See *Hunt v Severs* [1994].

Does this *save her* money or is it a loss? If she had to pay to alter the flat in any way to make it suitable for her to live in, these costs may be claimable as special damages.

Physical injuries may be more easy to quantify than non-pecuniary losses. What can she claim for here? If she gets a lump sum, what would the multiplier be for her continued pain and suffering?

These are additional earnings. A claim may be based on these, but unlike her other job, this may be less permanent—how long could someone like E expect to have a high profile on TV?

The object of a question like this is to get you to work out how much damages E will be able to claim. Negligence is not disputed so you need not talk about duty, breach, causation etc. Obviously, the amount of damages you end up with might not be the same as a court would award—the idea is for you to identify and discuss the various principles that apply to the different parts of the claim, not to get an exact figure. On the physical injuries, you may find the diagram on p 560 helpful. Consider also whether this is the kind of situation where the court might exercise its power to insist that the parties create a Periodical Payment Order to cover the future losses. If so, how would this work?

Index

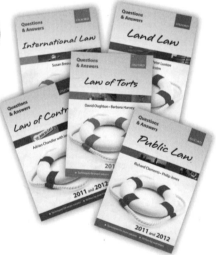